An Introduction to

POETRY

Seventh Edition

X. J. Kennedy

SCOTT, FORESMAN/LITTLE, BROWN HIGHER EDUCATION
A Division of Scott, Foresman and Company
Glenview, Illinois   London, England

An Instructor's Edition of *An Introduction to Poetry, Seventh Edition,* is available through your local Scott, Foresman representative or by writing the English Editor, Higher Education and Professional Division, Scott, Foresman and Company, 1900 East Lake Avenue, Glenview, Illinois 60025.

ISBN 0-673-52025-0 Student Edition
ISBN 0-673-49860-3 Instructor's Edition

Library of Congress Cataloging-in-Publication Data

Kennedy, X. J.
   An introduction to poetry/X. J. Kennedy.—7th ed.
     p. cm.
   Includes bibliographical references.
   ISBN 0-673-52025-0
   1. Poetics.   2. English poetry.   3. American poetry.   I. Title.
PN1042.K39   1990   89-10824
808.1—dc20

         3   4   5   6—RRC—95   94   93   92   91   90

Preface

What is poetry? Pressed for an answer, Robert Frost made a classic reply: "Poetry is the kind of thing poets write." In all likelihood, Frost was not trying merely to evade the question but to chide his questioner into thinking for himself. A trouble with definitions is that they may stop thought. If Frost had said, "Poetry is a rhythmical composition of words expressing an attitude, designed to surprise and delight, and to arouse an emotional response," the questioner might have settled back in his chair, content to have learned the truth about poetry. He would have learned nothing, or not so much as he might learn by continuing to wonder.

The nature of poetry eludes simple definitions. (In this respect it is rather like jazz. Asked after one of his concerts, "What is jazz?" Louis Armstrong replied, "Man, if you gotta ask, you'll never know.") Definitions will be of little help at first, if we are to know poetry and respond to it. We have to go to it willing to see and hear. For this reason, you are asked in reading this book not to be in any hurry to decide what poetry is, but instead to study poems and to let them grow in your mind. At the end of our discussions of poetry, the problem of definition will be taken up again (for those who may wish to pursue it).

Confronted with a formal introduction to poetry, you may be wondering, "Who needs it?" and you may well be right. It's unlikely that you have avoided meeting poetry before; and perhaps you already have a friendship, or at least a fair acquaintance, with some of the great English-speaking poets of all time. What this book provides is an introduction to the *study* of poetry. It tries to help you look at a poem closely, to offer you a wider and more accurate vocabulary with which to express what poems say to you. It will suggest ways to judge for yourself the poems you read. It may set forth some poems new to you.

A frequent objection is that poetry ought not to be studied at all. In this view, a poem is either a series of gorgeous noises to be funneled through one ear and out the other without being allowed to trouble the mind, or an experience so holy that to analyze it in a classroom is as cruel and mechanical as dissecting a hummingbird. To the first view, it might be countered that a good poem has something to say that is well worth listening to. To the second view, it might be argued that poems are much less perishable than humming-birds, and luckily, we can study them in flight. The risk of a poem's dying from observation is not nearly so great as the risk of not really seeing it at all. It is doubtful that any excellent poem has ever vanished from human memory because people have read it too closely. More likely, poems that vanish are poems that no one reads closely, for no one cares.

That poetry matters to the people who write it has been shown unmistakably by the ordeal of Soviet poet Irina Ratushinskaya, now living in the West. Sentenced to prison for three and a half years, she was given paper and pencil only twice a month to write letters to her husband and her parents and was not allowed to write anything else. Nevertheless, Ratushinskaya composed more than two hundred poems in her cell, engraving them with a burnt match in a bar of soap, then memorizing the lines. "I would read the poem and read it," she said, "until it was committed to memory—then with one washing of my hands, it would be gone."[1]

Good poetry is something that readers and listeners, too, can care about. In fact, an ancient persuasion of humankind is that the hearing of a poem, as well as the making of a poem, can be a religious act. Poetry, in speech and song, was part of classic Greek drama, which for playwright, actor, and spectator alike was a holy-day ceremony. The Greeks' belief that a poet writes a poem only by supernatural assistance is clear from the invocations to the Muse that begin the *Iliad* and the *Odyssey* and from the opinion of Socrates (in Plato's *Ion*) that a poet has no powers of invention until divinely inspired. Among the ancient Celts, poets were regarded as magicians and priests, and whoever insulted one of them might expect to receive a curse in rime potent enough to afflict him with boils and to curdle the milk of his cows. Such identifications between the poet and the magician are less common these days, although we know that poetry is involved in the primitive white-magic of children, who bring themselves good luck in a game with the charm "Roll, roll, Tootsie-roll! / Roll the marble in the hole!" and who warn against a hex while jumping along a sidewalk: "Step on a crack, / Break your mother's back." But in this age when we pride ourselves that a computer may solve the riddle of all creation as soon as it is programmed, magic seems to some people of small importance and so too does poetry. It is dangerous, however, to dismiss what we do not logically understand. To read a poem at all, we have to be willing to offer it responses *besides* a logical understanding. Whether we attribute the effect of a poem to a divine spirit or to the reactions of our glands and cortexes, we have to take the reading of poetry seriously (not solemnly), if only because—as some of the poems in this book may demonstrate—few other efforts can repay us so generously, both in wisdom and in joy.

If, as I hope you will do, you sometimes browse in the book for fun, you may be annoyed to see so many questions following the poems. Should you feel this way, try reading with a slip of paper to cover up the questions. You will then—if the Muse should inspire you—have paper in hand to write a poem.

[1]Reported in the *New York Times*, December 19, 1986.

A Word about Careers

Students tend to agree that to read poets such as Shakespeare, Keats, Emily Dickinson, and Robert Frost is probably good for the spirit, and most even take some pleasure in the experience. But many, if they aren't planning to teach English and are impatient to begin some other career, often wonder whether the study of poetry, however enjoyable, is not a waste of time or, at least, an annoying obstacle.

This objection may seem reasonable, but it rests on a shaky assumption. It can be argued that, on the contrary, success in a career is *not* mostly a matter of learning certain information and skills that belong exclusively to a certain profession. In most careers, according to a business executive, people often fail not because they don't understand their jobs, but because they don't understand the people they work with, or their clients or customers; and so they can't imagine another person's point of view. To leap outside the walls of your self, to see through another person's eyes—this is an experience that literature abundantly offers. Although, if you are lucky, you may never meet (or have to do business with) anyone *exactly* like the insanely jealous speaker of the poem "Soliloquy of the Spanish Cloister," you will probably learn much about the kind of person he is from Robert Browning's portrait of him. Who knows? Among your fellow students or coworkers may be a J. Alfred Prufrock (the central character of T. S. Eliot's poem), or someone like John Updike's "Ex-Basketball Player." What is it like to be black, a white may wonder? Perhaps Langston Hughes, Gwendolyn Brooks, Lucille Clifton, Rita Dove, Dudley Randall, James C. Kilgore, and others have something to tell. What is it like to be a woman? A man who would learn can read, for a start, Emily Dickinson, Sylvia Plath, Anne Sexton, Denise Levertov, Adrienne Rich, Anne Bradstreet, Sharon Olds, and many more.

Plodding singlemindedly toward careers, some people are like horses wearing blinders. For many, the goals look fixed and predictable. Competent nurses, accountants, and dental technicians seem always in demand. Others may find that in our society some careers, like waves in the sea, will rise or fall unexpectedly. Think how many professions we now take for granted, which only a few years ago didn't even exist: computer programming, energy conservation, tofu manufacture, videotape rental. Others that once looked like lifetime meal tickets have been cut back and nearly ruined: shoe repairing, commercial fishing, railroading.

In a society perpetually in change, it may be risky to lock yourself on one track to a career, refusing to consider any other. "We are moving," writes John Naisbitt in *Megatrends*, a study of our changing society, "from the specialist, soon obsolete, to the generalist who can adapt." Perhaps the greatest opportunity in your whole life lies in a career that has yet to be invented. If you do change your career as you go along, you will be like most people. According to U.S. Department of Labor statistics, the average person in a working life changes occupations three times. When for some unforeseen reason you have to make such a change, basic skills may be your most valuable credentials—and a knowledge of humanity.

Literature has much practical knowledge to offer you. An art of words, it can help you become more sensitive to language, both your own and other people's. It can make you aware of the difference between the word that is exactly right and the word that is merely good enough—Mark Twain calls it "the difference between the lightning and the lightning-bug." Read a fine work of literature alertly, and some of its writer's sensitivity to words may grow on you. A Supreme Court justice, John Paul Stevens, gave his opinion (informally) that the best preparation for law school is to study poetry. Why? George D. Gopen, an English professor with a law degree, says it may be because "no other discipline so closely replicates the central question asked in the study of legal thinking: Here is a text; in how many ways can it have meaning?" (By the way, if a career you plan has anything to do with advertising, whether writing it or buying it or resisting it, be sure to read Chapter 4, "Saying and Suggesting," on the hints inherent in words.)

Many careers today, besides law, call for close reading and for clear thinking expressed on paper. Lately, college placement directors have reported more demand for graduates who are good readers and writers. The reason is evident: employers need people who can handle words. In a recent survey conducted by Cornell University, business executives were asked to rank in importance the traits they look for when hiring. Leadership was first, but skill in writing and speaking came in fourth, ahead of managerial skill, ahead of skill in analysis. Times change, but to think cogently and to express yourself well are abilities the world still needs.

That is why most colleges, however thorough the career training they may provide, still insist on general training as well, including basic courses in the humanities. No one can promise that your study of literature will result in cash profit, but at least the kind of wealth that literature provides is immune to fluctuations of the Dow Jones average. A highly paid tool and die maker, asked by his community college English instructor why he had enrolled in an evening literature course, said, "Oh, I just decided there has to be more to life than work, a few beers, and the bowling alley." If you should discover in yourself a fondness for great reading, then in no season of your life are you likely to become incurably bored or feel totally alone—even after you make good in your career, even when there is nothing on television.

Changes in This Edition

Instructors familiar with this book from its earlier editions may be struck, first of all, by the new look of Chapter One. Following the wishes of many, this opening chapter now contains sections on Lyric Poetry and Narrative Poetry, to try to make these rough but serviceable distinctions clear from the start. A different array of poems has been called for, but if you are looking for Housman's "Loveliest of trees," Robert Hayden's "Those Winter Sundays," Linda Pastan's "Ethics," Robert Francis's "Catch," or Marvell's "To His Coy Mistress," please be assured that these poems are still aboard.

Once again, the book's representation of minority poets has been strengthened, and so has the number of woman poets, both earlier and contemporary. Now added to this edition are Jimmy Santiago Baca, Aphra Behn, Deborah Digges, Rita Dove, Mary Elizabeth Coleridge, Louise Erdrich, Linda Gregg, Elizabeth Jennings, Lorine Niedecker, Katherine Philips, Grace Schulman, Wole Soyinka, Ruth Stone, Emma Lee Warrior, Nancy Willard, and Eleanor Wylie. Several others who were in the last edition are represented now in greater depth.

This time the ample *Anthology: Poetry* has been lengthened by only two poems, bringing the total to 146. It now includes 44 new selections—traditional, modern, and contemporary. These fresh choices have been made with the help of dozens of instructors, in an effort to provoke livelier classes.

For those who want to give their students a little background information on the poets they read, a new feature has been added: *Lives of the Poets,* which follows the *Anthology.* This section offers brief biographies, tucked in one place for easy reference. While it seemed neither necessary nor workable to include a biography for every poet, there is one for each poet represented by two selections or more. Throughout the book, an asterisk (*) after a poet's by-line indicates a biographee.

For classes who have time for it, a knotty problem—how to evaluate an unfamiliar poem—is now treated in detail, with fresh (and almost certainly unfamiliar) poems given, and a list of questions supplied to help students make up their own minds. Users of the section of bad poetry will be happy to see that it now boasts major works by William McGonagall and Julia A. Moore, and other horrific new examples.

Since the sixth edition of *An Introduction to Poetry,* deep changes have been made in the "Supplement: Writing," especially in "Writing about Literature." In the past, our advice on writing has been conventional, not much nourished by recent advances in composition theory. In earlier editions, I used to see the writing of a paper as a lockstep trip through stages, with a foreseeable product at the end. This advice has now been recast, more accurately to reflect real life. Strategies for discovering material are given priority. Students are still told they may find it helpful to state a thesis, but this advice is given as only one possible way to write. Editing and mechanics, though given careful attention, take a back seat to more vital matters, such as the tendency of fresh ideas to arrive when it's time to revise. The directions for documenting sources now follow the latest *MLA Handbook for Writers of Research Papers.* At the end of each chapter you will now find a few "Suggestions for Writing," which may be of special use to anyone using this book in a writing course.

Not one old question has gone unquestioned. More details about these and other renovations may be found in the preface to the thoroughly revised and updated *Instructor's Manual to Accompany An Introduction to Poetry, Seventh*

Edition, now conveniently bound in with desk copies and so made part of the book itself.

THANKS

Once again, in revising this book and its manual, I have depended on the reactions, corrections, and suggestions of many instructors. (Some responded to it as part of *Literature, Fourth Edition.*) Deep thanks to Ila Abernathy, University of Arizona; Stephen Adams, University of Minnesota at Duluth; Jonathan Aldrich, Portland School of Art; R.M. Bedell, Virginia Military Institute; William W. Betts, Jr., Indiana University of Pennsylvania; Ellen Sternberg Bevan, St. John Fisher College; Peggy L. Brayfield, Eastern Illinois University; Laurel Brodsley, UCLA; Joyce Moss Brown, Catonsville Cummunity College; Mary M. Burns, South Central Community College; Ellen Miller Casey, University of Scranton; Joe R. Christopher, Tarleton State University; Robert F. Coleman, Palomar College; Ruth Corson, Norwalk Community College; LuDene Dallimore, Weber State College; Emanuel di Pasquale, Middlesex County Community College; Dan Doll, University of New Orleans; Judi Doumas, Old Dominion University; Charles Clay Doyle, University of Georgia; William D. Eisenberg, Bloomsburg University of Pennsylvania; Ed Eleazer, Albany (Georgia) Junior College; SallyAnn H. Ferguson, North Carolina A & T State University; Matthew A. Fike, University of Michigan, Eastern Michigan University; Robert Foster, SUNY College, Potsdam; G. Dale Gleason, Hutchinson Community College; Len Gougeon, University of Scranton; R.S. Gwynn, Lamar University; Diane Harris, Kent State University; Charles O. Hartman, Connecticut College; Norleen M. Healy, Sheridan College; James Heldman, Western Kentucky University; Randel Helms, Arizona State University; Leonard J. Leff, Oklahoma State University; Richard Lessa, University of Hawaii at Manoa; Stephen Shu-ning Liu, Clark County Community College; Joe Lostracco, Austin Community College; Kathy L. May, Virginia Polytechnic Institute and State University; Robert McGovern, Ashland College; Mary Nardo, Brevard Community College; Bruce Naschak, Mesa College; Janet C. Nosek, University of Alaska, Anchorage; L. Anderson Orr, Virginia Wesleyan College; Linda Pannill, Transylvania University; David Peck, California State University, Long Beach; Judith K. Powers, University of Wyoming; Helon H. Raines, Casper College; Linda C. Rollins, Motlow State Community College; Arthrell D. Sanders, North Carolina Central University; B. Sandlin, Scottsdale Community College; Ellery Sedgwick, Longwood College; Debra J. Sheffer, Central Missouri State University; Carol Sklenicka, Milwaukee Institute of Art and Design; Michael J. Smith, Highline Community College; Paul H. Stacy, University of Hartford; Al Starr, Essex Community College; Dabney Stuart, College of William & Mary; Joseph L. Swonk, Rappahannock Community College; Ray S. Williams, Brigham Young University; Stephen Caldwell Wright, Seminole Community College. Some of these instructors testified that they have used this book for twenty years. Others said that they never have used this book and don't intend to start. I am grateful to them, one and all.

Generously, many students wrote reactions and suggestions. I wish there were space to thank them all, but special thanks to D. D. Doner, Austin Community College; Stephania A. Ezell, University of Central Arkansas; Lawrence A. Ferguson, Centralia Community College; Christopher R. Lake, University of Wisconsin Center, Fond du Lac; Jack H. Marshall, Northeast Texas Community College; Tracy Martinez, Santa Barbara City College; Connie McMurray, Oakland Community College; and Jacqueline Waddington, University of Minnesota. In justice, I would have to name all the students at Tufts, Wellesley, Michigan, North Carolina (Greensboro), California (Irvine), and Leeds who in the past let me read poems in their company.

I owe thanks to many people on the publisher's staff, especially Anne E. Smith and Garret White for lending constant support, Ted Simpson for editing with a knowing hand, Marisa L. L'Heureux for zealously shaping and polishing, Guy Huff for battling with permissions, Debbie Costello for giving the book a fresh design, Kelly Mountain for locating poets' portraits, and Francis Byrne for inspired project editing. B. Dundee Holt recommended, and even transcribed, a rap song.

Finally, I remain grateful to hundreds of instructors named in prefaces past. Much of their thinking and experience is still here, as is that of Sylvan Barnet, who back in 1965 lent order to a confused manuscript. Dorothy M. Kennedy, co-author of the manual, has my lasting gratitude for certain of the questions and biographies, and for much besides.

Contents

3   *Words*   38

4 Saying and Suggesting 64

5 Imagery 73

6   *Figures of Speech*   88

7 Song   108

8 Sound   124

9 Rhythm 145

10 Closed Form, Open Form   164

11 Poems for the Eye   198

12 Symbol   205

13 Myth   217

16 What Is Poetry?   273

Anthology: Poetry   277

Lives of the Poets   407

Criticism: On Poetry   439

Supplement: Writing   459

TO THE MUSE

Give me leave, Muse, in plain view to array
Your shift and bodice by the light of day.
I would have brought an epic. Be not vexed
Instead to grace a niggling schoolroom text;
Let down your sanction, help me to oblige
Him who would lead fresh devots to your liege,
And at your altar, grant that in a flash
They, he and I know incense from dead ash.
                                        —X.J.K.

1 Reading a Poem

How do you read a poem? The literal-minded might say, "Just let your eye light on it"; but there is more to poetry than meets the eye. What Shakespeare called "the mind's eye" also plays a part. Many a reader who has no trouble understanding and enjoying prose finds poetry difficult. This is to be expected. At first glance, a poem usually will make some sense and give some pleasure, but it may not yield everything at once. Sometimes it only hints at meaning still to come if we will keep after it. Poetry is not to be galloped over like the daily news: a poem differs from most prose in that it is to be read slowly, carefully, and attentively. Not all poems are difficult, of course, and some can be understood and enjoyed on first seeing. But good poems yield more if read twice; and the best poems—after ten, twenty, or a hundred readings—still go on yielding.

Approaching a thing written in lines and surrounded with white space, we need not expect it to be a poem just because it is **verse.** (Any composition in lines of more or less regular rhythm, usually ending in rimes, is verse.) Here, for instance, is a specimen of verse that few will call poetry:

> Thirty days hath September,
> April, June, and November;
> All the rest have thirty-one
> Excepting February alone,
> To which we twenty-eight assign
> Till leap year makes it twenty-nine.

To a higher degree than that classic memory-tickler, poetry appeals to the mind and arouses feelings. Poetry may state facts, but, more important, it makes imaginative statements that we may value even if its facts are incorrect. Coleridge's error in placing a star within the horns of the crescent moon in "The Rime of the Ancient Mariner" does not stop the passage from being good poetry, though it is faulty astronomy. According to one poet, Gerard Manley Hopkins, poetry is "to be heard for its own sake and interest even over and above its interest of meaning." There are other elements in a poem besides plain prose sense: sounds, images, rhythms, figures of speech. These may strike us and please us even before we ask, "But what does it all mean?"

This is a truth not readily grasped by anyone who regards a poem as a kind of puzzle written in secret code with a message slyly concealed. The effect of a poem (one's whole mental and emotional response to it) consists in much more than simply a message. By its musical qualities, by its suggestions, it can work on the reader's unconscious. T. S. Eliot put it well when he said in *The Use of Poetry and the Use of Criticism* that the prose sense of a poem is chiefly useful in keeping the reader's mind "diverted and quiet, while the poem does its work upon him." Eliot went on to liken the meaning of a poem to the bit of meat a burglar brings along to throw to the family dog. What is the work of a poem? To touch us, to stir us, to make us glad, and possibly even to tell us something.

How to set about reading a poem? Here are a few suggestions.

To begin with, read the poem once straight through, with no particular expectations; read open-mindedly. Let yourself experience whatever you find, without worrying just yet about the large general and important ideas the poem contains (if indeed it contains any). Don't dwell on a troublesome word or difficult passage—just push on. Some of the difficulties may seem smaller when you read the poem for a second time; at least, they will have become parts of a whole for you.

On second reading, read for the exact sense of all the words; if there are words you don't understand, look them up in a dictionary. Dwell on any difficult parts as long as you need to.

If you read the poem silently to yourself, sound its words in your mind. (This is a technique that will get you nowhere in a speed-reading course, but it may help the poem to do its work on you.) Better still, read the poem aloud, or hear someone else read it. You may discover meanings you didn't perceive in it before. Even if you are no actor, to decide how to speak a poem can be an excellent method of getting to understand it. Some poems, like bells, seem heavy till heard. Listen while reading the following lines from Alexander Pope's *Dunciad*. Attacking the minor poet James Ralph, who had sung the praises of a mistress named Cynthia, Pope makes the goddess of Dullness exclaim:

"Silence, ye wolves! while Ralph to Cynthia howls,
And makes night hideous—answer him, ye owls!"

When *ye owls* slide together and become *yowls*, poor Ralph's serenade is turned into the nightly outcry of a cat.

Try to **paraphrase** the poem as a whole, or perhaps just the more difficult lines. In paraphrasing, we put into our own words what we understand the poem to say, restating ideas that seem essential, coming out and stating what the poem may only suggest. This may sound like a heartless thing to do to a poem, but good poems can stand it. In fact, to compare a poem to its paraphrase is a good way to see the distance between poetry and prose. In making a paraphrase, we generally work through a poem or a passage line by line. The statement that results may take as many words as the original, if not more. A paraphrase, then, is ampler than a **summary,** a brief condensation of gist, main idea, or story. (Summary of a horror film in *TV Guide*: "Demented biologist, coveting power over New York, swells sewer rats to hippopotamus-size.") Here is a poem worth considering line by line. The poet writes of an island in a lake in the west of Ireland, in a region where he spent many summers as a boy.

William Butler Yeats (1865 – 1939)*

THE LAKE ISLE OF INNISFREE   1892

I will arise and go now, and go to Innisfree,
And a small cabin build there, of clay and wattles made:
Nine bean-rows will I have there, a hive for the honey-bee,
And live alone in the bee-loud glade.

And I shall have some peace there, for peace comes dropping slow,   5
Dropping from the veils of the morning to where the cricket sings;
There midnight's all a glimmer, and noon a purple glow,
And evening full of the linnet's wings.

I will arise and go now, for always night and day
I hear lake water lapping with low sounds by the shore;   10
While I stand on the roadway, or on the pavements gray,
I hear it in the deep heart's core.

Though relatively simple, this poem is far from simple-minded. We need to absorb it slowly and thoughtfully. At the start, for most of us, it raises problems: what are *wattles,* from which the speaker's dream-cabin is to be made? We might guess, but in this case it will help to consult a dictionary: they are "poles interwoven with sticks or branches, formerly used in building as frameworks to support walls or roofs." Evidently, this getaway house will be built in an old-fashioned way: it won't be a prefabricated log cabin or A-frame house, nothing modern or citified. The phrase *bee-loud glade* certainly isn't commonplace language of the sort we find on a cornflake package, but right away, we can understand it, at least partially: it's a place loud with bees. What is a *glade*? Experience might tell us that it is an open space in woods, but if that word stops us, we can look it up. Although the *linnet* doesn't live in North America, it is a creature with wings—a songbird of the finch family, adds the dictionary. But even if we don't make a special trip to the dictionary to find *linnet,* we recognize that the word means "bird," and the line makes sense to us.

A paraphrase of the whole poem might go something like this (in language easier to forget than that of the original): "I'm going to get up now, go to Innisfree, build a cabin, plant beans, keep bees, and live peacefully by myself amid nature and beautiful light. I want to, because I can't forget the sound of that lake water. When I'm in the city, a gray and dingy place, I seem to hear it deep inside me."

These dull remarks, roughly faithful to what Yeats is saying, seem a long way from poetry. Nevertheless, they make certain things clear. For one, they spell out what the poet merely hints at in his choice of the word *gray:* that he finds the city dull and depressing. He stresses the word; instead of saying *gray pavements,* in the usual word-order, he turns the phrase around and makes *gray* stand at the end of the line, where it rimes with *day* and so takes extra emphasis. The grayness of the city therefore seems important to the poem, and the paraphrase tries to make its meaning obvious.

Whenever you paraphrase, you stick your neck out. You affirm what the poem gives you to understand. And making a paraphrase can help you see the central thought of the poem, its **theme.** Theme isn't the same as **subject,** the main topic, whatever the poem is "about." In Yeats's poem, the subject is the lake isle of Innisfree, or a wish to retreat to it. But the theme is, "I yearn for an ideal place where I will find perfect peace and happiness." Themes can be stated variously, depending on what you believe most matters in the poem. Taking a different view of the poem, placing more weight on the speaker's wish to escape the city, you might instead state the theme: "This city is getting me down—I want to get back to nature." But after taking a second look at that statement, you might want to sharpen it. After all, this Innisfree seems a special, particular place, where the natural world means more to the poet than just any old trees and birds he might see in a park. Perhaps a stronger statement of theme, one closer to what matters most in the poem, might be: "I want to quit the city for my heaven on earth." That, of course, is saying in an obvious way what Yeats says more subtly, more memorably.

Not all poems clearly assert a proposition, but many do; some even declare their themes in their opening lines: "Gather ye rose-buds while ye may!"—that is, enjoy love before it's too late. This theme, stated in that famous first line of Robert Herrick's "To the Virgins, to Make Much of Time" (page 329), is so familiar that we give it a name: **carpe diem,** Latin for "seize the day." It is a favorite argument of poets since Roman times. You will meet it in more than one poem in this book.

A paraphrase, of course, never tells *all* that a poem contains; nor will every reader agree that a particular paraphrase is accurate. We all make our own interpretations; and sometimes the total meaning of a poem evades even the poet who wrote it. Asked to explain his difficult *Sordello,* Robert Browning replied that when he had written the poem only God and he knew what it meant; but "Now, only God knows." Still, to analyze a poem *as if* we could be certain of its meaning is, in general, more fruitful than to proceed as if no certainty could ever be had. The latter approach is likely to end in complete subjectivity: the attitude of the reader who says, "Yeats's 'Lake Isle of Innisfree' is really about the lost island of Atlantis. It is, because I think it is. How can you prove me wrong?" Interpretations can't be proven "wrong." A more fruitful question might be, "What can we understand from the poem's very words?"

All of us bring personal associations to the poems we read. "The Lake Isle of Innisfree" might give you special pleasure if you have ever vacationed on a small island or on the shore of a lake. Such associations are inevitable, even to be welcomed, as long as they don't interfere with our reading the words on the page. We need to distinguish irrelevant responses from those the poem calls for. The reader who can't stand "The Lake Isle of Innisfree" because she is afraid of bees isn't reading a poem by Yeats, but one of her own invention.

Now and again we meet a poem—perhaps startling and memorable—into which the method of paraphrase won't take us far. Some portion of any deep poem resists explanation, but certain poems resist it almost entirely. Many poems of religious mystics seem closer to dream than waking. So do poems that record hallucinations or drug experiences, such as Coleridge's "Kubla Khan" (page 299), as well as poems that embody some private system of beliefs, such as Blake's "The Sick Rose" (page 291), or the same poet's lines from *Jerusalem*,

> For a Tear is an Intellectual thing,
> And a Sigh is the Sword of an Angel King.

So do nonsense poems, translations of primitive folk songs, and surreal poems.[1] Such poetry may move us and give pleasure (although not, perhaps, the pleasure of mental understanding). We do it no harm by trying to paraphrase it, though we may fail. Whether logically clear or strangely opaque, good poems appeal to the intelligence and do not shrink from it.

So far, we have taken for granted that poetry differs from prose; yet all our strategies for reading poetry—plowing straight on through and then going back, isolating difficulties, trying to paraphrase, reading aloud, using a dictionary—are no different from those we might employ in unraveling a complicated piece of prose. Poetry, after all, is similar to prose in most respects. At the very least, it is written in the same language. Like prose, poetry shares knowledge with us. It tells us, for instance, of a beautiful island in Lake Gill, County Sligo, Ireland, of how one man feels toward it. Maybe the poet knows no more about Innisfree than a writer of a travel guidebook knows. And yet Yeats's poem indicates a kind of knowledge that tourist guidebooks do not ordinarily reveal: that the human heart can yearn for peace and happiness, that the lake isle of Innisfree with its "low sounds by the shore" can echo and reecho in memory forever.

LYRIC POETRY

Originally, as its Greek name suggests, a *lyric* was a poem sung to the music of a lyre. This earlier meaning—a poem made for singing—is still current today, when we use *lyrics* to mean the words of a popular song. But the kind of printed poem we now call a *lyric* is usually something else, for over the past five hundred

---

[1]The French poet André Breton, founder of **surrealism,** a movement in art and writing, declared that a higher reality exists, which to mortal eyes looks absurd. To mirror that reality, surrealist poets are fond of bizarre and dreamlike objects such as soluble fish and white-haired revolvers.

years, the nature of lyric poetry has changed greatly. Ever since the rise of the printing press in the fifteenth century, poets have written less often for singers, more often for readers. In general, this tendency has made lyric poems contain less word-music and (since they can be pondered on a page) more thought—and perhaps more complicated feelings.

Here is a rough definition of a **lyric** as it is written today: a short poem expressing the thoughts and feelings of a single speaker. Probably, it won't report conversations between two or more speakers, as does a poem given later in this chapter, "Sir Patrick Spence." Often a poet will write a lyric in the first person ("I will arise and go now, and go to Innisfree"), but not always. Instead, a lyric might describe an object or recall an experience without the speaker's ever bringing himself or herself into it. (For an example of such a lyric, one in which the poet refrains from saying "I," see William Carlos Williams's "The Red Wheelbarrow" on page 25, Theodore Roethke's "Root Cellar" on page 75, or Gerard Manley Hopkins's "Pied Beauty" on page 80.)

Perhaps because, rightly or wrongly, some people still think of lyrics as lyre-strummings, they expect a lyric to be an outburst of feeling, somewhat resembling a song, at least containing musical elements such as rime, rhythm, or sound effects. Such expectations are fulfilled in "The Lake Isle of Innisfree," that impassioned lyric full of language rich in sound (as you will hear if you'll read it aloud). In practice, though, many contemporary poets write short poems in which they voice opinions or complicated feelings—poems that no reader would dream of trying to sing. Most people would call such poems lyrics, too; one recent commentator has argued that a lyric may contain an argument.[2]

But in the sense in which we use it, *lyric* will usually apply to a kind of poem you can easily recognize. Here, for instance, are two lyrics. They differ sharply in subject and theme, but they have traits in common: both are short, and (as you will find) both set forth one speaker's definite, unmistakable feelings.

D. H. Lawrence (1885 – 1930)*

PIANO   1918

Softly, in the dusk, a woman is singing to me;
Taking me back down the vista of years, till I see
A child sitting under the piano, in the boom of the tingling strings
And pressing the small, poised feet of a mother who smiles as she
    sings.

In spite of myself, the insidious mastery of song   5
Betrays me back, till the heart of me weeps to belong
To the old Sunday evenings at home, with winter outside
And hymns in the cozy parlor, the tinkling piano our guide.

[2]Jeffrey Walker, "Aristotle's Lyric," *College English* 51 (January, 1989) 5–26.

So now it is vain for the singer to burst into clamor
With the great black piano appassionato. The glamor   10
Of childish days is upon me, my manhood is cast
Down in the flood of remembrance, I weep like a child for the past.

Questions

1. Jot down a brief paraphrase of this poem. In your paraphrase, clearly show what the
   speaker says is happening at present and also what he finds himself remembering.
   Make clear which seems the more powerful in its effect on him.
2. What are the speaker's various feelings? What do you understand from the words
   insidious and *betrays*?
3. With what specific details does the poem make the past seem real?
4. What is the subject of Lawrence's poem? How would you state its theme?

Marianne Moore (1887 – 1972)*

THE WOOD-WEASEL   1944

emerges daintily, the skunk—
don't laugh—in sylvan black and white chipmunk
regalia. The inky thing
adaptively whited with glistening
goat-fur, is wood-warden. In his   5
ermined well-cuttlefish-inked wool, he is
determination's totem. Out-
lawed? His sweet face and powerful feet go about
in chieftain's coat of Chilkat cloth.
He is his own protection from the moth,   10

noble little warrior. That
otter-skin on it, the living pole-cat,
smothers anything that stings. Well,—
this same weasel's playful and his weasel
associates are too. Only   15
Wood-weasels shall associate with me.

THE WOOD-WEASEL. 9 *Chilkat cloth:* Fine cloth made by the Chilkats, a Native American people
of southeastern Alaska.

Questions

1. What traits and features does Marianne Moore find in her subject to admire?
2. In what ways does the language of "The Wood-Weasel" differ from most prose you've
   read lately? (Suggestion: read the poem aloud.)
3. The poet uses three different names for the same animal: *wood-weasel, skunk,* and
   pole-cat. What possible reasons might she have for preferring the first?
4. "To hell with people—I'll take skunks." How accurate would that be as a statement
   of the poem's theme?

Narrative Poetry

Although a lyric sometimes relates an incident, or like "Piano" draws a scene, it does not usually relate a series of events. That happens in a **narrative poem,** one whose main purpose is to tell a story.

In Western literature, narrative poetry dates back to the Babylonian epic of Gilgamesh (composed before 2000 B.C.) and Homer's epic *Iliad* and *Odyssey* (composed before 700 B.C.). It may well have originated much earlier. In England and Scotland, storytelling poems have long been popular; in the late Middle Ages, ballads—or storytelling songs—circulated widely. Some, like "Sir Patrick Spence" and "Bonny Barbara Allan," survive in our day, and folksingers sometimes perform them.

Evidently the art of narrative poetry invites the skills of a writer of fiction: the ability to draw characters and settings briefly, to engage attention, to shape a plot. Needless to say, it calls for all the skills of a poet besides. Here are two narrative poems: one medieval, one modern. How would you paraphrase the stories they tell? How do they hold your attention to their stories?

Anonymous (traditional Scottish ballad)

Sir Patrick Spence

The king sits in Dumferling toune,
    Drinking the blude-reid wine:
"O whar will I get guid sailor
    To sail this schip of mine?"

Up and spak an eldern knicht,   5
    Sat at the kings richt kne:
"Sir Patrick Spence is the best sailor
    That sails upon the se."

The king has written a braid letter,
    And signed it wi' his hand,   10
And sent it to Sir Patrick Spence,
    Was walking on the sand.

The first line that Sir Patrick red,
    A loud lauch lauchèd he;
The next line that Sir Patrick red,   15
    The teir blinded his ee.

"O wha° is this has don this deid,   *who*
    This ill deid don to me,
To send me out this time o' the yeir,
    To sail upon the se!   20

"Mak haste, mak haste, my mirry men all,
   Our guid schip sails the morne."
"O say na sae°, my master deir,   *so*
   For I feir a deadlie storme.

"Late late yestreen I saw the new moone,   25
   Wi' the auld moone in hir arme,
And I feir, I feir, my deir master,
   That we will cum to harme."

O our Scots nobles wer richt laith°   *loath*
   To weet° their cork-heild schoone°,   *wet; shoes* 30
Bot lang owre° a' the play wer playd,   *before*
   Their hats they swam aboone°.   *above (their heads)*

O lang, lang may their ladies sit,
   Wi' their fans into their hand,
Or ere° they se Sir Patrick Spence   *long before* 35
   Cum sailing to the land.

O lang, lang may the ladies stand,
   Wi' their gold kems° in their hair,   *combs*
Waiting for their ain° deir lords,   *own*
   For they'll se thame na mair.   40

Haf owre°, haf owre to Aberdour,   *halfway over*
   It's fiftie fadom deip,
And thair lies guid Sir Patrick Spence,
   Wi' the Scots lords at his feit.

SIR PATRICK SPENCE. 9 *braid:* Broad, but broad in what sense? Among guesses are *plain-spoken,*
official, and *on wide paper.*

QUESTIONS

1. That the king drinks "blood-red wine" (line 2)—what meaning do you find in that
   detail? What does it hint, or foreshadow?
2. What do you make of this king and his motives for sending Spence and the Scots
   lords out into an impending storm? Is he a fool, is he cruel and inconsiderate, is he
   deliberately trying to drown Sir Patrick and his crew, or can't we possibly know? Let
   your answer depend on the poem alone, not on anything you read into it.
3. Comment on this ballad's methods of storytelling. Is the story told too briefly for us
   to care what happens to Spence and his men, or does the poet by any means make
   us feel compassion for them? Do you resent the lack of a detailed account of the
   shipwreck?
4. Lines 25–28—the new moon with the old moon in her arm—has been much admired
   as poetry. What does this stanza contribute to the story as well?

Robert Frost (1874 – 1963)*

"Out, Out—"   1916

The buzz-saw snarled and rattled in the yard
And made dust and dropped stove-length sticks of wood,
Sweet-scented stuff when the breeze drew across it.
And from there those that lifted eyes could count
Five mountain ranges one behind the other   5
Under the sunset far into Vermont.
And the saw snarled and rattled, snarled and rattled,
As it ran light, or had to bear a load.
And nothing happened: day was all but done.
Call it a day, I wish they might have said   10
To please the boy by giving him the half hour
That a boy counts so much when saved from work.
His sister stood beside them in her apron
To tell them "Supper." At the word, the saw,
As if to prove saws knew what supper meant,   15
Leaped out at the boy's hand, or seemed to leap—
He must have given the hand. However it was,
Neither refused the meeting. But the hand!
The boy's first outcry was a rueful laugh,
As he swung toward them holding up the hand   20
Half in appeal, but half as if to keep
The life from spilling. Then the boy saw all—
Since he was old enough to know, big boy
Doing a man's work, though a child at heart—
He saw all spoiled. "Don't let him cut my hand off—   25
The doctor, when he comes. Don't let him, sister!"
So. But the hand was gone already.
The doctor put him in the dark of ether.
He lay and puffed his lips out with his breath.
And then—the watcher at his pulse took fright.   30
No one believed. They listened at his heart.
Little—less—nothing!—and that ended it.
No more to build on there. And they, since they
Were not the one dead, turned to their affairs.

"Out, Out—" The title of this poem echoes the words of Shakespeare's Macbeth on receiving news that his queen is dead: "Out, out, brief candle! / Life's but a walking shadow, a poor player / That struts and frets his hour upon the stage / And then is heard no more. It is a tale / Told by an idiot, full of sound and fury, / Signifying nothing" (Macbeth V, v, 23–28).

QUESTIONS

1. How does Frost make the buzz-saw appear sinister? How does he make it seem, in another way, like a friend?

2. What do you make of the people who surround the boy—the "they" of the poem? Who might they be? Do they seem to you concerned and compassionate, cruel, indifferent, or what?
3. What does Frost's reference to *Macbeth* contribute to your understanding of "Out, Out—"? How would you state the theme of Frost's poem?
4. Set this poem side by side with "Sir Patrick Spence." How does "Out, Out—" resemble that medieval folk ballad in subject, or differ from it? How is Frost's poem similar or different in its way of telling a story?

Today, lyrics in the English language seem more plentiful than other kinds of poetry. Long narrative poems still appear, but have a far smaller audience than Henry Wadsworth Longfellow's *Evangeline* and Alfred, Lord Tennyson's *Idylls of the King* enjoyed in the nineteenth century.

Also more fashionable in former times was a third variety of poetry, **didactic poetry:** that apparently written to state a message or teach a body of knowledge. In a lyric, a speaker may express sadness; in a didactic poem, he or she may explain that sadness is inherent in life. Poems that impart a body of knowledge, like Ovid's *Art of Love* and Lucretius's *On the Nature of Things,* are didactic. Such instructive poetry was favored especially by classical Latin poets and by English poets of the eighteenth century. In *The Fleece* (1757), John Dyer celebrated the British woolen industry and included practical advice on raising sheep:

> In cold stiff soils the bleaters oft complain
> Of gouty ails, by shepherds termed the halt:
> Those let the neighboring fold or ready crook
> Detain, and pour into their cloven feet
> Corrosive drugs, deep-searching arsenic,
> Dry alum, verdegris, or vitriol keen.

One might agree with Dr. Johnson's comment on Dyer's effort: "The subject, Sir, cannot be made poetical." But it may be argued that the subject of didactic poetry does not make it any less poetical. Good poems, it seems, can be written about anything under the sun. In a splendid poem, Robert Lowell tells of an encounter with a garbage-eating skunk, while in another fine poem, James Merrill shows us a woman dissecting live turtles in a laboratory. Like Dyer, John Milton also described sick sheep in "Lycidas," a poem few readers have thought unpoetic:

> The hungry sheep look up, and are not fed,
> But, swoll'n with wind and the rank mist they draw,
> Rot inwardly, and foul contagion spread . . .

What makes Milton's lines better poetry than Dyer's is, among other things, a difference in attitude. Sick sheep to Dyer mean the loss of a few shillings and pence; to Milton, whose sheep stand for English Christendom, they mean a moral catastrophe.

SUGGESTION FOR WRITING

Write a concise, accurate paraphrase of a poem from the Anthology: Poetry (pages 277–406). Your instructor may wish to suggest a poem or poems. Although your paraphrase should take in the entire poem, it need not mention everything. Just try to include the points that seem most vital and try to state the poem's main thought, or *theme*. Be ready to share your paraphrase with the rest of the class and to compare it with other paraphrases of the same poem. You may then be able to test yourself as a reader of poetry. What in the poem whizzed by you that other students noticed? What did you discover that others ignored?

2 Listening to a Voice

TONE

In late-show Westerns, when one hombre taunts another, it is customary for the second to drawl, "Smile when you say that, pardner" or "Mister, I don't like your tone of voice." Sometimes in reading a poem, although we can neither see a face nor hear a voice, we can infer the poet's attitude from other evidence.

Like tone of voice, **tone** in literature often conveys an attitude toward the person addressed. Like the manner of a person, the manner of a poem may be friendly or belligerent toward its reader, condescending or respectful. Again like tone of voice, the tone of a poem may tell us how the speaker feels about himself or herself: cocksure or humble, sad or glad. But usually when we ask, "What is the tone of a poem?" we mean, "What attitude does the poet take toward a theme or a subject?" Is the poet being affectionate, hostile, earnest, playful, sarcastic, or what? We may never be able to know, of course, the poet's personal feelings. All we need know is how to feel when we read the poem.

Strictly speaking, tone isn't an attitude; it is whatever in the poem makes an attitude clear to us: the choice of certain words instead of others, the picking out of certain details. In Housman's "Loveliest of trees," for example, the poet communicates his admiration for a cherry tree's beauty by singling out for attention its white blossoms; had he wanted to show his dislike for the tree, he might have concentrated on its broken branches, birdlime, or snails. Rightly to perceive the tone of a poem, we need to read the poem carefully, paying attention to whatever suggestions we find in it.

Theodore Roethke (1908 – 1963)*

My Papa's Waltz   1948

The whiskey on your breath
Could make a small boy dizzy;
But I hung on like death:
Such waltzing was not easy.

We romped until the pans   5
Slid from the kitchen shelf;
My mother's countenance
Could not unfrown itself.

The hand that held my wrist
Was battered on one knuckle;   10
At every step you missed
My right ear scraped a buckle.

You beat time on my head
With a palm caked hard by dirt,
Then waltzed me off to bed   15
Still clinging to your shirt.

What is the tone of this poem? Most readers find the speaker's attitude toward his father affectionate and take this recollection of childhood to be a happy one. But at least one reader, concentrating on certain details, once wrote: "Roethke expresses his resentment for his father, a drunken brute with dirty hands and a whiskey breath who carelessly hurt the child's ear and manhandled him." Although this reader accurately noticed some of the events in the poem and perceived that in the son's hanging on to the father "like death" there is something desperate, he missed the tone of the poem and so misunderstood it altogether. Among other things, this reader didn't notice the rollicking rhythms of the poem; the playfulness of a rime like *dizzy* and *easy*; the joyful suggestions of the words *waltz, waltzing,* and *romped.* Probably the reader didn't stop to visualize this scene in all its comedy, with kitchen pans falling and the father happily using his son's head for a drum. Nor did he stop to feel the suggestions in the last line, with the boy *still clinging* with persistent love.

Such a poem, though it includes lifelike details that aren't pretty, has a tone relatively easy to recognize. So does **satiric poetry,** a kind of comic poetry that generally conveys a message. Usually its tone is one of detached amusement, withering contempt, and implied superiority. In a satiric poem, the poet ridicules some person or persons (or perhaps some kind of human behavior), examining the victim by the light of certain principles and implying that the reader, too, ought to feel contempt for the victim.

Countee Cullen (1903 – 1946)

FOR A LADY I KNOW   1925

She even thinks that up in heaven
  Her class lies late and snores,
While poor black cherubs rise at seven
  To do celestial chores.

QUESTIONS
1. What is Cullen's message?
2. How would you characterize the tone of this poem? Wrathful? Amused?

    In some poems the poet's attitude may be plain enough; while in other poems attitudes may be so mingled that it is hard to describe them tersely without doing injustice to the poem. Does Andrew Marvell in "To His Coy Mistress" (page 350) take a serious or playful attitude toward the fact that he and his lady are destined to be food for worms? No one-word answer will suffice. And what of T. S. Eliot's "Love Song of J. Alfred Prufrock" (page 309)? In his attitude toward his redemption-seeking hero who wades with trousers rolled, Eliot is seriously funny. Such a mingled tone may be seen in the following poem by the wife of a governor of the Massachusetts Bay Colony and the earliest American poet of note. Anne Bradstreet's first book, *The Tenth Muse Lately Sprung Up in America* (1650), had been published in England without her consent. She wrote these lines to preface a second edition:

Anne Bradstreet (1612? – 1672)

THE AUTHOR TO HER BOOK   1678

Thou ill-formed offspring of my feeble brain,
Who after birth did'st by my side remain,
Till snatched from thence by friends, less wise than true,
Who thee abroad exposed to public view;
Made thee in rags, halting, to the press to trudge,   5
Where errors were not lessened, all may judge.
At thy return my blushing was not small,
My rambling brat (in print) should mother call;
I cast thee by as one unfit for light,
Thy visage was so irksome in my sight;   10
Yet being mine own, at length affection would
Thy blemishes amend, if so I could:
I washed thy face, but more defects I saw,
And rubbing off a spot, still made a flaw.
I stretched thy joints to make thee even feet,   15
Yet still thou run'st more hobbling than is meet;

In better dress to trim thee was my mind,
But nought save homespun cloth in the house I find.
In this array, 'mongst vulgars may'st thou roam;
In critics' hands beware thou dost not come;   20
And take thy way where yet thou are not known.
If for thy Father asked, say thou had'st none;
And for thy Mother, she alas is poor,
Which caused her thus to send thee out of door.

In the author's comparison of her book to an illegitimate ragamuffin, we may
be struck by the details of scrubbing and dressing a child: details that might
well occur to a mother who had scrubbed and dressed many. As she might feel
toward such a child, so she feels toward her book. She starts by deploring it
but, as the poem goes on, cannot deny it her affection. Humor enters (as in the
pun in line 15). She must dress the creature in *homespun cloth,* something both
crude and serviceable. By the end of her poem, Bradstreet seems to regard her
book-child with tenderness, amusement, and a certain indulgent awareness of
its faults. To read this poem is to sense its mingling of several attitudes.
Simultaneously, a poet can be merry and in earnest.

Walt Whitman (1819 – 1892)*

TO A LOCOMOTIVE IN WINTER   1881

Thee for my recitative,
Thee in the driving storm even as now, the snow, the winter-day
    declining,
Thee in thy panoply°, thy measur'd dual throbbing and thy   *suit of*
    beat convulsive,   *armor*
Thy black cylindric body, golden brass and silvery steel,
Thy ponderous side-bars, parallel and connecting rods, gyrating,
    shuttling at thy sides,   5
Thy metrical, now swelling pant and roar, now tapering in the
    distance,
Thy great protruding head-light fix'd in front,
Thy long, pale, floating vapor-pennants, tinged with delicate purple,
The dense and murky clouds out-belching from thy smoke-stack,
Thy knitted frame, thy springs and valves, the tremulous twinkle of
    thy wheels,   10
Thy train of cars behind, obedient, merrily following,
Through gale or calm, now swift, now slack, yet steadily careering;
Type of the modern — emblem of motion and power — pulse of the
    continent,
For once come serve the Muse and merge in verse, even as here I see
    thee,

With storm and buffeting gusts of wind and falling snow,   15
By day thy warning ringing bell to sound its notes,
By night thy silent signal lamps to swing.
Fierce-throated beauty!
Roll through my chant with all thy lawless music, thy swinging lamps
    at night,
Thy madly-whistled laughter, echoing, rumbling like an earthquake,
    rousing all,   20
Law of thyself complete, thine own track firmly holding,
(No sweetness debonair of tearful harp or glib piano thine,)
Thy trills of shrieks by rocks and hills return'd,
Launch'd o'er the prairies wide, across the lakes,
To the free skies unpent and glad and strong.   25

Emily Dickinson (1830 – 1886)*

I LIKE TO SEE IT LAP THE MILES   (about 1862)

I like to see it lap the Miles –
And lick the Valleys up –
And stop to feed itself at Tanks –
And then – prodigious step

Around a Pile of Mountains –   5
And supercilious peer
In Shanties – by the sides of Roads –
And then a Quarry pare

To fit its Ribs
And crawl between   10
Complaining all the while
In horrid – hooting stanza –
Then chase itself down Hill –

And neigh like Boanerges –
Then – punctual as a Star   15
Stop – docile and omnipotent
At its own stable door –

QUESTIONS

1. What differences in tone do you find between Whitman's and Dickinson's poems? Point out in each poem whatever contributes to these differences.
2. *Boanerges* in Dickinson's last stanza means "sons of thunder," a name given by Jesus to the disciples John and James (see Mark 3:17). How far should the reader work out the particulars of this comparison? Does it make the tone of the poem serious?
3. In Whitman's opening line, what is a *recitative*? What other specialized terms from the vocabulary of music and poetry does each poem contain? How do they help underscore Whitman's theme?

4. Poets and song-writers probably have regarded the locomotive with more affection than they have shown most other machines. Why do you suppose this to be? Can you think of any other poems or songs for example?
5. What do these two poems tell you about locomotives that you would not be likely to find in a technical book on railroading?
6. Are the subjects of the two poems identical? Discuss.

Langston Hughes (1902 – 1967)*

HOMECOMING   1959

I went back in the alley
And I opened up my door.
All her clothes was gone:
She wasn't home no more.

I pulled back the covers,   5
I made down the bed.
A *whole* lot of room
Was the only thing I had.

QUESTIONS

1. How does the speaker feel about this sudden disappearance? Exactly what in the poem makes his feelings clear?
2. Suppose the speaker had ranted, cried, felt sorry for himself, and discussed his anger, frustration, and grief at great length. Do you suppose a better poem might have resulted? What do you find to admire in the poem as it is?

John Milton (1608 – 1674)*

ON THE LATE MASSACRE IN PIEMONT   (1655)

Avenge, O Lord, thy slaughtered saints, whose bones
   Lie scattered on the Alpine mountains cold;
   Even them who kept thy truth so pure of old,
When all our fathers worshiped stocks and stones,
Forget not: in thy book record their groans   5
   Who were thy sheep, and in their ancient fold
   Slain by the bloody Piemontese, that rolled
Mother with infant down the rocks. Their moans
The vales redoubled to the hills, and they
   To heaven. Their martyred blood and ashes sow   10
O'er all the Italian fields, where still doth sway
   The triple Tyrant; that from these may grow
   A hundredfold, who, having learnt thy way,
Early may fly the Babylonian woe.

On the Late Massacre in Piemont. Despite hostility between Catholics and Protestants, the Waldenses, members of a Puritan sect, had been living in the Piemont, that region in northwest Italy bounded by the crests of the Alps. In 1655, ignoring a promise to observe religious liberty, troops of the Roman Catholic ruler of the Piemont put to death several members of the sect. 4 *When . . . stones:* Englishmen had been Catholics, worshiping stone and wooden statues (so Milton charges) when the Waldensian sect was founded in the twelfth century. 12 *The triple Tyrant:* The Pope, to whom is attributed authority over earth, heaven, and hell. 14 *Babylonian woe:* Destruction expected to befall the city of Babylon at the world's end as punishment for its luxury and other wickedness (see Revelation 18:1 – 24). Protestants took Babylon to mean the Church of Rome.

Question

What is Milton's attitude toward the massacre? Does he express a single feeling, or a mingling of feelings?

The Person in the Poem

The tone of a poem, we said, is like tone of voice in that both communicate feelings. Still, this comparison raises a question: When we read a poem, whose "voice" speaks to us?

"The poet's" is one possible answer; and in the case of many a poem, that answer may be right. Reading Anne Bradstreet's "The Author to Her Book," we can be reasonably sure that the poet speaks of her very own book, and of her own experiences. In order to read a poem, we seldom need to read a poet's biography; but in truth there are certain poems whose full effect depends upon our knowing at least a fact or two of the poet's life. In this poem, surely the poet refers to himself:

Trumbull Stickney (1874 – 1904)

Sir, say no more   1905

Sir, say no more,
Within me 'tis as if
The green and climbing eyesight of a cat
Crawled near my mind's poor birds.

The subject of Stickney's poem is not some nightmare or hallucination. The poem may mean more to you if you know that Stickney, who wrote it shortly before his death, had been afflicted by cancer of the brain. But the poem is not a prosaic entry in the diary of a dying man, nor is it a good poem because a dying man wrote it. Not only does it tell truth from experience, it speaks in memorable words.

Most of us can tell the difference between a person we meet in life and a person we meet in a work of art — unlike the moviegoer in the Philippines who, watching a villain in an exciting film, pulled out a revolver and peppered the screen. And yet, in reading poems, we are liable to temptation. When the poet says "I," we may want to assume that he or she, like Trumbull Stickney, is making a personal statement. But reflect: do all poems have to be personal? Here is a brief poem inscribed on the tombstone of an infant in Burial Hill cemetery, Plymouth, Massachusetts:

> Since I have been so quickly done for,
> I wonder what I was begun for.

We do not know who wrote those lines, but it is clear that the poet was not a short-lived infant writing from personal experience. In other poems, the speaker is obviously a **persona** or fictitious character: not the poet, but the poet's creation. As a grown man, William Blake, a skilled professional engraver, wrote a poem in the voice of a boy, an illiterate chimney sweeper. (The poem appears on page 36.) No law decrees that the speaker in a poem even has to be human: good poems have been uttered by clouds, pebbles, and cats. A **dramatic monologue** is a poem written as a speech made at some decisive or revealing moment. It is usually addressed by the speaker to some other character (who remains silent). Robert Browning, who developed the form, liked to put words into the mouths of characters stupider, weaker, or nastier than he: for instance, see "Soliloquy of the Spanish Cloister" (page 296), in which the speaker is an insanely proud and jealous monk.

Let's consider a poem spoken not by a poet but by a persona — in this case, a woman. The poem is a monologue, but not a dramatic monologue. (It gives us the spoken thoughts of one person, but the moment isn't particularly dramatic.)

Philip Larkin (1922 – 1985)*

WEDDING-WIND   1951

The wind blew all my wedding-day,
And my wedding-night was the night of the high wind;
And a stable door was banging, again and again,
That he must go and shut it, leaving me
Stupid in candlelight, hearing rain,   5
Seeing my face in the twisted candlestick,
Yet seeing nothing. When he came back
He said the horses were restless, and I was sad
That any man or beast that night should lack
The happiness I had.

                 Now in the day   10
All's ravelled under the sun by the wind's blowing.
He has gone to look at the floods, and I
Carry a chipped pail to the chicken-run,
Set it down, and stare. All is the wind
Hunting through clouds and forests, thrashing   15
My apron and the hanging cloths on the line.

Can it be borne, this bodying-forth by wind
Of joy my actions turn on, like a thread
Carrying beads? Shall I be let to sleep
Now this perpetual morning shares my bed?   20
Can even death dry up
These new delighted lakes, conclude
Our kneeling as cattle by all-generous waters?

QUESTIONS

1. Who is the speaker and what are her circumstances? Where does the poem take place?
2. Does the poet, in your view, exaggerate the joy of feeding chickens? What accounts
   for the intensity of the speaker's happiness?
3. How successful do you find this male poet in imagining a woman's feelings?

In a famous definition, William Wordsworth calls poetry "the spontaneous
overflow of powerful feelings . . . recollected in tranquillity."[1] But in the case
of the following poem, Wordsworth's feelings weren't all his; they didn't just
overflow spontaneously; and the process of tranquil recollection had to go on
for years.

William Wordsworth (1770 – 1850)*

I Wandered Lonely as a Cloud   1807

I wandered lonely as a cloud
    That floats on high o'er vales and hills,
When all at once I saw a crowd,
    A host, of golden daffodils,
Beside the lake, beneath the trees,   5
Fluttering and dancing in the breeze.

Continuous as the stars that shine
    And twinkle on the milky way,
They stretched in never-ending line
    Along the margin of a bay: 10
Ten thousand saw I at a glance,
Tossing their heads in sprightly dance.

The waves beside them danced; but they
    Out-did the sparkling waves in glee;
A poet could not but be gay,   15
    In such a jocund company;
I gazed — and gazed — but little thought
What wealth the show to me had brought:

[1] For a fuller text of Wordsworth's statement, see page 446.

For oft, when on my couch I lie
   In vacant or in pensive mood,
They flash upon that inward eye
   Which is the bliss of solitude;
And then my heart with pleasure fills,
And dances with the daffodils.

20

Between the first printing of the poem in 1807 and the version of 1815 given here, Wordsworth made several deliberate improvements. He changed *dancing* to *golden* in line 4, *Along* to *Beside* in line 5, *Ten thousand* to *Fluttering and* in line 6, *laughing* to *jocund* in line 16, and he added a whole stanza (the second). In fact, the writing of the poem was unspontaneous enough for Wordsworth, at a loss for lines 21 – 22, to take them from his wife Mary. It is likely that the experience of daffodil-watching was not entirely his to begin with but was derived in part from the recollections his sister Dorothy Wordsworth had set down in her journal of April 15, 1802, two years before he first drafted his poem:

> When we were in the woods beyond Gowbarrow Park we saw a few daffodils close to the water-side. We fancied that the lake had floated the seeds ashore, and that the little colony had so sprung up. But as we went along there were more and yet more; and at last, under the boughs of the trees, we saw that there was a long belt of them along the shore, about the breadth of a country turnpike road. I never saw daffodils so beautiful. They grew among the mossy stones about and about them; some rested their heads upon these stones as on a pillow for weariness; and the rest tossed and reeled and danced, and seemed as if they verily laughed with the wind, that flew upon them over the Lake; they looked so gay, ever glancing, ever changing. This wind blew directly over the Lake to them. There was here and there a little knot, and a few stragglers a few yards higher up; but they were so few as not to disturb the simplicity, unity, and life of that one busy highway.

Notice that Wordsworth's poem echoes a few of his sister's observations. Weaving poetry out of their mutual memories, Wordsworth has offered the experience as if altogether his own, made himself lonely, and left Dorothy out. The point is not that Wordsworth is a liar or a plagiarist but that, like any other good poet, he has transformed ordinary life into art. A process of interpreting, shaping, and ordering had to intervene between the experience of looking at daffodils and the finished poem.

We need not deny that a poet's experience can contribute to a poem nor that the emotion in the poem can indeed be the poet's. Still, to write a good poem one has to do more than live and feel. It seems a pity that, as Randall Jarrell has said, a cardinal may write verses worse than his youngest choirboy's. But writing poetry takes skill and imagination — qualities that extensive travel and wide experience do not necessarily give. For much of her life, Emily Dickinson seldom strayed from her family's house and grounds in Amherst,

Massachusetts; yet her rimed lifestudies of a snake, a bee, and a hummingbird contain more poetry than we find in any firsthand description (so far) of the surface of the moon.

James Stephens (1882 – 1950)*

A GLASS OF BEER   1918

The lanky hank of a she in the inn over there
Nearly killed me for asking the loan of a glass of beer;
May the devil grip the whey-faced slut by the hair,
And beat bad manners out of her skin for a year.

That parboiled ape, with the toughest jaw you will see   5
On virtue's path, and a voice that would rasp the dead,
Came roaring and raging the minute she looked at me,
And threw me out of the house on the back of my head!

If I asked her master he'd give me a cask a day;
But she, with the beer at hand, not a gill° would arrange!   *quarter-pint* 10
May she marry a ghost and bear him a kitten, and may
The High King of Glory permit her to get the mange.

QUESTIONS

1. Who do you take to be the speaker? Is it the poet? The speaker may be angry, but what is the tone of this poem?
2. Would you agree with a commentator who said, "To berate anyone in truly memorable language is practically a lost art in America"? How well does the speaker (an Irishman) succeed? Which of his epithets and curses strike you as particularly imaginative?

Mary Elizabeth Coleridge (1861 – 1907)

WE NEVER SAID FAREWELL   1897

We never said farewell, nor even looked
    Our last upon each other, for no sign
Was made when we the linkèd chain unhooked
    And broke the level line.

And here we dwell together, side by side,   5
    Our places fixed for life upon the chart.
Two islands that the roaring seas divide
    Are not more far apart.

1. In "We never said farewell," who do you suppose to be the *we*? How do you know? Are both persons speaking, or just one of them?
2. How would you state this poem's theme?

Paul Zimmer (b. 1934)

THE DAY ZIMMER LOST RELIGION   1976

The first Sunday I missed Mass on purpose
I waited all day for Christ to climb down
Like a wiry flyweight from the cross and
Club me on my irreverent teeth, to wade into
My blasphemous gut and drop me like a   5
Red hot thurible°, the devil roaring in   *vessel for incense*
Reserved seats until he got the hiccups.

It was a long cold way from the old days
When cassocked and surpliced I mumbled Latin
At the old priest and rang his obscure bell.   10
A long way from the dirty wind that blew
The soot like venial sins across the school yard
Where God reigned as a threatening,
One-eyed triangle high in the fleecy sky.

The first Sunday I missed Mass on purpose   15
I waited all day for Christ to climb down
Like the playground bully, the cuts and mice
Upon his face agleam, and pound me
Till my irreligious tongue hung out.
But of course He never came, knowing that   20
I was grown up and ready for Him now.

QUESTIONS

1. Who is the person in this poem? The mature poet? The poet as a child? Some fictitious character?
2. What do you understand to be the speaker's attitude toward religion at the present moment?

EXPERIMENT: *Reading with and without Biography*

Read the following poem and state what you understand from it. Then consider the circumstances in which it probably came to be written. (Some information is offered in a note on page 36.) Does the meaning of the poem change? To what extent does an appreciation of the poem need the support of biography?

William Carlos Williams (1883 – 1963)*

THE RED WHEELBARROW   1923

so much depends
upon

a red wheel
barrow

glazed with rain   5
water

beside the white
chickens.

IRONY

To see a distinction between the poet and the words of a fictitious character — between Philip Larkin and "Wedding-Wind" — is to be aware of **irony:**
a manner of speaking that implies a discrepancy. If the mask says one thing and
we sense that the writer is in fact saying something else, the writer has adopted
an **ironic point of view.** No finer illustration exists in English than Jonathan
Swift's "A Modest Proposal," an essay in which Swift speaks as an earnest,
humorless citizen who sets forth his reasonable plan to aid the Irish poor. The
plan is so monstrous no sane reader can assent to it: the poor are to sell their
children as meat for the tables of their landlords. From behind his falseface,
Swift is actually recommending not cannibalism but love and Christian charity.

A poem is often made complicated and more interesting by another kind
of irony. **Verbal irony** occurs whenever words say one thing but mean something else, usually the opposite. The word *love* means *hate* here: "I just *love* to
stay home and do my hair on a Saturday night!" If the verbal irony is conspicu-
ously bitter, heavy-handed, and mocking, it is **sarcasm:** "Oh, he's the biggest
spender in the world, all right!" (The sarcasm, if that statement were spoken,
would be underscored by the speaker's tone of voice.) A famous instance of
sarcasm is Mark Antony's line in his oration over the body of slain Julius
Caesar: "Brutus is an honorable man." Antony repeats this line until the
enraged populace begins shouting exactly what he means to call Brutus and the
other conspirators: traitors, villains, murderers. We had best be alert for irony
on the printed page, for if we miss it, our interpretations of a poem may go wild.

Robert Creeley (b. 1926)

OH NO   1959

If you wander far enough
you will come to it
and when you get there
they will give you a place to sit

for yourself only, in a nice chair,
and all your friends will be there
with smiles on their faces
and they will likewise all have places.

This poem is rich in verbal irony. The title helps point out that between the speaker's words and attitude lie deep differences. In line 2, what is *it?* Old age? The wandering suggests a conventional metaphor: the journey of life. Is *it* literally a rest home for "senior citizens," or perhaps some naïve popular concept of heaven (such as we meet in comic strips: harps, angels with hoops for halos) in which the saved all sit around in a ring, smugly congratulating one another? We can't be sure, but the speaker's attitude toward this final sitting-place is definite. It is a place for the selfish, as we infer from the phrase *for yourself only.* And *smiles on their faces* may hint that the smiles are unchanging and forced. There is a difference between saying "They had smiles on their faces" and "They smiled": the latter suggests that the smiles came from within. The word *nice* is to be regarded with distrust. If we see through this speaker, as Creeley implies we can do, we realize that, while pretending to be sweet-talking us into a seat, actually he is revealing the horror of a little hell. And the title is the poet's reaction to it (or the speaker's unironic, straightforward one): "Oh no! Not *that!*"

Dramatic irony, like verbal irony, contains an element of contrast, but it usually refers to a situation in a play wherein a character, whose knowledge is limited, says, does, or encounters something of greater significance than he or she knows. We, the spectators, realize the meaning of this speech or action, for the playwright has afforded us superior knowledge. In Sophocles' *King Oedipus,* when Oedipus vows to punish whoever has brought down a plague upon the city of Thebes, we know — as he does not — that the man he would punish is himself. (Referring to such a situation that precedes the downfall of a hero in a tragedy, some critics speak of **tragic irony** instead of dramatic irony.) Superior knowledge can be enjoyed not only by spectators in a theater but by readers of poetry as well. In *Paradise Lost,* we know in advance that Adam will fall into temptation, and we recognize his overconfidence when he neglects a warning. The situation of Oedipus contains also **cosmic irony,** or **irony of fate:** some Fate with a grim sense of humor seems cruelly to trick a human being. Cosmic irony clearly exists in poems in which fate or the Fates are personified and seen as hostile, as in Thomas Hardy's "The Convergence of the Twain" (page 320); and it may be said to occur too in Robinson's "Richard Cory" (page 114). Evidently it is a twist of fate for the most envied man in town to kill himself.

To sum up: the effect of irony depends upon the reader's noticing some incongruity or discrepancy between two things. In *verbal irony,* there is a contrast between the speaker's words and meaning; in an *ironic point of view,* between the writer's attitude and what is spoken by a fictitious character; in *dramatic irony,* between the limited knowledge of a character and the fuller knowledge of the reader or spectator; in *cosmic irony,* between a character's aspiration and the treatment he or she receives at the hands of Fate. Although in the work of an inept poet irony can be crude and obvious sarcasm, it is invaluable to a poet of more complicated mind, who imagines more than one perspective.

W. H. Auden (1907 – 1973)*

THE UNKNOWN CITIZEN   1940

(To JS/07/M/378
*This Marble Monument
Is Erected by the State)*

He was found by the Bureau of Statistics to be
One against whom there was no official complaint,
And all the reports on his conduct agree
That, in the modern sense of an old-fashioned word, he was a saint,
For in everything he did he served the Greater Community.   5
Except for the War till the day he retired
He worked in a factory and never got fired,
But satisfied his employers, Fudge Motors Inc.
Yet he wasn't a scab or odd in his views,
For his Union reports that he paid his dues,   10
(Our report on his Union shows it was sound)
And our Social Psychology workers found
That he was popular with his mates and liked a drink.
The Press are convinced that he bought a paper every day
And that his reactions to advertisements were normal in every way.   15
Policies taken out in his name prove that he was fully insured,
And his Health-card shows he was once in hospital but left it cured.
Both Producers Research and High-Grade Living declare
He was fully sensible to the advantages of the Installment Plan
And had everything necessary to the Modern Man,   20
A phonograph, a radio, a car and a frigidaire.
Our researchers into Public Opinion are content
That he held the proper opinions for the time of year;
When there was peace, he was for peace; when there was war, he
     went.
He was married and added five children to the population,   25
Which our Eugenist says was the right number for a parent of his
     generation,
And our teachers report that he never interfered with their
     education.
Was he free? Was he happy? The question is absurd:
Had anything been wrong, we should certainly have heard.

Questions

1. Read the three-line epitaph at the beginning of the poem as carefully as you read what follows. How does the epitaph help establish the voice by which the rest of the poem is spoken?
2. Who is speaking?
3. What ironic discrepancies do you find between the speaker's attitude toward the subject and that of the poet himself? By what is the poet's attitude made clear?
4. In the phrase "The Unknown Soldier" (of which "The Unknown Citizen" reminds us), what does the word *unknown* mean? What does it mean in the title of Auden's poem?
5. What tendencies in our civilization does Auden satirize?
6. How would you expect the speaker to define a Modern Man, if a phonograph, a radio, a car, and a refrigerator are "everything" a Modern Man needs?

Herbert Scott (b. 1931)

THE GROCER'S CHILDREN   1976

The grocer's children
eat day-old bread,
moldy cakes and cheese,
soft black bananas
on stale shredded wheat,   5
weeviled rice, their plates
heaped high with wilted
greens, bruised fruit,
surprise treats
from unlabeled cans,   10
tainted meat.
The grocer's children
never go hungry.

Questions

1. At what point, in reading "The Grocer's Children," do you realize that the poem is ironic?
2. Does the speaker reveal his own attitude toward what he reports? If so, how does he make it clear to us?

John Betjeman (1906 – 1984)

IN WESTMINSTER ABBEY   1940

Let me take this other glove off
    As the *vox humana* swells,
And the beauteous fields of Eden
    Bask beneath the Abbey bells.
Here, where England's statesmen lie,   5
Listen to a lady's cry.

Gracious Lord, oh bomb the Germans.
    Spare their women for Thy Sake,
And if that is not too easy
    We will pardon Thy Mistake.   10
But, gracious Lord, whate'er shall be,
Don't let anyone bomb me.

Keep our Empire undismembered,
    Guide our Forces by Thy Hand,
Gallant blacks from far Jamaica,   15
    Honduras and Togoland;
Protect them Lord in all their fights,
And, even more, protect the whites.

Think of what our Nation stands for:
    Books from Boots' and country lanes,   20
Free speech, free passes, class distinction,
    Democracy and proper drains.
Lord, put beneath Thy special care
One-eighty-nine Cadogan Square.

Although dear Lord I am a sinner,   25
    I have done no major crime;
Now I'll come to Evening Service
    Whensoever I have the time.
So, Lord, reserve for me a crown,
And do not let my shares° go down.   *stocks* 30

I will labor for Thy Kingdom,
    Help our lads to win the war,
Send white feathers to the cowards,
    Join the Women's Army Corps,
Then wash the Steps around Thy Throne   35
In the Eternal Safety Zone.

Now I feel a little better,
    What a treat to hear Thy Word,
Where the bones of leading statesmen
    Have so often been interred.   40
And now, dear Lord, I cannot wait
Because I have a luncheon date.

In Westminster Abbey. First printed during World War II. 2 *vox humana:* an organ stop that makes tones similar to those of the human voice. 20 *Boots':* a chain of pharmacies whose branches had lending libraries.

Questions

1. Who is the speaker? What do we know about her life style? About her prejudices?
2. Point out some of the places in which she contradicts herself.
3. How would you describe the speaker's attitude toward religion?
4. Through the medium of irony, what positive points do you believe Betjeman makes?

Sarah N. Cleghorn (1876 – 1959)

THE GOLF LINKS   1917

The golf links lie so near the mill
   That almost every day
The laboring children can look out
   And see the men at play.

QUESTIONS

1. Is this brief poem satiric? Does it contain any verbal irony? Is the poet making a matter-of-fact statement in words that mean just what they say?
2. What other kind of irony is present in the poem?
3. Sarah N. Cleghorn's poem dates from before the enactment of legislation against child labor. Is it still a good poem, or is it hopelessly dated?
4. How would you state its theme?
5. Would you call this poem lyric, narrative, or didactic?

EXERCISE: *Detecting Irony*

Point out the kinds of irony that occur in the following poem.

Thomas Hardy (1840 – 1928)*

THE WORKBOX   1914

"See, here's the workbox, little wife,
   That I made of polished oak."
He was a joiner°, of village life;   *carpenter*
   She came of borough folk.

He holds the present up to her   5
   As with a smile she nears
And answers to the profferer,
   " 'Twill last all my sewing years!"

"I warrant it will. And longer too.
   'Tis a scantling that I got   10
Off poor John Wayward's coffin, who
   Died of they knew not what.

"The shingled pattern that seems to cease
   Against your box's rim
Continues right on in the piece   15
   That's underground with him.

"And while I worked it made me think
   Of timber's varied doom:
One inch where people eat and drink,
   The next inch in a tomb.   20

"But why do you look so white, my dear,
	And turn aside your face?
You knew not that good lad, I fear,
	Though he came from your native place?"

"How could I know that good young man,			25
	Though he came from my native town,
When he must have left far earlier than
	I was a woman grown?"

"Ah, no. I should have understood!
	It shocked you that I gave				30
To you one end of a piece of wood
	Whose other is in a grave?"

"Don't, dear, despise my intellect,
	Mere accidental things
Of that sort never have effect				35
	On my imaginings."

Yet still her lips were limp and wan,
	Her face still held aside,
As if she had known not only John,
	But known of what he died.				40

Robert Burns (1759 – 1796)*

## THE TOAD-EATER				(1783?)

What of earls with whom you have supped,
	And of dukes that you dined with yestreen°?			*last night*
Lord! an insect's an insect at most,
	Though it crawl on the curls of a Queen.

QUESTIONS

1. A toad-eater was originally (according to the Oxford English Dictionary) "the attendant of a charlatan, employed to eat or pretend to eat toads (held to be poisonous)
to enable his master to exhibit his skill in expelling poison." Later, *toad-eater* was
shortened to *toady*. What does that word mean today? (If you don't know, infer what
it means from Burns's poem. The meaning hasn't changed.)
2. What ironic contrast does Burns draw in the last two lines?
3. How would you describe this speaker's tone of voice?

FOR REVIEW AND FURTHER STUDY

EXERCISE: *Telling Tone*

Here are two radically different poems on a similar subject. Try stating the theme of each
poem in your own words. How is tone (the speaker's attitude) different in the two poems?

Richard Lovelace (1618 – 1658)

To Lucasta   1649

On Going to the Wars

Tell me not, Sweet, I am unkind
   That from the nunnery
Of thy chaste breast and quiet mind,
   To war and arms I fly.

True, a new mistress now I chase,   5
   The first foe in the field;
And with a stronger faith embrace
   A sword, a horse, a shield.

Yet this inconstancy is such
   As you too shall adore;   10
I could not love thee, Dear, so much,
   Loved I not Honor more.

Wilfred Owen (1893 – 1918)*

Dulce et Decorum Est   1920

Bent double, like old beggars under sacks,
Knock-kneed, coughing like hags, we cursed through sludge,
Till on the haunting flares we turned our backs
And towards our distant rest began to trudge.
Men marched asleep. Many had lost their boots   5
But limped on, blood-shod. All went lame; all blind;
Drunk with fatigue; deaf even to the hoots
Of tired, outstripped Five-Nines° that dropped behind.   *gas-shells*

Gas! Gas! Quick, boys! — An ecstasy of fumbling,
Fitting the clumsy helmets just in time;   10
But someone still was yelling out and stumbling
And flound'ring like a man in fire or lime . . .
Dim, through the misty panes and thick green light,
As under a green sea, I saw him drowning.
In all my dreams, before my helpless sight,   15
He plunges at me, guttering, choking, drowning.

If in some smothering dreams you too could pace
Behind the wagon that we flung him in,
And watch the white eyes writhing in his face,
His hanging face, like a devil's sick of sin;   20

If you could hear, at every jolt, the blood
Come gargling from the froth-corrupted lungs,
Obscene as cancer, bitter as the cud
Of vile, incurable sores on innocent tongues, —
My friend, you would not tell with such high zest   25
To children ardent for some desperate glory,
The old Lie: Dulce et decorum est
Pro patria mori.

DULCE ET DECORUM EST. Owen was a British infantry officer in World War I. 17 *you too:* Some manuscript versions of this poem carry the dedication "To Jessie Pope" (a writer of patriotic verse) or "To a certain Poetess." 27 – 28 *Dulce et . . . mori:* a quotation from the Latin poet Horace, "It is sweet and fitting to die for one's country."

Bettie Sellers (b. 1926)

IN THE COUNSELOR'S WAITING ROOM   1981

The terra cotta girl
with the big flat farm feet
traces furrows in the rug
with her toes,
reads an existentialist paperback   5
from psychology class,
finds no ease there
from the guilt of loving
the quiet girl down the hall.
Their home soil has seen to this visit,   10
their Baptist mothers,
who weep for the waste of sturdy hips
ripe for grandchildren.

IN THE COUNSELOR'S WAITING ROOM. The poet is a teacher and administrator at a small college in Georgia. 1 *terra cotta:* fired clay, light brownish orange in hue. 5 *existentialist:* of the twentieth-century school of philosophy that holds (among other tenets) that an individual is alone and isolated, free and yet responsible, and ordinarily subject to guilt, anxiety, and dread.

QUESTIONS

1. For what sort of counseling is this girl waiting?
2. Point out all the words that refer to plowing, to clay and earth. Why are the mothers called "home soil"? How do these references to earth relate to the idea in the last line?
3. What irony inheres in this situation?
4. Does the poet appear to sympathize with the girls? With their weeping mothers? In what details does this poem hint at any of the poet's own attitude or attitudes?

Jonathan Swift (1667 – 1745)*

On Stella's Birthday   (1718 – 1719)

Stella this day is thirty-four
(We shan't dispute a year or more) —
However, Stella, be not troubled,
Although thy size and years are doubled,
Since first I saw thee at sixteen,   5
The brightest virgin on the green,
So little is thy form declined,
Made up so largely in thy mind.
Oh, would it please the gods, to split
Thy beauty, size, and years, and wit,   10
No age could furnish out a pair
Of nymphs so graceful, wise, and fair,
With half the luster of your eyes,
With half your wit, your years, and size.
And then, before it grew too late,   15
How should I beg of gentle Fate
(That either nymph might have her swain)
To split my worship too in twain.

On Stella's Birthday. For many years Swift made an annual birthday gift of a poem to his close friend Mrs. Esther Johnson, the degree of whose nearness to the proud and lonely Swift remains an enigma to biographers. 18 *my worship*: as Dean of St. Patrick's in Dublin, Swift was addressed as "Your Worship."

Questions

1. If you were Stella, would you be amused or insulted by the poet's references to your *size?*
2. According to Swift in lines 7 – 8, what has compensated Stella for what the years have taken away?
3. Comment on the last four lines. Does Swift exempt himself from growing old?
4. How would you describe the tone of this poem? Offensive (like the speaker's complaints in "A Glass of Beer")? Playfully tender? Sad over Stella's growing fat and old?

Robert Flanagan (b. 1941)

Reply to an Eviction Notice   1978

My mother and father camped in such apartments
in their time, landlord, promoter
of cramped endurances,
your rightful inheritance. Your father
purchased shrewdly and practiced ungiving   5
well. Mine did not.

So my sweaty bursts of living
are managed in rooms
gauged like parking meters, narrow as coin slots,
while from the landscaped, architect-designed   10
vantage of your home,
the town lies before you like a Monopoly board.
Ownership is your reward
and punishment; movement mine.

QUESTIONS

1. What does the poem tell us about this anonymous landlord? What is the speaker's attitude toward him or her?
2. Paraphrase, in your own words, the last two lines.

John Ciardi (1916 – 1986)

IN PLACE OF A CURSE   1959

At the next vacancy for God, if I am elected,
I shall forgive last the delicately wounded
who, having been slugged no harder than anyone else,
never got up again, neither to fight back,
nor to finger their jaws in painful admiration.   5

They who are wholly broken, and they in whom
mercy is understanding, I shall embrace at once
and lead to pillows in heaven. But they who are
the meek by trade, baiting the best of their betters
with the extortions of a mock-helplessness   10

I shall take last to love, and never wholly.
Let them all into Heaven—I abolish Hell—
but let it be read over them as they enter:
"Beware the calculations of the meek, who gambled nothing,
gave nothing, and could never receive enough."   15

QUESTIONS

1. What kinds of people does the speaker dislike? Whom does he feel compassion for?
2. How would you describe the tone of this poem? How can you tell it isn't entirely serious?

William Blake (1757 – 1827)*

The Chimney Sweeper   1789

When my mother died I was very young,
And my father sold me while yet my tongue
Could scarcely cry " 'weep! 'weep! 'weep! 'weep!"
So your chimneys I sweep, and in soot I sleep.

There's little Tom Dacre, who cried when his head,   5
That curled like a lamb's back, was shaved: so I said
"Hush, Tom! never mind it, for when your head's bare
You know that the soot cannot spoil your white hair."

And so he was quiet, and that very night,
As Tom was a-sleeping, he had such a sight!   10
That thousands of sweepers, Dick, Joe, Ned, and Jack,
Were all of them locked up in coffins of black.

And by came an Angel who had a bright key,
And he opened the coffins and set them all free;
Then down a green plain leaping, laughing, they run,   15
And wash in a river, and shine in the sun.

Then naked and white, all their bags left behind,
They rise upon clouds and sport in the wind;
And the Angel told Tom, if he'd be a good boy,
He'd have God for his father, and never want joy.   20

And so Tom awoke; and we rose in the dark,
And got with our bags and our brushes to work.
Though the morning was cold, Tom was happy and warm;
So if all do their duty they need not fear harm.

Questions

1. What does Blake's poem reveal about conditions of life in the London of his day?
2. What does this poem have in common with "The Golf Links" (page 30)?
3. Sum up your impressions of the speaker's character. What does he say and do that displays it to us?
4. What pun do you find in line 3? Is its effect comic or serious?
5. In Tom Dacre's dream (lines 11 – 20), what wishes come true? Do you understand them to be the wishes of the chimney sweepers, of the poet, or of both?
6. In the last line, what is ironic in the speaker's assurance that the dutiful *need not fear harm*? What irony is there in his urging all to *do their duty*? (Who have failed in their duty to *him*?)
7. What is the tone of Blake's poem? Angry? Hopeful? Sorrowful? Compassionate? (Don't feel obliged to sum it up in a single word.)

Information for Experiment: *Reading with and without Biography*

The Red Wheelbarrow (p. 25). Dr. Williams's poem reportedly contains a personal experience: he was gazing from the window of the house where one of his patients, a small girl, lay suspended between life and death. (This account, from the director of the public library in Williams's native Rutherford, N.J., is given by Geri M. Rhodes in "The Paterson Metaphor in William Carlos Williams' *Paterson*," master's essay, Tufts University, June 1965.)

SUGGESTIONS FOR WRITING

1. In a paragraph, sum up your initial reactions to "The Red Wheelbarrow." Then, taking another look at the poem in light of information noted above, write a second paragraph summing up your further reactions.
2. Write a short essay titled "What Thomas Hardy Leaves Unsaid in 'The Workbox'."
3. Write a verbal profile or short character sketch of the speaker of John Betjeman's "In Westminster Abbey."
4. In a brief essay, consider the tone of two poems on a similar subject. Compare and contrast Walt Whitman and Emily Dickinson as locomotive-fanciers; or, in the poems by Richard Lovelace and Wilfred Owen, compare and contrast attitudes toward war. (For advice on writing about poetry by the method of comparison and contrast, see page 485.)

3 *Words*

LITERAL MEANING: WHAT A POEM SAYS FIRST

Although successful as a painter, Edgar Degas struggled to produce sonnets, and found poetry discouragingly hard to write. To his friend, the poet Stéphane Mallarmé, he complained, "What a business! My whole day gone on a blasted sonnet, without getting an inch further . . . and it isn't ideas I'm short of . . . I'm full of them, I've got too many . . ."

"But Degas," said Mallarmé, "you can't make a poem with ideas — you make it with *words!*"[1]

Like the celebrated painter, some people assume that all it takes to make a poem is a bright idea. Poems state ideas, to be sure, and sometimes the ideas are invaluable; and yet the most impressive idea in the world will not make a poem unless its words are selected and arranged with loving art. Some poets take great pains to find the right word. Unable to fill a two-syllable gap in an unfinished line that went, "The seal's wide – – gaze toward Paradise," Hart Crane paged through an unabridged dictionary. When he reached S, he found the object of his quest in *spindrift:* "spray skimmed from the sea by a strong wind." The word is exact and memorable. Any word can be the right word, however, if artfully chosen and placed. It may be a word as ordinary as *from.* Consider the difference between "The sedge is withered *on* the lake" (a misquotation of a line by Keats) and "The sedge is withered *from* the lake" (what Keats in fact wrote). Keats's original line suggests, as the altered line doesn't, that because the sedge (a growth of grasslike plants) has withered *from* the lake, it has withdrawn mysteriously.

---

[1]Paul Valéry, *Degas . . . Manet . . . Morisot,* translated by David Paul (New York: Pantheon, 1960) 62.

In reading a poem, some people assume that its words can be skipped over rapidly, and they try to leap at once to the poem's general theme. It is as if they fear being thought clods unless they can find huge ideas in the poem (whether or not there are any). Such readers often ignore the literal meanings of words: the ordinary, matter-of-fact sense to be found in a dictionary. (As you will see in Chapter Four, "Saying and Suggesting," words possess not only dictionary meanings — **denotations** — but also many associations and suggestions — **connotations.**) Consider the following poem and see what you make of it.

William Carlos Williams (1883 – 1963)*

THIS IS JUST TO SAY   1934

I have eaten
the plums
that were in
the icebox
and which   5
you were probably
saving
for breakfast

Forgive me
they were delicious   10
so sweet
and so cold

Some readers distrust a poem so simple and candid. They think, "What's wrong with me? There has to be more to it than this!" But poems seldom are puzzles in need of solutions. We can begin by accepting the poet's statements, without suspecting the poet of trying to hoodwink us. On later reflection, of course, we might possibly decide that the poet is playfully teasing or being ironic; but Williams gives us no reason to think that. There seems no need to look beyond the literal sense of his words, no profit in speculating that the plums symbolize worldly joys and that the icebox stands for the universe. Clearly, a reader who held such a grand theory would have overlooked (in eagerness to find a significant idea) the plain truth that the poet makes clear to us: that ice-cold plums are a joy to taste, especially if one knows they'll be missed the next morning.

To be sure, Williams's small poem is simpler than most poems are; and yet in reading any poem, no matter how complicated, you will do well to reach slowly and reluctantly for a theory to explain it by. To find the general theme of a poem, you first need to pay attention to its words. Recall Yeats's "The Lake Isle of Innisfree" (page 3), a poem that makes a statement—crudely summed up, "I yearn to leave the city and retreat to a place of ideal peace and happiness." And yet before we can realize this theme, we have to notice details: nine bean rows, a glade loud with bees, "lake water lapping with low sounds by the shore," the gray of a pavement. These details and not some abstract remark make clear what the poem is saying: that the city is drab, while the island hideaway is sublimely beautiful.

Poets often strive for words that point to physical details and solid objects. They may do so even when speaking of an abstract idea:

> Beauty is but a flower
> Which wrinkles will devour;
> Brightness falls from the air,
> Queens have died young and fair,
> Dust hath closed Helen's eye.
> I am sick, I must die:
>   Lord, have mercy on us!

In these lines by Thomas Nashe, the abstraction *beauty* has grown petals that shrivel. Brightness may be a general name for light, but Nashe succeeds in giving it the weight of a falling body.

If a poem reads *daffodils* instead of *plant life*, *diaper years* instead of *infancy*, we call its **diction**, or choice of words, **concrete** rather than **abstract**. Concrete words refer to what we can immediately perceive with our senses: *dog*, *actor*, *chemical*, or particular individuals who belong to those general classes: *Bonzo the fox terrier*, *Clint Eastwood*, *hydrogen sulfate*. Abstract words express ideas or concepts: *love*, *time*, *truth*. In abstracting, we leave out some characteristics found in each individual, and instead observe a quality common to many. The word *beauty*, for instance, denotes what may be observed in numerous persons, places, and things. Most poets tend to favor concrete diction, at least part of the time. In an apt criticism, William Butler Yeats once took to task the poems of W. E. Henley for being "abstract, as even an actor's movement can be when the thought of doing is plainer to his mind than the doing itself: the straight line from cup to lip, let us say, more plain than the hand's own sensation weighed down by that heavy spillable cup."[2] To convey the sense of that heavy spillable cup was to Yeats a goal, one that surely he attained in "Among School Children" by describing a woman's stark face: "Hollow of cheek as though it drank the wind / And took a mess of shadows for its meat." A more abstract-minded poet might have written "Her hollow cheek and wasted, hungry look."

Ezra Pound gave a famous piece of advice to his fellow poets: "Go in fear of abstractions." This is not to say that a poet cannot employ abstract words, nor that all poems have to be about physical things. Much of T. S. Eliot's *Four Quartets* is concerned with time, eternity, history, language, reality, and other things that cannot be handled. But Eliot, however high he may soar for a larger view, keeps returning to earth. He makes us aware of *things*, as Thomas Carlyle said a good writer has to do: "Wonderful it is with what cutting words, now

---

[2]*The Trembling of the Veil* (1922), reprinted in *The Autobiography of William Butler Yeats* (New York: Macmillan, 1953) 177.

and then, he severs asunder the confusion; shears it down, were it furlongs deep, into the true center of the matter; and there not only hits the nail on the head, but with crushing force smites it home, and buries it." Like other good writers, good poets remind us of that smitten nail and that spillable cup.

Knute Skinner (b. 1929)

THE COLD IRISH EARTH   1968

I shudder thinking
of the cold Irish earth.
The firelighter flares
in the kitchen range,
but a cold rain falls   5
all around Liscannor.
It scours the Hag's face
on the Cliffs of Moher.
It runs through the bog
and seeps up into mounds   10
of abandoned turf.
My neighbor's fields are chopped
by the feet of cattle
sinking down to the roots
of winter grass.   15
That coat hangs drying now
by the kitchen range,
but down at Healy's cross
the Killaspuglonane graveyard
is wet to the bone.   20

QUESTIONS

1. To what familiar phrase does Skinner's poem lend fresh meaning? What is its usual meaning?
2. What details in the poem show us that, in using the old phrase, Skinner literally means what he says?

Henry Taylor (b. 1942)

RIDING A ONE-EYED HORSE   1975

One side of his world is always missing.
You may give it a casual wave of the hand
or rub it with your shoulder as you pass,
but nothing on his blind side ever happens.

Hundreds of trees slip past him into darkness,   5
drifting into a hollow hemisphere
whose sounds you will have to try to explain.
Your legs will tell him not to be afraid

if you learn never to lie. Do not forget
to turn his head and let what comes come seen: 10
he will jump the fences he has to if you swing
toward them from the side that he can see

and hold his good eye straight. The heavy dark
will stay beside you always; let him learn
to lean against it. It will steady him   15
and see you safely through diminished fields.

QUESTION

Do you read this poem as a fable in which the horse stands for something, or as a set
of instructions for riding a one-eyed horse?

Robert Graves (1895 – 1985)

DOWN, WANTON, DOWN!   1933

Down, wanton, down! Have you no shame
That at the whisper of Love's name,
Or Beauty's, presto! up you raise
Your angry head and stand at gaze?

Poor bombard-captain, sworn to reach   5
The ravelin and effect a breach —
Indifferent what you storm or why,
So be that in the breach you die!

Love may be blind, but Love at least
Knows what is man and what mere beast;   10
Or Beauty wayward, but requires
More delicacy from her squires.

Tell me, my witless, whose one boast
Could be your staunchness at the post,
When were you made a man of parts   15
To think fine and profess the arts?

Will many-gifted Beauty come
Bowing to your bald rule of thumb,
Or Love swear loyalty to your crown?
Be gone, have done! Down, wanton, down!   20

DOWN, WANTON, DOWN! 5 *bombard-captain:* officer in charge of a bombard, an early type of cannon
that hurled stones. 6 *ravelin:* fortification with two faces that meet in a protruding angle. *effect a
breach:* break an opening through (a fortification). 15 *man of parts:* man of talent or ability.

1. How do you define a wanton?
2. What wanton does the poet address?
3. Explain the comparison drawn in the second stanza.
4. In line 14, how many meanings do you find in *staunchness at the post*?
5. Explain any other puns you find in lines 15 – 19.
6. Do you take this to be a cynical poem making fun of Love and Beauty, or is Graves making fun of stupid, animal lust?

Peter Davison (b. 1928)

THE LAST WORD   1970

When I saw your head bow, I knew I had beaten you.
You shed no tears — not near me — but held your neck
Bare for the blow I had been too frightened
Ever to deliver, even in words. And now,
In spite of me, plummeting it came.   5
Frozen we both waited for its fall.

Most of what you gave me I have forgotten
With my mind but taken into my body,
But this I remember well: the bones of your neck
And the strain in my shoulders as I heaved up that huge   10
Double blade and snapped my wrists to swing
The handle down and hear the axe's edge
Nick through your flesh and creak into the block.

QUESTIONS

1. "The Last Word" stands fourth in a series titled "Four Love Poems." Sum up what happens in this poem. Do you take this to be *merely* a literal account of an execution? Explain the comparison.
2. Which words embody concrete things and show us physical actions? Which words have sounds that especially contribute to the poem's effectiveness?

Bruce Guernsey (b. 1944)

GLOVE   1987

If in this word
is love itself
then love is bone
and blood inside
the form that warms   5
your lovely hand—

your hand is love
and mine that takes
your love in mine
without your hand   10
is nothing but
an empty word.

Questions

1. What double meaning do you find in "the form that warms your lovely hand"?
2. What does this poem say about love? (Suggestion: How would you paraphrase lines 7–12?)

John Donne (1572 – 1631)*

BATTER MY HEART, THREE-PERSONED GOD, FOR YOU   (about 1610)

Batter my heart, three-personed God, for You
As yet but knock, breathe, shine, and seek to mend.
That I may rise and stand, o'erthrow me, and bend
Your force to break, blow, burn, and make me new.
I, like an usurped town to another due,   5
Labor to admit You, but Oh! to no end.
Reason, Your viceroy in me, me should defend,
But is captived, and proves weak or untrue.
Yet dearly I love You, and would be lovèd fain,
But am betrothed unto Your enemy;   10
Divorce me, untie or break that knot again;
Take me to You, imprison me, for I,
Except You enthrall me, never shall be free,
Nor ever chaste, except You ravish me.

Questions

1. In the last line of this sonnet, to what does Donne compare the onslaught of God's love? Do you think the poem weakened by the poet's comparing a spiritual experience to something so grossly carnal? Discuss.
2. Explain the seeming contradiction in the last line: in what sense can a ravished person be *chaste*? Explain the seeming contradictions in lines 3 – 4 and 12 – 13: how can a person thrown down and destroyed be enabled to *rise and stand*; an imprisoned person be *free*?
3. In lines 5 – 6 the speaker compares himself to a *usurped town* trying to throw off its conqueror by admitting an army of liberation. Who is the "usurper" in this comparison?
4. Explain the comparison of *Reason* to a *viceroy* (lines 7 – 8).
5. Sum up in your own words the message of Donne's poem. In stating its theme, did you have to read the poem for literal meanings, figurative comparisons, or both?

The Value of a Dictionary

If a poet troubles to seek out the best words available, the least we can do is to find out what the words mean. The dictionary is a firm ally in reading poems; if the poems are more than a century old, it is indispensable. Meanings change. When the Elizabethan poet George Gascoigne wrote, "O Abraham's brats, O brood of blessed seed," the word *brats* implied neither irritation nor contempt. When in the seventeenth century Andrew Marvell imagined two lovers' "vegetable love," he referred to a vegetative or growing love, not one resembling a lettuce. And when King George III called a building an "awful artificial spectacle," he was not condemning it but praising it as an awe-inspiring work of art.

In reading poetry, there is nothing to be done about this inevitable tendency of language except to watch out for it. If you suspect that a word has shifted in meaning over the years, most standard desk dictionaries will be helpful, an unabridged dictionary more helpful yet, and most helpful of all the *Oxford English Dictionary (OED)*, which gives, for each definition, successive examples of the word's written use through the past thousand years. You need not feel a grim obligation to keep interrupting a poem in order to rummage the dictionary; but if the poem is worth reading very closely, you may wish any aid you can find.

One of the valuable services of poetry is to recall for us the concrete, physical sense that certain words once had, but since have lost. As the English critic H. Coombes has remarked in *Literature and Criticism,*

> We use a word like *powerful* without feeling that it is really "power-full." We do not seem today to taste the full flavor of words as we feel that Falstaff (and Shakespeare, and probably his audience) tasted them when he was applauding the virtues of "good sherris-sack," which makes the brain "apprehensive, quick, forgetive, full of nimble, fiery, and delectable shapes." And being less aware of the life and substantiality of words, we are probably less aware of the things . . . that these words stand for.

"Every word which is used to express a moral or intellectual fact," said Emerson in his study *Nature,* "if traced to its root, is found to be borrowed from some material appearance. *Right* means straight; *wrong* means twisted. *Spirit* primarily means wind; *transgression,* the crossing of a line; *supercilious,* the raising of an eyebrow." Browse in a dictionary and you will discover such original concretenesses. These are revealed in your dictionary's etymologies, or brief notes on the derivation of words, given in most dictionaries near the beginning of an entry on a word; in some dictionaries, at the end of the entry. Look up *squirrel,* for instance, and you will find it comes from two Greek words meaning "shadow-tail." For another example of a common word that originally contained a poetic metaphor, look up the origin of *daisy.*

Much of the effect of the following poem depends upon our awareness of the precision with which the poet has selected his words. We can better see this by knowing their derivations. For instance, *potpourri* comes from French: *pot* plus *pourri.* What do these words mean? (If you do not know French, look up the etymology of the word in a dictionary.) Look up the definitions and etymologies of *revenance, circumstance, inspiration, conceptual, commotion, cordial,* and *azure;* and try to state the meanings these words have in Wilbur's poem.

Richard Wilbur (b. 1921)*

IN THE ELEGY SEASON   1950

Haze, char, and the weather of All Souls':
A giant absence mopes upon the trees:
Leaves cast in casual potpourris
Whisper their scents from pits and cellar-holes.

Or brewed in gulleys, steeped in wells, they spend   5
In chilly steam their last aromas, yield
From shallow hells a revenance of field
And orchard air. And now the envious mind

Which could not hold the summer in my head
While bounded by that blazing circumstance   10
Parades these barrens in a golden trance,
Remembering the wealthy season dead,

And by an autumn inspiration makes
A summer all its own. Green boughs arise
Through all the boundless backward of the eyes,   15
And the soul bathes in warm conceptual lakes.

Less proud than this, my body leans an ear
Past cold and colder weather after wings'
Soft commotion, the sudden race of springs,
The goddess' tread heard on the dayward stair,   20

Longs for the brush of the freighted air, for smells
Of grass and cordial lilac, for the sight
Of green leaves building into the light
And azure water hoisting out of wells.

An **allusion** is an indirect reference to any person, place, or thing — fictitious, historical, or actual. Sometimes, to understand an allusion in a poem, we have to find out something we didn't know before. But usually the poet asks of us only common knowledge. When Edgar Allan Poe refers to "the glory that was Greece / And the grandeur that was Rome," he assumes that we have heard of those places, and that we will understand his allusion to the cultural achievement of those nations (implicit in *glory* and *grandeur*).

Allusions not only enrich the meaning of a poem, they also save space. In "The Love Song of J. Alfred Prufrock" (page 310), T. S. Eliot, by giving a brief introductory quotation from the speech of a damned soul in Dante's *Inferno*, is able to suggest that his poem will be the confession of a soul in torment, who sees no chance of escape.

Often in reading a poem you will meet a name you don't recognize, on which the meaning of a line (or perhaps a whole poem) seems to depend. In this book, most such unfamiliar references and allusions are glossed or foot-noted, but when you venture out on your own in reading poems, you may find yourself needlessly perplexed unless you look up such names, the way you look up any other words. Unless the name is one that the poet made up, you will probably find it in one of the larger desk dictionaries, such as *Webster's New Collegiate Dictionary*, *The American Heritage Dictionary*, or *Webster's II*. If you don't solve your problem there, try an encyclopedia, a world atlas, or *The New Century Cyclopedia of Names*.

Some allusions are quotations from other poems. In L. E. Sissman's "In and Out: A Home Away from Home," the narrator, a male college student, describes his sleeping love,

> This Sally now does like a garment wear
> The beauty of the evening; silent, bare,
> Hips, shoulders, arms, tresses, and temples lie.

(For the source of these lines, see Wordsworth's "Composed upon Westminster Bridge," page 400.)

EXERCISE: *Catching Allusions*

From your knowledge, supplemented by a dictionary or other reference work if need be, explain the allusions in the following four poems.

J. V. Cunningham (1911 – 1985)*

FRIEND, ON THIS SCAFFOLD THOMAS MORE LIES DEAD   1960

Friend, on this scaffold Thomas More lies dead
Who would not cut the Body from the Head.

Herman Melville (1819 – 1891)

THE PORTENT   1859

Hanging from the beam,
  Slowly swaying (such the law),
Gaunt the shadow on your green,
  Shenandoah!

The cut is on the crown   5
    (Lo, John Brown),
And the stabs shall heal no more.

Hidden in the cap
    Is the anguish none can draw;
So your future veils its face,   10
    Shenandoah!

But the streaming beard is shown
    (Weird John Brown),
The meteor of the war.

Lucille Clifton (b. 1936)

WINNIE SONG   1987

a dark wind is blowing
the townships into town.
they have burned your house
winnie mandela
but your house has been on fire   5
a hundred years.
they have locked your husband
in a cage
and it has made him free.
Mandela. Mandala. Mandala   10
is the universe. the universe
is burning. a dark wind is blowing
the homelands into home.

Laurence Perrine (b. 1915)

JANUS   1984

Janus writes books for women's liberation;
His wife types up the scripts from his dictation.

John Clare (1793 – 1864)

MOUSE'S NEST   (about 1835)

I found a ball of grass among the hay
And progged it as I passed and went away;
And when I looked I fancied something stirred,
And turned again and hoped to catch the bird —

When out an old mouse bolted in the wheats   5
With all her young ones hanging at her teats;
She looked so odd and so grotesque to me,
I ran and wondered what the thing could be,
And pushed the knapweed bunches where I stood;
Then the mouse hurried from the craking° brood.   *crying*   10
The young ones squeaked, and as I went away
She found her nest again among the hay.
The water o'er the pebbles scarce could run
And broad old cesspools glittered in the sun.

Questions

1. "To prog" (line 2) means "to poke about for food, to forage." In what ways does this
   word fit more exactly here than *prodded, touched,* or *searched?*
2. Is *craking* (line 10) better than *crying?* Which word better fits the poem? Why?
3. What connections do you find between the last two lines and the rest of the poem?
   To what are water that *scarce could run* and *broad old cesspools* (lines 13 and 14)
   likened?

Word Choice and Word Order

Even if Samuel Johnson's famous *Dictionary* of 1755 had been as thick as
Webster's unabridged, an eighteenth-century poet searching through it for
words to use would have had a narrower choice. For in English literature of the
neoclassical period or **Augustan age** — that period from about 1660 into the
late eighteenth century — many poets subscribed to a belief in **poetic diction**:
"A system of words," said Dr. Johnson, "refined from the grossness of domestic
use." The system admitted into a serious poem only certain words and subjects,
excluding others as violations of **decorum** (propriety). Accordingly such common words as *rat, cheese, big, sneeze,* and *elbow,* although admissible to satire,
were thought inconsistent with the loftiness of tragedy, epic, ode, and elegy. Dr.
Johnson's biographer, James Boswell, tells how a poet writing an epic reconsid-
ered the word "rats" and instead wrote "the whiskered vermin race." Johnson
himself objected to Lady Macbeth's allusion to her "keen knife," saying that
"we do not immediately conceive that any crime of importance is to be committed with a knife; or who does not, at last, from the long habit of connecting
a knife with sordid offices, feel aversion rather than terror?" Probably Johnson
was here the victim of his age, and Shakespeare was right, but Johnson in one
of his assumptions was right too: there are inappropriate words as well as
appropriate ones.

Neoclassical poets chose their classical models more often from Roman
writers than from Greek, as their diction suggests by the frequency of Latin
derivatives. For example, a *net,* according to Dr. Johnson's dictionary, is "any
thing reticulated or decussated, at equal distances, with interstices between the
intersections." In company with Latinate words often appeared fixed combinations of adjective and noun ("finny prey" for "fish"), poetic names (a song to
a lady named Molly might rechristen her Parthenia), and allusions to classical
mythology. Neoclassical poetic diction was evidently being abused when, instead of saying "uncork the bottle," a poet could write,

Apply thine engine to the spongy door,
Set *Bacchus* from his glassy prison free,

in some bad lines ridiculed by Alexander Pope in *Peri Bathous, or, Of the Art of Sinking in Poetry.*

Not all poetic diction is excess baggage. To a reader who knew at first hand both living sheep and the pastoral poems of Virgil — as most readers nowadays do not — such a fixed phrase as "the fleecy care," which seems stilted to us, conveyed pleasurable associations. But "fleecy care" was more than a highfalutin way of saying "sheep"; as one scholar has pointed out, "when they wished, our poets could say 'sheep' as clearly and as often as anybody else. In the first place, 'fleecy' drew attention to wool, and demanded the appropriate visual image of sheep; for aural imagery the poets would refer to 'the bleating kind'; it all depended upon what was happening in the poem."[3]

Other poets have found some special kind of poetic language valuable: Old English poets, with their standard figures of speech ("whale-road" for the sea, "ring-giver" for a ruler); makers of folk ballads who, no less than neoclassicists, love fixed epithet-noun combinations ("milk-white steed," "blood-red wine," "steel-driving man"); and Edmund Spenser, whose example made popular the adjective ending in *-y* (*fleecy, grassy, milky*).

When Wordsworth, in his Preface to *Lyrical Ballads,* asserted that "the language really spoken by men," especially by humble rustics, is plainer, more emphatic, and conveys "elementary feelings . . . in a state of greater simplicity," he was, in effect, advocating a new poetic diction. Wordsworth's ideas invited freshness into English poetry and, by admitting words that neoclassical poets would have called "low" ("His poor old *ankles* swell"), helped rid poets of the fear of being thought foolish for mentioning a commonplace.

This theory of the superiority of rural diction was, as Coleridge pointed out, hard to adhere to, and, in practice, Wordsworth was occasionally to write a language as Latinate and citified as these lines on yew trees:

Huge trunks! — and each particular trunk a growth
Of intertwisted fibers serpentine
Up-coiling, and inveterately convolved . . .

Language so Latinate sounds pedantic to us, especially the phrase *inveterately convolved.* In fact, some poets, notably Gerard Manley Hopkins, have subscribed to the view that English words derived from Anglo-Saxon (Old English) have more force and flavor than their Latin equivalents. *Kingly,* one may feel, has more power than *regal.* One argument for this view is that so many words of Old English origin — *man, wife, child, house, eat, drink, sleep* — are basic to our living speech. It may be true that a language closer to Old English is particularly fit for rendering abstract notions concretely — as does the memorable title of a medieval work of piety, the *Ayenbite of Inwit* ("again-bite of inner

---

[3]Bonamy Dobrée, *English Literature in the Early Eighteenth Century, 1700 – 1740* (New York: Oxford UP, 1959) 161.

wisdom" or "remorse of conscience"). And yet this view, if accepted at all, must be accepted with reservations. Some words of Latin origin carry meanings both precise and physical. In the King James Bible is the admonition, "See then that ye walk circumspectly, not as fools, but as wise" (Ephesians 5:15). To be *circumspect* (a word from two Latin roots meaning "to look" and "around") is to be watchful on all sides — a meaning altogether lost in a modernized wording of the passage once printed on a subway poster for a Bible society: "Be careful how you live, not thoughtlessly but thoughtfully."

When E. E. Cummings begins a poem, "mr youse needn't be so spry / concernin questions arty," we recognize another kind of diction available to poetry: **vulgate** (speech not much affected by schooling). Handbooks of grammar sometimes distinguish various **levels of usage.** A sort of ladder is imagined, on whose rungs words, phrases, and sentences may be ranked in an ascending order of formality, from the curses of an illiterate thug to the commencement-day address of a doctor of divinity. These levels range from vulgate through **colloquial** (the casual conversation or informal writing of literate people) and **general English** (most literate speech and writing, more studied than colloquial but not pretentious), up to **formal English** (the impersonal language of educated persons, usually only written, possibly spoken on dignified occasions). Recently, however, lexicographers have been shunning such labels. The designation *colloquial* has been expelled (*bounced* would be colloquial; *trun out,* vulgate) from *Webster's Third New International Dictionary* on the grounds that "it is impossible to know whether a word out of context is colloquial or not" and that the diction of Americans nowadays is more fluid than the labels suggest. Aware that we are being unscientific, we may find the labels useful. They may help roughly to describe what happens when, as in the following poem, a poet shifts from one level of usage to another. This poem employs, incidentally, a colloquial device throughout: omitting the subjects of sentences. In keeping the characters straight, it may be helpful to fill in the speaker for each *said* and for the verbs *saw* and *ducked* (lines 9 and 10).

Josephine Miles (1911 – 1985)

REASON   1955

Said, Pull her up a bit will you, Mac, I want to unload there.
Said, Pull her up my rear end, first come first serve.
Said, Give her the gun, Bud, he needs a taste of his own bumper.
Then the usher came out and got into the act:
Said, Pull her up, pull her up a bit, we need this space, sir.   5
Said, For God's sake, is this still a free country or what?
You go back and take care of Gary Cooper's horse
And leave me handle my own car.

Saw them unloading the lame old lady,
Ducked out under the wheel and gave her an elbow,
Said, All you needed to do was just explain;
Reason, Reason is my middle name.

10

Language on more than one level enlivens this miniature comedy; the vulgate of the resentful driver ("Pull her up my rear end," "leave me handle my own car") and the colloquial of the bystander ("Give her the gun"). There is also a contrast in formality between the old lady's driver, who says "Mac," and the usher, who says "sir." These varied levels of language distinguish the speakers in the poem from one another.

The diction of "Reason" is that of speech; that of Coleridge's "Kubla Khan" (page 299) is more bookish. Coleridge is not at fault, however: the language of Josephine Miles's reasonable driver might not have contained Kubla Khan's stately pleasure dome. At present, most poetry in English appears to be shunning expressions such as "fleecy care" in favor of general English and the colloquial. In Scotland, there has been an interesting development: the formation of an active group of poets who write in Scots, a **dialect** (variety of language spoken by a social group or spoken in a certain locality). Perhaps, whether poets write in language close to speech or in language of greater formality, their poems will ring true if they choose appropriate words.

EXPERIMENT: *Wheeshts into Hushes*

Reword the following poem from Scots dialect into general English, using the closest possible equivalents. Then try to assess what the poem has gained or lost. (In line 4, a "ploy," as defined by *Webster's Third New International Dictionary,* is a pursuit or activity, "especially one that requires eagerness or finesse.")

Hugh MacDiarmid
[Christopher Murray Grieve] (1892 – 1978)

WHEESHT, WHEESHT   1926

Wheesht°, wheesht, my foolish hert,	*hush*
For weel ye ken°	*know*
I widna ha'e ye stert	
Auld ploys again.	
It's guid to see her lie	
Sae snod° an' cool,	*smooth*
A' lust o' lovin' by –	
Wheesht, wheesht, ye fule!	

Not only the poet's choice of words makes a poem seem more formal, or less, but also the way the words are arranged into sentences. Compare these lines,

> Jack and Jill went up the hill
> To fetch a pail of water.
> Jack fell down and broke his crown
> And Jill came tumbling after.

with Milton's account of a more significant downfall:

> Earth trembled from her entrails, as again
> In pangs, and Nature gave a second groan;
> Sky loured, and, muttering thunder, some sad drops
> Wept at completing of the mortal sin
> Original; while Adam took no thought
> Eating his fill, nor Eve to iterate
> Her former trespass feared, the more to soothe
> Him with her loved society, that now
> As with new wine intoxicated both
> They swim in mirth, and fancy that they feel
> Divinity within them breeding wings
> Wherewith to scorn the Earth.

Not all the words in Milton's lines are bookish: indeed, many of them can be found in nursery rimes. What helps, besides diction, to distinguish this account of the Biblical fall from "Jack and Jill" is that Milton's nonstop sentence seems further removed from usual speech in its length (83 words), in its complexity (subordinate clauses), and in its word order ("with new wine intoxicated both" rather than "both intoxicated with new wine"). Should we think less (or more highly) of Milton for choosing a style so elaborate and formal? No judgment need be passed: both Mother Goose and the author of *Paradise Lost* use language appropriate to their purposes.

Among languages, English is by no means the most flexible. English words must be used in fairly definite and inviolable patterns, and whoever departs too far from them will not be understood. In the sentence "Cain slew Abel," if you change the word order, you change the meaning: "Abel slew Cain." Such inflexibility was not true of Latin, in which a poet could lay down words in almost any sequence and, because their endings (inflections) showed what parts of speech they were, could trust that no reader would mistake a subject for an object or a noun for an adjective. (E. E. Cummings has striven, in certain of his poems, for the freedom of Latin. One such poem, "anyone lived in a pretty how town," appears on page 60.)

The rigidity of English word order invites the poet to defy it and to achieve unusual effects by inverting it. It is customary in English to place adjective in front of noun (*a blue mantle, new pastures*). But an unusual emphasis is achieved when Milton ends "Lycidas" by reversing the pattern:

> At last he rose, and twitched his mantle blue:
> Tomorrow to fresh woods, and pastures new.

Perhaps the inversion in *mantle blue* gives more prominence to the color associated with heaven (and in "Lycidas," heaven is of prime importance). Perhaps the inversion in *pastures new*, stressing the *new*, heightens the sense of a rebirth.

Coleridge offered two "homely definitions of prose and poetry; that is, *prose:* words in their best order; *poetry:* the best words in the best order." If all goes well, a poet may fasten the right word into the right place, and the result may be — as T. S. Eliot said in "Little Gidding" — a "complete consort dancing together."

Emma Lee Warrior (b. 1941)

How I Came to Have a Man's Name   1988

It's a good thing Dad deserted Mom
and all us kids for a cousin's wiles,
cause then we learned from Grampa
how to pray to the Sun, the Moon and Stars.

Before a January dawn, under a moondog sky,   5
Yellow Dust hitched up a team to a strawfilled sleigh.
Snow squeaked against the runners
in reply to the crisp crackling cottonwoods.
They bundled up bravely in buffalo robes,
their figures pronounced by the white of night;   10
the still distance of the Wolf Trail° greeted them,   *Milky Way*
and Ipisowahs,° the boy child of Natosi,°   *morning star/the sun*
and Kokomiikiisom° watched their hurry.   *the moon*
My momma's body was bent with pain.
Otohkostskaksin° sensed the Morning Star's   *Yellow Dust*   15
presence and so he beseeched him:

"Aayo, Ipisowahs, you see us now,
pitiful creatures.
We are thankful there is no wind.
We are thankful for your light.   20
Guide us safely to our destination.
May my daughter give birth in a warm place.
May her baby be a boy; may he have your name.
May he be fortunate because of your name.
May he live long and be happy.   25
Bestow your name upon him, Ipisowahs.
His name will be Ipisowahs.
Aayo, help us, we are pitiful."

And Ipisowahs led them that icy night
through the Old Man River Valley   30

and out onto the frozen prairie.
They rushed to the hospital
where my mother pushed me into this world
and nobody bothered to change my name.

How I Came to Have a Man's Name. The words glossed in the margin of the poem are the poet's translations from the Blackfoot language.

Questions

1. What do the words from the Blackfoot language contribute to this poem? (Suggestion: Try reading them aloud as best you can.)
2. If the unborn child was to be named Ipisowahs, "morning star," then why do you suppose the poet signs herself Emma Lee Warrior?

Thomas Hardy (1840 – 1928)*

THE RUINED MAID   1901

"O 'Melia, my dear, this does everything crown!
Who could have supposed I should meet you in Town?
And whence such fair garments, such prosperi-ty?" —
"O didn't you know I'd been ruined?" said she.

— "You left us in tatters, without shoes or socks,   5
Tired of digging potatoes, and spudding up docks°;   *spading up dockweed*
And now you've gay bracelets and bright feathers three!" —
"Yes: that's how we dress when we're ruined," said she.

— "At home in the barton° you said 'thee' and 'thou,'   *farmyard*
And 'thik oon,' and 'theäs oon,' and 't'other'; but now   10
Your talking quite fits 'ee for high compa-ny!" —
"Some polish is gained with one's ruin," said she.

— "Your hands were like paws then, your face blue and bleak
But now I'm bewitched by your delicate cheek,
And your little gloves fit as on any la-dy!" —   15
"We never do work when we're ruined," said she.

— "You used to call home-life a hag-ridden dream,
And you'd sigh, and you'd sock°; but at present you seem   *groan*
To know not of megrims° or melancho-ly!" —   *blues*
"True. One's pretty lively when ruined," said she.   20

— "I wish I had feathers, a fine sweeping gown,
And a delicate face, and could strut about Town!" —
"My dear — a raw country girl, such as you be,
Cannot quite expect that. You ain't ruined," said she.

1. Where does this dialogue take place? Who are the two speakers?
2. Comment on Hardy's use of the word *ruined*. What is the conventional meaning of the word when applied to a woman? As 'Melia applies it to herself what is its meaning?
3. Sum up the attitude of each speaker toward the other. What details of the new 'Melia does the first speaker most dwell upon? Would you expect Hardy to be so impressed by all these details, or is there, between his view of the characters and their view of themselves, any hint of an ironic discrepancy?
4. In losing her country dialect (*thik oon* and *theäs oon* for *this one* and *that one*), 'Melia is presumed to have gained in sophistication. What does Hardy suggest by her *ain't* in the last line?

Richard Eberhart (b. 1904)

THE FURY OF AERIAL BOMBARDMENT   1947

You would think the fury of aerial bombardment
Would rouse God to relent; the infinite spaces
Are still silent. He looks on shock-pried faces.
History, even, does not know what is meant.

You would feel that after so many centuries   5
God would give man to repent; yet he can kill
As Cain could, but with multitudinous will,
No farther advanced than in his ancient furies.

Was man made stupid to see his own stupidity?
Is God by definition indifferent, beyond us all?   10
Is the eternal truth man's fighting soul
Wherein the Beast ravens in its own avidity?

Of Van Wettering I speak, and Averill,
Names on a list, whose faces I do not recall
But they are gone to early death, who late in school   15
Distinguished the belt feed lever from the belt holding pawl.

QUESTIONS

1. As a naval officer during World War II, Richard Eberhart was assigned for a time as an instructor in a gunnery school. How has this experience apparently contributed to the diction of his poem?
2. In his *Life of John Dryden*, complaining about a description of a sea fight Dryden had filled with nautical language, Samuel Johnson argued that technical terms should be excluded from poetry. Is this criticism applicable to Eberhart's last line? Can a word succeed for us in a poem, even though we may not be able to define it? (For more evidence, see also the technical terms in Henry Reed's "Naming of Parts," p. 367.)
3. Some readers have found a contrast in tone between the first three stanzas of this poem and the last stanza. How would you describe this contrast? What does diction contribute to it?

Wole Soyinka (b. 1934)

LOST TRIBE   1988

Ants disturbed by every passing tread,
The wandering tribe still scurries round
In search of lost community. Love by rote,
Care by inscription. Incantations without magic.
Straws outstretched to suck at every passing broth,   5
Incessant tongues pretend to a way of thought—
Where language mints are private franchise,
The coins prove counterfeit on open markets.

Hard-sell pharmacies dispense all social pills:
"Have a nice day now." "Touch someone."   10
There's premium on the verb imperative—some
Instant fame psychologist pronounced it on TV—
He's now forgotten like tomorrow's guru,
Instant cult, disposable as paper diaper—
Firm commands denote sincerity;   15
The wish is wishy-washy, lacks "contact
Positive." The waiter barks: "Enjoy your meal,"
Or crisper still: *"Enjoy!"* You feel you'd better!
Buses, subway, park seats push the gospel,
Slogans like tickertapes emblazon foreheads—   20
"Talk it over with someone—now, not later!"
"Take down fences, not mend them."
"Give a nice smile to someone." But, a tear-duct
Variant: "Have you hugged your child today?"

QUESTIONS

1. What criticisms of our use of the English language is this Nigerian poet making?
2. What do you understand from lines 7–8, with their reference to "language mints" and counterfeit coins?
3. Explain the allusion in the title of this poem. How might it apply to Americans?

FOR REVIEW AND FURTHER STUDY

David B. Axelrod (b. 1943)

ONCE IN A WHILE A PROTEST POEM   1976

Over and over again the papers print
the dried-out tit of an African woman
holding her starving child. Over

and over, cropping it each time to one
prominent, withered tit, the feeble   5
infant face. Over and over to toughen
us, teach us to ignore the foam turned
dusty powder on the infant's lips,
the mother's sunken face (is cropped)
and filthy dress. The tit remains;   10
the tit held out for everyone to see,
reminding us only that we are not so hungry
ogling the tit, admiring it and in our
living rooms, making it a symbol of starving
millions; our sympathy as real as silicone.   15

QUESTIONS

1. Why is the last word in this poem especially meaningful?
2. What does the poet protest?

Lewis Carroll
[Charles Lutwidge Dodgson] (1832 – 1898)

JABBERWOCKY   1871

'Twas brillig, and the slithy toves
    Did gyre and gimble in the wabe:
All mimsy were the borogoves,
    And the mome raths outgrabe.

"Beware the Jabberwock, my son!   5
    The jaws that bite, the claws that catch!
Beware the Jubjub bird, and shun
    The frumious Bandersnatch!"

He took his vorpal sword in hand;
    Long time the manxome foe he sought —   10
So rested he by the Tumtum tree
    And stood awhile in thought.

And, as in uffish thought he stood,
    The Jabberwock, with eyes of flame,
Came whiffling through the tulgey wood,   15
    And burbled as it came!

One, two! One, two! And through and through
    The vorpal blade went snicker-snack!
He left it dead, and with its head
    He went galumphing back.   20

"And hast thou slain the Jabberwock?
  Come to my arms, my beamish boy!
O frabjous day! Callooh, Callay!"
  He chortled in his joy.

'Twas brillig, and the slithy toves   25
  Did gyre and gimble in the wabe:
All mimsy were the borogoves,
  And the mome raths outgrabe.

JABBERWOCKY. Fussy about pronunciation, Carroll in his preface to *The Hunting of the Snark* declares: "The first 'o' in 'borogoves' is pronounced like the 'o' in 'borrow.' I have heard people try to give it the sound of the 'o' in 'worry.' Such is Human Perversity." *Toves*, he adds, rimes with *groves*.

QUESTIONS

1. Look up *chortled* (line 24) in your dictionary and find out its definition and origin.
2. In *Through the Looking-Glass*, Alice seeks the aid of Humpty Dumpty to decipher the meaning of this nonsense poem. "*Brillig*," he explains, "means four o'clock in the afternoon — the time when you begin *broiling* things for dinner." Does *brillig* sound like any other familiar word?
3. "*Slithy*," the explanation goes on, "means 'lithe and slimy.' 'Lithe' is the same as 'active.' You see it's like a portmanteau — there are two meanings packed up into one word." *Mimsy* is supposed to pack together both "flimsy" and "miserable." In the rest of the poem, what other portmanteau — or packed suitcase — words can you find?

Wallace Stevens (1879 – 1955)*

METAMORPHOSIS   1942

Yillow, yillow, yillow,
Old worm, my pretty quirk,
How the wind spells out
Sep - tem - ber. . . .

Summer is in bones.   5
Cock-robin's at Caracas.
Make o, make o, make o,
Oto - otu - bre.

And the rude leaves fall.
The rain falls. The sky   10
Falls and lies with the worms.
The street lamps

Are those that have been hanged.
Dangling in an illogical
To and to and fro   15
Fro Niz - nil - imbo.

1. Explain the title. Of the several meanings of *metamorphosis* given in a dictionary, which best applies to the process that Stevens sees in the natural world?
2. What metamorphosis is also taking place in the *language* of the poem? How does it continue from line 4 to line 8 to line 16?
3. In the last line, which may recall the thickening drone of a speaker lapsing into sleep, *Niz - nil - imbo* seems not only a pun on the name of a month, but also a portmanteau word into which at least two familiar words are packed. Say it aloud. What are they?
4. What dictionary definitions of the word *quirk* seem relevant to line 2? How can a worm be a quirk? What else in this poem seems quirky?

E. E. Cummings (1894 – 1962)*

ANYONE LIVED IN A PRETTY HOW TOWN   1940

anyone lived in a pretty how town
(with up so floating many bells down)
spring summer autumn winter
he sang his didn't he danced his did.

Women and men (both little and small)   5
cared for anyone not at all
they sowed their isn't they reaped their same
sun moon stars rain

children guessed (but only a few
and down they forgot as up they grew   10
autumn winter spring summer)
that noone loved him more by more

when by now and tree by leaf
she laughed his joy she cried his grief
bird by snow and stir by still   15
anyone's any was all to her

someones married their everyones
laughed their cryings and did their dance
(sleep wake hope and then) they
said their nevers they slept their dream   20

stars rain sun moon
(and only the snow can begin to explain
how children are apt to forget to remember
with up so floating many bells down)

one day anyone died i guess   25
(and noone stooped to kiss his face)
busy folk buried them side by side
little by little and was by was

all by all and deep by deep
and more by more they dream their sleep   30
noone and anyone earth by april
wish by spirit and if by yes.

Women and men (both dong and ding)
summer autumn winter spring
reaped their sowing and went their came   35
sun moon stars rain

Questions

1. Summarize the story told in this poem. Who are the characters?
2. Rearrange the words in the two opening lines into the order you would expect them usually to follow. What effect does Cummings obtain by his unconventional word order?
3. Another of Cummings's strategies is to use one part of speech as if it were another; for instance, in line 4, *didn't* and *did* ordinarily are verbs, but here they are used as nouns. What other words in the poem perform functions other than their expected ones?

Exercise: *Different Kinds of English*

Read the following poems and see what kinds of diction and word order you find in them. Which poems are least formal in their language and which most formal? Is there any use of vulgate English? Any dialect? What does each poem achieve that its own kind of English makes possible?

Anonymous (American oral verse)

Carnation Milk   (about 1900?)

Carnation Milk is the best in the land;
Here I sit with a can in my hand —
No tits to pull, no hay to pitch,
You just punch a hole in the son of a bitch.

CARNATION MILK. "This quatrain is imagined as the caption under a picture of a rugged-looking cowboy seated upon a bale of hay," notes William Harmon in his *Oxford Book of American Light Verse* (New York: Oxford UP, 1979). Possibly the first to print this work was David Ogilvy (b. 1911), who quotes it in his *Confessions of an Advertising Man* (New York: Atheneum, 1963).

A. R. Ammons (b. 1926)

Spring Coming   1970

The caryophyllaceae
like a scroungy
frost are

rising through the lawn:
many-fingered as leggy
 copepods: 5
a suggestive delicacy,
lacework, like
the scent of wild plum
 thickets: 10
also the grackles
with their incredible
vertical, horizontal,
reversible
tails have arrived: 15
such nice machines.

William Wordsworth (1770 – 1850)*

MY HEART LEAPS UP WHEN I BEHOLD   1807

My heart leaps up when I behold
 A rainbow in the sky:
So was it when my life began;
So is it now I am a man;
So be it when I shall grow old,   5
 Or let me die!
The Child is father of the Man;
And I could wish my days to be
Bound each to each by natural piety.

William Wordsworth (1770 – 1850)*

MUTABILITY   1822

From low to high doth dissolution climb,
And sink from high to low, along a scale
Of awful notes, whose concord shall not fail;
A musical but melancholy chime,
Which they can hear who meddle not with crime, 5
Nor avarice, nor over-anxious care.
Truth fails not; but her outward forms that bear
The longest date do melt like frosty rime°,   *frozen dew*
That in the morning whitened hill and plain
And is no more; drop like the tower sublime 10
Of yesterday, which royally did wear
His crown of weeds, but could not even sustain
Some casual shout that broke the silent air,
Or the unimaginable touch of Time.

Anonymous

SCOTTSBORO   1936

Paper come out — done strewed de news
Seven po' chillun moan deat' house blues,
Seven po' chillun moanin' deat' house blues.
Seven nappy° heads wit' big shiny eye   *frizzy*
All boun' in jail and framed to die,   5
All boun' in jail and framed to die.

Messin' white woman — snake lyin' tale
Hang and burn and jail wit' no bail.
Dat hang and burn and jail wit' no bail.
Worse ol' crime in white folks' lan'   10
Black skin coverin' po' workin' man,
Black skin coverin' po' workin' man.

Judge and jury — all in de stan'
Lawd, biggety name for same lynchin' ban',
Lawd, biggety name for same lynchin' ban'.   15
White folks and nigger in great co't house
Like cat down cellar wit' nohole mouse.
Like cat down cellar wit' nohole mouse.

SCOTTSBORO. This folk blues, collected by Lawrence Gellert in *Negro Songs of Protest* (New York: Carl Fischer, Inc., 1936), is a comment on the Scottsboro case. In 1931 nine black youths of Scottsboro, Alabama, were arrested and charged with the rape of two white women. Though eventually, after several trials, they were found not guilty, some of them at the time this song was composed had been convicted and sentenced to death.

SUGGESTIONS FOR WRITING

1. Choosing a poem that strikes you as particularly inventive or unusual in its language, such as Wallace Stevens's "Metamorphosis" (page 59), E. E. Cummings's "anyone lived in a pretty how town" (page 60), or Gerard Manley Hopkins's "The Wind-hover" (page 334), write a brief analysis of it. Concentrate on the diction of the poem and its word order. For what possible purposes does the poet depart from standard English? (To find some pointers on writing about poetry by the method of analysis, see page 477.)
2. In a short essay, set forth the pleasures of browsing in a dictionary. As you browse, see if you can discover any "found poems".
3. "Printing poetry in dialect, such as 'Scottsboro,' insults the literacy of a people." Think about this critical charge and comment on it.
4. Write a short defense of a poet's right to employ the language of science and technology. Alternatively, point out some of the dangers and drawbacks of using such language in poetry. For evidence, see the poems in this chapter by Richard Eberhart and A. R. Ammons and those in the Anthology by James Merrill (page 352) and Henry Reed (page 367).

4 Saying and Suggesting

To write so clearly that they might bring "all things as near the mathematical plainness" as possible — that was the goal of scientists according to Bishop Thomas Sprat, who lived in the seventeenth century. Such an effort would seem bound to fail, because words, unlike numbers, are ambiguous indicators. Although it may have troubled Bishop Sprat, the tendency of a word to have multiplicity of meaning rather than mathematical plainness opens broad avenues to poetry.

Every word has at least one **denotation:** a meaning as defined in a dictionary. But the English language has many a common word with so many denotations that a reader may need to think twice to see what it means in a specific context. The noun *field,* for instance, can denote a piece of ground, a sports arena, the scene of a battle, part of a flag, a profession, and a number system in mathematics. Further, the word can be used as a verb ("he fielded a grounder") or an adjective ("field trip," "field glasses").

A word also has **connotations:** overtones or suggestions of additional meaning that it gains from all the contexts in which we have met it in the past. The word *skeleton,* according to a dictionary, denotes "the bony framework of a human being or other vertebrate animal, which supports the flesh and protects the organs." But by its associations, the word can rouse thoughts of war, of disease and death, or (possibly) of one's plans to go to medical school. Think, too, of the difference between "Old Doc Jones" and "Abner P. Jones, M.D." In the mind's eye, the former appears in his shirtsleeves; the latter has a gold nameplate on his door. That some words denote the same thing but have sharply different connotations is pointed out in this anonymous Victorian jingle:

Here's a little ditty that you really ought to know:
Horses "sweat" and men "perspire," but ladies only "glow."

The terms *druggist, pharmacist,* and *apothecary* all denote the same occupation, but apothecaries lay claim to special distinction.

Poets aren't the only people who care about the connotations of language. Advertisers know that connotations make money. Nowadays many automobile dealers advertise their secondhand cars not as "used" but as "pre-owned," as if fearing that "used car" would connote an old heap with soiled upholstery and mysterious engine troubles that somebody couldn't put up with. "Pre-owned," however, suggests that the previous owner has taken the trouble of breaking in the car for you. Not long ago prune-packers, alarmed by a slump in sales, sponsored a survey to determine the connotations of prunes in the public consciousness. Asked, "What do you think of when you hear the word *prunes?*" most people replied, "dried up," "wrinkled," or "constipated." Dismayed, the packers hired an advertising agency to create a new image for prunes, in hopes of inducing new connotations. Soon, advertisements began to show prunes in brightly colored settings, in the company of bikinied bathing beauties.

In imaginative writing, connotations are as crucial as they are in advertising. Consider this sentence: "A new brand of journalism is being born, or spawned" (Dwight Macdonald writing in *The New York Review of Books*). The last word, by its associations with fish and crustaceans, suggests that this new journalism is scarcely the product of human beings. And what do we make of Romeo's assertion that Juliet "is the sun"? Surely even a lovesick boy cannot mean that his sweetheart is "the incandescent body of gases about which the earth and other planets revolve" (a dictionary definition). He means, of course, that he thrives in her sight, that he feels warm in her presence or even at the thought of her, that she illumines his world and is the center of his universe. Because in the mind of the hearer these and other suggestions are brought into play, Romeo's statement, literally absurd, makes excellent sense.

Here is a famous poem that groups together things with similar connotations: certain ships and their cargoes. (A *quinquireme,* by the way, was an ancient Assyrian vessel propelled by sails and oars.)

John Masefield (1878 – 1967)

Cargoes   1902

Quinquireme of Nineveh from distant Ophir,
Rowing home to haven in sunny Palestine,
With a cargo of ivory,
And apes and peacocks,
Sandalwood, cedarwood, and sweet white wine.   5

Stately Spanish galleon coming from the Isthmus,
Dipping through the Tropics by the palm-green shores,
With a cargo of diamonds,
Emeralds, amethysts,
Topazes, and cinnamon, and gold moidores°.   *Portuguese coins* 10

Dirty British coaster with a salt-caked smoke stack,
Butting through the Channel in the mad March days,
With a cargo of Tyne coal,
Road-rails, pig-lead,
Firewood, iron-ware, and cheap tin trays.   15

To us, as well as to the poet's original readers, the place-names in the first two
stanzas suggest the exotic and faraway. Ophir, a vanished place, may have been
in Arabia; according to the Bible, King Solomon sent there for its celebrated
pure gold, also for ivory, apes, peacocks, and other luxury items. (See I Kings
9 – 10.) In his final stanza, Masefield groups commonplace things (mostly heavy
and metallic), whose suggestions of crudeness, cheapness, and ugliness he deliberately contrasts with those of the precious stuffs he has listed earlier. For
British readers, the Tyne is a stodgy and familiar river; the English Channel in
March, choppy and likely to upset a stomach. The quinquireme is *rowing,* the
galleon is *dipping,* but the dirty British freighter is *butting,* aggressively pushing.
Conceivably, the poet could have described firewood and even coal as beautiful,
but evidently he wants them to convey sharply different suggestions here, to go
along with the rest of the coaster's cargo. In drawing such a sharp contrast
between past and present, Masefield does more than merely draw up bills-of-
lading. Perhaps he even implies a wry and unfavorable comment upon life in
the present day. His meaning lies not so much in the dictionary definitions of
his words (*"moidores:* Portuguese gold coins formerly worth approximately five
pounds sterling") as in their rich and vivid connotations.

William Blake (1757 – 1827)*

LONDON   1794

I wander through each chartered street,
Near where the chartered Thames does flow,
And mark in every face I meet
Marks of weakness, marks of woe.

In every cry of every man,   5
In every infant's cry of fear,
In every voice, in every ban,
The mind-forged manacles I hear.

How the chimney-sweeper's cry
Every black'ning church appalls   10

And the hapless soldier's sigh
Runs in blood down palace walls.

But most through midnight streets I hear
How the youthful harlot's curse
Blasts the new born infant's tear   15
And blights with plagues the marriage hearse.

Here are only a few of the possible meanings of three of Blake's words:

chartered (lines 1, 2)

DENOTATIONS: Established by a charter (a written grant or a certificate of
incorporation); leased or hired.

CONNOTATIONS: Defined, limited, restricted, channeled, mapped, bound by
law; bought and sold (like a slave or an inanimate object); Magna Charta;
charters given crown colonies by the King.

OTHER WORDS IN THE POEM WITH SIMILAR CONNOTATIONS: *Ban*, which can
denote (1) a legal prohibition; (2) a churchman's curse or malediction;
(3) in medieval times, an order summoning a king's vassals to fight for
him. *Manacles*, or shackles, restrain movement. *Chimney-sweeper*, *soldier*,
and *harlot* are all hirelings.

INTERPRETATION OF THE LINES: The street has had mapped out for it the
direction in which it must go; the Thames has had laid down to it the
course it must follow. Street and river are channeled, imprisoned, enslaved (like every inhabitant of London).

black'ning (line 10)

DENOTATION: Becoming black.

CONNOTATIONS: The darkening of something once light, the defilement of
something once clean, the deepening of guilt, the gathering of darkness
at the approach of night.

OTHER WORDS IN THE POEM WITH SIMILAR CONNOTATIONS: Objects becoming
marked or smudged (*marks of weakness, marks of woe* in the faces of
passers-by; bloodied walls of a palace; marriage blighted with plagues);
the word *appalls* (denoting not only "to overcome with horror" but "to
make pale" and also "to cast a pall or shroud over"); *midnight streets*.

INTERPRETATION OF THE LINE: Literally, every London church grows black
from soot and hires a chimney-sweeper (a small boy) to help clean it. But
Blake suggests too that by profiting from the suffering of the child
laborer, the church is soiling its original purity.

Blasts, blights (lines 15 – 16)

DENOTATIONS: Both *blast* and *blight* mean "to cause to wither" or "to ruin
and destroy." Both are terms from horticulture. Frost *blasts* a bud and
kills it; disease *blights* a growing plant.

CONNOTATIONS: Sickness and death; gardens shriveled and dying; gusts of
wind and the ravages of insects; things blown to pieces or rotted and
warped.

OTHER WORDS IN THE POEM WITH SIMILAR CONNOTATIONS: Faces marked with weakness and woe; the child become a chimney-sweep; the soldier killed by war; blackening church and bloodied palace; young girl turned harlot; wedding carriage transformed into a hearse.

INTERPRETATION OF THE LINES: Literally, the harlot spreads the plague of syphilis, which, carried into marriage, can cause a baby to be born blind. In a larger and more meaningful sense, Blake sees the prostitution of even one young girl corrupting the entire institution of matrimony and endangering every child.

Some of these connotations are more to the point than others; the reader of a poem nearly always has the problem of distinguishing relevant associations from irrelevant ones. We need to read a poem in its entirety and, when a word leaves us in doubt, look for other things in the poem to corroborate or refute what we think it means. Relatively simple and direct in its statement, Blake's account of his stroll through the city at night becomes an indictment of a whole social and religious order. The indictment could hardly be this effective if it were "mathematically plain," its every word restricted to one denotation clearly spelled out.

Wallace Stevens (1879 – 1955)*

DISILLUSIONMENT OF TEN O'CLOCK   1923

The houses are haunted
By white night-gowns.
None are green,
Or purple with green rings,
Or green with yellow rings,   5
Or yellow with blue rings.
None of them are strange,
With socks of lace
And beaded ceintures.
People are not going   10
To dream of baboons and periwinkles.
Only, here and there, an old sailor,
Drunk and asleep in his boots,
Catches tigers
In red weather.   15

QUESTIONS

1. What are *beaded ceintures?* What does the phrase suggest?
2. What contrast does Stevens draw between the people who live in these houses and the old sailor? What do the connotations of *white night-gowns* and *sailor* add to this contrast?
3. What is lacking in these people who wear white night-gowns? Why should the poet's view of them be a "disillusionment"?

Gwendolyn Brooks (b. 1917)*

THE BEAN EATERS

1960

They eat beans mostly, this old yellow pair.
Dinner is a casual affair.
Plain chipware on a plain and creaking wood,
Tin flatware.

Two who are Mostly Good.   5
Two who have lived their day,
But keep on putting on their clothes
And putting things away.

And remembering . . .
Remembering, with tinklings and twinges,   10
As they lean over the beans in their rented back room that is full of
    beads and receipts and dolls and cloths, tobacco crumbs, vases
    and fringes.

QUESTIONS

1. What do we infer about this old couple and their life style from the details in lines
   1–4 about their diet, dishes, dinnertable, and cutlery?
2. In that long last line, what is suggested by the things they have saved and stored?

Timothy Steele (b. 1948)*

EPITAPH

1979

Here lies Sir Tact, a diplomatic fellow
Whose silence was not golden, but just yellow.

QUESTIONS

1. To what famous saying does the poet allude?
2. What are the connotations of *golden?* Of *yellow?*

Geoffrey Hill (b. 1932)

MERLIN

1959

I will consider the outnumbering dead:
For they are the husks of what was rich seed.
Now, should they come together to be fed,
They would outstrip the locusts' covering tide.

Arthur, Elaine, Mordred; they are all gone   5
Among the raftered galleries of bone.

By the long barrows of Logres they are made one,
And over their city stands the pinnacled corn.

MERLIN. In medieval legend, Merlin was a powerful magician and a seer, an aide of King Arthur.
5 *Elaine:* in Arthurian romance, the beloved of Sir Launcelot. *Mordred:* Arthur's treacherous
nephew by whose hand the king died. 7 *barrows:* earthworks for burial of the dead. *Logres:* name
of an ancient British kingdom, according to the twelfth-century historian Geoffrey of Monmouth,
who gathered legends of King Arthur.

QUESTIONS

1. What does the title "Merlin" contribute to this poem? Do you prefer to read the poem as though it is Merlin who speaks to us — or the poet?
2. Line 4 alludes to the plague of locusts that God sent upon Egypt (Exodus 10): "For they covered the face of the whole earth, so that the land was darkened . . ." With this allusion in mind, explain the comparison of the dead to locusts.
3. Why are the suggestions inherent in the names of *Arthur, Elaine,* and *Mordred* more valuable to this poem than those we might find in the names of other dead persons called, say, Gus, Tessie, and Butch?
4. Explain the phrase in line 6: *the raftered galleries of bone.*
5. In the last line, what *city* does the poet refer to? Does he mean some particular city, or is he making a comparison?
6. What is interesting in the adjective *pinnacled?* How can it be applied to corn?

Wallace Stevens (1879 – 1955)*

THE EMPEROR OF ICE-CREAM   1923

Call the roller of big cigars,
The muscular one, and bid him whip
In kitchen cups concupiscent curds.
Let the wenches dawdle in such dress
As they are used to wear, and let the boys   5
Bring flowers in last month's newspapers.
Let be be finale of seem.
The only emperor is the emperor of ice-cream.

Take from the dresser of deal,
Lacking the three glass knobs, that sheet   10
On which she embroidered fantails once
And spread it so as to cover her face.
If her horny feet protrude, they come
To show how cold she is, and dumb.
Let the lamp affix its beam.   15
The only emperor is the emperor of ice-cream.

THE EMPEROR OF ICE-CREAM. 9 *deal:* fir or pine wood used to make cheap furniture.

QUESTIONS

1. What scene is taking place in the first stanza? Describe it in your own words. What are your feelings about it?

2. Who do you suppose to be the dead person in the second stanza? What can you infer about her? What do you know about her for sure?
3. Make a guess about this mysterious emperor. Who do you take him to be?
4. What does ice cream mean to you? In this poem, what do you think it means to Stevens?

Walter de la Mare (1873 – 1956)

THE LISTENERS   1912

"Is there anybody there?" said the Traveller,
    Knocking on the moonlit door;
And his horse in the silence champed the grasses
    Of the forest's ferny floor:
And a bird flew up out of the turret,   5
    Above the Traveller's head:
And he smote upon the door again a second time;
    "Is there anybody there?" he said.
But no one descended to the Traveller;
    No head from the leaf-fringed sill   10
Leaned over and looked into his gray eyes,
    Where he stood perplexed and still.
But only a host of phantom listeners
    That dwelt in the lone house then
Stood listening in the quiet of the moonlight   15
    To that voice from the world of men:
Stood thronging the faint moonbeams on the dark stair
    That goes down to the empty hall,
Hearkening in an air stirred and shaken
    By the lonely Traveller's call.   20
And he felt in his heart their strangeness,
    Their stillness answering his cry,
While his horse moved, cropping the dark turf,
    'Neath the starred and leafy sky;
For he suddenly smote on the door, even   25
    Louder, and lifted his head: —
"Tell them I came, and no one answered,
    That I kept my word," he said.
Never the least stir made the listeners,
    Though every word he spake   30
Fell echoing through the shadowiness of the still house
    From the one man left awake:
Ay, they heard his foot upon the stirrup,
    And the sound of iron on stone,
And how the silence surged softly backward,   35
    When the plunging hoofs were gone.

1. Before you had read this poem, what suggestions did its title bring to mind?
2. Now that you have read the poem, what do you make of these "listeners"? Who or what do you imagine them to be?
3. Why is *the moonlit door* (in line 2) a phrase more valuable to this poem than if the poet had written simply "the door"?
4. What does *turret* (in line 5) suggest?
5. Reconstruct some earlier events that might have preceded the Traveller's visit. Who might this Traveller be? Who are the unnamed persons — "them" (line 27) — for whom the Traveller leaves a message? What promise has he kept? (The poet doesn't tell us; we can only guess.)
6. Do you think this poem any the worse for the fact that its setting, characters, and action are so mysterious? What does "The Listeners" gain from not telling us all?

Robert Frost (1874 – 1963)*

FIRE AND ICE   1923

Some say the world will end in fire,
Some say in ice.
From what I've tasted of desire
I hold with those who favor fire.
But if it had to perish twice,   5
I think I know enough of hate
To say that for destruction ice
Is also great
And would suffice.

QUESTIONS

1. To whom does Frost refer in line 1? In line 2?
2. What connotations of *fire* and *ice* contribute to the richness of Frost's comparison?

SUGGESTIONS FOR WRITING

1. In a short essay, analyze a poem full of words that radiate suggestions. Looking into the Anthology that begins on page 277, you might consider T. S. Eliot's "The Love Song of J. Alfred Prufrock," John Keats's "To Autumn," Sylvia Plath's "Daddy," or many others. Focus on particular words: explain their connotations and show how these suggestions are part of the poem's meaning. (For guidelines on writing about poetry by the method of analysis, see page 477.)
2. In a current newspaper or magazine, select an advertisement that tries to surround a product with an aura. A new car, for instance, might be described in terms of some powerful jungle cat ("purring power, ready to spring"). Likely hunting-grounds for such ads are magazines that cater to the affluent (*New Yorker, Vogue,* and others). Clip or photocopy the ad and circle words in it that seem especially suggestive. Then, in an accompanying paper, unfold the suggestions in these words and try to explain the ad's appeal. How is the purpose of connotative language used in advertising copy different from that of such language when used in poetry?

5 Imagery تشبیہ - صور, تشبیہ سبویر

Ezra Pound (1885 – 1972)*

IN A STATION OF THE METRO   1916

The apparition of these faces in the crowd;
Petals on a wet, black bough.

Pound said he wrote this poem to convey an experience: emerging one day from a train in the Paris subway *(Métro)*, he beheld "suddenly a beautiful face, and then another and another." Originally he had described his impression in a poem thirty lines long. In this final version, each line contains an **image,** which, like a picture, may take the place of a thousand words.

Though the term *image* suggests a thing seen, when speaking of images in poetry we generally mean *a word or sequence of words that refers to any sensory experience.* Often this experience is a sight (**visual imagery,** as in Pound's poem), but it may be a sound (**auditory imagery**) or a touch (**tactile imagery,** as a perception of roughness or smoothness). It may be an odor or a taste or perhaps a bodily sensation such as pain, the prickling of gooseflesh, the quenching of thirst, or — as in the following brief poem — the perception of something cold.

Taniguchi Buson (1715 – 1783)

THE PIERCING CHILL I FEEL   (about 1760)

The piercing chill I feel:
   my dead wife's comb, in our bedroom,
     under my heel . . .
              — Translated by Harold G. Henderson

As in this **haiku** (in Japanese, a poem of about seventeen syllables) an image can convey a flash of understanding. Had he wished, the poet might have spoken of the dead woman, of the contrast between her death and his memory of her, of his feelings toward death in general. But such a discussion would be quite different from the poem he actually wrote. Striking his bare foot against the comb, now cold and motionless but associated with the living wife (perhaps worn in her hair), the widower feels a shock as if he had touched the woman's corpse. A literal, physical sense of death is conveyed; the abstraction "death" is understood through the senses. To render the abstract in concrete terms is what poets often try to do; in this attempt, an image can be valuable.

An image may occur in a single word, a phrase, a sentence, or, as in this case, an entire short poem. To speak of the **imagery** of a poem — all its images taken together — is often more useful than to speak of separate images. To divide Buson's haiku into five images — *chill, wife, comb, bedroom, heel* — is possible, for any noun that refers to a visible object or a sensation is an image, but this is to draw distinctions that in themselves mean little and to disassemble a single experience.

Does an image cause a reader to experience a sense impression? Not quite. Reading the word *petals,* no one literally sees petals; but the occasion is given for imagining them. The image asks to be seen with the mind's eye. And although "In a Station of the Metro" records what Ezra Pound saw, it is of course not necessary for a poet actually to have lived through a sensory experience in order to write of it. Keats may never have seen a newly discovered planet through a telescope, despite the image in his sonnet on Chapman's Homer (p. 341).

It is tempting to think of imagery as mere decoration, particularly when we read Keats, who fills his poems with an abundance of sights, sounds, odors, and tastes. But a successful image is not just a dab of paint or a flashy bauble. When Keats opens "The Eve of St. Agnes" with what have been called the coldest lines in literature, he evokes by a series of images a setting and a mood:

St. Agnes' eve — Ah, bitter chill it was!
The owl, for all his feathers, was a-cold;
The hare limped trembling through the frozen grass,
And silent was the flock in woolly fold:
Numb were the Beadsman's fingers, while he told
His rosary, and while his frosted breath,
Like pious incense from a censer old,
Seemed taking flight for heaven, without a death, . . .

Indeed, some literary critics look for much of the meaning of a poem in its imagery, wherein they expect to see the mind of the poet more truly revealed than in whatever the poet explicitly claims to believe. In his investigation of Wordsworth's "Ode: Intimations of Immortality," the critic Cleanth Brooks devotes his attention to the imagery of light and darkness, which he finds carries on and develops Wordsworth's thought.[1]

[1]"Wordsworth and the Paradox of the Imagination," in *The Well Wrought Urn* (New York: Harcourt, 1956).

Though Shakespeare's Theseus (in *A Midsummer Night's Dream*) accuses poets of being concerned with "airy nothings," poets are usually very much concerned with what is in front of them. This concern is of use to us. Perhaps, as Alan Watts has remarked, Americans are not the materialists they are sometimes accused of being. How could anyone taking a look at an American city think that its inhabitants deeply cherish material things? Involved in our personal hopes and apprehensions, anticipating the future so hard that much of the time we see the present through a film of thought across our eyes, perhaps we need a poet occasionally to remind us that even the coffee we absentmindedly sip comes in (as Yeats put it) a "heavy spillable cup."

T. S. Eliot (1888 – 1965)*

THE WINTER EVENING SETTLES DOWN   1917

The winter evening settles down
With smell of steaks in passageways.
Six o'clock.
The burnt-out ends of smoky days.
And now a gusty shower wraps   5
The grimy scraps
Of withered leaves about your feet
And newspapers from vacant lots;
The showers beat
On broken blinds and chimney-pots,   10
And at the corner of the street
A lonely cab-horse steams and stamps.

And then the lighting of the lamps.

QUESTIONS

1. What mood is evoked by the images in Eliot's poem?
2. What kind of city neighborhood has the poet chosen to describe? How can you tell?

Theodore Roethke (1908 – 1963)*

ROOT CELLAR   1948

Nothing would sleep in that cellar, dank as a ditch,
Bulbs broke out of boxes hunting for chinks in the dark,
Shoots dangled and drooped,
Lolling obscenely from mildewed crates,
Hung down long yellow evil necks, like tropical snakes.   5
And what a congress of stinks! —

Roots ripe as old bait,
Pulpy stems, rank, silo-rich,
Leaf-mold, manure, lime, piled against slippery planks.
Nothing would give up life: 10
Even the dirt kept breathing a small breath.

Questions

1. As a boy growing up in Saginaw, Michigan, Theodore Roethke spent much of his
   time in a large commercial greenhouse run by his family. What details in his poem
   show more than a passing acquaintance with growing things?
2. What varieties of image does "Root Cellar" contain? Point out examples.
3. What do you understand to be Roethke's attitude toward the root cellar? Does he
   view it as a disgusting chamber of horrors? Pay special attention to the last two lines.

Elizabeth Bishop (1911 – 1979)*

The Fish   1946

I caught a tremendous fish
and held him beside the boat
half out of water, with my hook
fast in a corner of his mouth.
He didn't fight.   5
He hadn't fought at all.
He hung a grunting weight,
battered and venerable
and homely. Here and there
his brown skin hung in strips   10
like ancient wall-paper,
and its pattern of darker brown
was like wall-paper:
shapes like full-blown roses
stained and lost through age.   15
He was speckled with barnacles,
fine rosettes of lime,
and infested
with tiny white sea-lice,
and underneath two or three   20
rags of green weed hung down.
While his gills were breathing in
the terrible oxygen
— the frightening gills,
fresh and crisp with blood,   25

that can cut so badly —
I thought of the coarse white flesh كوزيت
packed in like feathers,
the big bones and the little bones,
the dramatic reds and blacks   30
of his shiny entrails, احشاء
and the pink swim-bladder
like a big peony.
I looked into his eyes
which were far larger than mine   35
but shallower, and yellowed,
the irises backed and packed
with tarnished tinfoil
seen through the lenses
of old scratched isinglass. شيشه ماهي   40
They shifted a little, but not
to return my stare.
    — It was more like the tipping
of an object toward the light.
I admired his sullen face,   45
the mechanism of his jaw,
and then I saw
that from his lower lip
    — if you could call it a lip —
grim, wet, and weapon-like,   50
hung five old pieces of fish-line,
or four and a wire leader
with the swivel still attached,
with all their five big hooks
grown firmly in his mouth.   55
A green line, frayed at the end
where he broke it, two heavier lines,
and a fine black thread
still crimped from the strain and snap
when it broke and he got away.   60
Like medals with their ribbons
frayed and wavering,
a five-haired beard of wisdom
trailing from his aching jaw.
I stared and stared   65
and victory filled up
the little rented boat,
from the pool of bilge
where oil had spread a rainbow
around the rusted engine   70
to the bailer rusted orange,

the sun-cracked thwarts,
the oarlocks on their strings,
the gunnels — until everything
was rainbow, rainbow, rainbow!   75
And I let the fish go.

1. How many abstract words does this poem contain? What proportion of the poem is imagery?
2. What is the speaker's attitude toward the fish? Comment in particular on lines 61 – 64.
3. What attitude do the images of the rainbow of oil (line 69), the orange bailer (bailing bucket, line 71), the *sun-cracked thwarts* (line 72) convey? Does the poet expect us to feel mournful because the boat is in such sorry condition?
4. What is meant by *rainbow, rainbow, rainbow*?
5. How do these images prepare us for the conclusion? Why does the speaker let the fish go?

Oscar Wilde (1854 – 1900)

SYMPHONY IN YELLOW   1889

An omnibus across the bridge
   Crawls like a yellow butterfly,
   And, here and there, a passer-by
Shows like a little restless midge°.   *a tiny fly*

Big barges full of yellow hay   5
   Are moored against the shadowy wharf,
   And, like a yellow silken scarf,
The thick fog hangs along the quay.

The yellow leaves begin to fade
   And flutter from the Temple elms,   10
   And at my feet the pale green Thames
Lies like a rod of rippled jade.

1. What season is it?
2. What is fresh and surprising in this view of an ordinary city scene?
3. To which of your senses does this poem most appeal?

John Haines (b. 1924)

WINTER NEWS   1966

They say the wells
are freezing
at Northway where
the cold begins.

Oil tins bang   5
as evening comes on,
and clouds of
steaming breath drift
in the street.

Men go out to feed   10
the stiffening dogs,

the voice of the snowman
calls the white-
haired children home.

QUESTIONS

1. Which of the images in this poem strike you as the most vivid? To which senses do
   Haines's images appeal?
2. Why are the children described as "white-haired"?

Emily Dickinson (1830 – 1886)*

A ROUTE OF EVANESCENCE   (1879)

A Route of Evanescence
With a revolving Wheel –
A Resonance of Emerald –
A Rush of Cochineal° –   *red dye*
And every Blossom on the Bush   5
Adjusts its tumbled Head –
The mail from Tunis, probably,
An easy Morning's Ride –

A ROUTE OF EVANESCENCE. 1 *Evanescence*; ornithologist's term for the luminous sheen of certain
birds' feathers. 7 *Tunis*: capital city of Tunisia, North Africa.

QUESTION

What is the subject of this poem? How can you tell?

Jean Toomer (1894 – 1967)

REAPERS   1923

Black reapers with the sound of steel on stones
Are sharpening scythes. I see them place the hones
In their hip-pockets as a thing that's done,
And start their silent swinging, one by one.
Black horses drive a mower through the weeds,   5
And there, a field rat, startled, squealing bleeds,
His belly close to ground. I see the blade,
Blood-stained, continue cutting weeds and shade.

QUESTIONS

1. Imagine the scene Jean Toomer describes. Which particulars most vividly strike the mind's eye?
2. What kind of image is *silent swinging*?
3. Read the poem aloud. Notice especially the effect of the words *sound of steel on stones* and *field rat, startled, squealing bleeds.* What interesting sounds are present in the very words that contain these images?
4. What feelings do you get from this poem as a whole? Would you agree with someone who said, "This poem gives us a sense of happy, carefree life down on the farm, close to nature"? Exactly what in "Reapers" makes you feel the way you do? Besides appealing to our auditory and visual imagination, what do the images contribute?

Gerard Manley Hopkins (1844 – 1889)*

PIED BEAUTY   (1877)
spotted

Glory be to God for dappled things —
    For skies of couple-color as a brinded° cow;   *streaked*
        For rose-moles all in stipple upon trout that swim;
Fresh-firecoal chestnut-falls; finches' wings;
    Landscape plotted and pieced — fold, fallow, and plow;   5
        And áll trádes, their gear and tackle and trim°.   *equipment*

All things counter, original, spare, strange;
    Whatever is fickle, freckled (who knows how?)
        With swift, slow; sweet, sour; adazzle, dim;
He fathers-forth whose beauty is past change: 10
        Praise him.

QUESTIONS

1. What does the word *pied* mean? (Hint: what does a Pied Piper look like?)
2. According to Hopkins, what do *skies, cow, trout, ripe chestnuts, finches' wings,* and *landscapes* all have in common? What landscapes can the poet have in mind? (Have you ever seen any *dappled* landscape while looking down from an airplane, or from a mountain or high hill?)

3. What do you make of line 6: what can carpenters' saws and ditch-diggers' spades possibly have in common with the dappled things in lines 2 – 4?
4. Does Hopkins refer only to contrasts that meet the eye? What other kinds of variation interest him?
5. Try to state in your own words the theme of this poem. How essential to our understanding of this theme are Hopkins's images?

ABOUT HAIKU

> On the one-ton temple bell
> a moonmoth, folded into sleep,
> sits still.
>   — Taniguchi Buson

The name *haiku* means "beginning-verse" — perhaps because the form may have originated in a game. Players, given a haiku, were supposed to extend its three lines into a longer poem. Haiku (the word can also be plural) tend to consist mainly of imagery, but as we saw in Buson's lines on the cold comb, their imagery is not always only pictorial.

> Heat-lightning streak —
> through darkness pierces
> the heron's shriek.
>   — Matsuo Basho

In the poet's account of his experience, are sight and sound neatly distinguished from each other?

Note that a haiku has little room for abstract thoughts or general observations. The following attempt, though in seventeen syllables, is far from haiku in spirit:

> Now that our love is gone
> I feel within my soul
> a nagging distress.

Unlike the author of those lines, haiku poets look out upon a literal world, seldom looking inward to *discuss* their feelings. Japanese haiku tend to be seasonal in subject, but because they are so highly compressed, they usually just *imply* a season: a blossom indicates spring; a crow on a branch, autumn; snow, winter. Not just pretty little sketches of nature (as some Westerners think), haiku assume a view of the universe in which observer and nature are not separated.

A haiku in Japanese is rimeless, its seventeen syllables usually arranged in three lines, often following a pattern of five, seven, and five syllables. Haiku written in English frequently ignore such a pattern; they may be rimed (like the English versions of Buson and Basho), or unrimed, as the poet prefers.

John Ridland (b. 1933)

THE LAZY MAN'S HAIKU   1975

out in the night
a wheelbarrowful
of moonlight

If you care to try your hand at haiku-writing, here are a few suggestions. Make every word matter. Include few adjectives, shun needless conjunctions. Set your poem in the present — "Haiku," said Basho, "is simply what is happening in this place at this moment." Confine your poem to what can be seen, heard, smelled, tasted, or touched. Mere sensory reports, however, will be meaningless unless they make the reader feel something — as a contemporary American writer points out in this spoof.

Richard Brautigan (1935 – 1985)

HAIKU AMBULANCE   1968

A piece of green pepper fell
off the wooden salad bowl:
so what?

Here, freely translated, are two more Japanese haiku to inspire you. The first is by master poet Basho (1644 – 1694), sometimes called the Shakespeare of the haiku.

In the old stone pool
a frogjump:
splishhhhh.

The second (in a translation by Cid Corman) is by Issa (1763 – 1827), a poet noted for wit.

only one guy and
only one fly trying to
make the guest room do

Finally, here are eight more recent haiku written in English. (Don't expect them all to observe a strict arrangement of seventeen syllables.) Haiku, in any language, is an art of few words, many suggestions. A haiku starts us thinking and feeling. "So the reader," Raymond Roseliep wrote, "keeps getting on where the poet got off."

Sprayed with strong poison
my roses are crisp this year
in the crystal vase
— Paul Goodman

After weeks of watching the roof leak
I fixed it tonight
by moving a single board
— Gary Snyder

Dusk over the lake;
　a turtle's head emerges
　　then silently sinks
　　　　— Virgil Hutton

broken bowl
the pieces
still rocking
　　　　— Penny Harter

campfire extinguished,
the woman washing dishes
in a pan of stars
　　　　— Raymond Roseliep

on the cardboard box
holding the frozen wino:
Fragile: Do not crush.
　　　　Nicholas A. Virgilio

The green cockleburs
Caught in the thick woolly hair
Of the black boy's head.
　　　　— Richard Wright

A dawn in a tree of birds.
Another.
And then another.
　　　　— Kenneth Rexroth

For Review and Further Study

John Keats (1795 – 1821)*

Bright star! would I were steadfast as thou art　　　　(1819)

Bright star! would I were steadfast as thou art —
　Not in lone splendor hung aloft the night,
And watching, with eternal lids apart,
　Like nature's patient, sleepless Eremite°　　　　　　　　　*hermit*
The moving waters at their priest-like task　　　　　　　　　5
　Of pure ablution round earth's human shores,
Or gazing on the new soft-fallen mask
　Of snow upon the mountains and the moors —
No — yet still steadfast, still unchangeable,
　Pillowed upon my fair love's ripening breast,　　　　　　　10
To feel for ever its soft fall and swell,
　Awake for ever in a sweet unrest,
Still, still to hear her tender-taken breath,
And so live ever — or else swoon to death.

Questions

1. Stars are conventional symbols for love and a loved one. (Love, Shakespeare tells us in a sonnet, "is the star to every wandering bark.") In this sonnet, why is it not possible for the star to have this meaning? How does Keats use it?
2. What seems concrete and particular in the speaker's observations?
3. Suppose Keats had said *slow and easy* instead of *tender-taken* in line 13? What would have been lost?

Timothy Steele (b. 1948)

WAITING FOR THE STORM   1986

Breeze sent a wrinkling darkness
Across the bay. I knelt
Beneath an upturned boat,
And, moment by moment, felt

The sand at my feet grow colder,   5
The damp air chill and spread.
Then the first raindrops sounded
On the hull above my head.

QUESTIONS

1. How many sensory experiences does this poem evoke?
2. By what means does the poem build an atmosphere of suspenseful expectation?
3. Read the poem aloud. What do you notice that differentiates "Waiting for the Storm" from prose?

EXPERIMENT: *Writing with Images*

Taking the following poems as examples from which to start rather than as models to be slavishly copied, try to compose a brief poem that consists largely of imagery.

Walt Whitman (1819 – 1892)*

THE RUNNER   1867

On a flat road runs the well-train'd runner;
He is lean and sinewy, with muscular legs;
He is thinly clothed — he leans forward as he runs,
With lightly closed fists, and arms partially rais'd.

T. E. Hulme (1883 – 1917)

IMAGE   (about 1910)

Old houses were scaffolding once
                              and workmen whistling.

William Carlos Williams (1883 – 1963)*

THE GREAT FIGURE   1921

Among the rain
and lights
I saw the figure 5
in gold
on a red   5
firetruck
moving
tense
unheeded
to gong clangs   10
siren howls
and wheels rumbling
through the dark city.

Robert Bly (b. 1926)*

DRIVING TO TOWN LATE TO MAIL A LETTER   1962

It is a cold and snowy night. The main street is deserted.
The only things moving are swirls of snow.
As I lift the mailbox door, I feel its cold iron.
There is a privacy I love in this snowy night.
Driving around, I will waste more time.

Gary Snyder (b. 1930)

MID-AUGUST AT SOURDOUGH MOUNTAIN LOOKOUT   1959

Down valley a smoke haze
Three days heat, after five days rain
Pitch glows on the fir-cones
Across rocks and meadows
Swarms of new flies.   5

I cannot remember things I once read
A few friends, but they are in cities.
Drinking cold snow-water from a tin cup
Looking down for miles
Through high still air.   10

MID-AUGUST AT SOURDOUGH MOUNTAIN LOOKOUT. *Sourdough Mountain:* in the state of Washington,
where the poet's job at the time was to watch for forest fires.

H. D. [Hilda Doolittle] (1886 – 1961)

HEAT   1916

O wind, rend open the heat,
cut apart the heat,
rend it to tatters.

Fruit cannot drop   5
through this thick air —
fruit cannot fall into heat
that presses up and blunts
the points of pears
and rounds the grapes.

Cut the heat —   10
plough through it,
turning it on either side
of your path.

Emanuel di Pasquale (b. 1943)

A SENSUAL, FOR EZRA POUND   1989

A girl is feeding
grapes to three leopards.
The leopards are black.
The grapes are also black.
Blue black.   5
And the girl is naked.
Like ripening grapes,
her breasts, her small breasts,
lean lightly into the air.

Linda Gregg (b. 1942)

THE GRUB   1981

The almost transparent white grub moves
slowly along the edge of the frying pan.
The grease makes the only sound, loud
in the empty room. Even the rim is cooking him.
The worm stops. Raises his head slightly.   5
Lowers it, moving tentatively down the side.
He seems to be moving on his own time,
but he is falling by definition. He moves forward
touching the frying grease with his whole face.

Mary Oliver (b. 1935)

RAIN IN OHIO   1983

The robin cries: *rain!*
The crow calls: *plunder!*

The blacksnake climbing
in the vines halts
his long ladder of muscle   5

while the thunderheads whirl up
out of the white west,

their dark hooves nicking
the tall trees as they come.

Rain, rain, rain! sings the robin   10
frantically, then flies for cover.

The crow hunches.
The blacksnake

pours himself swift and heavy
into the ground.   15

SUGGESTIONS FOR WRITING

1. Choose, from the Anthology that begins on page 277, a poem that appeals to you.
   Then write a brief account of your experience in reading it, paying special notice to
   its imagery. What images strike you, and why? What do they contribute to the poem
   as a whole? Poems rich in imagery include Samuel Taylor Coleridge's "Kubla Khan,"
   Robert Frost's "Birches," John Keats's "Ode on Melancholy," Charlotte Mew's "The
   Farmer's Bride," William Carlos Williams's "Spring and All (By the road to the
   contagious hospital)" and many more.
2. After you have read the haiku and the discussion of haiku-writing in this chapter,
   write three or four haiku of your own. Then write a brief prose account of your
   experience in writing them. What, if anything, did you find out?
3. Reflect on Samuel Johnson's famous remarks on "the business of the poet" (page
   445). Try applying Johnson's view to some recent poem — say, Elizabeth Bishop's
   "The Fish" (in this chapter). Would Johnson find Bishop a seer of "general and
   transcendental truths" or a counter of tulip-streaks? Then, in a short critical statement of your own, support or attack Johnson's view.

6 Figures of Speech

WHY SPEAK FIGURATIVELY?

"I will speak daggers to her, but use none," says Hamlet, preparing to confront his mother. His statement makes sense only because we realize that *daggers* is to be taken two ways: literally (denoting sharp, pointed weapons) and nonliterally (referring to something that can be used *like* weapons — namely, words). Reading poetry, we often meet comparisons between two things whose similarity we have never noticed before. When Marianne Moore observes that a fir tree has "an emerald turkey-foot at the top," the result is a pleasure that poetry richly affords: the sudden recognition of likenesses.

A treetop like a turkey-foot, words like daggers — such comparisons are called **figures of speech.** In its broadest definition, a figure of speech may be said to occur whenever a speaker or writer, for the sake of freshness or emphasis, departs from the usual denotations of words. Certainly, when Hamlet says he will speak daggers, no one expects him to release pointed weapons from his lips, for *daggers* is not to be read solely for its denotation. Its connotations — sharp, stabbing, piercing, wounding — also come to mind, and we see ways in which words and daggers work alike. (Words too can hurt: by striking through pretenses, possibly, or by wounding their hearer's self-esteem.) In the statement "A razor is sharper than an ax," there is no departure from the usual denotations of *razor* and *ax*, and no figure of speech results. Both objects are of the same class; the comparison is not offensive to logic. But in "How sharper than a serpent's tooth it is to have a thankless child," the objects — snake's tooth (fang) and ungrateful offspring — are so unlike that no reasonable comparison may be made between them. To find similarity, we attend to the connotations of *serpent's tooth* — biting, piercing, venom, pain — rather than to its denotations. If we are aware of the connotations of *red rose* (beauty, softness, freshness, and so forth), then the line "My love is like a red, red rose" need not call to mind a woman with a scarlet face and a thorny neck.

Figures of speech are not devices to state what is demonstrably untrue. Indeed they often state truths that more literal language cannot communicate; they call attention to such truths; they lend them emphasis.

Alfred, Lord Tennyson (1809 – 1892)*

THE EAGLE   1851

He clasps the crag with crooked hands;
Close to the sun in lonely lands,
Ringed with the azure world, he stands.

The wrinkled sea beneath him crawls;
He watches from his mountain walls,
And like a thunderbolt he falls.

This brief poem is rich in figurative language. In the first line, the phrase *crooked hands* may surprise us. An eagle does not have hands, we might protest; but the objection would be a quibble, for evidently Tennyson is indicating exactly how an eagle clasps a crag, in the way that human fingers clasp a thing. By implication, too, the eagle is a person. *Close to the sun,* if taken literally, is an absurd exaggeration, the sun being a mean distance of 93,000,000 miles from the earth. For the eagle to be closer to it by the altitude of a mountain is an approach so small as to be insignificant. But figuratively, Tennyson conveys that the eagle stands above the clouds, perhaps silhouetted against the sun, and for the moment belongs to the heavens rather than to the land and sea. The word *ringed* makes a circle of the whole world's horizons and suggests that we see the world from the eagle's height; the sea becomes an aged, sluggish animal; *mountain walls,* possibly literal, also suggests a fort or castle; and finally the eagle itself is likened to a thunderbolt in speed and in power, perhaps also in that its beak is — like our abstract conception of a lightning bolt — pointed. How much of the poem can be taken literally? Only *he clasps the crag, he stands, he watches, he falls.* The rest is made of figures of speech. The result is that, reading Tennyson's poem, we gain a bird's-eye view of sun, sea, and land — and even of bird. Like imagery, figurative language refers us to the physical world.

William Shakespeare (1564 – 1616)*

SHALL I COMPARE THEE TO A SUMMER'S DAY?   1609

Shall I compare thee to a summer's day? *a*
Thou art more lovely and more temperate. *b*
Rough winds do shake the darling buds of May, *a*
And summer's lease hath all too short a date. *b*

Sometime too hot the eye of heaven shines,   5
And often is his gold complexion dimmed;
And every fair° from fair sometimes declines,   *fair one*
By chance, or nature's changing course, untrimmed.
But thy eternal summer shall not fade,
Nor lose possession of that fair thou ow'st°;   *ownest, have* 10
Nor shall death brag thou wand'rest in his shade,
When in eternal lines to time thou grow'st.
   So long as men can breathe or eyes can see,
   So long lives this, and this gives life to thee.

English sonnet

Howard Moss (1922 – 1987)

SHALL I COMPARE THEE TO A SUMMER'S DAY?   1976

Who says you're like one of the dog days?
You're nicer. And better.
Even in May, the weather can be gray,
And a summer sub-let doesn't last forever.
Sometimes the sun's too hot;   5
Sometimes it is not.
Who can stay young forever?
People break their necks or just drop dead!
But you? Never!
If there's just one condensed reader left   10
Who can figure out the abridged alphabet,
   After you're dead and gone,
   In this poem you'll live on!

QUESTIONS

1. In Howard Moss's streamlined version of Shakespeare, from a series called "Modified Sonnets (Dedicated to adapters, abridgers, digesters, and condensers everywhere)," to what extent does the poet use figurative language? In Shakespeare's original sonnet, how high a proportion of Shakespeare's language is figurative?
2. Compare some of Moss's lines to the corresponding lines in Shakespeare's sonnet. Why is *Even in May, the weather can be gray* less interesting than the original? In the lines on the sun (5 – 6 in both versions), what has Moss's modification deliberately left out? Why is Shakespeare's seeing death as a braggart memorable? Why aren't you greatly impressed by Moss's last two lines?
3. Can you explain Shakespeare's play on the word *untrimmed* (line 8)? Evidently the word can mean "divested of trimmings," but what other suggestions do you find in it?
4. How would you answer someone who argued, "Maybe Moss's language isn't as good as Shakespeare's, but the meaning is still there. What's wrong with putting Shakespeare into up-to-date words that can be understood by everybody?"

Jon Stallworthy (b. 1935)

SINDHI WOMAN   1963

Barefoot through the bazaar,
and with the same undulant grace
as the cloth blown back from her face,
she glides with a stone jar
high on her head   5
and not a ripple in her tread.

Watching her cross erect
stones, garbage, excrement, and crumbs
of glass in the Karachi slums,
I, with my stoop, reflect   10
they stand most straight
who learn to walk beneath a weight.

SINDHI WOMAN. The Sindhi are the predominantly Moslem people of Sind, a former province of India now in Pakistan. 9 *Karachi:* located on the Arabian Sea, from 1948 to 1959 the capital of Pakistan.

QUESTION

Where in the poem does the most striking figurative language occur? What other figurative language does the poet use?

METAPHOR AND SIMILE

> Life, like a dome of many-colored glass,
> Stains the white radiance of Eternity.

The first of these lines (from Shelley's "Adonais") is a **simile:** a comparison of two things, indicated by some connective, usually *like, as, than,* or a verb such as *resembles.* A simile expresses a similarity. Still, for a simile to exist, the things compared have to be dissimilar in kind. It is no simile to say, "Your fingers are like mine," it is a literal observation. But to say, "Your fingers are like sausages" is to use a simile. Omit the connective — say, "Your fingers are sausages" — and the result is a **metaphor,** a statement that one thing *is* something else, which, in a literal sense, it is not. In the second of Shelley's lines, it is *assumed* that Eternity is light or radiance, and we have an **implied metaphor,** one that uses neither a connective nor the verb *to be.* Here are examples:

Oh, my love is like a red, red rose.	*Simile*
Oh, my love resembles a red, red rose.	*Simile*
Oh, my love is redder than a rose.	*Simile*
Oh, my love is a red, red rose.	*Metaphor*
Oh, my love has red petals and sharp thorns.	*Implied metaphor*
Oh, I placed my love into a long-stem vase	
And I bandaged my bleeding thumb.	*Implied metaphor*

Often you can tell a metaphor from a simile by much more than just the presence or absence of a connective. In general, a simile refers to only one characteristic that two things have in common, while a metaphor is not plainly limited in the number of resemblances it may indicate. To use the simile "He eats like a pig" is to compare man and animal in one respect: eating habits. But to say "He's a pig" is to use a metaphor that might involve comparisons of appearance and morality as well.

For scientists as well as poets, the making of metaphors is customary. In 1933 George Lemaitre, the Belgian priest and physicist credited with the Big Bang theory of the origin of the universe, conceived of a primal atom that existed before anything else, which expanded and produced everything. And so, he remarked, making a wonderful metaphor, the evolution of the cosmos as it is today "can be compared to a display of fireworks that has just ended." As astrophysicist and poet Alan Lightman has noted, we can't help envisioning scientific discoveries in terms of things we know from daily life—spinning balls, waves in water, pendulums, weights on springs. "We have no other choice," Lightman reasons. "We cannot avoid forming mental pictures when we try to grasp the meaning of our equations, and how can we picture what we have not seen?"[1] In science as well as in poetry, it would seem, metaphors are necessary instruments of understanding.

In everyday speech, simile and metaphor occur frequently. We use metaphors ("She's a doll") and similes ("The tickets are selling like hotcakes") without being fully conscious of them. If, however, we are aware that words possess literal meanings as well as figurative ones, we do not write *died in the wool* for *dyed in the wool* or *tow the line* for *toe the line,* nor do we use **mixed metaphors** as did the writer who advised, "Water the spark of knowledge and it will bear fruit," or the speaker who urged, "To get ahead, keep your nose to the grindstone, your shoulder to the wheel, your ear to the ground, and your eye on the ball." Perhaps the unintended humor of these statements comes from our seeing that the writer, busy stringing together stale metaphors, was not aware that they had any physical reference.

Unlike a writer who thoughtlessly mixes metaphors, a good poet can join together incongruous things and still keep the reader's respect. In his ballad "Thirty Bob a Week," John Davidson has a British workingman tell how it feels to try to support a large family on small wages:

It's a naked child against a hungry wolf;
    It's playing bowls upon a splitting wreck;
It's walking on a string across a gulf
    With millstones fore-and-aft about your neck;
But the thing is daily done by many and many a one;
    And we fall, face forward, fighting, on the deck.

Like the man with his nose to the grindstone, Davidson's wage-earner is in an absurd fix; but his balancing act seems far from merely nonsensical. For every

[1]"Physicists' Use of Metaphor," *The American Scholar* (Winter 1989) 99.

one of the poet's comparisons — of workingman to child, to bowler, to tight-rope walker, and to seaman — offer suggestions of a similar kind. All help us see (and imagine) the workingman's hard life: a brave and unyielding struggle against impossible odds.

A poem may make a series of comparisons, like Davidson's, or the whole poem may be one extended comparison:

Richard Wilbur (b. 1917)*

A Simile for Her Smile   1950

Your smiling, or the hope, the thought of it,
Makes in my mind such pause and abrupt ease
As when the highway bridgegates fall,
Balking the hasty traffic, which must sit
On each side massed and staring, while   5
Deliberately the drawbridge starts to rise:

Then horns are hushed, the oilsmoke rarifies,
Above the idling motors one can tell
The packet's smooth approach, the slip,
Slip of the silken river past the sides,   10
The ringing of clear bells, the dip
And slow cascading of the paddle wheel.

How much life metaphors bring to poetry may be seen by comparing two poems by Tennyson and Blake.

Alfred, Lord Tennyson (1809 – 1892)*

Flower in the Crannied Wall   1869

Flower in the crannied wall,
I pluck you out of the crannies,
I hold you here, root and all, in my hand,
Little flower — but *if* I could understand
What you are, root and all, and all in all,
I should know what God and man is.

How many metaphors does this poem contain? None. Compare it with a briefer poem on a similar theme: the quatrain that begins Blake's "Auguries of Inno-cence." (We follow here the opinion of W. B. Yeats, who, in editing Blake's poems, thought the lines ought to be printed separately.)

William Blake (1757 – 1827)*

TO SEE A WORLD IN A GRAIN OF SAND   (about 1803)

To see a world in a grain of sand
And a heaven in a wild flower,
Hold infinity in the palm of your hand
And eternity in an hour.

Set beside Blake's poem, Tennyson's — short though it is — seems lengthy.
What contributes to the richness of "To see a world in a grain of sand" is
Blake's use of a metaphor in every line. And every metaphor is loaded with
suggestion. Our world does indeed resemble a grain of sand: in being round,
in being stony, in being one of a myriad (the suggestions go on and on). Like
Blake's grain of sand, a metaphor holds much, within a small circumference.

Sylvia Plath (1932 – 1963)*

METAPHORS   1960

I'm a riddle in nine syllables,
An elephant, a ponderous house,
A melon strolling on two tendrils.
O red fruit, ivory, fine timbers!
This loaf's big with its yeasty rising.   5
Money's new-minted in this fat purse.
I'm a means, a stage, a cow in calf.
I've eaten a bag of green apples,
Boarded the train there's no getting off.

QUESTIONS

1. To what central fact do all the metaphors in this poem refer?
2. In the first line, what has the speaker in common with a riddle? Why does she say
   she has *nine* syllables?
3. How would you describe the tone of this poem? (Perhaps the poet expresses more
   than one attitude.) What attitude is conveyed in the metaphors of an elephant, "a
   ponderous house," "a melon strolling on two tendrils"? By the metaphors of red fruit,
   ivory, fine timbers, new-minted money? By the metaphor in the last line?

Emily Dickinson (1830 – 1886)*

IT DROPPED SO LOW – IN MY REGARD   (about 1863)

It dropped so low – in my Regard –
I heard it hit the Ground –
And go to pieces on the Stones
At bottom of my Mind –

Yet blamed the Fate that flung it—*less*
Than I denounced Myself,
For entertaining Plated Wares
Upon My Silver Shelf —

QUESTIONS

1. What is *it*? What two things are compared?
2. How much of the poem develops and amplifies this comparison?

James C. Kilgore (1928 – 1988)

THE WHITE MAN PRESSED THE LOCKS   1970

Driving down the concrete artery,
Away from the smoky heart,
Through the darkening, blighted body,
Pausing at varicose veins,
The white man pressed the locks   5
   on all the sedan's doors,
Sped toward the white corpuscles
   in the white arms
     hugging the black city.

QUESTIONS

1. Explain the two implied metaphors in this poem: what are the two bodies?
2. How do you take the word *hugging*? Is this a loving embrace or a stranglehold?
3. What, in your own words, is the poet's theme?

Peter Williams (b. 1937)

WHEN SHE WAS HERE, LI BO, SHE WAS
LIKE COLD SUMMER LAGER   1978

Her presence was a roomful of flowers,
Her absence is an empty bed.
         — *Li Bo (701 – 762)*

When she was here, Li Bo, she was like cold
   summer lager,
Like hot pastrami at Katz's on Houston Street,
Like a bright nickname on my downtown express,
Like every custardy honey from the old art books:
She was quadraphonic° Mahler   *four-channeled*   5
And the perfect little gymnast.

Now she's gone, it's like flat Coke on Sunday morning,
Like a melted Velveeta on white, eaten
Listening to Bobby Vinton —
Like the Philadelphia Eagles.   10

Questions

1. What do the lines from the Chinese poet Li Bo (in the **epigraph** or introductory quotation) have to do with the poem that ensues?
2. In the first six lines of the poem, what quality or qualities does the poet find in the things he likens to the presence of his lover? In the last lines, how are the four things that resemble her absence all alike?
3. This poem is full of allusions: in the first part, to a famous New York delicatessen and to a much-admired Austrian composer. Explain the allusions in part two.
4. What is the tone of the poem? (Sorrowful? Bitter? Or what?) How do the similes help communicate the poet's attitude?

Experiment: *Likening*

Write a two-part poem that follows the method of Peter Williams, finding your own similes to express a joyful experience in terms of things you admire, and a glum experience in terms of things you dislike. Possible subjects: Before meeting a loved one and after. Having a dull, badly paid job and then quitting it. Losing weight and putting it back on.

Ruth Whitman (b. 1922)

Castoff Skin   1973

She lay in her girlish sleep at ninety-six,
small as a twig.
Pretty good figure

for an old lady, she said to me once.
Then she crawled away, leaving   5
a tiny stretched transparence

behind her. When I kissed her paper cheek
I thought of the snake,
of his quick motion.

Questions

1. Explain the central metaphor in "Castoff Skin."
2. What other figures of speech does the poem contain?

Exercise: *What Is Similar?*

Each of these quotations contains a simile or a metaphor. In each of these figures of speech, what two things is the poet comparing? Try to state exactly what you understand the two things to have in common: the most striking similarity or similarities that the poet sees.

1. Think of the storm roaming the sky uneasily
   like a dog looking for a place to sleep in,
   listen to it growling.
   > — Elizabeth Bishop, "Little Exercise"
2. When the hounds of spring are on winter's traces . . .
   > — Algernon Charles Swinburne, "Atalanta in Calydon"
3. . . . the sun gnaws the night's bone
   down through the meat and gristle.
   > —John Ridland, "Elegy for My Aunt"
4. The scarlet of the maples can shake me like a cry
   Of bugles going by.
   > — Bliss Carman, "A Vagabond Song"
5. "Hope" is the thing with feathers –
   That perches in the soul –
   And sings the tune without the words –
   And never stops – at all –
   > — Emily Dickinson, an untitled poem
6. Work without Hope draws nectar in a sieve . . .
   > —Samuel Taylor Coleridge, "Work Without Hope"
7. A new electric fence,
   Its five barbed wires tight
   As a steel-stringed banjo.
   > — Van K. Brock, "Driving at Dawn"
8. Spring stirs Gossamer Beynon schoolmistress like a spoon.
   > — Dylan Thomas, *Under Milk Wood*

Other Figures

When Shakespeare asks, in a sonnet,

> O! how shall summer's honey breath hold out
> Against the wrackful siege of batt'ring days,

it might seem at first that he mixes metaphors. How can a *breath* confront the battering ram of an invading army? But it is summer's breath and, by giving it to summer, Shakespeare makes the season a man or woman. It is as if the fragrance of summer were the breath within a person's body, and winter were the onslaught of old age.

Such is one instance of **personification:** a figure of speech in which a thing, an animal, or an abstract term (*truth, nature*) is made human. A personification extends throughout this whole short poem:

James Stephens (1882 – 1950)*

THE WIND   1915

The wind stood up and gave a shout.
He whistled on his fingers and

Kicked the withered leaves about
And thumped the branches with his hand

And said he'd kill and kill and kill,
And so he will and so he will.

The wind is a wild man, and evidently it is not just any autumn breeze but a hurricane or at least a stiff gale. In poems that do not work as well as this one, personification may be employed mechanically. Hollow-eyed personifications walk the works of lesser English poets of the eighteenth century: Coleridge has quoted the beginning of one such neoclassical ode, "Inoculation! heavenly Maid, descend!" It is hard for the contemporary reader to be excited by William Collins's "The Passions, An Ode for Music" (1747), which personifies, stanza by stanza, Fear, Anger, Despair, Hope, Revenge, Pity, Jealousy, Love, Hate, Melancholy, and Cheerfulness, and has them listen to Music, until even "Brown Exercise rejoiced to hear, / And Sport leapt up, and seized his beechen spear." Still, the portraits of the Seven Deadly Sins in the fourteenth-century *Vision of Piers Plowman* remain memorable: "Thanne come Slothe al bislabered, with two slimy eiyen. . . ." In "Two Sonnets on Fame" John Keats makes an abstraction come alive in seeing Fame as "a wayward girl."

Hand in hand with personification often goes **apostrophe**: a way of addressing someone or something invisible or not ordinarily spoken to. In an apostrophe, a poet (in these examples Wordsworth) may address an inanimate object ("Spade! with which Wilkinson hath tilled his lands"), some dead or absent person ("Milton! thou shouldst be living at this hour"), an abstract thing ("Return, Delights!"), or a spirit ("Thou Soul that art the eternity of thought"). More often than not, the poet uses apostrophe to announce a lofty and serious tone. An "O" may even be put in front of it ("O moon!") since, according to W. D. Snodgrass, every poet has a right to do so at least once in a lifetime. But apostrophe doesn't have to be highfalutin. It is a means of giving life to the inanimate. It is a way of giving body to the intangible, a way of speaking to it person to person, as in the words of a moving American spiritual: "Death, ain't you got no shame?"

Most of us, from time to time, emphasize a point with a statement containing exaggeration: "Faster than greased lightning," "I've told him a thousand times." We speak, then, not literal truth but use a figure of speech called **overstatement** (or **hyperbole**). Poets too, being fond of emphasis, often exaggerate for effect. Instances are Marvell's profession of a love that should grow "Vaster than empires, and more slow" and Burgon's description of Petra: "A rose-red city, half as old as Time." Overstatement can be used also for humorous purposes, as in a fat woman's boast (from a blues song): "Every time I shake, some skinny gal loses her home."[2] The opposite is **understatement,** implying more than is said. Mark Twain in *Life on the Mississippi* recalls how, as an apprentice steamboat-pilot asleep when supposed to be on watch, he was roused by the pilot and sent clambering to the pilot house: "Mr. Bixby was close behind, commenting." Another example is Robert Frost's line "One could do worse than be a swinger of birches" — the conclusion of a poem that has

[2]Quoted by Amiri Baraka [LeRoi Jones] in *Blues People* (New York: Morrow, 1963).

suggested that to swing on a birch tree is one of the most deeply satisfying activities in the world.

In **metonymy,** the name of a thing is substituted for that of another closely associated with it. For instance, we say "The White House decided," and mean the president did. When John Dyer writes in "Grongar Hill,"

A little rule, a little sway,
A sun beam on a winter's day,
Is all the proud and mighty have
Between the cradle and the grave,

we recognize that *cradle* and *grave* signify birth and death. A kind of metonymy, **synecdoche** is the use of a part of a thing to stand for the whole of it or vice versa. We say "She lent a hand," and mean that she lent her entire presence. Similarly, Milton in "Lycidas" refers to greedy clergymen as "blind mouths." Another kind of metonymy is the **transferred epithet**: a device of emphasis in which the poet attributes some characteristic of a thing to another thing closely associated with it. When Thomas Gray observes that, in the evening pastures, "drowsy tinklings lull the distant folds," he well knows that sheep's bells do not drowse, but sheep do. When Hart Crane, describing the earth as seen from an airplane, speaks of "nimble blue plateaus," he attributes the airplane's motion to the earth.

Paradox occurs in a statement that at first strikes us as self-contradictory but that on reflection makes some sense. "The peasant," said G. K. Chesterton, "lives in a larger world than the globe-trotter." Here, two different meanings of *larger* are contrasted: "greater in spiritual values" versus "greater in miles." Some paradoxical statements, however, are much more than plays on words. In a moving sonnet, the blind John Milton tells how one night he dreamed he could see his dead wife. The poem ends in a paradox:

But oh, as to embrace me she inclined,
I waked, she fled, and day brought back my night.

EXERCISE: *Paradox*

What paradoxes do you find in the following poem? For each, explain the sense that underlies the statement.

Chidiock Tichborne (1568? – 1586)

ELEGY, WRITTEN WITH HIS OWN HAND
IN THE TOWER BEFORE HIS EXECUTION   1586

My prime of youth is but a frost of cares,
    My feast of joy is but a dish of pain,
My crop of corn is but a field of tares°,   *weeds*

And all my good is but vain hope of gain:
The day is past, and yet I saw no sun,
And now I live, and now my life is done.

My tale was heard, and yet it was not told,
    My fruit is fall'n, and yet my leaves are green,
My youth is spent, and yet I am not old,
    I saw the world, and yet I was not seen:
My thread is cut, and yet it is not spun,
And now I live, and now my life is done.

I sought my death, and found it in my womb,
    I looked for life, and saw it was a shade,
I trod the earth, and knew it was my tomb,
    And now I die, and now I was but made:
My glass is full, and now my glass is run,
And now I live, and now my life is done.

ELEGY, WRITTEN WITH HIS OWN HAND. Accused of taking part in the Babington Conspiracy, a plot by Roman Catholics against the life of Queen Elizabeth I, eighteen-year-old Chidiock Tichborne was hanged, drawn, and quartered at the Tower of London. That is virtually all we know about him.

Asked to tell the difference between men and women, Samuel Johnson replied, "I can't conceive, madam, can you?" The great dictionary-maker was using a figure of speech known to classical rhetoricians as *paronomasia*, better known to us as a **pun** or play on words. How does a pun operate? It reminds us of another word (or other words) of similar or identical sound but of very different denotation. Although puns at their worst can be mere piddling quibbles, at best they can sharply point to surprising but genuine resemblances. The name of a dentist's country estate, Tooth Acres, is accurate: aching teeth paid for the property. In his novel *Moby-Dick*, Herman Melville takes up questions about whales that had puzzled scientists: for instance, are the whale's spoutings water or gaseous vapor? And when Melville speaks pointedly of the great whale "sprinkling and mistifying the gardens of the deep," we catch his pun, and conclude that the creature both mistifies and mystifies at once.

In poetry, a pun may be facetious, as in Thomas Hood's ballad of "Faithless Nelly Gray":

Ben Battle was a soldier bold,
    And used to war's alarms;
But a cannon-ball took off his legs,
    So he laid down his arms!

Or it may be serious, as in these lines on war by E. E. Cummings:

the bigness of cannon
is skillful,

(*is skillful* becoming *is kill-ful* when read aloud), or perhaps, as in Shakespeare's song in *Cymbeline*, "Fear no more the heat o' th' sun," both facetious and serious at once:

Golden lads and girls all must,
As chimney-sweepers, come to dust.

George Herbert (1593 – 1633)*

THE PULLEY   1633

When God at first made man,
Having a glass of blessings standing by —
Let us (said he) pour on him all we can;
Let the world's riches, which dispersèd lie,
    Contract into a span.   5

So strength first made a way,
Then beauty flowed, then wisdom, honor, pleasure:
When almost all was out, God made a stay,
Perceiving that, alone of all His treasure,
    Rest in the bottom lay.   10

For if I should (said he)
Bestow this jewel also on My creature,
He would adore My gifts instead of Me,
And rest in Nature, not the God of Nature:
    So both should losers be.   15

Yet let him keep the rest,
But keep them with repining restlessness;
Let him be rich and weary, that at least,
If goodness lead him not, yet weariness
    May toss him to My breast.   20

QUESTIONS

1. What different senses of the word *rest* does Herbert bring into this poem?
2. How do God's words in line 16, *Yet let him keep the rest,* seem paradoxical?
3. What do you feel to be the tone of Herbert's poem? Does the punning make the poem seem comic?
4. Why is the poem called "The Pulley"? What is its implied metaphor?

To sum up: even though figures of speech are not to be taken *only* literally, they refer us to a tangible world. By *personifying* an eagle, Tennyson reminds us that the bird and humankind have certain characteristics in common. Through *metonymy*, a poet can focus our attention on a particular detail in a larger object; through *hyperbole* and *understatement*, make us see the physical actuality in back of words. *Pun* and *paradox* cause us to realize this actuality, too, and probably surprise us enjoyably at the same time. Through *apostrophe*, the poet animates the inanimate and asks it to listen — speaks directly to an immediate god or to the revivified dead. Put to such uses, figures of speech have power. They are more than just ways of playing with words.

Edmund Waller (1606 – 1687)

ON A GIRDLE   1645

That which her slender waist confined,
Shall now my joyful temples bind;
No monarch but would give his crown,
His arms might do what this has done.

It was my heaven's extremest sphere,   5
The pale° which held that lovely deer;   *enclosure*
My joy, my grief, my hope, my love,
Did all within this circle move!

A narrow compass! and yet there
Dwelt all that's good, and all that's fair!   10
Give me but what this riband bound,
Take all the rest the sun goes round!

ON A GIRDLE. This girdle is a waistband or sash — not, of course, a modern "foundation garment." 1 – 2 *That which . . . temples bind:* A courtly lover might bind his brow with a lady's ribbon, to signify he was hers. 5 *extremest sphere:* In Ptolemaic astronomy, the outermost of the concentric spheres that surround the earth. In its wall the farthest stars are set.

QUESTIONS

1. To what things is the girdle compared?
2. Explain the pun in line 4. What effect does it have upon the tone of the poem?
3. Why is the effect of this pun different from that of Thomas Hood's play on the same word in "Faithless Nelly Gray" (quoted on p. 100)?
4. What does *compass* denote in line 9?
5. What paradox occurs in lines 9 – 10?
6. How many of the poem's statements are hyperbolic? Is the compliment the speaker pays his lady too grandiose to be believed? Explain.

Theodore Roethke (1908 – 1963)*

I KNEW A WOMAN   1958

I knew a woman, lovely in her bones,
When small birds sighed, she would sigh back at them;
Ah, when she moved, she moved more ways than one:
The shapes a bright container can contain!
Of her choice virtues only gods should speak,   5
Or English poets who grew up on Greek
(I'd have them sing in chorus, cheek to cheek).

How well her wishes went! She stroked my chin,
She taught me Turn, and Counter-turn, and Stand;
She taught me Touch, that undulant white skin;   10

I nibbled meekly from her proffered hand;
She was the sickle; I, poor I, the rake,
Coming behind her for her pretty sake
(But what prodigious mowing we did make).

Love likes a gander, and adores a goose: 15
Her full lips pursed, the errant note to seize;
She played it quick, she played it light and loose;
My eyes, they dazzled at her flowing knees;
Her several parts could keep a pure repose,
Or one hip quiver with a mobile nose   20
(She moved in circles, and those circles moved).

Let seed be grass, and grass turn into hay:
I'm martyr to a motion not my own;
What's freedom for? To know eternity.
I swear she cast a shadow white as stone.   25
But who would count eternity in days?
These old bones live to learn her wanton ways:
(I measure time by how a body sways).

QUESTIONS

1. What outrageous puns do you find in Roethke's poem? Describe the effect of them.
2. What kind of figure of speech occurs in all three lines: *Of her choice virtues only gods should speak; My eyes, they dazzled at her flowing knees;* and *I swear she cast a shadow white as stone?*
3. What sort of figure is the poet's reference to himself as *old bones?*
4. Do you take *Let seed be grass, and grass turn into hay* as figurative language, or literal statement?
5. If you agree that the tone of this poem is witty and playful, do you think the poet is making fun of the woman? What is his attitude toward her? What part do figures of speech play in communicating it?

FOR REVIEW AND FURTHER STUDY

Robert Frost (1874 – 1963)*

THE SILKEN TENT   1942

She is as in a field a silken tent
At midday when a sunny summer breeze
Has dried the dew and all its ropes relent,
So that in guys° it gently sways at ease,   *attachments that steady it*
And its supporting central cedar pole,   5
That is its pinnacle to heavenward
And signifies the sureness of the soul,

Seems to owe naught to any single cord,
But strictly held by none, is loosely bound
By countless silken ties of love and thought   10
To everything on earth the compass round,
And only by one's going slightly taut
In the capriciousness of summer air
Is of the slightest bondage made aware.

QUESTIONS

1. Is Frost's comparison of woman and tent a simile or a metaphor?
2. What are the ropes or cords?
3. Does the poet convey any sense of this woman's character? What sort of person do you believe her to be?
4. Paraphrase the poem, trying to state its implied meaning. (If you need to be refreshed about paraphrase, turn back to pages 2 – 3.) Be sure to include the implications of the last three lines.

Denise Levertov (b. 1923)*

LEAVING FOREVER   1964

He says the waves in the ship's wake
are like stones rolling away.
I don't see it that way.
But I see the mountain turning,
turning away its face as the ship
takes us away.

QUESTIONS

1. What do you understand to be the man's feelings about leaving forever? How does the speaker feel? With what two figures of speech does the poet express these conflicting views?
2. Suppose that this poem had ended in another simile (instead of its three last lines):

   I see the mountain as a suitcase
   left behind on the shore
   as the ship takes us away.

   How is Denise Levertov's choice of a figure of speech a much stronger one?

Jane Kenyon (b. 1947)

THE SUITOR   1978

We lie back to back. Curtains
lift and fall,
like the chest of someone sleeping.
Wind moves the leaves of the box elder;
they show their light undersides,   5

turning all at once
like a school of fish.
Suddenly I understand that I am happy.
For months this feeling
has been coming closer, stopping 10
for short visits, like a timid suitor.

QUESTION
In each simile you find in this poem, exactly what is the similarity?

Richard Wilbur (b. 1921)*

SLEEPLESS AT CROWN POINT 1976

All night, this headland
Lunges into the rumpling
Capework of the wind.

Robert Frost (1874 – 1963)*

THE SECRET SITS 1936

We dance round in a ring and suppose,
But the Secret sits in the middle and knows.

Margaret Atwood (b. 1939)

YOU FIT INTO ME 1971

you fit into me
like a hook into an eye

a fish hook
an open eye

Grace Schulman

HEMISPHERES 1984

Our bodies, luminary under bedclothes,
fit tightly like the pieces of a broken
terra cotta vase that is newly mended,
smooth surfaces, no jagged edges visible.

I've read that countries were so interlocked 5
before the oceans fractured them and splayed
Mexico enfolding Mauritania;
Brazil's round shoulder hoisted to Nigeria;
Italy pressing Libya; Alaska
so linked with Russia in the Bering Straits 10
that fingers touched, like dead hands on a harp.
Our tremulous hands held fast in sleep at dawn;
legs, arms entwined, one continent, one mass.

John Tagliabue (b. 1923)

MAINE VASTLY COVERED WITH MUCH SNOW   1984

4 squirrels
are as busy as monks
looking for seeds; inside the seeds is a
            scripture;
nourishing themselves they trace their pre-history 5
            and future;
is theology something like the flourish of their tails?
            alert, aware of changing seasons,
            aware of other blokes about
            they persist in their 10
            scrutiny of syllables.

John Ashbery (b. 1927)*

THE CATHEDRAL IS   1979

Slated for demolition.

W. S. Merwin (b. 1927)

SONG OF MAN CHIPPING AN ARROWHEAD   1973

Little children you will all go
but the one you are hiding
will fly

Robert Burns (1759 – 1796)*

OH, MY LOVE IS LIKE A RED, RED ROSE (about 1788)

Oh, my love is like a red, red rose
    That's newly sprung in June;
My love is like the melody
    That's sweetly played in tune.

So fair art thou, my bonny lass,   5
    So deep in love am I;
And I will love thee still, my dear,
    Till a' the seas gang° dry.   *go*

Till a' the seas gang dry, my dear,
    And the rocks melt wi' the sun;   10
And I will love thee still, my dear,
    While the sands o' life shall run.

And fare thee weel, my only love!
    And fare thee weel awhile!
And I will come again, my love   15
    Though it were ten thousand mile.

SUGGESTIONS FOR WRITING

1. Freely using your imagination, write a paragraph in which you make as many hyperbolic statements as possible. Then write another version, changing all your exaggeration to understatement. Then, in a concluding paragraph, sum up what this experiment shows you about figurative language. Some possible topics are "The Most Gratifying (or Terrifying) Moment of My Life," "The Job I Almost Landed," "The Person I Most Admire."
2. Choose a short poem rich in figurative language: Sylvia Plath's "Metaphors," say, or Burns's "Oh, my love is like a red, red rose." Rewrite the poem, taking for your model Howard Moss's deliberately bepiddling version of "Shall I compare thee to a summer's day?" Eliminate every figure of speech. Turn the poem into language as flat and unsuggestive as possible. (Just ignore any rime or rhythm in the original.) Then, in a paragraph, indicate lines in your revised version that seem glaringly worsened. In conclusion, sum up what your barbaric rewrite tells you about the nature of poetry.

7 Song

SINGING AND SAYING

Most poems are more memorable than most ordinary speech, and when music is combined with poetry the result can be more memorable still. The differences between speech, poetry, and song may appear if we consider, first of all, this fragment of an imaginary conversation between two lovers:

> Let's not drink; let's just sit here and look at each other. Or put a kiss inside my goblet and I won't want anything to drink.

Forgettable language, we might think; but let's try to make it a little more interesting:

> Drink to me only with your eyes, and I'll pledge my love to you with my
>   eyes;
> Or leave a kiss within the goblet, that's all I'll want to drink.

The passage is closer to poetry, but still has a distance to go. At least we now have a figure of speech — the metaphor that love is wine, implied in the statement that one lover may salute another by lifting an eye as well as by lifting a goblet. But the sound of the words is not yet especially interesting. Here is another try, by Ben Jonson:

> Drink to me only with thine eyes,
>   And I will pledge with mine;
> Or leave a kiss but in the cup,
>   And I'll not ask for wine.

In these opening lines from Jonson's poem "To Celia," the improvement is noticeable. These lines are poetry; their language has become special. For one thing, the lines rime (with an additional rime sound on *thine*). There is interest, too, in the proximity of the words *kiss* and *cup:* the repetition (or alliteration) of the *k* sound. The rhythm of the lines has become regular; generally every other word (or syllable) is stressed:

> DRINK to me ON-ly WITH thine EYES,
>   And I will PLEDGE with MINE;
> OR LEAVE a KISS but IN the CUP,
>   And I'LL not ASK for WINE.

All these devices of sound and rhythm, together with metaphor, produce a pleasing effect — more pleasing than the effect of "Let's not drink; let's look at each other." But the words became more pleasing still when later set to music:

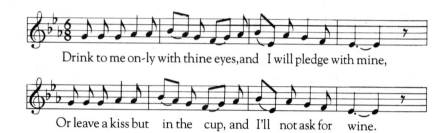

Drink to me on-ly with thine eyes, and I will pledge with mine,

Or leave a kiss but in the cup, and I'll not ask for wine.

In this memorable form, the poem is still alive today.

Ben Jonson (1573? – 1637)*

To Celia   1616

Drink to me only with thine eyes,
    And I will pledge with mine;
Or leave a kiss but in the cup,
    And I'll not ask for wine.
The thirst that from the soul doth rise   5
    Doth ask a drink divine;
But might I of Jove's nectar sup,
    I would not change for thine.

I sent thee late a rosy wreath,
    Not so much honoring thee   10
As giving it a hope that there
    It could not withered be.
But thou thereon didst only breathe,
    And sent'st it back to me;
Since when it grows, and smells, I swear,   15
    Not of itself but thee.

A compliment to a lady has rarely been put in language more graceful, more wealthy with interesting sounds. Other figures of speech besides metaphor make them unforgettable: for example, the hyperbolic tributes to the power of the lady's sweet breath, which can start picked roses growing again, and her kisses, which even surpass the nectar of the gods.

This song falls into stanzas — as many poems that resemble songs also do. A **stanza** (Italian for "station," "stopping-place," or "room") is a group of lines whose pattern is repeated throughout the poem. Most songs have more than one stanza. When printed, the stanzas of songs and poems usually are set off from one another by space. When sung, stanzas of songs are indicated by a pause or by the introduction of a refrain, or chorus (a line or lines repeated). The word **verse,** which strictly refers to one line of a poem, is sometimes loosely used to mean a whole stanza: "All join in and sing the second verse!" In speaking of a stanza, whether sung or read, it is customary to indicate by a convenient algebra its **rime scheme,** the order in which rimed words recur. For instance, the rime scheme of this stanza by Herrick is *a b a b*; the first and third lines rime and so do the second and fourth:

> Round, round, the roof doth run;
>   And being ravished thus,
> Come, I will drink a tun
>   To my Propertius.

Refrains are words, phrases, or lines repeated at intervals in a song or songlike poem. A refrain usually follows immediately after a stanza, and when it does, it is called **terminal refrain.** A refrain whose words change slightly with each recurrence is called an **incremental refrain.** Sometimes we also hear an **internal refrain:** one that appears within a stanza, generally in a position that stays fixed throughout a poem. Both internal refrains and terminal refrains are used to great effect in the traditional song "The Cruel Mother":

Anonymous (traditional Scottish ballad)

THE CRUEL MOTHER

She sat down below a thorn,
    Fine flowers in the valley,
And there she has her sweet babe born
    And the green leaves they grow rarely.

"Smile na sae° sweet, my bonny babe,"   *so*   5
    Fine flowers in the valley,
"And° ye smile sae sweet, ye'll smile me dead."   *if*
    And the green leaves they grow rarely.

She's taen out her little pen-knife,
    Fine flowers in the valley,   10
And twinned° the sweet babe o' its life,   *severed*
    And the green leaves they grow rarely.

She's howket° a grave by the light of the moon,   *dug*
    Fine flowers in the valley,
And there she's buried her sweet babe in   15
    And the green leaves they grow rarely.

As she was going to the church,
    Fine flowers in the valley,
She saw a sweet babe in the porch
    And the green leaves they grow rarely.   20

"O sweet babe, and thou were mine,"
    Fine flowers in the valley,
"I wad cleed° thee in the silk so fine."   *dress*
    And the green leaves they grow rarely.

"O mother dear, when I was thine,"   25
    Fine flowers in the valley,
"You did na prove to me sae kind."
    And the green leaves they grow rarely.

Taken by themselves, the refrain lines might seem mere pretty nonsense. But interwoven with the story of the murdered child, they form a terrible counterpoint. What do they come to mean? Possibly that Nature keeps going about her chores, unmindful of sin and suffering. The effect is an ironic contrast. Besides, by hearing the refrain over and over and over, we find it hard to forget.

    Unlike many poems we read on the printed page, songs tend to be written in language simple enough to understand on first hearing. This immediate clarity is essential to **rap**, a form of popular music in which words are recited to a driving rhythmic beat. In Black English, *rap* means "to talk" ("Let's rap about it"), and in most current rap songs, the singer talks or recites at top speed, dazzling us with long, rhythmic, four-stress lines that end in rimes. Although today many rap singers and groups use electronic backgrounds, rap began on city streets in the game of "signifying," in which two poets aim rimed insults at each other, sometimes accompanying their tirades with a beat made by clapping or finger-snapping. Anyone interested in the form will enjoy listening to Run DMC, Grandmaster Flash, L. L. Cool J, the Fat Boys, and other performers currently popular. Here, for instance, is the opening of a rap lyric, "Parents Just Don't Understand," by W. Smith, J. Townes, and Pete Q. Harris, and performed by D. J. Jazzy Jeff and The Fresh Prince on a recent recording.[1] We listen in on a high school lad's lament:

> You know, parents are the same, no matter time nor place.
> They don't understand that us kids are gonna make *some* mistakes.
> So, to you other kids, all across the land—
> There's no need to argue, parents just don't understand.

---

[1]*He's the DJ, I'm the Rapper* (Jive LP album 1091-1-J, 1988. Copyright © 1988 by Zomba Enterprises, Inc., ASCAP).

I remember one year, my mom took me school shopping—
It was me, my brother, my mom—oh, my pop and
My little sister all hopped in the car.
We headed downtown to the gallery mall.
My mom started buggin' with the clothes she chose.
I didn't say nothing at first, I just turned up my nose.
She said, "What's wrong? This shirt cost twenty dollars!"
I said, "Mom, the shirt is plaid, with a butterfly collar."
The next half-hour was the same old thing,
My mother buying me clothes from nineteen sixty-three,
And then she lost her mind and did the ultimate:
I asked her for Adidas and she bought me Zips!
I said, "Mom, what are you doing? You'll ruin my rep!"
She said, "You're only sixteen, you don't *have* a rep yet."
I said, "Mom, let's put these clothes back, please?"
She said, "No! You go to school to learn, not for a fashion show."
I said, "Decision time, and now—come on, Mom, I'm not Bowser.
Mom, please put back the bell-bottom Brady Bunch trousers.
But if you don't want to, I can live with that,
But you gotta put back the double-knit reversible slacks."

She wasn't givin' in, everything stayed the same.
Inevitably the first day of school came.
I thought I could get over. I tried to play sick,
But my mom said, "No, no way—uh uh—forget it!"
There was nothing I could do. I tried to relax.
I got dressed up in those ancient artifacts
And when I walked in the school, it was just as I thought:
The kids were cracking up laughing at the clothes Mom bought.
And those who weren't laughing still had a ball
'Cause they were pointing and whispering as I walked down the hall.
I got home and told my mom how my day went—
She said, "If they were laughing you don't need them 'cause they're not
    good friends."
For the next six hours, I tried to explain to my mom
That I was gonna have to go through this about two hundred more times.
So to you other kids, all across the land—
There's no need to argue, parents just don't understand.

As the story continues, the speaker takes a joyride in his parents' Porsche with a twelve-year-old runaway until a police car catches him. Although some of these rimes are clever and unexpected (*Bowser / trousers, relax / artifacts*), most of this language sounds ordinary, written to be talked fast and understood at once.

Not all popular songs are so plainspoken: Bob Dylan, Sting, Bono, Elvis Costello, Michelle Shocked, and others have written complicated lyrics full of strange, dreamlike imagery. To unravel them, a listener may have to play a recording many times, with the treble turned up all the way.

Many familiar poems began life as songs, but today, their tunes forgotten, they survive only in poetry anthologies. Shakespeare studded his plays with songs, and many of his contemporaries wrote verse to fit existing tunes. Some poets, themselves musicians (like Thomas Campion), composed both words and music. In Shakespeare's day, **madrigals,** short secular songs for three or more voice-parts arranged in counterpoint, enjoyed great favor. A madrigal by Chidiock Tichborne is given on page 99 and another by an anonymous poet, "The Silver Swan," on page 122.

Some poets who were not composers printed their work in madrigal books for others to set to music. In the seventeenth century, however, poetry and song seem to have fallen away from each other. By the end of the century, much new poetry, other than songs for plays, was written to be printed and to be silently read. Poets who wrote popular songs — like Thomas D'Urfey, compiler of the collection *Pills to Purge Melancholy* — were considered somewhat disreputable. With the notable exceptions of John Gay, who took existing popular tunes for *The Beggar's Opera,* and Robert Burns, who rewrote folk songs or made completely new words for them, few important English poets since Campion have been first-rate song-writers.

Occasionally, a poet has learned a thing or two from music. "But for the opera I could never have written *Leaves of Grass,*" said Walt Whitman, who loved the Italian art form for its expansiveness. Coleridge, Hardy, Auden, and many others have learned from folk ballads, and T. S. Eliot patterned his thematically repetitive *Four Quartets* after the structure of a quartet in classical music. "Poetry," said Ezra Pound, "begins to atrophy when it gets too far from music." Still, even in the twentieth century, the poet has been more often a corrector of printer's proofs than a tunesmith or performer.

Some people think that to make a poem and to travel about singing it, as many rock singer-composers now do, is a return to the venerable tradition of the **troubadours,** minstrels of the late Middle Ages. But there are differences. No doubt the troubadours had to please their patrons, but for better or worse their songs were not affected by a stopwatch in a producer's hand or by the technical resources of a sound studio. Bob Dylan has denied that he is a poet, and Paul Simon once told an interviewer, "If you want poetry read Wallace Stevens." Nevertheless, much has been made lately of current song lyrics as poetry. Are rock songs poems? Clearly some, but not all, are. That the lyrics of a song cannot stand the scrutiny of a reader does not necessarily invalidate them, though; song-writers do not usually write in order to be read. Pete Seeger has quoted a saying of his father: "A printed folk song is like a photograph of a bird in flight." Still there is no reason not to photograph birds, or to read song lyrics. If the words seem rich and interesting, we may possibly increase our enjoyment of them and perhaps be able to sing them more accurately. Like most poems and songs of the past, most current songs may end in the trash can of time. And yet, certain memorable rimed and rhythmic lines may live on, especially if music has served them for a base and if singers have given them wide exposure.

Compare the following poem by Edwin Arlington Robinson and a popular song lyric based on it. Notice what Paul Simon had to do to Robinson's original in order to make it into a song, and how Simon altered Robinson's conception.

Edwin Arlington Robinson (1869 – 1935)

RICHARD CORY   1897

Whenever Richard Cory went down town,
We people on the pavement looked at him:
He was a gentleman from sole to crown,
Clean favored, and imperially slim.

And he was always quietly arrayed,   5
And he was always human when he talked;
But still he fluttered pulses when he said,
"Good-morning," and he glittered when he walked.

And he was rich — yes, richer than a king —
And admirably schooled in every grace: 10
In fine°, we thought that he was everything   *in short*
To make us wish that we were in his place.

So on we worked, and waited for the light,
And went without the meat, and cursed the bread;
And Richard Cory, one calm summer night,   15
Went home and put a bullet through his head.

Paul Simon (b. 1942)

RICHARD CORY   1966

With Apologies to E. A. Robinson

They say that Richard Cory owns
One half of this old town,
With elliptical connections
To spread his wealth around.
Born into Society,   5
A banker's only child,
He had everything a man could want:
Power, grace and style.

Refrain:

But I, I work in his factory
And I curse the life I'm livin'   10
And I curse my poverty
And I wish that I could be
Oh I wish that I could be
Oh I wish that I could be
Richard Cory.   15

The papers print his picture
Almost everywhere he goes:
Richard Cory at the opera,
Richard Cory at a show
And the rumor of his party   20
And the orgies on his yacht —
Oh he surely must be happy
With everything he's got.   *(Refrain.)*

He freely gave to charity,
He had the common touch,   25
And they were grateful for his patronage
And they thanked him very much,
So my mind was filled with wonder
When the evening headlines read:
    "Richard Cory went home last night   30
    And put a bullet through his head."   *(Refrain.)*

RICHARD CORY by Paul Simon. If possible, listen to the ballad sung by Simon and Garfunkel on
Sounds of Silence (Columbia recording CL 2469, stereo CS 9269), © 1966 by Paul Simon. Used
by permission.

BALLADS

Any narrative song, like Paul Simon's "Richard Cory," may be called a **ballad.**
In English, some of the most famous ballads are **folk ballads,** loosely defined
as anonymous story-songs transmitted orally before they were ever written
down. Sir Walter Scott, a pioneer collector of Scottish folk ballads, drew the
ire of an old woman whose songs he had transcribed: "They were made for
singing and no' for reading, but ye ha'e broken the charm now and they'll never
be sung mair." The old singer had a point. Print freezes songs and tends to hold
them fast to a single version. If Scott and others had not written them down,
however, many would have been lost.

In his monumental work *The English and Scottish Popular Ballads*
(1882 – 1898), the American scholar Francis J. Child winnowed out 305 folk
ballads he considered authentic — that is, creations of illiterate or semiliterate
people who had preserved them orally. Child, who worked by insight as well
as by learning, did such a good job of telling the difference between folk ballads
and other kinds that later scholars have added only about a dozen ballads to

his count. Often called **Child ballads,** his texts include "The Three Ravens," "Sir Patrick Spence," "The Twa Corbies," "Edward," "The Cruel Mother," and many others still on the lips of singers. Here is one of the best-known Child ballads.

Anonymous (traditional Scottish ballad)

BONNY BARBARA ALLAN

It was in and about the Martinmas time,
  When the green leaves were afalling,
That Sir John Graeme, in the West Country,
  Fell in love with Barbara Allan.

He sent his men down through the town,   5
  To the place where she was dwelling;
"O haste and come to my master dear,
  Gin° ye be Barbara Allan."   *if*

O hooly°, hooly rose she up,   *slowly*
  To the place where he was lying,   10
And when she drew the curtain by:
  "Young man, I think you're dying."

"O it's I'm sick, and very, very sick,
  And 'tis a' for Barbara Allan." —
"O the better for me ye's never be,   15
  Tho your heart's blood were aspilling.

"O dinna ye mind°, young man," said she,   *don't you remember*
  "When ye was in the tavern adrinking,
That ye made the health° gae round and round,   *toasts*
  And slighted Barbara Allan?"   20

He turned his face unto the wall,
  And death was with him dealing:
"Adieu, adieu, my dear friends all,
  And be kind to Barbara Allan."

And slowly, slowly raise she up,   25
  And slowly, slowly left him,
And sighing said she could not stay,
  Since death of life had reft him.

She had not gane a mile but twa,
  When she heard the dead-bell ringing,   30
And every jow° that the dead-bell geid,   *stroke*
  It cried, "Woe to Barbara Allan!"

"O mother, mother, make my bed!
  O make it saft and narrow!
Since my love died for me today,   35
  I'll die for him tomorrow."

BONNY BARBARA ALLAN. 1 *Martinmas:* Saint Martin's day, November 11.

QUESTIONS

1. In any line does the Scottish dialect cause difficulty? If so, try reading the line aloud.
2. Without ever coming out and explicitly calling Barbara hard-hearted, this ballad reveals that she is. In which stanza and by what means is her cruelty demonstrated?
3. At what point does Barbara evidently have a change of heart? Again, how does the poem dramatize this change without explicitly talking about it?
4. In many American versions of this ballad, noble knight John Graeme becomes an ordinary citizen. The gist of the story is the same, but at the end are these further stanzas, incorporated from a different ballad:

They buried Willie in the old churchyard
  And Barbara in the choir;
And out of his grave grew a red, red rose,
  And out of hers a briar.

They grew and grew to the steeple top
  Till they could grow no higher;
And there they locked in a true love's knot,
  The red rose round the briar.

Do you think this appendage heightens or weakens the final impact of the story? Can the American ending be defended as an integral part of a new song? Explain.
5. Paraphrase lines 9, 15 – 16, 22, 25 – 28. By putting these lines into prose, what has been lost?

As you can see from "Bonny Barbara Allan," in a traditional English or Scottish folk ballad the storyteller speaks of the lives and feelings of others. Even if the pronoun "I" occurs, it rarely has much personality. Characters often exchange dialogue, but no one character speaks all the way through. Events move rapidly, perhaps because some of the dull transitional stanzas have been forgotten. The events themselves, as ballad scholar Albert B. Friedman has said, are frequently "the stuff of tabloid journalism — sensational tales of lust, revenge and domestic crime. Unwed mothers slay their newborn babes; lovers unwilling to marry their pregnant mistresses brutally murder the poor women, for which, without fail, they are justly punished."[2] There are also many ballads of the supernatural ("The Twa Corbies") and of gallant knights ("Sir Patrick Spence"), and there are a few humorous ballads, usually about unhappy marriages.

The ballad-spinner has at hand a fund of ready-made epithets: steeds are usually "milk-white" or "berry-brown," lips "rosy" or "ruby-red," corpses and graves "clay-cold," beds (like Barbara Allan's) "soft and narrow." At the least,

[2]Introduction to *The Viking Book of Folk Ballads of the English-Speaking World,* edited by Albert B. Friedman (New York: Viking, 1956).

these conventional phrases are terse and understandable. Sometimes they add meaning: the king who sends Sir Patrick Spence to his doom drinks "blood-red wine." The clothing, steeds, and palaces of ladies and lords are always luxurious: a queen may wear "grass-green silk" or "Spanish leather" and ride a horse with "fifty silver bells and nine." Such descriptions are naive, for as Friedman points out, ballad-singers were probably peasants imagining what they had seen only from afar: the life of the nobility. This may be why the skin of ladies in folk ballads is ordinarily "milk-white," "lily-white," or "snow-white." In an agrarian society, where most people worked in the fields, not to be suntanned was a sign of gentility.

A favorite pattern of ballad-makers is the so-called **ballad stanza,** four lines rimed *a b c b,* tending to fall into 8, 6, 8, and 6 syllables:

Clerk Saunders and Maid Margaret
   Walked owre yon garden green,
And deep and heavy was the love
   That fell thir twa between°.   *between those two*

Though not the only possible stanza for a ballad, this easily singable quatrain has continued to attract poets since the Middle Ages. Close kin to the ballad stanza is **common meter,** a stanza found in hymns such as "Amazing Grace," by the eighteenth-century English hymnist John Newton:

Amazing grace! how sweet the sound
   That saved a wretch like me!
I once was lost, but now am found,
   Was blind, but now I see.

Notice that its pattern is that of the ballad stanza except for its *two* pairs of rimes. That all its lines rime is probably a sign of more literate artistry than we usually hear in folk ballads. Another sign of schoolteachers' influence is that Newton's rimes are exact. (Rimes in folk ballads are often rough-and-ready, as if made by ear, rather than polished and exact, as if the riming words had been matched for their similar spellings. In "Barbara Allan," for instance, the hard-hearted lover's name rimes with *afalling, dwelling, aspilling, dealing,* and even with *ringing* and *adrinking.*) That so many hymns were written in common meter may have been due to convenience. If a congregation didn't know the tune to a hymn in common meter, they readily could sing its words to the tune of another such hymn they knew. Besides hymnists, many poets have favored common meter, among them A. E. Housman and Emily Dickinson.

Related to traditional folk ballads but displaying characteristics of their own, **broadside ballads** (so called because they were printed on one sheet of paper) often were set to traditional tunes. Most broadside ballads were an early form of journalism made possible by the development of cheap printing and by the growth of audiences who could read, just barely. Sometimes merely humorous or tear-jerking, often they were rimed accounts of sensational news events. That they were widespread and often scorned in Shakespeare's day is attested by the character of Autolycus in *A Winter's Tale,* an itinerant hawker of ballads about sea monsters and strange pregnancies ("a usurer's wife was brought to bed of twenty money-bags"). Although many broadsides tend to be **doggerel** (verse full of irregularities due not to skill but to incompetence), many excellent poets had their work taken up and peddled in the streets — among them Marvell, Swift, and Byron.[3]

Literary ballads, not meant for singing, are written by sophisticated poets for book-educated readers who enjoy being reminded of folk ballads. Literary ballads imitate certain features of folk ballads: they may tell of dramatic conflicts or of mortals who encounter the supernatural; they may use conventional figures of speech or ballad stanzas. Well-known poems of this kind include Keats's "La Belle Dame Sans Merci," Coleridge's "Rime of the Ancient Mariner," and (in our time) Dudley Randall's "Ballad of Birmingham."

Dudley Randall (b. 1914)

BALLAD OF BIRMINGHAM   1966

(On the Bombing of a Church in
Birmingham, Alabama, 1963)

"Mother dear, may I go downtown
Instead of out to play,
And march the streets of Birmingham
In a Freedom March today?"

"No, baby, no, you may not go,   5
For the dogs are fierce and wild,
And clubs and hoses, guns and jail
Aren't good for a little child."

"But, mother, I won't be alone.
Other children will go with me,   10
And march the streets of Birmingham
To make our country free."

"No, baby, no, you may not go,
For I fear those guns will fire.
But you may go to church instead   15
And sing in the children's choir."

She has combed and brushed her night-dark hair,
And bathed rose petal sweet,

[3]A generous collection of broadsides has been assembled by Vivian de Sola Pinto and A. E. Rodway in *The Common Muse: An Anthology of Popular British Ballad Poetry, XVth – XXth Century* (St. Clair Shores, Mich.: Scholarly Press, 1957). See also *Irish Street Ballads,* edited by Colm O. Lochlainn (New York: Corinth Books, 1960), and Olive Woolley Burt, *American Murder Ballads and Their Stories* (New York: Oxford UP, 1958).

And drawn white gloves on her small brown hands,
And white shoes on her feet.   20

The mother smiled to know her child
Was in the sacred place,
But that smile was the last smile
To come upon her face.

For when she heard the explosion,   25
Her eyes grew wet and wild.
She raced through the streets of Birmingham
Calling for her child.

She clawed through bits of glass and brick,
Then lifted out a shoe.   30
"O here's the shoe my baby wore,
But, baby, where are you?"

QUESTIONS

1. This poem, about a dynamite blast set off in a black people's church by a racial terrorist (later convicted), delivers a message without preaching. How would you sum up this message, its implied theme?
2. What is ironic in the mother's denying her child permission to take part in a protest march?
3. How does this modern poem resemble a traditional ballad?

EXPERIMENT: *Seeing the Traits of Ballads*

In the Anthology at the back of this book, read the Child ballads "Edward," "The Three Ravens," and "The Twa Corbies" (pages 278 – 280). With these ballads in mind, consider one or more of these modern poems:

W. H. Auden, "As I Walked Out One Evening" (page 285)
William Jay Smith, "American Primitive" (page 383)
William Butler Yeats, "Crazy Jane Talks with the Bishop" (page 405).

What characteristics of folk ballads do you find in them? In what ways do these modern poets depart from the traditions of folk ballads of the Middle Ages?

FOR REVIEW AND FURTHER STUDY

John Lennon (1940 – 1980)
Paul McCartney (b. 1942)

ELEANOR RIGBY   1966

Ah, look at all the lonely people!
Ah, look at all the lonely people!

Eleanor Rigby
Picks up the rice in the church where a wedding has been,
Lives in a dream,   5

Waits at the window
Wearing the face that she keeps in a jar by the door.
Who is it for?

All the lonely people,
Where do they all come from? 10
All the lonely people,
Where do they all belong?

Father McKenzie,
Writing the words of a sermon that no one will hear,
No one comes near 15
Look at him working,
Darning his socks in the night when there's nobody there.
What does he care?

All the lonely people
Where do they all come from? 20
All the lonely people
Where do they all belong?

Eleanor Rigby
Died in the church and was buried along with her name.
Nobody came. 25
Father McKenzie,
Wiping the dirt from his hands as he walks from the grave,
No one was saved.

All the lonely people,
Where do they all come from? 30
All the lonely people,
Where do they all belong?

Ah, look at all the lonely people!
Ah, look at all the lonely people!

ELEANOR RIGBY by John Lennon and Paul McCartney. This song first appeared in 1966 on the Beatles' album *Revolver* (Capital ST 2576).
    Copyright © 1966 Northern Songs Ltd. All rights for the United States, Canada, and Mexico controlled and administered by Blackwood Music, Inc. under license from ATV Music (Maclen). All rights reserved. International copyright secured. Used by permission.

QUESTION

Is there any reason to call this famous song lyric a ballad? Compare it with a traditional ballad, such as "Bonny Barbara Allan." Do you notice any similarity? What are the differences?

EXERCISE: *Songs or Poems or Both?*

Consider each of the following song lyrics. Which do you think can stand not only to be sung but to be read as poetry? Which probably should not be seen but only heard?

Anonymous (English madrigal)

FA, MI, FA, RE, LA, MI   1609

   Fa, mi, fa, re, la, mi,
Begin, my son, and follow me;
     Sing flat, fa mi,
   So shall we well agree.
     Hey tro loly lo.   5
     Hold fast, good son,
   With hey tro lily lo.
O sing this once again, lustily.

Anonymous (English madrigal)

THE SILVER SWAN, WHO LIVING HAD NO NOTE   1612

The silver swan, who living had no note,
When death approached unlocked her silent throat;
Leaning her breast against the reedy shore,
Thus sung her first and last, and sung no more.
Farewell, all joys; O death, come close mine eyes;
More geese than swans now live, more fools than wise.

Bruce Springsteen (b. 1949)

BORN TO RUN   1975

In the day we sweat it out in the streets
     of a runaway American dream
At night we ride through mansions of
     glory in suicide machines
Sprung from cages out on Highway 9
Chrome wheeled, fuel injected
And steppin' out over the line   5
Baby this town rips the bones from your back
It's a death trap, it's a suicide rap
We gotta get out while we're young
'Cause tramps like us, baby we were born to run.

Wendy, let me in, I wanna be your friend   10
I want to guard your dreams and visions
Just wrap your legs round these velvet rims
And strap your hands across my engines
Together we could break this trap
We'll run till we drop, baby we'll never go back   15

Will you walk with me out on the wire
'Cause baby I'm just a scared and lonely rider
But I gotta know how it feels
I want to know if your love is wild
Girl I want to know if love is real   20

Beyond the Palace hemi-powered drones
        scream down the boulevard
The girls comb their hair in rear-view mirrors
And the boys try to look so hard
The amusement park rises bold and stark
Kids are huddled on the beach in a mist   25
I wanna die with you out on the streets tonight
In an everlasting kiss

The highways jammed with broken heroes
On a last chance power drive
Everybody's out on the run tonight   30
But there's no place left to hide
Together, Wendy, we can live with the sadness
I'll love you with all the madness in my soul
Someday girl, I don't know when,
        we're gonna get to that place
Where we really want to go   35
And we'll walk in the sun
But till then tramps like us
Baby we were born to run

Suggestions for Writing

1. Write a short study of a lyric (or lyrics) by a recent popular song-writer. Show why you believe the song-writer's work deserves the name of poetry.
2. Compare and contrast the English folk ballad "The Three Ravens" with the Scottish folk ballad "The Twa Corbies" (both in the Anthology).
3. Compare the versions of "Richard Cory" by Edwin Arlington Robinson and by Paul Simon. Point out changes Simon apparently made in the poem to render it singable. What other changes did he make? How did he alter Robinson's story and its characters?
4. After listening to some recent examples of rap (see page 111), compose a short rap lyric of your own, one that tells a story.

8 *Sound*

SOUND AS MEANING

Isak Dinesen, in a memoir of her life on a plantation in East Africa, tells how some Kikuyu tribesmen reacted to their first hearing of rimed verse:

> The Natives, who have a strong sense of rhythm, know nothing of verse, or at least did not know anything before the times of the schools, where they were taught hymns. One evening out in the maize-field, where we had been harvesting maize, breaking off the cobs and throwing them on to the ox-carts, to amuse myself, I spoke to the field laborers, who were mostly quite young, in Swahili verse. There was no sense in the verses, they were made for the sake of rime — "Ngumbe na-penda chumbe, Malaya mbaya. Wakamba na-kula mamba." The oxen like salt — whores are bad — The Wakamba eat snakes. It caught the interest of the boys, they formed a ring round me. They were quick to understand that meaning in poetry is of no consequence, and they did not question the thesis of the verse, but waited eagerly for the rime, and laughed at it when it came. I tried to make them themselves find the rime and finish the poem when I had begun it, but they could not, or would not, do that, and turned away their heads. As they had become used to the idea of poetry, they begged: "Speak again. Speak like rain." Why they should feel verse to be like rain I do not know. It must have been, however, an expression of applause, since in Africa rain is always longed for and welcomed.[1]

What the tribesmen had discovered is that poetry, like music, appeals to the ear. However limited it may be in comparison with the sound of an orchestra — or a tribal drummer — the sound of words in itself gives pleasure. However,

[1] Isak Dinesen, *Out of Africa* (New York: Random, 1972).

we might doubt Isak Dinesen's assumption that "meaning in poetry is of no consequence." "Hey nonny-nonny" and such nonsense has a place in song lyrics and other poems, and we might take pleasure in hearing rimes in Swahili; but most good poetry has meaningful sound as well as musical sound. Certainly the words of a song have an effect different from that of wordless music: they go along with their music and, by making statements, add more meaning. The French poet Isidore Isou, founder of a literary movement called *lettrisme*, maintained that poems can be written not only in words but in letters (sample lines: *xyl, xyl, / prprali dryl / znglo trpylo pwi*). But the sound of letters alone, without denotation and connotation, has not been enough to make Letterist poems memorable. In the response of the Kikuyu tribesmen, there may have been not only the pleasure of hearing sounds but also the agreeable surprise of finding that things not usually associated had been brought together.

More powerful when in the company of meaning, not apart from it, the sounds of consonants and vowels can contribute greatly to a poem's effect. The sound of *s*, which can suggest the swishing of water, has rarely been used more accurately than in Surrey's line "Calm is the sea, the waves work less and less." When, in a poem, the sound of words working together with meaning pleases mind and ear, the effect is **euphony,** as in the following lines from Tennyson's "Come down, O maid":

> Myriads of rivulets hurrying through the lawn,
> The moan of doves in immemorial elms,
> And murmuring of innumerable bees.

Its opposite is **cacophony:** a harsh, discordant effect. It too is chosen for the sake of meaning. We hear it in Milton's scornful reference in "Lycidas" to corrupt clergymen whose songs "Grate on their scrannel pipes of wretched straw." (Read that line and one of Tennyson's aloud and see which requires lips, teeth, and tongue to do more work.) But note that although Milton's line is harsh in sound, the line (when we meet it in his poem) is pleasing because it is artful. In a famous passage from his *Essay on Criticism,* Pope has illustrated both euphony and cacophony. (Given here as Pope printed it, the passage relies heavily on italics and capital letters, for particular emphasis. If you will read these lines aloud, dwelling a little longer or harder on the words italicized, you will find that Pope has given you very good directions for a meaningful reading.)

Alexander Pope (1688 – 1744)*

TRUE EASE IN WRITING COMES FROM ART, NOT CHANCE   1711

True Ease in Writing comes from Art, not Chance,
As those move easiest who have learned to dance.
'Tis not enough no Harshness gives Offence,
The *Sound* must seem an *Echo* to the *Sense.*
Soft is the strain when *Zephyr°* gently blows,   *the west wind*   5

And the *smooth Stream* in *smoother Numbers*° flows;   *metrical rhythm*
But when loud Surges lash the sounding Shore,
The *hoarse, rough Verse* should like the *Torrent* roar.
When *Ajax* strives, some Rock's vast Weight to throw,
The Line too *labors,* and the Words move *slow;*   10
Not so, when swift *Camilla* scours the Plain,
Flies o'er th' unbending Corn, and skims along the Main°.   *expanse (of sea)*
Hear how *Timotheus'* varied Lays surprise,
And bid Alternate Passions fall and rise!
While, at each Change, the Son of *Lybian Jove*   15
Now *burns* with Glory, and then *melts* with Love;
Now his *fierce Eyes* with *sparkling Fury* glow;
Now *Sighs* steal out, and *Tears begin to flow:*
Persians and Greeks like *Turns of Nature* found,
And the *World's Victor* stood subdued by *Sound!*   20
The Pow'rs of Music all our Hearts allow;
And what *Timotheus* was, is *Dryden* now.

TRUE EASE IN WRITING COMES FROM ART, NOT CHANCE (*An Essay on Criticism,* lines 362 – 383). 9
Ajax: Greek hero, almost a superman, who in Homer's account of the siege of Troy hurls an
enormous rock that momentarily flattens Hector, the Trojan prince (*Iliad* VII, 268 – 272). 11
Camilla: a kind of Amazon or warrior woman of the Volcians, whose speed and lightness of step
are praised by the Roman poet Virgil: "She could have skimmed across an unmown grainfield /
Without so much as bruising one tender blade; / She could have sped across an ocean's surge /
Without so much as wetting her quicksilver soles" (*Aeneid* VII, 808 – 811). 13 *Timotheus:* favorite
musician of Alexander the Great. In "Alexander's Feast, or The Power of Music," John Dryden
imagines him: "Timotheus, placed on high / Amid the tuneful choir, / With flying fingers touched
the lyre: / The trembling notes ascend the sky, / And heavenly joys inspire." 15 *Lybian Jove:* name
for Alexander. A Libyan oracle had declared the king to be the son of the god Zeus Ammon.

Notice the pleasing effect of all the *s* sounds in the lines about the west wind
and the stream, and in another meaningful place, the effect of the consonants
in *Ajax strives,* a phrase that makes our lips work almost as hard as Ajax
throwing the rock.

Is sound identical with meaning in lines such as these? Not quite. In the
passage from Tennyson, for instance, the cooing of doves is not *exactly* a moan.
As John Crowe Ransom pointed out, the sound would be almost the same but
the meaning entirely different in "The murdering of innumerable beeves."
While it is true that the consonant sound *sl-* will often begin a word that
conveys ideas of wetness and smoothness — *slick, slimy, slippery, slush* — we are
so used to hearing it in words that convey nothing of the kind — *slave, slow,
sledgehammer* — that it is doubtful whether, all by itself, the sound communicates anything definite. The most beautiful phrase in the English language,
according to Dorothy Parker, is *cellar door.* Another wit once nominated, as our
most euphonious word, not *sunrise* or *silvery* but *syphilis.*

Relating sound more closely to meaning, the device called **onomatopoeia**
is an attempt to represent a thing or action by a word that imitates the sound
associated with it: *zoom, whiz, crash, bang, ding-dong, pitter-patter, yakety-yak.*
Onomatopoeia is often effective in poetry, as in Emily Dickinson's line about
the fly with its "uncertain stumbling Buzz," in which the nasal sounds *n, m, ng*

and the sibilants *c, s* help make a droning buzz, and in Robert Lowell's transcription of a bird call, "yuck-a, yuck-a, yuck-a" (in "Falling Asleep over the Aeneid").

Like the Kikuyu tribesmen, others who care for poetry have discovered in the sound of words something of the refreshment of cool rain. Dylan Thomas, telling how he began to write poetry, said that from early childhood words were to him "as the notes of bells, the sounds of musical instruments, the noises of wind, sea, and rain, the rattle of milkcarts, the clopping of hooves on cobbles, the fingering of branches on the window pane, might be to someone, deaf from birth, who has miraculously found his hearing."[2] For readers, too, the sound of words can have a magical spell, most powerful when it points to meaning. James Weldon Johnson in *God's Trombones* has told of an old-time preacher who began his sermon, "Brothers and sisters, this morning I intend to explain the unexplainable — find out the indefinable — ponder over the imponderable — and unscrew the inscrutable!" The repetition of sound in *unscrew* and *inscrutable* has appeal, but the magic of the words is all the greater if they lead us to imagine the mystery of all Creation as an enormous screw that the preacher's mind, like a screw-driver, will loosen. Though the sound of a word or the meaning of a word may have value all by itself, both become more memorable when taken together.

William Butler Yeats (1865 – 1939)*

WHO GOES WITH FERGUS?   1892

Who will go drive with Fergus now,
And pierce the deep wood's woven shade,
And dance upon the level shore?
Young man, lift up your russet brow,
And lift your tender eyelids, maid,   5
And brood on hopes and fear no more.

And no more turn aside and brood
Upon love's bitter mystery;
For Fergus rules the brazen cars°,   *chariots*
And rules the shadows of the wood,   10
And the white breast of the dim sea
And all dishevelled wandering stars.

WHO GOES WITH FERGUS? *Fergus:* Irish king who gave up his throne to be a wandering poet.

QUESTIONS

1. In what lines do you find euphony? *good sound*
2. In what line do you find cacophony? *bad sound*
3. How do the sounds of these lines stress what is said in them?

[2]"Notes on the Art of Poetry," *Modern Poetics,* ed. James Scully (New York: McGraw-Hill, 1965).

EXERCISE: *Listening to Meaning*

Read aloud the following brief poems. In the sounds of which particular words are meanings well captured? In which of the poems below do you find onomatopoeia?

John Updike (b. 1932)*

WINTER OCEAN   1960

Many-maned scud-thumper, tub
of male whales, maker of worn wood, shrub-
ruster, sky-mocker, rave!
portly pusher of waves, wind-slave.

Frances Cornford (1886 – 1960)

THE WATCH   1923

I wakened on my hot, hard bed,
Upon the pillow lay my head;
Beneath the pillow I could hear
My little watch was ticking clear.
I thought the throbbing of it went   5
Like my continual discontent. *dissatisfied*
I thought it said in every tick: *restless*
I am so sick, so sick, so sick.
O death, come quick, come quick, come quick,
Come quick, come quick, come quick, come quick!   10

[handwritten annotations: "Pal Pitation" and "regular" near line 5]

William Wordsworth (1770 – 1850)*

A SLUMBER DID MY SPIRIT SEAL   1800

A slumber did my spirit seal;
    I had no human fears —
She seemed a thing that could not feel
    The touch of earthly years.

No motion has she now, no force;   5
    She neither hears nor sees;
Rolled round in earth's diurnal course,
    With rocks, and stones, and trees.

Emanuel di Pasquale (b. 1943)*

RAIN   1971

Like a drummer's brush,
the rain hushes the surface of tin porches.

Aphra Behn (1640?–1689)

WHEN MAIDENS ARE YOUNG   1687

When maidens are young, and in their spring,
Of pleasure, of pleasure let 'em take their full swing,
   Full swing, full swing,
And love, and dance, and play, and sing,
For Silvia, believe it, when youth is done,   5
There's nought but hum-drum, hum-drum, hum-drum,
There's nought but hum-drum, hum-drum, hum-drum.

ALLITERATION AND ASSONANCE

Listening to a symphony in which themes are repeated throughout each
movement, we enjoy both their recurrence and their variation. We take similar
pleasure in the repetition of a phrase or a single chord. Something like this
pleasure is afforded us frequently in poetry.

Analogies between poetry and wordless music, it is true, tend to break
down when carried far, since poetry — to mention a single difference — has
denotation. But like musical compositions, poems have patterns of sounds.
Among such patterns long popular in English poetry is **alliteration**, which has
been defined as a succession of similar sounds. Alliteration occurs in the
repetition of the same consonant sound at the beginning of successive
words — "round and round the rugged rocks the ragged rascal ran" — or
inside the words, as in Milton's description of the gates of Hell:

> On a sudden open fly
> With impetuous recoil and jarring sound
> The infernal doors, and on their hinges grate
> Harsh thunder, that the lowest bottom shook
> Of Erebus.

The former kind is called **initial alliteration**, the latter **internal alliteration**
or **hidden alliteration**. We recognize alliteration by sound, not by spelling:
know and *nail* alliterate, *know* and *key* do not. In a line by E. E. Cummings,

"colossal hoax of clocks and calendars," the sound of *x* within *hoax* alliterates with the *cks* in *clocks*. Incidentally, the letter *r* does not *always* lend itself to cacophony: elsewhere in *Paradise Lost* Milton said that

> Heaven opened wide
> Her ever-during gates, harmonious sound
> On golden hinges moving . . .

By itself, a letter-sound has no particular meaning. This is a truth forgotten by people who would attribute the effectiveness of Milton's lines on the Heavenly Gates to, say, "the mellow *o*'s and liquid *l* of *harmonious* and *golden*." Mellow *o*'s and liquid *l*'s occur also in the phrase *moldy cold oatmeal*, which may have a quite different effect. Meaning depends on larger units of language than letters of the alphabet.

Today good prose writers usually avoid alliteration; in the past, some cultivated it. "There is nothing more swifter than time, nothing more sweeter," wrote John Lyly in *Euphues* (1579), and he went on — playing especially with the sounds of *v, n, t, s, l,* and *b* — "we have not, as Seneca saith, little time to live, but we lose much; neither have we a short life by nature, but we make it shorter by naughtiness." Poetry, too, formerly contained more alliteration than it usually contains today. In Old English verse, each line was held together by alliteration, a basic pattern still evident in the fourteenth century, as in the following description of the world as a "fair field" in *Piers Plowman:*

> A *f*eir *f*eld *f*ul of *f*olk *f*ond I ther bi-twene,
> Of alle *m*aner of *m*en, the *m*ene and the riche . . .

Most poets nowadays save alliteration for special occasions. They may use it to give emphasis, as Edward Lear does: "*F*ar and *f*ew, *f*ar and *f*ew, / Are the *l*ands where the Jumblies *l*ive." With its aid they can point out the relationship between two things placed side by side, as in Pope's line on things of little worth: "The courtier's *p*romises, and sick man's *p*rayers." Alliteration, too, can be a powerful aid to memory. It is hard to forget such tongue twisters as "Peter Piper picked a peck of pickled peppers," or common expressions like "green as grass," "tried and true," and "from stem to stern." In fact, because alliteration directs our attention to something, it had best be used neither thoughtlessly nor merely for decoration, lest it call attention to emptiness. A case in point may be a line by Philip James Bailey, a reaction to a lady's weeping: "I saw, but *sp*ared to *sp*eak." If the poet chose the word *spared* for any meaningful reason other than that it alliterates with *speak,* the reason is not clear.

As we have seen, to repeat the sound of a consonant is to produce alliteration, but to repeat the sound of a *vowel* is to produce **assonance.** Like alliteration, assonance may occur either initially — "*a*ll the *aw*ful *au*guries"[3] — or internally — Edmund Spenser's "Her goodly *eyes* like sapph*i*res sh*i*ning

---

[3]Some prefer to call the repetition of an initial vowel-sound by the name of alliteration: "apt alliteration's artful aid."

bright, / Her forehead *ivory white* . . ." and it can help make common phrases unforgettable: "eager beaver," "holy smoke." Like alliteration, it slows the reader down and focuses attention.

A. E. Housman (1859 – 1936)*

EIGHT O'CLOCK   1922

He stood, and heard the steeple
   Sprinkle the quarters on the morning town.
One, two, three, four, to market-place and people
   It tossed them down.

Strapped, noosed, nighing his hour,   5
   He stood and counted them and cursed his luck;
And then the clock collected in the tower
   Its strength, and struck.

QUESTIONS

1. Why does the protagonist in this brief drama curse his luck? What is his situation?
2. For so short a poem, "Eight O'Clock" carries a great weight of alliteration. What patterns of initial alliteration do you find? What patterns of internal alliteration? What effect is created by all this heavy emphasis?

Robert Herrick (1591 – 1674)*

UPON JULIA'S VOICE   1648

So smooth, so sweet, so silv'ry is thy voice,
As, could they hear, the damned would make no noise,
But listen to thee (walking in thy chamber)
Melting melodious words, to lutes of amber.

UPON JULIA'S VOICE. 4 *amber:* either the fossilized resin from which pipestems are sometimes made today, and which might have inlaid the body of a lute; or an alloy of four parts silver and one part gold.

QUESTIONS

1. Is Julia speaking or singing? How do we know for sure?
2. In what moments in this brief poem does the sound of words especially help convey meaning?
3. Does Herrick's reference to *the damned* (presumably howling from Hell's torments) seem out of place?

Janet Lewis (b. 1899)

GIRL HELP   1927

Mild and slow and young,
She moves about the room,
And stirs the summer dust
With her wide broom.

In the warm, lofted air,   5
Soft lips together pressed,
Soft wispy hair,
She stops to rest,

And stops to breathe,
Amid the summer hum,   10
The great white lilac bloom
Scented with days to come.

QUESTIONS

1. What assonance and alliteration do you find in this poem? (Suggestion: It may help to read the poem aloud.)
2. In this particular poem, how are these repetitions (or echoes) of sound valuable?

EXERCISE: *Hearing How Sound Helps*

Which of these translations of the same passage from Petrarch do you think is better poetry? Why? What do assonance and alliteration have to do with your preference?

1. Love that liveth and reigneth in my thought,
   That built his seat within my captive breast,
   Clad in the arms wherein with me he fought,
   Oft in my face he doth his banner rest.
          —Henry Howard, Earl of Surrey (1517? – 1547)
2. The long love that in my thought doth harbor,
   And in mine heart doth keep his residence,
   Into my face presseth with bold pretense
   And therein campeth, spreading his banner.
          —Sir Thomas Wyatt (1503? – 1542)

EXPERIMENT: *Reading for Assonance*

Try reading aloud as rapidly as possible the following poem by Tennyson. From the difficulties you encounter, you may be able to sense the slowing effect of assonance. Then read the poem aloud a second time, with consideration.

THE SPLENDOR FALLS ON CASTLE WALLS   1850

The splendor falls on castle walls
    And snowy summits old in story;
The long light shakes across the lakes,
    And the wild cataract leaps in glory.
Blow, bugle, blow, set the wild echoes flying,   5
Blow, bugle; answer, echoes, dying, dying, dying.

    O hark, O hear! how thin and clear,
        And thinner, clearer, farther going!
    O sweet and far from cliff and scar°   *jutting rock*
        The horns of Elfland faintly blowing!   10
Blow, let us hear the purple glens replying:
Blow, bugle; answer, echoes, dying, dying, dying.

    O love, they die in yon rich sky,
        They faint on hill or field or river;
    Our echoes roll from soul to soul,   15
        And grow for ever and for ever.
Blow, bugle, blow, set the wild echoes flying,
And answer, echoes, answer, dying, dying, dying.

RIME

Isak Dinesen's tribesmen, to whom rime was a new phenomenon, recognized at once that rimed language is special language. So do we, for, although much English poetry is unrimed, rime is one means to set poetry apart from ordinary conversation and bring it closer to music. A **rime** (or rhyme), defined most narrowly, occurs when two or more words or phrases contain an identical or similar vowel-sound, usually accented, and the consonant-sounds (if any) that follow the vowel-sound are identical: *hay* and *sleigh, prairie schooner* and *piano tuner.*[4] From these examples it will be seen that rime depends not on spelling but on sound.

    Excellent rimes surprise. It is all very well that a reader may anticipate which vowel-sound is coming next, for patterns of rime give pleasure by satisfying expectations; but riming becomes dull clunking if, at the end of each line, the reader can predict the word that will end the next. Hearing many a jukebox song for the first time, a listener can do so: *charms* lead to *arms, skies above* to *love.* As Alexander Pope observes of the habits of dull rimesters,

[4]Some definitions of *rime* would apply the term to the repetition of any identical or similar sound, not only a vowel-sound. In this sense, assonance is a kind of rime; so is alliteration (called **initial rime**).

Where'er you find "the cooling western breeze,"
In the next line it "whispers through the trees";
If crystal streams "with pleasing murmurs creep,"
The reader's threatened (not in vain) with "sleep" . . .

But who — given the opening line of this comic poem — could predict the lines that follow?

William Cole (b. 1919)

ON MY BOAT ON LAKE CAYUGA   1985

On my boat on Lake Cayuga
I have a horn that goes "Ay-oogah!"
I'm not the modern kind of creep
Who has a horn that goes "beep beep."

Robert Herrick, in a more subtle poem, made good use of rime to indicate a startling contrast:

Then while time serves, and we are but decaying,
Come, my Corinna, come, let's go a-Maying.

Though good rimes seem fresh, not all will startle, and probably few will call to mind things so unlike as *May* and *decay*, *Cayuga* and *Ay-oogah*. Some masters of rime often link words that, taken out of text, might seem common and unevocative. Here, for instance, is Alexander Pope's comment on a trifling courtier:

Yet let me flap this bug with gilded wings,
This painted child of dirt, that stinks and stings;
Whose buzz the witty and the fair annoys,
Yet wit ne'er tastes, and beauty ne'er enjoys:
So well-bred spaniels civilly delight
In mumbling of the game they dare not bite.
Eternal smiles his emptiness betray,
As shallow streams run dimpling all the way.

Pope's rime-words are not especially memorable — and yet these lines are, because (among other reasons) they rime. Wit may be driven home without rime, but it is rime that rings the doorbell. Admittedly, some rimes wear thin from too much use. More difficult to use freshly than before the establishment of Tin Pan Alley, rimes such as *moon, June, croon* seem leaden and to ring true would need an extremely powerful context. *Death* and *breath* are a rime that poets have used with wearisome frequency; another is *birth, earth, mirth*. And yet we cannot exclude these from the diction of poetry, for they might be the very words a poet would need in order to say something new and original. The following brief poem seems fresher than its rimes (if taken out of context) would lead us to expect.

William Blake (1757 – 1827)*

THE ANGEL THAT PRESIDED O'ER MY BIRTH   (1808 – 1811)

The Angel that presided o'er my birth
Said, "Little creature, formed of Joy and Mirth,
Go love without the help of any thing on earth."

What matters to rime is freshness — not of a word but of the poet's way of seeing.

Good poets, said John Dryden, learn to make their rime "so properly a part of the verse, that it should never mislead the sense, but itself be led and governed by it." The comment may remind us that skillful rime — unlike poor rime — is never a distracting ornament. "Rime the rudder is of verses, / With which, like ships, they steer their courses," wrote the seventeenth-century poet Samuel Butler. Like other patterns of sound, rime can help a poet to group ideas, emphasize particular words, and weave a poem together. It can start reverberations between words and can point to connections of meaning.

To have an **exact rime,** sounds following the vowel sound have to be the same: *red* and *bread, wealthily* and *stealthily, walk to her* and *talk to her.* If final consonant sounds are the same but the vowel sounds are different, the result is **slant rime,** also called **near rime, off rime,** or **imperfect rime:** *sun* riming with *bone, moon, rain, green, gone, thin.* By not satisfying the reader's expectation of an exact chime, but instead giving a clunk, a slant rime can help a poet say some things in a particular way. It works especially well for disappointed let-downs, negations, and denials, as in Blake's couplet:

He who the ox to wrath has moved
Shall never be by woman loved.

Many poets have admired the unexpected and arresting effect of a slant rime. As a student in high school, Kenneth Burke (later to become known as a critic, poet, and fiction writer) decided that "the most nearly perfect possible imperfect rime" was the combination of *widow-shadow-meadow.* "Ever since then," he wrote, "I have been trying to fit them just right into a poem—and maybe some day I'll succeed." Here is one attempt.

Kenneth Burke (b. 1897)

THE HABIT OF IMPERFECT RHYMING   1968

Lips now rhyme with slops
Hips with blobs
Passion with nuclear fission
And beauty with shoddy.
The word for lovely leisure, *school,*   5

Is now in line with urban sprawl.
Are we blunted or haunted?
Is last year's auto a dodo?
Let widow be bedded
With shadow and meadow.   10

All this is necessary
Says the secretary—
Else moan, groan, bone must go with alone,
As breath must go with death.

Consonance, a kind of slant rime, occurs when the rimed words or phrases have the same consonant sounds but a different vowel, as in *chitter* and *chatter*. It is used in a traditional nonsense poem, "The Cutty Wren": " 'O where are you going?' says *Milder* to *Malder.*" (W. H. Auden wrote a variation on it that begins, " 'O where are you going?' said *reader* to *rider,*" thus keeping the consonance.)

End rime, as its name indicates, comes at the ends of lines, **internal rime** within them. Most rime tends to be end rime. Few recent poets have used internal rime so heavily as Wallace Stevens in the beginning of "Bantams in Pine-Woods": "Chieftain Iffucan of Azcan in caftan / Of tan with henna hackles, halt!" (lines also heavy on alliteration). A poet may employ both end rime and internal rime in the same poem, as in Robert Burns's satiric ballad "The Kirk's Alarm":

> Orthodox, Orthodox, wha believe in John Knox,
>   Let me sound an alarm to your conscience:
> There's a heretic blast has been blawn i' the wast°,   *west*
>   "That what is not sense must be nonsense."

Masculine rime is a rime of one-syllable words (*jail, bail*) or (in words of more than one syllable) stressed final syllables: *di-VORCE, re-MORSE,* or *horse, re-MORSE.* **Feminine rime** is a rime of two or more syllables, with stress on a syllable other than the last: *TUR-tle, FER-tile,* or (to take an example from Byron) *in-tel-LECT-u-al, hen-PECKED you all.* Often it lends itself to comic verse, but can occasionally be valuable to serious poems, as in Wordsworth's "Resolution and Independence":

> We poets in our youth begin in gladness,
> But thereof come in the end despondency and madness.

or as in Anne Sexton's seriously witty "Eighteen Days Without You":

> and of course we're not married, we are a pair of scissors
> who come together to cut, without towels saying His. Hers.

Serious poems containing feminine rimes of three syllables have been attempted, notably by Thomas Hood in "The Bridge of Sighs":

Take her up tenderly,
Lift her with care;
Fashioned so slenderly,
Young, and so fair!

But the pattern is hard to sustain without lapsing into unintended comedy, as in the same poem:

Still, for all slips of hers,
One of Eve's family —
Wipe those poor lips of hers,
Oozing so clammily.

It works better when comedy is wanted:

Hilaire Belloc (1870 – 1953)

THE HIPPOPOTAMUS   1896

I shoot the Hippopotamus
    with bullets made of platinum,
Because if I use leaden ones
    his hide is sure to flatten 'em.

In **eye rime,** spellings look alike but pronunciations differ — *rough* and *dough*, *idea* and *flea*, *Venus* and *menus*. Strictly speaking, eye rime is not rime at all.

In the early 1960s in American poetry, rime suffered a tremendous fall from favor. A new generation of poets took for models the open forms of Whitman and William Carlos Williams. Only lately has skilled rime prominently reappeared, in the work of new poets such as R. L. Barth, Amy Clampitt, Dana Gioia, R. S. Gwynn, Marilyn Hacker, Gjertrud Schnackenberg, and Timothy Steele. Here is a recent sample:

Brad Leithauser (b. 1953)

TRAUMA   1982

You will carry this suture
    Into the future.
The past never passes.
    It simply amasses.

Still, most American poets don't write in rime; some even consider it exhausted. Such a view may be a reaction against the wearing-thin of rimes by overuse or the mechanical and meaningless application of a rime scheme. Yet anyone who listens to children skipping rope in the street, making up rimes to delight themselves as they go along, may doubt that the pleasures of rime are ended; and certainly the practice of Yeats and Emily Dickinson, to name only two, suggests that the possibilities of slant rime may be nearly infinite. If successfully employed, as it has been at times by a majority of English-speaking poets whose work we care to save, rime runs through its poem like a spine: the creature moves by means of it.

William Butler Yeats (1865 – 1939)*

LEDA AND THE SWAN   1924

A sudden blow: the great wings beating still
Above the staggering girl, her thighs caressed
By the dark webs, her nape caught in his bill,
He holds her helpless breast upon his breast.

How can those terrified vague fingers push   5
The feathered glory from her loosening thighs?
And how can body, laid in that white rush,
But feel the strange heart beating where it lies?

A shudder in the loins engenders there
The broken wall, the burning roof and tower   10
And Agamemnon dead.
                         Being so caught up,
So mastered by the brute blood of the air,
Did she put on his knowledge with his power
Before the indifferent beak could let her drop?

QUESTIONS

1. According to Greek mythology, the god Zeus in the form of a swan descended upon Leda, a Spartan queen. Among the offspring of this union were Clytemnestra, Agamemnon's unfaithful wife who conspired in his murder, and Helen, on whose account the Trojan war was fought. What does a knowledge of these allusions contribute to our understanding of the poem's last two lines?
2. The slant rime *up / drop* (lines 11, 14) may seem accidental or inept. Is it? Would this poem have ended nearly so well if Yeats had made an exact rime like *up / cup* or like *stop / drop*?

Gerard Manley Hopkins (1844 – 1889)*

GOD'S GRANDEUR   (1877)

The world is charged with the grandeur of God.
   It will flame out, like shining from shook foil;
   It gathers to a greatness, like the ooze of oil
Crushed. Why do men then now not reck his rod?
Generations have trod, have trod, have trod;   5
   And all is seared with trade; bleared, smeared with toil;
   And wears man's smudge and shares man's smell: the soil
Is bare now, nor can foot feel, being shod.

And for all this, nature is never spent;
   There lives the dearest freshness deep down things;   10
And though the last lights off the black West went
   Oh, morning, at the brown brink eastward, springs —
Because the Holy Ghost over the bent
   World broods with warm breast and with ah! bright wings.

GOD'S GRANDEUR. 1 *charged:* as though with electricity. 3–4 *It gathers . . . Crushed:* The grandeur of God will rise and be manifest, as oil rises and collects from crushed olives or grain. 4 *reck his rod:* heed His law. 10 *deep down things:* Tightly packing the poem, Hopkins omits the preposition *in* or *within* before *things.* 11 *last lights . . . went:* When in 1534 Henry VIII broke ties with the Roman Catholic Church and created the Church of England?

QUESTIONS

1. In a letter Hopkins explained *shook foil* (line 2): "I mean foil in its sense of leaf or tinsel. . . . Shaken goldfoil gives off broad glares like sheet lightning and also, and this is true of nothing else, owing to its zigzag dints and creasings and network of small many cornered facets, a sort of fork lightning too." What do you think he meant by the phrase *ooze of oil* (line 3)? Would you call this phrase an example of alliteration?
2. What instances of internal rime does the poem contain? How would you describe their effects?
3. Point out some of the poet's uses of alliteration and assonance. Do you believe that Hopkins perhaps goes too far in his heavy use of devices of sound, or would you defend his practice?
4. Why do you suppose Hopkins, in the last two lines, says *over the bent / World* instead of (as we might expect) *bent over the world?* How can the world be bent? Can you make any sense out of this wording, or is Hopkins just trying to get his rime scheme to work out?

James Whitehead (b. 1936)

THE COUNTRY MUSIC STAR BEGINS HIS POLITICS   1979

There are no deadlier Americas
Than those I see from stages where I work,
And over coffee in the bad cafes,
Which is how everyone is going broke
Investing in good times and sentiment   5
Which pays my wages.
                        Squandering their love
The size of death and a revival tent
A troubled pride is what I have to give.

Whatever else they want they hardly say,
And I don't either. I am paid to strum   10
And make up songs that help grown children play.
The thing I do has prospered and gone wrong.
Lord, we are multiplied and we mean well.
There's murder in the darkness I can't kill.

QUESTIONS

1. What ironies trouble the speaker in this sonnet?
2. What suggestions emanate from Whitehead's title?
3. Notice the off-rimes, especially *work / broke*, *strum / wrong*, and *well / kill*. To what
   extent do they help to illuminate the poem's theme?

Robert Frost (1874 – 1963)*

DESERT PLACES   1936

Snow falling and night falling fast, oh, fast
In a field I looked into going past,
And the ground almost covered smooth in snow,
But a few weeds and stubble showing last.

The woods around it have it — it is theirs.   5
All animals are smothered in their lairs,
I am too absent-spirited to count;
The loneliness includes me unawares.

And lonely as it is, that loneliness
Will be more lonely ere it will be less —   10
A blanker whiteness of benighted snow
With no expression, nothing to express.

They cannot scare me with their empty spaces
Between stars — on stars where no human race is.
I have it in me so much nearer home   15
To scare myself with my own desert places.

1. What are these desert places that the speaker finds in himself? (More than one theory is possible. What is yours?)
2. Notice how many times, within the short space of lines 8 – 10, Frost says *lonely* (or *loneliness*). What other words in the poem contain similar sounds that reinforce these words?
3. In the closing stanza, the feminine rimes *spaces, race is,* and *places* might well occur in light or comic verse. Does "Desert Places" leave you laughing? If not, what does it make you feel?

READING AND HEARING POEMS ALOUD

Thomas Moore's "The light that lies in women's eyes" — a line rich in internal rime, alliteration, and assonance — is harder to forget than "The light burning in the gaze of a woman." Because of sound, it is possible to remember the obscure line Christopher Smart wrote while in an insane asylum: "Let Ross, house of Ross rejoice with the Great Flabber Dabber Flat Clapping Fish with hands." Such lines, striking as they are even when read silently, become still more effective when said out loud. Reading poems aloud is a way to understand them. For this reason, practice the art of lending poetry your voice.

Before trying to read a poem aloud to other people, understand its meaning as thoroughly as possible. If you know what the poet is saying and the poet's attitude toward it, you will be able to find an appropriate tone of voice and to give each part of the poem a proper emphasis.

Except in the most informal situations and in some class exercises, read a poem to yourself before trying it on an audience. No actor goes before the footlights without first having studied the script, and the language of poems usually demands even more consideration than the language of most contemporary plays. Prepare your reading in advance. Check pronunciations you are not sure of. Underline things to be emphasized.

Read deliberately, more slowly than you would read aloud from a newspaper. Keep in mind that you are saying something to somebody. Don't race through the poem as if you are eager to get it over with.

Don't lapse into singsong. A poem may have a definite swing, but swing should never be exaggerated at the cost of sense. If you understand what the poem is saying and utter the poem as if you do, the temptation to fall into such a mechanical intonation should not occur. Observe the punctuation, making slight pauses for commas, longer pauses for full stops (periods, question marks, exclamation points).

If the poem is rimed, don't raise your voice and make the rimes stand out unnaturally. They should receive no more volume than other words in the poem, though a faint pause at the end of each line will call the listener's attention to them. This advice is contrary to a school that holds that, if a line does not end in any punctuation, one should not pause but run it together with the line following. The trouble is that, from such a reading, a listener may not be able to identify the rimes; besides, the line, that valuable unit of rhythm, is destroyed.

In some older poems rimes that look like slant rimes may have been exact rimes in their day:

> Still so perverse and opposite,
> As if they worshiped God for spite.
> — Samuel Butler, *Hudibras* (1663)

> Soft yielding minds to water glide away,
> And sip, with nymphs, their elemental tea.
> — Alexander Pope, "The Rape of the Lock" (1714)

You may wish to establish a consistent policy toward such shifting usage: is it worthwhile to distort current pronunciation for the sake of the rime?

Listening to a poem, especially if it is unfamiliar, calls for concentration. Merciful people seldom read poetry uninterruptedly to anyone for more than a few minutes at a time. Robert Frost, always kind to his audiences, used to intersperse poems with many silences and seemingly casual remarks — shrewdly giving his hearers a chance to rest from their labors and giving his poems a chance to settle in.

If, in first listening to a poem, you don't take in all its meaning, don't be discouraged. With more practice in listening, your attention span and your ability to understand poems read aloud will increase. Incidentally, following the text of poems in a book while hearing them read aloud may increase your comprehension, but it may not necessarily help you to *listen*. At least some of the time, close your book and let your ears make the poems welcome. That way, their sounds may better work for you.

Hearing recordings of poets reading their work can help both your ability to read aloud and your ability to listen. Not all poets read their poems well, but there is much to be relished in both the highly dramatic reading style of a Dylan Thomas and the quiet underplay of a Robert Frost. You need feel no obligation, of course, to imitate the poet's reading of a poem. You have to feel about the poem in your own way, in order to read it with conviction and naturalness.

Even if you don't have an audience, the act of speaking poetry can have its own rewards. Perhaps that is what James Wright is driving at in the following brief prose poem.

James Wright (1927 – 1980)*

SAYING DANTE ALOUD   1976

You can feel the muscles and veins rippling in widening and rising
    circles,
like a bird in flight under your tongue.

EXERCISE: *Reading for Sound and Meaning*

Read these brief poems aloud. What devices of sound do you find in each of them? Try to explain what sound contributes to the total effect of the poem and how it reinforces what the poet is saying.

Michael Stillman (b. 1940)

IN MEMORIAM JOHN COLTRANE   1972

Listen to the coal
rolling, rolling through the cold
    steady rain, wheel on

wheel, listen to the
turning of the wheels this night   5
    black as coal dust, steel

on steel, listen to
these cars carry coal, listen
    to the coal train roll.

IN MEMORIAM JOHN COLTRANE. John Coltrane (1926 – 1967) was a saxophonist whose originality, passion, and technical wizardry have had a deep influence on the history of modern jazz.

William Shakespeare (1564 – 1616)*

FULL FATHOM FIVE THY FATHER LIES   (about 1611)

Full fathom five thy father lies;
    Of his bones are coral made;
Those are pearls that were his eyes:
    Nothing of him that doth fade,
But doth suffer a sea change   5
Into something rich and strange.
Sea nymphs hourly ring his knell:
    Ding-dong.
Hark! now I hear them — *Ding-dong, bell.*

FULL FATHOM FIVE THY FATHER LIES. The spirit Ariel sings this song in *The Tempest* to Ferdinand, prince of Naples, who mistakenly thinks his father is drowned.

A. E. Housman (1859 – 1936)*

WITH RUE MY HEART IS LADEN   1896

With rue my heart is laden
    For golden friends I had,
For many a rose-lipt maiden
    And many a lightfoot lad.

By brooks too broad for leaping   5
    The lightfoot boys are laid;
The rose-lipt girls are sleeping
    In fields where roses fade.

T. S. Eliot (1888 – 1965)*

VIRGINIA   1934

Red river, red river,
Slow flow heat is silence
No will is still as a river
Still. Will heat move
Only through the mocking-bird   5
Heard once? Still hills
Wait. Gates wait. Purple trees,
White trees, wait, wait,
Delay, decay. Living, living,
Never moving. Ever moving   10
Iron thoughts came with me
And go with me:
Red river, river, river.

VIRGINIA. This poem is one of a series entitled "Landscapes."

SUGGESTIONS FOR WRITING

1. Write about a personal experience with reading poems aloud.
2. Explain why contemporary poets are right (or wrong) to junk rime.
3. Consider the verbal music in W. H. Auden's "As I Walked Out One Evening" (or another selection from the Anthology). Analyze the poem for language with ear-appeal and show how the poem's sound is of a piece with its meaning.

9 *Rhythm*

STRESSES AND PAUSES

Rhythms affect us powerfully. We are lulled by a hammock's sway, awakened by an alarm clock's repeated yammer. Long after we come home from a beach, the rising and falling of waves and tides continue in memory. How powerfully the rhythms of poetry also move us may be felt in folk songs of railroad workers and chain gangs whose words were chanted in time to the lifting and dropping of a sledgehammer, and in verse that marching soldiers shout, putting a stress on every word that coincides with a footfall:

> Your LEFT! TWO! THREE! FOUR!
> Your LEFT! TWO! THREE! FOUR!
> You LEFT your WIFE and TWEN-ty-one KIDS
> And you LEFT! TWO! THREE! FOUR!
> You'll NEV-er get HOME to-NIGHT!

A rhythm is produced by a series of recurrences: the returns and departures of the seasons, the repetitions of an engine's stroke, the beats of the heart. A rhythm may be produced by the recurrence of a sound (the throb of a drum, a telephone's busy-signal), but rhythm and sound are not identical. A totally deaf person at a parade can sense rhythm from the motions of the marchers' arms and feet, from the shaking of the pavement as they tramp. Rhythms inhere in the motions of the moon and stars, even though when they move we hear no sound.

In poetry, several kinds of recurrent *sound* are possible, including (as we saw in the last chapter) rime, alliteration, and assonance. But most often when we speak of the **rhythm** of a poem we mean the recurrence of stresses and pauses in it. When we hear a poem read aloud, stresses and pauses are, of course, part of its sound. It is possible to be aware of rhythms in poems read silently, too.

A **stress** (or **accent**) is a greater amount of force given to one syllable in speaking than is given to another. We favor a stressed syllable with a little more breath and emphasis, with the result that it comes out slightly louder, higher in pitch, or longer in duration than other syllables. In this manner we place a stress on the first syllable of words such as *eagle, impact, open,* and *statue,* and on the second syllable in *cigar, mystique, precise,* and *until.* Each word in English carries at least one stress, except (usually) for the articles *a, an,* and *the,* and one-syllable prepositions: *at, by, for, from, of, to, with.* Even these, however, take a stress once in a while: "Get WITH it!" "You're not THE Dolly Parton?" One word by itself is seldom long enough for us to notice a rhythm in it. Usually a sequence of at least a few words is needed for stresses to establish their pattern: a line, a passage, a whole poem. Strong rhythms may be seen in most Mother Goose rimes, to which children have been responding for hundreds of years. This rime is for an adult to chant while jogging a child up and down on a knee:

> Here goes my lord
> A trot, a trot, a trot, a trot!
> Here goes my lady
> A canter, a canter, a canter, a canter!
> Here goes my young master
> Jockey-hitch, jockey-hitch, jockey-hitch, jockey-hitch!
> Here goes my young miss
> An amble, an amble, an amble, an amble!
> The footman lags behind to tipple ale and wine
> And goes gallop, a gallop, a gallop, to make up his time.

More than one rhythm occurs in these lines, as the make-believe horse changes pace. How do these rhythms differ? From one line to the next, the interval between stresses lengthens or grows shorter. In "a TROT a TROT a TROT a TROT," the stress falls on every other syllable. But in the middle of the line "A CAN-ter a CAN-ter a CAN-ter a CAN-ter," the stress falls on every third syllable. When stresses recur at fixed intervals as in these lines, the result is called a **meter.** The line "A trot a trot a trot a trot" is in **iambic** meter, a succession of alternate unstressed and stressed syllables.[1] Of all rhythms in the English language, this one is most familiar; most of our traditional poetry is written in it and ordinary speech tends to resemble it. Most poems, less obvious in rhythm than nursery rimes are, rarely stick to their meters with such jog-trot regularity. The following lines also contain a horseback-riding rhythm. (The poet, Gerard Manley Hopkins, is comparing the pell-mell plunging of a burn — Scottish word for a brook — to the motion of a wild horse.)

> This darksome burn, horseback brown,
> His rollrock highroad roaring down,
> In coop and in comb the fleece of his foam
> Flutes and low to the lake falls home.

[1] Another kind of meter is possible, in which the intervals between stresses vary. This is **accentual** meter, not often found in contemporary poetry. It is discussed in the second part of this chapter.

In the third line, when the brook courses through coop and comb ("hollow" and "ravine"), the passage breaks into a gallop; then, with the two-beat *falls home*, almost seems reined to a sudden halt.

Stresses embody meanings. Whenever two or more fall side by side, words gain in emphasis. Consider these hard-hitting lines from John Donne, in which accent marks have been placed, dictionary-fashion, to indicate the stressed syllables:

> Bat'ter my heart', three'-per'soned God', for You'
> As yet' but knock', breathe', shine', and seek' to mend';
> That I may rise' and stand', o'er'throw' me, and bend'
> Your force' to break', blow', burn', and make' me new'.

Unstressed (or **slack**) syllables also can direct our attention to what the poet means. In a line containing few stresses and a great many unstressed syllables, there can be an effect not of power and force but of hesitation and uncertainty. Yeats asks in "Among School Children" what young mother, if she could see her baby grown to be an old man, would think him

> A com'pen·sa'tion for the pang' of his birth'
> Or the un·cer'tain·ty of his set'ting forth'?

When unstressed syllables recur in pairs, the result is a rhythm that trips and bounces, as in Robert Service's rollicking line:

> A bunch' of the boys' were whoop'ing it up' in the Mal'a·mute sa·loon'
> . . .

or in Poe's lines — also light but probably supposed to be serious:

> For the moon' nev·er beams' with·out bring'ing me dreams'
> Of the beau'ti·ful An'na·bel Lee'.

Apart from the words that convey it, the rhythm of a poem has no meaning. There are no essentially sad rhythms, nor any essentially happy ones. But some rhythms enforce certain meanings better than others do. The bouncing rhythm of Service's line seems fitting for an account of a merry night in a Klondike saloon; but it may be distracting when encountered in Poe's wistful elegy.

EXERCISE: *Appropriate and Inappropriate Rhythms*

In each of the following passages decide whether rhythm enforces meaning and tone or works against these elements and consequently against the poem's effectiveness.

1. Alfred, Lord Tennyson, "Break, break, break":

> Break, break, break,
> On thy cold gray stones, O Sea!

2. Edgar Allan Poe, "Ulalume":

> Then my heart it grew ashen and sober
>   As the leaves that were crispèd and sere —
>   As the leaves that were withering and sere,

And I cried: "It was surely October
    On *this* very night of last year
    That I journey — I journeyed down here —
    That I brought a dread burden down here —
    On this night of all nights in the year,
    Ah, what demon has tempted me here?"

3. Greg Keeler, "There Ain't No Such Thing as a Montana Cowboy" (a song lyric):

I couldn't be cooler, I come from Missoula,
And I rope and I chew and I ride.
But I'm a heroin dealer, and I drive a four-wheeler
With stereo speakers inside.
My ol' lady Phoebe's out rippin' off C.B.'s
From the rigs at the Wagon Wheel Bar,
Near a Montana truck stop and a shit-outta-luck stop
For a trucker who's driven too far.

4. Eliza Cook, "Song of the Sea-Weed":

Many a lip is gaping for drink,
    And madly calling for rain;
And some hot brains are beginning to think
    Of a messmate's opened vein.

5. William Shakespeare, song from *The Tempest:*

The master, the swabber, the boatswain, and I,
The gunner and his mate
Loved Moll, Meg, and Marian, and Margery,
But none of us cared for Kate;
For she had a tongue with a tang
Would cry to a sailor "Go hang!" —
She loved not the savor of tar nor of pitch
Yet a tailor might scratch her where'er she did itch;
Then to sea, boys, and let her go hang!

Rhythms in poetry are due not only to stresses but also to pauses. "Every nice ear," observed Alexander Pope (*nice* meaning "finely tuned"), "must, I believe, have observed that in any smooth English verse of ten syllables, there is naturally a pause either at the fourth, fifth, or sixth syllable." Such a light but definite pause within a line is called a **cesura** (or caesura), "a cutting." More liberally than Pope, we apply the name to any pause in a line of any length, after any word in the line. In studying a poem, we often indicate a cesura by double lines(‖). Usually, a cesura will occur at a mark of punctuation, but there can be a cesura even if no punctuation is present. Sometimes you will find it at the end of a phrase or clause or, as in these lines by William Blake, after an internal rime:

And priests in black gowns‖were walking their rounds
And binding with briars‖my joys and desires.

Lines of ten or twelve syllables (as Pope knew) tend to have just one cesura, though sometimes there are more:

Cover her face:‖mine eyes dazzle:‖she died young.

Pauses also tend to recur at more prominent places — namely, after each line. At the end of a verse (from *versus*, "a turning"), the reader's eye, before turning to go on to the next line, makes a pause, however brief. If a line ends in a full pause — usually indicated by some mark of punctuation — we call it **end-stopped.** All the lines in this stanza by Theodore Roethke are end-stopped:

> Let seed be grass and grass turn into hay:
> I'm martyr to a motion not my own;
> What's freedom for? To know eternity.
> I swear she cast a shadow white as stone.
> But who would count eternity in days?
> These old bones live to learn her wanton ways:
> (I measure time by how a body sways).[2]

A line that does not end in punctuation and that therefore is read with only a slight pause after it is called a **run-on line.** Because a run-on line gives us only part of a phrase, clause, or sentence, we have to read on to the line or lines following, in order to complete a thought. All these lines from Robert Browning's "My Last Duchess" are run-on lines:

> . . . Sir, 'twas not
> Her husband's presence only, called that spot
> Of joy into the Duchess' cheek: perhaps
> Frà Pandolf chanced to say "Her mantle laps
> Over my lady's wrist too much," or "Paint
> Must never hope to reproduce the faint
> Half-flush that dies along her throat." Such stuff
> Was courtesy, she thought . . .

A passage in run-on lines has a rhythm different from that of a passage like Roethke's in end-stopped lines. When emphatic pauses occur in the quotation from Browning, they fall within a line rather than at the end of one. The passage by Roethke and that by Browning are in lines of the same meter (iambic) and the same length (ten syllables). What makes the big difference in their rhythms is the running on, or lack of it.

To sum up: rhythm is recurrence. In poems, it is made of stresses and pauses. The poet can produce it by doing any of several things: making the intervals between stresses fixed or varied, long or short; indicating pauses (cesuras) within lines; end-stopping lines or running them over; writing in short or long lines. Rhythm in itself cannot convey meaning. And yet if a poet's words have meaning, their rhythm must be one with it.

---

[2]The complete poem, "I Knew a Woman," appears on page 102.

Gwendolyn Brooks (b. 1917)*

We Real Cool   1960

The Pool Players.
Seven at the Golden Shovel.

We real cool. We
Left school. We

Lurk late. We
Strike straight. We

Sing sin. We   5
Thin gin. We

Jazz June. We
Die soon.

Question

Describe the rhythms of this poem. By what techniques are they produced?

Robert Frost (1874 – 1963)*

Never Again Would Birds' Song Be the Same   1942

He would declare and could himself believe
That the birds there in all the garden round
From having heard the daylong voice of Eve
Had added to their own an oversound,
Her tone of meaning but without the words.   5
Admittedly an eloquence so soft
Could only have had an influence on birds
When call or laughter carried it aloft.
Be that as may be, she was in their song.
Moreover her voice upon their voices crossed   10
Had now persisted in the woods so long
That probably it never would be lost.
Never again would birds' song be the same.
And to do that to birds was why she came.

Questions

1. Who is *he?*
2. In reading aloud line 9, do you stress *may?* (Do you say "as MAY be" or "as may BE"?) What guide do we have to the poet's wishes here?
3. Which lines does Frost cast mostly or entirely into monosyllables? How would you describe the impact of these lines?
4. In his *Essay on Criticism*, Alexander Pope made fun of poets who wrote mechanically, without wit: "And ten low words oft creep in one dull line." Do you think this criticism applicable to Frost's lines of monosyllables? Explain.

Ben Jonson (1573? – 1637)*

SLOW, SLOW, FRESH FOUNT, KEEP TIME WITH MY SALT TEARS   1600

Slow, slow, fresh fount, keep time with my salt tears;
   Yet slower yet, oh faintly, gentle springs;
List to the heavy part the music bears,
    Woe weeps out her division° when she sings.   *a part in a song*
      Droop herbs and flowers,   5
      Fall grief in showers;
      Our beauties are not ours;
        Oh, I could still,
Like melting snow upon some craggy hill,
   Drop, drop, drop, drop,   10
Since nature's pride is now a withered daffodil.

SLOW, SLOW, FRESH FOUNT. The nymph Echo sings this lament over the youth Narcissus in Jonson's play *Cynthia's Revels*. In mythology, Nemesis, goddess of vengeance, to punish Narcissus for loving his own beauty, caused him to pine away and then transformed him into a narcissus (another name for a *daffodil*, line 11).

QUESTIONS

1. Read the first line aloud rapidly. Why is it difficult to do so?
2. Which lines rely most heavily on stressed syllables?
3. In general, how would you describe the rhythm of this poem? How is it appropriate to what is said?

Alexander Pope (1688 – 1744)*

ATTICUS   1735

How did they fume, and stamp, and roar, and chafe!
And swear, not Addison himself was safe.
   Peace to all such! but were there one whose fires
True genius kindles, and fair fame inspires;
Blest with each talent, and each art to please,   5
And born to write, converse, and live with ease,
Should such a man, too fond to rule alone,
Bear, like the Turk, no brother near the throne,
View him with scornful, yet with jealous eyes,
And hate for arts that caused himself to rise;   10
Damn with faint praise, assent with civil leer,
And, without sneering, teach the rest to sneer;
Willing to wound, and yet afraid to strike,
Just hint a fault, and hesitate dislike;
Alike reserved to blame, or to commend,   15
A timorous foe, and a suspicious friend;

Dreading e'en fools, by flatterers besieged,
And so obliging, that he ne'er obliged;
Like Cato, give his little Senate laws,
And sit attentive to his own applause: 20
While wits and Templars every sentence raise,
And wonder with a foolish face of praise —
Who but must laugh, if such a man there be?
Who would not weep, if Atticus were he?

Atticus. In this selection from "An Epistle to Dr. Arbuthnot," Pope has been referring to dull
versifiers and their angry reception of his satiric thrusts at them. With *Peace to all such!* (line 3)
he turns to his celebrated portrait of a rival man of letters, Joseph Addison. 19 *Cato:* Roman
senator about whom Addison had written a tragedy. 21 *Templars:* London lawyers who dabbled
in literature.

QUESTIONS

1. In these lines — one of the most famous damnations in English poetry — what
   positive virtues, in Pope's view, does Addison lack?
2. Which lines are end-stopped? What is the effect of these lines upon the rhythm of
   this passage? (Suggestion: Read "Atticus" aloud.)

EXERCISE: *Two Kinds of Rhythm*

The following compositions in verse have lines of similar length, yet they differ greatly
in rhythm. Explain how they differ and why.

Sir *Thomas Wyatt* (1503? – 1542)*

WITH SERVING STILL   (1528 – 1536)

With serving still°   *continually*
  This have I won,
For my goodwill
  To be undone;

And for redress   5
  Of all my pain,
Disdainfulness
  I have again°;   *in return*

And for reward
  Of all my smart   10
Lo, thus unheard,
  I must depart!

Wherefore all ye
  That after shall
By fortune be,   15
  As I am, thrall,

Example take
    What I have won,
Thus for her sake
    To be undone!   20

Dorothy Parker (1893 – 1967)

RÉSUMÉ   1926

Razors pain you;
Rivers are damp;
Acids stain you;
And drugs cause cramp.
Guns aren't lawful;   5
Nooses give;
Gas smells awful;
You might as well live.

METER

To enjoy the rhythms of a poem, no special knowledge of meter is necessary. All you need do is pay attention to stresses and where they fall, and you will perceive the basic pattern, if there is any. However, there is nothing occult about the study of meter. Most people find they can master its essentials in no more time than it takes to learn a complicated game such as chess. If you take the time, you will then have the pleasure of knowing what is happening in the rhythms of many a fine poem, and pleasurable knowledge may even deepen your insight into poetry. The following discussion, then, will be of interest only to those who care to go deeper into **prosody**, the study of metrical structures in poetry.

Far from being artificial constructions found only in the minds of poets, meters occur in everyday speech and prose. As the following example will show, they may need only a poet to recognize them. The English satirist Max Beerbohm, after contemplating the title page of his first book, took his pen and added two more lines.

Max Beerbohm (1872 – 1956)

ON THE IMPRINT OF THE FIRST ENGLISH EDITION OF
THE WORKS OF MAX BEERBOHM   (1896)

"London: JOHN LANE, *The Bodley Head*
    New York: Charles Scribner's Sons."
This plain announcement, nicely read,
    Iambically runs.

In everyday life, nobody speaks or writes in perfect iambic rhythm, except at moments: "a HAM on RYE and HIT the MUStard HARD!" (As we have seen, iambic rhythm consists of a series of syllables alternately unstressed and stressed.) Poets rarely speak in it for long, either — at least, not with absolute consistency. If you read aloud Max Beerbohm's lines, you'll hear an iambic rhythm, but not an unvarying one. And yet all of us speak with a rising and falling of stress *somewhat like* iambic meter. Perhaps, as the poet and scholar John Thompson has maintained, "The iambic metrical pattern has dominated English verse because it provides the best symbolic model of our language."[3]

To make ourselves aware of a meter, we need only listen to a poem, or sound its words to ourselves. If we care to work out exactly what a poet is doing, we *scan* a line or a poem by indicating the stresses in it. **Scansion**, the art of so doing, is not just a matter of pointing to syllables; it is also a matter of listening to a poem and making sense of it. To scan a poem is one way to indicate how to read it aloud; in order to see where stresses fall, you have to see the places where the poet wishes to put emphasis. That is why, when scanning a poem, you may find yourself suddenly understanding it.

An objection might be raised against scanning: isn't it too simple to pretend that all language (and poetry) can be divided neatly into stressed syllables and unstressed syllables? Indeed it is. As the linguist Otto Jespersen has said, "In reality there are infinite gradations of stress, from the most penetrating scream to the faintest whisper."[4] However, the idea in scanning a poem is not to reproduce the sound of a human voice. For that we would do better to buy a tape recorder. To scan a poem, rather, is to make a diagram of the stresses (and absences of stress) we find in it. Various marks are used in scansion; in this book we use ´ for a stressed syllable and ˘ for an unstressed syllable. Some scanners, wishing a little more precision, also use the **half-stress** (`); this device can be helpful in many instances when a syllable usually not stressed comes at a place where it takes some emphasis, as in the last syllable in a line:

Bŏúnd eách tŏ eách with nát·ŭ·ral pí·e·ty.

Here, with examples, are some of the principal meters we find in English poetry. Each is named for its basic **foot,** or molecule (usually one stressed and one or two unstressed syllables).

1. **Iambic** (foot: the **iamb,** ˘´):
   Thĕ fáll·ĭng oút ŏf fáith·fŭl friĕnds, rĕ·néw·ĭng ís ŏf lóve

2. **Anapestic** (foot: the **anapest,** ˘˘´):
   Ĭ ăm món·ărch ŏf áll Ĭ sŭr·véy

3. **Trochaic** (foot: the **trochee,** ´˘):
   Dóu·blĕ, dóu·blĕ, tóil ănd tróu·blĕ

[3]*The Founding of English Metre* (New York: Columbia UP, 1966) 12.
[4]"Notes on Metre," (1933), reprinted in *The Structure of Verse: Modern Essays on Prosody,* ed. Harvey Gross, 2nd ed. (New York: Echo Press, 1978).

4. **Dactylic** (foot: the **dactyl**, ´˘˘):

    Táke hĕr ŭp tén·dĕr·lў

Iambic and anapestic meters are called **rising** meters because their movement rises from unstressed syllable (or syllables) to stress; trochaic and dactylic meters are called **falling.** In the twentieth century, the bouncing meters — anapestic and dactylic — have been used more often for comic verse than for serious poetry. Called feet, though they contain no unaccented syllables, are the **monosyllabic foot** (´) and the **spondee** (″). Meters are not ordinarily made up of them; if one were, it would be like the steady impact of nails being hammered into a board — no pleasure to hear or to dance to. But inserted now and then, they can lend emphasis and variety to a meter, as Yeats well knew when he broke up the predominantly iambic rhythm of "Who Goes with Fergus?" (page 000) with the line,

    Ănd thĕ white breast ŏf thĕ dim séa,

in which occur two spondees. Meters are classified also by line lengths: *trochaic monometer,* for instance, is a line one trochee long, as in this anonymous brief comment on microbes:

    Adam
    Had 'em.

A frequently heard metrical description is **iambic pentameter:** a line of five iambs, a meter especially familiar because it occurs in all blank verse (such as Shakespeare's plays and Milton's *Paradise Lost*), heroic couplets, and sonnets. The commonly used names for line lengths follow:

monometer	one foot	**pentameter**	five feet
dimeter	two feet	**hexameter**	six feet
trimeter	three feet	**heptameter**	seven feet
tetrameter	four feet	**octameter**	eight feet

Lines of more than eight feet are possible but are rare. They tend to break up into shorter lengths in the listening ear.

    When Yeats chose the spondees *white breast* and *dim sea,* he was doing what poets who write in meter do frequently for variety — using a foot other than the expected one. Often such a substitution will be made at the very beginning of a line, as in the third line of this passage from Christopher Marlowe's *Tragical History of Doctor Faustus:*

    Wăs this thĕ fáce thăt láunched ă thou·sănd ships

    Ănd búrnt thĕ tóp·lĕss tów'rs ŏf Íl·ĭ·um?

    Swéet Hél·ĕn, máke mĕ ĭm·mór·tăl with ă kiss.

How, we might wonder, can that last line be called iambic at all? But it is, just as a waltz that includes an extra step or two, or leaves a few steps out, remains a waltz. In the preceding lines the basic iambic pentameter is established, and though in the third line the regularity is varied from, it does not altogether disappear. It continues for a while to run on in the reader's mind, where (if the poet does not stay away from it for too long) the meter will be when the poem comes back to it.

Like a basic dance step, a meter is not to be slavishly adhered to. The fun in reading a metrical poem often comes from watching the poet continually departing from perfect regularity, giving a few heel-kicks to display a bit of joy or ingenuity, then easing back into the basic step again. Because meter is orderly and the rhythms of living speech are unruly, poets can play one against the other, in a sort of counterpoint. Robert Frost, a master at pitting a line of iambs against a very natural-sounding and irregular sentence, declared, "I am never more pleased than when I can get these into strained relation. I like to drag and break the intonation across the meter as waves first comb and then break stumbling on a shingle."[5]

Evidently Frost's skilled effects would be lost to a reader who, scanning a Frost poem or reading it aloud, distorted its rhythms to fit the words exactly to the meter. With rare exceptions, a good poem can be read and scanned the way we would speak its sentences if they were ours. This, for example, is an unreal scansion:

That's mў lăst Dúch·ĕss paint·ĕd ŏn thĕ wáll.

— because no speaker of English would say that sentence in that way. We are likely to stress *That's* and *last*.

Variety in rhythm is not merely desirable in poetry, it is a necessity, and the poem that fails to depart often enough from absolute regularity is in trouble. If the beat of its words slips into a mechanical pattern, the poem marches robot-like right into its grave. Luckily, few poets, except writers of greeting cards, favor rhythms that go "a TROT a TROT a TROT a TROT" for very long. Robert Frost told an audience one time that if when writing a poem he found its rhythm becoming monotonous, he knew that the poem was going wrong and that he himself didn't believe what it was saying.

Although in good poetry we seldom meet a very long passage of absolute metrical regularity, we sometimes find (in a line or so) a monotonous rhythm that is effective. Words fall meaningfully in Macbeth's famous statement of world-weariness: "Tomorrow and tomorrow and tomorrow . . ." and in the opening lines of Thomas Gray's "Elegy":

The cúr·fĕw tólls thĕ knéll ŏf párt·ĭng dáy,
The lów·ĭng hérd wĭnd slów·lĭ o'er thĕ léa,
The plów·măn hóme·wărd plóds hĭs wéar·ў wáy,
Ănd léaves thĕ wórld tŏ dárk·nĕss ănd tŏ mé.[6]

Although certain unstressed syllables in these lines seem to call for more emphasis than others — you might, for instance, care to throw a little more

[5]Letter to John Cournos in 1914, in *Selected Letters of Robert Frost,* ed. Lawrance Thompson (New York: Holt, 1964) 128.
[6]The complete poem, "Elegy Written in a Country Churchyard," appears on page 264.

weight on the second syllable of *curfew* in the opening line — we can still say the lines are notably iambic. Their almost unvarying rhythm seems just right to convey the tolling of a bell and the weary setting down of one foot after the other.

Besides the two rising meters (iambic, anapestic) and the two falling meters (trochaic, dactylic), English poets have another valuable meter. It is **accentual meter,** in which the poet does not write in feet (as in the other meters) but instead counts accents (stresses). The idea is to have the same number of stresses in every line. The poet may place them anywhere in the line and may include practically any number of unstressed syllables, which do not count. In "Christabel," for instance, Coleridge keeps four stresses to a line, though the first line has only eight syllables and the last line has eleven:

> There is not wind e·nough to twirl
> The one red leaf, the last of its clan,
> That dan·ces as of·ten as dance it can,
> Hang·ing so light, and hang·ing so high,
> On the top-most twig that looks up at the sky.

The history of accentual meter is long and honorable. Old English poetry was written in a kind of accentual meter, but its line was more rule-bound than Coleridge's: four stresses arranged two on either side of a cesura, plus alliteration of three of the stressed syllables. In "Junk," Richard Wilbur revives the pattern:

> An axe an·gles ‖ from my neigh·bor's ash·can . . .

Many poets, from the authors of Mother Goose rimes to Gerard Manley Hopkins, have sometimes found accentual meters congenial.

It has been charged that the importation of Greek names for meters and of the classical notion of feet was an unsuccessful attempt to make a Parthenon out of English wattles. The charge is open to debate, but at least it is certain that Greek names for feet cannot mean to us what they meant to Aristotle. Greek and Latin poetry is measured not by stressed and unstressed syllables but by long and short vowel sounds. An iamb in classical verse is one short syllable followed by a long syllable. Such a meter constructed on the principle of vowel length is called a **quantitative meter.** Campion's "Rose-cheeked Laura" was an attempt to demonstrate it in English, but probably we enjoy the rhythm of the poem's well-placed stresses whether or not we notice its vowel sounds.

Thomas Campion (1567 – 1620)*

ROSE-CHEEKED LAURA, COME   1602

Rose-cheeked Laura, come,
Sing thou smoothly with thy beauty's
Silent music, either other
           Sweetly gracing.

Lovely forms do flow   5
From concent° divinely framèd;   *harmony*
Heav'n is music, and thy beauty's
        Birth is heavenly.

These dull notes we sing
Discords need for helps to grace them;   10
Only beauty purely loving
        Knows no discord,

But still moves delight,
Like clear springs renewed by flowing,
Ever perfect, ever in them-   15
        Selves eternal.

Although less popular among poets today than formerly, meter endures. Major poets from Shakespeare through Yeats have fashioned their work by it, and if we are to read their poems with full enjoyment, we need to be aware of it. To enjoy metrical poetry — even to write it — you do not have to slice lines into feet; you do need to recognize when a meter is present in a line, and when the line departs from it. An argument in favor of meter is that it reminds us of body rhythms such as breathing, walking, the beating of the heart. In an effective metrical poem, these rhythms cannot be separated from what the poet is saying — or, in the words of an old jazz song, "It don't mean a thing if you ain't got that swing." As critic Paul Fussell has put it: "No element of a poem is more basic — and I mean physical — in its effect upon the reader than the metrical element, and perhaps no technical triumphs reveal more readily than the metrical the poet's sympathy with that universal human nature . . . which exists outside his own."[7]

Walter Savage Landor (1775 – 1864)

On Seeing a Hair of Lucretia Borgia   (1825)

Borgia, thou once wert almost too august
And high for adoration; now thou'rt dust.
All that remains of thee these plaits unfold,
Calm hair, meandering in pellucid gold.

Questions

1. Who was Lucretia Borgia and when did she live? Because of her reputation, what connotations does her name add to Landor's poem?
2. What does *meander* mean? How can a hair meander?

[7]*Poetic Meter and Poetic Form* (New York: Random, 1965) 110.

3. Scan the poem, indicating stressed syllables. What is the basic meter of most of the poem? What happens to this meter in the last line? Note especially *meandering in pel-*. How many light, unstressed syllables are there in a row? Does rhythm in any way reinforce what Landor is saying?

EXERCISE: *Meaningful Variation*

At what place or places in each of these passages does the poet depart from basic iambic meter? How does each departure help underscore the meaning?

1. John Dryden, "Mac Flecknoe" (speech of Flecknoe, prince of Nonsense, referring to Thomas Shadwell, poet and playwright):

   Shadwell alone of all my sons is he
   Who stands confirmed in full stupidity.
   The rest to some faint meaning make pretense,
   But Shadwell never deviates into sense.

2. Alexander Pope, *An Essay on Criticism:*

   A needless Alexandrine ends the song
   That, like a wounded snake, drags its slow length along.

3. Henry King, "The Exequy" (an apostrophe to his wife):

   'Tis true, with shame and grief I yield,
   Thou like the van° first tookst the field,   *vanguard*
   And gotten hath the victory
   In thus adventuring to die
   Before me, whose more years might crave
   A just precedence in the grave.
   But hark! my pulse like a soft drum
   Beats my approach, tells thee I come;
   And slow howe'er my marches be,
   I shall at last sit down by thee.

4. Henry Wadsworth Longfellow, "Mezzo Cammin":

   Half-way up the hill, I see the Past
       Lying beneath me with its sounds and sights, —
   A city in the twilight dim and vast,
       With smoking roofs, soft bells, and gleaming lights, —
   And hear above me on the autumnal blast
       The cataract of Death far thundering from the heights.

5. Wallace Stevens, "Sunday Morning":

   Deer walk upon our mountains, and the quail
   Whistle about us their spontaneous cries;
   Sweet berries ripen in the wilderness;
   And, in the isolation of the sky,
   At evening, casual flocks of pigeons make
   Ambiguous undulations as they sink,
   Downward to darkness, on extended wings.

Which of the following poems contain predominant meters? Which poems are not wholly metrical, but are metrical in certain lines? Point out any such lines. What reasons do you see, in such places, for the poet's seeking a metrical effect?

Edna St. Vincent Millay (1892 – 1950)*

COUNTING-OUT RHYME   1928

Silver bark of beech, and sallow
Bark of yellow birch and yellow
  Twig of willow.

Stripe of green in moosewood maple,
Color seen in leaf of apple,   5
  Bark of popple.

Wood of popple pale as moonbeam,
Wood of oak for yoke and barn-beam,
  Wood of hornbeam.

Silver bark of beech, and hollow   10
Stem of elder, tall and yellow
  Twig of willow.

A. E. Housman (1859 – 1936)*

WHEN I WAS ONE-AND-TWENTY   1896

When I was one-and-twenty
  I heard a wise man say,
"Give crowns and pounds and guineas,
  But not your heart away;
Give pearls away and rubies   5
  But keep your fancy free."
But I was one-and-twenty,
  No use to talk to me.

When I was one-and-twenty
  I heard him say again,   10
"The heart out of the bosom
  Was never given in vain;
'Tis paid with sighs a plenty
  And sold for endless rue."
And I am two-and-twenty,   15
  And oh, 'tis true, 'tis true.

William Carlos Williams (1883 – 1963)*

THE DESCENT OF WINTER (SECTION 10/30)   1934

To freight cars in the air

all the slow
   clank, clank
   clank, clank
moving about the treetops   5

the
   wha, wha
of the hoarse whistle

   pah, pah, pah
   pah, pah, pah, pah, pah   10
   piece and piece
   piece and piece
moving still trippingly
through the morningmist

long after the engine   15
has fought by
             and disappeared
in silence
           to the left

Walt Whitman (1819 – 1892)*

BEAT! BEAT! DRUMS!   (1861)

Beat! beat! drums! — blow! bugles! blow!
Through the windows — through doors — burst like a ruthless force,
Into the solemn church, and scatter the congregation,
Into the school where the scholar is studying;
Leave not the bridegroom quiet — no happiness must he have now
    with his bride,   5
Nor the peaceful farmer any peace, ploughing his field or gathering
    his grain,
So fierce you whirr and pound you drums — so shrill you bugles
    blow.

Beat! beat! drums! — blow! bugles! blow!
Over the traffic of cities — over the rumble of wheels in the streets;
Are beds prepared for sleepers at night in the houses? no sleepers
    must sleep in those beds,   10

No bargainer's bargains by day — no brokers or speculators — would
  they continue?
Would the talkers be talking? would the singer attempt to sing?
Would the lawyer rise in the court to state his case before the judge?
Then rattle quicker, heavier drums — you bugles wilder blow.

Beat! beat! drums! — blow! bugles! blow!   15
Make no parley — stop for no expostulation,
Mind not the timid — mind not the weeper or prayer,
Mind not the old man beseeching the young man,
Let not the child's voice be heard, nor the mother's entreaties,
Make even the trestles to shake the dead where they lie awaiting the
  hearses.   20
So strong you thump O terrible drums — so loud you bugles blow.

Langston Hughes (1902–1967)*

DREAM BOOGIE   1951

Good morning, daddy!
Ain't you heard
The boogie-woogie rumble
Of a dream deferred?

Listen closely: 5
You'll hear their feet
Beating out and beating out a—

  You think
  It's a happy beat?

Listen to it closely: 10
Ain't you heard
something underneath
like a—

  What did I say?

Sure,   15
I'm happy!
Take it away!

  Hey, pop!
  Re-bop!
  Mop!   20

    Y-e-a-h!

Suggestions for Writing

1. When has a rhythm of any kind (whether or not in poetry) stirred you, picked you up, and carried you along with it? Write an account of your experience.
2. The fact that most contemporary poets have given up meter, in the view of Stanley Kunitz, has made poetry "easier to write, but harder to remember." Why so? Comment on Kunitz's remark, or quarrel with it, in two or three paragraphs.
3. Ponder Robert Frost's idea of "the sound of sense" (page 449). Then, in a paragraph or two, try to show what light this idea sheds upon Frost's "Never Again Would Birds' Song Be the Same" (or any other Frost poem in this book).

10 *Closed Form, Open Form*

Form, as a general idea, is the design of a thing as a whole, the configuration of all its parts. No poem can escape having some kind of form, whether its lines are as various in length as broomstraws, or all in hexameter. To put this point in another way: if you were to listen to a poem read aloud in a language unknown to you, or if you saw the poem printed in that foreign language, whatever in the poem you could see or hear would be the form of it.[1]

Writing in **closed form,** a poet follows (or finds) some sort of pattern, such as that of a sonnet with its rime scheme and its fourteen lines of iambic pentameter. On a page, poems in closed form tend to look regular and symmetrical, often falling into stanzas that indicate groups of rimes. Along with William Butler Yeats, who held that a successful poem will "come shut with a click, like a closing box," the poet who writes in closed form apparently strives for a kind of perfection — seeking, perhaps, to lodge words so securely in place that no word can be budged without a worsening. For the sake of meaning, though, a competent poet often will depart from a symmetrical pattern. As Robert Frost observed, there is satisfaction to be found in things not mechanically regular: "We enjoy the straight crookedness of a good walking stick."

The poet who writes in **open form** usually seeks no final click. Often, such a poet views the writing of a poem as a process, rather than a quest for an absolute. Free to use white space for emphasis, able to shorten or lengthen lines as the sense seems to require, the poet lets the poem discover its shape as it goes along, moving as water flows downhill, adjusting to its terrain, engulfing obstacles.

Most poetry of the past is in closed form, exhibiting at least a pattern of rime or meter, but since the early 1960s most American poets have preferred forms that stay open. Lately, the situation has been changing yet again, with

---

[1]For a good summary of the uses of the term **form** in criticism of poetry, see the article "Form" by G. N. G. Orsini in *Princeton Encyclopedia of Poetry and Poetics,* 2nd ed., eds. Preminger, Warnke, and Hardison (Princeton: Princeton UP, 1975).

closed form reappearing in much recent poetry. Whatever the fashion of the moment, the reader who seeks a wide understanding of poetry of both the present and the past will need to know both the closed and open varieties.

Closed Form: Blank Verse, Stanza, Sonnet

Closed form gives some poems a valuable advantage: it makes them more easily memorable. The **epic** poems of nations — long narratives tracing the adventures of popular heroes: the Greek *Iliad* and *Odyssey,* the French *Song of Roland,* the Spanish *Cid* — tend to occur in patterns of fairly consistent line length or number of stresses because these works were sometimes transmitted orally. Sung to the music of a lyre or chanted to a drumbeat, they may have been easier to memorize because of their patterns. If a singer forgot something, the song would have a noticeable hole in it, so rime or fixed meter probably helped prevent an epic from deteriorating when passed along from one singer to another. It is no coincidence that so many English playwrights of Shakespeare's day favored iambic pentameter. Companies of actors, often called upon to perform a different play daily, could count on a fixed line length to aid their burdened memories.

Some poets complain that closed form is a straitjacket, a limit to free expression. Other poets, however, feel that, like fires held fast in a narrow space, thoughts stated in a tightly binding form may take on a heightened intensity. "Limitation makes for power," according to one contemporary practitioner of closed form, Richard Wilbur; "the strength of the genie comes of his being confined in a bottle." Compelled by some strict pattern to arrange and rearrange words, delete, and exchange them, poets must focus on them the keenest attention. Often they stand a chance of discovering words more meaningful than the ones they started out with. And at times, in obedience to a rime scheme, the poet may be surprised by saying something quite unexpected. Composing a poem is like walking blindfolded down a dark road, with one's hand in the hand of an inexorable guide. With the conscious portion of the mind, the poet may wish to express what seems to be a good idea. But a line ending in *year* must be followed by another ending in *atmosphere, beer, bier, bombardier, cashier, deer, frictiongear, frontier,* or some other rime word that otherwise might not have entered the poem. That is why rime schemes and stanza patterns can be mighty allies and valuable disturbers of the unconscious. As Rolfe Humphries has said about strict form: "It makes you think of better things than you would all by yourself."

The best-known one-line pattern for a poem in English is **blank verse:** unrimed iambic pentameter. (This pattern is not a stanza: stanzas have more than one line.) Most portions of Shakespeare's plays are in blank verse, and so are Milton's *Paradise Lost,* Tennyson's "Ulysses," certain dramatic monologues of Browning and Frost, and thousands of other poems. Here is a poem in blank verse that startles us by dropping out of its pattern in the final line. Keats appears to have written it late in his life to his fiancée Fanny Brawne.

John Keats (1795 – 1821)*

THIS LIVING HAND, NOW WARM AND CAPABLE   (1819?)

This living hand, now warm and capable
Of earnest grasping, would, if it were cold
And in the icy silence of the tomb,
So haunt thy days and chill thy dreaming nights
That thou wouldst wish thine own heart dry of blood   5
So in my veins red life might stream again,
And thou be conscience-calmed — see here it is —
I hold it towards you.

The **couplet** is a two-line stanza, usually rimed. Its lines often tend to be equal in length, whether short or long. Here are two examples:

Blow,
Snow!

As I in hoary winter's night stood shivering in the snow,
Surprised I was with sudden heat which made my heart to glow.

Actually, any pair of rimed lines that contains a complete thought is called a couplet, even if it is not a stanza, such as the couplet that ends a sonnet by Shakespeare. Unlike other stanzas, couplets are often printed solid, one couplet not separated from the next by white space. This practice is usual in printing the **heroic couplet** — or **closed couplet** — two rimed lines of iambic pentameter, the first ending in a light pause, the second more heavily end-stopped. George Crabbe, in *The Parish Register,* described a shotgun wedding:

Next at our altar stood a luckless pair,
Brought by strong passions and a warrant there:
By long rent cloak, hung loosely, strove the bride,
From every eye, what all perceived, to hide;
While the boy bridegroom, shuffling in his place,
Now hid awhile and then exposed his face.
As shame alternately with anger strove
The brain confused with muddy ale to move,
In haste and stammering he performed his part,
And looked the rage that rankled in his heart.

Though employed by Chaucer, the heroic couplet was named from its later use by Dryden and others in poems, translations of classical epics, and verse plays of epic heroes. It continued in favor through most of the eighteenth century. Much of our pleasure in reading good heroic couplets comes from the seemingly easy precision with which a skilled poet unites statements and strict pattern. In doing so, the poet may place a pair of words, phrases, clauses, or sentences side by side in agreement or similarity, forming a **parallel,** or in contrast and opposition, forming an **antithesis.** The effect is neat. For such skill in manipulating parallels and antitheses, John Denham's lines on the river Thames were much admired:

O could I flow like thee, and make thy stream
My great example, as it is my theme!
Though deep, yet clear; though gentle, yet not dull;
Strong without rage, without o'erflowing full.

These lines were echoed by Pope, ridiculing a poetaster, in two heroic couplets in *The Dunciad:*

Flow, Welsted, flow! like thine inspirer, Beer:
Though stale, not ripe; though thin, yet never clear;
So sweetly mawkish, and so smoothly dull;
Heady, not strong; o'erflowing, though not full.

Reading long poems in so exact a form, one may feel like a spectator at a ping-pong match unless the poet skillfully keeps varying rhythms. One way of escaping such metronome-like monotony is to keep the cesura (see page 148) shifting about from place to place — now happening early in a line, now happening late — and at times unexpectedly to hurl in a second or third cesura. This skill, among other things, distinguishes the work of Dryden and Pope. If you care to see it in action, try working through Dryden's elegy for Oldham (page 307) or Pope's acid portrait of Atticus (page 151), noticing where the cesuras fall. You'll find that the pauses skip around with lively variety.

A **tercet** is a group of three lines. If rimed, they usually keep to one rime sound, as in this anonymous English children's jingle:

Julius Caesar,
The Roman geezer,
Squashed his wife with a lemon-squeezer.

(That, by the way, is a great demonstration of surprising and unpredictable rimes.) **Terza rima,** the form Dante employs in *The Divine Comedy,* is made of tercets linked together by the rime scheme *a b a, b c b, c d c, d e d, e f e,* and so on. Harder to do in English than in Italian — with its greater resources of riming words — the form nevertheless has been managed by Shelley in "Ode to the West Wind" (with the aid of some slant rimes):

Make me thy lyre, even as the forest is:
What if my leaves are falling like its own!
The tumult of thy mighty harmonies

Will take from both a deep, autumnal tone,
Sweet though in sadness. Be thou, spirit fierce,
My spirit! Be thou me, impetuous one!

The workhorse of English stanzas is the **quatrain,** used for more rimed poems than any other form. It comes in many line lengths, and sometimes contains lines of varying length, as in the ballad stanza (see page 118).

Longer and more complicated stanzas are, of course, possible, but couplet, tercet, and quatrain have been called the building blocks of our poetry because most longer stanzas are made up of them. What short stanzas does John Donne mortar together to make the longer stanza of his "Song"?

Song   1633

Go and catch a falling star,
   Get with child a mandrake root,
Tell me where all past years are,
   Or who cleft the Devil's foot,
Teach me to hear mermaids singing,   5
   Or to keep off envy's stinging,
      And find
      What wind
Serves to advance an honest mind.

If thou be'st borne to strange sights,   10
   Things invisible to see,
Ride ten thousand days and nights,
   Till age snow white hairs on thee,
Thou, when thou return'st, wilt tell me
   All strange wonders that befell thee,   15
      And swear
      Nowhere
Lives a woman true, and fair.

If thou findst one, let me know,
   Such a pilgrimage were sweet —   20
Yet do not, I would not go,
   Though at next door we might meet;
Though she were true, when you met her,
   And last, till you write your letter,
      Yet she   25
      Will be
False, ere I come, to two, or three.

Recently in vogue is a form known as **syllabic verse**, in which the poet establishes a pattern of a certain number of syllables to a line. Either rimed or rimeless but usually stanzaic, syllabic verse has been hailed as a way for poets to escape "the tyranny of the iamb" and discover less conventional rhythms, since, if they take as their line length an *odd* number of syllables, then iambs, being feet of *two* syllables, cannot fit perfectly into it. Offbeat victories have been scored in syllabics by such poets as W. H. Auden, W. D. Snodgrass, Donald Hall, Thom Gunn, and Marianne Moore. A well-known syllabic poem is Dylan Thomas's "Fern Hill" (page 390). Notice its shape on the page, count the syllables in its lines, and you'll perceive its perfect symmetry. Although like playing a game, the writing of such a poem is apparently more than finger exercise: the discipline can help a poet to sing well, though (with Thomas) singing "in . . . chains like the sea."

Poets who write in demanding forms seem to enjoy taking on an arbitrary task for the fun of it, as ballet dancers do, or weightlifters. Much of our pleasure in reading such poems comes from watching words fall into a shape. It is the pleasure of seeing any hard thing done skillfully — a leap executed in a dance, a basketball swished through a basket. Still, to be excellent, a poem needs more than skill; and to enjoy a poem it isn't always necessary for the reader to be aware of the skill that went into it. Unknowingly, the editors of *The New Yorker* once printed an **acrostic** — a poem in which the initial letter of each line, read downward, spells out a word or words — that named (and insulted) a well-known anthologist. Evidently, besides being ingenious, the acrostic was a printable poem. In the Old Testament book of Lamentations, profoundly moving songs tell of the sufferings of the Jews after the destruction of Jerusalem. Four of the songs are written as an alphabetical acrostic, every stanza beginning with a letter of the Hebrew alphabet. However ingenious, such sublime poetry cannot be dismissed as merely witty; nor can it be charged that a poet who writes in such a form does not express deep feeling.

Patterns of sound and rhythm can, however, be striven after in a dull mechanical way, for which reason many poets today think them dangerous. Swinburne, who loved alliterations and tripping meters, had enough detachment to poke fun at his own excessive patterning:

> From the depth of the dreamy decline of the dawn through a notable
>   nimbus of nebulous noonshine,
>   Pallid and pink as the palm of the flag-flower that flickers with fear of
>   the flies as they float,
> Are the looks of our lovers that lustrously lean from a marvel of mystic
>   miraculous moonshine,
>   These that we feel in the blood of our blushes that thicken and
>   threaten with throbs through the throat?

This is bad, but bad deliberately. Viewed mechanically, as so many empty boxes somehow to be filled up, stanzas can impose the most hollow sort of discipline, and a poem written in these stanzas becomes no more than finger-exercise. If any good at all, a poem in a fixed pattern, such as a sonnet, is created not only by the craftsman's chipping away at it but by the explosion of a sonnet-shaped *idea*.

Ronald Gross (b. 1935)

YIELD   1967

Yield.
No Parking.
Unlawful to Pass.
Wait for Green Light.
Yield.   5

Stop.
Narrow Bridge.
Merging Traffic Ahead
Yield.

Yield.   10

QUESTIONS

1. This poem by Ronald Gross is a "found poem." After reading it, how would you
   define **found poetry**?
2. Does "Yield" have a theme? If so, how would you state it?
3. What makes "Yield" mean more than traffic signs ordinarily mean to us?

Ronald Gross, who produces his "found poetry" by arranging prose from such
unlikely places as traffic signs and news stories into poem-like lines, has told of
making a discovery:

> As I worked with labels, tax forms, commercials, contracts, pin-up cap-
> tions, obituaries, and the like, I soon found myself rediscovering all the
> traditional verse forms in found materials: ode, sonnet, epigram, haiku,
> free verse. Such finds made me realize that these forms are not mere
> artifices, but shapes that language naturally takes when carrying powerful
> thoughts or feelings.[2]

Though Gross is a playful experimenter, his remark is true of serious
poetry. Traditional verse forms like sonnets and haiku aren't a lot of hollow
pillowcases for a poet to stuff with verbiage. At best, in the hands of a skilled
poet, they can be shapes into which living language seems to fall naturally.

It is fun to see words tumble gracefully into such a shape. Consider, for
instance, one famous "found poem," a sentence discovered in a physics textbook: "And so no force, however great, can stretch a cord, however fine, into
a horizontal line which shall be absolutely straight."[3] What a good clear sentence containing effective parallels ("however great . . . however fine"), you
might say, taking pleasure in it. Yet this plain statement gives extra pleasure
if arranged like this:

And so no force, however great,
   Can stretch a cord, however fine,
   Into a horizontal line
Which shall be absolutely straight.

So spaced, in lines that reveal its built-in rimes and rhythms, the sentence
would seem one of those "shapes that language naturally takes" that Ronald
Gross finds everywhere. (It is possible, of course, that the textbook writer was

[2]"Speaking of Books: Found Poetry," *The New York Times Book Review*, June 11, 1967. See also
Gross's *Pop Poems* (New York: Simon, 1967).
[3]William Whewell, *Elementary Treatise on Mechanics* (Cambridge, England, 1819).

gleefully planting a quatrain for someone to find; but perhaps it is more likely that he knew much rimed, metrical poetry by heart and couldn't help writing it unconsciously.) Inspired by pop artists who reveal fresh vistas in Brillo boxes and comic strips, found poetry has had a recent flurry of activity. Earlier practitioners include William Carlos Williams, whose long poem *Paterson* quotes historical documents and statistics. Prose, wrote Williams, can be a "laboratory" for poetry: "It throws up jewels which may be cleaned and grouped." Such a jewel may be the sentence Rosmarie Waldrop found in *The Joy of Cooking* and arranged as verse.

Rosmarie Waldrop (b. 1935)

THE RELAXED ABALONE   1970

Abalone, like inkfish,
needs prodigious pounding
if it has died in a state
of tension.

EXPERIMENT: *Finding a Poem*

In a newspaper, magazine, catalogue, textbook, or advertising throwaway, find a sentence or passage that (with a little artistic manipulation on your part) shows promise of becoming a poem. Copy it into lines like poetry, being careful to place what seem to be the most interesting words at the ends of lines to give them greatest emphasis. According to the rules of found poetry, you may excerpt, delete, repeat, and rearrange elements but not add anything. What does this experiment tell you about poetic form? About ordinary prose?

When we speak, with Ronald Gross, of "traditional verse forms," we usually mean **fixed forms.** If written in a fixed form a poem inherits from other poems certain familiar elements of structure: an unvarying number of lines, say, or a stanza pattern. In addition, it may display certain **conventions:** expected features such as themes, subjects, attitudes, or figures of speech. In medieval folk ballads a "milk-white steed" is a conventional figure of speech; and if its rider be a cruel and beautiful witch who kidnaps mortals, she is a conventional character. (*Conventional* doesn't necessarily mean uninteresting.)

In the poetry of western Europe and America, the **sonnet** is the fixed form that has attracted for the longest time the largest number of noteworthy practitioners. Originally an Italian form (*sonnetto:* "little song"), the sonnet owes much of its prestige to Petrarch (1304 – 1374), who wrote in it of his love for the unattainable Laura. So great was the vogue for sonnets in England at the end of the sixteenth century that a gentleman might have been thought a boor if he couldn't turn out a decent one. Not content to adopt merely the sonnet's fourteen-line pattern, English poets also tried on its conventional mask of the tormented lover. They borrowed some of Petrarch's similes (a lover's heart, for instance, is like a storm-tossed boat) and invented others. (If you would like more illustrations of Petrarchan conventions, see Shakespeare's sonnet on page 260.)

Soon after English poets imported the sonnet into the middle of the sixteenth century, they worked out their own rime scheme — one easier for them to follow than Petrarch's, which calls for a greater number of riming words than English can readily provide. (In Italian, according to an exaggerated report, practically everything rimes.) In the following **English sonnet,** sometimes called a **Shakespearean sonnet,** the rimes cohere in four clusters: *a b a b, c d c d, e f e f, g g.* Because a rime scheme tends to shape the poet's statements to it, the English sonnet has three places where the procession of thought is likely to turn in another direction. Within its form, a poet may pursue one idea throughout the three quatrains and then in the couplet end with a surprise.

Michael Drayton (1563 – 1631)

SINCE THERE'S NO HELP, COME LET US KISS AND PART   1619

Since there's no help, come let us kiss and part; *a*
Nay, I have done, you get no more of me, *b*
And I am glad, yea, glad with all my heart *a*
That thus so cleanly I myself can free; *b*
Shake hands for ever, cancel all our vows, *c*
And when we meet at any time again, *d*
Be it not seen in either of our brows *c*
That we one jot of former love retain. *d*
Now at the last gasp of Love's latest breath, *e*
When, his pulse failing, Passion speechless lies, *f*   10
When Faith is kneeling by his bed of death, *e*
And Innocence is closing up his eyes, *f*
    Now if thou wouldst, when all have given him over, *g*
    From death to life thou mightst him yet recover. *g*

[handwritten margin note: English or Shakespearean sonnet]

Less frequently met in English poetry, the **Italian sonnet,** or **Petrarchan sonnet,** follows the rime scheme *a b b a, a b b a* in its first eight lines, the **octave,** and then adds new rime sounds in the last six lines, the **sestet.** The sestet may rime *c d c d c d, c d e c d e, c d c c d c,* or in almost any other variation that doesn't end in a couplet. This organization into two parts sometimes helps arrange the poet's thoughts. In the octave, the poet may state a problem, and then, in the sestet, may offer a resolution. A lover, for example, may lament all octave long that a loved one is neglectful, then in line 9 begin to foresee some outcome: the speaker will die, or accept unhappiness, or trust that the beloved will have a change of heart.

Elizabeth Barrett Browning (1806 – 1861)

GRIEF   1844

I tell you, hopeless grief is passionless;   *a*
    That only men incredulous of despair,   *b*
    Half-taught in anguish, through the midnight air   *b*
Beat upward to God's throne in loud access   *a*
Of shrieking and reproach. Full desertness   *a*
    In souls, as countries, lieth silent-bare   *b*   5
    Under the blanching, vertical eye-glare   *b*
Of the absolute Heavens. Deep-hearted man, express   *a*
Grief for the Dead in silence like to death: *c*
    Most like a monumental statue set   *d*   10
In everlasting watch and moveless woe   *e*
Till itself crumble to the dust beneath.   *c*
    Touch it: the marble eyelids are not wet   *d*
If it could weep, it could arise and go.   *e*

[handwritten margin note: Italian op Petrarchan Sonnet]

In this Italian sonnet, the division in thought comes a bit early — in the middle of line 8. Few English-speaking poets who have used the form seem to feel strictly bound by it.

    "The sonnet," in the view of Robert Bly, a modern critic, "is where old professors go to die." And yet the use of the form by such twentieth-century poets as Yeats, Frost, Auden, Thomas, Pound, Cummings, Berryman, and Lowell suggests that it may be far from exhausted. Like the hero of the popular ballad "Finnegan's Wake," literary forms (though not professors) declared dead have a habit of springing up again. No law compels sonnets to adopt an exalted tone, or confines them to an Elizabethan vocabulary, as this sonnet by a contemporary poet makes clear.

R. S. Gwynn (b. 1948)

SCENES FROM THE PLAYROOM   1986

Now Lucy with her family of dolls   *a*
Disfigures Mother with an emery board,   *b*
While Charles, with match and rubbing alcohol,   *a*
Readies the struggling cat, for Chuck is bored.   *b*

The young ones pour more ink into the water *a*   5
Through which the latest goldfish gamely swims, *b*
Laughing, pointing at naked, neutered Father. *a*
The toy chest is a Buchenwald of limbs. *b*

Mother is so lovely; Father, so late. *c*
The cook is off, yet dinner must go on. *d*   10
With onions as her only cause for tears *e*
She hacks the red meat from the slippery bone, *d*
Setting the table, where the children wait, *c*
Her grinning babies, clean behind the ears. *e*

QUESTIONS

1. Explain the allusion to Buchenwald in line 8.
2. What do we know about this family and their life-style? What is revealed by the word
   latest (line 6)?
3. What do you think of these children and their parents? What does the poet think
   of them? By what details is his attitude made clear?

EXERCISE: *Knowing Two Kinds of Sonnet*

Find other sonnets in this book. Which are English in form? Which are Italian? Which
are variations on either form or combinations of the two? You may wish to try your hand
at writing both kinds of sonnet and experience the difference for yourself.

Oscar Wilde said that a cynic is "a man who knows the price of everything
and the value of nothing." Such a terse, pointed statement is called an epigram.
In poetry, however, an **epigram** is a form: "A short poem ending in a witty
or ingenious turn of thought, to which the rest of the composition is intended
to lead up" (according to the *Oxford English Dictionary*). Often it is a malicious
gibe with an unexpected stinger in the final line — perhaps in the very last
word:

Alexander Pope (1688 – 1744)*

EPIGRAM ENGRAVED ON THE COLLAR OF A DOG
WHICH I GAVE TO HIS ROYAL HIGHNESS   1738

I am his Highness' dog at Kew;
Pray tell me, sir, whose dog are you?

Cultivated by the Roman poet Martial — for whom the epigram was a short poem, sometimes satiric but not always — this form has been especially favored by English poets who love Latin. Few characteristics of the English epigram seem fixed. Its pattern tends to be brief and rimed, its tone playfully merciless.

Martial (A.D. 40?–102?)

READERS AND LISTENERS PRAISE MY BOOKS   A.D. 90

Readers and listeners praise my books;
You swear they're worse than a beginner's.
Who cares? I always plan my dinners
To please the diners, not the cooks.
                    — Translated by R. L. Barth

Sir John Harrington (1561? – 1612)

OF TREASON   1618

Treason doth never prosper; what's the reason?
For if it prosper, none dare call it treason.

William Blake (1757 – 1827)*

HER WHOLE LIFE IS AN EPIGRAM   (1793)

Her whole life is an epigram: smack smooth°, and   *perfectly smooth*
     neatly penned,
Platted° quite neat to catch applause, with a sliding   *plaited, woven*
     noose at the end.

E. E. Cummings (1894 – 1962)*

A POLITICIAN   1944

a politician is an arse upon
which everyone has sat except a man

Langston Hughes (1902–1967)*

Green Memory   1951

A wonderful time—the War:
when money rolled in
and blood rolled out.

But blood
was far away   5
from here—

Money was near.

J. V. Cunningham (1911–1985)*

This *Humanist* whom no beliefs constrained   1947

This *Humanist* whom no beliefs constrained
Grew so broad-minded he was scatter-brained.

John Frederick Nims (b. 1914)*

Contemplation   1967

"I'm Mark's alone!" you swore. Given cause to doubt you,
I think less of you, dear. But more about you.

Stevie Smith (1902–1971)*

This Englishwoman   1937

This Englishwoman is so refined
She has no bosom and no behind.

Robert Crawford (b. 1959)

My Iambic Pentameter Lines   1986

Three drunks, a leg on one quite gone, bereft
Of sense, and traveling on five feet, all left.

Paul Ramsey (b. 1924)

A POET DEFENDED   1984

You claim his poems are garbage. Balderdash!
Garbage includes some meat. His poems are trash.

R. L. Barth (b. 1947)*

DEFINITION   1984

The epigram is not artillery,
Blockbusters, automatic weaponry,
Napalm or rockets; but, hunkered in mire,
The sniper-scoped guerilla's small-arms fire.

Bruce Bennett (b. 1940)

LEADER   1984

      A man shot himself
in the foot.

      "OW!" he howled,
hopping this way and
that. "Do something!   5
Do something!"

      "We are! We are!"
shouted those around
him. "We're hopping!
We're hopping!"   10

EXPERIMENT: Expanding an Epigram

Rewrite any of the preceding epigrams, taking them out of rime (if they are in rime) and adding a few more words to them. See if your revisions have nearly the same effect as the originals.

EXERCISE: Reading for Couplets

Read all the sonnets by Shakespeare in this book. How do the final couplets of some of them resemble epigrams? Does this similarity diminish their effect of "seriousness"?

In English the only other fixed form to rival the sonnet and the epigram in favor is the **limerick:** five anapestic lines usually riming *a a b b a.* Here is a sample, attributed to W. R. Inge (1860 – 1954):

> There was an old man of Khartoum
> Who kept a tame sheep in his room,
>   "To remind me," he said,
>   "Of someone who's dead,
> But I never can recollect whom."

The limerick was made popular by Edward Lear (1812 – 1888), English painter and author of nonsense, whose own custom was to make the last line hark back to the first: "That oppressive old man of Khartoum."

EXPERIMENT: *Contriving a Clerihew*

The **clerihew,** a fixed form named for its inventor, Edmund Clerihew Bentley (1875 – 1956), has straggled behind the limerick in popularity. Here are four examples: how would you define the form and what are its rules? Who or what is its conventional subject matter? Try writing your own example.

> James Watt
> Was the hard-boiled kind of Scot:
> He thought any dream
> Sheer waste of steam.
>   — W. H. Auden

> Sir Christopher Wren
> Said, "I am going to dine with some men.
> If anybody calls
> Say I am designing St. Paul's."
>   — Edmund Clerihew Bentley

> Etienne de Silhouette
> (It's a good bet)
> Has the shadiest claim
> To fame.
>   — Cornelius J. Ter Maat

Dylan Thomas (1914 – 1953)*

DO NOT GO GENTLE INTO THAT GOOD NIGHT   1952

Do not go gentle into that good night, *a*
Old age should burn and rave at close of day; *b*
Rage, rage against the dying of the light. *a*

Though wise men at their end know dark is right, *a*
Because their words had forked no lightning they *b*   5
Do not go gentle into that good night. *a*

Good men, the last wave by, crying how bright *a*
Their frail deeds might have danced in a green bay, *b*
Rage, rage against the dying of the light. *a*

Wild men who caught and sang the sun in flight, *d*
And learn, too late, they grieved it on its way, *b*
Do not go gentle into that good night. *d*   10

Grave men, near death, who see with blinding sight *d*
Blind eyes could blaze like meteors and be gay, *b*
Rage, rage against the dying of the light. *d*   15

And you, my father, there on the sad height, *d*
Curse, bless, me now with your fierce tears, I pray, *b*
Do not go gentle into that good night. *d*
Rage, rage against the dying of the light. *d*

There are lots of spondee in this villanella

QUESTIONS

1. "Do not go gentle into that good night" is a **villanelle:** a fixed form originated by
   French courtly poets of the Middle Ages. What are its rules?
2. Is Thomas's poem, like many another villanelle, just an elaborate and trivial exercise?
   Whom does the poet address? What is he saying?   اسم الوالد ؟   ذكر.

OPEN FORM

Writing in **open form,** a poet seeks to discover a fresh and individual arrangement for words in every poem. Such a poem, generally speaking, has neither
a rime scheme nor a basic meter informing the whole of it. Doing without those
powerful (some would say hypnotic) elements, the poet who writes in open form
relies on other means to engage and to sustain the reader's attention. Novice
poets often think that open form looks easy, not nearly so hard as riming
everything; but in truth, formally open poems are easy to write only if written
carelessly. To compose lines with keen awareness of open form's demands, and
of its infinite possibilities, calls for skill: at least as much as that needed to write
in meter and rime, if not more. Should the poet succeed, then the discovered
arrangement will seem exactly right for what the poem is saying. Words will
seem at home in their positions, as naturally as the words of a decent sonnet.

Denise Levertov (b. 1923)*

SIX VARIATIONS (PART III)   1961

Shlup, shlup, the dog
as it laps up
water
makes intelligent
music, resting   5
now and then to take breath in irregular
measure.

Open form, in this brief poem, affords Denise Levertov certain advantages. Able to break off a line at whatever point she likes (a privilege not available to the poet writing, say, a conventional sonnet, who has to break off each line after its tenth syllable), she selects her pauses artfully. Line-breaks lend emphasis: a word or phrase at the end of a line takes a little more stress (and receives a little more attention), because the ending of the line compels the reader to make a slight pause, if only for the brief moment it takes to sling back one's eyes (like a typewriter carriage) and fix them on the line following. Slight pauses, then, follow the words and phrases *the dog / laps up / water / intelligent / resting / irregular / measure* — all of these being elements that apparently the poet wishes to call our attention to. (The pause after a line-break also casts a little more weight upon the *first* word or phrase of each succeeding line.) Levertov makes the most of white space — another means of calling attention to things, as any good picture-framer knows. By setting a word all alone on a line *(water / measure)*, she makes it stand out more than it would do in a line of pentameter. She feels free to include a bit of rime *(Shlup, shlup / up)*. She creates rhythms: if you will read aloud the phrases *intelligent / music* and *irregular / measure,* you will sense that in each phrase the arrangement of pauses and stresses is identical. Like the dog's halts to take breath, the lengths of the lines seem naturally irregular. The result is a fusion of meaning and form: indeed, an "intelligent music."

Poetry in open form used to be called **free verse** (from the French **vers libre**), suggesting a kind of verse liberated from the shackles of rime and meter. "Writing free verse," said Robert Frost, who wasn't interested in it, "is like playing tennis with the net down." And yet, as Denise Levertov and many other poets demonstrate, high scores can be made in such an unconventional game, provided it doesn't straggle all over the court. For a successful poem in open form, the term *free verse* seems inaccurate. "Being an art form," said William Carlos Williams, "verse cannot be 'free' in the sense of having *no* limitations or guiding principles."[4] Various substitute names have been suggested: organic poetry, composition by field, raw (as against cooked) poetry, open form poetry. "But what does it matter what you call it?" remark the editors of an anthology called *Naked Poetry.* The best poems of the last twenty years "don't rhyme (usually) and don't move on feet of more or less equal duration (usually). That nondescription moves toward the only technical principle they all have in common."[5]

And yet many poems in open form have much more in common than absences and lacks. One positive principle has been Ezra Pound's famous suggestion that poets "compose in the sequence of the musical phrase, not in the sequence of the metronome" — good advice, perhaps, even for poets who write inside fixed forms. In Charles Olson's influential theory of **projective verse**, poets compose by listening to their own breathing. On paper, they indicate the rhythms of a poem by using a little white space or a lot, a slight

[4]"Free Verse," article in *Princeton Encyclopedia of Poetry and Poetics.*
[5]Stephen Berg and Robert Mezey, eds., foreword to *Naked Poetry: Recent American Poetry in Open Forms* (Indianapolis: Bobbs, 1969).

indentation or a deep one, depending on whether a short pause or a long one is intended. Words can be grouped in clusters on the page (usually no more words than a lungful of air can accommodate). Heavy cesuras are sometimes shown by breaking a line in two and lowering the second part of it.[6] (An Olson poem appears on page 196.)

To the poet working in open form, no less than to the poet writing a sonnet, line length can be valuable. Walt Whitman, who loved to expand vast sentences for line after line, knew well that an impressive rhythm can accumulate if the poet will keep long lines approximately the same length, causing a pause to recur at about the same interval after every line. Sometimes, too, Whitman repeats the same words at each line's opening. An instance is the masterly sixth section of "When Lilacs Last in the Dooryard Bloom'd," an elegy for Abraham Lincoln:

Coffin that passes through lanes and streets,
Through day and night with the great cloud darkening the land,
With the pomp of the inloop'd flags with the cities draped in black,
With the show of the States themselves as of crape-veil'd women standing,
With processions long and winding and the flambeaus of the night,
With the countless torches lit, with the silent sea of faces and the unbared
    heads,
With the waiting depot, the arriving coffin, and the somber faces,
With dirges through the night, with the thousand voices rising strong and
    solemn,
With all the mournful voices of the dirges pour'd around the coffin,
The dim-lit churches and the shuddering organs — where amid these you
    journey,
With the tolling tolling bells' perpetual clang,
Here, coffin that slowly passes,
I give you my sprig of lilac.

There is music in such solemn, operatic arias. Whitman's lines echo another model: the Hebrew **psalms**, or sacred songs, as translated in the King James Version of the Bible. In Psalm 150, repetition also occurs inside of lines:

Praise ye the Lord. Praise God in his sanctuary: praise him in the firmament of his power.

Praise him for his mighty acts: praise him according to his excellent greatness.

Praise him with the sound of the trumpet: praise him with the psaltery and harp.

Praise him with the timbrel and dance: praise him with stringed instruments and organs.

Praise him upon the loud cymbals: praise him upon the high sounding cymbals.

Let every thing that hath breath praise the Lord. Praise ye the Lord.

[6]See Olson's essays "Projective Verse" and "Letter to Elaine Feinstein" in *Selected Writings*, edited by Robert Creeley (New York: New Directions, 1966). Olson's letters to Cid Corman are fascinating: *Letters for Origin, 1950 – 1955*, edited by Albert Glover (New York: Grossman, 1970).

In Biblical Psalms, we are in the presence of (as Robert Lowell has said) "supreme poems, written when their translators merely intended prose and were forced by the structure of their originals to write poetry."[7]

Whitman was a more deliberate craftsman than he let his readers think, and to anyone interested in writing in open form, his work will repay close study. He knew that repetitions of any kind often make memorable rhythms, as in this passage from "Song of Myself," with every line ending on an *-ing* word (a stressed syllable followed by an unstressed syllable):

> Here and there with dimes on the eyes walking,
> To feed the greed of the belly the brains liberally spooning,
> Tickets buying, taking, selling, but in to the feast never once going,
> Many sweating, ploughing, thrashing, and then the chaff for payment
>   receiving,
> A few idly owning, and they the wheat continually claiming.

Much more than simply repetition, of course, went into the music of those lines — the internal rime *feed, greed,* the use of assonance, the trochees that begin the third and fourth lines, whether or not they were calculated.

In such classics of open form poetry, sound and rhythm are positive forces. When speaking a poem in open form, you often may find that it makes a difference for the better if you pause at the end of each line. Try pausing there, however briefly; but don't allow your voice to drop. Read just as you would normally read a sentence in prose (except for the pauses, of course). Why do the pauses matter? Open form poetry usually has no meter to lend it rhythm. *Some* lines in an open form poem, as we have seen in Whitman's "dimes on the eyes" passage, do fall into metrical feet; sometimes the whole poem does. Usually lacking meter's aid, however, open form, in order to have more and more noticeable rhythms, has need of all the recurring pauses it can get. When reading their own work aloud, open form poets like Robert Creeley and Allen Ginsberg often pause very definitely at each line break. Such a habit makes sense only in reading artful poems.

Some poems, to be sure, seem more widely open in form than others. A poet, for instance, may employ rime, but have the rimes recur at various intervals; or perhaps rime lines of various lengths. (See T. S. Eliot's famous "Love Song of J. Alfred Prufrock" on page 310. Is it a closed poem left ajar or an open poem trying to slam itself?) No law requires a poet to split thoughts into verse lines at all. Charles Baudelaire, Rainer Maria Rilke, Jorge Luis Borges, Alexander Solzhenitsyn, T. S. Eliot, and many others have written **prose poems**, in which, without caring that eye appeal and some of the rhythm of a line structure may be lost, the poet prints words in a block like a prose paragraph. For an example see Karl Shapiro's "The Dirty Word" (page 377).[8]

"Farewell, pale skunky pentameters (the only honest English meter, gloop! gloop!)," Kenneth Koch has gleefully exclaimed, suggesting that it was high time

---

[7]"On Freedom in Poetry," in Berg and Mezey, *Naked Poetry*.
[8]For more examples see *The Prose Poem, An International Anthology,* edited by Michael Benedikt (New York: Dell, 1976).

to junk such stale conventions. Many poets who agree with him believe that it is wrong to fit words into any pattern that already exists, and instead believe in letting a poem seek its own shape as it goes along. (Traditionalists might say that that is what all good poems do anyway: sonnets rarely know they are going to be sonnets until the third line has been written. However, there is no doubt that the sonnet form already exists, at least in the back of the head of any poet who has ever read sonnets.) Some open form poets offer a historical motive: they want to reflect the nervous, staccato, disconnected pace of our bumper-to-bumper society. Others see open form as an attempt to suit thoughts and words to a more spontaneous order than the traditional verse forms allow. "Better," says Gary Snyder, quoting from Zen, "the perfect, easy discipline of the swallow's dip and swoop, 'without east or west.' "[9]

At the moment, much exciting new poetry is being written in both open form and closed. Today, many younger poets (labeled New Formalists) have taken up rime and meter and have been writing sonnets, epigrams, and poems in rimed stanzas, giving "pale skunky pentameters" a fresh lease on life.[10]

E. E. Cummings (1894 – 1962)*

BUFFALO BILL 'S   1923

Buffalo Bill 's
defunct
        who used to
        ride a watersmooth-silver
                                stallion   5
and break onetwothreefourfive pigeonsjustlikethat
                                Jesus
he was a handsome man
                        and what i want to know is
how do you like your blueeyed boy   10
Mister Death

QUESTION

Cummings's poem would look like this if given conventional punctuation and set in a solid block like prose:

Buffalo Bill's defunct, who used to ride a water-smooth silver stallion and break one, two, three, four, five pigeons just like that. Jesus, he was a handsome man. And what I want to know is: "How do you like your blue-eyed boy, Mister Death?"

If this were done, by what characteristics would it still be recognizable as poetry? But what would be lost?

[9]"Some Yips & Barks in the Dark," in Berg and Mezey, *Naked Poetry*.
[10]For more samples of recent formal poetry than this book provides, see *The Direction of Poetry* ed. Robert Richman (Boston: Houghton, 1988), *Ecstatic Occasions, Expedient Forms* ed. David Lehman (New York: Collier, 1987), and *Strong Measures: Contemporary American Poetry in Traditional Forms* ed. Philip Dacey and David Jauss (New York: Harper, 1986).

Emily Dickinson (1830 – 1886)*

VICTORY COMES LATE   (1861)

Victory comes late –
And is held low to freezing lips –
Too rapt with frost
To take it –
How sweet it would have tasted –   5
Just a Drop –
Was God so economical?
His Table's spread too high for Us –
Unless We dine on tiptoe –
Crumbs – fit such little mouths –   10
Cherries – suit Robins –
The Eagle's Golden Breakfast strangles – Them –
God keep His Oath to Sparrows –
Who of little Love – know how to starve –

QUESTIONS

1. In this specimen of poetry in open form, can you see any other places at which the
   poet might have broken off any of her lines? To place a word last in a line gives it
   a greater emphasis; she might, for instance, have ended line 12 with *Breakfast* and
   begun a new line with the word *strangles*. Do you think she knows what she is doing
   here or does the pattern of this poem seem decided by whim? Discuss.
2. Read the poem aloud. Try pausing for a fraction of a second at every dash. Is there
   any justification for the poet's unorthodox punctuation?

"THE KERMESS" by Pieter Breughel (1520? – 1569)

William Carlos Williams (1883 – 1963)*

THE DANCE   1944

In Breughel's great picture, The Kermess,
the dancers go round, they go round and
around, the squeal and the blare and the
tweedle of bagpipes, a bugle and fiddles
tipping their bellies (round as the thick-   5
sided glasses whose wash they impound)
their hips and their bellies off balance
to turn them. Kicking and rolling about
the Fair Grounds, swinging their butts, those
shanks must be sound to bear up under such   10
rollicking measures, prance as they dance
in Breughel's great picture, The Kermess.

THE DANCE. Breughel, a Flemish painter known for his scenes of peasant activities, represented in "The Kermess" a celebration on the feast day of a local patron saint.

QUESTIONS

1. Scan this poem and try to describe the effect of its rhythms.
2. Williams, widely admired for his free verse, insisted for many years that what he sought was a form not in the least bit free. What effect does he achieve by ending lines on such weak words as the articles *and* and *the*? By splitting *thick- / sided*? By splitting a prepositional phrase with the break at the end of line 8? By using line breaks to split *those* and *such* from what they modify? What do you think he is trying to convey?
3. Is there any point in his making line 12 a repetition of the opening line?
4. Look at the reproduction of Breughel's painting "The Kermess" (also called "Peasants Dancing"). Aware that the rhythms of dancers, the rhythms of a painting, and the rhythms of a poem are not all the same, can you put in your own words what Breughel's dancing figures have in common with Williams's descriptions of them?
5. Compare with "The Dance" another poem that refers to a Breughel painting: W. H. Auden's "Musée des Beaux Arts" on page 287. What seems to be each poet's main concern: to convey in words a sense of the painting, or to visualize the painting in order to state some theme?

Stephen Crane (1871 – 1900)

THE HEART   1895

In the desert
I saw a creature, naked, bestial,
Who, squatting upon the ground,
Held his heart in his hands,
And ate of it.   5

I said, "Is it good, friend?"
"It is bitter — bitter," he answered;
"But I like it
Because it is bitter,
And because it is my heart."   10

Walt Whitman (1819 – 1892)*

Cavalry Crossing a Ford   (1865)

A line in long array where they wind betwixt green islands,
They take a serpentine course, their arms flash in the sun — hark to
    the musical clank,
Behold the silvery river, in it the splashing horses loitering stop to
    drink,
Behold the brown-faced men, each group, each person a picture, the
    negligent rest on the saddles,
Some emerge on the opposite bank, others are just entering the
    ford — while,   5
Scarlet and blue and snowy white,
The guidon flags flutter gayly in the wind.

Questions

The following nit-picking questions are intended to help you see exactly what makes these two open form poems by Crane and Whitman so different in their music.
1. What devices of sound occur in Whitman's phrase *silvery river* (line 3)? Where else in his poem do you find these devices?
2. Does Crane use any such devices?
3. In number of syllables, Whitman's poem is almost twice as long as Crane's. Which poem has more pauses in it? (Count pauses at the ends of lines, at marks of punctuation.)
4. Read the two poems aloud. In general, how would you describe the effect of their sounds and rhythms? Is Crane's poem necessarily an inferior poem for having less music?

Wallace Stevens (1879 – 1955)*

Thirteen Ways of Looking at a Blackbird   1923

I

Among twenty snowy mountains,
The only moving thing
Was the eye of the blackbird.

II

I was of three minds,
Like a tree
In which there are three blackbirds.

III

The blackbird whirled in the autumn winds.
It was a small part of the pantomime.

IV

A man and a woman
Are one.
A man and a woman and a blackbird
Are one.

V

I do not know which to prefer,
The beauty of inflections
Or the beauty of innuendoes,
The blackbird whistling
Or just after.

VI

Icicles filled the long window
With barbaric glass.
The shadow of the blackbird
Crossed it, to and fro.
The mood
Traced in the shadow
An indecipherable cause.

VII

O thin men of Haddam,
Why do you imagine golden birds?
Do you not see how the blackbird
Walks around the feet
Of the women about you?

VIII

I know noble accents 30
And lucid, inescapable rhythms;
But I know, too,
That the blackbird is involved
In what I know.

IX

When the blackbird flew out of sight, 35
It marked the edge
Of one of many circles.

X

At the sight of blackbirds
Flying in a green light,
Even the bawds of euphony 40
Would cry out sharply.

XI

He rode over Connecticut
In a glass coach.
Once, a fear pierced him,
In that he mistook 45
The shadow of his equipage
For blackbirds.

XII

The river is moving.
The blackbird must be flying.

XIII

It was evening all afternoon. 50
It was snowing
And it was going to snow.
The blackbird sat
In the cedar-limbs.

THIRTEEN WAYS OF LOOKING AT A BLACKBIRD. 25 *Haddam:* This Biblical-sounding name is that of
a town in Connecticut.

QUESTIONS

1. What is the speaker's attitude toward the men of Haddam? What attitude toward this
   world does he suggest they lack? What is implied by calling them *thin* (line 25)?

2. What do the landscapes of winter contribute to the poem's effectiveness? If Stevens had chosen images of summer lawns, what would have been lost?

3. In which sections of the poem does Stevens suggest that a unity exists between human being and blackbird, between blackbird and the entire natural world? Can we say that Stevens "philosophizes"? What role does imagery play in Stevens's statement of his ideas?

4. What sense can you make of Part X? Make an enlightened guess.

5. Consider any one of the thirteen parts. What patterns of sound and rhythm do you find in it? What kind of structure does it have?

6. If the thirteen parts were arranged in some different order, would the poem be just as good? Or can we find a justification for its beginning with Part I and ending with Part XIII?

7. Does the poem seem an arbitrary combination of thirteen separate poems? Or is there any reason to call it a whole?

Gary Gildner (b. 1938)

First Practice   1969

After the doctor checked to see
we weren't ruptured,
the man with the short cigar took us
under the grade school,
where we went in case of attack   5
or storm, and said
he was Clifford Hill, he was
a man who believed dogs
ate dogs, he had once killed
for his country, and if   10
there were any girls present
for them to leave now.
                No one
left. OK, he said, he said I take
that to mean you are hungry
men who hate to lose as much   15
as I do. OK. Then
he made two lines of us
facing each other,
and across the way, he said,
is the man you hate most   20
in the world,
and if we are to win
that title I want to see how.
But I don't want to see
any marks when you're dressed,   25
he said. He said, *Now.*

1. What do you make of Hill and his world-view?
2. How does the speaker reveal his own view? Why, instead of quoting Hill directly ("This is a dog-eat-dog world"), does he call him *a man who believed dogs ate dogs* (lines 8 – 9)?
3. What effect is made by breaking off and lowering *No one* at the end of line 12?
4. What is gained by having a rime on the poem's last word?
5. For the sake of understanding how right the form of Gildner's poem is for it, imagine the poem in meter and a rime scheme, and condensed into two stanzas:

> Then he made two facing lines of us
> And he said, Across the way,
> Of all the men there are in the world
> Is the man you most want to slay,
>
> And if we are to win that title, he said,
> I want you to show me how.
> But I don't want to see any marks when you're dressed,
> He said. Go get him. *Now.*

Why would that rewrite be so unfaithful to what Gildner is saying?
6. How would you answer someone who argued, "This can't be a poem — its subject is ugly and its language isn't beautiful"?

Michael Heffernan (b. 1942)

LIVING ROOM   1988

Christmas Eve at Beitzinger's Hardware
John & Phil had bourbon in the backroom for the customers
along with a cooker full of braised raccoon.

I would have eaten some, only Bill Allen,
who was in there replumbing his toilet,   5
said This coon is a little blue,

and John had referred to cooking it long enough
to get the strangeness out.
So I drank my bourbon and stepped into the light

on Broadway and went next door to buy   10
Kathy a wristwatch from Bud Benelli,
who was delighted to see me buy something for a change.

The great thing is, I thought,
that down here in the real world nobody's gods win
and nobody's demons either.   15

Which is why Phil had placed that poor beast's forepaw
on a piece of hardcrust bread
and laid it in the scalepan where they weigh the nails

and Uncle Bud had seen fit that she should come
into the living room with that watch on   20
dancing to something on the radio.

1. What do you take to be the setting of this poem? Is this Broadway, New York? Point to evidence.
2. What contrasts do you find between the feast in the backroom and what followed after the speaker "stepped into the light"?
3. In your own words, what is the theme of the poem? Where is this theme summed up? How do the last two stanzas illustrate it?
4. Comment on the form of this poem. How does it differ from prose?

FOR REVIEW AND FURTHER STUDY

Leigh Hunt (1784 – 1859)

RONDEAU   1838

Jenny kissed me when we met,
　　Jumping from the chair she sat in;
Time, you thief, who love to get
　　Sweets into your list, put that in:
Say I'm weary, say I'm sad,   5
　　Say that health and wealth have missed me,
Say I'm growing old, but add,
　　Jenny kissed me.

QUESTION

Here is a fresh contemporary version of Hunt's "Rondeau" that yanks open the form of the rimed original:

Jenny kissed me when we met,
jumping from her chair;
Time, you thief, who love to add
sweets into your list, put that in:
say I'm weary, say I'm sad,
say I'm poor and in ill health,
say I'm growing old — but note, too,
Jenny kissed me.

That revised version says approximately the same thing as Hunt's original, doesn't it? Why is it less effective?

Keith Waldrop (b. 1932)*

PROPOSITION II   1975

Each grain of sand has an architecture, but
a desert displays the structure of the wind.

1. How is this poem like an epigram?
2. How is it dissimilar?

Elizabeth Bishop (1911 – 1979)*

SESTINA   1965

September rain falls on the house.
In the failing light, the old grandmother
sits in the kitchen with the child
beside the Little Marvel Stove,
reading the jokes from the almanac,   5
laughing and talking to hide her tears.

She thinks that her equinoctial tears
and the rain that beats on the roof of the house
were both foretold by the almanac,
but only known to a grandmother.   10
The iron kettle sings on the stove.
She cuts some bread and says to the child,

It's time for tea now; but the child
is watching the teakettle's small hard tears
dance like mad on the hot black stove,   15
the way the rain must dance on the house.
Tidying up, the old grandmother
hangs up the clever almanac

on its string. Birdlike, the almanac
hovers half open above the child,   20
hovers above the old grandmother
and her teacup full of dark brown tears.
She shivers and says she thinks the house
feels chilly, and puts more wood in the stove.

It was to be, says the Marvel Stove.   25
I know what I know, says the almanac.
With crayons the child draws a rigid house
and a winding pathway. Then the child
puts in a man with buttons like tears
and shows it proudly to the grandmother.   30

But secretly, while the grandmother
busies herself about the stove,
the little moons fall down like tears

from between the pages of the almanac
into the flower bed the child
has carefully placed in the front of the house.

Time to plant tears, says the almanac.
The grandmother sings to the marvellous stove
and the child draws another inscrutable house.

SESTINA. As its title indicates, this poem is written in the trickiest of medieval fixed forms, that of
the **sestina** (or "song of sixes"), said to have been invented in Provence in the thirteenth century
by the troubadour poet Arnaut Daniel. In six six-line stanzas, the poet repeats six end-words (in
a prescribed order), then reintroduces the six repeated words (in any order) in a closing **envoy**
of three lines. Elizabeth Bishop strictly follows the troubadour rules for the order in which the
end-words recur. (If you care, you can figure out the formula: in the first stanza, the six words are
arranged A B C D E F; in the second, F A E B D C; and so on.) Notable sestinas in English have
been written also by Sir Philip Sidney, Algernon Charles Swinburne, and Rudyard Kipling, more
recently by Ezra Pound ("Sestina: Altaforte"), by W. H. Auden ("Hearing of Harvests Rotting in
the Valleys" and others), and by contemporary poets, among them John Ashbery, Dana Gioia,
Marilyn Hacker, Michael Heffernan, Donald Justice, Peter Klappert, William Meredith, Howard
Nemerov, John Frederick Nims, Robert Pack, Henry Taylor, and Mona Van Duyn.

QUESTIONS

1. A perceptive comment from a student: "Something seems to be going on here that
   the child doesn't understand. Maybe some terrible loss has happened." Test this
   guess by reading the poem closely.
2. Then consider this possibility. We don't know that "Sestina" is autobiographical;
   still, does any information about the poet's early life contribute to your reading of
   the poem? (See "Lives of the Poets," page 410).
3. In the "little moons" that fall from the almanac (line 33), does the poem introduce
   dream or fantasy, or do you take these to be small round pieces of paper?
4. What is the tone of this poem — the speaker's apparent attitude toward the scene
   described?
5. In an essay, "The Sestina," in *A Local Habitation* (U of Michigan P, 1985), John
   Frederick Nims defends the form against an obvious complaint against it:

   A shallow view of the sestina might suggest that the poet writes a stanza, and then
   is stuck with six words which he has to juggle into the required positions through
   five more stanzas and an envoy — to the great detriment of what passion and
   sincerity would have him say. But in a good sestina the poet has six words, six images,
   six ideas so urgently in his mind that he cannot get away from them; he wants to
   test them in all possible combinations and come to a conclusion about their relationship.

   How well does this description of a good sestina fit "Sestina"?

EXPERIMENT: *Urgent Repetition*

Write a sestina and see what you find out by doing so. (Even if you fail in the attempt,
you just might learn something interesting.) To start, pick six words you think worth
repeating six times. This elaborate pattern gives you much help: as John Ashbery has
pointed out, writing a sestina is "like riding downhill on a bicycle and having the pedals
push your feet." Here is some encouragement from a poet and critic, John Heath-Stubbs:
"I have never read a sestina that seemed to me a total failure."

Geoffrey Chaucer (1340? – 1400)

YOUR ŸEN TWO WOL SLEE ME SODENLY   (late fourteenth century)

Your ÿen° two wol slee° me sodenly;   *eyes; slay*
I may the beautee of hem° not sustene°,   *them; resist*
So woundeth hit thourghout my herte kene.

And but° your word wol helen° hastily   *unless, heal*
My hertes wounde, while that hit is grene°,   *new*   5
    Your ÿen two wol slee me sodenly;
    I may the beautee of hem not sustene.

Upon my trouthe° I sey you feithfully   *word*
That ye ben of my lyf and deeth the quene;
For with my deeth the trouthe° shal be sene.   *truth*   10
    Your ÿen two wol slee me sodenly;
    I may the beautee of hem not sustene,
    So woundeth it thourghout my herte kene.

YOUR ŸEN TWO WOL SLEE ME SODENLY. This poem is one of a group of three in the same fixed form, entitled "Merciles Beaute." 3 *so woundeth . . . kene:* "So deeply does it wound me through the heart."

QUESTIONS

1. This is a **roundel** (or **rondel**), an English form. What are its rules? How does it remind you of French courtly forms such as the villanelle, employed by Dylan Thomas (page 178)?
2. Try writing a roundel of your own in modern English. Although tricky, the form isn't extremely difficult: write only three lines and your poem is already eight-thirteenths finished. Here are some possible opening lines:

   Baby, your eyes will slay me. Shut them tight.
   Against their glow, I can't hold out for long. . . .

   Your eyes present a pin to my balloon:
   One pointed look and I start growing small. . . .

   Since I escaped from love, I've grown so fat,
   I barely can remember being thin. . . .

EXERCISE: *Seeing the Logic of Open Form Verse*

Read the following poems in open form silently to yourself, noticing what each poet does with white space, repetitions, line breaks, and indentations. Then read the poems aloud, trying to indicate by slight pauses where lines end and also pausing slightly at any space inside a line. Can you see any reasons for the poet's placing his words in this arrangement rather than in a prose paragraph? Do any of these poets seem to care also about visual effect? (As with other kinds of poetry, there may not be any obvious logical reason for everything that happens in these poems.)

E. E. Cummings (1894 – 1962)*

IN JUST-   1923

in Just-
spring   when the world is mud-
luscious the little
lame balloonman

whistles   far   and wee   5

and eddieandbill come
running from marbles and
piracies and it's
spring

when the world is puddle-wonderful   10

the queer
old balloonman whistles
far   and   wee
and bettyandisbel come dancing

from hop-scotch and jump-rope and   15

it's
spring
and
     the

          goat-footed   20

balloonMan   whistles
far
and
wee

Linda Pastan (b. 1932)*

JUMP CABLING   1984

When our cars   touched
When you lifted the hood   of mine
To see the intimate workings   underneath,
When we were bound   together
By a pulse of pure   energy,   5
When my car like the   princess
In the tale woke with a   start,
I thought why not ride the rest of the way together?

Donald Finkel (b. 1929)

GESTURE   1970

My arm sweeps down
    a pliant arc
        whatever I am
            streams through my
                negligent wrist: 5

the poem
        uncoils
           like a
               whip, and
snaps   10
softly   an inch from your enchanted face.

Charles Olson (1910 – 1970)

LA CHUTE   1967

my drum, hollowed out thru the thin slit,
carved from the cedar wood, the base I took
when the tree was felled

o my lute, wrought from the tree's crown

my drum, whose lustiness   5
was not to be resisted
            my lute,

from whose pulsations
not one could turn away

                    They   10
are where the dead are, my drum fell
where the dead are, who
will bring it up, my lute
who will bring it up where it fell in the face of them
where they are, where my lute and drum have fallen?   15

LA CHUTE. The French title means "The Fall."

SUGGESTIONS FOR WRITING

1. William Carlos Williams, in an interview, delivered this blast:

> Forcing twentieth-century America into a sonnet—gosh, how I hate sonnets—is like putting a crab into a square box. You've got to cut his legs off to make him fit. When you get through, you don't have a crab any more.

In a two-page essay, defend the modern American sonnet against Williams's charge. Or instead, open fire on it, using Williams's view for ammunition. Some sonnets to consider: R. S. Gwynn's "Scenes from the Playroom" (page 173), Gwendolyn Brooks's "The Rites for Cousin Vit" (page 295), and Archibald MacLeish's "The End of the World" (page 349).

2. Write an unserious argument for or against the abolition of limericks. Give illustrations of limericks you think worthy of abolition (or preservation).

3. Is "free verse" totally free? Argue this question in a short essay, drawing evidence from open-form poems that interest you.

11 Poems for the Eye

Let's look at a famous poem with a distinctive visible shape. In the seventeenth century, ingenious poets trimmed their lines into the silhouettes of altars and crosses, pillars and pyramids. Here is one. Is it anything more than a demonstration of ingenuity?

George Herbert (1593 – 1633)*

EASTER WINGS   1633

Lord, who createdst man in wealth and store,
Though foolishly he lost the same,
Decaying more and more,
Till he became
Most poor;
With thee
Oh, let me rise
As larks, harmoniously,
And sing this day thy victories;
Then shall the fall further the flight in me.

My tender age in sorrow did begin;
And still with sicknesses and shame
Thou didst so punish sin,
That I became
Most thin.
With thee
Let me combine,
And feel this day thy victory;
For if I imp my wing on thine,
Affliction shall advance the flight in me.

In the next-to-last line, *imp* is a term from falconry meaning to repair the wing of an injured bird by grafting feathers into it.

If we see it merely as a picture, we will have to admit that Herbert's word design does not go far. It renders with difficulty shapes that a sketcher's pencil could set down in a flash, in more detail, more accurately. Was Herbert's effort wasted? It might have been, were there not more to his poem than meets the eye. The mind, too, is engaged by the visual pattern, by the realization that the words *most thin* are given emphasis by their narrow form. Here, visual pattern points out meaning. Heard aloud, too, "Easter Wings" gives further pleasure. Its rimes, its rhythm are perceptible.

Ever since George Herbert's day, poets have continued to experiment with the looks of printed poetry. Notable efforts to entertain the eye are Lewis Carroll's rimed mouse's tail in *Alice in Wonderland*; and the *Calligrammes* of Guillaume Apollinaire, who arranged words in the shapes of a necktie, of the Eiffel Tower, of spears of falling rain. Here is a bird-shaped poem of more recent inspiration than Herbert's. What does its visual form have to do with what the poet is saying?

John Hollander (b. 1929)

SWAN AND SHADOW   1969

<pre>
                        Dusk
                      Above the
                  water hang the
                         loud
                         flies
                         Here
                         O so
                         gray
                         then
                      What   A pale signal will appear
                      When   Soon before its shadow fades
                      Where   Here in this pool of opened eye
                      In us   No Upon us As at the very edges
                    of where we take shape in the dark air
                      this object bares its image awakening
                        ripples of recognition that will
                          brush darkness up into light
        even after this bird this hour both drift by atop the perfect sad instant now
                          already passing out of sight
                      toward yet-untroubled reflection
                    this image bears its object darkening
                  into memorial shades Scattered bits of
                  light   No of water Or something across
                  water   Breaking up No Being regathered
                  soon   Yet by then a swan will have
                   gone   Yet out of mind into what
                    vast
                     pale
                     hush
                     of a
                     place
                      past
              sudden dark as
                if a swan
                    sang
</pre>

A whole poem doesn't need to be such a verbal silhouette, of course, for its appearance on the page to seem meaningful. In some lines of a longer poem, William Carlos Williams has conveyed the way an energetic bellhop (or hotel porter) runs downstairs:

> ta tuck a
> > ta tuck a
> > > ta tuck a
> > > > ta tuck a
> > > > > ta tuck a

This is not only good onomatopoeia and an accurate description of a rhythm; the steplike appearance of the lines goes together with their meaning.

At least some of our pleasure in silently reading a poem derives from the way it looks upon its page. A poem in an open form can engage the eye with snowfields of white space and thickets of close-set words. A poem in stanzas can please us by its visual symmetry. And, far from being merely decorative, the visual devices of a poem can be meaningful, too. White space — as poets demonstrate who work in open forms — can indicate pauses. If white space entirely surrounds a word or phrase or line, then that portion of the poem obviously takes special emphasis. Typographical devices such as capital letters and italics also can lay stress upon words. In most traditional poems, a capital letter at the beginning of each new line helps indicate the importance the poet places upon line-divisions, whose regular intervals make a rhythm out of pauses. And the poet may be trying to show us that certain lines rime by indenting them.

Though too much importance can be given to the visual element of poetry and though many poets seem hardly to care about it, it can be another dimension that sets apart poetry from prose. It is at least arguable that some of Walt Whitman's long-line, page-filling descriptions of the wide ocean, open landscapes, and broad streets of his America, which meet the eye as wide expanses of words, would lose something — besides rhythm — if couched in lines only three or four syllables long. Another poet who deeply cared about visual appearance was William Blake (1757 – 1827), graphic artist and engraver as well as a master artist in words. By publishing his *Songs of Innocence* and *Songs of Experience* (among other works) with illustrations and accompanying hand-lettered poems, often interwoven with the lines of the poems, Blake apparently strove to make poem and appearance of poem a unity, striking mind and eye at the same time.

Some poets who write in English have envied poets who write in Chinese, a language in which certain words look like the things they represent. Consider this Chinese poem:

Wang Wei (701 – 761)

BIRD-SINGING STREAM   (about 750)

人靜月時　閒夜出鳴　桂春驚春　花山山澗　落空鳥中

Substituting English words for ideograms, the poem becomes:

man	leisure	cassia	flower	fall
quiet	night	spring	mountain	empty
moon	rise	startle	mountain	bird
at times	sing	spring	stream	middle

Even without the aid of English crib-notes, all of us can read some Chinese if we can recognize a picture of a man. What resemblances can you see between any of the other ideograms and the things they stand for?[1]

Wai-lim Yip, the poet and critic who provided the Chinese text and translation, has also translated the poem into more usual English word order, still keeping close to the original sequence of ideas:

Man at leisure. Cassia flowers fall.
Quiet night. Spring mountain is empty.
Moon rises. Startles — a mountain bird.
It sings at times in the spring stream.

One envious Western poet was Ezra Pound, who included a few Chinese ideograms in his *Cantos* as illustrations. From the scholar Ernest Fenollosa, Pound said he had come to understand why a language written in ideograms "simply *had to stay poetic*; simply couldn't help being and staying poetic in a way that a column of English type might very well not stay poetic."[2] Having an imperfect command of Chinese, Pound greatly overestimated the tendency of the language to depict things. (Only a small number of characters in modern Chinese are pictures; Chinese characters, like Western alphabets, also indicate the sounds of words.) Still, Pound's misunderstanding was fruitful. Thanks to his influence, many other recent poets were encouraged to consider the appearance of words.[3] E. E. Cummings, in a poem that begins "mOOn Over tOwns mOOn," has reveled in the fact that O's are moonshaped. Aram Saroyan, in a poem entitled "crickets," makes capital of the fact that the word *cricket* somewhat resembles the snub-nosed insect of approximately the same length. The poem begins,

crickets
crickets
crickets
crickets

[1]To help you compare English and Chinese, the Chinese original has been arranged in Western word-order. (Ordinarily, in Chinese, the word for "man" would appear at the upper right.)
[2]*The ABC of Reading* (Norfolk, Conn., 1960) 22.
[3]For a brief discussion of Pound's misunderstanding and its influence, see Milton Klonsky's introduction to his anthology *Speaking Pictures: A Gallery of Pictorial Poetry from the Sixteenth Century to the Present* (New York: Harmony, 1975).

and goes on down its page like that, for thirty-seven lines. (Read aloud, by the way, the poem sounds somewhat like crickets chirping!)

In recent years, a movement called **concrete poetry** has traveled far and wide. Though practitioners of the art disagree over its definition, what most concretists seem to do is make designs out of letters and words. Other concrete poets wield typography like a brush dipped in paint, using such techniques as blow-up, montage, and superimposed elements (the same words printed many times on top of the same impression, so that the result is blurriness). They may even keep words in a usual order, perhaps employing white space as freely as any writer of open form verse. (More freely sometimes — Aram Saroyan has a concrete poem that consists of a page blank except for the word *oxygen.*) Poet Richard Kostelanetz has suggested that a more accurate name for concrete poetry might be "word-imagery." He sees it occupying an area somewhere between conventional poetry and visual art.[4]

Admittedly, some concrete poems mean less than meets the eye. That many pretentious doodlers have taken up concretism may have caused a *Time* writer to sneer: did Joyce Kilmer miss all that much by never having seen a poem lovely as a

```
       t
      ttt
     rrrrr
    rrrrrrr
  eeeeeeeee
      ???
```

Like other structures of language, however, concrete poems evidently can have the effect of poetry, if written by poets. Whether or not it ought to be dubbed "poetry," this art can do what poems traditionally have done: use language in delightful ways that reveal meanings to us.

Edwin Morgan (b. 1920)

SIESTA OF A HUNGARIAN SNAKE   1968

s   sz   sz   SZ   sz   SZ   sz   ZS   zs   ZS   zs   zs   z

QUESTIONS

1. What do you suppose Morgan is trying to indicate by reversing the order of the two letters in mid line?
2. What, if anything, about this snake seems Hungarian?
3. Does the sound of its consonants matter?

---

[4]Introduction to his anthology *Imaged Words and Worded Images* (New York: Outerbridge and Dienstfrey, 1970).

Dorthi Charles (b. 1963)

CONCRETE CAT   1971

```
      A           A
    e   ɾ       e   ɾ
   e Y e     e Y e      stripestripestripestripe      ɾ
  whisker        whisker    stripestripestripe      ə           \
 whisker  m    h  whisker   stripestripestripestripes    ɪ  /  ɾ  a  ɪ  \
        o   ɾ              stripestripestripe        / ɾ
       U              stripestripestripestripe

      paw paw        paw paw              əsnoɯ

   dishdish                        litterbox
                                   litterbox
```

QUESTIONS

1. What does this writer indicate by capitalizing the *a* in *ear?* The *y* in *eye?* The *u* in mouth? By using spaces between the letters in the word *tail?*
2. Why is the word *mouse* upside down?
3. What possible pun might be seen in the cat's middle stripe?
4. What is the tone of "Concrete Cat"? How is it made evident?
5. Do these words seem chosen for their connotations or only for their denotations? Would you call this work of art a poem?

EXPERIMENT: *Do It Yourself*

Make a concrete poem of your own. If you need inspiration, pick some familiar object or animal and try to find words that look like it. For more ideas, study the typography of a magazine or newspaper; cut out interesting letters and numerals and try pasting them into arrangements. What (if anything) do your experiments tell you about familiar letters and words?

SUGGESTIONS FOR WRITING

1. Consider whether concrete poetry is a vital new art form or merely visual trivia.
2. Should a poem be illustrated, or is it better left to the mind's eye? Discuss this question in a brief essay. You might care to consider William Blake's illustration for "A Poison Tree" or the illustrations in a collection of poems for children.

12 *Symbol*

The national flag is supposed to bestir our patriotic feelings. When a black cat crosses his path, a superstitious man shivers, foreseeing bad luck. To each of these, by custom, our society expects a standard response. A flag, a black cat's crossing one's path — each is a **symbol:** a visible object or action that suggests some further meaning in addition to itself. In literature, a symbol might be the word *flag* or the words *a black cat crossed his path* or every description of flag or cat in an entire novel, story, play, or poem.

A flag and the crossing of a black cat may be called **conventional symbols,** since they can have a conventional or customary effect on us. Conventional symbols are also part of the language of poetry, as we know when we meet the red rose, emblem of love, in a lyric, or the Christian cross in the devotional poems of George Herbert. More often, however, symbols in literature have no conventional, long-established meaning, but particular meanings of their own. In Melville's novel *Moby-Dick,* to take a rich example, whatever we associate with the great white whale is *not* attached unmistakably to white whales by custom. Though Melville tells us that men have long regarded whales with awe and relates Moby Dick to the celebrated fish that swallowed Jonah, the reader's response is to one particular whale, the creature of Herman Melville. Only the experience of reading the novel in its entirety can give Moby Dick his particular meaning.

We should say *meanings,* for as Eudora Welty has observed, it is a good thing Melville made Moby Dick a whale, a creature large enough to contain all that critics have found in him. A symbol in literature, if not conventional, has more than just one meaning. In "The Raven," by Edgar Allan Poe, the appearance of a strange black bird in the narrator's study is sinister; and indeed, if we take the poem seriously, we may even respond with a sympathetic shiver of dread. Does the bird mean death, fate, melancholy, the loss of a loved one, knowledge in the service of evil? All these, perhaps. Like any well-chosen symbol, Poe's raven sets going within the reader an unending train of feelings and associations.

We miss the value of a symbol, however, if we think it can mean absolutely anything we wish. If a poet has any control over our reactions, the poem will guide our responses in a certain direction.

T. S. Eliot (1888 – 1965)*

THE *BOSTON EVENING TRANSCRIPT*   1917

The readers of the *Boston Evening Transcript*
Sway in the wind like a field of ripe corn.

When evening quickens faintly in the street,
Wakening the appetites of life in some
And to others bringing the *Boston Evening Transcript*,   5
I mount the steps and ring the bell, turning
Wearily, as one would turn to nod good-bye to La Rochefoucauld,
If the street were time and he at the end of the street,
And I say, "Cousin Harriet, here is the *Boston Evening Transcript.*"

The newspaper, whose name Eliot purposely repeats so monotonously, indicates what this poem is about. Now defunct, the *Transcript* covered in detail the slightest activity of Boston's leading families and was noted for the great length of its obituaries. Eliot, then, uses the newspaper as a symbol for an existence of boredom, fatigue (*Wearily*), petty and unvarying routine (since an evening newspaper, like night, arrives on schedule). The *Transcript* evokes a way of life without zest or passion, for, opposed to people who read it, Eliot sets people who do not: those whose desires revive, not expire, when the working day is through. Suggestions abound in the ironic comparison of the *Transcript*'s readers to a cornfield late in summer. To mention only a few: the readers sway because they are sleepy; they vegetate; they are drying up; each makes a rattling sound when turning a page. It is not necessary that we know the remote and similarly disillusioned friend to whom the speaker might nod: La Rochefoucauld, whose cynical *Maxims* entertained Parisian society under Louis XIV (sample: "All of us have enough strength to endure the misfortunes of others"). We understand that the nod is symbolic of an immense weariness of spirit. We know nothing about Cousin Harriet, whom the speaker addresses, but imagine from the greeting she inspires that she is probably a bore.

If Eliot wishes to say that certain Bostonians lead lives of sterile boredom, why does he couch his meaning in symbols? Why doesn't he tell us directly what he means? These questions imply two assumptions not necessarily true: first, that Eliot has a message to impart; second, that he is concealing it. We have reason to think that Eliot did not usually have a message in mind when beginning a poem, for as he once told a critic: "The conscious problems with which one is concerned in the actual writing are more those of a quasi musical nature . . . than of a conscious exposition of ideas." Poets sometimes discover what they have to say while in the act of saying it. And it may be that in his *Transcript* poem, Eliot is saying exactly what he means. By communicating his meaning through symbols instead of statements, he may be choosing the only kind of language appropriate to an idea of great subtlety and complexity. (The paraphrase "Certain Bostonians are bored" hardly begins to describe the poem in all its possible meaning.) And by his use of symbolism, Eliot affords us the pleasure of finding our own entrances to his poem. Another great strength of a symbol is that, like some figures of speech, it renders the abstract in concrete terms, and, like any other image, refers to what we can perceive — an object like a newspaper, a gesture like a nod. Eliot might, like Robert Frost, have called himself a "synecdochist." Frost explained: "Always a larger significance. A little thing touches a larger thing."

This power of suggestion that a symbol contains is, perhaps, its greatest advantage. Sometimes, as in the following poem by Emily Dickinson, a symbol will lead us from a visible object to something too vast to be perceived.

Emily Dickinson (1830 – 1886)*

THE LIGHTNING IS A YELLOW FORK   (about 1870)

The Lightning is a yellow Fork
From Tables in the sky
By inadvertent fingers dropt
The awful Cutlery

Of mansions never quite disclosed   5
And never quite concealed
The Apparatus of the Dark
To ignorance revealed.

If the lightning is a fork, then whose are the fingers that drop it, the table from which it slips, the household to which it belongs? The poem implies this question without giving an answer. An obvious answer is "God," but can we be sure? We wonder, too, about these partially lighted mansions: if our vision were clearer, what would we behold?[1]

"But how am I supposed to know a symbol when I see one?" The best approach is to read poems closely, taking comfort in the likelihood that it is better not to notice symbols at all than to find significance in every literal stone

[1] In its suggestion of an infinite realm that mortal eyes cannot quite see, but whose nature can be perceived fleetingly through things visible, Emily Dickinson's poem, by coincidence, resembles the work of late-nineteenth-century French poets called **symbolists.** To a symbolist the shirt-tail of Truth is continually seen disappearing around a corner. With their Neoplatonic view of ideal realities existing in a great beyond, whose corresponding symbols are the perceptible cats that bite us and tangible stones we stumble over, French poets such as Charles Baudelaire, Jules Laforgue, and Stéphane Mallarmé were profoundly to affect poets writing in English, notably Yeats (who said a poem "entangles . . . a part of the Divine essence") and Eliot. But we consider in this chapter symbolism as an element in certain poems, not Symbolism, the literary movement.

and huge meanings in every thing. In looking for the symbols in a poem, pick out all the references to concrete objects — newspapers, black cats, twisted pins. Consider these with special care. Notice any that the poet emphasizes by detailed description, by repetition, or by placing at the very beginning or end of the poem. Ask: What is the poem about, what does it add up to? If, when the poem is paraphrased, the paraphrase depends primarily upon the meaning of certain concrete objects, these richly suggestive objects may be the symbols.

There are some things a literary symbol usually is *not*. A symbol is not an abstraction. Such terms as *truth, death, love,* and *justice* cannot work as symbols (unless personified, as in the traditional figure of Justice holding a scale). Most often, a symbol is something we can see in the mind's eye: a newspaper, a lightning bolt, a gesture of nodding good-bye.

In narratives, a well-developed character who speaks much dialogue and is not the least bit mysterious is usually not a symbol. But watch out for an executioner in a black hood; a character, named for a Biblical prophet, who does little but utter a prophecy; a trio of old women who resemble the Three Fates. (It has been argued, with good reason, that Milton's fully rounded character of Satan in *Paradise Lost* is a symbol embodying evil and human pride, but a narrower definition of symbol is more frequently useful.) A symbol *may* be a part of a person's body (the baleful eye of the murder victim in Poe's story "The Tell-Tale Heart") or a look, a voice, a mannerism.

A symbol usually is not the second term of a metaphor. In the line "The lightning is a yellow fork," the symbol is the lightning, not the fork.

Sometimes a symbol addresses a sense other than sight: the sound of a mysterious harp at the end of Chekhov's play *The Cherry Orchard;* or, in William Faulkner's tale "A Rose for Emily," the odor of decay that surrounds the house of the last survivor of a town's leading family — suggesting not only physical dissolution but also the decay of a social order. A symbol is a special kind of image, for it exceeds the usual image in the richness of its connotations. The dead wife's cold comb in the haiku of Buson (discussed on page 73) works symbolically, suggesting among other things the chill of the grave, the contrast between the living and the dead.

Holding a narrower definition than that used in this book, some readers of poetry prefer to say that a symbol is always a concrete object, never an act. They would deny the label "symbol" to Ahab's breaking his tobacco pipe before setting out to pursue Moby Dick (suggesting, perhaps, his determination to allow no pleasure to distract him from the chase) or to any large motion (as Ahab's whole quest). This distinction, while confining, does have the merit of sparing one from seeing all motion to be possibly symbolic. Some would call Ahab's gesture not a symbol but a **symbolic act.**

To sum up: a symbol radiates hints or casts long shadows (to use Henry James's metaphor). We are unable to say it "stands for" or "represents" a meaning. It evokes, it suggests, it manifests. It demands no single necessary interpretation, such as the interpretation a driver gives to a red traffic light.

Rather, like Emily Dickinson's lightning bolt, it points toward an indefinite meaning, which may lie in part beyond the reach of words. In a symbol, as Thomas Carlyle said in *Sartor Resartus*, "the Infinite is made to blend with the Finite, to stand visible, and as it were, attainable there."

Thomas Hardy (1840 – 1928)*

NEUTRAL TONES   1898

We stood by a pond that winter day,
And the sun was white, as though chidden of God,
And a few leaves lay on the starving sod;
  — They had fallen from an ash, and were gray.

Your eyes on me were as eyes that rove   5
Over tedious riddles of years ago;
And some words played between us to and fro
  On which lost the more by our love.

The smile on your mouth was the deadest thing
Alive enough to have strength to die;   10
And a grin of bitterness swept thereby
  Like an ominous bird a-wing. . . .

Since then, keen lessons that love deceives,
And wrings with wrong, have shaped to me
Your face, and the God-curst sun, and a tree,   15
  And a pond edged with grayish leaves.

QUESTIONS

1. Sum up the story told in this poem. In lines 1 – 12, what is the dramatic situation? What has happened in the interval between the experience related in these lines and the reflection in the last stanza?
2. What meanings do you find in the title?
3. Explain in your own words the metaphor in line 2.
4. What connotations appropriate to this poem does the *ash* (line 4) have, that *oak* or *maple* would lack?
5. What visible objects in the poem function symbolically? What actions or gestures?

If we read of a ship, its captain, its sailors, and the rough seas, and we realize we are reading about a commonwealth and how its rulers and workers keep it going even in difficult times, then we are reading an **allegory.** Closely akin to symbolism, allegory is a description — usually narrative — in which persons, places, and things are employed in a continuous system of equivalents.

Although more strictly limited in its suggestions than symbolism, allegory need not be thought inferior. Few poems continue to interest readers more than Dante's allegorical *Divine Comedy*. Sublime evidence of the appeal of allegory may be found in Christ's use of the **parable:** a brief narrative — usually allegorical but sometimes not — that teaches a moral.

Matthew 13:24–30 (Authorized or King James Version, 1611)

THE PARABLE OF THE GOOD SEED

The kingdom of heaven is likened unto a man which sowed good seed in his field:

But while men slept, his enemy came and sowed tares among the wheat, and went his way.

But when the blade was sprung up, and brought forth fruit, then appeared the tares also.

So the servants of the householder came and said unto him, Sir, didst not thou sow good seed in thy field? From whence then hath it tares?

He said unto them, An enemy hath done this. The servants said unto him, Wilt thou then that we go and gather them up?   5

But he said, Nay; lest while ye gather up the tares, ye root up also the wheat with them.

Let both grow together until the harvest: and in the time of harvest I will say to the reapers, Gather ye together first the tares, and bind them in bundles to burn them: but gather the wheat into my barn.

The sower is the Son of man, the field is the world, the good seed are the children of the Kingdom, the tares are the children of the wicked one, the enemy is the devil, the harvest is the end of the world, the reapers are angels. "As therefore the tares are gathered and burned in the fire; so shall it be in the end of this world" (Matthew 13:36 – 42).

Usually, as in this parable, the meanings of an allegory are plainly labeled or thinly disguised. In John Bunyan's allegorical narrative *The Pilgrim's Progress,* it is clear that the hero Christian, on his journey through places with such pointed names as Vanity Fair, the Valley of the Shadow of Death, and Doubting Castle, is the soul, traveling the road of life on the way toward Heaven. An allegory, when carefully built, is systematic. It makes one principal comparison, the working out of whose details may lead to further comparisons, then still further comparisons: Christian, thrown by Giant Despair into the dungeon of Doubting Castle, escapes by means of a key called Promise. Such a complicated design may take great length to unfold, as in Spenser's *Faerie Queene;* but the method may be seen in a short poem:

George Herbert (1593 – 1633)*

REDEMPTION   1633

Having been tenant long to a rich Lord,
  Not thriving, I resolvèd to be bold,
And make a suit unto him to afford
  A new small-rented lease and cancel th' old.
In Heaven at his manor I him sought.   5
  They told me there that he was lately gone
About some land which he had dearly bought
  Long since on earth, to take possessiòn.
I straight returned, and knowing his great birth,
  Sought him accordingly in great resorts,   10
  In cities, theaters, gardens, parks, and courts.
At length I heard a ragged noise and mirth
  Of thieves and murderers; there I him espied,
Who straight "Your suit is granted," said, and died.

QUESTIONS

1. In this allegory, what equivalents does Herbert give each of these terms: *tenant, Lord, not thriving, suit, new lease, old lease, manor, land, dearly bought, take possession, his great birth?*
2. What scene is depicted in the last three lines?

   An object in allegory is like a bird whose cage is clearly lettered with its identity — "RAVEN, *Corvus corax*; habitat of specimen, Maine." A symbol, by contrast, is a bird with piercing eyes that mysteriously appears one evening in your library. It is there; you can touch it. But what does it mean? You look at it. It continues to look at you.

   Whether an object in literature is a symbol, part of an allegory, or no such thing at all, it has at least one sure meaning. Moby Dick is first a whale, the *Boston Evening Transcript* a newspaper. Besides deriving a multitude of intangible suggestions from the title symbol in Eliot's long poem *The Waste Land,* its readers cannot fail to carry away a sense of the land's physical appearance: a river choked with sandwich papers and cigarette ends, London Bridge "under the brown fog of a winter dawn." A virtue of *The Pilgrim's Progress* is that its walking abstractions are no mere abstractions but are also human: Giant Despair is a henpecked husband. The most vital element of a literary work may pass us by, unless before seeking further depths in a thing, we look to the thing itself.

Emily Dickinson (1830 – 1886)*

I HEARD A FLY BUZZ – WHEN I DIED   (about 1862)

I heard a Fly buzz – when I died –
The Stillness in the Room
Was like the Stillness in the Air –
Between the Heaves of Storm –

The Eyes around – had wrung them dry –   5
And Breaths were gathering firm
For that last Onset – when the King
Be witnessed – in the Room –

I willed my Keepsakes – Signed away
What portion of me be   10
Assignable – and then it was
There interposed a Fly –

With Blue – uncertain stumbling Buzz –
Between the light – and me –
And then the Windows failed – and then   15
I could not see to see –

QUESTIONS

1. Why is the poem written in the past tense? Where is the speaker at present?
2. What do you understand from the repetition of the word *see* in the last line?
3. What does the poet mean by *Eyes around* (line 5), *that last Onset* (line 7), *the King* (line 7), and *What portion of me be / Assignable* (lines 10 – 11)?
4. In line 13, how can a sound be called *Blue* and *stumbling*?
5. What further meaning might *the Windows* (line 15) suggest, in addition to denoting the windows of the room?
6. What connotations of the word *fly* seem relevant to an account of a death?
7. Summarize your interpretation of the poem. What does the fly mean?

Robert Frost (1874–1963)*

THE ROAD NOT TAKEN   1916

Two roads diverged in a yellow wood,
And sorry I could not travel both
And be one traveler, long I stood
And looked down one as far as I could
To where it bent in the undergrowth;   5

Then took the other, as just as fair,
And having perhaps the better claim,
Because it was grassy and wanted wear;
Though as for that the passing there
Had worn them really about the same,   10

And both that morning equally lay
In leaves no step had trodden black.
Oh, I kept the first for another day!
Yet knowing how way leads on to way,
I doubted if I should ever come back.   15

I shall be telling this with a sigh
Somewhere ages and ages hence:
Two roads diverged in a wood, and I—
I took the one less traveled by,
And that has made all the difference.   20

QUESTION

What symbolism do you find in this poem, if any? Back up your claim with evidence.

Christina Rossetti (1830 – 1894)

UPHILL   1862

Does the road wind uphill all the way?
    Yes, to the very end.
Will the day's journey take the whole long day?
    From morn to night, my friend.

But is there for the night a resting-place?   5
    A roof for when the slow dark hours begin.
May not the darkness hide it from my face?
    You cannot miss that inn.

Shall I meet other wayfarers at night?
    Those who have gone before.   10
Then must I knock, or call when just in sight?
    They will not keep you standing at that door.

Shall I find comfort, travel-sore and weak?
    Of labor you shall find the sum.
Will there be beds for me and all who seek?   15
    Yea, beds for all who come.

QUESTIONS

1. At what line in reading this poem did you tumble to the fact that the poet is building
   an allegory?
2. For what does each thing stand?
3. What does the title of the poem suggest to you?
4. Recast the meaning of line 14, a knotty line, in your own words.
5. Discuss the possible identities of the two speakers — the apprehensive traveler and
   the character with all the answers. Are they specific individuals? Allegorical figures?
6. Compare "Uphill" with Robert Creeley's "Oh No" (page 25). What striking similarities do you find in these two dissimilar poems?

Gjertrud Schnackenberg (b. 1953)

SIGNS   1974

Threading the palm, a web of little lines
Spells out the lost money, the heart, the head,
The wagging tongues, the sudden deaths, in signs
We would smooth out, like imprints on a bed,

In signs that can't be helped, geese heading south,   5
In signs read anxiously, like breath that clouds
A mirror held to a barely open mouth,
Like telegrams, the gathering of crowds —

The plane's X in the sky, spelling disaster:
Before the whistle and hit, a tracer flare;   10
Before rubble, a hairline crack in plaster
And a housefly's panicked scribbling on the air.

QUESTIONS

1. What are "signs" in this poet's sense of the word?
2. The poem gives a list of signs. What unmistakable meaning does each indicate?
3. Compare Schnackenberg's fly and Emily Dickinson's (page 212). Which insect seems loaded with more suggestions?
4. Can you think of any familiar signs that *aren't* ominous?
5. This poem was written when the poet was a student at Mount Holyoke College. Knowing this fact, do you like it any less, or any more?

EXERCISE: *Symbol Hunting*

After you have read each of these poems, decide which description best suits it:
1. The poem has a central symbol.
2. The poem contains no symbolism, but is to be taken literally.

Sir Philip Sidney (1554 – 1586)

YOU THAT WITH ALLEGORY'S CURIOUS FRAME   1591

You that with allegory's curious frame
    Of others' children changelings use to make,
    With me those pains, for God's sake, do not take;
I list not° dig so deep for brazen fame.   *I do not choose to*
When I say Stella, I do mean the same   5
    Princess of beauty for whose only sake
    The reins of love I love, though never slake,
And joy therein, though nations count it shame.
I beg no subject to use eloquence,
    Nor in hid ways do guide philosophy;   10

Look at my hands for no such quintessence,
But know that I in pure simplicity
Breathe out the flames which burn within my heart,
Love only reading unto me this art.

William Carlos Williams (1883 – 1963)*

POEM   1934

As the cat
climbed over
the top of

the jamcloset
first the right   5
forefoot

carefully
then the hind
stepped down
into the pit of   10
the empty
flowerpot

Theodore Roethke (1908 – 1963)*

NIGHT CROW   1948

When I saw that clumsy crow
Flap from a wasted tree,
A shape in the mind rose up:
Over the gulfs of dream
Flew a tremendous bird   5
Further and further away
Into a moonless black,
Deep in the brain, far back.

John Donne (1572 – 1631)*

A BURNT SHIP   1633

Out of a fired ship which by no way
But drowning could be rescued from the flame
Some men leaped forth, and ever as they came
Near the foe's ships, did by their shot decay;
So all were lost, which in the ship were found,
     They in the sea being burnt, they in the burnt ship drowned.

Wallace Stevens (1879 – 1955)*

ANECDOTE OF THE JAR   1923

I placed a jar in Tennessee,
And round it was, upon a hill.
It made the slovenly wilderness
Surround that hill.

The wilderness rose up to it,   5
And sprawled around, no longer wild.
The jar was round upon the ground
And tall and of a port in air.

It took dominion everywhere.
The jar was gray and bare.   10
It did not give of bird or bush,
Like nothing else in Tennessee.

SUGGESTIONS FOR WRITING

1. Write a paraphrase of Emily Dickinson's "I heard a Fly buzz — when I died." Make clear whatever meanings you find in the fly (and other concrete objects).
2. Discuss the symbolism in a poem in the Anthology: Poetry beginning on page 277. Likely poems to study (among many) are Louise Bogan's "The Dream," T. S. Eliot's "The Love Song of J. Alfred Prufrock," Robert Lowell's "Skunk Hour," Howard Nemerov's "The Snow Globe," and Adrienne Rich's "Aunt Jennifer's Tigers."
3. Take some relatively simple, straightforward poem, such as William Carlos Williams's "This Is Just to Say" (page 39), and write a burlesque critical interpretation of it. Claim to discover symbols in the poem that it doesn't contain. While letting your ability to "read into" a poem run wild, don't invent anything that you can't somehow support from the text of the poem itself. At the end of your burlesque, add a paragraph summing up what this exercise indicates about how to read poems, or how not to.

13 Myth

Poets have long been fond of retelling **myths,** narrowly defined as traditional stories of immortal beings. Such stories taken collectively may also be called **myth** or **mythology.** In one of the most celebrated collections of myth ever assembled, the *Metamorphoses,* the poet Ovid has told — to take one example from many — how Phaeton, child of the sun god, rashly tried to drive his father's fiery chariot on its daily round, lost control of the horses, and caused disaster both to himself and to the world. Our use of the term *myth* in discussing poetry, then, differs from its use in expressions such as "the myth of communism" and "the myth of democracy." In these examples, myth, in its broadest sense, is any idea people believe in, whether true or false. Nor do we mean — to take another familiar use of the word — a cock-and-bull story: "Judge Rapp doesn't roast speeders alive; that's just a *myth.*" In the following discussion, *myth* will mean — as critic Northrop Frye has put it — "the imitation of actions near or at the conceivable limits of desire." Myths tell us of the exploits of the gods — their battles, the ways in which they live, love, and perhaps suffer — all on a scale of magnificence larger than our life. We envy their freedom and power; they enact our wishes and dreams. Whether we believe in them or not, their adventures are myths: Ovid, it seems, placed no credence in the stories he related, for he declared, "I prate of ancient poets' monstrous lies."

And yet it is characteristic of a myth that it *can* be believed. Throughout history, myths have accompanied religious doctrines and rituals. They have helped sanction or recall the reasons for religious observances. A sublime instance is the New Testament account of the Last Supper. Because of it and its record of the words of Jesus, "This do in remembrance of Me," Christians have continued to re-enact the offering and partaking of the body and blood of their Lord, under the appearances of bread and wine. It is essential to recall that, just because a myth narrates the acts of a god, we do not necessarily mean by the term a false or fictitious narrative. When we speak of the "myth of Islam" or "the Christian myth," we do so without implying either belief or disbelief.

Myths can also help sanction customs and institutions other than religious ones. At the same time as the baking of bread was introduced to ancient Greece — one theory goes — there was introduced the myth of Demeter, goddess of grain, who had kindly sent her emissary Triptolemus to teach humankind this valuable art — thus helping to persuade the distrustful that bread was a good thing. Some myths seem made to divert and regale, not to sanction anything. Such may be the story of the sculptor Pygmalion, who fell in love with his statue of a woman; so exquisite was his work, so deep was his feeling, that Aphrodite brought the statue to life. And yet perhaps the story goes deeper than mere diversion: perhaps it is a way of saying that works of art achieve a reality of their own, that love can transform or animate its object.

How does a myth begin? Several theories have been proposed, none universally accepted. One is that a myth is a way to explain some natural phenomenon. Winter comes and the vegetation perishes because Persephone, child of Demeter, must return to the underworld for four months every year. This theory, as classical scholar Edith Hamilton has pointed out, may lead us to think incorrectly that Greek mythology was the creation of a primitive people. Tales of the gods of Mount Olympus may reflect an earlier inheritance, but Greek myths known to us were transcribed in an era of high civilization. Anthropologists have questioned whether primitive people generally find beauty in the mysteries of nature. "From my own study of living myths among savages," wrote Bronislaw Malinowski, "I should say that primitive man has to a very limited extent the purely artistic or scientific interest in nature; there is but little room for symbolism in his ideas and tales; and myth, in fact, is not an idle rhapsody . . . but a hard-working, extremely important cultural force."[1] Such a practical function was seen by Sir James Frazer in *The Golden Bough:* myths were originally expressions of human hope that nature would be fertile. Still another theory is that, once upon a time, heroes of myth were human prototypes. The Greek philosopher Euhemerus declared myths to be tales of real persons, which poets had exaggerated. Most present-day historians of myth would seek no general explanation but would say that different myths probably have different origins.

Poets have many coherent mythologies on which to draw; perhaps those most frequently consulted by British and American poets are the classical, the Christian, the Norse, and folk myth of the American frontier (embodying the deeds of superhuman characters such as Paul Bunyan). Some poets have taken inspiration from other myths as well: T. S. Eliot's *The Waste Land,* for example, is enriched by allusions to Buddhism and to pagan vegetation-cults.

As a tour through any good art museum will demonstrate, myth pervades much of the graphic art of Western civilization. In literature, one evidence of its continuing value to recent poets and storytellers is the frequency with which myths — both primitive and civilized — are retold. William Faulkner's story

---

[1]Bronislaw Malinowski, *Myth in Primitive Psychology* (1926); reprinted in *Magic, Science and Religion* (New York: Doubleday, 1954) 97.

"The Bear" recalls tales of Indian totem animals; John Updike's novel *The Centaur* presents the horse-man Chiron as a modern high school teacher; Hart Crane's poem "For the Marriage of Faustus and Helen" unites two figures of different myths, who dance to jazz; T. S. Eliot's plays bring into the drawing room the myths of Alcestis (*The Cocktail Party*) and the Eumenides (*The Family Reunion*); Jean Cocteau's film *Orphée* shows us Eurydice riding to the underworld with an escort of motorcycles. Popular interest in such works may testify to the profound appeal myths continue to hold for us. Like any other large body of knowledge that can be alluded to, myth offers the poet an instant means of communication — if the reader also knows the particular myth cited. Writing "Lycidas," John Milton could depend upon his readers — mostly persons of similar classical learning — to understand him without footnotes. Today, a poet referring to a traditional myth must be sure to choose a reasonably well-known one, or else write as well as T. S. Eliot, whose work has compelled his readers to single out his allusions and look them up. Like other varieties of poetry, myth is a kind of knowledge, not at odds with scientific knowledge but existing in addition to it.

D. H. Lawrence (1885 – 1930)*

BAVARIAN GENTIANS   1932

Not every man has gentians in his house
in soft September, at slow, sad Michaelmas.

Bavarian gentians, big and dark, only dark
darkening the daytime, torch-like with the smoking blueness of
    Pluto's gloom,
ribbed and torch-like, with their blaze of darkness spread blue   5
down flattening into points, flattened under the sweep of white day
torch-flower of the blue-smoking darkness, Pluto's dark-blue daze,
black lamps from the halls of Dis, burning dark blue,
giving off darkness, blue darkness, as Demeter's pale lamps give off
    light,
lead me then, lead the way.   10

Reach me a gentian, give me a torch!
let me guide myself with the blue, forked torch of this flower
down the darker and darker stairs, where blue is darkened on
    blueness
even where Persephone goes, just now, from the frosted September
to the sightless realm where darkness is awake upon the dark   15
and Persephone herself is but a voice

or a darkness invisible enfolded in the deeper dark
of the arms Plutonic, and pierced with the passion of dense gloom,
among the splendor of torches of darkness, shedding darkness on the
    lost bride and her groom.

BAVARIAN GENTIANS. 4 *Pluto:* Roman name for Hades, in Greek mythology the ruler of the underworld, who abducted Persephone to be his bride. Each spring Persephone returns to earth and is
welcomed by her mother Demeter, goddess of fruitfulness; each winter she departs again, to dwell
with her husband below. 8 *Dis:* Pluto's realm.

QUESTIONS

1. Read this poem aloud. What devices of sound do you hear in it?
2. What characteristics of gentians appear to remind Lawrence of the story of Persephone? What significance do you attach to the poem's being set in September? How
   does the fact of autumn matter to the gentians and to Persephone?

Thomas Hardy (1840 – 1928)*

THE OXEN   1915

Christmas Eve, and twelve of the clock.
    "Now they are all on their knees,"
An elder said as we sat in a flock
    By the embers in hearthside ease.

We pictured the meek mild creatures where   5
    They dwelt in their strawy pen,
Nor did it occur to one of us there
    To doubt they were kneeling then.

So fair a fancy few would weave
    In these years! Yet, I feel,   10
If someone said on Christmas Eve,
    "Come; see the oxen kneel

"In the lonely barton° by yonder coomb°   *farmyard; a hollow*
    Our childhood used to know,"
I should go with him in the gloom,   15
    Hoping it might be so.

THE OXEN. This ancient belief has had wide currency among peasants and farmers of Western
Europe. Some also say that on Christmas Eve the beasts can speak.

QUESTIONS

1. What body of myth is Hardy's subject and what are his speaker's attitudes toward
   it? Perhaps, in Hardy's view, the pious report about oxen is only part of it.
2. Read this poem aloud and notice its sound and imagery. What contrast do you find
   between the sounds of the first stanza and the sounds of the last stanza? Which words

make the difference? What images enforce a contrast in tone between the beginning of the poem and its ending?
3. G. K. Chesterton, writing as a defender of Christian faith, called Hardy's writings "the mutterings of the village atheist." See other poems by Hardy (particularly "Four Satires of Circumstance," page 323). What do you think Chesterton might have meant? Can "The Oxen" be called a hostile mutter?

William Wordsworth (1770 – 1850)*

THE WORLD IS TOO MUCH WITH US   1807

The world is too much with us; late and soon, *a*
Getting and spending, we lay waste our powers; *b*
Little we see in Nature that is ours; *b*
We have given our hearts away, a sordid boon! *a*
This Sea that bares her bosom to the moon; *a*   5
The winds that will be howling at all hours, *b*
And are up-gathered now like sleeping flowers; *b*
For this, for everything, we are out of tune; *a*
It moves us not. Great God! I'd rather be *c*
A Pagan suckled in a creed outworn; *d*   10
So might I, standing on this pleasant lea, *c*
Have glimpses that would make me less forlorn; *d*
Have sight of Proteus rising from the sea; *c*
Or hear old Triton blow his wreathèd horn. *d*

[handwritten annotations: "Italian Sonnet" ; "change starts here in the middle of sestet not at the begining of six lines this is the only deviation from the original form of italian sonnet"]

QUESTIONS

1. In this sonnet by Wordsworth what condition does the poet complain about? To what does he attribute this condition?
2. How does it affect him as an individual?

When Plato in *The Republic* relates the Myth of Er, he introduces supernatural characters he himself originated. Poets, too, have been inspired to make up myths of their own, for their own purposes. "I must create a system or be enslaved by another man's," said William Blake, who in his "prophetic books" peopled the cosmos with supernatural beings having names like Los, Urizen, and Vala (side by side with recognizable figures from the Old Testament and New Testament). This kind of system-making probably has advantages and drawbacks. T. S. Eliot, in his essay on Blake, wishes that the author of *The Four Zoas* had accepted traditional myths, and he compares Blake's thinking to a piece of homemade furniture whose construction diverted valuable energy from the writing of poems. Others have found Blake's untraditional cosmos an achievement — notably William Butler Yeats, himself the author of an elaborate personal mythology. Although we need not know all of Yeats's mythology to enjoy his poems, to know of its existence can make a few great poems deeper for us and less difficult.

William Butler Yeats (1865 – 1939)*

THE SECOND COMING   1921

Turning and turning in the widening gyre°   *spiral*
The falcon cannot hear the falconer;
Things fall apart; the center cannot hold;
Mere anarchy is loosed upon the world,
The blood-dimmed tide is loosed, and everywhere   5
The ceremony of innocence is drowned;
The best lack all conviction, while the worst
Are full of passionate intensity.

Surely some revelation is at hand;
Surely the Second Coming is at hand;   10
The Second Coming! Hardly are those words out
When a vast image out of *Spiritus Mundi*
Troubles my sight: somewhere in sands of the desert
A shape with lion body and the head of a man,
A gaze blank and pitiless as the sun,   15
Is moving its slow thighs, while all about it
Reel shadows of the indignant desert birds.
The darkness drops again; but now I know
That twenty centuries of stony sleep
Were vexed to nightmare by a rocking cradle,   20
And what rough beast, its hour come round at last,
Slouches towards Bethlehem to be born?

What kind of Second Coming does Yeats expect? Evidently it is not to be
a Christian one. Yeats saw human history as governed by the turning of a Great
Wheel, whose phases influence events and determine human personalities —
rather like the signs of the Zodiac in astrology. Every two thousand years comes
a horrendous moment: the Wheel completes a turn; one civilization ends and
another begins. Strangely, a new age is always announced by birds and by acts
of violence. Thus the Greek-Roman world arrives with the descent of Zeus in
swan's form and the burning of Troy, the Christian era with the descent of the
Holy Spirit — traditionally depicted as a dove — and the Crucifixion. In 1919
when Yeats wrote "The Second Coming," his Ireland was in the midst of
turmoil and bloodshed; the Western Hemisphere had been severely shaken by
World War I. A new millennium seemed imminent. What sphinxlike, savage
deity would next appear on earth, with birds proclaiming it angrily? Yeats
imagines it emerging from *Spiritus Mundi*, Soul of the World, a collective
unconscious from which a human being (since the individual soul touches it)
receives dreams, nightmares, and racial memories.[2]

[2]Yeats fully explains his system in *A Vision* (1938; reprinted New York: Macmillan, 1956).

It is hard to say whether a poet who discovers a personal myth does so to have something to live by or to have something to write about. Robert Graves, who professed his belief in a White Goddess ("Mother of All Living, the ancient power of love and terror"), declared that he wrote his poetry in a trance, inspired by his Goddess-Muse.[3] Luckily, we do not have to know a poet's religious affiliation before we can read the poems. Perhaps most personal myths that enter poems are not acts of faith but works of art: stories that resemble traditional mythology.

Dick Allen (b. 1939)

NIGHT DRIVING   1987

Cold hands on the cold wheel of his car,
Driving from Bridgeport, he watches
The long line of red taillights
Curving before him, remembers
How his father used to say they were cats' eyes   5
Staring back at them, a long line of cats
Watching from the distance—never Fords,
Buicks, Chevrolets, filled with the heads
Of children, lovers, lonely businessmen,
But cats in the darkness. Half asleep,   10
He can believe, or make himself believe
The truth of his father—all the lies
Not really lies: images which make
The world come closer, cats' eyes up ahead.

QUESTIONS

1. How does personal myth function in this poem?
2. What suggestions can you find in the poem's title?

Harvey Shapiro (b. 1924)

NATIONAL COLD STORAGE COMPANY   1966

The National Cold Storage Company contains
More things than you can dream of.
Hard by the Brooklyn Bridge it stands
In a litter of freight cars,
Tugs to one side; the other, the traffic   5
Of the Long Island Expressway.

[3]See Graves's *The White Goddess*, rev. ed. (New York: Farrar, 1966), or for a terser statement of his position, see his lecture "The Personal Muse" in *On Poetry: Collected Talks and Essays* (New York: Doubleday, 1969).

I myself have dropped into it in seven years
Midnight tossings, plans for escape, the shakes.
Add this to the national total—
Grant's tomb, the Civil War, Arlington, 10
The young President dead.
Above the warehouse and beneath the stars
The poets creep on the harp of the Bridge.
But see,
They fall into the National Cold Storage Company 15
One by one. The wind off the river is too cold,
Or the times too rough, or the Bridge
Is not a harp at all. Or maybe
A monstrous birth inside the warehouse
Must be fed by everything—ships, poems, 20
Stars, all the years of our lives.

QUESTIONS

1. Do you take the National Cold Storage Company to be a real company, some imagined afterworld, or both? What different things is it said to keep?
2. In line 13, Brooklyn Bridge is a harp; in lines 17–18 it is not a harp. Does the poet contradict himself?
3. What do you make of this monster—the "monstrous birth"—about whose existence the poet speculates in his closing lines?

John Milton (1608 – 1674)*

LYCIDAS   1637

In this monody the author bewails a learned friend, unfortunately drowned in his passage from Chester on the Irish Seas, 1637. And by occasion foretells the ruin of our corrupted clergy then in their height.

Yet once more, O ye laurels, and once more,
Ye myrtles brown°, with ivy never sere,   *dark*
I come to pluck your berries harsh and crude°,   *immature*
And with forced fingers rude
Shatter your leaves before the mellowing year.   5
Bitter constraint and sad occasion dear
Compels me to disturb your season due;
For Lycidas is dead, dead ere his prime,
Young Lycidas, and hath not left his peer.

Lycidas. A *monody* is a song for a single voice, generally a lament. Milton's *learned friend* was Edward King, scholar and poet, a fellow student at Cambridge University, where King had been preparing for the ministry. In calling him Lycidas, Milton employs a conventional name for a young shepherd in **pastoral poetry** (which either portrays the world of shepherds with some realism, as in Virgil's *Eclogues,* or makes it a prettified Eden, as in Marlowe's "The Passionate Shepherd to His Love"). 1 – 2 *laurels, myrtles:* Evergreens in the crowns traditionally bestowed upon poets.

Who would not sing for Lycidas? he knew   10
Himself to sing, and build the lofty rhyme.
He must not float upon his wat'ry bier
Unwept, and welter° to the parching wind,   *toss about*
Without the meed° of some melodious tear.   *tribute*
    Begin, then, Sisters of the Sacred Well   15
That from beneath the seat of Jove doth spring,
Begin, and somewhat loudly sweep the string.
Hence with denial vain and coy excuse:
So may some gentle Muse°   *poet*
With lucky words favor my destined urn,   20
And, as he passes, turn,
And bid fair peace be to my sable shroud!
For we were nursed upon the self-same hill,
Fed the same flocks, by fountain, shade, and rill;
    Together both, ere the high lawns appeared   25
Under the opening eyelids of the Morn,
We drove a-field, and both together heard
What time the gray-fly winds° her sultry horn,   *sounds*
Batt'ning° our flocks with the fresh dews of night,   *feeding*
Oft till the star that rose at evening bright   30
Toward Heav'n's descent had sloped his westering wheel.
Meanwhile the rural ditties were not mute,
Tempered to the oaten° flute,   *made of an oat stalk*
Rough satyrs danced, and fauns with cloven heel
From the glad sound would not be absent long;   35
And old Damoetas loved to hear our song.
    But, O the heavy change, now thou art gone,
Now thou art gone, and never must return!
Thee, Shepherd, thee the woods and desert caves,
With wild thyme and the gadding° vine o'ergrown,   *wandering*   40
And all their echoes mourn.
The willows, and the hazel copses green,
Shall now no more be seen
Fanning their joyous leaves to thy soft lays.
As killing as the canker to the rose,   45
Or taint-worm to the weanling herds that graze,
Or frost to flowers, that their gay wardrobe wear
When first the white thorn blows°;   *blossoms*
Such, Lycidas, thy loss to shepherd's ear.
    Where were ye, Nymphs, when the remorseless deep   50
Closed o'er the head of your loved Lycidas?
For neither were ye playing on the steep
Where your old bards, the famous Druids, lie,
Nor on the shaggy top of Mona high,

---

36 *Damoetas:* Perhaps some Cambridge tutor. 53 *Druids:* priests and poets of the Celts in pre-Christian Britain. 54 *Mona:* Roman name for the Isle of Man, near which King was drowned.

Nor yet where Deva spreads her wizard stream.   55
Ay me! I fondly° dream!   *foolishly*
"Had ye been there" — for what could that have done?
What could the Muse herself that Orpheus bore,
The Muse herself, for her enchanting son,
Whom universal Nature did lament,   60
When, by the rout° that made the hideous roar,   *mob*
His gory visage down the stream was sent,
Down the swift Hebrus to the Lesbian shore?
    Alas! What boots it° with uncessant care   *what good does it do*
To tend the homely, slighted shepherd's trade,   65
And strictly meditate the thankless Muse?
Were it not better done, as others use°,   *do*
To sport with Amaryllis in the shade,
Or with the tangles of Neaera's hair?
Fame is the spur that the clear spirit doth raise   70
(That last infirmity of noble mind)
To scorn delights and live laborious days;
But the fair guerdon when we hope to find,
And think to burst out into sudden blaze
Comes the blind Fury with th' abhorrèd shears,   75
And slits the thin-spun life. "But not the praise,"
Phoebus replied, and touched my trembling ears:
"Fame is no plant that grows on mortal soil,
Nor in the glistering° foil,   *glittering*
Set off to the world, nor in broad rumor° lies,   *reputation* 80
But lives and spreads aloft by those pure eyes
And perfect witness of all-judging Jove;
As he pronounces lastly on each deed,
Of so much fame in Heav'n expect thy meed."
    O fountain Arethuse, and thou honored flood,   85
Smooth-sliding Mincius, crowned with vocal reeds,
That strain I heard was of a higher mood:
But now my oat proceeds,
And listens to the Herald of the Sea,
That came in Neptune's plea.   90
He asked the waves, and asked the felon winds,
What hard mishap hath doomed this gentle swain?
And questioned every gust of rugged wings
That blows from off each beakèd promontory:
They knew not of his story;   95

55 *Deva*: the River Dee, flowing between England and Wales. Its shifts in course were said to augur good luck for one country or the other. 68 – 69 *Amaryllis, Neaera*: conventional names for shepherdesses. 70 *the clear spirit doth raise*: doth raise the clear spirit. 77 *touched . . . ears*: gesture signifying "Remember!" 79 *foil*: a setting of gold or silver leaf, used to make a gem appear more brilliant. 85 – 86 *Arethuse, Mincius*: a fountain and river near the birthplaces of Theocritus and Virgil, respectively, hence recalling the most celebrated writer of pastorals in Greek and the most celebrated in Latin. 90 *in Neptune's plea*: bringing the sea-god's plea, "not guilty."

And sage Hippotades their answer brings,
That not a blast was from his dungeon strayed:
The air was calm, and on the level brine
Sleek Panope with all her sisters played.
It was that fatal and perfidious bark,   100
Built in th' eclipse, and rigged with curses dark,
That sunk so low that sacred head of thine.
    Next, Camus, reverend sire, went footing slow,
His mantle hairy, and his bonnet sedge,
Inwrought with figures dim, and on the edge   105
Like to that sanguine flower inscribed with woe.
"Ah! who hath reft," quoth he, "my dearest pledge?"
Last came, and last did go,
The pilot of the Galilean lake;
Two massy keys he bore of metals twain   110
(The golden opes, the iron shuts amain°).   *with force*
He shook his mitered locks, and stern bespake: —
"How well could I have spared for thee, young swain,
Enow° of such as for their bellies' sake,   *enough*
Creep, and intrude, and climb into the fold!   115
Of other care they little reck'ning make
Than how to scramble at the shearers' feast,
And shove away the worthy bidden guest.
Blind mouths! that scarce themselves know how to hold
A sheep-hook, or have learned aught else the least   120
That to the faithful herdsman's art belongs!
What recks it them? What need they? they are sped°;   *prosperous*
And, when they list°, their lean and flashy songs   *so incline*
Grate on their scrannel° pipes of wretched straw;   *feeble, harsh*
The hungry sheep look up, and are not fed,   125
But, swoll'n with wind and the rank mist they draw,
Rot inwardly, and foul contagion spread;
Besides what the grim wolf with privy° paw   *stealthy*
Daily devours apace, and nothing said;
But that two-handed engine at the door   130
Stands ready to smite once, and smite no more."

99 *Panope:* a sea nymph. Her name means "one who sees all." 101 *eclipse:* thought to be an omen of evil fortune. 103 *Camus:* spirit of the river Cam and personification of Cambridge University. 109–112 *pilot:* Saint Peter, once a fisherman in Galilee, to whom Jesus gave the keys of Heaven (Matthew 16:19). As first Bishop of Rome, he wears the miter, a bishop's emblematic head-covering. 115 *fold:* the Church of England. 120 *sheep-hook:* a bishop's staff or crozier, which resembles a shepherd's crook. 128 *wolf:* probably the Church of Rome. Jesuits in England at the time were winning converts. 130 *two-handed engine:* This disputed phrase may refer (among other possibilities) to the punishing sword of The Word of God (Revelation 19:13–15 and Hebrews 4:12). Perhaps Milton sees it as a lightning bolt, as does Spenser, to whom Jove's wrath is a "three-forked engine" (*Faerie Queene*, VIII, 9). 131 *smite once . . . no more:* Because, in the proverb, lightning never strikes twice in the same place?

Return, Alpheus; the dread voice is past
That shrunk thy streams; return, Sicilian Muse,
And call the vales, and bid them hither cast
Their bells and flow'rets of a thousand hues.   135
Ye valleys low, where the mild whispers use°   *resort*
Of shades, and wanton winds, and gushing brooks,
On whose fresh lap the swart star sparely looks,
Throw hither all your quaint enameled eyes,
That on the green turf suck the honied showers,   140
And purple all the ground with vernal flowers.
Bring the rathe° primrose that forsaken dies,   *early*
The tufted crow-toe, and pale jessamine,
The white pink, and the pansy freaked° with jet,   *streaked*
The glowing violet,   145
The musk-rose, and the well-attired woodbine,
With cowslips wan that hang the pensive head,
And every flower that sad embroidery wears;
Bid amaranthus all his beauty shed,
And daffadillies fill their cups with tears,   150
To strew the laureate hearse where Lycid lies.
For so, to interpose a little ease,
Let our frail thoughts dally with false surmise,
Ay me! whilst thee the shores and sounding seas
Wash far away, where'er thy bones are hurled;   155
Whether beyond the stormy Hebrides,
Where thou, perhaps, under the whelming tide
Visit'st the bottom of the monstrous° world;   *full of sea monsters*
Or whether thou, to our moist vows° denied,   *prayers*
Sleep'st by the fable of Bellerus old,   160
Where the great Vision of the guarded mount
Looks toward Namancos and Bayona's hold°:   *stronghold*
Look homeward, angel, now, and melt with ruth°;   *pity*
And, O ye dolphins, waft the hapless youth.

    Weep no more, woeful shepherds, weep no more,   165
For Lycidas, your sorrow, is not dead,
Sunk though he be beneath the wat'ry floor:
So sinks the day-star in the ocean bed
And yet anon repairs his drooping head,
And tricks° his beams, and with new-spangled ore°   *arrays; gold* 170
Flames in the forehead of the morning sky:
So Lycidas sunk low, but mounted high,

---

133 *Sicilian Muse:* who inspired Theocritus, a native of Sicily. 138 *swart star:* Sirius, at its zenith in summer, was thought to turn vegetation black. 153 *false surmise:* futile hope that the body of Lycidas could be recovered. 160 *Bellerus:* legendary giant of Land's End, the far tip of Cornwall. 161 *guarded mount:* Saint Michael's Mount, off Land's End, said to be under the protection of the archangel. 162 *Namancos, Bayona:* on the coast of Spain. 164 *dolphins:* In Greek legend, these kindly mammals carried the spirits of the dead to the Blessed Isles.

Through the dear might of Him that walked the waves,
Where, other groves and other streams along,
With nectar pure his oozy locks he laves,   175
And hears the unexpressive nuptial song,
In the blest kingdoms meek of Joy and Love.
There entertain him all the Saints above,
In solemn troops, and sweet societies,
That sing, and singing in their glory move,   180
And wipe the tears forever from his eyes.
Now, Lycidas, the shepherds weep no more;
Henceforth thou art the Genius° of the shore,   guardian spirit
In thy large recompense, and shalt be good
To all that wander in that perilous flood.   185

    Thus sang the uncouth° swain to th' oaks and rills,   rustic (or little-known)
While the still Morn went out with sandals gray;
He touched the tender stops of various quills°,   reeds of a shepherd's pipe
With eager thought warbling his Doric lay:
And now the sun had stretched out all the hills,   190
And now was dropped into the western bay.
At last he rose, and twitched° his mantle blue: donned
Tomorrow to fresh woods and pastures new.

176 *unexpressive nuptial song:* inexpressibly beautiful song for the marriage feast of the Lamb (Revelation 19:9). 189 *Doric lay:* pastoral poem. Doric is the dialect of Greek employed by Theocritus.

Questions and Exercises

1. With the aid of an encyclopedia or a handbook of classical mythology (such as Bulfinch's *Mythology*, Edith Hamilton's *Mythology*, or H. J. Rose's *Handbook of Greek Mythology*) learn more about the following myths or mythical figures and places to which Milton alludes:

    Line 15   Sisters of the Sacred Well (Muses)
         16   seat of Jove (Mount Olympus)
         58   the Muse . . . that Orpheus bore (Calliope)
    61 – 63   (the death of Orpheus)
         75   Fury with the . . . shears (Atropos, one of the three Fates)
         77   Phoebus
         89   Herald of the Sea (Triton)
         90   Neptune
         96   Hippotades
      106   (Hyacinthus)
      132   Alpheus

    Then reread Milton's poem. As a result of your familiarity with these myths, what details become clear?
2. Read the parable of the Good Shepherd (John 10:1 – 18). What relationships does Milton draw between the Christian idea of the shepherd and pastoral poetry?

3. "With these trifling fictions [allusions to classical mythology]," wrote Samuel Johnson about "Lycidas," "are mingled the most awful and sacred truths, such as ought never to be polluted with such irreverend combinations." Does this mingling of paganism and Christianity detract from Milton's poem? Discuss.
4. In "Lycidas" does Milton devise any new myth or myths?

SUGGESTIONS FOR WRITING

1. Write an explication of D. H. Lawrence's "Bavarian Gentians" or Thomas Hardy's "The Oxen." (For hints on writing about poetry by the method of explication, see page 477.)
2. In a brief essay, either serious or otherwise, invent a brand new personal myth.

14 Alternatives

THE POET'S REVISIONS

"He / Who casts to write a living line must sweat, / . . . and strike the second heat / Upon the Muse's anvil," wrote Ben Jonson. Indeed, few if any immortal poems can have been perfected with the first blow. As a result, a poet may leave us two or more versions of a poem — perhaps (as Robert Graves has said of his work drafts) "hatched and cross-hatched by puzzling layers of ink."

We need not, of course, rummage the poet's wastebasket in order to evaluate a poem. If we wish, we can follow a suggestion of the critic Austin Warren: take any fine poem and make changes in it. Then compare the changes with the original. We may then realize why the poem is as it is instead of something else. However, there is a certain undeniable pleasure in watching a poem go through its growth stages. Some readers have claimed that the study of successive versions gives them insight into the process by which poems come to be. More important to a reader whose concern is to read poems with appreciation, we stand to learn something about the rightness of a finished poem from seeing what alternatives occurred to the poet. To a critic who protested two lines in Wordsworth's "The Thorn," a painfully flat description of an infant's grave,

> I've measured it from side to side;
> 'Tis three feet long and two feet wide,

Wordsworth retorted, "They ought to be liked." However, he thought better of them and later made this change:

> Though but of compass small, and bare
> To thirsty suns and parching air.

William Butler Yeats, who enjoyed revision, kept trying to improve the poems of his youth. A merciless self-critic, Yeats discarded lines that a lesser poet would have been grateful for. In some cases his final version was practically a new poem.

William Butler Yeats (1865 – 1939)*

THE OLD PENSIONER   1890

I had a chair at every hearth,
When no one turned to see
With "Look at that old fellow there;
And who may he be?"
And therefore do I wander on,   5
And the fret is on me.

The road-side trees keep murmuring —
Ah, wherefore murmur ye
As in the old days long gone by,
Green oak and poplar tree!   10
The well-known faces are all gone,
And the fret is on me.

William Butler Yeats (1865 – 1939)

THE LAMENTATION OF THE OLD PENSIONER   1939

Although I shelter from the rain
Under a broken tree
My chair was nearest to the fire
In every company
That talked of love or politics,   5
Ere Time transfigured me.

Though lads are making pikes again
For some conspiracy,
And crazy rascals rage their fill
At human tyranny,   10
My contemplations are of Time
That has transfigured me.

There's not a woman turns her face
Upon a broken tree,
And yet the beauties that I loved   15
Are in my memory;
I spit into the face of Time
That has transfigured me.

QUESTIONS

1. "The Old Pensioner" is this poem's first printed version; "Lamentation," its last.
   From the original, what elements has Yeats in the end retained?
2. What does the final version add to our knowledge of the old man (his character,
   attitudes, circumstances)?

3. Compare in sound and rhythm the refrain in the "Lamentation" with the original refrain.
4. Why do the statements in the final version seem to follow one another more naturally, and the poem as a whole seem more tightly woven together?

Yeats's practice seems to document the assertion of critic A. F. Scott that "the work of correction is often quite as inspired as the first onrush of words and ideas." Yeats made a revealing comment on his methods of revision:

> In dream poetry, in "Kubla Khan," . . . every line, every word can carry its unanalyzable, rich associations; but if we dramatize some possible singer or speaker we remember that he is moved by one thing at a time, certain words must be dull and numb. Here and there in correcting my early poems I have introduced such numbness and dullness, turned, for instance, the "curd-pale moon" into the "brilliant moon," that all might seem, as it were, remembered with indifference, except some one vivid image. When I began to rehearse a play I had the defects of my early poetry; I insisted upon obvious all-pervading rhythm. Later on I found myself saying that only in those lines or words where the beauty of the passage came to its climax, must rhythm be obvious.[1]

In changing colorful words for "dull and numb" ones, in breaking up and varying rhythms, Yeats evidently is trying for improvement not in a particular line, but in an entire poem.

Not all revisions are successful. An instance might be the alterations Keats made in "La Belle Dame sans Merci," in which a stanza with "wild wild eyes" and exactly counted kisses,

> She took me to her elfin grot,
>   And there she wept and sighed full sore,
> And there I shut her wild wild eyes
>   With kisses four.

was scrapped in favor of:

> She took me to her elfin grot,
>   And there she gazed and sighèd deep,
> And there I shut her wild sad eyes —
>   So kissed to sleep.

When Mark Antony begins his funeral oration, "Friends, Romans, countrymen: lend me your ears," Shakespeare makes him ask something quite different from the modernized version in one high school English textbook: "Friends, Romans, countrymen: listen to me." Strictly speaking, any revised version of a poem is a different poem, even if its only change is a single word.

[1]"Dramatis Personae, 1896–1902," in *The Autobiography of William Butler Yeats* (New York: Macmillan, 1953).

EXERCISE: *Early and Late Versions*

In each of the following pairs, which details of the revised version show an improvement of the earlier one? Exactly what makes the poet's second thoughts seem better (if you agree that they are)? Italics indicate words of one text not found in the other. Notice that in some cases, the poet has also changed word order.

1. Samuel Taylor Coleridge, "The Rime of the Ancient Mariner," from Part III:

   a. One after one, by the hornèd Moon
         (Listen, O Stranger! to me)
      Each turn'd his face with a ghastly pang
         And curs'd me with his *ee*.
                    (1799 version)

   b. One after one, by the *star-dogged* Moon,
      Too quick for groan or sigh,
      Each turned his face with a ghastly pang
      And cursed me with his *eye*.
                    (1817 version)

2. William Blake, last stanza of "London" (complete poem given on 000):

   a. But most the midnight harlot's curse
      From every *dismal* street I hear,
      Weaves around the marriage hearse
      And blasts the new born infant's tear.
                    (first draft, 1793)

   b. But most *through* midnight streets I hear
      How the *youthful* harlot's curse
      Blasts the new born infant's tear
      And *blights with plagues* the marriage hearse.
                    (1794 version)

3. Edward FitzGerald, *The Rubáiyát of Omar Khayyám,* a quatrain:

   a. *For in and out, above, about, below,*
         'Tis nothing but a Magic Shadow-show,
            Play'd in a Box whose Candle is the Sun,
         Round *which* we *Phantom Figures* come and go.
                    (first version, 1859 edition)

   b. We *are no other than a moving row*
         Of Magic Shadow-*shapes that* come and go
         Round *with* the Sun-*illumined Lantern held*
         In Midnight by the Master of the Show; . . .
                    (fifth version, 1889 edition)

Walt Whitman (1819 – 1892)*

A NOISELESS PATIENT SPIDER

A noiseless patient spider,
I mark'd where on a little promontory it stood isolated,
Mark'd how to explore the vacant vast surrounding,
It launch'd forth filament, filament, filament, out of itself,

Ever unreeling them, ever tirelessly speeding them.   5
And you O my soul where you stand,
Surrounded, detached, in measureless oceans of space,
Ceaselessly musing, venturing, throwing, seeking the spheres to
    connect them,
Till the bridge you will need be form'd, till the ductile anchor hold,
Till the gossamer thread you fling catch somewhere, O my soul.   10

Walt Whitman (1819 – 1892)

THE SOUL, REACHING, THROWING OUT FOR LOVE

The Soul, reaching, throwing out for love,
As the spider, from some little promontory, throwing out filament
    after filament, tirelessly out of itself, that one at least may catch
    and form a link, a bridge, a connection
O I saw one passing along, saying hardly a word — yet full of love I
    detected him, by certain signs
O eyes wishfully turning! O silent eyes!
For then I thought of you o'er the world,   5
O latent oceans, fathomless oceans of love!
O waiting oceans of love! yearning and fervid! and of you sweet souls
    perhaps in the future, delicious and long:
But Death, unknown on the earth — ungiven, dark here, unspoken,
    never born:
You fathomless latent souls of love — you pent and unknown oceans
    of love!

QUESTIONS

1. One of these two versions of a poem by Whitman is an early draft from the poet's
   notebook. The other is the final version completed in 1871, about ten years later.
   Which is the final version?
2. In the final version, what has Whitman done to render his central metaphor (the
   comparison of soul and spider) more vivid and exact? What proportion of the final
   version is devoted to this metaphor?
3. In the early draft, what lines seem distracting or nonessential?

TRANSLATIONS

Poetry, said Robert Frost, is what gets lost in translation. If absolutely true, the
comment is bad news for most of us, who have to depend on translations for
our only knowledge of great poems in many other languages. However, some
translators seem able to save a part of their originals and bring it across the
language gap. At times they may even add more poetry of their own, as if to
try to compensate for what is lost.

Unlike the writer of an original poem, the translator begins with a meaning that already exists. To convey it, the translator may decide to stick closely to the denotations of the original words or else to depart from them, more or less freely, after something he or she values more. The latter aim is evident in the *Imitations* of Robert Lowell, who said he had been "reckless with literal meaning" and instead had "labored hard to get the tone." Particularly defiant of translation are poems in dialect, uneducated speech, and slang: what can be used for English equivalents? Ezra Pound, in a bold move, translates the song of a Chinese peasant in *The Classic Anthology Defined by Confucius:*

> Yaller bird, let my corn alone,
> Yaller bird, let my crawps alone,
> These folks here won't let me eat,
> I wanna go back whaar I can meet
> the folks I used to know at home,
>   I got a home an' I wanna' git goin'.

Here, it is our purpose to judge a translation not by its fidelity to its original, but by the same standards we apply to any other poem written in English. To do so may be another way to see the difference between appropriate and inappropriate words.

Federico García Lorca (1899 – 1936)

La guitarra 1921	Guitar 1967	
Empieza el llanto	Begins the crying	
de la guitarra.	of the guitar.	
Se rompen las copas	From earliest dawn	
de la madrugada.	the strokes are breaking.	
Empieza el llanto	Begins the crying	5
de la guitarra.	of the guitar.	
Es inútil	It is futile	
callarla.	to stop its sound.	
Es imposible	It is impossible	
callarla.	to stop its sound.	10
Llora monótona	It is crying a monotone	
como llora el agua,	like the crying of water,	
como llora el viento	like the crying of wind	
sobre la nevada.	over fallen snow.	
Es imposible	It is impossible	15
callarla.	to stop its sound.	
Llora por cosas	It is crying over things	
lejanas.	far off.	

Arena del Sur caliente
que pide camelias blancas.
Llora flecha sin blanco,
la tarde sin mañana,
y el primer pájaro muerto
sobre la rama.
¡Oh, guitarra!
Corazón malherido
por cinco espadas.

Burning sand of the South
which covets white camelias.   20
It is crying the arrow without aim,
the evening without tomorrow,
and the first dead bird on the branch.
O guitar!
Heart heavily wounded   25
by five sharp swords.

— Translated by Keith Waldrop

QUESTIONS

1. Someone who knows Spanish should read aloud the original and the translation. Although it is impossible for any translation fully to capture the resonance of García Lorca's poem, in what places is the English version most nearly able to approximate it?
2. Another translation renders line 21: "It mourns for the targetless arrow." What is the difference between mourning for something and being the cry of it?
3. Throughout his translation, Waldrop closely follows the line divisions of the original, but in line 23 he combines García Lorca's lines 23 and 24. Can you see any point in his doing so? Would "on the branch" by itself be a strong line of English poetry?

EXERCISE: *Comparing Translations*

Which English translation of each of the following poems is the best poetry? The originals may be of interest to some. For those who do not know the foreign language, the editor's line-by-line prose paraphrases may help indicate what the translator had to work with and how much of the translation is the translator's own idea. In which do you find the diction most felicitous? In which do pattern and structure best move as one? What differences in tone are apparent? It is doubtful that any one translation will surpass the others in every detail.

Horace (65 – 8 B.C.)

ODES I (38)   (about 20 B.C.)

Persicos odi, puer, apparatus,
Displicent nexae philyra coronae;
Mitte sectari, rosa quo locorum
         Sera moretur.
Simplici myrto nihil allabores   5
Sedulus curo: neque te ministrum
Dedecet myrtus neque me sub arta
         Vite bibentem.

ODES I (38). Prose translation: (1) Persian pomp, boy, I detest, (2) garlands woven of linden bark displease me; (3 – 4) give up searching for the place where the late-blooming rose is. (5 – 6) Put no laborious trimmings on simple myrtle: (6 – 7) for myrtle is unbecoming neither to you, a servant, nor to me, under the shade of this (8) vine, drinking.

1. SIMPLICITY   (about 1782)

> Boy, I hate their empty shows,
>   Persian garlands I detest,
> Bring me not the late-blown rose
>   Lingering after all the rest:
> Plainer myrtle pleases me   5
>   Thus outstretched beneath my vine,
> Myrtle more becoming thee,
>   Waiting with thy master's wine.
>   — William Cowper

2. FIE ON EASTERN LUXURY!   (about 1830)

> Nay, nay, my boy — 'tis not for me,
>   This studious pomp of Eastern luxury;
> Give me no various garlands — fine
>   With linden twine,
> Nor seek, where latest lingering blows,   5
>   The solitary rose.
>
> Earnest I beg — add not with toilsome pain,
> One far-sought blossom to the myrtle plain,
> For sure, the fragrant myrtle bough
>   Looks seemliest on thy brow;   10
> Nor me mis-seems, while, underneath the vine,
> Close interweaved, I quaff the rosy wine.
>   — Hartley Coleridge

3. THE PREFERENCE DECLARED   1892

> Boy, I detest the Persian pomp;
>   I hate those linden-bark devices;
> And as for roses, holy Moses!
>   They can't be got at living prices!
> Myrtle is good enough for us, —   5
>   For *you*, as bearer of my flagon;
> For *me*, supine beneath this vine,
>   Doing my best to get a jag on!
>   — Eugene Field

Charles Baudelaire (1821 – 1867)

RECUEILLEMENT   1866

Sois sage, ô ma Douleur, et tiens-toi plus tranquille.
Tu réclamais le Soir; il descend; le voici:
Une atmosphère obscure enveloppe la ville,
Aux uns portant la paix, aux autres le souci.

"MEDITATION." Prose translation: (1) Behave yourself [as a mother would say to her child], O my
Sorrow, and keep calmer. (2) You called for Evening; it descends; here it is: (3) a dim atmosphere
envelops the city, (4) Bringing peace to some; to others anxiety.

Pendant que des mortels la multitude vile,   5
Sous le fouet du Plaisir, ce bourreau sans merci,
Va cueillir des remords dans la fête servile,
Ma Douleur, donne-moi la main; viens par ici,

Loin d'eux. Vois se pencher les défuntes Années,
Sur les balcons du ciel, en robes surannées;   10
Surgir du fond des eaux le Regret souriant;

Le Soleil moribond s'endormir sous une arche,
Et, comme un long linceul traînant à l'Orient,
Entends, ma chère, entends la douce Nuit qui marche.

(5) While the vile multitude of mortals (6) under the whip of Pleasure, that merciless executioner, (7) go to gather remorse in the servile festival, (8) my Sorrow, give me your hand; come this way, (9) far from them. See the dead years lean (10) on the balconies of the sky, in old-fashioned dresses; (11) [see] Regret, smiling, emerge from the depths of the waters; (12) [see] the dying Sun go to sleep under an arch; (13) and like a long shroud trailing in the East, (14) hear, my darling, hear the soft Night who is walking.

1. Peace, be at peace, O thou my heaviness   1919

Peace, be at peace, O thou my heaviness,
Thou callèdst for the evening, lo! 'tis here,
The City wears a somber atmosphere
That brings repose to some, to some distress.
Now while the heedless throng make haste to press   5
Where pleasure drives them, ruthless charioteer,
To pluck the fruits of sick remorse and fear,
Come thou with me, and leave their fretfulness.
See how they hang from heaven's high balconies,
The old lost years in faded garments dressed,   10
And see Regret with faintly smiling mouth;
And while the dying sun sinks in the west,
Hear how, far off, Night walks with velvet tread,
And her long robe trails all about the south.
    — Lord Alfred Douglas

2. Inward Conversation   1961

Be reasonable, my pain, and think with more detachment.
You asked to see the dusk; it descends; it is here:
A sheath of dark light robes the city,
To some bringing peace, to some the end of peace.
Now while the rotten herds of mankind,   5
Flogged by pleasure, that lyncher without touch,
Go picking remorse in their filthy holidays,
Let us join hands, my pain; come this way,

Far from them. Look at the dead years that lean on
The balconies of the sky, in their clothes long out of date;   10
The sense of loss that climbs from the deep waters with a smile;

The sun, nearly dead, that drops asleep beneath an arch;
And listen to the night, like a long shroud being dragged
Toward the east, my love, listen, the soft night is moving.
    — Robert Bly

3. MEDITATION

Calm down, my Sorrow, we must move with care.
You called for evening; it descends; it's here.
The town is coffined in its atmosphere,
bringing relief to some, to others care.

Now while the common multitude strips bare,   5
feels pleasure's cat o' nine tails on its back,
and fights off anguish at the great bazaar,
give me your hand, my Sorrow. Let's stand back;

back from these people! Look, the dead years dressed
in old clothes crowd the balconies of the sky.   10
Regret emerges smiling from the sea,

the sick sun slumbers underneath an arch,
and like a shroud strung out from east to west,
listen, my Dearest, hear the sweet night march!
  — Robert Lowell

4. MEDITATION

1982

Behave, my Sorrow! let's have no more scenes.
Evening's what you wanted — Evening's here:
a gradual darkness overtakes the town,
bringing peace to some, to others pain.

Now, while humanity racks up remorse   5
in low distractions under Pleasure's lash,
grovelling for a ruthless master — come
away, my Sorrow, leave them! Give me your hand . . .

See how the dear departed dowdy years
crowd the balconies of heaven, leaning down,   10
while smiling out of the sea appears Regret;

the Sun will die in its sleep beneath a bridge,
and trailing westward like a winding-sheet —
listen, my dear — how softly Night arrives.
  — Richard Howard

PARODY

In a **parody**, one writer imitates another writer or another work, for the purpose of poking fun. Parody is a favorite medium for child poets, as shown in this jingle made up by children on the streets of Edinburgh.

Anonymous

WE FOUR LADS FROM LIVERPOOL ARE   (about 1963)

We four lads from Liverpool are—
Paul in a taxi, John in a car,
George on a scooter, tootin' his hooter,
Following Ringo Starr.

Skillfully written, parody can be a devastating form of literary criticism. Rather than merely flinging abuse, the wise parodist imitates with understanding, even with sympathy. The many crude parodies of T. S. Eliot's difficult poem *The Waste Land* show parodists mocking what they cannot fathom, with the result that, instead of illuminating the original, they belittle it (and themselves). Good parodists have an ear for the sounds and rhythms of their originals, as does James Camp, who echoes Walt Whitman's stately "Out of the Cradle Endlessly Rocking" in his line "Out of the crock endlessly ladling" (what a weary teacher feels he is doing). Parody can be aimed at poems good or bad; yet there are poems of such splendor and dignity that no parodist seems able to touch them without looking like a small dog defiling a cathedral, and others so illiterate that good parody would be squandered on them. In the following original by T. E. Brown, what failings does the parodist, J. A. Lindon, jump upon? (*God wot,* by the way, is an archaism for "God knows.")

T. E. Brown (1830 – 1897)

MY GARDEN   1887

A garden is a lovesome thing,
  God wot!
Rose plot,
Fringed pool,
Ferned grot —
The veriest school
Of peace; and yet the fool
Contends that God is not —
Not God! in gardens! when the eve
  is cool?
Nay, but I have a sign;
'Tis very sure God walks in mine.

J. A. Lindon (b. 1914)

My GARDEN   1959

A garden is a *lovesome* thing?
  What rot!
Weed plot,
Scum pool,
Old pot,   5
Snail-shiny stool
In pieces; yet the fool
Contends that snails are not —
Not snails! in gardens! when
  the eve is cool?
Nay, but I see their trails!   10
'Tis very sure *my* garden's full
  of snails!

Hugh Kingsmill
[Hugh Kingsmill Lunn] (1889 – 1949)

WHAT, STILL ALIVE AT TWENTY-TWO?   (about 1920)

What, still alive at twenty-two,
A clean, upstanding chap like you?
Sure, if your throat 'tis hard to slit,
Slit your girl's, and swing for it.

Like enough, you won't be glad   5
When they come to hang you, lad:

But bacon's not the only thing
That's cured by hanging from a string.

So, when the spilt ink of the night
Spreads o'er the blotting-pad of light,   10
Lads whose job is still to do
Shall whet their knives, and think of you.

QUESTIONS

1. A. E. Housman considered this the best of many parodies of his poetry. Read his
   poems in this book, particularly "Eight O'Clock" (page 131), "When I was one-and-
   twenty" (page 160), and "To an Athlete Dying Young" (page 336). What characteristics of theme, form, and language does Hugh Kingsmill's parody convey?
2. What does Kingsmill exaggerate?

Kenneth Koch (b. 1925)

MENDING SUMP   1960

"Hiram, I think the sump is backing up.
The bathroom floor boards for above two weeks
Have seemed soaked through. A little bird, I think,
Has wandered in the pipes, and all's gone wrong."
"Something there is that doesn't hump a sump,"   5
He said; and through his head she saw a cloud
That seemed to twinkle. "Hiram, well," she said,
"Smith is come home! I saw his face just now
While looking through your head. He's come to die
Or else to laugh, for hay is dried-up grass   10
When you're alone." He rose, and sniffed the air.
"We'd better leave him in the sump," he said.

QUESTIONS

1. What poet is the object of this parody? Which of his poems are echoed in it?
2. Koch gains humor by making outrageous statements in the tone and language of his
   original. Looking at other poems in this book by the poet being parodied, how would
   you describe their tone? Their language?
3. Suppose, instead of casting his parody into blank verse, Koch had written:

   "Hiram, the sump is backing up.
   The bathroom floor boards
   For above two weeks
   Have been soaking through. A little bird,
   I think, has wandered in
   The pipes, and all's gone wrong."

   Why would the biting edge of his parody have been blunted?
4. What, by the way, is a *sump*?

In the following parody, what poem or poet is being kidded? Does the parodist seem only to be having fun, or is he making any critical point?

George Starbuck (b. 1931)

MARGARET ARE YOU DRUG   1966

Cool it Mag.
Sure it's a drag
With all that green flaked out.
Next thing you know they'll be changing the color of bread.

But look, Chick,   5
Why panic?
Sevennyeighty years, we'll *all* be dead.

Roll with it, Kid.
I did.
Give it the old benefit of the doubt.   10

I mean leaves
Schmeaves.
You sure you aint just feeling sorry for yourself?

MARGARET ARE YOU DRUG. This is one of a series of "Translations from the English."

SUGGESTIONS FOR WRITING

1. Write a poem in the manner of Emily Dickinson, William Carlos Williams, E. E. Cummings, or any other modern poet whose work interests you and which you feel able to imitate. Decide, before you start, whether to write a serious imitation (that could be slipped into the poet's *Collected Poems* without anyone being the wiser), or a humorous parody. Read all the poet's poems included in this book; perhaps you will find it helpful also to consult a larger selection or collection of the poet's work. It might be simplest to choose a particular poem as your model; but, if you like, you may echo any number of poems. Choose a model within the range of your own skill: to imitate a sonnet, for instance, you need to be able to rime and to write in meter. Probably, if your imitation is serious, and not a parody, it is a good idea to pick a subject or theme characteristic of the poet. This is a difficult project, but if you can do it even fairly well, you will know a great deal more about poetry and your poet.
2. Compare and contrast the earlier version of Robert Frost's poem originally titled "In White" with the finished version "Design" (page 478). What specific improvements did the poet make? Why do you think he made them? What was the matter with his first thoughts?
3. Word-processing systems, it is claimed, now enable writers to revise swiftly and efficiently. If you are familiar with word processors or computers, point out any possible advantages and disadvantages to poetry that may result from this recent development in technology.

15 Evaluating a Poem

Telling Good from Bad

Why do we call some poems "bad"? We are talking not about their moral implications. Rather, we mean that, for one or more of many possible reasons, the poem has failed to move us or to engage our sympathies. Instead, it has made us doubt that the poet is in control of language and vision; perhaps it has aroused our antipathies or unwittingly appealed to our sense of the comic, though the poet is serious. Some poems can be said to succeed despite burdensome faults. But in general such faults are symptoms of deeper malady: some weakness in a poem's basic conception or in the poet's competence.

Nearly always, a bad poem reveals only a dim and distorted awareness of its probable effect on its audience. Perhaps the sound of words may clash with what a poem is saying, as in the jarring last word of this opening line of a tender lyric (author unknown, quoted by Richard Wilbur): "Come into the tent, my love, and close the flap." Perhaps a metaphor may fail by calling to mind more differences than similarities, as in Emily Dickinson's lines "Our lives are Swiss — / So still — so cool." A bad poem usually overshoots or falls short of its mark by the poet's thinking too little or too much. Thinking too much, a poet contrives an excess of ingenuity like that quoted by Alexander Pope in *Peri Bathous, or Of the Art of Sinking in Poetry:* a hounded stag who "Hears his own feet, and thinks they sound like more; / And fears the hind feet will o'ertake the fore." Thinking too little, a poet writes redundantly, as Wordsworth in "The Thorn": "And they had fixed the wedding-day, / The morning that must wed them both."

In a poem that has a rime scheme or a set line length, when all is well, pattern and structure move inseparably with the rest of their poem, the way a tiger's skin and bones move with their tiger. But sometimes, in a poem that fails, the poet evidently has had difficulty in fitting the statements into a formal pattern. English poets have long felt free to invert word order for a special effect (Milton: "ye myrtles brown"), but the poet having trouble keeping to a rime scheme may invert words for no apparent reason but convenience. Needing a rime for *barge* may lead to ending a line with a *policedog large* instead of *a large policedog.* Another sign of trouble is a profusion of adjectives. If a line of iambic pentameter reads, "Her lovely skin, like dear sweet white old silk," we suspect the poet of stuffing the line to make it long enough. (But no one suspects Matthew Arnold of padding the last line of "To Marguerite": "The unplumbed, salt, estranging sea.")

Because, over his or her dead body, even a poet's slightest and feeblest efforts may be collected, some lines in the canon of celebrated bards make us wonder, "How could they have written this?" Wordsworth, Shelley, Whitman, and Browning are among the great whose failures can be painful, and sometimes an excellent poem will have a bad spot in it. To be unwilling to read them, though, would be as ill advised as to refuse to see Venice just because the Grand Canal is said to contain impurities. The seasoned reader of poetry thinks no less of Tennyson for having written, "Form, Form, Riflemen Form! . . . Look to your butts, and take good aims!" The collected works of a duller poet may contain no such lines of unconscious double meaning, but neither do they contain any poem as good as "Ulysses." If the duller poet never had a spectacular failure, it may be because of failure to take risks. "In poetry," said Ronsard, "the greatest vice is mediocrity."

Often, inept poems fall into familiar categories. At one extreme is the poem written entirely in conventional diction, dimly echoing Shakespeare, Wordsworth, and the Bible, but garbling them. Couched in a rhythm that ticks along like a metronome, this kind of poem shows no sign that its author has ever taken a hard look at anything that can be tasted, handled, and felt. It employs loosely and thoughtlessly the most abstract of words: *love, beauty, life, death, time, eternity.* Littered with old-fashioned contractions (*'tis, o'er, where'er*), it may end in a simple preachment or platitude. George Orwell's complaint against much contemporary writing (not only poetry) is applicable: "As soon as certain topics are raised" — and one thinks of such standard topics for poetry as spring, a first kiss, and stars — "the concrete melts into the abstract and no one seems able to think of turns of speech that are not hackneyed." Writers, Orwell charged, too often make their sentences out of tacked-together phrases "like the sections of a prefabricated hen-house."[1] Versifiers often do likewise.

At the opposite extreme is the poem that displays no acquaintance with poetry of the past but manages, instead, to fabricate its own clichés. Slightly paraphrased, a manuscript once submitted to *The Paris Review* began:

Vile
    rottenflush

        o   — *screaming* —
      f CORPSEBLOOD!!   ooze
STRANGLE my

        eyes . . .

                    HELL's
      O, ghastly   stench***!!!

[1]George Orwell, "Politics and the English Language," from *Shooting an Elephant and Other Essays* (New York: Harcourt, 1945).

At most, such a work has only a private value. The writer has vented personal frustrations upon words, instead of kicking stray dogs. In its way, "Vile Rotten-flush" is as self-indulgent as the oldfangled "first kiss in spring" kind of poem. "I dislike," said John Livingston Lowes, "poems that black your eyes, or put up their mouths to be kissed."

As jewelers tell which of two diamonds is fine by seeing which scratches the other, two poems may be tested by comparing them. This method works only on poems similar in length and kind: an epigram cannot be held up to test an epic. Most poems we meet are neither sheer trash nor obvious master-pieces. Because good diamonds to be proven need softer ones to scratch, in this chapter you will find a few clear-cut gems and a few clinkers.

Anonymous (English)

O MOON, WHEN I GAZE ON THY BEAUTIFUL FACE   (about 1900)

O Moon, when I gaze on thy beautiful face,
Careering along through the boundaries of space,
The thought has often come into my mind
If I ever shall see thy glorious behind.

O MOON. Sir Edmund Gosse, the English critic (1849 – 1928), offered this quatrain as the work of his maidservant, but there is reason to suspect him of having written it.

QUESTIONS

1. To what fact of astronomy does the last line refer?
2. Which words seem chosen with too little awareness of their denotations and connotations?
3. Even if you did not know that these lines probably were deliberately bad, how would you argue with someone who maintained that the opening *O* in the poem was admirable as a bit of concrete poetry? (See the quotation from E. E. Cummings on page 202.)

Grace Treasone

LIFE   (about 1963)

Life is like a jagged tooth
that cuts into your heart;
fix the tooth and save the root,
and laughs, not tears, will start.

QUESTIONS

1. Try to paraphrase this poem. What is the poet saying?
2. How consistent is the working out of the comparison of life to a tooth?

Stephen Tropp (b. 1930)

MY WIFE IS MY SHIRT   1960

My wife is my shirt
I put my hands through her armpits
slide my head through her mouth
& finally button her blood around my hands

QUESTIONS

1. How consistently is the metaphor elaborated?
2. Why can this metaphor be said to work in exactly the opposite way from a personification?
3. A paraphrase might discover this simile: "My wife is as intimate, familiar, and close to me as the shirt on my back." If this is the idea and the poem is supposed to be a love poem, how precisely is its attitude expressed?

William McGonagall (1830? – 1902)

THE ALBION BATTLESHIP CALAMITY   (1898)

'Twas in the year of 1898, and on the 21st of June,
The launching of the Battleship Albion caused a great gloom,
Amongst the relatives of many persons who were drowned in the
    River Thames,
Which their relatives will remember while life remains.

The vessel was christened by the Duchess of York,   5
And the spectators' hearts felt as light as cork
As the Duchess cut the cord that was holding the fine ship,
Then the spectators loudly cheered as the vessel slid down the slip.

The launching of the vessel was very well carried out,
While the guests on the stands cheered without any doubt,   10
Under the impression that everything would go well;
But, alas! instantaneously a bridge and staging fell.

Oh! little did the Duchess of York think that day
That so many lives would be taken away
At the launching of the good ship Albion,   15
But when she heard of the catastrophe she felt woebegone.

But accidents will happen without any doubt,
And often the cause thereof is hard to find out;
And according to report, I've heard people say,
'Twas the great crowd on the bridge caused it to give way.   20

Just as the vessel entered the water the bridge and staging gave way,
Immersing some three hundred people which caused great dismay

Amongst thousands of spectators that were standing there,
And in the faces of the bystanders were depicted despair.

Then the police boats instantly made for the fatal spot,   25
And with the aid of dockyard hands several people were got,
While some scrambled out themselves, the best way they could—
And the most of them were the inhabitants of the neighborhood.

Part of them were the wives and daughters of the dockyard hands,
And as they gazed upon them they in amazement stands;   30
And several bodies were hauled up quite dead,
Which filled the onlookers' hearts with pity and dread.

One of the first rescued was a little baby,
Which was conveyed away to a mortuary;
And several were taken to the fitter's shed, and attended to there   35
By the firemen and several nurses with the greatest care.

Meanwhile heartrending scenes were taking place,
Whilst the tears ran down many a Mother and Father's face,
That had lost their children in the River Thames,
Which they will remember while life remains.   40

Oh, Heaven! it was horrible to see the bodies laid out in rows,
And as Fathers and Mothers passed along, adown their cheeks the
    tears flows,
While their poor, sickly hearts were throbbing with fear.

A great crowd had gathered to search for the missing dead,
And many strong men broke down because their heart with pity bled,   45
As they looked upon the distorted faces of their relatives dear,
While adown their cheeks flowed many a silent tear.

The tenderest sympathy, no doubt, was shown to them,
By the kind hearted Police and Firemen;
The scene in fact was most sickening to behold,   50
And enough to make one's blood run cold,
To see tear-stained men and women there
Searching for their relatives, and in their eyes a pitiful stare.

There's one brave man in particular I must mention,
And I'm sure he's worthy of the people's attention: 55
His name is Thomas Cooke, of No. 6 Percy Road, Canning Town,
Who's name ought to be to posterity handed down,
Because he leapt into the River Thames, and heroically did behave,
And rescued five persons from a watery grave.

Mr. Wilson, a young Electrician, got a terrible fright,   60
When he saw his mother and sister dead—he was shocked at the
    sight,
Because his sister had not many days returned from her honeymoon,
And in his countenance, alas! there was a sad gloom.

Her Majesty has sent a message of sympathy to the bereaved ones in
    distress,
And the Duke and Duchess of York have sent 25 guineas I must
    confess,   65
And £1000 from the Directors of the Thames Ironworks and
    Shipbuilding Company,
Which I hope will help to fill the bereaved one's hearts with glee.

And in conclusion I will venture to say,
That accidents will happen by night and by day;
And I will say without any fear,   70
Because to me it appears quite clear,
That the stronger we our houses do build,
The less chance we have of being killed.

THE ALBION BATTLESHIP CALAMITY. The poetry of McGonagall, handloom weaver and amateur Shakespearean actor of Dundee, Scotland, has become popular not for its merits but for its flamboyant faults. Like a writer of broadside ballads, McGonagall revels in fires, accidents, bridge disasters, shipwrecks, mine cave-ins, and other catastrophes. In England and Scotland, his *Poetic Gems* (1890, reprinted 1934) and *More Poetic Gems* (1966) are classics.

QUESTIONS

1. With a pencil, delete anything in this poem that seems to you repetitious. What would you remove? (Don't say "The whole poem"; look for glaring redundancies.)
2. In what places does the poet appear to make a remark for no reason other than to round out his rime?
3. How vivid and exact is McGonagall's description of the sudden collapse of the bridge and staging? How clear and detailed are his portraits of victims and relatives? What words or phrases seem particularly vague and woolly?
4. Inspect the lines about Mr. Wilson (60–63). Why is the word *shocked* such an unlucky choice? Even granting that this might be a deliberate pun, why is it bad?
5. In the next-to-last stanza, what is the poet's attitude toward money?
6. Comment on the wisdom of the last two lines.
7. As best you can tell from this poem, how sharp is the poet's awareness of his readers and their possible reactions?

Emily Dickinson (1830 – 1886)*

A DYING TIGER – MOANED FOR DRINK   (ABOUT 1862)

A Dying Tiger – moaned for Drink –
I hunted all the Sand –
I caught the Dripping of a Rock
And bore it in my Hand –

His Mighty Balls – in death were thick –   5
But searching – I could see
A Vision on the Retina
Of Water – and of me –

'Twas not my blame – who sped too slow –
'Twas not his blame – who died   10
While I was reaching him –
But 'twas – the fact that He was dead –

QUESTION

How does this poem compare in success with other poems of Emily Dickinson that you
know? Justify your opinion by pointing to some of this poem's particulars.

EXERCISE: *Seeing What Went Wrong*

Here is a small anthology of bad moments in poetry. For what reasons does each
selection fail? In which passages do you attribute the failure to inappropriate sound or
diction? To awkward word order? To inaccurate metaphor? To excessive overstatement?
To forced rime? To monotonous rhythm? To redundancy? To simple-mindedness or
excessive ingenuity?

1. Last lines of *Enoch Arden* by Alfred, Lord Tennyson:

   So passed the strong heroic soul away.
   And when they buried him, the little port
   Had seldom seen a costlier funeral.

2. From *Purely Original Verse* (1891) by J. Gordon Coogler (1865–1901), of Columbia,
   South Carolina:

   Alas for the South, her books have grown fewer—
   She never was much given to literature.

3. From "Lines Written to a Friend on the Death of His Brother, Caused by a Railway
   Train Running Over Him Whilst He Was in a State of Inebriation" by James Henry
   Powell:

   Thy mangled corpse upon the rails in frightful shape was found.
   The ponderous train had killed thee as its heavy wheels went round,
   And thus in dreadful form thou met'st a drunkard's awful death
   And I, thy brother, mourn thy fate, and breathe a purer breath.

4. From *Dolce Far Niente* by the American poet Francis Saltus Saltus, who flourished
   in the 1890s:

   Her laugh is like sunshine, full of glee,
   And her sweet breath smells like fresh-made tea.

5. From another gem by Francis Saltus Saltus, "The Spider":

   Then all thy feculent majesty recalls
       The nauseous mustiness of forsaken bowers,
   The leprous nudity of deserted halls—
       The positive nastiness of sullied flowers.

   And I mark the colours yellow and black
       That fresco thy lithe, dictatorial thighs,
   I dream and wonder on my drunken back
       How God could possibly have created flies!

6. From "Song to the Suliotes" by George Gordon, Lord Byron:

   Up to battle! Sons of Suli
   Up, and do your duty duly!
   There the wall—and there the moat is:

Bouwah! Bouwah! Suliotes,
There is booty—there is beauty!
Up my boys and do your duty!

7. From a juvenile poem of John Dryden, "Upon the Death of the Lord Hastings" (a victim of smallpox):

Each little pimple had a tear in it,
To wail the fault its rising did commit . . .

8. From "I Kissed Pa Twice After His Death" by Mattie J. Peterson (1866–1947), the self-styled "Poetissima Laureatissima of Bladen County":

I saw him coming stepping high,
Which was of his walk the way . . .

9. From "The Abbey Mason" by Thomas Hardy:

When longer yet dank death had wormed
The brain wherein the style had germed

From Gloucester church it flew afar—
The style called Perpendicular.—

To Winton and to Westminster
It ranged, and grew still beautifuller . . .

10. A metaphor from "The Crucible of Life" by the once-popular American newspaper poet Edgar A. Guest:

Sacred and sweet is the joy that must come
From the furnace of life when you've poured off the scum.

11. From an elegy for Queen Victoria by one of her subjects:

Dust to dust, and ashes to ashes,
Into the tomb the Great Queen dashes.

Sentimentality is a failure of writers who seem to feel a great emotion but who fail to give us sufficient grounds for sharing it. The emotion may be an anger greater than its object seems to call for, as in these lines to a girl who caused scandal (the exact nature of her act never being specified): "The gossip in each hall / Will curse your name . . . / Go! better cast yourself right down the falls!"[2] Or it may be an enthusiasm quite unwarranted by its subject: in *The Fleece* John Dyer temptingly describes the pleasures of life in a workhouse for the poor. The sentimental poet is especially prone to tenderness. Great tears fill his eyes at a glimpse of an aged grandmother sitting by a hearth. For all the poet knows, she may be the manager of a casino in Las Vegas who would be startled to find herself an object of pity, but the sentimentalist doesn't care to know about the woman herself. She is a general excuse for feeling maudlin. Any other conventional object will serve as well: a faded valentine, the strains of an old song, a baby's cast-off pacifier. An instance of such emotional self-indulgence is "The Old Oaken Bucket," by Samuel Woodworth, a stanza of which goes:

[2] Ali. S. Hilmi, "The Preacher's Sermon," in *Verse at Random* (Larnaca, Cyprus: Ohanian Press, 1953).

How sweet from the green, mossy brim to receive it,
   As, poised on the curb, it inclined to my lips!
Not a full-flushing goblet could tempt me to leave it,
   Tho' filled with the nectar that Jupiter sips.
And now, far removed from the loved habitation,
   The tear of regret will intrusively swell,
As fancy reverts to my father's plantation,
   And sighs for the bucket that hung in the well.

The staleness of the phrasing and imagery (Jove's nectar, *tear of regret*) suggests that the speaker is not even seeing the actual physical bucket, and the tripping meter of the lines is inappropriate to an expression of tearful regret. Perhaps the poet's nostalgia is genuine. Indeed, as Keith Waldrop has put it, "a bad poem is always sincere." However sincere in their feelings, sentimental poets are insincere in their art — otherwise, wouldn't they trouble to write better poems? Wet-eyed and sighing for a bucket, Woodworth achieves not pathos but **bathos:** a description that can move us to laughter instead of tears.[3] Tears, of course, can be shed for good reason. A piece of sentimentality is not to be confused with a well-wrought poem whose tone is tenderness.

Rod McKuen (b. 1933)

THOUGHTS ON CAPITAL PUNISHMENT   1954

There ought to be capital punishment for cars
that run over rabbits and drive into dogs
and commit the unspeakable, unpardonable crime
of killing a kitty cat still in his prime.

Purgatory, at the very least   5
                    should await the driver
   driving over a beast.

Those hurrying headlights coming out of the dark
that scatter the scampering squirrels in the park
should await the best jury that one might compose   10
of fatherless chipmunks and husbandless does.

And then found guilty, after too fair a trial
should be caged in a cage with a hyena's smile
or maybe an elephant with an elephant gun
should shoot out his eyes when the verdict is done.   15

[3]*Bathos* in poetry can also mean an abrupt fall from the sublime to the trivial or incongruous. A sample, from Nicholas Rowe's play *The Fair Penitent:* "Is it the voice of thunder, or my father?" Another, from John Close, a minor Victorian: "Around their heads a dazzling halo shone, / No need of mortal robes, or any hat." When, however, such a letdown is used for a *desirable* effect of humor or contrast, it is usually called an **anticlimax:** as in Alexander Pope's lines on the queen's palace, "Here thou, great Anna! whom three realms obey, / Dost sometimes counsel take — and sometimes tea."

There ought to be something, something that's fair
to avenge Mrs. Badger as she waits in her lair
for her husband who lies with his guts spilling out
cause he didn't know what automobiles are about.

Hell on the highway, at the very least   20
                    should await the driver
    driving over a beast.

Who kills a man kills a bit of himself
But a cat too is an extension of God.

William Stafford (b. 1914)*

TRAVELING THROUGH THE DARK   1962

Traveling through the dark I found a deer
dead on the edge of the Wilson River road.
It is usually best to roll them into the canyon:
that road is narrow; to swerve might make more dead.

By glow of the tail-light I stumbled back of the car   5
and stood by the heap, a doe, a recent killing;
she had stiffened already, almost cold.
I dragged her off; she was large in the belly.

My fingers touching her side brought me the reason —
her side was warm; her fawn lay there waiting,   10
alive, still, never to be born.
Beside that mountain road I hesitated.

The car aimed ahead its lowered parking lights;
under the hood purred the steady engine.
I stood in the glare of the warm exhaust turning red;   15
around our group I could hear the wilderness listen.

I thought hard for us all — my only swerving —
then pushed her over the edge into the river.

QUESTIONS

1. Compare these poems by Rod McKuen and William Stafford. How are they similar?
2. Explain Stafford's title. Who are all those traveling through the dark?
3. Comment on McKuen's use of language. Consider especially: *unspeakable, unpardonable crime* (line 3), *kitty cat* (4), *scatter the scampering squirrels* (9), and *cause he didn't know* (19).
4. Compare the meaning of Stafford's last two lines and McKuen's last two. Does either poem have a moral? Can either poem be said to moralize?
5. Which poem might be open to the charge of sentimentality? Why?

EXERCISE: *Fine or Shoddy Tenderness*

Which of the following five poems do you find sentimental? Which would you defend? At least one kind of evidence to look for is minute, detailed observation of physical objects. In a successful poem, the poet is likely at least occasionally to notice the world beyond his or her own skin; in a sentimental poem, this world is likely to be ignored.

Julia A. Moore (1847 – 1920)

LITTLE LIBBY   1876

One more little spirit to Heaven has flown,
    To dwell in that mansion above,
Where dear little angels, together roam,
    In God's everlasting love.

One little flower has withered and died,   5
    A bud nearly ready to bloom,
Its life on earth is marked with pride;
    Oh, sad it should die so soon.

Sweet little Libbie, that precious flower
    Was a pride in her parents' home,   10
They miss their little girl *every* hour,
    Those friends that are left to mourn.

Her sweet silvery voice no more is heard
    In the home where she once roamed;
Her place is *vacant* around the hearth,   15
    Where her friends are mourning lone.

They are mourning the loss of a little girl,
    With black eyes and auburn hair,
She was a treasure to them in this world,
    This beautiful child so fair.   20

One morning in April, a short time ago,
    Libbie was active and gay;
Her Saviour called her, she had to go,
    E're the close of that pleasant day.

While eating dinner, this dear little child   25
    Was choked on a piece of beef.
Doctors came, tried their skill awhile,
    But none could give relief.

She was ten years of age, I am told,
    And in school stood very high.   30
Her little form now the earth enfolds,
    In her embrace it must ever lie.

Her friends and schoolmates will not forget
    Little Libbie that is no more;
She is waiting on the shining step,   35
    To welcome home friends once more.

Bill Knott (b. 1940)

POEM   1968

The only response
to a child's grave is
to lie down before it and play dead

Dabney Stuart (b. 1937)

CRIB DEATH   1987

Kisses are for the living.
Even if the terrible breath of the dead
Never rose from the earth's mouth,
Dread of it would turn our heads aside
As relatives at a funeral meet and kiss.   5
Living in such air is what the living have,
Less choice than a stone what's cut into its face.

Leo Connellan (b. 1928)

SCOTT HUFF   1978

Think tonight of sixteen
year old Scott Huff of
Maine driving home fell asleep at
the wheel, his car sprang awake
from the weight of his foot head on   5
into a tree. God, if you need him
take him asking me to believe in
you because there are yellow buttercups,
salmon for my heart in the rivers,
fresh springs of ice cold water running away.   10
You can have all these back for Scott Huff.

Ted Kooser (b. 1939)

A Child's Grave Marker   1985

A small block of granite
engraved with her name and the dates
just wasn't quite pretty enough
for this lost little girl
or her parents, who added a lamb   5
cast in plaster of paris,
using the same kind of cake mold
my grandmother had—iron,
heavy and black as a skillet.
The lamb came out coconut-white,   10
and seventy years have proven it
soft in the rain. On this hill,
overlooking a river in Iowa,
it melts in its own sweet time.

Knowing Excellence

How can we tell an excellent poem from any other? To give reasons for excellence in poetry is harder than to give reasons for failure in poetry (so often due to familiar kinds of imprecision and sentimentality). A bad poem tends to be stereotyped, an excellent poem unique. In judging either, we can have no absolute specifications. A poem is not like an electric toaster that an inspector can test by a check-off list. It has to be judged on the basis of what it is trying to be and how well it succeeds in the effort.

To judge a poem, we first have to understand it. At least, we need to understand it *almost* all the way; there is, to be sure, a poem such as Hopkins's "The Windhover" (page 334), which most readers probably would call excellent even though its meaning is still being debated. Although it is a good idea to give a poem at least a couple of considerate readings before judging it, sometimes our first encounter starts turning into an act of evaluation. Moving along into the poem, becoming more deeply involved in it, we may begin forming an opinion. In general, the more a poem contains for us to understand, the more rewarding we are likely to find it. Of course, an obscure and highly demanding poem is not always to be preferred to a relatively simple one. Difficult poems can be pretentious and incoherent; still, there is something to be said for the poem complicated enough to leave us something to discover on our fifteenth reading (unlike most limericks, which yield their all at a look). Here is such a poem, one not readily fathomed and exhausted.

William Butler Yeats (1865 – 1939)*

SAILING TO BYZANTIUM   1927

That is no country for old men. The young
In one another's arms, birds in the trees
— Those dying generations — at their song,
The salmon-falls, the mackerel-crowded seas,
Fish, flesh, or fowl, commend all summer long   5
Whatever is begotten, born, and dies.
Caught in that sensual music all neglect
Monuments of unaging intellect.

An aged man is but a paltry thing,
A tattered coat upon a stick, unless   10
Soul clap its hands and sing, and louder sing
For every tatter in its mortal dress,
Nor is there singing school but studying
Monuments of its own magnificence;
And therefore I have sailed the seas and come   15
To the holy city of Byzantium.

O sages standing in God's holy fire
As in the gold mosaic of a wall,
Come from the holy fire, perne in a gyre°,   *spin down a spiral*
And be the singing-masters of my soul.   20
Consume my heart away; sick with desire
And fastened to a dying animal
It knows not what it is; and gather me
Into the artifice of eternity.

Once out of nature I shall never take   25
My bodily form from any natural thing,
But such a form as Grecian goldsmiths make
Of hammered gold and gold enameling
To keep a drowsy Emperor awake;
Or set upon a golden bough to sing   30
To lords and ladies of Byzantium
Of what is past, or passing, or to come.

SAILING TO BYZANTIUM. Byzantium was the capital of the Byzantine Empire, the city now called
Istanbul. Yeats means, though, not merely the physical city. Byzantium is also a name for his
conception of paradise.

Though *salmon-falls* (line 4) suggests Yeats's native Ireland, the poem, as we
find out in line 25, is about escaping from the entire natural world. If the poet
desires this escape, then probably the *country* mentioned in the opening line
is no political nation but the cycle of birth and death in which human beings

are trapped; and, indeed, the poet says his heart is "fastened to a dying animal." Imaginary landscapes, it would seem, are merging with the historical Byzantium. Lines 17 – 18 refer to mosaic images, adornments of the Byzantine cathedral of St. Sophia, in which the figures of saints are inlaid against backgrounds of gold. The clockwork bird of the last stanza is also a reference to something actual. Yeats noted: "I have read somewhere that in the Emperor's palace at Byzantium was a tree made of gold and silver, and artificial birds that sang." This description of the role the poet would seek — that of a changeless, immortal singer — directs us back to the earlier references to music and singing. Taken all together, they point toward the central metaphor of the poem: the craft of poetry can be a kind of singing. One kind of everlasting monument is a great poem. To study masterpieces of poetry is the only "singing school" — the only way to learn to write a poem.

We have no more than skimmed through a few of this poem's suggestions, enough to show that, out of allusion and imagery, Yeats has woven at least one elaborate metaphor. Surely one thing the poem achieves is that, far from merely puzzling us, it makes us aware of relationships between what a person can imagine and the physical world. There is the statement that a human heart is bound to the body that perishes, and yet it is possible to see consciousness for a moment independent of flesh, to sing with joy at the very fact that the body is crumbling away. Expressing a similar view of mortality, the Japanese artist Hokusai has shown a withered tree letting go of its few remaining leaves, while under it two graybeards shake with laughter. Like Hokusai's view, that of Yeats is by no means simple. Much of the power of Yeats's poem comes from the physical terms with which he states the ancient quarrel between body and spirit, body being a "tattered coat upon a stick." There is all the difference in the world between the work of the poet like Yeats whose eye is on the living thing and whose mind is awake and passionate, and that of the slovenly poet whose dull eye and sleepy mind focus on nothing more than some book read hastily long ago. The former writes a poem out of compelling need, the latter as if it seems a nice idea to write something.

Yeats's poem has the three qualities essential to beauty, according to the definition of Thomas Aquinas: wholeness, harmony, and radiance. The poem is all one; its parts move in peace with one another; it shines with emotional intensity. There is an orderly progression going on in it: from the speaker's statement of his discontent with the world of "sensual music," to his statement that he is quitting this world, to his prayer that the sages will take him in, and his vision of future immortality. And the images of the poem relate to one another — *dying generations* (line 3), *dying animal* (line 22), and the undying golden bird (lines 27 – 32) — to mention just one series of related things. "Sailing to Byzantium" is not the kind of poem that has, in Pope's words, "One simile, that solitary shines / In the dry desert of a thousand lines." Rich in figurative language, Yeats's whole poem develops a metaphor, with further metaphors as its tributaries.

"Sailing to Byzantium" has a theme that matters to us. What human being does not long, at times, to shed timid, imperfect flesh, to live in a state of absolute joy, unperishing? Being human, perhaps we too are stirred by Yeats's prayer: "Consume my heart away, sick with desire / And fastened to a dying animal. . . ." If it is true that in poetry (as Ezra Pound declared) "only emotion endures," then Yeats's poem ought to endure. (No reasons to be moved by a poem, however, can be of much use. If you happen not to feel moved by this poem, try another — but come back to "Sailing to Byzantium" after a while.)

Most excellent poems, it might be argued, contain significant themes, as does "Sailing to Byzantium." But the presence of such a theme is not enough to render a poem excellent. Not theme alone makes an excellent poem, but how well a theme is stated.

Yeats's poem, some would say, is the match for any lyric in our language. Some might call it inferior to an epic (to Milton's *Paradise Lost*, say, or to the *Iliad*), but this claim is to lead us into a different argument: whether certain genres are innately better than others. Such an argument usually leads to a dead end. Evidently, *Paradise Lost* has greater range, variety, matter, length, and ambitiousness. But any poem — whether an epic or an epigram — may be judged by how well it fulfills the design it undertakes. God, who created both fleas and whales, pronounced all good. Fleas, like epigrams, have no reason to feel inferior.

EXERCISE: *Two Poems to Compare*

Here are two poems with a similar theme. Which contains more qualities of excellent poetry? Decide whether the other is bad or whether it may be praised for achieving something different.

Arthur Guiterman (1871 – 1943)

ON THE VANITY OF EARTHLY GREATNESS   1936

The tusks that clashed in mighty brawls
Of mastodons, are billiard balls.

The sword of Charlemagne the Just
Is ferric oxide, known as rust.

The grizzly bear whose potent hug   5
Was feared by all, is now a rug.

Great Caesar's bust is on the shelf,
And I don't feel so well myself.

Percy Bysshe Shelley (1792 – 1822)

OZYMANDIAS   1818

I met a traveler from an antique land
Who said: Two vast and trunkless legs of stone
Stand in the desert. Near them, on the sand,
Half sunk, a shattered visage lies, whose frown,
And wrinkled lip, and sneer of cold command,   5
Tell that its sculptor well those passions read
Which yet survive, stamped on these lifeless things,
The hand that mocked° them and the heart that fed;   *imitated*
And on the pedestal these words appear:
"My name is Ozymandias, king of kings: 10
Look on my works, ye Mighty, and despair!"
Nothing beside remains. Round the decay
Of that colossal wreck, boundless and bare
The lone and level sands stretch far away.

Some excellent poems of the past will remain sealed to us unless we are willing to sympathize with their conventions. Pastoral poetry, for instance — Marlowe's "Passionate Shepherd" and Milton's "Lycidas" — asks us to accept certain conventions and situations that may seem old-fashioned: idle swains, oaten flutes. We are under no grim duty, of course, to admire poems whose conventions do not appeal to us. But there is no point in blaming a poet for playing a particular game or for observing its rules.

Bad poems, of course, can be woven together out of conventions, like patchwork quilts made of old unwanted words. In Shakespeare's England, poets were busily imitating the sonnets of Petrarch, the Italian poet whose praise of his beloved Laura had become well known. The result of their industry was a surplus of Petrarchan **conceits,** or elaborate comparisons (from the Italian *concetto:* concept, bright idea). In the following sonnet, Shakespeare, who at times helped himself generously from the Petrarchan stockpile, pokes fun at poets who thoughtlessly use such handed-down figures of speech.

William Shakespeare (1564 – 1616)*

MY MISTRESS' EYES ARE NOTHING LIKE THE SUN   1609

My mistress' eyes are nothing like the sun;   *a*
Coral is far more red than her lips' red;   *b*   ~Tan color~   ~English~
If snow be white, why then her breasts are dun;   *a*   ~sonnet~
If hairs be wires, black wires grow on her head.   *b*
I have seen roses damasked red and white,   *c*   5
But no such roses see I in her cheeks;   *d*

And in some perfumes is there more delight *C*
Than in the breath that from my mistress reeks. *d*
I love to hear her speak, yet well I know *e*
That music hath a far more pleasing sound; *f*   10
I grant I never saw a goddess go: *e*
My mistress, when she walks, treads on the ground. *f*
    And yet, by heaven, I think my love as rare *g*
    As any she°, belied with false compare. *g*   *woman*

Contrary to what you might expect, for years after Shakespeare's time, poets
continued to write fine poems with Petrarchan conventions.

Thomas Campion (1567 – 1620)*

THERE IS A GARDEN IN HER FACE   1617

There is a garden in her face
Where roses and white lilies grow;
    A heav'nly paradise is that place
Wherein all pleasant fruits do flow.
    There cherries grow which none may buy   5
    Till "Cherry-ripe" themselves do cry.

Those cherries fairly do enclose
Of orient pearl a double row,
    Which when her lovely laughter shows,
They look like rose-buds filled with snow;   10
    Yet them nor° peer nor prince can buy,   *neither*
    Till "Cherry-ripe" themselves do cry.

Her eyes like angels watch them still;
Her brows like bended bows do stand,
    Threat'ning with piercing frowns to kill   15
All that attempt, with eye or hand
    Those sacred cherries to come nigh
    Till "Cherry-ripe" themselves do cry.

THERE IS A GARDEN IN HER FACE. 6 *"Cherry-ripe"*: cry of fruit-peddlers in London streets.

QUESTIONS

1. What does Campion's song owe to Petrarchan tradition?
2. What in it strikes you as fresh observation of actual life?
3. Comment in particular on the last stanza. Does the comparison of eyebrows to threatening bowmen seem too silly or far-fetched? What sense do you find in it?
4. Try to describe the tone of this poem. What do you understand, from this portrait of a young girl, to be the poet's feelings?

Excellent poetry might be easier to recognize if each poet had a fixed position on the slopes of Mount Parnassus, but from one century to the next, the reputations of some poets have taken humiliating slides, or made impressive clambers. We decide for ourselves which poems to call excellent, but readers of the future may reverse our opinions. Most of us no longer would share this popular view of Walt Whitman by one of his contemporaries:

> Walt Whitman (1819 – 1892), by some regarded as a great poet; by others, as no poet at all. Most of his so-called poems are mere catalogues of things, without meter or rime, but in a few more regular poems and in lines here and there he is grandly poetical, as in "O Captain! My Captain!"[1]

Walt Whitman (1819 – 1892)*

O Captain! My Captain!   1865

O Captain! my Captain! our fearful trip is done,
The ship has weather'd every rack, the prize we sought is won,
The port is near, the bells I hear, the people all exulting,
While follow eyes the steady keel, the vessel grim and daring;
    But O heart! heart! heart!   5
      O the bleeding drops of red,
        Where on the deck my Captain lies,
        Fallen cold and dead.

O Captain! my Captain! rise up and hear the bells;
Rise up — for you the flag is flung — for you the bugle trills,   10
For you bouquets and ribbon'd wreaths — for you the shores
    a-crowding,
For you they call, the swaying mass, their eager faces turning;
    Here Captain! dear father!
      This arm beneath your head!
      It is some dream that on the deck,   15
        You've fallen cold and dead.

My Captain does not answer, his lips are pale and still,
My father does not feel my arm, he has no pulse nor will,
The ship is anchor'd safe and sound, its voyage closed and done,
From fearful trip the victor ship comes in with object won;   20
    Exult O shores, and ring O bells!
      But I with mournful tread,
        Walk the deck my Captain lies,
        Fallen cold and dead.

O CAPTAIN! MY CAPTAIN! Written soon after the death of Abraham Lincoln, this was, in Whitman's lifetime, by far the most popular of his poems.

[1]J. Willis Westlake, A.M., in Common-school Literature, English and American, with Several Hundred Extracts to be Memorized (Philadelphia, 1898).

1. Compare this with other Whitman poems. (See another elegy for Lincoln, "When Lilacs Last in the Dooryard Bloom'd.") In what ways is "O Captain! My Captain!" uncharacteristic of his works? Do you agree with J. Willis Westlake that this is one of the few occasions on which Whitman is "grandly poetical?"
2. Comment on the appropriateness to its subject of the poem's rhythms.
3. Do you find any evidence in this poem that an excellent poet wrote it?

There is nothing to do but commit ourselves and praise or blame and, if need be, let time erase our error. In a sense, all readers of poetry are constantly reexamining the judgments of the past by choosing those poems they care to go on reading. In the end, we have to admit that the critical principles set forth in this chapter are all very well for admiring excellent poetry we already know, but they cannot be carried like a yardstick in the hand, to go out looking for it. As Ezra Pound said in his *ABC of Reading*, "A classic is classic not because it conforms to certain structural rules, or fits certain definitions (of which its author had quite probably never heard). It is classic because of a certain eternal and irrepressible freshness."

The best poems, like "Sailing to Byzantium," may offer a kind of religious experience. In the last decade of the twentieth century, some of us rarely set foot outside an artificial environment. Whizzing down four-lane superhighways, we observe lakes and trees in the distance. In a way our cities are to us as anthills are to ants: no less than anthills, they are "natural" structures. But the "unnatural" world of school or business is, as Wordsworth says, too much with us. Locked in the shells of our ambitions, our self-esteem, we forget our kinship to earth and sea. We fabricate self-justifications. But a great poem shocks us into another order of perception. It points beyond language to something still more essential. It ushers us into an experience so moving and true that we feel (to quote King Lear) "cut to the brain." In bad or indifferent poetry, words are all there is.

Carl Sandburg (1878 – 1967)

FOG   1916

The fog comes
on little cat feet.
It sits looking
over harbor and city
on silent haunches
and then moves on.

QUESTION

In lines 15–22 of "The Love Song of J. Alfred Prufrock" (page 310), T.S. Eliot also likens fog to a cat. Compare Sandburg's lines and Eliot's. Which passage tells us more about fogs and cats?

Thomas Gray (1716 – 1771)*

ELEGY WRITTEN IN A COUNTRY CHURCHYARD   1753

The curfew tolls the knell of parting day,
   The lowing herd wind slowly o'er the lea,
The plowman homeward plods his weary way,
   And leaves the world to darkness and to me.

Now fades the glimmering landscape on the sight,   5
   And all the air a solemn stillness holds,
Save where the beetle wheels his droning flight,
   And drowsy tinklings lull the distant folds;

Save that from yonder ivy-mantled tower
   The moping owl does to the moon complain   10
Of such, as wand'ring near her secret bower,
   Molest her ancient solitary reign.

Beneath those rugged elms, that yew tree's shade,
   Where heaves the turf in many a mold'ring heap,
Each in his narrow cell forever laid,   15
   The rude° forefathers of the hamlet sleep.   *simple, ignorant*

The breezy call of incense-breathing morn,
   The swallow twitt'ring from the straw-built shed,
The cock's shrill clarion, or the echoing horn°,   *fox-hunters' horn*
   No more shall rouse them from their lowly bed.   20

For them no more the blazing hearth shall burn,
   Or busy housewife ply her evening care;
No children run to lisp their sire's return,
   Or climb his knees the envied kiss to share.

Oft did the harvest to their sickle yield,   25
   Their furrow oft the stubborn glebe° has broke;   *turf*
How jocund did they drive their team afield!
   How bowed the woods beneath their sturdy stroke!

Let not Ambition mock their useful toil,
   Their homely joys, and destiny obscure;   30
Nor Grandeur hear with a disdainful smile
   The short and simple annals of the poor.

The boast of heraldry°, the pomp of pow'r,   *noble birth*
   And all that beauty, all that wealth e'er gave,
Awaits alike th' inevitable hour.   35
   The paths of glory lead but to the grave.

ELEGY WRITTEN IN A COUNTRY CHURCHYARD. In English poetry, an **elegy** has come to mean a lament or a sadly meditative poem, sometimes written on the occasion of a death. Other elegies in this book include Chidiock Tichborne's "Elegy," Milton's "Lycidas," A. E. Housman's "To an Athlete Dying Young," and in more recent poetry, "The Rites for Cousin Vit" by Gwendolyn Brooks and "Elegy for Jane" by Theodore Roethke.

Nor you, ye proud, impute to these the fault,
    If Mem'ry o'er their tomb no trophies raise,
Where through the long-drawn aisle and fretted° vault   *inlaid with designs*
    The pealing anthem swells the note of praise.   40

Can storied urn or animated bust
    Back to its mansion call the fleeting breath?
Can Honor's voice provoke the silent dust,
    Or Flatt'ry soothe the dull cold ear of Death?

Perhaps in this neglected spot is laid   45
    Some heart once pregnant with celestial fire;
Hands that the rod of empire might have swayed,
    Or waked to ecstasy the living lyre.

But knowledge to their eyes her ample page
    Rich with the spoils of time did ne'er unroll;   50
Chill Penury° repressed their noble rage,   *Poverty*
    And froze the genial current of the soul.

Full many a gem of purest ray serene,
    The dark unfathomed caves of ocean bear:
Full many a flower is born to blush unseen,   55
    And waste its sweetness on the desert air.

Some village Hampden, that with dauntless breast
    The little tyrant of his field withstood;
Some mute inglorious Milton here may rest,
    Some Cromwell, guiltless of his country's blood.   60

Th' applause of list'ning senates to command,
    The threats of pain and ruin to despise,
To scatter plenty o'er a smiling land,
    And read their hist'ry in a nation's eyes,

Their lot forbade; nor circumscribed alone   65
    Their growing virtues, but their crimes confined;
Forbade to wade through slaughter to a throne,
    And shut the gates of mercy on mankind,

The struggling pangs of conscious truth to hide,
    To quench the blushes of ingenuous° shame,   *innocent*   70
Or heap the shrine of Luxury and Pride
    With incense kindled at the Muse's flame.

41 *storied urn:* vessel holding the ashes of the dead after cremation. *Storied* can mean (1) decorated with scenes; (2) inscribed with a life's story; or (3) celebrated in story or history. The *animated bust* is a lifelike sculpture of the dead, placed on a tomb. 57 *Hampden:* John Hampden (1594 – 1643), member of Parliament, had resisted illegal taxes on his lands imposed by Charles I. 60 *Cromwell . . . his country's blood:* Gray blames Oliver Cromwell (1599 – 1658) for strife and tyranny. As general of the armies of Parliament, Cromwell had won the Civil War against Charles I and had signed the king's death warrant. As Lord Protector of England (1653 – 1658), he had ruled with an iron hand. 71 – 72 *heap the shrine . . . Muse's flame:* Gray chides mercenary poets who write poems to please their rich, high-living patrons.

Far from the madding° crowd's ignoble strife,   *frenzied*
    Their sober wishes never learned to stray;
Along the cool sequestered vale of life   75
    They kept the noiseless tenor° of their way.   *ongoing motion*

Yet ev'n these bones from insult to protect
    Some frail memorial still erected nigh,
With uncouth rhymes and shapeless sculpture decked,
    Implores the passing tribute of a sigh.   80

Their name, their years, spelt by th' unlettered Muse,
    The place of fame and elegy supply:
And many a holy text around she strews,
    That teach the rustic moralist to die.

For who to dumb Forgetfulness a prey,   85
    This pleasing anxious being e'er resigned,
Left the warm precincts of the cheerful day,
    Nor cast one longing ling'ring look behind?

On some fond breast the parting soul relies,
    Some pious drops the closing eye requires;   90
Ev'n from the tomb the voice of Nature cries,
    Ev'n in our ashes live their wonted° fires.   *customary*

For thee, who mindful of th' unhonored dead
    Dost in these lines their artless tale relate;
If chance°, by lonely contemplation led,   *if by chance* 95
    Some kindred spirit shall inquire thy fate,

Haply° some hoary-headed swain° may say,   *perhaps; gray-haired shepherd*
    "Oft have we seen him at the peep of dawn
Brushing with hasty steps the dews away
    To meet the sun upon the upland lawn.   100

"There at the foot of yonder nodding beech
    That wreathes its old fantastic roots so high,
His listless length at noontide would he stretch,
    And pore upon the brook that babbles by.

"Hard by yon wood, now smiling as in scorn,   105
    Mutt'ring his wayward fancies he would rove,
Now drooping, woeful wan, like one forlorn,
    Or crazed with care, or crossed in hopeless love.

"One morn I missed him, on the customed hill,
    Along the heath and near his fav'rite tree;   110
Another came; not yet beside the rill°,   *brook*
    Nor up the lawn, nor at the wood was he;

"The next with dirges due in sad array
  Slow through the churchway path we saw him borne.
Approach and read (for thou canst read) the lay°,   *song or poem* 115
  Graved on the stone beneath yon aged thorn."

The Epitaph

Here rests his head upon the lap of Earth
  A youth to Fortune and to Fame unknown.
Fair Science° frowned not on his humble birth,   *Knowledge*
  And Melancholy marked him for her own.   120

Large was his bounty, and his soul sincere,
  Heav'n did a recompense as largely send:
He gave to Mis'ry all he had, a tear,
  He gained from Heav'n ('twas all he wished) a friend.

No farther seek his merits to disclose,   125
  Or draw his frailties from their dread abode,
(There they alike in trembling hope repose),
  The bosom of His Father and his God.

QUESTIONS

1. In contrasting the unknown poor buried in this village churchyard and famous men buried in cathedrals (in *fretted vault*, line 39), what is Gray's theme? What do you understand from the line, *The paths of glory lead but to the grave?*

2. Carl J. Weber thinks that Gray's compassion for the village poor anticipates the democratic sympathies of the American Revolution: "Thomas Gray is the pioneer literary spokesman for the Ordinary Man." But another critic, Lyle Glazier, argues that the "Elegy" isn't political at all: that we misread if we think the poet meant "to persuade the poor and obscure that their barren lives are meaningful"; and also misread if we think he meant to assure the privileged classes "in whose ranks Gray was proud to consider himself" that they need not worry about the poor, "who have already all essential riches." How much truth do you find in either of these views?

3. Cite lines and phrases that show Gray's concern for the musical qualities of words.

4. Who is the *youth* of the closing Epitaph? By *thee* (line 93) does Gray mean himself? Does he mean some fictitious poet supposedly writing the "Elegy" — the first-person speaker (line 4)? Does he mean some village stonecutter, a crude poet whose illiterate Muse (line 81) inspired him to compose tombstone epitaphs? Or could the Epitaph possibly refer to Gray's close friend of school and undergraduate days, the promising poet Richard West, who had died in 1742? Which interpretation seems to you the most reasonable? (Does our lack of absolute certainty negate the value of the poem?)

5. Walter Savage Landor called the Epitaph a tin kettle tied to the tail of a noble dog. Do you agree that the Epitaph is inferior to what has gone before it? What is its function in Gray's poem?

6. Many sources for Gray's phrases and motifs have been found in earlier poets: Virgil, Horace, Dante, Milton, and many more. Even if it could be demonstrated that

Gray's poem has not one original line in it, would it be possible to dismiss the "Elegy" as a mere rag-bag of borrowings?

7. Gray's poem, a pastoral elegy, is in the same genre as another famous English poem: John Milton's "Lycidas." What conventions are common to both?

8. In the earliest surviving manuscript of Gray's poem, lines 73 – 76 read:

No more with Reason and thyself at strife;
Give anxious cares and endless wishes room
But through the cool sequester'd vale of Life
Pursue the silent tenor of thy doom.

In what ways does the final version of those lines seem superior?

9. Perhaps the best-known poem in English, Gray's "Elegy" has inspired hundreds of imitations, countless parodies, and translations into eighteen or more languages. (Some of these languages contain dozens of attempts to translate it.) To what do you attribute the poem's fame? What do you suppose has proved so universally appealing in it?

10. Compare Gray's "Elegy" with Shelley's "Ozymandias" and Arthur Guiterman's "On the Vanity of Earthly Greatness." What do the three poems have in common? How would you rank them in order of excellence?

EXERCISE: *Evaluating the Unfamiliar*

In this exercise you will read work by two American poets who differ in many ways. At present, they are seldom included in literature textbooks and anthologies. For each, you will find not one but three short poems, to give you a deeper sense of their work than a lone poem might supply. (Brief biographies for these poets appear in the Lives of the Poets section, but before you look at their facts, read the poems.)

Read the poems carefully and make your own personal, tentative evaluation of the poet's work—what you now know of it. Here are some questions you might ask yourself (taking the poets one at a time):

Do these poems at all engage your sympathies? Do they stir you and touch your feelings?

What, if anything, might make them memorable? Do they have any vivid images? Any metaphors, understatement, overstatement, or other figures of speech? Do these poems appeal to the ear?

What are the poets saying? Do they tell you anything?

Do the poems exhibit any wild incompetence such as you found in William McGonagall's "Albion Battleship Calamity"? Do you find any forced rimes, inappropriate words, or other unintentionally comic features? Can the poems be accused of bathos or sentimentality, or do you trust the poet to report honest feelings?

How well does the poet seem in control of language? Does the poet's language reflect in any detail the physical world we know?

Do these poems seem entirely drawn from other poetry of the past, or do you have a sense that the poet is thinking and feeling on her (or his) own? Does the poet show any evidence of having read other poets' poetry?

Try setting these poems side by side with any similar poems you know and admire. (You might try, for instance, comparing Lorine Niedecker's work with that of William Carlos Williams, or James Hayford's with that of Robert Frost.) Are they fit to be seen in the same company?

Are these poems sufficiently rich and interesting to repay more than one reading?

What do you suppose the poet is trying to do? How successful is the attempt, in your opinion?

Do you or don't you think this poet's work deserving of a larger audience?

Lorine Niedecker

Lorine Niedecker (1903 – 1970)*

POPCORN-CAN COVER   (c. 1959)

Popcorn-can cover
screwed to the wall
over a hole
     so the cold
can't mouse in   5

Lorine Niedecker (1903–1970)*

I TAKE IT SLOW   (c. 1950)

I take it slow
  alone the river
wild sunflowers
  over my head
the dead   5
  who gave me life
give me this
  our relative the air
floods
  our rich friend   10
silt

Lorine Niedecker (1903 – 1970)*

SORROW MOVES IN WIDE WAVES   (c. 1950)

Sorrow moves in wide waves,
    it passes, lets us be.
It uses us, we use it,
    it's blind while we see.

Consciousness is illimitable,   5
    too good to forsake
tho what we feel be misery
    and we know will break.

Old Mother turns blue and from us,
    "Don't let my head drop to the earth.   10
I'm blind and deaf." Death from the heart,
    a thimble in her purse.

"It's a long day since last night.
    Give me space. I need
floors. Wash the floors, Lorine!   15
    Wash clothes! Weed!"

James Hayford (b. 1913)

BEHIND THE WALL   1983

What shall we find behind this wall,
Only the room next door?
I never went in from here before.
Better stand by in case I call—

In case when I pry off this lath   5
We find a sealed staircase
Or someone's secret burial place,
Or even a charmed garden path—

A pocket of old night is all.
Wait; what's this down in the dark?   10
A carpenter's hammer old as the ark—
The hand long dead that let you fall.

James Hayford

James Hayford (b. 1913)

UNDER THE HOLY EYE   1983

The world and I when young
And backward and content
Were visible among
The several bodies hung
About the firmament   5

Under the holy eye.
Though we all strove alone,
Some cloistered behind stone,
Some under the wide sky,
Our struggles yet were known,   10

Our Bibles still were true.
Then everything proved vast,
And numerous, and fast,
And, Father, either you
Or we flew out of view.   15

James Hayford (b. 1913)

DRY NOON   1983

Their low house nooning in the maple shade,
The pair inside remember having hayed.

The day today is dry and very fine—
Good haying weather, he has said, yes sir—
He who will hay no more, come rain or shine.   5

In all the valley, not a breeze to stir
The old man's breeches drying on the line.

SUGGESTIONS FOR WRITING

1. Write your brief evaluation of the poems of Lorine Niedecker, or those of James Hayford.
2. Concoct the worst poem you can write and, in a brief accompanying essay, recount the difficulties you met and overcame in writing it. Quote, for instance, any lines you thought of but had to discard for not being bad enough.
3. In the Anthology: Poetry that begins on page 277, find a poem you especially admire, or dislike. In a brief essay (300 – 500 words), evaluate it. Refer to particulars in the poem to support your opinion of it.

16 *What Is Poetry?*

Robert Francis (1901 – 1987)

CATCH   1950

Two boys uncoached are tossing a poem together,
Overhand, underhand, backhand, sleight of hand, every hand,
Teasing with attitudes, latitudes, interludes, altitudes,
High, make him fly off the ground for it, low, make him stoop,
Make him scoop it up, make him as-almost-as-possible miss it,   5
Fast, let him sting from it, now, now fool him slowly,
Anything, everything tricky, risky, nonchalant,
Anything under the sun to outwit the prosy,
Over the tree and the long sweet cadence down,
Over his head, make him scramble to pick up the meaning,   10
And now, like a posy, a pretty one plump in his hands.

As Robert Francis hints in this playful poem, the pitching poet keeps the
catching reader alert by creating little difficulties. Reading some of the poems
in this book, you have probably felt like the boy or girl on the receiving end:
sometimes having to work to make the catch, once in a while encountering a
poem that lands with an easy *plump* right in the middle of your understanding.

What, then, is poetry? By now, perhaps, you have formed your own idea,
whether or not you can define it. Robert Frost made a try at a definition: "A
poem is an idea caught in the act of dawning." Just in case further efforts at
definition can be useful, here are a few memorable ones (including, for a second
look, some given earlier):

> the art of uniting pleasure with truth by calling imagination to the help
> of reason.
> — Samuel Johnson

the best words in the best order.
                    — Samuel Taylor Coleridge

the record of the best and happiest moments of the happiest and best minds.
                    — Percy Bysshe Shelley

musical Thought.
                    — Thomas Carlyle

at bottom a criticism of life.
                    — Matthew Arnold

If I read a book and it makes my whole body so cold no fire can ever warm me, I know that it is poetry. If I feel physically as if the top of my head were taken off, I know that it is poetry. These are the only ways I know it. Is there any other way?
                    — Emily Dickinson

speech framed . . . to be heard for its own sake and interest even over and above its interest of meaning.
                    — Gerard Manley Hopkins

a revelation in words by means of the words.
                    — Wallace Stevens

not the assertion that something is true, but the making of that truth more fully real to us.
                    — T. S. Eliot

the body of linguistic constructions that men usually refer to as poems.
                    — J. V. Cunningham

anything said in such a way, or put on the page in such a way, as to invite from the hearer or the reader a certain kind of attention.
                    — William Stafford

the clear expression of mixed feelings.
                    — W. H. Auden

A poem differs from most prose in several ways. For one, both writer and reader tend to regard it differently. The poet's attitude is something like this: I offer this piece of writing to be read not as prose but as a poem — that is, more perceptively, thoughtfully, and considerately, with more attention to sounds and connotations. This is a great deal to expect, but in return, the reader, too, has a right to certain expectations. Approaching the poem in the anticipation of out-of-the-ordinary knowledge and pleasure, the reader assumes that the poem may use certain enjoyable devices not available to prose: rime, alliteration, meter, and rhythms — definite, various, or emphatic. (The poet may not *always* decide to use these things.) The reader expects the poet to make greater use, perhaps, of resources of meaning such as figurative language, allusion, symbol, and imagery. As readers of prose we might seek no more than meaning: no more than what could be paraphrased without serious loss. Meeting any figurative language or graceful turns of word order, we think them pleasant extras. But in poetry all these "extras" matter as much as the paraphraseable content, if not more. For, when we finish reading a good poem, we cannot explain precisely to ourselves what we have experienced — without repeating, word for word, the language of the poem itself. Archibald MacLeish makes this point memorably in his "Ars Poetica":

A poem should not mean
But be.

"Poetry is to prose as dancing is to walking," remarked Paul Valéry. It is doubtful, however, that anyone can draw an immovable boundary between poetry and prose. Certain prose needs only to be arranged in lines to be seen as poetry — especially prose that conveys strong emotion in vivid, physical imagery and in terse, figurative, rhythmical language. Even in translation the words of Chief Joseph of the Nez Percé tribe, at the moment of his surrender to the U.S. Army in 1877, still move us and are memorable:

Hear me, my warriors, my heart is sick and sad:
Our chiefs are killed,
The old men all are dead,
It is cold and we have no blankets.

The little children freeze to death.

Hear me, my warriors, my heart is sick and sad:
From where the sun now stands I will fight no more forever.

It may be that a poem can point beyond words to something still more essential. Language has its limits, and probably Edgar Allan Poe was the only poet ever to claim he could always find words for whatever he wished to express. For, of all a human being can experience and imagine, words say only part. "Human speech," said Flaubert, who strove after the best of it, "is like a cracked kettle on which we hammer out tunes to make bears dance, when what we long for is the compassion of the stars."

Like Yeats's chestnut-tree in "Among School Children" (which when asked whether it is leaf, blossom, or bole, has no answer), a poem is to be seen not as a confederation of form, rime, image, metaphor, tone, and theme, but as a whole. We study a poem one element at a time because the intellect best comprehends what it can separate. But only our total attention, involving the participation of our blood and marrow, can see all elements in a poem fused, all dancing together. Yeats knew how to make poems and how to read them:

God guard me from those thoughts men think
In the mind alone;
He that sings a lasting song
Thinks in a marrow-bone.

Throughout this book, we have been working on the assumption that the patient and conscious explication of poems will sharpen unconscious perceptions. We can only hope that it will; the final test lies in whether you care to go on by yourself, reading other poems, finding in them pleasure and enlightenment. Pedagogy must have a stop; so too must the viewing of poems as if their elements fell into chapters. For the total experience of reading a poem surpasses the mind's categories. The wind in the grass, says a proverb, cannot be taken into the house.

ANTHOLOGY: POETRY

Sit a while dear son,
Here are biscuits to eat and here is milk to drink,
But as soon as you sleep and renew yourself in sweet clothes,
I kiss you with a good-by kiss and open the gates for your egress
    hence.

Long enough have you dream'd contemptible dreams,
Now I wash the gum from your eyes,
You must habit yourself to the dazzle of the light and of every
    moment of your life.

Long have you timidly waded holding a plank by the shore,
Now I will you to be a bold swimmer,
To jump off in the midst of the sea, rise again, nod to me, shout, and
    laughingly dash with your hair.
            — Walt Whitman, "Song of Myself"

EDWARD

"Why dois your brand° sae° drap wi' bluid,   *sword; so*
  Edward, Edward?
Why dois your brand sae drap wi' bluid?
 And why sae sad gang° yee, O?"   *go*
"O, I hae killed my hauke sae guid,   5
  Mither, mither,
O, I hae killed my hauke sae guid,
 And I had nae mair bot° hee, O."   *but*

"Your haukis bluid was nevir sae reid
  Edward, Edward,   10
Your haukis bluid was nevir sae reid,
 My deir son I tell thee, O."
"O, I hae killed my reid-roan steid,
  Mither, mither,
O, I hae killed my reid-roan steid,   15
 That erst° was sa fair and frie°, O."   *once; free*

"Your steid was auld, and ye hae gat mair,
  Edward, Edward,
Your steid was auld, and ye hae gat mair,
 Sum other dule° ye drie°, O."   *sorrow; suffer* 20
"O, I hae killed my fadir deir,
  Mither, mither,
O, I hae killed my fadir deir,
 Alas, and wae° is mee, O!"   *woe*

"And whatten penance wul ye drie for that,   25
  Edward, Edward?
And whatten penance will ye drie for that?
 My deir son, now tell me, O."
"Ile set my feit in yonder boat,
  Mither, mither,   30
Ile set my feit in yonder boat,
 And Ile fare ovir the sea, O."

"And what wul ye doe wi' your towirs and your ha'°, *hall*
  Edward, Edward,
And what wul ye doe wi' your towirs and your ha', 35
 That were sae fair to see, O?"
"Ile let thame stand tul they doun fa',
  Mither, mither,
Ile let thame stand tul they doun fa',
 For here nevir mair maun° I bee, O."   *must* 40

"And what wul ye leive to your bairns° and your wife,   *children*
    Edward, Edward?
And what wul ye leive to your bairns and your wife,
    When ye gang ovir the sea, O?"
"The warldis° room, late° them beg thrae° life,   *world's; let; through*   45
    Mither, mither
The warldis room, late them beg thrae life,
    For thame nevir mair wul I see, O."

"And what wul ye leive to your ain° mither deir,   *own*
    Edward, Edward?   50
And what wul ye leive to your ain mither deir?
    My deir son, now tell me, O."
"The curse of hell frae me sall ye beir,
    Mither, mither,
The curse of hell frae me sall ye beir,   55
    Sic° counseils° ye gave to me, O."   *such; counsel*

COMPARE:

"Edward" with a modern ballad such as "Ballad of Birmingham" by Dudley Randall
(page 119).

Anonymous (traditional English ballad)

THE THREE RAVENS

There were three ravens sat on a tree,
    Down a down, hay down, hay down,
There were three ravens sat on a tree,
    With a down,
There were three ravens sat on a tree,   5
They were as black as they might be.
    With a down derry, derry, derry, down, down.

The one of them said to his mate,
"Where shall we our breakfast take?"

"Down in yonder greene field,   10
There lies a knight slain under his shield.

"His hounds they lie down at his feet,
So well they can their master keep.

"His hawks they fly so eagerly,
There's no fowl dare him come nigh."   15

Down there comes a fallow doe,
As great with young as she might go.

She lift up his bloody head,
And kist his wounds that were so red.

She got him up upon her back,   20
And carried him to earthen lake°.   *the grave*

She buried him before the prime,
She was dead herself ere evensong time.

God send every gentleman
Such hawks, such hounds, and such a leman°.   *lover* 25

THE THREE RAVENS. The lines of refrain are repeated in each stanza. "Perhaps in the folk mind the doe is the form the soul of a human mistress, now dead, has taken," Albert B. Friedman has suggested (in *The Viking Book of Folk Ballads*). "Most probably the knight's beloved was understood to be an enchanted woman who was metamorphosed at certain times into an animal." 22 – 23 *prime, evensong:* two of the canonical hours set aside for prayer and worship. Prime is at dawn, evensong at dusk.

Anonymous (traditional Scottish ballad)

THE TWA CORBIES

As I was walking all alane,
I heard twa corbies° making a mane°;   *ravens; moan*
The tane° unto the t'other say,   *one*
"Where sall we gang° and dine today?"   *go*

"In behint yon auld fail dyke°,   *turf wall* 5
I wot° there lies a new slain knight;   *know*
And naebody kens° that he lies there,   *knows*
But his hawk, his hound, and lady fair.

"His hound is to the hunting gane,
His hawk to fetch the wild-fowl hame,   10
His lady's ta'en another mate,
So we may mak our dinner sweet.

"Ye'll sit on his white hause-bane°,   *neck bone*
And I'll pike out his bonny blue een;
Wi' ae° lock o' his gowden hair   *one* 15
We'll theek° our nest when it grows bare.   *thatch*

"Mony a one for him makes mane,
But nane sall ken where he is gane;
O'er his white banes, when they are bare,
The wind sall blaw for evermair."   20

THE TWA CORBIES. Sir Walter Scott, the first to print this ballad in his *Minstrelsy of the Scottish Border* (1802 – 1803), calls it "rather a counterpart than a copy" of "The Three Ravens." M. J. C. Hodgart and other scholars think he may have written most of it himself.

Anonymous (English lyric)

SUMER IS ICUMEN IN   (thirteenth century)

Sumer is icumen in	Summer is acoming in —
Lhude sing cuccu	Loudly sing, cuckoo!
Groweþ sed and bloweþ med	Groweth seed and bloweth mead
and springþ þe wde nu	And springeth the wood new.
Sing cuccu	Sing, cuckoo! 5
Awe bleteþ after lomb	Ewe bleateth after lamb,
Ihouþ after calue cu	Loweth after calf cow,
Bulluc sterteþ bucke uerteþ	Bullock starteth, buck farteth —
Murie sing cuccu	Merrily sing, cuckoo!
Cuccu cuccu	Cuckoo, cuckoo, 10
Wel singes þu cuccu	Well singest thou, cuckoo!
ne swik þu nauer nu	Cease thou never now.
Sing cuccu nu Sing cuccu	Sing, cuckoo now! Sing, cuckoo!
Sing cuccu Sing cuccu nu	Sing, cuckoo! Sing, cuckoo, now!

SUMER IS ICUMEN IN. On the left, this famous song is printed as it appears in a thirteenth-century manuscript: a commonplace book, or book of songs and obituaries set down by various monks at Reading Abbey (Harley manuscript 978, now in the British Museum). On the right, words and spellings have been modernized and punctuation added, but word-order kept unaltered. In the opening line, *acoming* is not quite a faithful translation: *is icumen* means "has come." Summer is already here. The character þ is called a *thorn*, and is pronounced like the spelling *th*. 8 *starteth:* starts, jumps up and runs.

Anonymous (English lyric)

I SING OF A MAIDEN   (fifteenth century)

I sing of a maiden	that is makeless°,	*matchless (or mateless)*
King of alle kinges	to° her son che ches°.	*to be; she chose*
He cam all so stille	there° his moder was	*where*
As dew in Aprille	that falleth on the grass.	

| He cam all so stille | to his moderes bower | | 5 |
| As dew in Aprille | that falleth on the flower. | | |

He cam all so stille   there his moder lay
As dew in Aprille   that falleth on the spray.

Moder and maiden   was never none but she —
Well may swich° a lady   Godes moder be.   *such*   10

I SING OF A MAIDEN. To keep the rhythm, pronounce the final *e* in *alle, stille,* and *Aprille* like *e* in *the*. 5 *bower:* dwelling place, room, or bedchamber.

Anonymous (English lyric)

WESTERN WIND   (about 1500)

Western wind, when wilt thou blow,
The° small rain down can rain?   *(so that) the*
Christ, if my love were in my arms,
And I in my bed again!

COMPARE:

"Western Wind" with "Wedding-Wind" by Philip Larkin (page 20).

Matthew Arnold (1822 – 1888)

DOVER BEACH   1867

The sea is calm tonight.
The tide is full, the moon lies fair
Upon the straits; — on the French coast the light
Gleams and is gone; the cliffs of England stand,
Glimmering and vast, out in the tranquil bay.   5
Come to the window, sweet is the night-air!
Only, from the long line of spray
Where the sea meets the moon-blanched land,
Listen! you hear the grating roar
Of pebbles which the waves draw back, and fling,   10
At their return, up the high strand,
Begin, and cease, and then again begin,
With tremulous cadence slow, and bring
The eternal note of sadness in.

Sophocles long ago 15
Heard it on the Aegean, and it brought
Into his mind the turbid ebb and flow
Of human misery; we
Find also in the sound a thought,
Hearing it by this distant northern sea. 20

The Sea of Faith
Was once, too, at the full, and round earth's shore
Lay like the folds of a bright girdle furled.
But now I only hear
Its melancholy, long, withdrawing roar, 25
Retreating, to the breath
Of the night-wind, down the vast edges drear
And naked shingles° of the world. *gravel beaches*

Ah, love, let us be true
To one another! for the world, which seems 30
To lie before us like a land of dreams,
So various, so beautiful, so new,
Hath really neither joy, nor love, nor light,
Nor certitude, nor peace, nor help for pain;
And we are here as on a darkling° plain *darkened or darkening* 35
Swept with confused alarms of struggle and flight,
Where ignorant armies clash by night.

John Ashbery (b. 1927)*

AT NORTH FARM 1984

Somewhere someone is traveling furiously toward you,
At incredible speed, traveling day and night,
Through blizzards and desert heat, across torrents, through narrow
    passes.
But will he know where to find you,
Recognize you when he sees you, 5
Give you the thing he has for you?

Hardly anything grows here,
Yet the granaries are bursting with meal,
The sacks of meal piled to the rafters.
The streams run with sweetness, fattening fish; 10
Birds darken the sky. Is it enough
That the dish of milk is set out at night,
That we think of him sometimes,
Sometimes and always, with mixed feelings?

Margaret Atwood

Margaret Atwood (b. 1939)*

ALL BREAD   1978

All bread is made of wood,
cow dung, packed brown moss,
the bodies of dead animals, the teeth
and backbones, what is left
after the ravens. This dirt   5
flows through the stems into the grain,
into the arm, nine strokes
of the axe, skin from a tree,
good water which is the first
gift, four hours.   10

Live burial under a moist cloth,
a silver dish, the row
of white famine bellies
swollen and taut in the oven,
lungfuls of warm breath stopped   15
in the heat from an old sun.

Good bread has the salt taste
of your hands after nine
strokes of the axe, the salt
taste of your mouth, it smells   20
of its own small death, of the deaths
before and after.

Lift these ashes
into your mouth, your blood;
to know what you devour   25
is to consecrate it,
almost. All bread must be broken
so it can be shared. Together
we eat this earth.

W. H. Auden

W. H. Auden (1907 – 1973)*

As I Walked Out One Evening   1940

As I walked out one evening,
   Walking down Bristol Street,
The crowds upon the pavement
   Were fields of harvest wheat.

And down by the brimming river   5
   I heard a lover sing
Under an arch of the railway:
   "Love has no ending.

"I'll love you, dear, I'll love you
   Till China and Africa meet,   10
And the river jumps over the mountain
   And the salmon sing in the street,

"I'll love you till the ocean
   Is folded and hung up to dry
And the seven stars go squawking   15
   Like geese about the sky.

"The years shall run like rabbits,
   For in my arms I hold
The Flower of the Ages,
   And the first love of the world."   20

But all the clocks in the city
    Began to whirr and chime:
"O let not Time deceive you,
    You cannot conquer Time.

"In the burrows of the Nightmare   25
    Where Justice naked is,
Time watches from the shadow
    And coughs when you would kiss.

"In headaches and in worry
    Vaguely life leaks away,   30
And Time will have his fancy
    Tomorrow or today.

"Into many a green valley
    Drifts the appalling snow;
Time breaks the threaded dances   35
    And the diver's brilliant bow.

"O plunge your hands in water,
    Plunge them in up to the wrist;
Stare, stare in the basin
    And wonder what you've missed.   40

"The glacier knocks in the cupboard,
    The desert sighs in the bed,
And the crack in the teacup opens
    A lane to the land of the dead.

"Where the beggars raffle the banknotes   45
    And the Giant is enchanting to Jack,
And the Lily-white Boy is a Roarer,
    And Jill goes down on her back.

"O look, look in the mirror,
    O look in your distress;   50
Life remains a blessing
    Although you cannot bless.

"O stand, stand at the window
    As the tears scald and start;
You shall love your crooked neighbor   55
    With your crooked heart."

It was late, late in the evening,
    The lovers they were gone;
The clocks had ceased their chiming,
    And the deep river ran on.   60

"The Fall of Icarus" by Pieter Breughel (1520? – 1569)

W. H. Auden (1907 – 1973)*

Musée des Beaux Arts   1940

About suffering they were never wrong,
The Old Masters: how well they understood
Its human position; how it takes place
While someone else is eating or opening a window or just walking
    dully along;
How, when the aged are reverently, passionately waiting   5
For the miraculous birth, there always must be
Children who did not specially want it to happen, skating
On a pond at the edge of the wood:
They never forgot
That even the dreadful martyrdom must run its course   10
Anyhow in a corner, some untidy spot
Where the dogs go on with their doggy life and the torturer's horse
Scratches its innocent behind on a tree.

In Brueghel's *Icarus,* for instance: how everything turns away
Quite leisurely from the disaster; the ploughman may   15
Have heard the splash, the forsaken cry,
But for him it was not an important failure; the sun shone
As it had to on the white legs disappearing into the green
Water; and the expensive delicate ship that must have seen
Something amazing, a boy falling out of the sky,   20
Had somewhere to get to and sailed calmly on.

COMPARE:

"Musée des Beaux Arts" with "The Dance" by William Carlos Williams (page 185) and
the painting by Pieter Breughel to which each poem refers.

Jimmy Santiago Baca (b. 1952)

SPLICED WIRE   1982

I filled your house with light.
There was warmth in all corners
of the house. My words I gave you
like soft warm toast in early morning.
I brewed your tongue   5
to a rich dark coffee, and drank
my fill. I turned on the music for you,
playing notes along the crest
of your heart, like birds,
eagles, ravens, owls on rim of red canyon,   10

I brought reception clear to you,
and made the phone ring at your request,
from Paris or South America,
you could talk to any of the people,
as my words gave them life,   15
from a child in a boat with his father,
to a prisoner in a concentration camp,
all at your bedside.

And then you turned away, wanted
a larger mansion. I said no. I left you.   20
The plug pulled out, the house blinked out,
Into a quiet darkness, swallowing wind,
collecting autumn leaves like stamps
between its old boards where they stick.

You say, or carry the thought with you   25
to comfort you, that faraway somewhere,
lightning knocked down all the power lines.
But no my love, it was I,

pulling the plug. Others will come, plug in,
but often the lights will dim weakly   30
in storms, the music stop to a drawl,
the warmth shredded by cold drafts.

R. L. Barth (b. 1947)*

THE INSERT   1981

Our view of sky, jungle, and fields constricts
Into a sink hole covered with sawgrass

Undulating, soon whipped slant as the chopper
Hovers at four feet. Rapt, boot-deep in slime,

We deploy ourselves in a loose perimeter,   5
Listening for incoming rockets above

The thump of rotor blades; edgy for contact,
Junkies of terror impatient to shoot up.

Nothing moves, nothing sounds: then, single file,
We move across a streambed toward high ground.   10

The terror of the insert's quickly over.
Too quickly . . . and more quickly every time . . .

THE INSERT. R. L. Barth, a U.S. Marine in 1966 – 69, served as a long-range reconnaissance leader
in Vietnam. An *insert* is the dropping of troops into an area by helicopter.

COMPARE:

"The Insert" with the poems of Wilfred Owen: "Dulce et Decorum Est" (page 32) and
"Anthem for Doomed Youth" (page 358).

Elizabeth Bishop (1911 – 1979)*

FILLING STATION   1965

Oh, but it is dirty!
— this little filling station,
oil-soaked, oil-permeated
to a disturbing, over-all
black translucency.   5
Be careful with that match!

Father wears a dirty,
oil-soaked monkey suit
that cuts him under the arms,
and several quick and saucy   10
and greasy sons assist him
(it's a family filling station),
all quite thoroughly dirty.

Do they live in the station?
It has a cement porch
behind the pumps, and on it
a set of crushed and grease-
impregnated wickerwork;
on the wicker sofa
a dirty dog, quite comfy.

Some comic books provide
the only note of color —
of certain color. They lie
upon a big dim doily
draping a taboret
(part of the set), beside
a big hirsute begonia.

Why the extraneous plant?
Why the taboret?
Why, oh why, the doily?
(Embroidered in daisy stitch
with marguerites, I think,
and heavy with gray crochet.)

Somebody embroidered the doily.
Somebody waters the plant,
or oils it, maybe. Somebody
arranges the rows of cans
so that they softly say:
ESSO — SO — SO — SO
to high-strung automobiles.
Somebody loves us all.

COMPARE:

"Filling Station" with "MECANIC ON DUTY AT ALL TIMES" by Miller Williams (page 397).

Elizabeth Bishop

Elizabeth Bishop (1911–1979)*

ONE ART   1976

The art of losing isn't hard to master;
so many things seem filled with the intent
to be lost that their loss is no disaster.

Lose something every day. Accept the fluster
of lost door keys, the hour badly spent.   5
The art of losing isn't hard to master.

Then practice losing farther, losing faster:
places, and names, and where it was you meant
to travel. None of these will bring disaster.

I lost my mother's watch. And look! my last, or   10
next-to-last, of three loved houses went.
The art of losing isn't hard to master.

I lost two cities, lovely ones. And, vaster,
some realms I owned, two rivers, a continent.
I miss them, but it wasn't a disaster.   15

—Even losing you (the joking voice, a gesture
I love) I shan't have lied. It's evident
the art of losing's not too hard to master
though it may look like (*Write* it!) like disaster.

COMPARE:

"One Art" with "Do not go gentle into that good night" by Dylan Thomas (page 178)
and "Sestina" by Elizabeth Bishop (page 192).

William Blake (1757 – 1827)*

THE SICK ROSE   1794

O Rose, thou art sick!
The invisible worm
That flies in the night,
In the howling storm,

Has found out thy bed   5
Of crimson joy,
And his dark secret love
Does thy life destroy.

Joseph Brodsky (b. 1940)*

BELFAST TUNE   1988

Here's a girl from a dangerous town.
   She crops her dark hair short
so that less of her has to frown
   when someone gets hurt.

She folds her memories like a parachute.   5
   Dropped, she collects the peat
and cooks her veggies at home: they shoot
   here where they eat.

Ah, there's more sky in these parts than, say,
   ground. Hence her voice's pitch,   10
and her stare stains your retina like a gray
   bulb when you switch

hemispheres, and her knee-length quilt
   skirt's cut to catch the squall.
I dream of her either loved or killed   15
   because the town's too small.

Gwendolyn Brooks (b. 1917)*

A BLACK WEDDING SONG   1981

This love is a rich cry over
the deviltries and the death.
A weapon-song. Keep it strong.

Keep it strong.
Keep it logic and magic and lightning and muscle.   5

Strong hand in strong hand, stride to
the Assault that is promised you (knowing
no armor assaults a pudding or a mush.)

Here is your Wedding Day.
Here is your launch.   10

Come to your Wedding Song.

For you
I wish the kindness that romps or sorrows along.
Or kneels.

I wish you the daily forgiveness of each other.   15
For war comes in from the World
and puzzles a darling duet—
tangles tongues,
tears hearts, mashes minds;
there will be the need to forgive.   20

I wish you jewels of Black love.
Come to your Wedding Song.

Gwendolyn Brooks (b. 1917)*

THE RITES FOR COUSIN VIT   1949

Carried her unprotesting out the door.
Kicked back the casket-stand. But it can't hold her,
That stuff and satin aiming to enfold her,
The lid's contrition nor the bolts before.
Oh oh. Too much. Too much. Even now, surmise,   5
She rises in the sunshine. There she goes,
Back to the bars she knew and the repose
In love-rooms and the things in people's eyes.
Too vital and too squeaking. Must emerge.
Even now she does the snake-hips with a hiss,   10
Slops the bad wine across her shantung, talks
Of pregnancy, guitars and bridgework, walks
In parks or alleys, comes haply on the verge
Of happiness, haply hysterics. Is.

Gwendolyn Brooks

Robert Browning (1812 – 1889)*

SOLILOQUY OF THE SPANISH CLOISTER   1842

Gr-r-r — there go, my heart's abhorrence!
    Water your damned flower-pots, do!
If hate killed men, Brother Lawrence,
    God's blood, would not mine kill you!
What? your myrtle-bush wants trimming?   5
    Oh, that rose has prior claims —
Needs its leaden vase filled brimming?
    Hell dry you up with its flames!

At the meal we sit together;
    Salve tibi!° I must hear   *Hail to thee!*   10
Wise talk of the kind of weather,
    Sort of season, time of year:
Not a plenteous cork-crop: scarcely
    Dare we hope oak-galls, I doubt;
What's the Latin name for "parsley"?   15
    What's the Greek name for "swine's snout"?

Whew! We'll have our platter burnished,
    Laid with care on our own shelf!
With a fire-new spoon we're furnished,
    And a goblet for ourself,   20
Rinsed like something sacrificial
    Ere 'tis fit to touch our chaps —
Marked with L. for our initial!
    (He-he! There his lily snaps!)

Saint, forsooth! While Brown Dolores   25
    Squats outside the Convent bank
With Sanchicha, telling stories,
    Steeping tresses in the tank,
Blue-black, lustrous, thick like horsehairs,
    — Can't I see his dead eye glow,   30
Bright as 'twere a Barbary corsair's?
    (That is, if he'd let it show!)

When he finishes refection,
    Knife and fork he never lays
Cross-wise, to my recollection,   35
    As I do, in Jesu's praise.
I the Trinity illustrate,
    Drinking watered orange-pulp —
In three sips the Arian frustrate;
    While he drains his at one gulp!   40

SOLILOQUY OF THE SPANISH CLOISTER. 3 *Brother Lawrence:* one of the speaker's fellow monks. 31 *Barbary corsair:* a pirate operating off the Barbary coast of Africa. 39 *Arian:* a follower of Arius, heretic who denied the doctrine of the Trinity.

Oh, those melons! if he's able
    We're to have a feast; so nice!
One goes to the Abbot's table,
    All of us get each a slice.
How go on your flowers? None double?   45
    Not one fruit-sort can you spy?
Strange! — And I, too, at such trouble,
    Keep them close-nipped on the sly!

There's a great text in Galatians,
    Once you trip on it, entails   50
Twenty-nine distinct damnations,
    One sure, if another fails;
If I trip him just a-dying,
    Sure of heaven as sure can be,
Spin him round and send him flying   55
    Off to hell, a Manichee?

Or, my scrofulous French novel
    On grey paper with blunt type!
Simply glance at it, you grovel
    Hand and foot in Belial's gripe;   60
If I double down its pages
    At the woeful sixteenth print,
When he gathers his greengages,
    Ope a sieve and slip it in't?

Or, there's Satan! — one might venture   65
    Pledge one's soul to him, yet leave
Such a flaw in the indenture
    As he'd miss till, past retrieve,
Blasted lay that rose-acacia
    We're so proud of! *Hy, Zy, Hine.* . . .   70
'St, there's Vespers! *Plena gratia*
    Ave, Virgo!° Gr-r-r — you swine!   *Hail, Virgin, full of grace!*

49 *a great text in Galatians:* a difficult verse in this book of the Bible. Brother Lawrence will be damned as a heretic if he wrongly interprets it. 56 *Manichee:* another kind of heretic, one who (after the Persian philosopher Mani) sees in the world a constant struggle between good and evil, neither able to win. 60 *Belial:* Here, not specifically Satan but (as used in the Old Testament) a name for wickedness. 70 *Hy, Zy, Hine:* Possibly the sound of a bell to announce evening devotions.

Thomas Carew (1594? – 1640)

ASK ME NO MORE WHERE JOVE BESTOWS   1640

Ask me no more where Jove bestows,
When June is past, the fading rose;
For in your beauty's orient deep
These flowers, as in their causes, sleep.

Ask me no more whither do stray
The golden atoms of the day;
For in pure love heaven did prepare
Those powders to enrich your hair.

Ask me no more whither doth haste
The nightingale when May is past,
For in your sweet dividing throat
She winters, and keeps warm her note.

Ask me no more where those stars light
That downwards fall in dead of night,
For in your eyes they sit, and there
Fixèd become, as in their sphere.

Ask me no more if east or west
The phoenix builds her spicy nest,
For unto you at last she flies
And in your fragrant bosom dies.

5

10

15

20

ASK ME NO MORE WHERE JOVE BESTOWS. 3 *orient:* radiant, glowing. (In our time, this sense of the word is obsolete.) 4 *These flowers . . . sleep:* as they slept before they came into existence. (A *cause*, that which gives being, is a term from Aristotle and the Scholastic philosophers.) 11 *dividing:* singing, uttering a "division" or melodic phrase added to a basic tune. 18 *phoenix:* In legend, an Arabian bird believed to subsist on incense and perfumes. It was supposed to reproduce by going up in flames, to rise again out of its ashes.

Fred Chappell (b. 1936)

SKIN FLICK   1971

The selfsame surface that billowed once with
The shapes of Trigger and Gene. New faces now
Are in the saddle. Tits and buttocks
Slide rattling down the beam as down
A coal chute; in the splotched light
The burning bush strikes dumb.
Different sort of cattle drive:
No water for miles and miles.

In the aisles, new bugs and rats
Though it's the same Old Paint.
Audience of lepers, hopeless and homeless,
Or like the buffalo, at home
In the wind only. No
Mushy love stuff for them.

They eye the violent innocence they always knew.
Is that the rancher's palomino daughter?
Is this her eastern finishing school?
Same old predicament:
No water for miles and miles,
The horizon breeds no cavalry.

Men, draw your wagons in a circle. Be ready.

5

10

15

20

G. K. Chesterton (1874 – 1936)

THE DONKEY 1900

When fishes flew and forests walked
    And figs grew upon thorn,
Some moment when the moon was blood
    Then surely I was born;

With monstrous head and sickening cry   5
    And ears like errant wings,
The devil's walking parody
    On all four-footed things.

The tattered outlaw of the earth,
    Of ancient crooked will;   10
Starve, scourge, deride me: I am dumb,
    I keep my secret still.

Fools! For I also had my hour;
    One far fierce hour and sweet:
There was a shout about my ears,   15
    And palms before my feet.

THE DONKEY. For more details of the donkey's hour of triumph see Matthew 21:1 – 8.

Samuel Taylor Coleridge (1772 – 1834)*

KUBLA KHAN (1797 – 1798)

Or, a Vision in a Dream. A Fragment.

In Xanadu did Kubla Khan
A stately pleasure-dome decree:
Where Alph, the sacred river, ran
Through caverns measureless to man
    Down to a sunless sea.   5
So twice five miles of fertile ground
With walls and towers were girdled round;
And there were gardens bright with sinuous rills,
Where blossomed many an incense-bearing tree;
And here were forests ancient as the hills,   10
Enfolding sunny spots of greenery.

But oh! that deep romantic chasm which slanted
Down the green hill athwart a cedarn cover!
A savage place! as holy and enchanted
As e'er beneath a waning moon was haunted   15
By woman wailing for her demon-lover!

And from this chasm, with ceaseless turmoil seething,
As if this earth in fast thick pants were breathing,
A mighty fountain momently was forced:
Amid whose swift half-intermitted burst   20
Huge fragments vaulted like rebounding hail,
Or chaffy grain beneath the thresher's flail:
And 'mid these dancing rocks at once and ever
It flung up momently the sacred river.
Five miles meandering with a mazy motion   25
Through wood and dale the sacred river ran,
Then reached the caverns measureless to man,
And sank in tumult to a lifeless ocean:
And 'mid this tumult Kubla heard from far
Ancestral voices prophesying war!   30

   The shadow of the dome of pleasure
   Floated midway on the waves;
   Where was heard the mingled measure
   From the fountain and the caves.
It was a miracle of rare device,   35
A sunny pleasure-dome with caves of ice!

   A damsel with a dulcimer
   In a vision once I saw:
   It was an Abyssinian maid,
   And on her dulcimer she played,   40
   Singing of Mount Abora.
   Could I revive within me
   Her symphony and song,
   To such a deep delight 'twould win me,
That with music loud and long,   45
I would build that dome in air,
That sunny dome! those caves of ice!
And all who heard should see them there,
And all should cry, Beware! Beware!
His flashing eyes, his floating hair!   50
Weave a circle round him thrice,
And close your eyes with holy dread,
For he on honey-dew hath fed,
And drunk the milk of Paradise.

KUBLA KHAN. There was an actual Kublai Khan, a thirteenth-century Mongol emperor, and a Chinese city of Xamdu; but Coleridge's dream vision also borrows from travelers' descriptions of such other exotic places as Abyssinia and America. 51 *circle:* a magic circle drawn to keep away evil spirits.

Emily Dickinson

Emily Dickinson (1830 – 1886)*

BECAUSE I COULD NOT STOP FOR DEATH   (1863)

Because I could not stop for Death –
He kindly stopped for me –
The Carriage held but just Ourselves –
And Immortality.

We slowly drove – He knew no haste   5
And I had put away
My labor and my leisure too,
For His Civility –

We passed the School, where Children strove
At Recess – in the Ring –   10
We passed the Fields of Gazing Grain –
We passed the Setting Sun –

Or rather – He passed Us –
The Dews drew quivering and chill –
For only Gossamer, my Gown –   15
My Tippet° – only Tulle –   *cape*

We paused before a House that seemed
A Swelling of the Ground –

BECAUSE I COULD NOT STOP FOR DEATH. In the version of this poem printed by Emily Dickinson's first editors in 1890, stanza four was left out. In line 9 *strove* was replaced by *played*; line 10 **was** made to read "Their lessons scarcely done".

The Roof was scarcely visible –
The Cornice – in the Ground –

Since then – 'tis Centuries – and yet
Feels shorter than the Day
I first surmised the Horses' Heads
Were toward Eternity –

20

20, "The cornice but a mound"; 21, "Since then 'tis centuries, but each"; and capitalization and punctuation were made conventional.

Emily Dickinson (1830 – 1886)*

I STARTED EARLY – TOOK MY DOG   (1862)

I started Early – Took my Dog –
And visited the Sea –
The Mermaids in the Basement
Came out to look at me –

And Frigates – in the Upper Floor   5
Extended Hempen Hands –
Presuming Me to be a Mouse –
Aground – upon the Sands –

But no Man moved Me – till the Tide
Went past my simple Shoe –   10
And past my Apron – and my Belt
And past my Bodice – too –

And made as He would eat me up –
As wholly as a Dew
Upon a Dandelion's Sleeve –   15
And then – I started – too –

And He – He followed – close behind –
I felt His Silver Heel
Upon my Ankle – Then my Shoes
Would overflow with Pearl –   20

Until We met the Solid Town –
No One He seemed to know –
And bowing – with a Mighty look –
At me – The Sea withdrew –

MY LIFE HAD STOOD – A LOADED GUN   (about 1863)

My Life had stood – a Loaded Gun –
In Corners – till a Day
The Owner passed – identified –
And carried Me away –

And now We roam in Sovreign Woods –   5
And now We hunt the Doe –
And every time I speak for Him –
The Mountains straight reply –

And do I smile, such cordial light
Upon the Valley glow –   10
It is as a Vesuvian face
Had let its pleasure through –

And when at Night – Our good Day done –
I guard My Master's Head –
'Tis better than the Eider-Duck's   15
Deep Pillow – to have shared –

To foe of His – I'm deadly foe –
None stir the second time –
On whom I lay a Yellow Eye –
Or an emphatic Thumb –   20

Though I than He – may longer live
He longer must – than I –
For I have but the power to kill,
Without – the power to die –

Deborah Digges (b. 1950)

FOR *The Daughters of Hannah Bible Class* OF TIPTON, MISSOURI'S WOMEN'S PRISON: MOTHER'S DAY, 1959   1986

I remember the gifts we brought that Sunday.
We were no one to them.
We were another woman's children.
The number of blossoms they chose from the red
carnations we'd bound with wire at the stems   5
told how many children they had.

But today, driving through Tipton,
I couldn't remember their faces.
I must have been afraid if I looked too long
I might take on the expression of the thief   10
or the murderess—I had my own sins to contend with
that bloomed in dreams like bruises,
like corsages pinned to faded identical dresses
or strapped like watches to their wrists.
We'd fan ourselves with hymnals, out of rhythm,   15
while my mother's piano played out songs of forgiveness.
The afternoon went sunblind as an old grief,
the way my small son coming from sleep now
sees the last dream above him erased.
Still, they must have felt something break   20
open inside they didn't know had sealed
each spring when the roads cleared.
For the first time in months they could hold
their children, they could lift them up
onto the prison's ageless yard toys   25
and feel their own full weight all visiting hour—
so that the evening that followed would be blessed
somehow as each one waited for sleep,
when the voices along the corridors were only echoes,
the static on guardhouse radios, their weather.   30
Once they were every young girl escaping,
driving fast past these small towns.
Here, on the sun-side the last ice lining the eaves
catches the light cleanly, and hits ground,
the sound unmistakable, or hangs on,   35
shining, through the first thaw.

John Donne (1572 – 1631)*

THE FLEA Carpe diem Poem   1633

Mark but this flea, and mark in this
How little that which thou deny'st me is;
It sucked me first, and now sucks thee,
And in this flea our two bloods mingled be;
Thou know'st that this cannot be said   5
A sin, nor shame, nor loss of maidenhead,
    Yet this enjoys before it woo,
    And pampered swells with one blood made of two,
    And this, alas, is more than we would do.

Oh stay, three lives in one flea spare,   10
Where we almost, yea more than married are.
This flea is you and I, and this
Our marriage bed, and marriage temple is;
Though parents grudge, and you, we're met
And cloistered in these living walls of jet.   15
    Though use° make you apt to kill me,   *custom*
    Let not to that, self-murder added be,
    And sacrilege, three sins in killing three.

Cruel and sudden, hast thou since
Purpled thy nail in blood of innocence?   20
Wherein could this flea guilty be,
Except in that drop it sucked from thee?
Yet thou triumph'st, and say'st that thou
Find'st not thyself, nor me, the weaker now;
    'Tis true; then learn how false, fears be;   25
    Just so much honor, when thou yield'st to me,
    Will waste, as this flea's death took life from thee.

John Donne

John Donne (1572 – 1631)*

A VALEDICTION: FORBIDDING MOURNING   (1611)

As virtuous men pass mildly away,
    And whisper to their souls to go,
Whilst some of their sad friends do say
    The breath goes now, and some say no:

So let us melt, and make no noise,   5
    No tear-floods, nor sigh-tempests move;
'Twere profanation of our joys
    To tell the laity° our love.   *common people*

Moving of th' earth° brings harms and fears;   *earthquake*
    Men reckon what it did and meant;   10
But trepidation of the spheres,
    Though greater far, is innocent°.   *harmless*

Dull sublunary lovers' love
    (Whose soul is sense) cannot admit
Absence, because it doth remove   15
    Those things which elemented° it.   *constituted*

But we, by a love so much refined
    That ourselves know not what it is,
Inter-assurèd of the mind,
    Care less, eyes, lips, and hands to miss.   20

Our two souls, therefore, which are one,
    Though I must go, endure not yet
A breach, but an expansiòn,
    Like gold to airy thinness beat.

If they be two, they are two so   25
    As stiff twin compasses are two:
Thy soul, the fixed foot, makes no show
    To move, but doth, if th' other do.

And though it in the center sit,
    Yet when the other far doth roam,   30
It leans and harkens after it,
    And grows erect as that comes home.

Such wilt thou be to me, who must,
    Like th' other foot, obliquely run;
Thy firmness makes my circle just°,   *perfect* 35
    And makes me end where I begun.

A VALEDICTION: FORBIDDING MOURNING. According to Donne's biographer Izaak Walton, Donne's wife received this poem as a gift before the poet departed on a journey to France. 11 *spheres:* In Ptolemaic astronomy, the concentric spheres surrounding the earth. The trepidation or motion of the ninth sphere was thought to change the date of the equinox. 19 *Inter-assurèd of the mind:* each sure in mind that the other is faithful. 24 *gold to airy thinness:* Gold is so malleable that, if beaten to the thickness of gold leaf (1/250,000 of one inch), one ounce of gold would cover 250 square feet.

Rita Dove (b. 1952)

DAYSTAR   1986

She wanted a little room for thinking:
but she saw diapers steaming on the line,
a doll slumped behind the door.

So she lugged a chair behind the garage
to sit out the children's naps.   5

Sometimes there were things to watch—
the pinched armor of a vanished cricket,
a floating maple leaf. Other days
she stared until she was assured
when she closed her eyes   10
she'd see only her own vivid blood.

She had an hour, at best, before Liza appeared
pouting from the top of the stairs.
And just *what* was mother doing
out back with the field mice? Why,   15

building a palace. Later
that night when Thomas rolled over and
lurched into her, she would open her eyes
and think of the place that was hers
for an hour—where   20
she was nothing,
pure nothing, in the middle of the day.

John Dryden (1631 – 1700)*

To the Memory of Mr. Oldham   1684

Farewell, too little and too lately known,
Whom I began to think and call my own;
For sure our souls were near allied, and thine
Cast in the same poetic mold with mine.
One common note on either lyre did strike,   5
And knaves and fools we both abhorred alike.
To the same goal did both our studies drive:
The last set out the soonest did arrive.
Thus Nissus fell upon the slippery place,
While his young friend performed and won the race.   10
O early ripe! to thy abundant store
What could advancing age have added more?
It might (what Nature never gives the young)
Have taught the numbers° of thy native tongue.   *meters*
But satire needs not those, and wit will shine   15
Through the harsh cadence of a rugged line.
A noble error, and but seldom made,

To the Memory of Mr. Oldham. John Oldham, poet best remembered for his *Satires upon the Jesuits*, had died at thirty. 9 – 10 *Nissus; his young friend:* These two close friends, as Virgil tells us in the *Aeneid*, ran a race for the prize of an olive crown.

When poets are by too much force betrayed.
Thy gen'rous fruits, though gathered ere their
    prime,
Still showed a quickness; and maturing time   20
But mellows what we write to the dull sweets of
    rhyme.
Once more, hail, and farewell! farewell, thou young
But ah! too short, Marcellus of our tongue!
Thy brows with ivy and with laurels bound;
But fate and gloomy night encompass thee around.   25

23 *Marcellus:* Had he not died in his twentieth year, he would have succeeded the Roman emperor Augustus. 25 This line echoes the *Aeneid* (VI, 886), in which Marcellus is seen walking under the black cloud of his impending doom.

COMPARE:

"To the Memory of Mr. Oldham" with "Lycidas" by John Milton (page 224).

T. S. Eliot (1888 – 1965)*

JOURNEY OF THE MAGI   1927

"A cold coming we had of it,
Just the worst time of the year
For a journey, and such a long journey:
The ways deep and the weather sharp,
The very dead of winter."   5
And the camels galled, sore-footed, refractory,
Lying down in the melting snow.
There were times we regretted
The summer palaces on slopes, the terraces,
And the silken girls bringing sherbet.   10
Then the camel men cursing and grumbling
And running away, and wanting their liquor and women,
And the night-fires going out, and the lack of shelters,
And the cities hostile and the towns unfriendly
And the villages dirty and charging high prices: 15
A hard time we had of it.
At the end we preferred to travel all night,
Sleeping in snatches,
With the voices singing in our ears, saying
That this was all folly.   20

Then at dawn we came down to a temperate valley,
Wet, below the snow line, smelling of vegetation;
With a running stream and a water-mill beating the darkness,
And three trees on the low sky,
And an old white horse galloped away in the meadow.   25

Then we came to a tavern with vine-leaves over the lintel,
Six hands at an open door dicing for pieces of silver,
And feet kicking the empty wine-skins.
But there was no information, and so we continued
And arrived at evening, not a moment too soon   30
Finding the place; it was (you may say) satisfactory.
All this was a long time ago, I remember,
And I would do it again, but set down
This set down
This: were we led all that way for   35
Birth or Death? There was a Birth, certainly,
We had evidence and no doubt. I had seen birth and death,
But had thought they were different; this Birth was
Hard and bitter agony for us, like Death, our death.
We returned to our places, these Kingdoms,   40
But no longer at ease here, in the old dispensation,
With an alien people clutching their gods.
I should be glad of another death.

JOURNEY OF THE MAGI. The story of the Magi, the three wise men who traveled to Bethlehem to
behold the baby Jesus, is told in Matthew 2:1 – 12. That the three were kings is a later tradition.
1 – 5 *A cold coming . . . winter:* Eliot quotes with slight changes from a sermon preached on
Christmas day, 1622, by Bishop Lancelot Andrewes. 24 *three trees:* foreshadowing the three crosses
on Calvary (see Luke 23:32 – 33). 25 *white horse:* perhaps the steed that carried the conquering
Christ in the vision of St. John the Divine (Revelation 19:11 – 16). 41 *old dispensation:* older, pagan
religion about to be displaced by Christianity.

COMPARE:

"Journey of the Magi" with "The Magi" by William Butler Yeats (page 406).

T. S. Eliot

T. S. Eliot (1888 – 1965)*

The Love Song of J. Alfred Prufrock   1917

S'io credessi che mia risposta fosse
A persona che mai tornasse al mondo,
Questa fiamma staria senza piu scosse.
Ma perciocche giammai di questo fondo
Non torno vivo alcun, s'i'odo il vero,
Senza tema d'infamia ti rispondo.

Let us go then, you and I,
When the evening is spread out against the sky
Like a patient etherized upon a table;
Let us go, through certain half-deserted streets,
The muttering retreats   5
Of restless nights in one-night cheap hotels
And sawdust restaurants with oyster-shells:
Streets that follow like a tedious argument
Of insidious intent
To lead you to an overwhelming question . . .   10
Oh, do not ask, "What is it?"
Let us go and make our visit.

In the room the women come and go
Talking of Michelangelo.

The yellow fog that rubs its back upon the window-panes,   15
The yellow smoke that rubs its muzzle on the window-panes
Licked its tongue into the corners of the evening,
Lingered upon the pools that stand in drains,
Let fall upon its back the soot that falls from chimneys,
Slipped by the terrace, made a sudden leap,   20
And seeing that it was a soft October night,
Curled once about the house, and fell asleep.

And indeed there will be time
For the yellow smoke that slides along the street,
Rubbing its back upon the window-panes;   25
There will be time, there will be time
To prepare a face to meet the faces that you meet;
There will be time to murder and create,
And time for all the works and days of hands
That lift and drop a question on your plate;   30
Time for you and time for me,
And time yet for a hundred indecisions,
And for a hundred visions and revisions,
Before the taking of a toast and tea.

In the room the women come and go   35
Talking of Michelangelo.

And indeed there will be time
To wonder, "Do I dare?" and, "Do I dare?"
Time to turn back and descend the stair,
With a bald spot in the middle of my hair — 40
(They will say: "How his hair is growing thin!")
My morning coat, my collar mounting firmly to the chin,
My necktie rich and modest, but asserted by a simple pin —
(They will say: "But how his arms and legs are thin!")
Do I dare 45
Disturb the universe?
In a minute there is time
For decisions and revisions which a minute will reverse.

For I have known them all already, known them all: —
Have known the evenings, mornings, afternoons, 50
I have measured out my life with coffee spoons;
I know the voices dying with a dying fall
Beneath the music from a farther room.
    So how should I presume?

And I have known the eyes already, known them all — 55
The eyes that fix you in a formulated phrase,
And when I am formulated, sprawling on a pin,
When I am pinned and wriggling on the wall,
Then how should I begin
To spit out all the butt-ends of my days and ways? 60
    And how should I presume?

And I have known the arms already, known them all —
Arms that are braceleted and white and bare
(But in the lamplight, downed with light brown hair!)
Is it perfume from a dress 65
That makes me so digress?
Arms that lie along a table, or wrap about a shawl.
    And should I then presume?
    And how should I begin?

                .   .   .   .   .   .

Shall I say, I have gone at dusk through narrow streets 70
And watched the smoke that rises from the pipes
Of lonely men in shirt-sleeves, leaning out of windows? . . .

I should have been a pair of ragged claws
Scuttling across the floors of silent seas.

And the afternoon, the evening, sleeps so peacefully! 75
Smoothed by long fingers,
Asleep . . . tired . . . or it malingers,
Stretched on the floor, here beside you and me.
Should I, after tea and cakes and ices,
Have the strength to force the moment to its crisis? 80

But though I have wept and fasted, wept and prayed,
Though I have seen my head (grown slightly bald) brought in upon a
    platter,
I am no prophet — and here's no great matter;
I have seen the moment of my greatness flicker,
And I have seen the eternal Footman hold my coat, and snicker,   85
And in short, I was afraid.

And would it have been worth it, after all,
After the cups, the marmalade, the tea,
Among the porcelain, among some talk of you and me,
Would it have been worth while,   90
To have bitten off the matter with a smile,
To have squeezed the universe into a ball
To roll it toward some overwhelming question,
To say: "I am Lazarus, come from the dead,
Come back to tell you all, I shall tell you all" —   95
If one, settling a pillow by her head,
    Should say: "That is not what I meant at all.
    That is not it, at all."

And would it have been worth it, after all,
Would it have been worth while,   100
After the sunsets and the dooryards and the sprinkled streets,
After the novels, after the teacups, after the skirts that trail along the
    floor —
And this, and so much more? —
It is impossible to say just what I mean!
But as if a magic lantern threw the nerves in patterns on a screen: 105
Would it have been worth while
If one, settling a pillow or throwing off a shawl,
And turning toward the window, should say:
    "That is not it at all,
    That is not what I meant, at all."   110

                    .   .   .   .   .   .

No! I am not Prince Hamlet, nor was meant to be;
Am an attendant lord, one that will do
To swell a progress, start a scene or two,
Advise the prince; no doubt, an easy tool,
Deferential, glad to be of use,   115
Politic, cautious, and meticulous;
Full of high sentence, but a bit obtuse;
At times, indeed, almost ridiculous —
Almost, at times, the Fool.

I grow old . . . I grow old . . .   120
I shall wear the bottoms of my trousers rolled.

Shall I part my hair behind? Do I dare to eat a peach?
I shall wear white flannel trousers, and walk upon the beach.
I have heard the mermaids singing, each to each.

I do not think that they will sing to me.   125

I have seen them riding seaward on the waves
Combing the white hair of the waves blown back
When the wind blows the water white and black.

We have lingered in the chambers of the sea
By sea-girls wreathed with seaweed red and brown   130
Till human voices wake us, and we drown.

THE LOVE SONG OF J. ALFRED PRUFROCK. The epigraph, from Dante's *Inferno,* is the speech of one
dead and damned, who thinks that his hearer also is going to remain in Hell. Count Guido da
Montefeltro, whose sin has been to give false counsel after a corrupt prelate had offered him prior
absolution and whose punishment is to be wrapped in a constantly burning flame, offers to tell
Dante his story: "If I thought my reply were to someone who could ever return to the world, this
flame would waver no more. But since, I'm told, nobody ever escapes from this pit, I'll tell you
without fear of ill fame." 29 *works and days:* title of a poem by Hesiod (eighth century B.C.), depicting
his life as a hard-working Greek farmer and exhorting his brother to be like him. 82 *head . . . platter:*
like that of John the Baptist, prophet and praiser of chastity, whom King Herod beheaded at the
demand of Herodias, his unlawfully wedded wife (see Mark 6:17 – 28). 92 – 93 *squeezed . . . To roll
it:* an echo from Marvell's "To His Coy Mistress," lines 41 – 42 (see p. 350). 94 *Lazarus:* Probably
the Lazarus whom Jesus called forth from the tomb (John 11:1 – 44), but possibly the beggar seen
in Heaven by the rich man in Hell (Luke 16:19 – 25).

Louise Erdrich (b. 1954)

INDIAN BOARDING SCHOOL: THE RUNAWAYS   1984

Home's the place we head for in our sleep.
Boxcars stumbling north in dreams
don't wait for us. We catch them on the run.
The rails, old lacerations that we love,
shoot parallel across the face and break   5
just under Turtle Mountains. Riding scars
you can't get lost. Home is the place they cross.

The lame guard strikes a match and makes the dark
less tolerant. We watch through cracks in boards
as the land starts rolling, rolling till it hurts   10
to be here, cold in regulation clothes.
We know the sheriff's waiting at midrun
to take us back. His car is dumb and warm.
The highway doesn't rock, it only hums
like a wing of long insults. The worn-down welts   15
of ancient punishments lead back and forth.

All runaways wear dresses, long green ones,
the color you would think shame was. We scrub
the sidewalks down because it's shameful work.
Our brushes cut the stone in watered arcs   20
and in the soak frail outlines shiver clear
a moment, things us kids pressed on the dark
face before it hardened, pale, remembering
delicate old injuries, the spines of names and leaves.

INDIAN BOARDING SCHOOL: THE RUNAWAYS. 6. *Turtle Mountains:* in North Dakota and Manitoba.
The poet, of German and Native American descent, belongs to the Turtle Mountain Band of the
Chippewa.

Robert Frost (1874–1963)*

AWAY!   1962

Now I out walking
The world desert,
And my shoe and my stocking
Do me no hurt.

I leave behind   5
Good friends in town.
Let them get well-wined
And go lie down.

Don't think I leave
For the outer dark   10
Like Adam and Eve
Put out of the Park.

Forget the myth.
There is no one I
Am put out with   15
Or put out by.

Unless I'm wrong
I but obey
The urge of a song:
I'm—bound—away!   20

And I may return
If dissatisfied
With what I learn
From having died.

Robert Frost (1874–1963)*

BIRCHES   1916

When I see birches bend to left and right
Across the lines of straighter darker trees,
I like to think some boy's been swinging them.
But swinging doesn't bend them down to stay
As ice storms do. Often you must have seen them   5
Loaded with ice a sunny winter morning
After a rain. They click upon themselves
As the breeze rises, and turn many-colored
As the stir cracks and crazes their enamel.
Soon the sun's warmth makes them shed crystal shells   10
Shattering and avalanching on the snow crust—
Such heaps of broken glass to sweep away
You'd think the inner dome of heaven had fallen.
They are dragged to the withered bracken by the load,
And they seem not to break; though once they are bowed   15
So low for long, they never right themselves:
You may see their trunks arching in the woods
Years afterwards, trailing their leaves on the ground
Like girls on hands and knees that throw their hair
Before them over their heads to dry in the sun.   20
But I was going to say when Truth broke in
With all her matter of fact about the ice storm,
I should prefer to have some boy bend them
As he went out and in to fetch the cows—
Some boy too far from town to learn baseball,   25
Whose only play was what he found himself,
Summer or winter, and could play alone.
One by one he subdued his father's trees
By riding them down over and over again
Until he took the stiffness out of them,   30
And not one but hung limp, not one was left
For him to conquer. He learned all there was
To learn about not launching out too soon
And so not carrying the tree away
Clear to the ground. He always kept his poise   35
To the top branches, climbing carefully
With the same pains you use to fill a cup
Up to the brim, and even above the brim.
Then he flung outward, feet first, with a swish,
Kicking his way down through the air to the ground.   40

So was I once myself a swinger of birches.
And so I dream of going back to be.
It's when I'm weary of considerations,
And life is too much like a pathless wood
Where your face burns and tickles with the cobwebs 45
Broken across it, and one eye is weeping
From a twig's having lashed across it open.
I'd like to get away from earth awhile
And then come back to it and begin over.
May no fate willfully misunderstand me 50
And half grant what I wish and snatch me away
Not to return. Earth's the right place for love:
I don't know where it's likely to go better.
I'd like to go by climbing a birch tree,
And climb black branches up a snow-white trunk 55
Toward heaven, till the tree could bear no more,
But dipped its top and set me down again.
That would be good both going and coming back.
One could do worse than be a swinger of birches.

Robert Frost (1874 – 1963)*

Stopping by Woods on a Snowy Evening 1923

Whose woods these are I think I know.
His house is in the village though;
He will not see me stopping here
To watch his woods fill up with snow.

My little horse must think it queer 5
To stop without a farmhouse near
Between the woods and frozen lake
The darkest evening of the year.

He gives his harness bells a shake
To ask if there is some mistake. 10
The only other sound's the sweep
Of easy wind and downy flake.

The woods are lovely, dark and deep,
But I have promises to keep,
And miles to go before I sleep, 15
And miles to go before I sleep.

Compare:

"Stopping by Woods on a Snowy Evening" with "Desert Places" by Robert Frost (page 140).

Allen Ginsberg (b. 1926)

A SUPERMARKET IN CALIFORNIA   1956

What thoughts I have of you tonight, Walt Whitman, for I walked down the sidestreets under the trees with a headache self-conscious looking at the full moon.

In my hungry fatigue, and shopping for images, I went into the neon fruit supermarket, dreaming of your enumerations!

What peaches and what penumbras! Whole families shopping at night! Aisles full of husbands! Wives in the avocados, babies in the tomatoes! — and you, Garcia Lorca, what were you doing down by the watermelons?

I saw you, Walt Whitman, childless, lonely old grubber, poking among the meats in the refrigerator and eyeing the grocery boys.

I heard you asking questions of each: Who killed the pork chops? What price bananas? Are you my Angel?   5

I wandered in and out of the brilliant stacks of cans following you, and followed in my imagination by the store detective.

We strode down the open corridors together in our solitary fancy tasting artichokes, possessing every frozen delicacy, and never passing the cashier.

Where are we going, Walt Whitman? The doors close in an hour. Which way does your beard point tonight?

(I touch your book and dream of our odyssey in the supermarket and feel absurd.)

Will we walk all night through solitary streets? The trees add shade to shade, lights out in the houses, we'll both be lonely.   10

Will we stroll dreaming of the lost America of love past blue automobiles in driveways, home to our silent cottage?

Ah, dear father, graybeard, lonely old courage-teacher, what America did you have when Charon quit poling his ferry and you got out on a smoking bank and stood watching the boat disappear on the black waters of Lethe?

A SUPERMARKET IN CALIFORNIA. 2 *enumerations:* Many of Whitman's poems contain lists of observed details. 3 *Garcia Lorca:* modern Spanish poet who wrote an "Ode to Walt Whitman" in his booklength sequence *Poet in New York.* (A poem by Lorca appears on page 236.) 12 *Charon . . . Lethe:* Is the poet confusing two underworld rivers? Charon, in Greek and Roman mythology, is the boatman who ferries the souls of the dead across the River Styx. The River Lethe also flows through Hades, and a drink of its waters makes the dead lose their painful memories of loved ones thay have left behind.

COMPARE:

"A Supermarket in California" with Walt Whitman's "To a Locomotive in Winter" (page 16) and "I Saw in Louisiana a Live-Oak Growing" (page 394).

Dana Gioia (b. 1950)

CALIFORNIA HILLS IN AUGUST   1982

I can imagine someone who found
these fields unbearable, who climbed
the hillside in the heat, cursing the dust,
cracking the brittle weeds underfoot,
wishing a few more trees for shade.   5

An Easterner especially, who would scorn
the meagreness of summer, the dry
twisted shapes of black elm,
scrub oak, and chaparral — a landscape
August has already drained of green.   10

One who would hurry over the clinging
thistle, foxtail, golden poppy,
knowing everything was just a weed,
unable to conceive that these trees
and sparse brown bushes were alive.   15

And hate the bright stillness of the noon,
without wind, without motion,
the only other living thing
a hawk, hungry for prey, suspended
in the blinding, sunlit blue.   20

And yet how gentle it seems to someone
raised in a landscape short of rain —
the skyline of a hill broken by no more
trees than one can count, the grass,
the empty sky, the wish for water.   25

H. D. [Hilda Doolittle] (1886–1961)*

HELEN   1924

All Greece hates
the still eyes in the white face,
the lustre as of olives
where she stands,
and the white hands.   5

All Greece reviles
the wan face when she smiles,
hating it deeper still
when it grows wan and white,
remembering past enchantments   10
and past ills.

Greece sees unmoved,
God's daughter, born of love,
the beauty of cool feet
and slenderest knees,   15
could love indeed the maid,
only if she were laid,
white ash amid funereal cypresses.

HELEN. In Greek mythology, Helen, most beautiful of all women, was the daughter of a mortal, Leda, by the god Zeus. Her kidnapping set off the long and devastating Trojan War. While married to Menelaus, king of the Greek city-state of Sparta, Helen was carried off by Paris, prince of Troy. Menelaus and his brother Agammemnon raised an army, besieged Troy for ten years, and eventually recaptured her. One episode of the Trojan War is related in the *Iliad*, Homer's epic poem, composed before 700 B.C.

COMPARE:

"Helen" with "Long-legged Fly" by William Butler Yeats (page 404).

H. D.

Donald Hall (b. 1928)

NAMES OF HORSES   1978

All winter your brute shoulders strained against collars, padding
and steerhide over the ash hames, to haul
sledges of cordwood for drying through spring and summer,
for the Glenwood stove next winter, and for the simmering range.

In April you pulled cartloads of manure to spread on the fields,   5
dark manure of Holsteins, and knobs of your own clustered with oats.
All summer you mowed the grass in meadow and hayfield, the
      mowing machine
clacketing beside you, while the sun walked high in the morning;

and after noon's heat, you pulled a clawed rake through the same
    acres,
gathering stacks, and dragged the wagon from stack to stack,   10
and the built hayrack back, uphill to the chaffy barn,
three loads of hay a day from standing grass in the morning.

Sundays you trotted the two miles to church with the light load
of a leather quartertop buggy, and grazed in the sound of hymns.
Generation on generation, your neck rubbed the windowsill   15
of the stall, smoothing the wood as the sea smooths glass.

When you were old and lame, when your shoulders hurt bending to
    graze,
one October the man, who fed you and kept you, and harnessed you
    every morning,
led you through corn stubble to sandy ground above Eagle Pond,
and dug a hole beside you where you stood shuddering in your skin,   20

and lay the shotgun's muzzle in the boneless hollow behind your ear,
and fired the slug into your brain, and felled you into your grave,
shoveling sand to cover you, setting goldenrod upright above you,
where by next summer a dent in the ground made your monument.

For a hundred and fifty years, in the pasture of dead horses,   25
roots of pine trees pushed through the pale curves of your ribs,
yellow blossoms flourished above you in autumn, and in winter
frost heaved your bones in the ground — old toilers, soil makers:

O Roger, Mackerel, Riley, Ned, Nellie, Chester, Lady Ghost.

COMPARE:
"Names of Horses" with "The Bull Calf" by Irving Layton (page 344).

Thomas Hardy (1840 – 1928)*

THE CONVERGENCE OF THE TWAIN   1912

Lines on the Loss of the "Titanic"

I
        In a solitude of the sea
        Deep from human vanity,
And the Pride of Life that planned her, stilly couches she.

II
        Steel chambers, late the pyres
        Of her salamandrine fires,   5
Cold currents thrid°, and turn to rhythmic tidal lyres.   *thread*

III

           Over the mirrors meant
           To glass the opulent
The sea-worm crawls — grotesque, slimed, dumb, indifferent.

IV

           Jewels in joy designed   10
           To ravish the sensuous mind
Lie lightless, all their sparkles bleared and black and blind.

V

           Dim moon-eyed fishes near
           Gaze at the gilded gear
And query: "What does this vaingloriousness down here?"   15

VI

           Well: while was fashioning
           This creature of cleaving wing,
The Immanent Will that stirs and urges everything

VII

           Prepared a sinister mate
           For her — so gaily great —   20
A Shape of Ice, for the time far and dissociate.

VIII

           And as the smart ship grew
           In stature, grace, and hue,
In shadowy silent distance grew the Iceberg too.

IX

           Alien they seemed to be: 25
           No mortal eye could see
The intimate welding of their later history,

X

           Or sign that they were bent
           By paths coincident
On being anon twin halves of one august event.   30

XI

           Till the Spinner of the Years
           Said "Now!" And each one hears,
And consummation comes, and jars two hemispheres.

THE CONVERGENCE OF THE TWAIN. The luxury liner *Titanic,* supposedly unsinkable, went down in 1912 after striking an iceberg, on its first Atlantic voyage. 5 *salamandrine:* like the salamander, a lizard that supposedly thrives in fires, or like a spirit of the same name that inhabits fire (according to alchemists).

COMPARE:

"The Convergence of the Twain" with "Titanic" by David R. Slavitt (page 379).

Thomas Hardy

Thomas Hardy (1840–1928)*

DURING WIND AND RAIN   1917

They sing their dearest songs—
He, she, all of them—yea,
Treble and tenor and bass,
   And one to play;
With the candles mooning each face. . . .   5
   Ah, no; the years O!
How the sick leaves reel down in throngs!

They clear the creeping moss—
Elders and juniors—aye,
Making the pathways neat   10
   And the garden gay;
And they build a shady seat. . . .
   Ah, no; the years, the years;
See, the white storm-birds wing across!

They are blithely breakfasting all—   15
Men and maidens—yea,
Under the summer tree,
   With a glimpse of the bay,
While pet fowl come to the knee. . . .
   Ah, no! the years O!   20
And the rotten rose is ripped from the wall.

They change to a high new house,
He, she, all of them—aye,
Clocks and carpets and chairs
    On the lawn all day,   25
And brightest things that are theirs. . . .
    Ah, no; the years, the years;
Down their carved names the rain-drop plows.

COMPARE:

"During Wind and Rain" with "anyone lived in a pretty how town" by E. E. Cummings
(page 60).

Thomas Hardy (1840 – 1928)*

FOUR SATIRES OF CIRCUMSTANCE   1914

In Church

"And now to God the Father," he ends,
And his voice thrills up to the topmost tiles:
Each listener chokes as he bows and bends,
And emotion pervades the crowded aisles.
Then the preacher glides to the vestry-door,   5
And shuts it, and thinks he is seen no more.

The door swings softly ajar meanwhile,
And a pupil of his in the Bible class,
Who adores him as one without gloss or guile
Sees her idol stand with a satisfied smile   10
And re-enact at the vestry-glass
Each pulpit gesture in deft dumb-show
That had moved the congregation so.

In the Room of the Bride-elect

"Would it had been the man of our wish!"
Sighs her mother. To whom with vehemence she   15
In the wedding-dress — the wife to be —
"Then why were you so mollyish
As not to insist on him for me!"
The mother, amazed: "Why, dearest one,
Because you pleaded for this or none!"   20

"But Father and you should have stood out strong!
Since then, to my cost, I have lived to find
That you were right and that I was wrong;

This man is a dolt to the one declined. . . .
Ah! — here he comes with his button-hole rose.   25
Good God — I must marry him I suppose!"

In the Cemetery

"You see those mothers squabbling there?"
Remarks the man of the cemetery.
"One says in tears, ' 'Tis mine lies here!'
Another, *'Nay, mine, you Pharisee°!'*   *hypocrite* 30
Another, *'How dare you move my flowers*
And put your own on this grave of ours!'
But all their children were laid therein
At different times, like sprats in a tin°.   *sardines in a can*

"And then the main drain had to cross,   35
And we moved the lot some nights ago,
And packed them away in the general foss°   *ditch*
With hundreds more. But their folks don't know,
And as well cry over a new-laid drain
As anything else, to ease your pain!"   40

In the Nuptial Chamber

"O that mastering tune!" And up in the bed
Like a lace-robed phantom springs the bride;
"And why?" asks the man she had that day wed,
With a start, as the band plays on outside.
"It's the townsfolk's cheery compliment   45
Because of our marriage, my Innocent."

"O but you don't know! 'Tis the passionate air
To which my old Love waltzed with me,
And I swore as we spun that none should share
My home, my kisses, till death, save he!   50
And he dominates me and thrills me through,
And it's he I embrace while embracing you!"

FOUR SATIRES OF CIRCUMSTANCE. The series "Satires of Circumstance" consists of fifteen short poems; this is a sampling of them.

COMPARE:

"Four Satires of Circumstance" with Thomas Hardy's "The Workbox" (page 30) and "The Ruined Maid" (page 55).

Robert Hayden (1913–1980)

THOSE WINTER SUNDAYS   1962

Sundays too my father got up early
and put his clothes on in the blueblack cold,
then with cracked hands that ached
from labor in the weekday weather made
banked fires blaze. No one ever thanked him.   5

I'd wake and hear the cold splintering, breaking.
When the rooms were warm, he'd call,
and slowly I would rise and dress,
fearing the chronic angers of that house,

Speaking indifferently to him,   10
who had driven out the cold
and polished my good shoes as well.
What did I know, what did I know
of love's austere and lonely offices?

COMPARE:

"Those Winter Sundays" with "My Father's Martial Art" by Stephen Shu-ning Liu (page 347) and "Daddy" by Sylvia Plath (page 361).

Seamus Heaney (b. 1939)*

DIGGING   1966

Between my finger and my thumb
The squat pen rests; snug as a gun.

Under my window, a clean rasping sound
When the spade sinks into gravelly ground.
My father, digging. I look down   5

Till his straining rump among the flowerbeds
Bends low, comes up twenty years away
Stooping in rhythm through potato drills
Where he was digging.

The coarse boot nestled on the lug, the shaft   10
Against the inside knee was levered firmly.
He rooted out tall tops, buried the bright edge deep
To scatter new potatoes that we picked
Loving their cool hardness in our hands.

By God, the old man could handle a spade.   15
Just like his old man.

My grandfather cut more turf in a day
Than any other man on Toner's bog.
Once I carried him milk in a bottle
Corked sloppily with paper. He straightened up   20
To drink it, then fell to right away

Nicking and slicing neatly, heaving sods
Over his shoulder, going down and down
For the good turf. Digging.

The cold smell of potato mould, the squelch and slap   25
Of soggy peat, the curt cuts of an edge
Through living roots awaken in my head.
But I've no spade to follow men like them.

Between my finger and my thumb
The squat pen rests.   30
I'll dig with it.

Seamus Heaney (b. 1939)*

MOTHER OF THE GROOM   1972

What she remembers
Is his glistening back
In the bath, his small boots
In the ring of boots at her feet.

Hands in her voided lap,   5
She hears a daughter welcomed.
It's as if he kicked when lifted
And slipped her soapy hold.

Once soap would ease off
The wedding ring   10
That's bedded forever now
In her clapping hand.

Anthony Hecht (b. 1923)

THE VOW   1967

In the third month, a sudden flow of blood.
The mirth of tabrets ceaseth, and the joy
Also of the harp. The frail image of God
Lay spilled and formless. Neither girl nor boy,

But yet blood of my blood, nearly my child.   5
                     All that long day
Her pale face turned to the window's mild
                     Featureless grey.

And for some nights she whimpered as she dreamed
The dead thing spoke, saying: "Do not recall   10
Pleasure at my conception. I am redeemed
From pain and sorrow. Mourn rather for all
Who breathlessly issue from the bone gates,
                     The gates of horn,
For truly it is best of all the fates   15
                     Not to be born.

"Mother, a child lay gasping for bare breath
On Christmas Eve when Santa Claus had set
Death in the stocking, and the lights of death
Flamed in the tree. O, if you can, forget   20
You were the child, turn to my father's lips
                     Against the time
When his cold hand puts forth its fingertips
                     Of jointed lime."

Doctors of Science, what is man that he   25
Should hope to come to a good end? *The best
Is not to have been born.* And could it be
That Jewish diligence and Irish jest
The consent of flesh and a midwinter storm
                     Had reconciled,   30
Was yet too bold a mixture to inform
                     A simple child?

Even as gold is tried, Gentile and Jew.
If that ghost was a girl's, I swear to it:
Your mother shall be far more blessed than you.   35
And if a boy's, I swear: The flames are lit
That shall refine us; they shall not destroy
                     A living hair.
Your younger brothers shall confirm in joy
                     This that I swear.   40

THE VOW. 2 *tabrets:* small drums used to accompany traditional Jewish dances. 14 *gates of horn:*
According to Homer and Virgil pleasant, lying dreams emerge from the underworld through gates
of ivory; ominous, truth-telling dreams, through gates of horn.

George Herbert

George Herbert (1593 – 1633)*

LOVE   1633

Love bade me welcome; yet my soul drew back,
          Guilty of dust and sin.
But quick-eyed Love, observing me grow slack
          From my first entrance in,
Drew nearer to me, sweetly questioning   5
          If I lacked anything.

"A guest," I answered, "worthy to be here";
          Love said, "You shall be he."
"I, the unkind, ungrateful? Ah, my dear,
          I cannot look on Thee."   10
Love took my hand, and smiling did reply,
          "Who made the eyes but I?"

"Truth, Lord, but I have marred them; let my shame
          Go where it doth deserve."
"And know you not," says Love, "who bore the blame?"   15
          "My dear, then I will serve."
"You must sit down," says Love, "and taste My meat."
          So I did sit and eat.

COMPARE
"Love" with "Batter my heart, three-personed God" by John Donne (page 44).

Robert Herrick (1591–1674)*

THE BAD SEASON MAKES THE POET SAD   1648

Dull to myself and almost dead to these
My many fresh and fragrant mistresses,
Lost to all music now, since everything
Puts on the semblance here of sorrowing.
Sick is the land to th' heart, and doth endure   5
More dangerous faintings by her desp'rate cure.
But if that golden age would come again
And Charles here rule, as he before did reign,
If smooth and unperplexed the seasons were
As when the sweet Maria lived here,   10
I should delight to have my curls half drowned
In Tyrian dews, and head with roses crowned,
And once more yet, ere I am laid out dead,
Knock at a star with my exalted head.

THE BAD SEASON MAKES THE POET SAD. 1–2 *these . . . mistresses:* This line may appear to suggest that Herrick was a Don Juan, but see his brief biography in *Lives of the Poets* (page 419). To what "mistresses" might he refer? 5 *Sick is the land:* Civil War had erupted in England in 1642. 6 *desp'rate cure:* Herrick probably means rule by Parliament, which had brought an uneasy peace. In 1645 the forces of Parliament, led by Oliver Cromwell, had defeated the armies of Charles I, and the king had fled the country. 10 *Maria:* Henrietta Maria, wife of Charles. 12 *Tyrian dews:* perfumes from Tyre, in ancient Phoenicia.

Robert Herrick (1591 – 1674)*

TO THE VIRGINS, TO MAKE MUCH OF TIME   1648

Gather ye rose-buds while ye may,
    Old Time is still a-flying;
And this same flower that smiles today,
    Tomorrow will be dying.

The glorious lamp of heaven, the sun,   5
    The higher he's a-getting,
The sooner will his race be run,
    And nearer he's to setting.

That age is best which is the first,
    When youth and blood are warmer;   10
But being spent, the worse, and worst
    Times still succeed the former.

Then be not coy, but use your time,
  And while ye may, go marry;
For having lost but once your prime,   15
  You may for ever tarry.

COMPARE:

"To the Virgins, to Make Much of Time" with "To His Coy Mistress" by Andrew
Marvell (page 350) and "Go, Lovely Rose" by Edmund Waller (page 393).

Garrett Hongo (b. 1951)*

THE CADENCE OF SILK   1988

When I lived in Seattle, I loved watching
the Sonics play basketball; something
about that array of trained and energetic
bodies set in motion to attack a more
sluggish, less physically intelligent opponent   5
appealed to me, taught me about cadence
and play, the offguard breaking free
before the rebound, "releasing," as is said
in the parlance of the game, getting to
the center's downcourt pass and streaking   10
to the basket for a scoopshot layup
off the glass, all in rhythm, all in
perfect declensions of action, smooth
and strenuous as Gorgiasian rhetoric.
I was hooked on the undulant ballet   15
of the pattern offense, on the set play
back-door under the basket, and, at times,
even on the auctioneer's pace and elocution
of the play-by-play man. Now I watch
the Lakers, having returned to Los Angeles   20
some years ago, love them even more than
the Seattle team, long since broken up and aging.
The Lakers are incomparable, numerous
options for any situation, their players
the league's quickest, most intelligent,   25
and, it is my opinion, frankly, the most *cool.*

Few bruisers, they are sleek as arctic seals,
especially the small forward
as he dodges through the key, away from
the ball, rubbing off his man on the screen,   30
setting for his shot. Then, slick as spit,
comes the ball from the point guard,
and my man goes up, cradling the ball
in his right hand like a waiter balancing
a tray piled with champagne in stemmed glasses,   35
cocking his arm and bringing the ball
back behind his ear, pumping, letting fly then
as he jumps, popcorn-like, in the corner,
while the ball, launched, slung dextrously
with a slight backspin, slashes through   40
the basket's silk net with a small,
sonorous splash of completion.

THE CADENCE OF SILK. 14 *Gorgiasian rhetoric:* art of persuasive speaking as practiced by Gorgias
(485?–380? B.C.), Greek Sophist philosopher, who argued that nothing exists.

COMPARE:

"The Cadence of Silk" with "Ex-Basketball Player" by John Updike (page 392).

Garrett Hongo

Garrett Hongo (b. 1951)*

THE HONGO STORE
29 MILES VOLCANO
HILO, HAWAII   1982

From a photograph

My parents felt those rumblings
Coming deep from the earth's belly,
Thudding like the bell of the Buddhist Church.
Tremors in the ground swayed the bathinette
Where I lay squalling in soapy water.   5

My mother carried me around the house,
Back through the orchids, ferns, and plumeria
Of that greenhouse world behind the store,
And jumped between gas pumps into the car.

My father gave it the gun   10
And said, "Be quiet," as he searched
The frequencies, flipping for the right station
(The radio squealing more loudly than I could cry).

And then even the echoes stopped —
The only sound the Edsel's grinding   15
And the bark and crackle of radio news
Saying stay home or go to church.

"Dees time she no blow!"
My father said, driving back
Over the red ash covering the road.   20
"I worried she went go for broke already!"

So in this print the size of a matchbook,
The dark skinny man, shirtless and grinning,
A toothpick in the corner of his smile,
Lifts a naked baby above his head —   25
Behind him the plate glass of the store only
        cracked.

Gerard Manley Hopkins

Gerard Manley Hopkins (1844 – 1889)*

SPRING AND FALL   (1880)

To a Young Child

Márgarét, are you grieving
Over Goldengrove unleaving°?   *shedding its leaves*
Leáves, like the things of man, you
With your fresh thoughts care for, can you?
Ah! ás the heart grows older   5
It will come to such sights colder
By and by, nor spare a sigh
Though worlds of wanwood leafmeal lie;
And yet you will weep and know why.
Now no matter, child, the name: 10
Sórrow's springs áre the same.
Nor mouth had, no nor mind, expressed
What heart heard of, ghost° guessed: *spirit*
It is the blight man was born for,
It is Margaret you mourn for.   15

COMPARE:

"Spring and Fall" with "Margaret Are You Drug" by George Starbuck (page 243).

Gerard Manley Hopkins (1844 – 1889)*

THOU ART INDEED JUST, LORD, IF I CONTEND (1889)

Justus quidem tu es, Domine, si disputem tecum: verumtamen justa
    loquar ad te: Quare via impiorum prosperatur? &c.

Thou art indeed just, Lord, if I contend
With thee; but, sir, so what I plead is just.
Why do sinners' ways prosper? and why must
Disappointment all I endeavor end?
Wert thou my enemy, O thou my friend,   5
How wouldst thou worse, I wonder than thou dost
Defeat, thwart me? Oh, the sots and thralls of lust
Do in spare hours more thrive than I that spend,

Sir, life upon thy cause. See, banks and brakes°   *ferny marshes*
Now, leavèd how thick! lacèd they are again   10
With fretty chervil°, look, and fresh wind shakes   *wild herb*

Them; birds build — but not I build; no, but strain,
Time's eunuch, and not breed one work that wakes.
Mine, O thou lord of life, send my roots rain.

THOU ART INDEED JUST, LORD, IF I CONTEND. In the first two sentences of this poem, Hopkins
translates the Latin quotation from the Vulgate Bible (Jeremiah 12:1).

COMPARE:

"Thou art indeed just, Lord . . ." with "When I consider how my light is spent" by John
Milton (page 354).

Gerard Manley Hopkins (1844 – 1889)*

THE WINDHOVER (1877)

To Christ Our Lord

I caught this morning morning's minion, kingdom of daylight's
    dauphin, dapple-dawn-drawn Falcon, in his riding
    Of the rolling level underneath him steady air, and striding
High there, how he rung upon the rein of a wimpling wing
In his ecstasy! then off, off forth on swing,   5

As a skate's heel sweeps smooth on a bow-bend: the hurl and
   gliding
Rebuffed the big wind. My heart in hiding
Stirred for a bird, — the achieve of, the mastery of the thing!

Brute beauty and valor and act, oh, air, pride, plume, here
   Buckle! and the fire that breaks from thee then, a billion   10
Times told lovelier, more dangerous, O my chevalier!

   No wonder of it: shéer plód makes plow down sillion°   *furrow*
Shine, and blue-bleak embers, ah my dear,
   Fall, gall themselves, and gash gold-vermilion.

THE WINDHOVER. A windhover is a kestrel, or small falcon, so called because it can hover upon the wind. 4 *rung . . . wing:* A horse is "rung upon the rein" when its trainer holds the end of a long rein and has the horse circle him. The possible meanings of *wimpling* include (1) curving; (2) pleated, arranged in many little folds one on top of another; (3) rippling or undulating like the surface of a flowing stream.

A. E. Housman (1859 – 1936)*

LOVELIEST OF TREES, THE CHERRY NOW   1896

Loveliest of trees, the cherry now
Is hung with bloom along the bough,
And stands about the woodland ride°   *path*
Wearing white for Eastertide.
Now, of my threescore years and ten,   5
Twenty will not come again,
And take from seventy springs a score,
It only leaves me fifty more.

And since to look at things in bloom
Fifty springs are little room,   10
About the woodlands I will go
To see the cherry hung with snow.

COMPARE:

"Loveliest of trees, the cherry now" with "To the Virgins, to Make Much of Time" by Robert Herrick (page 329) and "Spring and Fall" by Gerard Manley Hopkins (page 333).

A. E. Housman

A. E. Housman (1859 – 1936)*

To an Athlete Dying Young   1896

The time you won your town the race
We chaired you through the market-place;
Man and boy stood cheering by,
And home we brought you shoulder-high.

Today, the road all runners come,   5
Shoulder-high we bring you home,
And set you at your threshold down,
Townsman of a stiller town.

Smart lad, to slip betimes away
From fields where glory does not stay,   10
And early though the laurel grows
It withers quicker than the rose.

Eyes the shady night has shut
Cannot see the record cut,
And silence sounds no worse than cheers   15
After earth has stopped the ears.

Now you will not swell the rout
Of lads that wore their honors out,
Runners whom renown outran
And the name died before the man.   20

So set, before its echoes fade,
The fleet foot on the sill of shade,
And hold to the low lintel up
The still-defended challenge-cup.

And round that early-laureled head 25
Will flock to gaze the strengthless dead,
And find unwithered on its curls
The garland briefer than a girl's.

COMPARE:

"To an Athlete Dying Young" with "Ex-Basketball Player" by John Updike (page 392).

Langston Hughes (1902 – 1967)*

DREAM DEFERRED 1951

What happens to a dream deferred?

Does it dry up
like a raisin in the sun?
Or fester like a sore —
And then run? 5
Does it stink like rotten meat?
Or crust and sugar over —
like a syrupy sweet?

Maybe it just sags
like a heavy load. 10

Or does it explode?

COMPARE:

"Dream Deferred" with Langston Hughes's "Dream Boogie" (page 162) and "Ballad of Birmingham" by Dudley Randall (page 119).

Langston Hughes

Langston Hughes (1902–1967)*

ISLAND   1959

Wave of sorrow,
Do not drown me now:

I see the island
Still ahead somehow.

I see the island   5
And its sands are fair:

Wave of sorrow,
Take me there.

COMPARE:

"Island" with "The Lake Isle of Innisfree" by William Butler Yeats (page 3).

Randall Jarrell (1914 – 1965)

THE DEATH OF THE BALL TURRET GUNNER   1945

From my mother's sleep I fell into the State
And I hunched in its belly till my wet fur froze.
Six miles from earth, loosed from its dream of life,
I woke to black flak and the nightmare fighters.
When I died they washed me out of the turret with a hose.

Randall Jarrell

THE DEATH OF THE BALL TURRET GUNNER. Jarrell has written: "A ball turret was a plexiglass sphere set into the belly of a B-17 or B-24, and inhabited by two .50 caliber machine-guns and one man, a short small man. When this gunner tracked with his machine-guns a fighter attacking his bomber from below, he revolved with the turret; hunched in his little sphere, he looked like the fetus in the womb. The fighters which attacked him were armed with cannon firing explosive shells. The hose was a steam hose."

COMPARE:

"The Death of the Ball Turret Gunner" with "Dulce et Decorum Est" by Wilfred Owen (page 338) and "The Insert" by R. L. Barth (page 289).

Robinson Jeffers (1887–1962)

TO THE STONE-CUTTERS   1925

Stone-cutters fighting time with marble, you foredefeated
Challengers of oblivion
Eat cynical earnings, knowing rock splits, records fall down,
The square-limbed Roman letters
Scale in the thaws, wear in the rain. The poet as well   5
Builds his monument mockingly;
For man will be blotted out, the blithe earth die, the brave
    sun
Die blind, his heart blackening:
Yet stones have stood for a thousand years, and pained
    thoughts found
The honey peace in old poems.   10

COMPARE:

"To the Stone-cutters" with "Not marble nor the gilded monuments" by William Shakespeare (page 374).

Elizabeth Jennings (b. 1926)

DELAY   1953

The radiance of that star that leans on me
Was shining years ago. The light that now
Glitters up there my eye may never see,
And so the time lag teases me with how

Love that loves now may not reach me until   5
Its first desire is spent. The star's impulse
Must wait for eyes to claim it beautiful
And love arrived may find us somewhere else.

COMPARE:

"Delay" with "Bright star! would I were steadfast as thou art" by John Keats (page 83).

Ben Jonson (1573? – 1637)*

ON MY FIRST SON   (1603)

Farewell, thou child of my right hand, and joy.
My sin was too much hope of thee, loved boy;
Seven years thou wert lent to me, and I thee pay,
Exacted by thy fate, on the just day.
Oh, could I lose all father° now. For why   *fatherhood*   5
Will man lament the state he should envỳ? —
To have so soon 'scaped world's and flesh's rage,
And, if no other misery, yet age.
Rest in soft peace, and asked, say, "Here doth lie
Ben Jonson his best piece of poetry,"   10
For whose sake henceforth all his vows be such
As what he loves may never like° too much.   *thrive*

ON MY FIRST SON. 1 *child of my right hand:* Jonson's son was named Benjamin; this phrase translates
the Hebrew name. 4 *the just day:* the very day. The boy had died on his seventh birthday.

COMPARE:

"On My First Son" with "To Her Son, H. P." by Katherine Philips (page 360).

Donald Justice (b. 1925)

ON THE DEATH OF FRIENDS IN CHILDHOOD   1960

We shall not ever meet them bearded in heaven,
Nor sunning themselves among the bald of hell;
If anywhere, in the deserted schoolyard at twilight,
Forming a ring, perhaps, or joining hands
In games whose very names we have forgotten.   5
Come, memory, let us seek them there in the shadows.

COMPARE:

"On the Death of Friends in Childhood" and "With rue my heart is laden" by A. E.
Housman (page 143).

John Keats (1795 – 1821)*

ON FIRST LOOKING INTO CHAPMAN'S HOMER   1816

Much have I traveled in the realms of gold,
   And many goodly states and kingdoms seen;
   Round many western islands have I been
Which bards in fealty to Apollo hold.
Oft of one wide expanse had I been told   5
   That deep-browed Homer ruled as his demesne°,   *domain*
   Yet did I never breathe its pure serene
Till I heard Chapman speak out loud and bold.
Then felt I like some watcher of the skies
   When a new planet swims into his ken;   10
Or like stout Cortez when with eagle eyes
   He stared at the Pacific — and all his men
Looked at each other with a wild surmise —
   Silent, upon a peak in Darien.

ON FIRST LOOKING INTO CHAPMAN'S HOMER. When one evening in October 1816 Keats's friend and former teacher Cowden Clarke introduced the young poet to George Chapman's vigorous Elizabethan translations of the *Iliad* and the *Odyssey*, Keats stayed up all night reading and discussing them in high excitement; then went home at dawn to compose this sonnet, which Clarke received at his breakfast table. 4 *fealty:* in feudalism, the loyalty of a vassal to his lord; *Apollo:* classical god of poetic inspiration. 11 *stout Cortez:* the best-known boner in English poetry. (What Spanish explorer *was* the first European to view the Pacific?) 14 *Darien:* old name for the Isthmus of Panama.

John Keats

John Keats (1795–1821)*

WHEN I HAVE FEARS THAT I MAY CEASE TO BE (1818)

When I have fears that I may cease to be
  Before my pen has gleaned my teeming brain,
Before high-pilèd books, in charact'ry°,   *written language*
  Hold like rich garners° the full-ripened grain;   *storehouses*
When I behold, upon the night's starred face,   5
  Huge cloudy symbols of a high romance,
And think that I may never live to trace
  Their shadows with the magic hand of chance;
And when I feel, fair creature of an hour,
  That I shall never look upon thee .nore,   10
Never have relish in the fairy° power   *supernatural*
  Of unreflecting love—then on the shore
Of the wide world I stand alone, and think
  Till love and fame to nothingness do sink.

WHEN I HAVE FEARS THAT I MAY CEASE TO BE. 12 *unreflecting:* thoughtless and spontaneous, rather than deliberate.

John Keats (1795 – 1821)*

TO AUTUMN   1820

I

Season of mists and mellow fruitfulness,
  Close bosom-friend of the maturing sun;
Conspiring with him how to load and bless
  With fruit the vines that round the thatch-eaves run;
To bend with apples the mossed cottage-trees,   5
  And fill all fruit with ripeness to the core;
    To swell the gourd, and plump the hazel shells
  With a sweet kernel; to set budding more,
  And still more, later flowers for the bees,
  Until they think warm days will never cease,   10
    For Summer has o'er-brimmed their clammy cells.

II

Who hath not seen thee oft amid thy store?
  Sometimes whoever seeks abroad may find
Thee sitting careless on a granary floor,
  Thy hair soft-lifted by the winnowing wind;   15

Or on a half-reaped furrow sound asleep,
   Drowsed with the fume of poppies, while thy hook°   *sickle*
     Spares the next swath and all its twinèd flowers:
And sometimes like a gleaner thou dost keep
   Steady thy laden head across a brook;   20
   Or by a cider-press, with patient look,
     Thou watchest the last oozings hours by hours.

III

Where are the songs of Spring? Ay, where are they?
   Think not of them, thou hast thy music too, —
While barrèd clouds bloom the soft-dying day,   25
   And touch the stubble-plains with rosy hue;
Then in a wailful choir the small gnats mourn
   Among the river sallows°, borne aloft   *willows*
     Or sinking as the light wind lives or dies;
And full-grown lambs loud bleat from hilly bourn;   30
   Hedge-crickets sing; and now with treble soft
The red-breast whistles from a garden-croft°   *garden plot*
     And gathering swallows twitter in the skies.

ODE TO AUTUMN. 12 *thee:* Autumn personified. 14 *Thy hair . . . winnowing wind:* Autumn's hair is a billowing cloud of straw. In winnowing, whole blades of grain were laid on a granary floor and beaten with wooden flails, then the beaten mass was tossed in a blanket until the yellow straw (or *chaff*) drifted away on the air, leaving kernels of grain. 30 *bourn:* perhaps meaning a brook. In current English, the word is a cousin of *burn,* as in the first line of Gerard Manley Hopkins's "Inversnaid"; but in archaic English, which Keats sometimes liked, a *bourn* can also be a boundary, or a destination. What possible meaning makes most sense to you?

COMPARE:

"To Autumn" with "In the Elegy Season" by Richard Wilbur (page 46).

Philip Larkin (1922 – 1985)*

HOME IS SO SAD   1964

Home is so sad. It stays as it was left,
Shaped to the comfort of the last to go
As if to win them back. Instead, bereft
Of anyone to please, it withers so,
Having no heart to put aside the theft   5

And turn again to what it started as,
A joyous shot at how things ought to be,
Long fallen wide. You can see how it was:
Look at the pictures and the cutlery.
The music in the piano stool. That vase.   10

Philip Larkin (1922–1985)*

POETRY OF DEPARTURES   1955

Sometimes you hear, fifth-hand,
As epitaph:
He chucked up everything
And just cleared off,
And always the voice will sound   5
Certain you approve
This audacious, purifying,
Elemental move.

And they are right, I think.
We all hate home   10
And having to be there:
I detest my room,
Its specially-chosen junk,
The good books, the good bed,
And my life, in perfect order: 15
So to hear it said

He walked out on the whole crowd
Leaves me flushed and stirred,
Like *Then she undid her dress*
Or *Take that you bastard;*   20
Surely I can, if he did?
And that helps me stay
Sober and industrious.
But I'd go today,

Yes, swagger the nut-strewn roads,   25
Crouch in the fo'c'sle
Stubbly with goodness, if
It weren't so artificial,
Such a deliberate step backwards
To create an object: 30
Books; china; a life
Reprehensibly perfect.

Irving Layton (b. 1912)

THE BULL CALF   1959

The thing could barely stand. Yet taken
from his mother and the barn smells
he still impressed with his pride,

with the promise of sovereignty in the way
his head moved to take us in.   5
The fierce sunlight tugging the maize from the ground
licked at his shapely flanks.
He was too young for all that pride.
I thought of the deposed Richard II.

"No money in bull calves," Freeman had said.   10
The visiting clergyman rubbed the nostrils
now snuffing pathetically at the windless day.
"A pity," he sighed.
My gaze slipped off his hat toward the empty sky
that circled over the black knot of men,   15
over us and the calf waiting for the first blow.

Struck,
the bull calf drew in his thin forelegs
as if gathering strength for a mad rush . . .
tottered . . . raised his darkening eyes to us,   20
and I saw we were at the far end
of his frightened look, growing smaller and smaller
till we were only the ponderous mallet
that flicked his bleeding ear
and pushed him over on his side, stiffly,   25
like a block of wood.

Below the hill's crest
the river snuffled on the improvised beach.
We dug a deep pit and threw the dead calf into it.
It made a wet sound, a sepulchral gurgle,   30
as the warm sides bulged and flattened.
Settled, the bull calf lay as if asleep,
one foreleg over the other,
bereft of pride and so beautiful now,
without movement, perfectly still in the cool pit,   35
I turned away and wept.

COMPARE:

"The Bull Calf" with "Names of Horses" by Donald Hall (page 319).

Denise Levertov

Denise Levertov (b. 1923)*

DIVORCING   1975

>   One garland
>   of flowers, leaves, thorns
> was twined round our two necks.
>   Drawn tight, it could choke us,
>   yet we loved its scratchy grace,   5
>   our fragrant yoke.
>
>   We were Siamese twins.
>   Our blood's not sure
>   if it can circulate,
>   now we are cut apart.   10
> Something in each of us is waiting
>   to see if we can survive,
>   severed.

COMPARE:

"Divorcing" with "You fit into me" by Margaret Atwood and "Hemispheres" by Grace
Schulman (both on page 105).

Philip Levine (b. 1928)

ANIMALS ARE PASSING FROM OUR LIVES   1968

It's wonderful how I jog
on four honed-down ivory toes
my massive buttocks slipping
like oiled parts with each light step.

I'm to market. I can smell   5
the sour, grooved block, I can smell
the blade that opens the hole
and the pudgy white fingers

that shake out the intestines
like a hankie. In my dreams   10
the snouts drool on the marble,
suffering children, suffering flies,

suffering the consumers
who won't meet their steady eyes
for fear they could see. The boy   15
who drives me along believes

that any moment I'll fall
on my side and drum my toes
like a typewriter or squeal
and shit like a new housewife   20

discovering television,
or that I'll turn like a beast
cleverly to hook his teeth
with my teeth. No. Not this pig.

COMPARE:

"Animals Are Passing from Our Lives" with "Butcher Shop" by Charles Simic (page 379).

Stephen Shu-ning Liu (b. 1930)

MY FATHER'S MARTIAL ART   1982

When he came home Mother said he looked
like a monk and stank of green fungus.
At the fireside he told us about life
at the monastery: his rock pillow,
his cold bath, his steel-bar lifting   5
and his wood-chopping. He didn't see
a woman for three winters, on Mountain O Mei.

"My Master was both light and heavy.
He skipped over treetops like a squirrel.
Once he stood on a chair, one foot tied   10
to a rope. We four pulled; we couldn't
move him a bit. His kicks could split
a cedar's trunk."

I saw Father break into a pumpkin
with his fingers. I saw him drop a hawk   15
with bamboo arrows. He rose before dawn, filled
our backyard with a harsh sound *hah, hah, hah:*
there was his Black Dragon Sweep, his Crane Stand,
his Mantis Walk, his Tiger Leap, his Cobra Coil . . .
Infrequently he taught me tricks and made me   20
fight the best of all the village boys.

From a busy street I brood over high cliffs
on O Mei, where my father and his Master sit:
shadows spread across their faces as the smog
between us deepens into a funeral pyre.   25

But don't retreat into night, my father.
Come down from the cliffs. Come
with a single Black Dragon Sweep and hush
this oncoming traffic with your *hah, hah, hah.*

Robert Lowell (1917 – 1977)*

SKUNK HOUR   1959

For Elizabeth Bishop

Nautilus Island's hermit
heiress still lives through winters in her Spartan cottage;
her sheep still graze above the sea.
Her son's a bishop. Her farmer
is first selectman in our village;   5
she's in her dotage.

Thirsting for
the hierarchic privacy
of Queen Victoria's century,
she buys up all   10
the eyesores facing her shore,
and lets them fall.

The season's ill —
we've lost our summer millionaire,
who seemed to leap from an L. L. Bean   15
catalogue. His nine-knot yawl
was auctioned off to lobstermen.
A red fox stain covers Blue Hill.

And now our fairy
decorator brightens his shop for fall;   20
his fishnet's filled with orange cork,

orange, his cobbler's bench and awl;
there is no money in his work,
he'd rather marry.

One dark night, 25
my Tudor Ford climbed the hill's skull;
I watched for love-cars. Lights turned down,
they lay together, hull to hull,
where the graveyard shelves on the town. . . .
My mind's not right. 30

A car radio bleats,
"Love, O careless Love. . . ." I hear
my ill-spirit sob in each blood cell,
as if my hand were at its throat. . . .
I myself am hell; 35
nobody's here —

only skunks, that search
in the moonlight for a bite to eat.
They march on their soles up Main Street:
white stripes, moonstruck eyes' red fire 40
under the chalk-dry and spar spire
of the Trinitarian Church.

I stand on top
of our back steps and breathe the rich air —
a mother skunk with her column of kittens swills the garbage pail. 45
She jabs her wedge-head in a cup
of sour cream, drops her ostrich tail,
and will not scare.

COMPARE:

"Skunk Hour" with "The Wood-Weasel" by Marianne Moore (page 7).

Archibald MacLeish (1892 – 1982)

THE END OF THE WORLD 1926

Quite unexpectedly as Vasserot
The armless ambidextrian was lighting
A match between his great and second toe,
And Ralph the lion was engaged in biting
The neck of Madame Sossman while the drum 5
Pointed, and Teeny was about to cough
In waltz-time swinging Jocko by the thumb —
Quite unexpectedly the top blew off:

And there, there overhead, there, there hung over
Those thousands of white faces, those dazed eyes,   10
There in the starless dark the poise, the hover,
There with vast wings across the canceled skies,
There in the sudden blackness the black pall
Of nothing, nothing, nothing — nothing at all.

Charles Martin (b. 1942)

ROUGH DRAFT   1987

     Popping gum, cracking wise,
       At poolside she defies
Gravity: lifted in her not quite skin-
   tight pink maillol, she shrieks uproar-
iously as the boyfriend starts to spin   5
   Her across one brawny shoulder:

     No Rogers, no Astaire:
      Her legs scissor the air
With an unglamorously panicked glee,
   And he's too stocky and too short   10
For idoldom: set down, she lurches free:
   Her taunting cry, his low retort:

     Ignoring the cold print
      Forbidding it, they sprint
Outrageously around the pool: arrive   15
   In a final burst of laughter
At the deep end: turn without pause and dive
   Into enveloping water:

     Explode at the other
      End, breathless, together.   20
Dripping, subdued, they recompose themselves
   And then go walking off. Traces
Of a distant light lie broken on the waves
   Their passage scribbles and erases.

Andrew Marvell (1621 – 1678)

TO HIS COY MISTRESS   1681

Had we but world enough and time,
This coyness°, lady, were no crime.   *modesty, reluctance*
We would sit down and think which way
To walk, and pass our long love's day.
Thou by the Indian Ganges' side   5
Should'st rubies find; I by the tide
Of Humber would complain°. I would   *sing sad songs*

Love you ten years before the Flood,
And you should, if you please, refuse
Till the conversion of the Jews.   10
My vegetable° love should grow   *vegetative, flourishing*
Vaster than empires, and more slow.
An hundred years should go to praise
Thine eyes, and on thy forehead gaze,
Two hundred to adore each breast,   15
But thirty thousand to the rest.
An age at least to every part,
And the last age should show your heart.
For, lady, you deserve this state°,   *pomp, ceremony*
Nor would I love at lower rate.   20
   But at my back I always hear
Time's wingèd chariot hurrying near,
And yonder all before us lie
Deserts of vast eternity.
Thy beauty shall no more be found,   25
Nor in thy marble vault shall sound
My echoing song; then worms shall try
That long preserved virginity,
And your quaint honor turn to dust,
And into ashes all my lust.   30
The grave's a fine and private place,
But none, I think, do there embrace.
   Now therefore, while the youthful hue
Sits on thy skin like morning glew°   *glow*
And while thy willing soul transpires   35
At every pore with instant° fires,   *eager*
Now let us sport us while we may;
And now, like amorous birds of prey,
Rather at once our time devour
Than languish in his slow-chapped° power.   *slow-jawed*   40
Let us roll all our strength and all
Our sweetness up into one ball
And tear our pleasures with rough strife
Thorough° the iron gates of life.   *through*
Thus, though we cannot make our sun   45
Stand still, yet we will make him run.

To His Coy Mistress. 7 *Humber:* a river that flows by Marvell's town of Hull (on the side of the
world opposite from the Ganges). 10 *conversion of the Jews:* an event that, according to St. John
the Divine, is to take place just before the end of the world. 35 *transpires:* exudes, as a membrane
lets fluid or vapor pass through it.

COMPARE:

"To His Coy Mistress" with "To the Virgins, to Make Much of Time" by Robert
Herrick (page 329).

George Meredith (1828 – 1909)

LUCIFER IN STARLIGHT   1883

On a starred night Prince Lucifer uprose,
   Tired of his dark dominion, swung the fiend
   Above the rolling ball in cloud part screened,
Where sinners hugged their specter of repose.
Poor prey to his hot fit of pride were those.   5
   And now upon his western wing he leaned,
   Now his huge bulk o'er Afric's sands careened,
Now the black planet shadowed Arctic snows.
Soaring through wider zones that pricked his scars
   With memory of the old revolt from Awe,   10
He reached a middle height, and at the stars,
Which are the brain of heaven, he looked, and sank.
Around the ancient track marched, rank on rank,
   The army of unalterable law.

James Merrill (b. 1926)

LABORATORY POEM   1958

Charles used to watch Naomi, taking heart
And a steel saw, open up turtles, live.
While she swore they felt nothing, he would gag
At blood, at the blind twitching, even after
The murky dawn of entrails cleared, revealing   5
Contours he knew, egg-yellows like lamps paling.

Well then. She carried off the beating heart
To the kymograph and rigged it there, a rag
In fitful wind, now made to strain, now stopped
By her solutions tonic or malign   10
Alternately in which it would be steeped.
What the heart bore, she noted on a chart,

For work did not stop only with the heart.
He thought of certain human hearts, their climb
Through violence into exquisite disciplines   15
Of which, as it now appeared, they all expired.
Soon she would fetch another and start over,
Easy in the presence of her lover.

LABORATORY POEM. 8 *kymograph*: device to record wavelike motions or pulsations on a piece of paper fastened to a revolving drum.

Charlotte Mew (1869–1928)

THE FARMER'S BRIDE   1916

Three Summers since I chose a maid,
Too young maybe—but more's to do
At harvest-time than bide and woo.
    When us was wed she turned afraid
Of love and me and all things human;   5
Like the shut of a winter's day.
Her smile went out, and 'twasn't a woman—
    More like a little frightened fay.°   *elf*
        One night, in the Fall, she runned away.

"Out 'mong the sheep, her be," they said,   10
'Should properly have been abed;
But sure enough she wasn't there
Lying awake with her wide brown stare.
So over seven-acre field and up-along across the down
We chased her, flying like a hare   15
Before our lanterns. To Church-Town
    All in a shiver and a scare
We caught her, fetched her home at last
    And turned the key upon her, fast.

She does the work about the house   20
As well as most, but like a mouse:
    Happy enough to chat and play
    With birds and rabbits and such as they,
    So long as men-folk keep away.
"Not near, not near!" her eyes beseech   25
When one of us comes within reach.
    The women say that beasts in stall
    Look round like children at her call.
    I've hardly heard her speak at all.
Shy as a leveret, swift as he,   30
Straight and slight as a young larch tree,
Sweet as the first wild violets, she,
To her wild self. But what to me?

The short days shorten and the oaks are brown,
    The blue smoke rises to the low gray sky,   35
One leaf in the still air falls slowly down,
    A magpie's spotted feathers lie
On the black earth spread white with rime,°   *frost*
The berries redden up to Christmas-time.

What's Christmas-time without there be   40
Some other in the house than we!

She sleeps up in the attic there
Alone, poor maid. 'Tis but a stair
Betwixt us. Oh! my God! the down,
The soft young down of her, the brown,   45
The brown of her—her eyes, her hair, her hair!

Edna St. Vincent Millay (1892–1950)*

Recuerdo   1920

We were very tired, we were very merry—
We had gone back and forth all night on the ferry.
It was bare and bright, and smelled like a stable—
But we looked into a fire, we leaned across a table,
We lay on a hill-top underneath the moon;   5
And the whistles kept blowing, and the dawn came soon.

We were very tired, we were very merry—
We had gone back and forth all night on the ferry;
And you ate an apple, and I ate a pear,
From a dozen of each we had bought somewhere;   10
And the sky went wan, and the wind came cold,
And the sun rose dripping, a bucketful of gold.

We were very tired, we were very merry,
We had gone back and forth all night on the ferry.
We hailed, "Good morrow, mother!" to a shawl-covered head, 15
And bought a morning paper, which neither of us read;
And she wept, "God bless you!" for the apples and pears,
And we gave her all our money but our subway fares.

Recuerdo. The Spanish title means "a recollection" or "a memory."

John Milton (1608 – 1674)*

When I consider how my light is spent   (1655?)

When I consider how my light is spent,
    Ere half my days in this dark world and wide,
    And that one talent which is death to hide
Lodged with me useless, though my soul more bent
To serve therewith my Maker, and present   5
    My true account, lest He returning chide;
    "Doth God exact day-labor, light denied?"

I fondly° ask. But Patience, to prevent   *foolishly*
That murmur, soon replies, "God doth not need
    Either man's work or His own gifts. Who best   10
    Bear His mild yoke, they serve Him best. His state
Is kingly: thousands at His bidding speed,
    And post o'er land and ocean without rest;
    They also serve who only stand and wait."

WHEN I CONSIDER HOW MY LIGHT IS SPENT. 1 *my light is spent:* Milton had become blind. 3 *that one talent:* For Jesus's parable of the talents (measures of money), see Matthew 25:14 – 30.

COMPARE:

"When I consider how my light is spent" with "Thou art indeed just, Lord, if I contend"
by Gerard Manley Hopkins (page 334).

Marianne Moore

Marianne Moore (1887 – 1972)*

THE MIND IS AN ENCHANTING THING   1944

is an enchanted thing
    like the glaze on a
katydid-wing
        subdivided by sun
        till the nettings are legion.   5
Like Gieseking playing Scarlatti;

like the apteryx-awl
    as a beak, or the
kiwi's rain-shawl
        of haired feathers, the mind   10
        feeling its way as though blind,
walks along with its eyes on the ground.

It has memory's ear
        that can hear without
having to hear.   15
                Like the gyroscope's fall,
                truly unequivocal
because trued by regnant certainty,

it is a power of
        strong enchantment. It   20
is like the dove-
                neck animated by
                sun; it is memory's eye;
it's conscientious inconsistency.

It tears off the veil; tears   25
        the temptation, the
mist the heart wears,
                from its eyes, — if the heart
                has a face; it takes apart
dejection. It's fire in the dove-neck's   30

iridescence; in the
        inconsistencies
of Scarlatti.
                Unconfusion submits
                its confusion to proof; it's   35
not a Herod's oath that cannot change.

THE MIND IS AN ENCHANTING THING. 6 *Gieseking . . . Scarlatti:* Walter Gieseking (1895 – 1956),
German pianist, was a celebrated performer of the difficult sonatas of Italian composer Domenico
Scarlatti (1685 – 1757). 7 *apteryx-awl:* awl-shaped beak of the apteryx, one of the kiwi family. (An
awl is a pointed tool for piercing wood or leather.) 36 *Herod's oath:* King Herod's order condemning
to death all infants in Bethlehem (Matthew 2:1 – 16). In one medieval English version of the Herod
story, a pageant play, the king causes the death of his own child by refusing to withdraw his
command.

Howard Nemerov (b. 1920)

THE SNOW GLOBE   1955

A long time ago, when I was a child,
They left my light on while I went to sleep,
As though they would have wanted me beguiled
By brightness if at all; dark was too deep.

And they left me one toy, a village white   5
With the fresh snow and silently in glass
Frozen forever. But if you shook it,
The snow would rise up in the rounded space

And from the limits of the universe
Snow itself down again. O world of white,   10
First home of dreams! Now that I have my dead,
I want so cold an emblem to rehearse
How many of them have gone from the world's light,
As I have gone, too, from my snowy bed.

John Frederick Nims (b. 1914)*

LOVE POEM   1947

My clumsiest dear, whose hands shipwreck vases, *a*
At whose quick touch all glasses chip and ring, *b*
Whose palms are bulls in china, burs in linen, *c*
And have no cunning with any soft thing *D*

Except all ill-at-ease fidgeting people: 5
The refugee uncertain at the door
You make at home; deftly you steady
The drunk clambering on his undulant floor.

Unpredictable dear, the taxi drivers' terror,
Shrinking from far headlights pale as a dime   10
Yet leaping before red apoplectic streetcars —
Misfit in any space. And never on time.

A wrench in clocks and the solar system. Only
With words and people and love you move at ease.
In traffic of wit expertly manoeuvre   15
And keep us, all devotion, at your knees.

Forgetting your coffee spreading on our flannel,
Your lipstick grinning on our coat,
So gayly in love's unbreakable heaven
Our souls on glory of spilt bourbon float.   20

Be with me, darling, early and late. Smash glasses —
I will study wry music for your sake.
For should your hands drop white and empty
All the toys of the world would break.

Sharon Olds (b. 1942)

THE ONE GIRL AT THE BOYS PARTY   1983

When I take my girl to the swimming party
I set her down among the boys. They tower and
bristle, she stands there smooth and sleek,
her math scores unfolding in the air around her.
They will strip to their suits, her body hard and   5
indivisible as a prime number,
they'll plunge in the deep end, she'll subtract
her height from ten feet, divide it into
hundreds of gallons of water, the numbers
bouncing in her mind like molecules of chlorine   10
in the bright blue pool. When they climb out,
her ponytail will hang its pencil lead
down her back, her narrow silk suit
with hamburgers and french fries printed on it
will glisten in the brilliant air, and they will   15
see her sweet face, solemn and
sealed, a factor of one, and she will
see their eyes, two each,
their legs, two each, and the curves of their sexes,
one each, and in her head she'll be doing her   20
wild multiplying, as the drops
sparkle and fall to the power of a thousand from her body.

Wilfred Owen (1893 – 1918)*

ANTHEM FOR DOOMED YOUTH   (1917?)

What passing-bells for these who die as cattle?
        Only the monstrous anger of the guns.
Only the stuttering rifles' rapid rattle
Can patter out their hasty orisons.
No mockeries now for them; no prayers nor bells,   5
        Nor any voice of mourning save the choirs, —
The shrill, demented choirs of wailing shells;
        And bugles calling for them from sad shires°.   counties

What candles may be held to speed them all?
        Not in the hands of boys, but in their eyes   10
        Shall shine the holy glimmers of good-byes.
The pallor of girls' brows shall be their pall;
Their flowers the tenderness of patient minds,
And each slow dusk a drawing-down of blinds.

Linda Pastan

Linda Pastan (b. 1932)*

ETHICS   1980

In ethics class so many years ago
our teacher asked this question every fall:
if there were a fire in a museum
which would you save, a Rembrandt painting
or an old woman who hadn't many   5
years left anyhow? Restless on hard chairs
caring little for pictures or old age
we'd opt one year for life, the next for art
and always half-heartedly. Sometimes
the woman borrowed my grandmother's face   10
leaving her usual kitchen to wander
some drafty, half imagined museum.
One year, feeling clever, I replied
why not let the woman decide herself?
Linda, the teacher would report, eschews   15
the burdens of responsibility.
This fall in a real museum I stand
before a real Rembrandt, old woman,
or nearly so, myself. The colors
within this frame are darker than autumn,   20
darker even than winter — the browns of earth,
though earth's most radiant elements burn
through the canvas. I know now that woman
and painting and season are almost one
and all beyond saving by children.   25

Katherine Philips (1632–1664)

ON HER SON, H.P.   (1655?)

What on earth deserves our trust?
Youth and beauty both are dust.
Long we gathering are with pain
What one moment calls again.
Seven years' childless marriage past,   5
A son, a son is born at last:
So exactly limned and fair,
Full of good spirits, mien, and air,
As a long life promisèd,
Yet, in less than six weeks, dead.   10
Too promising, too great a mind
In so small room to be confined;
Therefore, fit in Heaven to dwell,
He quickly broke the prison shell.
So the subtle° alchemist   *ingenious* 15
Can't with Hermes' seal resist
The powerful spirit's subtler flight,
But 'twill bid him long good night.
So the sun, if it arise
Half so glorious as his eyes,   20
Like this infant takes a shroud,
Buried in a morning cloud.

ON HER SON, H. P. In 1655, after seven years of marriage, the poet gave birth to her first child, Hector Philips, who lived only a few days. When this poem was first published (posthumously, in 1667), Philips's friend and editor Sir Charles Cotterell called it "EPITAPH. On Her Son H.P. at St. Syth's Church where her body also lies Interred." 7 *limned:* drawn or outlined in sharp detail (also a pun on *limbed*). 16 *Hermes' seal:* hermetic seal, such as might render an alchemist's bottle or beaker airtight (but still, in Philips's simile, fail to prevent its contents from leaking or evaporating). 22 *morning:* another pun.

COMPARE:

"On Her Son, H.P." with "On My First Son" by Ben Jonson (page 340).

Robert Phillips (b. 1938)

RUNNING ON EMPTY   1981

As a teenager I would drive Father's
Chevrolet cross-county, given me

reluctantly: "Always keep the tank
half full, boy, half full, ya hear?"

The fuel gauge dipping, dipping   5
toward Empty, hitting Empty, then

— thrilling! — 'way below Empty,
myself driving cross-county

mile after mile, faster and faster,
all night long, this crazy kid driving   10

the earth's rolling surface,
against all laws, defying chemistry,

rules, and time, riding on nothing
but fumes, pushing luck harder

than anyone pushed before, the wind   15
screaming past like the Furies . . .

I stranded myself only once, a white
night with no gas station open, ninety miles

from nowhere. Panicked for a while,
at standstill, myself stalled.   20

At dawn the car and I both refilled. But,
Father, I am running on empty still.

RUNNING ON EMPTY. 16 *Furies:* In Greek mythology, deities who pursue and torment evildoers.

Sylvia Plath (1932 – 1963)*

DADDY   1965

You do not do, you do not do
Any more, black shoe
In which I have lived like a foot
For thirty years, poor and white,
Barely daring to breathe or Achoo.   5

Daddy, I have had to kill you.
You died before I had time —
Marble-heavy, a bag full of God,
Ghastly statue with one grey toe
Big as a Frisco seal   10

And a head in the freakish Atlantic
Where it pours bean green over blue
In the waters off beautiful Nauset.
I used to pray to recover you.
Ach, du.   15

In the German tongue, in the Polish town
Scraped flat by the roller
Of wars, wars, wars.
But the name of the town is common.
My Polack friend   20

Says there are a dozen or two.
So I never could tell where you
Put your foot, your root,
I never could talk to you.
The tongue stuck in my jaw.   25

It stuck in a barb wire snare.
Ich, ich, ich, ich,
I could hardly speak.
I thought every German was you.
And the language obscene   30

An engine, an engine
Chuffing me off like a Jew.
A Jew to Dachau, Auschwitz, Belsen.
I began to talk like a Jew.
I think I may well be a Jew.   35

The snows of the Tyrol, the clear beer of Vienna
Are not very pure or true.
With my gypsy ancestress and my weird luck
And my Taroc pack and my Taroc pack
I may be a bit of a Jew.   40

I have always been scared of *you*,
With your Luftwaffe, your gobbledygoo.
And your neat moustache
And your Aryan eye, bright blue.
Panzer-man, panzer-man, O You —   45

Not God but a swastika
So black no sky could squeak through.
Every woman adores a Fascist,
The boot in the face, the brute
Brute heart of a brute like you.   50

You stand at the blackboard, daddy,
In the picture I have of you,
A cleft in your chin instead of your foot
But no less a devil for that, no not
Any less the black man who   55

15 *Ach, du:* Oh, you. 27 *Ich, ich, ich, ich:* I, I, I, I. 51 *blackboard:* Otto Plath had been a professor
of biology at Boston University.

Bit my pretty red heart in two.
I was ten when they buried you.
At twenty I tried to die
And get back, back, back to you.
I thought even the bones will do.   60

But they pulled me out of the sack,
And they stuck me together with glue.
And then I knew what to do.
I made a model of you,
A man in black with a Meinkampf look   65

And a love of the rack and the screw.
And I said I do, I do.
So daddy, I'm finally through.
The black telephone's off at the root,
The voices just can't worm through.   70

If I've killed one man, I've killed two —
The vampire who said he was you
And drank my blood for a year,
Seven years, if you want to know.
Daddy, you can lie back now.   75

There's a stake in your fat black heart
And the villagers never liked you.
They are dancing and stamping on you.
They always *knew* it was you.
Daddy, daddy, you bastard, I'm through.   80

DADDY. Introducing this poem in a reading, Sylvia Plath remarked:

The poem is spoken by a girl with an Electra complex. Her father died while she thought he was
God. Her case is complicated by the fact that her father was also a Nazi and her mother very possibly
part Jewish. In the daughter the two strains marry and paralyze each other — she has to act out
the awful little allegory before she is free of it.

(Quoted by A. Alvarez, *Beyond All This Fiddle,* New York, 1971.) In some details "Daddy" is
autobiography: the poet's father, Otto Plath, a German, had come to the United States from
Grabow, Poland. He had died following amputation of a gangrened foot and leg, when Sylvia was
eight years old. Politically, Otto Plath was a Republican, not a Nazi; but was apparently a somewhat
domineering head of the household. (See the recollections of the poet's mother, Aurelia Schober
Plath, in her edition of *Letters Home* by Sylvia Plath, New York, 1975.)

65 *Meinkampf:* Adolf Hitler entitled his autobiography *Mein Kampf* ("My Struggle").

COMPARE:
"Daddy" with "American Primitive" by William Jay Smith (page 383).

Sylvia Plath

Sylvia Plath (1932 – 1963)*

MORNING SONG   1965

Love set you going like a fat gold watch.
The midwife slapped your footsoles, and your bald cry
Took its place among the elements.

Our voices echo, magnifying your arrival. New statue.
In a drafty museum, your nakedness   5
Shadows our safety. We stand round blankly as walls.

I'm no more your mother
Than the cloud that distills a mirror to reflect its own slow
Effacement at the wind's hand.

All night your moth-breath   10
Flickers among the flat pink roses. I wake to listen:
A far sea moves in my ear.

One cry, and I stumble from bed, cow-heavy and floral
In my Victorian nightgown.
Your mouth opens clean as a cat's. The window square   15

Whitens and swallows its dull stars. And now you try
Your handful of notes;
The clear vowels rise like balloons.

Ezra Pound

Ezra Pound (1885 – 1972)*

THE RIVER-MERCHANT'S WIFE: A LETTER   1915

While my hair was still cut straight across my forehead
I played about the front gate, pulling flowers.
You came by on bamboo stilts, playing horse,
You walked about my seat, playing with blue plums.
And we went on living in the village of Chokan: 5
Two small people, without dislike or suspicion.
At fourteen I married My Lord you.
I never laughed, being bashful.
Lowering my head, I looked at the wall.
Called to, a thousand times, I never looked back.   10

At fifteen I stopped scowling,
I desired my dust to be mingled with yours
Forever and forever and forever.
Why should I climb the lookout?

At sixteen you departed,   15
You went into far Ku-to-yen, by the river of swirling eddies,
And you have been gone five months.
The monkeys make sorrowful noise overhead.

You dragged your feet when you went out.
By the gate now, the moss is grown, the different mosses,   20
Too deep to clear them away!
The leaves fall early this autumn, in wind.
The paired butterflies are already yellow with August
Over the grass in the West garden;
They hurt me. I grow older.   25

If you are coming down through the narrows of the river Kiang,
Please let me know before hand,
And I will come out to meet you
        As far as Cho-fu-sa.

THE RIVER-MERCHANT'S WIFE: A LETTER. A free translation from the Chinese poet Li Po (eighth century).

Dudley Randall (b. 1914)*

OLD WITHERINGTON   1966

Old Witherington had drunk too much again.
The children changed their play and packed around him
To jeer his latest brawl. Their parents followed.

Prune-black, with bloodshot eyes and one white tooth,
He tottered in the night with legs spread wide   5
Waving a hatchet. "Come on, come on," he piped,
"And I'll baptize these bricks with bloody kindling.
I may be old and drunk, but not afraid
To die. I've died before. A million times
I've died and gone to hell. I live in hell.   10
If I die now I die, and put an end
To all this loneliness. Nobody cares
Enough to even fight me now, except
This crazy bastard here."

                    And with these words
He cursed the little children, cursed his neighbors,   15
Cursed his father, mother, and his wife,
Himself, and God, and all the rest of the world,
All but his grinning adversary, who, crouched,
Danced tenderly around him with a jag-toothed bottle,
As if the world compressed to one old man   20
Who was the sun, and he sole faithful planet.

Dudley Randall

John Crowe Ransom (1888 – 1974)

BELLS FOR JOHN WHITESIDE'S DAUGHTER   1924

There was such speed in her little body,
And such lightness in her footfall,
It is no wonder her brown study
Astonishes us all.

Her wars were bruited in our high window.   5
We looked among orchard trees and beyond,
Where she took arms against her shadow,
Or harried unto the pond

The lazy geese, like a snow cloud
Dripping their snow on the green grass,   10
Tricking and stopping, sleepy and proud,
Who cried in goose, Alas,

For the tireless heart within the little
Lady with rod that made them rise
From their noon apple-dreams, and scuttle   15
Goose-fashion under the skies!

But now go the bells, and we are ready;
In one house we are sternly stopped
To say we are vexed at her brown study,
Lying so primly propped.   20

COMPARE:

"Bells for John Whiteside's Daughter" with "Elegy for Jane" by Theodore Roethke (page 371).

Henry Reed (1914 – 1986)

NAMING OF PARTS   1946

Today we have naming of parts. Yesterday,
We had daily cleaning. And tomorrow morning,
We shall have what to do after firing. But today,
Today we have naming of parts. Japonica
Glistens like coral in all of the neighboring gardens,   5
          And today we have naming of parts.

This is the lower sling swivel. And this
Is the upper sling swivel, whose use you will see,
When you are given your slings. And this is the piling swivel,
Which in your case you have not got. The branches   10
Hold in the gardens their silent, eloquent gestures,
          Which in our case we have not got.

This is the safety-catch, which is always released
With an easy flick of the thumb. And please do not let me
See anyone using his finger. You can do it quite easy   15
If you have any strength in your thumb. The blossoms
Are fragile and motionless, never letting anyone see
   Any of them using their finger.

And this you can see is the bolt. The purpose of this
Is to open the breech, as you see. We can slide it   20
Rapidly backwards and forwards: we call this
Easing the spring. And rapidly backwards and forwards
The early bees are assaulting and fumbling the flowers:
   They call it easing the Spring.

They call it easing the Spring: it is perfectly easy   25
If you have any strength in your thumb: like the bolt,
And the breech, and the cocking-piece, and the point of balance,
Which in our case we have not got; and the almond-blossom
Silent in all of the gardens and the bees going backwards and
  forwards,
   For today we have naming of parts.   30

COMPARE:

"Naming of Parts" with "The Fury of Aerial Bombardment" by Richard Eberhart (page
56).

Adrienne Rich (b. 1929)*

AUNT JENNIFER'S TIGERS   1951

Aunt Jennifer's tigers prance across a screen,
Bright topaz denizens of a world of green.
They do not fear the men beneath the tree;
They pace in sleek chivalric certainty.

Aunt Jennifer's fingers fluttering through her wool   5
Find even the ivory needle hard to pull.
The massive weight of Uncle's wedding band
Sits heavily upon Aunt Jennifer's hand.

When Aunt is dead, her terrified hands will lie
Still ringed with ordeals she was mastered by.   10
The tigers in the panel that she made
Will go on prancing, proud and unafraid.

Adrienne Rich

Adrienne Rich (b. 1929)*

THE NINTH SYMPHONY OF BEETHOVEN UNDERSTOOD AT LAST AS A SEXUAL MESSAGE   1973

A man in terror of impotence
or infertility, not knowing the difference
a man trying to tell something
howling from the climacteric
music of the entirely   5
isolated soul
yelling at Joy from the tunnel of the ego
music without the ghost
of another person in it, music
trying to tell something the man   10
does not want out, would keep if he could
gagged and bound and flogged with chords of Joy
where everything is silence and the
beating of a bloody fist upon
a splintered table   15

THE NINTH SYMPHONY OF BEETHOVEN UNDERSTOOD AT LAST AS A SEXUAL MESSAGE. In 1824, three years before his death, Ludwig van Beethoven (1770–1827), increasingly isolated by severe deafness, wrote his final (and, some say, greatest) symphony. 4 *climacteric music:* music written at a turning point or critical stage in life. In women, the *climacteric* is menopause; in men, it is that corresponding time when sexual activity and potency decline. 7 *yelling at Joy:* In the symphony's closing movement, four leading singers and a full chorus sing poet Friedrich von Schiller's ode "An die freude" ("To Joy"). This triumphant, rousing finale (in the words of critic Stefan Kunze) makes "an ecstatic, enthusiastic appeal to all humanity to unite in honor of a joy that shall flood every soul alive."

Adrienne Rich (b. 1929)*

TRYING TO TALK WITH A MAN   1973

Out in this desert we are testing bombs,
that's why we came here.

Sometimes I feel an underground river
forcing its way between deformed cliffs
an acute angle of understanding   5
moving itself like a locus of the sun
into this condemned scenery.

What we've had to give up to get here—
whole LP collections, films we starred in
playing in the neighborhoods, bakery windows   10
full of dry, chocolate-filled Jewish cookies,
the language of love-letters, of suicide notes,
afternoons on the riverbank
pretending to be children

Coming out to this desert   15
we meant to change the face of
driving among dull green succulents
walking at noon in the ghost town
surrounded by a silence

that sounds like the silence of the place   20
except that it came with us
and is familiar
and everything we were saying until now
was an effort to blot it out—
coming out here we are up against it   25

Out here I feel more helpless
with you than without you

You mention the danger
and list the equipment
we talk of people caring for each other   30
in emergencies—laceration, thirst—
but you look at me like an emergency

Your dry heat feels like power
your eyes are stars of a different magnitude
they reflect lights that spell out: EXIT   35
when you get up and pace the floor

talking of the danger
as if it were not ourselves
as if we were testing anything else.

COMPARE:

"TRYING TO TALK WITH A MAN" with "Once in a While a Protest Poem" by David B.
Axelrod (page 57).

Theodore Roethke

Theodore Roethke (1908 – 1963)*

Elegy for Jane   1953

My Student, Thrown by a Horse

I remember the neckcurls, limp and damp as tendrils;
And her quick look, a sidelong pickerel smile;
And how, once startled into talk, the light syllables leaped for her,
And she balanced in the delight of her thought,
A wren, happy, tail into the wind,   5
Her song trembling the twigs and small branches.
The shade sang with her;
The leaves, their whispers turned to kissing;
And the mold sang in the bleached valleys under the rose.

Oh, when she was sad, she cast herself down into such a pure depth,   10
Even a father could not find her:
Scraping her cheek against straw;
Stirring the clearest water.

My sparrow, you are not here,
Waiting like a fern, making a spiny shadow.   15
The sides of wet stones cannot console me,
Nor the moss, wound with the last light.

If only I could nudge you from this sleep,
My maimed darling, my skittery pigeon.
Over this damp grave I speak the words of my love: 20
I, with no rights in this matter,
Neither father nor lover.

COMPARE:

"Elegy for Jane" with "Bells for John Whiteside's Daughter" by John Crowe Ransom
(page 367).

Gibbons Ruark (b. 1941)

WAITING FOR YOU WITH THE SWALLOWS   1983

I was waiting for you
Where the four lanes wander
Into a city street,
Listening to the freight
Train's whistle and thunder   5
Come racketing through,

And I saw beyond black
Empty branches the light
Turn swiftly to a flurry
Of wingbeats in a hurry   10
For nowhere but the flight
From steeple-top and back

To steeple-top again.
I thought of how the quick
Hair shadows your lit face   15
Till laughter in your voice
Awoke and brought me back
And you stepped from the train.

I was waiting for you
Not a little too long   20
To learn what swallows said
Darkening overhead:
When we had time, we sang.
After we sang, we flew.

Paul Ruffin (b. 1941)

HOTEL FIRE: NEW ORLEANS   1980

From first light we fear falling:
after the fever of birth, impetus
toward that natural window, we
reach, cling, our fingers and toes
curled to grip, after the fire   5
that tempers us for the sun.

There I saw them — I see them still —
thrust from windows,
flailing like children
who know the earth has failed them: 10
they snatch at chinks, to ledges,
tumble to the wet street below,
the fire an old and certain death,
the leap the only faith that's left.

Anne Sexton

Anne Sexton (1928–1974)

THE KISS   1969

My mouth blooms like a cut.
I've been wronged all year, tedious
nights, nothing but rough elbows in them
and delicate boxes of Kleenex calling *crybaby*
crybaby, you fool!   5

Before today my body was useless.
Now it's tearing at its square corners.
It's tearing old Mary's garments off, knot by knot
and see—Now it's shot full of these electric bolts.
Zing! A resurrection!   10

Once it was a boat, quite wooden
and with no business, no salt water under it
and in need of some paint. It was no more
than a group of boards. But you hoisted her, rigged her.
She's been elected.   15

My nerves are turned on. I hear them like
musical instruments. Where there was silence
the drums, the strings are incurably playing. You did this.
Pure genius at work. Darling, the composer has stepped
into fire.   20

COMPARE:

"The Kiss" with "The Ninth Symphony of Beethoven Understood at Last as a Sexual
Message" by Adrienne Rich (page 369).

William Shakespeare (1564–1616)*

NOT MARBLE NOR THE GILDED MONUMENTS   1609

Not marble, nor the gilded monuments
Of princes, shall outlive this powerful rhyme;
But you shall shine more bright in these contents
Than unswept stone, besmeared with sluttish time.
When wasteful war shall statues overturn,   5
And broils root out the work of masonry,
Nor Mars his sword nor war's quick fire shall burn
The living record of your memory.
'Gainst death and all-oblivious enmity
Shall you pace forth; your praise shall still find room   10
Even in the eyes of all posterity
That wear this world out to the ending doom.
    So, till the judgment that yourself arise.
    You live in this, and dwell in lovers' eyes.

COMPARE:

"Not marble nor the gilded monuments" with "To the Stone-cutters" by Robinson
Jeffers (page 339).

William Shakespeare

William Shakespeare (1564 – 1616)*

THAT TIME OF YEAR THOU MAYST IN ME BEHOLD   1609

That time of year thou mayst in me behold
When yellow leaves, or none, or few, do hang
Upon those boughs which shake against the cold,
Bare ruined choirs where late the sweet birds sang.
In me thou see'st the twilight of such day   5
As after sunset fadeth in the west,
Which by-and-by black night doth take away,
Death's second self that seals up all in rest.
In me thou see'st the glowing of such fire
That on the ashes of his youth doth lie,   10
As the deathbed whereon it must expire,
Consumed with that which it was nourished by.
   This thou perceiv'st, which makes thy love more strong,
   To love that well which thou must leave ere long.

William Shakespeare (1564 – 1616)*

WHEN, IN DISGRACE WITH FORTUNE AND MEN'S EYES   1609

When, in disgrace with Fortune and men's eyes,
I all alone beweep my outcast state,
And trouble deaf heaven with my bootless° cries,   *futile*
And look upon myself and curse my fate,
Wishing me like to one more rich in hope,   5
Featured like him, like him with friends possessed,
Desiring this man's art, and that man's scope,
With what I most enjoy contented least,
Yet in these thoughts myself almost despising,
Haply° I think on thee, and then my state,   *luckily*   10
Like to the lark at break of day arising
From sullen earth, sings hymns at heaven's gate;
    For thy sweet love rememb'red such wealth brings
    That then I scorn to change my state with kings.

William Shakespeare (1564 – 1616)*

WHEN DAISIES PIED AND VIOLETS BLUE   1598

When daisies pied and violets blue
    And lady-smocks all silver-white
And cuckoo-buds° of yellow hue   *buttercups*
    Do paint the meadows with delight,
The cuckoo then, on every tree,   5
Mocks married men; for thus sings he,
         "Cuckoo,
Cuckoo, cuckoo!" — O word of fear,
Unpleasing to a married ear!

When shepherds pipe on oaten straws,   10
    And merry larks are ploughmen's clocks,
When turtles tread°, and rooks, and daws,   *turtledoves mate*
    And maidens bleach their summer smocks,
The cuckoo then, on every tree,
Mocks married men; for thus sings he,   15
         "Cuckoo,
Cuckoo, cuckoo!" — O word of fear,
Unpleasing to a married ear!

WHEN DAISIES PIED. This song and "When icicles hang by the wall" conclude the play *Love's Labor's Lost*. 2 *lady-smocks:* also named cuckoo-flowers. 8 O *word of fear:* because it sounds like *cuckold*, a man whose wife has deceived him.

William Shakespeare (1564 – 1616)*

WHEN ICICLES HANG BY THE WALL   1598

When icicles hang by the wall,
 And Dick the shepherd blows his nail,
And Tom bears logs into the hall,
 And milk comes frozen home in pail,
When blood is nipped and ways° be foul,   *roads* 5
 Then nightly sings the staring owl:
   "Tu-whit, to-who!"
  A merry note,
While greasy Joan doth keel° the pot.   *cool (as by skimming or stirring)*

When all aloud the wind doth blow,   10
 And coughing drowns the parson's saw°, *old saw, platitude*
And birds sit brooding in the snow,
 And Marian's nose looks red and raw,
When roasted crabs° hiss in the bowl,   *crab apples*
 Then nightly sings the staring owl: 15
   "Tu-whit, to-who!"
  A merry note,
While greasy Joan doth keel the pot.

Karl Shapiro (b. 1913)

THE DIRTY WORD   1947

 The dirty word hops in the cage of the mind like the Pondicherry vulture, stomping with its heavy left claw on the sweet meat of the brain and tearing it with its vicious beak, ripping and chopping the flesh. Terrified, the small boy bears the big bird of the dirty word into the house, and grunting, puffing, carries it up the stairs to his own room in 5 the skull. Bits of black feather cling to his clothes and his hair as he locks the staring creature in the dark closet.

 All day the small boy returns to the closet to examine and feed the bird, to caress and kick the bird, that now snaps and flaps its wings savagely whenever the door is opened. How the boy trembles and delights 10 at the sight of the white excrement of the bird! How the bird leaps and rushes against the walls of the skull, trying to escape from the zoo of the vocabulary! How wildly snaps the sweet meat of the brain in its rage.

 And the bird outlives the man, being freed at the man's death-funeral by a word from the rabbi.   15

 (But I one morning went upstairs and opened the door and entered the closet and found in the cage of my mind the great bird dead. Softly I wept it and softly removed it and softly buried the body of the bird in

the hollyhock garden of the house I lived in twenty years before. And out
of the worn black feathers of the wing have I made these pens to write   20
these elegies, for I have outlived the bird, and I have murdered it in my
early manhood.)

Richard Shelton (b. 1933)

MEXICO   1978

once each year
after a warm day in April
when darkness comes to the desert
uninvited but planning to spend the night
something hits me like a shovel   5
and I am stunned into believing
anything is possible

there is no overture to frenzy
I simply look up and see Scorpio
most dangerous of friends   10
with the last two stars in his tail
blinking like lights at a railroad crossing
while in one claw he holds the top
of a mountain in Mexico

and suddenly I know   15
everything I need is waiting for me
south of here in another country
and I have been walking through empty
rooms and talking to furniture

then I say to myself   20
why should I stay home and listen to Bach
such precision could have happened
to anyone to an infinite number
of monkeys with harpsichords

and next morning I start south   25
with my last chances flapping their wings
while birds of passage stream over me
in the opposite direction

I never find what I am looking for
and each time I return older   30
with my ugliness intact
but with the knowledge that if it isn't there
in the darkness under Scorpio
it isn't anywhere

Charles Simic (b. 1938)

BUTCHER SHOP   1971

Sometimes walking late at night
I stop before a closed butcher shop.
There is a single light in the store
Like the light in which the convict digs his tunnel.

An apron hangs on the hook: 5
The blood on it smeared into a map
Of the great continents of blood,
The great rivers and oceans of blood.

There are knives that glitter like altars
In a dark church   10
Where they bring the cripple and the imbecile
To be healed.

There's a wooden block where bones are broken,
Scraped clean—a river dried to its bed
Where I am fed,   15
Where deep in the night I hear a voice.

COMPARE:

"Butcher Shop" with "Animals Are Passing from Our Lives" by Philip Levine (page 346).

David R. Slavitt (b. 1935)

TITANIC   1983

Who does not love the *Titanic?*
If they sold passage tomorrow for that same crossing,
who would not buy?

To go down . . . We all go down, mostly
alone. But with crowds of people, friends, servants,   5
well fed, with music, with lights! Ah!

And the world, shocked, mourns, as it ought to do
and almost never does. There will be the books and movies
to remind our grandchildren who we were
and how we died, and give them a good cry.   10

Not so bad, after all. The cold
water is anaesthetic and very quick.
The cries on all sides must be a comfort.

We all go: only a few, first-class.

COMPARE:

"Titanic" with "The Convergence of the Twain" by Thomas Hardy (page 320).

Christopher Smart (1722 – 1771)*

FOR I WILL CONSIDER MY CAT JEOFFRY   (1759 – 1763)

For I will consider my Cat Jeoffry.
For he is the servant of the Living God, duly and daily serving him.
For at the first glance of the glory of God in the East he worships in
    his way.
For is this done by wreathing his body seven times round with
    elegant quickness.
For then he leaps up to catch the musk°, which is the   *catnip*
    blessing of God upon his prayer.   5
For he rolls upon prank to work it in.
For having done duty and received blessing he begins to consider
    himself.
For this he performs in ten degrees.
For first he looks upon his fore-paws to see if they are clean.
For secondly he kicks up behind to clear away there.   10
For thirdly he works it upon stretch° with the fore-paws   *he works his*
    extended.   *muscles, stretching*
For fourthly he sharpens his paws by wood.
For fifthly he washes himself.
For sixthly he rolls upon wash.
For seventhly he fleas himself, that he may not be interrupted upon
    the beat°.   *his patrol* 15
For eighthly he rubs himself against a post.
For ninthly he looks up for his instructions.
For tenthly he goes in quest of food.
For having considered God and himself he will consider his neighbor.
For if he meets another cat he will kiss her in kindness.   20
For when he takes his prey he plays with it to give it a chance.
For one mouse in seven escapes by his dallying.
For when his day's work is done his business more properly begins.
For he keeps the Lord's watch in the night against the Adversary.
For he counteracts the powers of darkness by his electrical skin and
    glaring eyes.   25
For he counteracts the Devil, who is death, by brisking about the life.
For in his morning orisons he loves the sun and the sun loves him.
For he is of the tribe of Tiger.
For the Cherub Cat is a term of the Angel Tiger.
For he has the subtlety and hissing of a serpent, which in goodness
    he suppresses.   30
For he will not do destruction if he is well-fed, neither will he spit
    without provocation.
For he purrs in thankfulness when God tells him he's a good Cat.

For he is an instrument for the children to learn benevolence upon.
For every house is incomplete without him, and a blessing is lacking
in the spirit.
For the Lord commanded Moses concerning the cats at the departure
of the Children of Israel from Egypt. 35
For every family had one cat at least in the bag.
For the English cats are the best in Europe.
For he is the cleanest in the use of his fore-paws of any quadruped.
For the dexterity of his defense is an instance of the love of God to
him exceedingly.
For he is the quickest to his mark of any creature. 40
For he is tenacious of his point.
For he is a mixture of gravity and waggery.
For he knows that God is his Savior.
For there is nothing sweeter than his peace when at rest.
For there is nothing brisker than his life when in motion. 45
For he is of the Lord's poor, and so indeed is he called by
benevolence perpetually — Poor Jeoffry! poor Jeoffry! the rat has
bit thy throat.
For I bless the name of the Lord Jesus that Jeoffry is better.
For the divine spirit comes about his body to sustain it in complete
cat.
For his tongue is exceeding pure so that it has in purity what it wants
in music.
For he is docile and can learn certain things. 50
For he can sit up with gravity which is patience upon approbation.
For he can fetch and carry, which is patience in employment.
For he can jump over a stick which is patience upon proof positive.
For he can spraggle upon waggle at the word of command.
For he can jump from an eminence into his master's bosom. 55
For he can catch the cork and toss it again.
For he is hated by the hypocrite and miser.
For the former is afraid of detection.
For the latter refuses the charge.
For he camels his back to bear the first notion of business. 60
For he is good to think on, if a man would express himself neatly.
For he made a great figure in Egypt for his signal services.
For he killed the Icneumon-rat, very pernicious by land.
For his ears are so acute that they sting again.

FOR I WILL CONSIDER MY CAT JEOFFRY. This is a self-contained extract from Smart's long poem
Jubilate Agno ("Rejoice in the Lamb"), written during his confinement for insanity. 35 *For the Lord
commanded Moses concerning the cats:* No such command is mentioned in Scripture. 54 *spraggle upon
waggle:* W. F. Stead, in his edition of Smart's poem, suggests that this means Jeoffry will sprawl when
his master waggles a finger or a stick. 59 *the charge:* perhaps the cost of feeding a cat.

For from this proceeds the passing quickness of his attention. 65
For by stroking of him I have found out electricity.
For I perceived God's light about him both wax and fire.
For the electrical fire is the spiritual substance which God sends from
    heaven to sustain the bodies both of man and beast.
For God has blessed him in the variety of his movements.
For, though he cannot fly, he is an excellent clamberer. 70
For his motions upon the face of the earth are more than any other
    quadruped.
For he can tread to all the measures upon the music.
For he can swim for life.
For he can creep.

Stevie Smith (1902 – 1971)*

I REMEMBER   1957

It was my bridal night I remember,
An old man of seventy-three
I lay with my young bride in my arms,
A girl with t.b.
It was wartime, and overhead   5
The Germans were making a particularly heavy raid on Hampstead.
What rendered the confusion worse, perversely
Our bombers had chosen that moment to set out for Germany.
Harry, do they ever collide?
I do not think it has ever happened,   10
Oh my bride, my bride.

Stevie Smith

William Jay Smith (b. 1918)

AMERICAN PRIMITIVE   1953

Look at him there in his stovepipe hat,
His high-top shoes, and his handsome collar;
Only my Daddy could look like that,
And I love my Daddy like he loves his Dollar.

The screen door bangs, and it sounds so funny —   5
There he is in a shower of gold;
His pockets are stuffed with folding money,
His lips are blue, and his hands feel cold.

He hangs in the hall by his black cravat,
The ladies faint, and the children holler: 10
Only my Daddy could look like that,
And I love my Daddy like he loves his Dollar.

COMPARE:

"American Primitive" with "Daddy" by Sylvia Plath (page 361).

W. D. Snodgrass (b. 1926)

SEEING YOU HAVE . . .   1959

Seeing you have a woman
Whose loves grow thick as the weeds
That keep songsparrows through the year,
Why are you envious of boys
Who prowl the streets all night in packs   5
So they are equal to the proud
Slender girls they fear?

She's like the tall grass, common,
That sends roots, where it needs,
Six feet into the prairies.   10
Why do you teach yourself the loud
Hankering voices of blue jays
That quarrel branch by branch to peck
And spoil the bitter cherries?

William Stafford (b. 1914)*

AT THE KLAMATH BERRY FESTIVAL   1966

The war chief danced the old way —
the eagle wing he held before his mouth —
and when he turned the boom-boom
stopped. He took two steps. A sociologist
was there; the Scout troop danced.   5
I envied him the places where he had not been.

The boom began again. Outside he heard
the stick game, and the Blackfoot gamblers
arguing at poker under lanterns.
Still-moccasined and bashful, holding   10
the eagle wing before his mouth,
listening and listening, he danced after others stopped.

He took two steps, the boom caught up,
the mountains rose, the still deep river
slid but never broke its quiet.   15
I looked back when I left:
he took two steps, he took two steps,
past the sociologist.

AT THE KLAMATH BERRY FESTIVAL. The Klamath Indians have a reservation at the base of the
Cascade Range in southern Oregon.

Wallace Stevens (1879 – 1955)*

PETER QUINCE AT THE CLAVIER   1923

I

Just as my fingers on these keys
Make music, so the selfsame sounds
On my spirit make a music, too.

Music is feeling, then, not sound;
And thus it is that what I feel,   5
Here in this room, desiring you,

Thinking of your blue-shadowed silk,
Is music. It is like the strain
Waked in the elders by Susanna.

Of a green evening, clear and warm,   10
She bathed in her still garden, while
The red-eyed elders watching, felt

The basses of their beings throb
In witching chords, and their thin blood
Pulse pizzicati of Hosanna.   15

II

In the green water, clear and warm,
Susanna lay.
She searched
The touch of springs,

And found   20
Concealed imaginings.
She sighed,
For so much melody.

Upon the bank, she stood
In the cool   25
Of spent emotions.
She felt, among the leaves,
The dew
Of old devotions.

She walked upon the grass,   30
Still quavering.
The winds were like her maids,
On timid feet,
Fetching her woven scarves,
Yet wavering.   35

A breath upon her hand
Muted the night.
She turned —
A cymbal crashed,
And roaring horns.   40

III

Soon, with a noise like tambourines,
Came her attendant Byzantines.

They wondered why Susanna cried
Against the elders by her side;

And as they whispered, the refrain   45
Was like a willow swept by rain.

Anon, their lamps' uplifted flame
Revealed Susanna and her shame.

And then, the simpering Byzantines
Fled, with a noise like tambourines.   50

IV

Beauty is momentary in the mind —
The fitful tracing of a portal;
But in the flesh it is immortal.

The body dies; the body's beauty lives.
So evenings die, in their green going,   55
A wave, interminably flowing.
So gardens die, their meek breath scenting
The cowl of winter, done repenting.
So maidens die, to the auroral
Celebration of a maiden's choral.   60

Susanna's music touched the bawdy strings
Of those white elders; but, escaping,
Left only Death's ironic scraping.
Now, in its immortality, it plays
On the clear viol of her memory,   65
And makes a constant sacrament of praise.

PETER QUINCE AT THE CLAVIER. In Shakespeare's *Midsummer Night's Dream*, Peter Quince is a
clownish carpenter who stages a mock-tragic play. In The Book of Susanna in the Apocrypha, two
lustful elders who covet Susanna, a virtuous married woman, hide in her garden, spy on her as
she bathes, then threaten to make false accusations against her unless she submits to them. When
she refuses, they cry out, and her servants come running. All ends well when the prophet Daniel
cross-examines the elders and proves them liars. 15 *pizzicati:* thin notes made by plucking a stringed
instrument. 42 *Byzantines:* Susanna's maidservants.

Wallace Stevens

Ruth Stone (b. 1915)

SECOND HAND COAT   1982

I feel
in her pockets; she wore nice cotton gloves,
kept a handkerchief box, washed her undies,
ate at the Holiday Inn, had a basement freezer,
belonged to a bridge club.   5
I think when I wake in the morning
that I have turned into her.
She hangs in the hall downstairs,
a shadow with pulled threads.
I slip her over my arms, skin of a matron.   10
Where are you? I say to myself, to the orphaned body,
and her coat says,
Get your purse, have you got your keys?

Jonathan Swift (1667 – 1745)*

A DESCRIPTION OF THE MORNING   1711

Now hardly here and there an hackney-coach°,   *horse-drawn cab*
Appearing, showed the ruddy morn's approach.
Now Betty from her master's bed had flown
And softly stole to discompose her own.
The slipshod 'prentice from his master's door   5
Had pared the dirt, and sprinkled round the floor.
Now Moll had whirled her mop with dextrous airs,
Prepared to scrub the entry and the stairs.
The youth with broomy stumps began to trace
The kennel°-edge, where wheels had worn the place.   *gutter* 10
The small-coal man was heard with cadence deep
Till drowned in shriller notes of chimneysweep,
Duns° at his lordship's gate began to meet,   *bill-collectors*
And Brickdust Moll had screamed through half the street.
The turnkey° now his flock returning sees,   *jailkeeper* 15
Duly let out a-nights to steal for fees;
The watchful bailiffs° take their silent stands;   *constables*
And schoolboys lag with satchels in their hands.

A DESCRIPTION OF THE MORNING. 9 *youth with broomy stumps:* a young man sweeping the gutter's
edge with worn-out brooms, looking for old nails fallen from wagonwheels, which were valuable.
14 *Brickdust Moll:* woman selling brickdust to be used for scouring.

Alfred, Lord Tennyson

Alfred, Lord Tennyson (1809 – 1892)*

DARK HOUSE, BY WHICH ONCE MORE I STAND 1850

Dark house, by which once more I stand
   Here in the long unlovely street,
   Doors, where my heart was used to beat
So quickly, waiting for a hand,

A hand that can be clasped no more — 5
   Behold me, for I cannot sleep,
   And like a guilty thing I creep
At earliest morning to the door.

He is not here; but far away
   The noise of life begins again, 10
   And ghastly through the drizzling rain
On the bald street breaks the blank day.

DARK HOUSE. This poem is one part of the series *In Memoriam*, an elegy for Tennyson's friend
Arthur Henry Hallam.

Alfred, Lord Tennyson (1809 – 1892)*

ULYSSES   (1833)

It little profits that an idle king,
By this still hearth, among these barren crags,
Matched with an agèd wife, I mete and dole
Unequal laws unto a savage race
That hoard, and sleep, and feed, and know not me.   5
I cannot rest from travel; I will drink
Life to the lees. All times I have enjoyed
Greatly, have suffered greatly, both with those
That loved me, and alone; on shore, and when
Through scudding drifts the rainy Hyades   10
Vexed the dim sea. I am become a name;
For always roaming with a hungry heart
Much have I seen and known — cities of men
And manners, climates, councils, governments,
Myself not least, but honored of them all —   15
And drunk delight of battle with my peers,
Far on the ringing plains of windy Troy.
I am a part of all that I have met;
Yet all experience is an arch wherethrough
Gleams that untraveled world whose margin fades   20
Forever and forever when I move.
How dull it is to pause, to make an end,
To rust unburnished, not to shine in use!
As though to breathe were life! Life piled on life
Were all too little, and of one to me   25
Little remains; but every hour is saved
From that eternal silence, something more,
A bringer of new things; and vile it were
For some three suns to store and hoard myself,
And this grey spirit yearning in desire   30
To follow knowledge like a sinking star,
Beyond the utmost bound of human thought.
    This is my son, mine own Telemachus,
To whom I leave the scepter and the isle —
Well-loved of me, discerning to fulfill   35
This labor, by slow prudence to make mild
A rugged people, and through soft degrees
Subdue them to the useful and the good.
Most blameless is he, centered in the sphere
Of common duties, decent not to fail   40
In offices of tenderness, and pay
Meet adoration to my household gods,
When I am gone. He works his work, I mine.

There lies the port; the vessel puffs her sail;
There gloom the dark, broad seas. My mariners,   45
Souls that have toiled, and wrought, and thought with me —
That ever with a frolic welcome took
The thunder and the sunshine, and opposed
Free hearts, free foreheads — you and I are old;
Old age hath yet his honor and his toil.   50
Death closes all; but something ere the end,
Some work of noble note, may yet be done,
Not unbecoming men that strove with Gods.
The lights begin to twinkle from the rocks;
The long day wanes; the low moon climbs; the deep   55
Moans round with many voices. Come, my friends,
'Tis not too late to seek a newer world.
Push off, and sitting well in order smite
The sounding furrows; for my purpose holds
To sail beyond the sunset, and the baths   60
Of all the western stars, until I die.
It may be that the gulfs will wash us down;
It may be we shall touch the Happy Isles,
And see the great Achilles, whom we knew.
Though much is taken, much abides; and though   65
We are not now that strength which in old days
Moved earth and heaven, that which we are, we are —
One equal temper of heroic hearts,
Made weak by time and fate, but strong in will
To strive, to seek, to find, and not to yield.   70

ULYSSES. 10 *Hyades:* daughters of Atlas, who were transformed into a group of stars. Their rising
with the sun was thought to be a sign of rain. 63 *Happy Isles:* Elysium, a paradise believed to be
attainable by sailing west.

COMPARE:

"Ulysses" with "Sir Patrick Spence" (page 8).

Dylan Thomas (1914 – 1953)*

FERN HILL   1946

Now as I was young and easy under the apple boughs
About the lilting house and happy as the grass was green,
          The night above the dingle° starry,   *wooded valley*
               Time let me hail and climb
          Golden in the heydays of his eyes,   5

And honored among wagons I was prince of the apple towns
And once below a time I lordly had the trees and leaves
                  Trail with daisies and barley
                Down the rivers of the windfall light.

And as I was green and carefree, famous among the barns   10
About the happy yard and singing as the farm was home,
              In the sun that is young once only,
                    Time let me play and be
                Golden in the mercy of his means,
And green and golden I was huntsman and herdsman, the calves   15
Sang to my horn, the foxes on the hills barked clear and cold,
                  And the sabbath rang slowly
                In the pebbles of the holy streams.

All the sun long it was running, it was lovely, the hay
Fields high as the house, the tunes from the chimneys, it was air   20
                And playing, lovely and watery
                    And fire green as grass.
                  And nightly under the simple stars
As I rode to sleep the owls were bearing the farm away,
All the moon long I heard, blessed among stables, the nightjars   25
                Flying with the ricks, and the horses
                  Flashing into the dark.

And then to awake, and the farm, like a wanderer white
With the dew, come back, the cock on his shoulder: it was all
                Shining, it was Adam and maiden,   30
                    The sky gathered again
                And the sun grew round that very day.
So it must have been after the birth of the simple light
In the first, spinning place, the spellbound horses walking warm
                  Out of the whinnying green stable   35
                  On to the fields of praise.

And honored among foxes and pheasants by the gay house
Under the new made clouds and happy as the heart was long,
              In the sun born over and over,
                    I ran my heedless ways,   40
                My wishes raced through the house high hay
And nothing I cared, at my sky blue trades, that time allows
In all his tuneful turning so few and such morning songs
                Before the children green and golden
                  Follow him out of grace,   45

Nothing I cared, in the lamb white days, that time would take me
Up to the swallow thronged loft by the shadow of my hand,
       In the moon that is always rising,
          Nor that riding to sleep
     I should hear him fly with the high fields   50
And wake to the farm forever fled from the childless land.
Oh as I was young and easy in the mercy of his means,
       Time held me green and dying
     Though I sang in my chains like the sea.

John Updike (b. 1932)*

EX-BASKETBALL PLAYER   1958

Pearl Avenue runs past the high-school lot,
Bends with the trolley tracks, and stops, cut off
Before it has a chance to go two blocks,
At Colonel McComsky Plaza. Berth's Garage
Is on the corner facing west, and there,   5
Most days, you'll find Flick Webb, who helps Berth out.

Flick stands tall among the idiot pumps —
Five on a side, the old bubble-head style,
Their rubber elbows hanging loose and low.
One's nostrils are two S's, and his eyes   10
An E and O. And one is squat, without
A head at all — more of a football type.

Once Flick played for the high-school team, the Wizards.
He was good: in fact, the best. In '46
He bucketed three hundred ninety points,   15
A county record still. The ball loved Flick.
I saw him rack up thirty-eight or forty
In one home game. His hands were like wild birds.

He never learned a trade, he just sells gas,
Checks oil, and changes flats. Once in a while,   20
As a gag, he dribbles an inner tube,
But most of us remember anyway.
His hands are fine and nervous on the lug wrench.
It makes no difference to the lug wrench, though.

Off work, he hangs around Mae's luncheonette.   25
Grease-gray and kind of coiled, he plays pinball,
Smokes those thin cigars, nurses lemon phosphates.
Flick seldom says a word to Mae, just nods
Beyond her face toward bright applauding tiers
Of Necco Wafers, Nibs, and Juju Beads.   30

COMPARE:

"Ex-Basketball Player" with "The Cadence of Silk" by Garrett Hongo (page 330) and
"To an Athlete Dying Young" by A. E. Housman (page 336).

Edmund Waller (1606 – 1687)*

GO, LOVELY ROSE   1645

 Go, lovely rose,
Tell her that wastes her time and me
 That now she knows,
When I resemble° her to thee,   *compare*
How sweet and fair she seems to be.   5

 Tell her that's young
And shuns to have her graces spied,
 That hadst thou sprung
In deserts where no men abide,
Thou must have uncommended died.   10

 Small is the worth
Of beauty from the light retired:
 Bid her come forth,
Suffer herself to be desired,
And not blush so to be admired.   15

 Then die, that she
The common fate of all things rare
 May read in thee,
How small a part of time they share
That are so wondrous sweet and fair.   20

COMPARE:

"Go, Lovely Rose" with "To the Virgins, to Make Much of Time" by Robert Herrick
(page 329) and "To His Coy Mistress" by Andrew Marvell (page 350).

Walt Whitman

Walt Whitman (1819 – 1892)*

I Saw in Louisiana a Live-Oak Growing   1867

I saw in Louisiana a live-oak growing,
All alone stood it and the moss hung down from the branches,
Without any companion it grew there uttering joyous leaves of dark
    green,
And its look, rude, unbending, lusty, made me think of myself,
But I wonder'd how it could utter joyous leaves standing alone there
    without its friend near, for I knew I could not,   5
And I broke off a twig with a certain number of leaves upon it, and
    twined around it a little moss,
And brought it away, and I have placed it in sight in my room,
It is not needed to remind me as of my own dear friends,
(For I believe lately I think of little else than of them,)
Yet it remains to me a curious token, it makes me think of manly
    love;   10
For all that, and though the live-oak glistens there in Louisiana
    solitary in a wide flat space,
Uttering joyous leaves all its life without a friend a lover near,
I know very well I could not.

COMPARE:

"I Saw in Louisiana a Live-Oak Growing" with "A Supermarket in California" by Allen
Ginsberg (page 317).

Richard Wilbur

Richard Wilbur (b. 1921)*

TRANSIT   1988

A woman I have never seen before
Steps from the darkness of her town-house door
At just that crux of time when she is made
So beautiful that she or time must fade.

What use to claim that as she tugs her gloves   5
A phantom heraldry of all the loves
Blares from the lintel? That the staggered sun
Forgets, in his confusion, how to run?

Still, nothing changes as her perfect feet
Click down the walk that issues in the street.   10
Leaving the stations of her body there
As a whip maps the countries of the air.

Richard Wilbur (b. 1921)*

THE WRITER   1976

In her room at the prow of the house
Where light breaks, and the windows are tossed with linden,
My daughter is writing a story.

I pause in the stairwell, hearing
From her shut door a commotion of typewriter-keys
Like a chain hauled over a gunwale.

Young as she is, the stuff
Of her life is a great cargo, and some of it heavy:
I wish her a lucky passage.

But now it is she who pauses,
As if to reject my thought and its easy figure.
A stillness greatens, in which

The whole house seems to be thinking,
And then she is at it again with a bunched clamor
Of strokes, and again is silent.

I remember the dazed starling
Which was trapped in that very room, two years ago;
How we stole in, lifted a sash

And retreated, not to affright it;
And how for a helpless hour, through the crack of the door,
We watched the sleek, wild, dark

And iridescent creature
Batter against the brilliance, drop like a glove
To the hard floor, or the desk-top.

And wait then, humped and bloody,
For the wits to try it again; and how our spirits
Rose when, suddenly sure,

It lifted off from a chair-back,
Beating a smooth course for the right window
And clearing the sill of the world.

It is always a matter, my darling,
Of life or death, as I had forgotten. I wish
What I wished you before, but harder.

5

10

15

20

25

30

Nancy Willard (b. 1936)

MARRIAGE AMULET   1974

You are polishing me like old wood.
At night we curl together like two rings
on a dark hand. After many nights,
the rough edges wear down.

If this is aging, it is warm as fleece.   5
I will gleam like ancient wood.
I will wax smooth, my crags and cowlicks
well-rubbed to show my grain.

Some sage will keep us in his hand for peace.

Miller Williams (b. 1930)

MECANIC ON DUTY AT ALL TIMES   1986

The license plate was another state and year.
The man's slow hands, as if they had no part
in whatever happened here, followed the hollows
and hills of his broad belt. Inside the car
four children, his face again, with eyes like washers,   5
were as still as the woman, two fingers touching her cheek.
"How much?" he said. "Well maybe fifty dollars
if I can find a used one. I guess I can."
The hands paid no attention. Out in the sun
light wires dipped and rose and dipped again   10
until they disappeared. *Flats fixed* and *Gas*
and *Quaker State* squeaked in the wind. Just that.
And the speeding trucks, wailing through their tires.

COMPARE:

"MECANIC ON DUTY AT ALL TIMES" with "Filling Station" by Elizabeth Bishop
(page 289).

William Carlos Williams (1883 – 1963)*

SPRING AND ALL   1923

By the road to the contagious hospital
under the surge of the blue
mottled clouds driven from the
northeast — a cold wind. Beyond, the
waste of broad, muddy fields   5
brown with dried weeds, standing and fallen

patches of standing water
the scattering of tall trees

All along the road the reddish
purplish, forked, upstanding, twiggy   10

stuff of bushes and small trees
with dead, brown leaves under them
leafless vines —

Lifeless in appearance, sluggish
dazed spring approaches —   15

They enter the new world naked,
cold, uncertain of all
save that they enter. All about them
the cold, familiar wind —

Now the grass, tomorrow   20
the stiff curl of wildcarrot leaf
One by one objects are defined —
It quickens: clarity, outline of leaf

But now the stark dignity of
entrance — Still, the profound change   25
has come upon them: rooted, they
grip down and begin to awaken

COMPARE:

"Spring and All" with "in Just-" by E. E. Cummings (page 195) and "Root Cellar" by
Theodore Roethke (page 75).

William Carlos Williams

William Carlos Williams (1883 – 1963)*

To Waken an Old Lady   1921

Old age is
a flight of small
cheeping birds
skimming
bare trees   5
above a snow glaze.
Gaining and failing
they are buffeted
by a dark wind —
But what?   10
On harsh weedstalks
the flock has rested,
the snow
is covered with broken
seedhusks   15
and the wind tempered
by a shrill
piping of plenty.

COMPARE:

"To Waken an Old Lady" with "Castoff Skin" by Ruth Whitman (page 96).

Yvor Winters (1900 – 1968)

At the San Francisco Airport   1960

To My Daughter, 1954

This is the terminal: the light
Gives perfect vision, false and hard;
The metal glitters, deep and bright.
Great planes are waiting in the yard —
They are already in the night.   5

And you are here beside me, small,
Contained and fragile, and intent
On things that I but half recall —
Yet going whither you are bent.
I am the past, and that is all.   10

But you and I in part are one:
The frightened brain, the nervous will,
The knowledge of what must be done,
The passion to acquire the skill
To face that which you dare not shun.   15

The rain of matter upon sense
Destroys me momently. The score:
There comes what will come. The expense
Is what one thought, and something more —
One's being and intelligence. 20

This is the terminal, the break.
Beyond this point, on lines of air,
You take the way that you must take;
And I remain in light and stare —
In light, and nothing else, awake. 25

William Wordsworth (1770 – 1850)*

COMPOSED UPON WESTMINSTER BRIDGE   1807

Earth has not anything to show more fair:
Dull would he be of soul who could pass by
A sight so touching in its majesty:
This City now doth, like a garment, wear
The beauty of the morning; silent, bare, 5
Ships, towers, domes, theatres, and temples lie
Open unto the fields, and to the sky;
All bright and glittering in the smokeless air.
Never did sun more beautifully steep
In his first splendor, valley, rock, or hill; 10
Ne'er saw I, never felt, a calm so deep!
The river glideth at his own sweet will:
Dear God! the very houses seem asleep;
And all that mighty heart is lying still!

William Wordsworth

James Wright

James Wright (1927 – 1980)*

A BLESSING   1961

Just off the highway to Rochester, Minnesota,
Twilight bounds softly forth on the grass.
And the eyes of those two Indian ponies
Darken with kindness.
They have come gladly out of the willows   5
To welcome my friend and me.
We step over the barbed wire into the pasture
Where they have been grazing all day, alone.
They ripple tensely, they can hardly contain their happiness
That we have come.   10
They bow shyly as wet swans. They love each other.
There is no loneliness like theirs.
At home once more,
They begin munching the young tufts of spring in the darkness.
I would like to hold the slenderer one in my arms,   15
For she has walked over to me
And nuzzled my left hand.
She is black and white,
Her mane falls wild on her forehead,
And the light breeze moves me to caress her long ear   20
That is delicate as the skin over a girl's wrist.
Suddenly I realize
That if I stepped out of my body I would break
Into blossom.

James Wright (1927 – 1980)*

AUTUMN BEGINS IN MARTINS FERRY, OHIO 1963

In the Shreve High football stadium,
I think of Polacks nursing long beers in Tiltonsville,
And gray faces of Negroes in the blast furnace at Benwood,
And the ruptured night watchman of Wheeling Steel,
Dreaming of heroes.   5

All the proud fathers are ashamed to go home.
Their women cluck like starved pullets,
Dying for love.

Therefore,
Their sons grow suicidally beautiful   10
At the beginning of October,
And gallop terribly against each other's bodies.

Sir Thomas Wyatt (1503? – 1542)*

THEY FLEE FROM ME THAT SOMETIME DID ME SEKË   (ABOUT 1535)

They flee from me that sometime did me sekë
   With naked fotë° stalking in my chamber.   *foot*
I have seen them gentle, tame and mekë
   That now are wild, and do not remember
   That sometime they put themself in danger   5
To take bread at my hand; and now they range
Busily seeking with a continual change.

Thankèd be fortune, it hath been otherwise
   Twenty times better; but once in speciàll,
In thin array, after a pleasant guise,   10
   When her loose gown from her shoulders did fall,
   And she me caught in her armës long and small,
Therëwith all sweetly did me kiss,
And softly said, *Dear heart, how like you this?*

It was no dremë: I lay broadë waking.   15
   But all is turned thorough° my gentleness   *through*

Into a strangë fashion of forsaking;
   And I have leave to go of her goodness,
   And she also to use newfangleness°.   *to seek novelty*
But since that I so kindëly am served   20
I would fain knowë what she hath deserved.

THEY FLEE FROM ME THAT SOMETIME DID ME SEKë. Some latter-day critics have called Sir Thomas Wyatt a careless poet because some of his lines appear faltering and metrically inconsistent; others have thought he knew what he was doing. It is uncertain whether the final *e*'s in English spelling were still pronounced in Wyatt's day as they were in Chaucer's, but if they were, perhaps Wyatt has been unjustly blamed. In this text, spellings have been modernized except in words where the final *e* would make a difference in rhythm. To sense how it matters, try reading the poem aloud leaving out the *e*'s and then putting them in wherever indicated. Sound them like the *a* in *sofa*. 20 *kindëly:* according to my kind (or hers); that is, as befits the nature of man (or woman). Perhaps there is also irony here, and the word means "unkindly."

Elinor Wylie (1885–1928)

THE EAGLE AND THE MOLE   1921

Avoid the reeking herd,
Shun the polluted flock,
Live like that stoic bird,
The eagle of the rock.

The huddled warmth of crowds   5
Begets and fosters hate;
He keeps, above the clouds,
His cliff inviolate.

When flocks are folded warm,
And herds to shelter run,   10
He sails above the storm,
He stares into the sun.

If in the eagle's track
Your sinews cannot leap,
Avoid the lathered pack,   15
Turn from the steaming sheep.

If you would keep your soul
From spotted sight or sound,
Live like the velvet mole;
Go burrow underground.   20

And there hold intercourse
With roots of trees and stones,
With rivers at their source,
And disembodied bones.

William Butler Yeats

William Butler Yeats (1865–1939)

Long-legged Fly   1940

That civilization may not sink,
Its great battle lost,
Quiet the dog, tether the pony
To a distant post;
Our master Caesar is in the tent   5
Where the maps are spread,
His eyes fixed upon nothing,
A hand under his head.

Like a long-legged fly upon the stream
His mind moves upon silence.   10

That the topless towers be burnt
And men recall that face,
Move most gently if move you must
In this lonely place.
She thinks, part woman, three parts a child,   15
That nobody looks; her feet
Practice a tinker shuffle
Picked up on the street.

Like a long-legged fly upon the stream
Her mind moves upon silence.   20

That girls at puberty may find
The first Adam in their thought,
Shut the door of the Pope's chapel,
Keep those children out.
There on that scaffolding reclines   25
Michael Angelo.
With no more sound than the mice make
His hand moves to and fro.

Like a long-legged fly upon the stream
His mind moves upon silence.   30

LONG-LEGGED FLY. This "fly" is the fresh-water insect also known as the water strider. 11 *topless towers:* of Troy, burned by the Greeks. Yeats echoes the description of Helen of Troy (whose abduction started the war) given in Christopher Marlowe's play *The Tragical History of Doctor Faustus:* "Was this the face that launched a thousand ships, / And burnt the topless towers of Ilium?" 23 *the Pope's Chapel:* Michelangelo had to lie on his back to paint upon the ceiling of the Sistine Chapel his celebrated frescoes depicting the creation, fall, and final judgment of humankind.

COMPARE:
"Long-legged Fly" with "Helen" by H.D. (page 319).

William Butler Yeats (1865–1939)

CRAZY JANE TALKS WITH THE BISHOP   1933

I met the Bishop on the road
And much said he and I.
"Those breasts are flat and fallen now,
Those veins must soon be dry;
Live in a heavenly mansion,   5
Not in some foul sty."

"Fair and foul are near of kin,
And fair needs foul," I cried.
"My friends are gone, but that's a truth
Nor° grave nor bed denied,   neither   10
Learned in bodily lowliness
And in the heart's pride.

"A woman can be proud and stiff
When on love intent;
But Love has pitched his mansion in   15
The place of excrement;
For nothing can be sole or whole
That has not been rent."

William Butler Yeats (1865 – 1939)*

The Magi   1914

Now as at all times I can see in the mind's eye,
In their stiff, painted clothes, the pale unsatisfied ones
Appear and disappear in the blue depth of the sky
With all their ancient faces like rain-beaten stones,
And all their helms of silver hovering side by side,   5
And all their eyes still fixed, hoping to find once more,
Being by Calvary's turbulence unsatisfied,
The uncontrollable mystery on the bestial floor.

COMPARE:

"The Magi" with "Journey of the Magi" by T. S. Eliot (page 308).

LIVES OF THE POETS

Here you will find a brief biographical note for each poet represented in the book by more than one selection. There is also a note for Thomas Gray, author of the long poem "Elegy in a Country Churchyard."

John Ashbery

John Ashbery, born in Rochester, New York, in 1927, was educated at Deerfield Academy, Harvard, and Columbia. In 1960 he became an art critic in Paris for the *New York Herald Tribune,* and from 1966 to 1972 served as executive editor of the magazine *Art News* in New York. His first full collection of poetry, *Some Trees* (1956), was chosen by W. H. Auden for publication in the Yale Series of Younger Poets; his *Self-Portrait in a Convex Mirror* (1976) garnered praise and three leading literary prizes, and sold well for a book of serious poetry. Ashbery has written plays and a novel (with James Schuyler), *A Nest of Ninnies* (1969). He now lives in New York and teaches part time in the writing program at Brooklyn College. Some critics have speculated that Ashbery's experience as an art critic has tinged his poetry: that he performs in words what an abstract expressionist performs on canvas in oils. His work can annoy readers who expect poems to make clear statements to be taken in only one way; others think him the foremost living American poet and major heir to the tradition of Wallace Stevens — that is, to the art of suggesting rather than depicting, of arranging words primarily for their own sake.

Margaret Atwood

Margaret Atwood, born in Ottawa in 1939, is a staunchly Canadian poet, short story writer, and novelist whose literary reputation has extended well beyond the borders of her native country. She published her first book of poems, *Double Persephone,* in 1962, the same year she was graduated from the University of Toronto. She went on to earn a master's degree at Radcliffe and to study Victorian fantasy at Harvard. She has advanced her country's cultural identity by publishing *Survival* (1972), a book about Canadian literature, and has edited *The Oxford Book of Canadian Verse* (1982). Her fiction and poetry, at once comic and grim, often deal with alienation and the destructive nature of human relationships. Her most recent novel, *Cat's Eye* (1989), has won attention on both sides of the Canadian border. The cream of her poetry has been skimmed in *Selected Poems* (1976) and *Selected Poems II* (1987).

W. H. Auden

W. H. Auden (1907 – 1973), born in York, England, in 1907, as a young man in the 1930s became the acknowledged spokesman for a generation of English poets that included Stephen Spender, C. Day Lewis, Christopher Isherwood, and Louis MacNeice. His early work was characterized by blithe wit, a Marxist outlook, and a knowledge of Freudian psychology; in later life, he professed Christianity and (in his views of poetry) increasing conservatism. In 1939 Auden emigrated to America, and in 1946 became a United States citizen. A prolific editor, anthologist, and translator of poetry, he collaborated on verse plays, travel memoirs, and (with his longtime friend Chester Kallman) librettos for operas, including Igor Stravinsky's *The Rake's Progress* (1951). He wrote influential criticism, notably that collected in *The Dyer's Hand* (1962). Auden divided his last years among England, Italy, Austria, and New York.

R. L. Barth

R. L. Barth was born in 1947 in Covington, Kentucky. From 1966 until 1969 he served as a patrol leader with the First Reconnaissance Battalion of the U.S. Marines in Vietnam. Later he held a Wallace Stegner fellowship in creative writing at Stanford. He now teaches English at Xavier University in Cincinnati, and has twice been a visiting lecturer at the University of California, Santa Barbara. As Robert L. Barth, he operates a small publishing house in Florence, Kentucky, issuing books and chapbooks of poetry by contemporary formalists Edgar Bowers, Turner Cassity, Dick Davis, Timothy Dekin, Thom Gunn, Charles Gullans, Warren Hope, Janet Lewis, Raymond Oliver, John Ridland, Don Stanford, Timothy Steele, Wesley Trimpi, William Wilborn, and others. His own classically taut poems of the Vietnam war have been gathered in *A Soldier's Time* (1987), and his work as a translator includes *Earthenware: XLVI Epigrams from Martial* (1988).

Elizabeth Bishop

Elizabeth Bishop (1911 – 1979) was born in Worcester, Massachusetts. After her father died (in her first year) and her mother was stricken with mental illness, she lived until age six with her grandmother in a coastal village in Nova Scotia. A sufferer from asthma, she received scant elementary schooling, but she read widely and deeply at home. At sixteen she entered Walnut Hill, a boarding school, and later graduated from Vassar. Her undergraduate poems won her the friendship of the poet Marianne Moore, who persuaded her not to go on to medical school, but instead to write. Fond of travel and flower-filled climates, Bishop lived for nine years in Key West, Florida, then for fifteen years in Brazil, dividing her time between the mountains and Rio de Janeiro. In 1966 she returned to the United States to teach: first at the University of Washington, then at Harvard from 1969 until 1977, when she retired. Most of her sparely disciplined work is contained in two volumes: *Complete Poems 1927 – 1979* (1983) and *Collected Prose* (1984). Her sharp-eyed poems, full of vivid images and apt metaphors, have affected the work of other poets, among them her friends Randall Jarrell and Robert Lowell.

William Blake

William Blake (1757 – 1827), poet, painter, and visionary, was born in the Soho district of London and early in life was apprenticed to an engraver. Becoming a skilled craftsman, he earned his living illustrating books, among them Dante's *Divine Comedy*, Milton's poems, and the Book of Job. A remarkable and original graphic artist whose only formal training came from a few months at the Royal Academy, Blake published his own poems, engraving them in a careful script embellished with hand-colored illustrations and decorations. His wife Catherine Boucher, whom he taught to read and write, shared his visions and helped him do the coloring. *Songs of Innocence* (1789) and *Songs of Experience* (1794), brief lyrics written from a child's point of view, are easy to enjoy; but anyone deeply interested in Blake copes also with the longer, more demanding "Prophetic Books," among them *The Book of Thel* (1789), *The Marriage of Heaven and Hell* (1790), and *Jerusalem* (1804 – 20). In these later works, out of his readings in alchemy, the Bible, and the works of Plato and Swedenborg, Blake derived support for his lifelong hatred of scientific rationalism and created his own mythology, complete with devils and deities. A sympathizer with both American and French revolutions, Blake was once accused of sedition, but the charges were dismissed. In his lifetime, Wordsworth and Coleridge were among the few admirers of his short lyrics; his "Prophetic Books" have had to wait until our century for compassionate readers.

Robert Bly

Robert Bly was born on a farm in Madison, Minnesota, in 1926, and continued to live there for most of his life. He was graduated from Harvard, where he began studies in mathematics before deciding to devote his life to poetry. Rather than teaching, Bly has preferred to support himself and his family by giving poetry readings and by translating books and poems from Scandinavian and other languages. In 1958 he launched a poetry magazine, *The Fifties* (later renamed, as decades went by, *The Sixties* and *The Seventies*). In it he spoofed academic critics, urged American poets to open their work to dream and surrealism, and introduced in translation the work of important poets of Europe and Latin America. Bly has vitally influenced the work of James Wright, Donald Hall, and many younger poets. His readings, in which he sometimes chants and dons primitive masks, have drawn throngs. In the 1960s he organized (with David Ray) American Writers Against the Vietnam War, and over the years has championed many causes, usually pacifist and antinuclear. Lately he has been leading retreats for men, trying to help them understand their male natures.

Gwendolyn Brooks

Gwendolyn Brooks, born in 1917 in Topeka, Kansas, moved early in life to Chicago's South Side, whose people she has commemorated in her poetry and in a novel, *Maud Martha* (1953). Recipient of the Pulitzer prize for poetry in 1950, for *Annie Allen*, Brooks has long been recognized as a leading voice in modern American letters. She has combined several teaching positions with raising two children. Since 1967, when she took part in a conference for black writers at Fisk University and was impressed with young black poets' views, she has increasingly been an activist, teaching teen-age black writers in Chicago and addressing her work especially to black audiences. Instead of continuing to publish with a mainstream New York publishing house, she switched her work to Broadside, a small literary press in Detroit founded by black poet Dudley Randall. Her memoir *Report from Part One* (1972) discusses her altered outlook. In 1985 she was named Consultant in Poetry to the Library of Congress. Her goals in life, she has declared, are "to be clean of heart, clear of mind, and claiming of what is right and just."

Robert Browning

Robert Browning (1812 – 1889), born in a suburb of London, was educated mainly in his father's six-thousand-volume library. With *Pauline* (1833), he began to print his poetry. After the death of his wife Elizabeth Barrett Browning, with whom he had lived in Italy, he returned to England to become (Henry James wrote) an "accomplished, saturated, sane, sound man of the London world." There, as he neared sixty, he enjoyed late but loud applause and the adulation of the Browning Society: faithful readers whose local groups met over their teacups to explicate him. Readers have most greatly favored Browning's story-poems in a form he perfected, the dramatic monologue — such as "My Last Duchess" and "Soliloquy of the Spanish Cloister" — in which he brings to life persons from the past (some of them famous), has them speak their inmost thoughts and reveal their characters. His masterpiece, *The Ring and the Book* (1868 – 69), is a long narrative poem in twelve monologues, based on a seventeenth-century Roman murder trial. Browning also wrote several plays, among them *A Blot in the 'Scutcheon* (1842). Through the praise and emulation of his later admirers Ezra Pound and T. S. Eliot, Browning has profoundly affected modern poetry. A formal experimenter, he speaks to us in energetic, punchy words — and like many later poets he introduces learning into his poems without apology. More important, Browning is among the great yea-sayers in English poetry: an affirmer and celebrant of life.

Robert Burns

Robert Burns (1759 – 1796), the preeminent poet of Scotland, was born in a two-room farm cottage in Alloway, a hamlet on the River Doon, the son of a farmer who worked himself to death. For most of his days Burns too struggled to farm poor soil. Though his schooling lasted only three years, he eagerly read Shakespeare and Pope as a boy and let poetry pour from his own pen. Only in 1786, when he felt he needed money to emigrate to Jamaica, did he publish his *Poems, Chiefly in the Scottish Dialect,* depicting Scottish rural life with warm humor, tender compassion, and rugged exuberance. The book scored an immediate hit and Burns remained in Scotland for the rest of his days. After Edinburgh's stylish society, which had lionized him for a time, let him drop, he returned to his plough, married Jean Armour (who earlier had borne him two sets of twins), and continued to farm until 1791, when he retired to the easier life of a tax official. But worn from toil, hardship, and poverty, Burns died at thirty-seven. Among his legacies are songs, such as "Flow Gently, Sweet Afton," "Comin' Through the Rye," and a song still heard in this country each New Year's eve, "Auld Lang Syne." Like Hugh MacDiarmid, Burns wrote poetry in both standard English and Scots dialect — in the latter whenever, as in "The Jolly Beggars" and "Address to the Unco Guid," he expressed defiantly unconventional views.

Thomas Campion

Thomas Campion (1567 – 1620), Elizabethan courtier, physician, musician, and poet, was the author of several books of solo songs with lute accompaniment, much admired for their masterly unity of words and music. In 1602 Campion wrote a tract, *Observations in the Art of English Poesy,* in which he argued in favor of writing quantitative verse in English, after the example of the ancient Greek and Latin poets. "Rose-cheeked Laura" was apparently written to illustrate his theories. In the same tract, he opposed the writing of any more poetry in rime and traditional English meters — in which, however, he excelled.

Samuel Taylor Coleridge

Samuel Taylor Coleridge (1772 – 1834) was born in Devonshire, England, a clergyman's fourteenth child. With poet Robert Southey, a fellow student at Cambridge University, he once planned to go to the United States and found a utopian community, but the scheme was never fulfilled. A zealous traveler, brilliant talker, and sometime professional lecturer, Coleridge wrote ably on philosophy and religion as well as on literature. As a young man, he collaborated with William Wordsworth on the influential *Lyrical Ballads* (1798), a milestone of English Romantic poetry. Among Coleridge's contributions were "The Rime of the Ancient Mariner," "Cristabel," and "Kubla Khan" — ornate poems of the exotic and supernatural. His *Biographia Literaria* (1817) combines literary criticism with autobiography, and sets forth views of poetry and the imagination (see page 000) heavily indebted to German idealist philosophy. Long troubled by an addiction to opium, Coleridge went to London in 1816 to live in the household of Dr. James Gilman, under whose care he passed the rest of his days.

E. E. Cummings

E[dward] E[stlin] Cummings (1894 – 1962) was born in Cambridge, Massachusetts, the son of a minister. As a young man at Harvard, he studied Greek and Latin. In World War I, while serving as an ambulance driver, he was mistakenly arrested and confined to a French prison — an experience that gave rise to a novel filled with vivid portraits of his fellow prisoners, *The Enormous Room* (1922). Off and on throughout the 1920s, Cummings lived in Paris. In *Eimi* (1933) he scathingly and satirically reported on a trip to the Soviet Union. Although many of his lyric poems revel in typographical experiment, in theme and sentiment they are often more conventional than they appear. Besides poetry Cummings wrote essays, plays including *Him* (1927) and *Santa Claus* (1946), and the ballet *Tom* (1935), and produced substantial work as a painter and a graphic artist. Throughout his career, he upheld simple themes: love is good, pomp is silly, one individual is worth a thousand faceless societies.

J. V. Cunningham

J[ames] V[incent] Cunningham (1911 – 1985) was born in Maryland, but spent his early life in Montana. A Shakespeare scholar with a Stanford Ph.D., Cunningham taught English at Brandeis for many years (1953 – 80) and for eight years served as chairman of the department. A reader of Latin and Greek, he became the modern master of the terse, pithy English verse epigram in the classical manner. All his poems have a similar brevity, firm control, and a cold, hardboiled manner. "Poetry is what looks like poetry, what sounds like poetry," he stated. "It is metrical composition." His relatively slim *Collected Poems and Epigrams* (1971) gathers most of his work in verse; his *Collected Essays* (1976), most of his work in prose, including an earlier study, *Woe and Wonder: The Emotional Effect of Shakespearean Tragedy.* In a late critical work, *Dickinson: Lyric and Legend* (1980), Cunningham took a withering look at the bard of Amherst.

Emily Dickinson

Emily Dickinson (1830 – 1886) passed nearly all her life in her family home in Amherst, Massachusetts. Her father was a prominent lawyer and for a time a United States congressman. One trip to Washington, D.C. and a short, unhappy period as a college student at New England Female Seminary (later

Mount Holyoke) were the extent of her distant travels, and as the years passed Dickinson withdrew from town activities and retired into deeper seclusion. Though she wrote more than a thousand poems, she published only seven. The extent of her work was known only after her death, when her manuscripts were discovered in a trunk in the homestead attic, stitched into little booklets and peppered with an idiosyncratic system of punctuation. From 1890 until midcentury, nine posthumous collections of her poems were assembled by friends and relatives, some of whom rewrote her work to make it more conventional. Thomas H. Johnson's three-volume edition of the *Poems* (1955) established a better text. In relatively few and simple forms clearly indebted to the hymns she heard in church, Dickinson succeeded in being a true visionary and a poet of colossal originality.

Emanuel di Pasquale

Emanuel di Pasquale, born in Sicily in 1943, emigrated to America with his mother after his father died. Although he did not learn English until he was sixteen, he began to write poetry at an early age and is now an English professor at Middlesex Community College in New Jersey. For years, di Pasquale has published poetry in *The Nation, New York Times, Sewanee Review,* and other places, but has only recently brought out a first collection, *Genesis* (1989). Lately, he has become known for his poems for children, which appear in several anthologies.

John Donne

John Donne (1572 – 1631), English poet and divine, wrote his subtle, worldly love lyrics as a young man in the court of Queen Elizabeth I. At the time, he came to be known in London as (wrote his contemporary, Richard Baker) "a great visitor of ladies, a great frequenter of plays, a great writer of conceited verses." The poems of his *Songs and Sonnets* were first circulated in manuscript, for in his lifetime Donne printed little. When in 1601 he married without the consent of his bride's father, he was dismissed from his secretarial post at court. For several years he endured poverty. His longer poems, *The First Anniversary* and *The Second Anniversary* (1611, 1612), suffused with gloom, see the order of the universe shaken by science and doubt. In 1615 Donne — apparently with some reluctance, for he had been raised a Catholic — became a priest of the Anglican church. From 1621 until he died he was dean of St. Paul's Cathedral in London, where he preached sermons known for their eloquence. His "Holy Sonnets" date from later life. Almost forgotten for two centuries, Donne's work has had much influence in our time. H. J. C. Grierson brought out a great scholarly edition of it in 1912; shortly thereafter it was championed by T. S. Eliot.

T. S. Eliot

T[homas] S[tearns] Eliot (1888 – 1965) was born of a New England family who had moved to St. Louis. After study at Harvard, Eliot emigrated to London, became a bank clerk and later an influential editor for the publishing house of Faber. In 1927 he became a British citizen and joined the Church of England. During the fire bombings of London in World War II, he served as an air raid warden. Although Eliot strove to keep his private life private, a recent biographer, Peter Ackroyd in *T. S. Eliot* (1984), throws light upon his troubled early marriage. Early poems such as "The Love Song of J. Alfred Prufrock" (1917) and *The Waste Land* (1922), an allusive and seemingly disconnected complaint about the sterility of contemporary city life, enormously influenced young poets. Eliot was mainly responsible for bringing French Symbolism into English poetry, and as a critic he helped revive interest in John Donne and other Metaphysical poets. In an early essay, "Tradition and the Individual Talent" (1919), he finds a necessary continuity in Western civilization. *Four Quartets*, completed in 1943, was Eliot's last major work of poetry: an attempt to structure a long thematic poem like a work of music. In later years he devoted himself to writing verse plays for the London stage; the best received was *The Cocktail Party* (1950), in which Alec Guinness played a psychiatrist. In 1948 Eliot received the Nobel Prize for Literature.

Robert Frost

Robert Frost (1874 – 1963), though born in San Francisco, came to be popularly known as a spokesman of rural New England. In periods of farming, teaching school, and raising chickens and writing for poultry journals, Frost struggled until his late thirties to support his family and to publish his poems, with little success. Moving to England to write and farm in 1912 – 15, he had his first book published in London: *A Boy's Will* (1913). Returning to America, he settled in New Hampshire, later teaching for many years (in a casual way) at Amherst College in Massachusetts. Audiences responded warmly to the poet's public readings; he was awarded four Pulitzer prizes. In late years the white-haired Frost became a sort of elder statesman and poet laureate of the John F. Kennedy administration: invited to read a poem at President Kennedy's inauguration, dispatched to Russia as a cultural emissary. Frost is sometimes admired for putting colloquial Yankee speech into poetry — and he did, but more essentially he mastered the art of laying conversational American speech along a metrical line. In a three-volume biography (1966 – 76), Lawrance Thompson made Frost out to be an overweening egotist who tormented his family, and we are only now coming around again to seeing him as more than that.

Thomas Gray

Thomas Gray (1716 – 1771), author of the most often quoted poem in English, was born in London into a middle-class home (his father was a scrivener, his mother kept a hat shop). He was the only one of twelve children to survive infancy. He attended Eton and later Cambridge University, where he studied for four years but did not take a degree. After a tour of Europe with his schoolmate Horace Walpole (the first Gothic novelist) and a short sojourn with his mother in the village of Stoke Poges, Gray returned to Cambridge to spend the rest of his life in seclusion as a sort of perpetual graduate student. He stayed around the university so long and became so widely learned in architecture, heraldry, botany, Greek, Old Norse, and other matters that in 1768, at fifty-two, he was appointed Regius Professor of History. So retiring was Gray that he first published his "Elegy in a Country Churchyard" anonymously — and only when friends browbeat him into printing it. He seems to have suffered from a constitutional lack of energy. He dreaded being known, and when the post of poet laureate was offered him, he rejected it. A dilettante, Gray considered himself an amateur in whatever he did. Poetry was only one of his interests, but in his "Elegy" and his Pindaric odes "The Bard" and "The Progress of Poesy," he spurred English poetry to break away from neoclassicism and move toward plainer speech, more various forms, infatuation with the colorful, primitive Old English past, and love of nature and countryside. Gray is buried in Stoke Poges, in the churchyard for which we remember him.

H. D. (Hilda Doolittle)

Hilda Doolittle (1886 – 1961), daughter of a Moravian mother and a professor of mathematics and astronomy, spent her first eight years in Bethlehem, Pennsylvania. At Bryn Mawr, she failed English and suffered a nervous collapse. By 1911, she had become a confirmed expatriate, living in London. At one time she was engaged to Ezra Pound, who submitted her early poems to Harriet Monroe's magazine *Poetry* and signed them "H. D. Imagiste." In 1913, she married poet and translator Richard Aldington, and in 1916 published *Sea Change,* her first book of poems. During World War I, H. D. went through a marital breakup and a number of misfortunes recalled in her novel *Palimpsest* (1926). Alone and in poor health, she was rescued by Winifred Ellerman, a writer signing herself Bryher, who adopted the poet's daughter by Cecil Gray and befriended H. D. for life. During 1933 and 1934, H. D. was a patient of Sigmund Freud, an experience she recalls in *Tribute to Freud* (1956). After World War II, the poet moved to Switzerland. Her last works of poetry were epic-long: *Trilogy* (1944 – 46) and the dramatic monologue *Helen in Egypt* (1961). Her earlier poems are available in *Collected Poems 1912 – 1944* (1983), edited by Louis L. Martz. In 1960, back in the United States for the last time, H. D. was given the American Academy of Arts and Letters Award of Merit for Poetry.

Thomas Hardy

Thomas Hardy (1840 – 1928) was both a major Victorian novelist and a great poet of the twentieth century. After his novel *Jude the Obscure* (1896) was trounced by critics who objected to its dismal morbidity, Hardy, who by then had made a modest fortune from his fiction, switched exclusively to his first love, poetry. Hardy was born in the English county of Dorsetshire ("Wessex" in his fiction and poetry), and as a young man worked as an architect. Determined to be a novelist, he first won success with *Far from the Madding Crowd* (1874), followed by *The Return of the Native* (1878), *The Mayor of Casterbridge* (1886), and his masterpiece *Tess of the D'Urbervilles* (1891). After the death of his first wife Emma, with whom he appears to have had had a rather cold and troubled relationship, Hardy was inspired to write a great spate of love poems in her memory. In old age he wrote a two-volume autobiography and charged his second wife, Florence, to publish it after his death under her own name. In both fiction and poetry, Hardy's view of the universe is somber: God appears to have forgotten us, and happiness usually arrives too late. *The Dynasts* (1903 – 08), a long epic poem, makes amused gods sneer down on the Napoleonic wars. Many modern poets have credited Hardy with teaching them a good deal, probably about irony and the use of spoken language, among them W. H. Auden, Philip Larkin, Dylan Thomas, and W. D. Snodgrass.

James Hayford

James Hayford has lived most of his life in Vermont: born in Montpelier in 1913, he now makes his home in Orleans, near the Canadian border. On his graduation from Amherst, he received a Robert Frost Fellowship, given him by the elder poet himself. Hayford has earned a living mainly as a teacher of English, history, and music; he has also worked as a carpenter, raised goats, and edited textbooks. As choirmaster for the Orleans Federated Church, Hayford has composed music for poems by Frost, Herbert, and himself. His work has appeared in *Harper's, The New Yorker,* and other magazines. The poet Robert Francis, an admirer of his work, published his collection *Processional with Wheelbarrow* in 1970; later, Hayford self-published his own collections. Recently the New England Press of Shelburne, Vermont, has brought out his children's novel *Gridley Firing* (1987) with woodcuts by Mary Azarian, and his *Star in the Shed Window: Collected Poems* (1989).

Seamus Heaney

Seamus Heaney, the best-known living Irish poet, was born on a farm in County Derry, Northern Ireland, in 1939. He taught at Queens University, Belfast, before leaving Northern Ireland in 1972 to make his home in Dublin. A guest lecturer at the University of California in Berkeley during the 1971 – 1972 academic year, he now divides his time between Dublin and America, where he teaches at Harvard. Among his recent books of verse are *Station Island* (1985) and *The Haw Lantern* (1987). Rich with images of love and loss, Heaney's poetry draws inventively on the history of Ireland and the Irish from ancient times to the violent present.

George Herbert

George Herbert (1593 – 1633), English devotional poet, the son of an aristocratic family, began writing poems as an undergraduate at Cambridge University. After dabbling for a time in worldly affairs, he entered the priesthood of the Church of England, to live out his days in a country parish. Herbert's poems have many references to music; according to his contemporary John Aubrey, he "had a very good hand on the lute, and set [to music] his own lyrics and sacred poems." Herbert did not publish his poems in his lifetime, but after his death friends collected them in *The Temple* (1633). The book is said to have stimulated Henry Vaughan to follow in Herbert's footsteps as a poet. Herbert makes the religious experience personal, definite, and familiar. For his use of startling "metaphysical" figures of speech, he has been compared with John Donne; but a rare sweetness and plain-spokenness make him unique among poets in English.

Robert Herrick

Robert Herrick (1591 – 1674), after serving as a goldsmith's apprentice, entered Cambridge University at twenty-two, then a late age. For nine years he seems to have lived in London, consorting with a group of poets and wits whose chief was Ben Jonson. In 1629 he became parish priest in Dean Prior, in rural Devonshire, where he lived out his days, sometimes chafing about the boorishness of his parishioners. When in 1647 the Puritans temporarily ousted him from his pulpit, Herrick returned to London. There at fifty-six he brought out his first book, *Noble Numbers* (1647), pious poems; then reprinted them together with five times as many sportive, secular poems in *Hesperides* (1648). Unluckily, the books came too late to cause a stir, Herrick's early fame as a poet having withered and the vogue for chiseled classical lyrics having gone by. Like his master Jonson, Herrick writes songlike poems inspired by Greek and Latin pastoral (or shepherd-and-shepherdess) poetry. We go to him not for profound ideas, but for fresh, tough speech and resonant music. Herrick, who remained a bachelor clergyman, probably imagined the mistresses he praised. He declared in *Hesperides,* "To his book's end this last line he'd have placed: / Jocund his Muse was, but his life was chaste."

Garrett Hongo

Garrett Hongo was born of Japanese ancestry in Volcano, Hawaii, in 1951, and grew up in Oahu and Los Angeles. He earned a B.A. degree at Pomona College and, after doing graduate work in Japanese at the University of Michigan, received an M.F.A. degree from the University of California, Irvine. Hongo has taught at the University of Southern California, the University of California, Irvine, and, most recently, at the University of Missouri, Columbia. His books of poetry include *Yellow Light* (1982) and *The River of Heaven* (1988), which won the Lamont Poetry Prize of the Academy of American Poets.

Gerard Manley Hopkins

Gerard Manley Hopkins (1844 – 1889), born in Essex, England, was, like Emily Dickinson, a major poet not known until our century. At twenty, a student at Oxford, he was converted to Roman Catholicism and received into that church by Cardinal Newman. Ordained a Jesuit, Hopkins at first served as parish priest and teacher in working-class sections of large cities (London, Glasgow, Liverpool, Manchester), where poverty and suffering distressed him. But his sermons were reportedly so strange (in one, he likened the church to a cow we milk and whose moo we follow) that his superiors removed him from public view, making him Professor of Greek at University College, Dublin. He died of typhoid fever at forty-four. Nearly thirty years after Hopkins's death, his friend Robert Bridges published his *Poems* (1918), having thought them too demanding for earlier readers. That much of Hopkins's work sounds odd to us may be due to the poet's admiration for Old English, with its gutsy monosyllables, and for Welsh poetry, rich in patterns of sound. Hopkins developed his own theory of versification: "sprung rhythm" — in brief, a kind of accentual verse. Though on entering the priesthood he had renounced poetry, he welcomed the suggestion of a superior that he contribute to a Jesuit magazine a poem on the drowning of five Franciscan nuns. The result, "The Wreck of the *Deutschland,*" received a rejection slip. This challenging poem has been called "the dragon guarding the door to Hopkins's poetry," but most readers have gone in by the back door of his more quickly accessible nature poems. In these, the sensuous world bursts forth in irrepressible testimony to its Maker's glory.

A. E. Housman

A. E. Housman (1859 – 1936), English poet and professor of Latin, was born in a village in rural Shropshire, England. Although as a student at Oxford he distinguished himself as a promising scholar of the classics, he failed his exams, apparently because of some inner crisis precipitated by his love for a fellow male student. Determined to overcome this setback, Housman, while working as a clerk in the British Patent Office, at night wrote scholarly articles. Within ten years these academic writings, bristling with cold sarcasms and scathing put-downs of rival scholars, had won him such high repute that he was invited to be Professor of Latin at the University of London. Later he stepped up to Cambridge University, to spend the rest of his days living a retiring academic life befitting his shy temperament. Though Housman published only two slim collections of poems — the instantly and enormously popular *A Shropshire Lad* (1898) and the conclusively titled *Last Poems* (1922) — his place as a minor master of the English lyric seems unshakable. Like many Latin poets he admired, he insists in well-turned lines that life is short and comes to a bad end.

Langston Hughes

Langston Hughes (1902 – 1967), who dropped his first name, James, was born in Joplin, Missouri. As a high school senior in Cleveland, he wrote a poem still often reprinted, "The Negro Speaks of Rivers." When a young man, Hughes worked as a merchant seaman, visited Africa, and lived for a time in Rome and Paris. While working as a busboy at a Washington, D.C., hotel, he showed his poems to hotel guest Vachel Lindsay, a poet then celebrated, and Lindsay urged them on a publisher. *The Weary Blues* (1926) earned him a considerable reputation. Hughes's work in poetry won him a scholarship to Lincoln University, from which he was graduated in 1929. He became a major figure in the Harlem Renaissance of the 1920s and early 1930s — a period when that district of New York City became a lively center for black writers, artists, and musicians. A versatile writer and teacher, Hughes, one of the first practicing poets to teach poetry writing in elementary schools, was also among the few poets to earn a living by giving readings and lecturing. Among his other works are novels, stories, plays, song lyrics, children's books, memoirs, translations, and essays reporting conversations with a Harlem dweller called Simple, a streetwise philosopher. *A Langston Hughes Reader* (1958) gives some idea of his richness and variety.

Randall Jarrell

Randall Jarrell (1914 – 1965) was born in Nashville, Tennessee, and served as a private in the army air force in World War II, an experience that gave rise to several of his best early poems. Much of his life was spent in academe. At

Vanderbilt, a psychology major, he studied literature with poet-critic John Crowe Ransom, who changed the direction of Jarrell's career. When Ransom moved to Kenyon College, Jarrell followed as an English instructor. At Kenyon, he formed another lifelong friendship: with a student who was to become a distinguished poet, Robert Lowell. Later Jarrell taught at the University of Texas, Sarah Lawrence, Princeton, Illinois, and for many years (1947 – 65) at the Woman's College of the University of North Carolina (now the U.N.C., Greensboro). His one novel, *Pictures from an Institution* (1954), is a satire set on a campus. As poetry editor for *The Nation* in the mid-1940s, Jarrell drew attention for his witty, astute, outspoken reviews of poetry. *Poetry and the Age* (1953) includes especially brilliant essays on Robert Frost and Wallace Stevens. Jarrell, who loved the German language, translated Goethe's *Faust* (Part I) and some of the Grimm fairy tales. In late years he wrote four books for children (with beautiful drawings by Maurice Sendak) including *The Bat Poet* (1964) and the posthumous *Fly by Night* (1976).

Ben Jonson

Ben Jonson (1573? – 1637), posthumous son of a Scottish minister, was a native Londoner. As a boy he received a firm grounding in Latin and Greek at Westminster School, but instead of enrolling in a university, took up bricklaying, then served as a soldier in Flanders. Home from the wars, he married and became an actor and playwright in London. Although a coolly rational classicist by persuasion, Jonson seems to have been an outspoken hothead, given to quarrels and brawls. In 1598 he killed a fellow actor in a duel and escaped the gallows only by claiming an ancient law that forbade hanging anyone who could read. From about 1606, Jonson frequented the Mermaid Tavern in London's Fleet Street, a favorite hangout of writers and actors. There, on the first Friday of each month, he presided over famed literary discussions; according to one report, his friend Shakespeare would take part at times and match wits with him. Later changing pubs (to the Devil and St. Dunstan), Jonson and his circle became known as the "Tribe of Ben"; Thomas Carew and Robert Herrick were younger members. Later Jonson became the leading writer of masks, elaborate plays with music and dancing produced at court. As a poet Jonson, in his precise Latinate lyrics, odes, and epigrams, helped get rid of worn-out Petrarchan conventions (those Shakespeare mocks in "My mistress' eyes are nothing like the sun"). As a playwright, he excelled; his comedies, especially *Volpone, or The Fox* (1606) and *The Alchemist* (1610), are among the crown jewels of the English stage.

John Keats

John Keats (1795 – 1821), son of a London stable keeper, studied to become a physician and served as a surgeon's apprentice before deciding on poetry as a career. In 1817 he published his first book, *Poems,* including "On First Looking into Chapman's Homer." Despite critics' hostility to his narrative poem *Endymion* (1818), Keats persisted. In 1818 he fell in love with sixteen-year-old Fanny Brawne, but, stricken with tuberculosis, postponed plans for marriage. In 1820, shortly after publication of his third and last book, Keats went to Italy in hopes of regaining his health, but his poetry soon slowed to a stop. In the following year, at twenty-five, he died in Rome and was buried there beneath the epitaph he wrote for himself: "Here lies one whose name was writ in water." His name, however, has continued to endure. No English poet wrote poems richer in sensuous imagery (as in his great odes, among them "Ode on Melancholy" and "To Autumn"), nor quite so beautifully reimagined the Middle Ages (in poems such as "La Belle Dame sans Merci" and "The Eve of St. Agnes"). He wrote several of the finest sonnets in the language, an unfinished epic of great interest, *Hyperion,* hilarious light verse, and scores of superb letters.

Philip Larkin

Philip Larkin (1922 – 1985), born in Coventry, England, has been called the most influential British poet since World War II. After studies at Oxford, he drifted into being a librarian, and for many years was head librarian for the University of Hull. Early in his career Larkin wrote two novels, *Jill* (1946) and *A Girl in Winter* (1947). He also reviewed jazz recordings for a London newspaper. A self-declared foe of modernism in music, art, and literature, he published only four slim volumes of poems, traditional in form. The earliest collection was heavily indebted to Yeats: *The North Ship* (1945, reissued in 1966 with a preface making fun of it). With *The Less Deceived* (1955), Larkin hit his characteristic stride, writing most of the poems in the voice of a tough-minded, disillusioned, self-deprecating man facing a dreary urban landscape of quiet frustration. This voice drew an immediate response from readers in postwar England.

D. H. Lawrence

David Herbert Lawrence (1885 – 1930) was born in Nottinghamshire, England, child of a coalminer and a schoolteacher who hated her husband's toil and vowed that her son should escape it. He took up fiction writing, attaining early success. During World War I, Lawrence and his wife were unjustly suspected of treason (he because of his pacifism, she because of her aristocratic German birth). After the armistice they left England and, seeking a climate healthier for Lawrence, who suffered from tuberculosis, wandered in Italy, France, Australia, Mexico, and the American Southwest. Lawrence is an impassioned spokesman for our unconscious, instinctive natures, which we moderns (he argues) have neglected in favor of our overweening intellects. In *Lady Chatterley's Lover* (1928), he strove to restore explicit sexuality to English fiction. The book, which today seems tame and repetitious, was long banned in Britain and the United States. Deeper Lawrence novels include *Sons and Lovers* (1913), a veiled account of his breaking away from his fiercely possessive mother; *The Rainbow* (1915); *Women in Love* (1921); and *The Plumed Serpent* (1926), about a revival of pagan religion in Mexico. Besides fiction, Lawrence left a rich legacy of poetry, essays, criticism (*Studies in Classic American Literature*, 1923, is especially shrewd and funny), and travel writing. Lawrence exerted deep influence on others, both by the message in his work and by his personal magnetism.

Denise Levertov

Denise Levertov was born in 1923 in Essex, England, daughter of a Welsh mother and a Russian Jewish-born priest of the Anglican church. She was educated at home, reading in her father's library. She served as a nurse in World War II. In 1947 she married an American novelist, Mitchell Goodman, and in the following year came to the United States. Her first book, published in England, had observed traditional poetic conventions (including rime and meter), but in America she discovered the work of William Carlos Williams and other open-form poets, and began to write in a different, freer mode. With Robert Creeley and others of the Black Mountain group, she has exerted much influence among younger poets. Her critical essays have been collected in *The Poet in the World* (1973) and *Light up the Cave* (1981). Levertov has been a tireless political activist, prominent in peace movements of the 1960s, 1970s, and 1980s. She now makes her home in Somerville, Massachusetts, and recently has been teaching poetry writing at Stanford on one coast and at Brandeis on the other.

Robert Lowell

Robert Lowell (1917 – 1977), born in Boston, came from a famous New England family that included three distinguished poets: James Russell, Maria, and Amy. He attended Harvard, then on the advice of his psychiatrist transferred to Kenyon, where he studied with poet-critics John Crowe Ransom and Randall Jarrell. During World War II he served time in a federal prison for resisting the draft. Lowell's early poems in *Lord Weary's Castle* (1946) were violent in imagery and tightly traditional in form. With the deliberately looser *Life Studies* (1959), he showed that he had learned from William Carlos Williams and the Beat poets, and his work became more open in form, more colloquial in speech, and more direct in its use of his own experience. Some of these poems were labeled "confessional poetry." As "Skunk Hour" tells us, Lowell's mind was sometimes "not right"; he suffered from recurrent manic depression that required him to spend periods in a hospital. Besides poetry, he wrote plays based on stories by Hawthorne and Melville: *The Old Glory* (1964, enlarged edition 1968) —

as well as English versions of the *Phaedra* of Racine (1961) and the *Prometheus Bound* of Aeschylus (1969). Lowell was also a remarkable critic of poetry.

Edna St. Vincent Millay

Edna St. Vincent Millay (1892 – 1950), born in Rockland, Maine, was the eldest of three daughters. When she was twelve, her father deserted the family. At twenty, she had already published "Renascence," one of her most celebrated poems. In 1917, she was graduated from Vassar College and settled in Greenwich Village, where she became as famous for her vivacious personality, her bohemian life-style, her acting and playwriting, and her feminism, as for her verse. Even as she wrote *The Harp Weaver*, a serious volume of verse that won her a Pulitzer Prize in 1923, Millay did hack writing to pay her bills. Among other work for which she is known are verse dramas such as *Aria da Capo* (1920) and the sonnet cycle *Fatal Interview* (1931). In 1923, she married Eugen Jan Boissevain, Dutch businessman and widower of feminist Inez Milholland. In 1927, Millay's political activism expressed itself in poems about Sacco and Vanzetti, two anarchists accused of murder, and involved her in an unsuccessful campaign to prevent their execution. Though she kept writing poetry well into the 1940s and received several honorary degrees, her reputation waned. Darkened by a nervous breakdown in 1944 and the poet's growing sense that the public had deserted her, Millay's life ended with a heart attack.

John Milton

John Milton (1608 – 1674), author of *Paradise Lost*, the greatest English epic, was born in London, the son of a scrivener who composed music. His mother early began schooling him to be a minister. He studied zealously. As he later recalled: "From my twelfth year I scarcely ever went to bed before midnight, which was the first cause of injury to my eyes." After he received his B.A. from Cambridge University in 1629, his father supported him through eight years of further study. "Lycidas" (1638), a poem of this period, shows his deepening seriousness about religion and his growing resentment of corruptions in the church, which were to lead him to the Puritan cause. Milton wrote much prose in the service of causes. In *Areopagitica* (1644), he argues for freedom of the press and opposes the strict censorship that had been imposed by Parliament. His unhappy marriage to Mary Powell led him to write tracts in favor of divorce. When Oliver Cromwell and the Puritans ousted King Charles and declared England a commonwealth, Milton's writings were remembered, and earned him a post as Cromwell's foreign secretary. His eyesight strained by years of hard study, Milton went blind and had to dictate his correspondence (in Latin) to clerks, one of whom was fellow poet Andrew Marvell. With the Restoration of Charles II in 1660, Milton's world came crashing down. In retirement, at last he turned to a project he had planned as a young man: his major heroic poem, *Paradise Lost* (1667), about Satan's rebellion and the Fall of Adam and Eve. This epic was followed by *Paradise Regained* (1671) and a verse drama modeled on a Greek tragedy, *Samson Agonistes* (1671).

Marianne Moore

Marianne Moore (1887 – 1972), whose poems earned praise from fellow poets as dissimilar as William Carlos Williams and T.S. Eliot, was born in Kirkwood, Missouri, a suburb of St. Louis. Her father abandoned the family in 1894, and Moore moved to Pennsylvania. In 1909, she was graduated from Bryn Mawr, where a classmate was the poet H.D. For a time, Moore taught business courses at the U.S. Indian School in Carlisle, Pennsylvania, where the athlete Jim Thorpe was among her students. By 1915, her poems — witty, satirical, intellectual, disruptive, and innovative — had begun to appear in *Poetry* magazine. Until her mother died in 1947, Moore, a dutiful daughter, lived with her in Brooklyn, supporting herself by a series of conventional jobs. From 1925 to 1929 she edited *The Dial*, a literary magazine in whose pages she published many of the best poets of her day. Besides poems, Moore wrote essays, reviews, and translations including *The Fables of La Fontaine* (1945). For her *Collected Poems* (1951), she won a Pulitzer Prize, the Bollingen Prize, and a National Book Award; her *Complete Poems* appeared in 1967. Late in life, Moore became a media figure for her fondness for the Brooklyn Dodgers and her penchant for three-cornered hats. She stayed in Brooklyn, writing and rewriting, through an active and vigorous old age.

Lorine Niedecker

Lorine Niedecker (1903 – 1970) spent nearly all her life on Blackhawk Island near Fort Atkinson, Wisconsin, where her father worked as a carp fisherman. After two years at Beloit College, she returned home to care for her ailing mother. Following a brief marriage in 1928, Niedecker held jobs as proofreader, librarian's helper, and cleaning worker in a hospital. After her marriage in 1963 she lived in Milwaukee, but on her husband's retirement the couple moved into a house they had built by the Rock River, and the poet returned to her native grounds. Although she lived an outwardly quiet life remote from publishing centers, Niedecker read widely and maintained a vigorous life of the mind. In the early 1930s she struck up a correspondence with poet and teacher Louis Zukofsky, who encouraged her poetry. In the 1950s poet Cid Corman printed her work in his avant garde little magazine *Origin*. During her lifetime she published sparingly, but *From This Condensery: The Complete Writing of Lorine Niedecker* (1985) contains a large body of poems, as well as critical essays, experimental prose, and five radio plays. Her life and work are the subject of Kristine Thatcher's play *Niedecker,* given an off-Broadway production in 1989.

John Frederick Nims

John Frederick Nims, born in 1913 in Muskegon, Michigan, has had a distinguished career as poet and translator, teacher and editor. He has taught at Florida, Illinois (Urbana and Chicago), Missouri, Notre Dame, Toronto, and other universities, and has held visiting professorships at Harvard and in Florence, Milan, and Madrid. The poems in his first book *The Iron Pastoral* (1947) deal wittily with jukeboxes, penny arcades, poolrooms, and other features of the contemporary scene. In *Of Flesh and Bone* (1967) Nims shows his mastery of the epigram. His *Selected Poems* appeared in 1982. A translator of poetry from languages as varied as classical Greek, Catalan, and Galacian, Nims has splendidly rendered into English *The Poems of St. John of the Cross* (1959, revised edition 1968). For several years (1978 – 85) he was editor of *Poetry* magazine. He is the author of an introduction to poetry, *Western Wind,* and editor of *The Harper Anthology of Poetry* (1981).

Wilfred Owen

Wilfred Owen (1893 – 1918) was, like A. E. Housman, a native of Shropshire, England. He attended London University and for a time served as lay assistant to a minister, helping the sick and poor. In 1916, during World War I, he enlisted in the British army, became a company commander, and in less than two years wrote all his famous antiwar poems of life in the trenches. The army seems suddenly to have changed Owen from a competent minor poet with little to say into a powerful voice of pacifism. At age twenty-five, while trying to get his men across a canal under enemy fire on the French front, he was killed in action only a week before the war ended. Though Owen published only four poems, after his death a collection of his work was edited by another front-line war poet, Siegfried Sassoon (1920). Owen is preeminent among English poets who wrote of that conflict, and the reputation of his work has continued to grow.

Linda Pastan

Linda Pastan was born Linda Olenik in New York in 1932. After her graduation from Radcliffe, she took two master's degrees at Simmons (M.L.S.) and Brandeis (M.A.). She married in 1953 and has a daughter and two sons. Her first book, *A Perfect Circle of the Sun* (1971), established her as an up-and-comer; *Selected Poems* appeared in 1979, confirming her accomplishment. Her subtle, often powerful poems are exceptionally clear and accessible.

Sylvia Plath

Sylvia Plath (1932 – 1963), one of the most remarkable poets in English of the past half-century, was born in Boston, the daughter of German immigrants who both taught at Boston University. The death of her father when the poet was eight came as a trauma from which she seems never quite to have recovered. As a scholarship-winning student at Smith College, Plath revealed early promise, and her work received early publication. Like Esther Greenwood, protagonist of her one novel *The Bell Jar* (1963), Plath won a student contest that sent her to work in New York for a national magazine, and struggled with a year-long siege of mental illness for which she underwent shock treatments. Returning to Smith, she was graduated with top honors. Later she studied at Cambridge University in England, where she met and in 1956 married the poet Ted Hughes. Estranged from her husband, she died a suicide in London, leaving two children and, in manuscript, the intense, powerful poems that went into her posthumous, highly acclaimed collection, *Ariel* (1965).

Alexander Pope

Alexander Pope (1688 – 1744), the leading English poet of the early eighteenth century, was born in London, son of a Roman Catholic linen merchant. A sickly, stunted, pockmarked child, he suffered from weak health and continual exhaustion throughout his life, and was said to have worn padded clothes to disguise his misshapen frame. Pope early excelled as a poet, composing his *Pastorals* (1709) at age sixteen. His rimed translations of the *Iliad* (1720) and the *Odyssey* (1725 – 26) and his edition of Shakespeare (1725), bestsellers in their day, made him independently wealthy, and he was able to buy an estate at Twickenham and live in style. Pope did not write an epic, but instead translated epics and wrote great mock epics: *The Rape of the Lock* (1714), in which he voices compassion for women transformed into wives, and *The Dunciad* (1728 – 43), in which he mocks his many literary enemies. He was a master satirist and splendid craftsman of the heroic couplet. Romantic critics generally think him no poet at all, but G. K. Chesterton remarked, "If Pope be not a poet, then who is?"

Ezra Pound

Ezra Pound (1885 – 1972), among the most influential (and still controversial) poets of our century, was born in Hailey, Idaho. He readied himself for a teaching career, but when in 1907 he lost his job at Wabash College for sheltering a penniless prostitute, he left America. Settling in England and later in Paris, he wielded influence on the work of T. S. Eliot, whose long poem *The*

Waste Land he edited; W. B. Yeats, whom he served as secretary and critic; and James Joyce. Pound was perpetually championing writers then unknown, like Robert Frost. In 1924 Pound settled permanently in Italy, where he came to admire Mussolini's economic policies. During World War II he made broadcasts to America by Italian radio, deemed treasonous. When American armed forces arrested him in 1944, Pound spent three weeks in a cage in an army camp in Pisa. Flown to the United States to stand trial, he was declared incompetent and for twelve years was confined in St. Elizabeth's in Washington, a hospital for the criminally insane. In 1958, at the intervention of Robert Frost, Archibald MacLeish, and other old friends, he was pronounced incurable and allowed to return to Italy to spend his last, increasingly silent years. In his prime, Pound is a swaggeringly confident critic, a berater of smugness and mediocrity, a delectable humorist. Among his lasting books are *Personae* (enlarged edition, 1949), short poems; his *ABC of Reading* (1934), an introduction to poetry; and *Literary Essays* (1954). His *Cantos,* a vast poem woven of historical themes published in instalments over forty years, Pound never finished. He is a great translator of poetry from Italian, Provençal, Chinese, and other languages. Pare away his delusions, and a remarkable human being and splendid poet remains.

Dudley Randall

Dudley Randall was born in 1914 in Washington, D.C. He was graduated from Wayne State University and the University of Michigan, and has worked as librarian and poet-in-residence at the University of Detroit. A pioneer in the modern movement to publish the work of black writers, Randall founded what has been called the most influential small publishing house in America, Broadside Press. He also edited an important anthology, *The Black Poets* (1971). Randall's *A Litany of Friends: New and Selected Poems* was published in 1981.

Adrienne Rich

Adrienne Rich was born in Baltimore in 1929, into a father-dominated Jewish family of comfortable means. While still an undergraduate at Radcliffe, she published her first book of poems, *A Change of World* (1951), with an introduction by W. H. Auden. Later she studied at Oxford. In 1953 she married an economist and soon bore three sons — an experience she said had been "radicalizing." During the Vietnam War, she took an active part in the peace movement. In 1970 after the suicide of her estranged husband, perhaps obliquely referred to in the poem "Diving into the Wreck," Rich turned increasingly to feminist matters, expressed not only in poetry but in prose: in *Of Woman Born* (1976), a study of the institution of motherhood. With Michelle Cliff, she has coedited *Sinister Wisdom,* a lesbian little magazine. Rich has taught at City College of New York, Columbia, Brandeis, Smith, Douglass, and elsewhere. Few woman poets in recent years have commanded a more devoted audience.

Theodore Roethke

Theodore Roethke (1908 – 1963) was born in Saginaw, Michigan, where his family ran a large greenhouse. (No poet seems wealthier in his knowledge of vegetation.) He went to the University of Michigan and (for a year) to Harvard. As a young poet teaching college at a time when creative writing teachers without Ph.D.s were suspect, Roethke held impermanent jobs before coming to rest at the University of Washington in Seattle. There, from 1947 until his death, he was an influential teacher of poetry and poetry writing; among his students were Carolyn Kizer, David Wagoner, and James Wright. Roethke was a large, heavyset man light on his feet (he once coached varsity tennis at Lafayette), and would sometimes prepare for a poetry reading by pacing the stage like an athlete warming up. His poetry developed from rather conventional and imitative lyrics through a phase of disconnected stream of consciousness into (at the end) a meditative poetry reminiscent in its open lines of Walt Whitman's.

William Shakespeare

William Shakespeare (1564 – 1616), the supreme writer of English, was born, baptized, and buried in the market town of Stratford-on-Avon, eighty miles from London. Son of a glovemaker and merchant who was high bailiff (or mayor) of the town, he probably attended grammar school and learned to read Latin authors in the original. At eighteen he married Anne Hathaway, twenty-six, by whom he had three children, including twins. By 1592 he had become well known and envied as an actor and playwright in London. From 1594 until he retired, he belonged to the same theatrical company, the Lord Chamberlain's Men (later renamed the King's Men in honor of their patron, James I), for whom he wrote thirty-six plays — some of them, such as *Hamlet* and *King Lear*, profound reworkings of old plays. As an actor, Shakespeare is believed to have played supporting roles, such as Hamlet's father's ghost. The company prospered, moved into the Globe in 1599, and in 1608 bought the fashionable Blackfriars as well; Shakespeare owned an interest in both theaters. When plagues shut down the theaters from 1592 to 1594, Shakespeare turned to poetry; his great Sonnets (published only in 1609) probably date from the 1590s. Plays were regarded as entertainments of little literary merit, like comic books today, and Shakespeare did not bother to supervise their publication. He did, however, carefully see through press his sonnets and the narrative poems *Venus and Adonis* (1593) and *The Rape of Lucrece* (1594).

Percy Bysshe Shelley

Percy Bysshe Shelley (1792 – 1822) married his first wife, sixteen-year-old Harriet Westbrook, in 1811, the same year he was expelled from Oxford for coauthoring a pamphlet defending atheism. His first major poem, *Queen Mab*, which advocated the abolishment of a number of established institutions, was privately printed in 1813. In 1814 Shelley went to France with Mary Wollstonecraft, later famous as the author of *Frankenstein* (1818). They were married after Harriet's suicide in 1816. In 1818 they settled in Italy, where Shelley wrote some of his best lyrics, including "Ode to the West Wind," "To a Skylark," and "Ozymandias"; poetic dramas; and *Adonais*, an elegy to his friend John Keats. "A Defense of Poetry," the poet's most important prose work, was written in 1821. While sailing during a storm, Shelley was drowned. He is remembered as a staunch believer in the eighteenth-century ideals of reason and the perfectibility of the human race.

Stevie Smith

Stevie Smith (1902 – 1971), was born in Hull, Yorkshire, christened Florence Margaret Smith. Being wiry and short, she acquired her nickname from a popular jockey, Stevie Donahue. For more than sixty years, beginning at age three, Smith lived with her aunt in Palmers Green, a suburb of London, and worked for thirty years as a publisher's secretary. Of her three novels, *Novel on Yellow Paper* (1936) is the best known. Her poetry readings, in public and on BBC radio, widened her audience. *Collected Poems* (1976) is illustrated with her own witty, slapdash, and rakishly charming drawings. *Me Again: Uncollected Writings* (1982) contains poems, stories, essays, and a play for radio. In a film, *Stevie* (1978), based on a stage play by Hugh Whitemore, Glenda Jackson plays the poet with keen empathy.

William Stafford

William Stafford, born in 1914 in Hutchinson, Kansas, was graduated from the University of Kansas and later took a doctorate at the University of Iowa. During World War II he was interned as a conscientious objector, an experience he recalls in his prose memoir *Down in My Heart* (1947). For many years he taught at Lewis and Clark College in Portland, Oregon, and in 1970 – 71 he served as Consultant in Poetry for the Library of Congress. *Traveling Through the Dark* (1962) won the National Book Award, and in 1977 Stafford published a large volume of his collected poems, *Stories That Could Be True*. In much of his work he traces the landscapes of the Midwest and of the Pacific Northwest, where he has long lived. He describes his poetry as "much like talk, with some enhancement."

Timothy Steele

Timothy Steele, born in Burlington, Vermont, in 1948, took his doctorate in English at Brandeis, where he studied literature with J. V. Cunningham. A Californian by adoption, he has taught and held a Wallace Stegner fellowship in creative writing at Stanford, and currently teaches at California State University, Los Angeles. His first collection, *Uncertainties and Rest,* appeared in 1979, and his most recent, *Sapphics Against Anger and Other Poems,* in 1986. *Missing Measures: Modern Poetry and the Revolt against Meter* (1990) is a critical study in literary history. His poems wear a Yankee reticence and a tendency toward precise understatement, holding much power within their strict limits. Steele writes exclusively in traditional forms, in which he demonstrates mastery.

James Stephens

James Stephens (1882 – 1950), born in Dublin, Ireland, was a famous member of the Irish Literary Renaissance, a movement early in the century that included William Butler Yeats and the playwrights Lady Gregory, J. M. Synge, and Sean O'Casey. As a young man Stephens took a job as a typist in a lawyer's office, where access to a typewriter started him writing fantastic fiction, some of it based on Irish folklore, such as his most popular novel, *The Crock of Gold* (1912). Other imaginative novels followed, including *The Demi-Gods* (1914) and *Deirdre* (1923). *Irish Fairy Tales* (1920) retells classic legends for young readers. Although best remembered for such books, Stephens was a considerable poet as well. His first collection appeared in 1909, and in 1926 he published his *Collected Poems.* Some of his poems are actually free translations from the Irish: "A Glass of Beer," for instance, is a version of a poem by Dáibhí Ó Bruadair (about 1625 – 98).

Wallace Stevens

Wallace Stevens (1879 – 1955) was born in Reading, Pennsylvania; his father was a successful lawyer; his mother, a former schoolteacher. As a special student at Harvard, he became president of the student literary magazine, the *Harvard Advocate,* but he did not want a liberal arts degree. Instead, he became a lawyer in New York City, and in 1916 joined the legal staff of the Hartford Accident and Indemnity Company. In 1936 he was elected a vice-president. Stevens, who would write poems in his head while walking to work and then dictate them to his secretary, was a leading expert on surety claims. Once asked how he was able to combine poetry and insurance, he replied that the two occupations had an element in common: "calculated risk." As a young man in New York, Stevens made lasting friendships with poets Marianne Moore and William Carlos Williams, but he did not seek literary society. Though his poems are full of references to Europe and remote places, his only travels were annual vacation trips to Key West. He printed his early poems in *Poetry* magazine, but did not publish a book until *Harmonium* appeared in 1923, when he was forty-four. Living quietly in Hartford, Connecticut, Stevens sought to discover order in a chaotic world with his subtle and exotic imagination. His critical essays, collected in *The Necessary Angel* (1951), and his *Letters* (1966), edited by his daughter Holly Stevens, reveal a penetrating, philosophic mind. His *Collected Poems* (1954), published on his seventy-fifth birthday, garnered major prizes and belated recognition for Stevens as a major American poet.

Jonathan Swift

Jonathan Swift (1667 – 1745), Anglo-Irish poet, satirist, journalist, and clergy-man, was born in Dublin, said to have been sired by an English steward. Uncles helped him attend Trinity College, Dublin, from which he was graduated "by special grace," having shone only in his studies of the classics. In 1694 Swift entered the Church of England and held parish appointments in Ireland, finally becoming Dean of St. Patrick's Cathedral, Dublin — to his disappointment, for he loved London and had hoped for a position there. His cousin John Dryden is reported to have told him, "Cousin Swift, you will never be a poet," a prophecy that time has proved inaccurate. In a life crowded with church duties, political agitation, literary society, and long and perhaps sexless love affairs, especially with his former pupil Esther Johnson (whom he called Stella), Swift found occasion to write much excellent verse. Still, he is best remembered for *Gulliver's Travels* (1726), an affectionate tribute to the reasoning part of "that animal called man," a scathing and scatological rebuke to the rest of him.

Alfred, Lord Tennyson

Alfred, Lord Tennyson (1809 – 1892), was born Alfred Tennyson in Lincoln-shire, England, the son of an alcoholic rural minister. When Queen Victoria made him a baron in 1883 (at seventy-five), he added the "Lord" to his byline. A precocious poet, Tennyson began writing verse at five, and when still in his teens collaborated with his brother Charles on *Poems by Two Brothers* (1827). As a student at Cambridge, he was unusual: he kept a snake for a pet, won a medal for poetry, and went home without taking a degree. But in college he made influential friendships, especially that of Arthur Hallam, whose death in 1833 inspired Tennyson's *In Memoriam* (1850), the elegiac sequence that con-tains "Dark house by which once more I stand." The year 1850 was a banner one for Tennyson in other ways: he at last felt prosperous enough to marry Emily Sellwood, who had remained engaged to him for fourteen years, and Queen Victoria named him poet laureate, in which capacity he served for four decades, writing poems for state occasions. Between 1859 and 1888 Tennyson completed *Idylls of the King,* a twelve-part narrative poem of Arthur and his Round Table. In his mid-sixties he wrote several plays. A spokesman for the Victorian age and its militant colonialism, Tennyson is still respected as a poet of varied assets, including an excellent ear.

Dylan Thomas

Dylan Thomas (1914 – 1953) was born in the coastal town of Swansea, Wales, the son of a teacher of English. Much of Thomas's life was a bitter struggle to support his wife and children, a struggle intensified by fondness for spending freely. Lacking a university education, Thomas found most paying literary work barred to him in Britain, although late in life he received many assignments to write film and radio scripts. A resonant reader-aloud of poetry, he made broadcasts for BBC radio and undertook several immensely popular reading tours of America, preceded by a reputation for heavy drinking and gustatorial lovemaking. He died in a hospital in New York City after drinking a procession of straight whiskeys, apparently courting the end. Thomas wrote not only poems (in the early ones he brought surrealism into English poetry), he also wrote remarkable stories and a "play for voices," *Under Milk Wood* (1954), based on memories of his home town in Wales.

John Updike

John Updike, born in Shillingford, Pennsylvania, in 1932, is primarily regarded as a novelist. But his first book was verse, *The Carpentered Hen* (1954), from which we take "Ex-Basketball Player"; and ever since, he has continued to produce verse both light and serious. He received his B.A. from Harvard, then went to Oxford to study drawing and fine art. From 1955 to 1957 he worked on the staff of *The New Yorker.* Though he left the magazine to write full-time, he has continued to supply it with bright stories and searching book reviews. Hardly a fall goes by without a new Updike novel. *The Witches of Eastwick* (1984) was recently a made into a successful motion picture.

Keith Waldrop

Keith Waldrop, born in 1932 in Emporia, Kansas, grew up in a family divided by his father's militant atheism and his mother's pious Christian fundamentalism. He took his doctorate at the University of Michigan with a thesis on obscenity in literature, and has since taught at Wesleyan University and at Brown. Waldrop has directed and acted in films and plays. His first book of poems, *A Windmill near Calvary* (1968), was nominated for the National Book Award. He lives in Providence, Rhode Island, with his wife, the poet and translator Rosmarie Waldrop, thousands of books and recordings, and a basement printing press that produces more books under the imprint Burning Deck.

Edmund Waller

Edmund Waller (1606 – 1687), born into a rich country family, is remembered in England not only as a poet but also as a member of Parliament. In 1643 he hatched "Waller's Plot," an attempt to turn London over to the exiled Charles I; it failed, but Parliament later pardoned him. His smooth, elegant poems included tributes to important public figures as well as courtly love lyrics. Written chiefly in iambic pentameter couplets, these later helped establish the heroic couplet as a favorite poetic form among English poets of the eighteenth century.

Walt Whitman

Walt Whitman (1819 – 1892) was born on Long Island, son of an impoverished farmer. He spent his early years as a school teacher, a temperance propagandist, a carpenter, a printer, and a newspaper editor on the Brooklyn *Eagle.* He began writing poetry in youth, sometimes declaiming his lines above the crash of waves on New York beaches. Apparently he was also inspired to write wide, spacious, confident lines by attending performances of Italian opera. His self-published *Leaves of Grass* (1855) won praise from Ralph Waldo Emerson and gained Whitman readers in England. For the rest of his life, he kept revising and enlarging it, ceasing with a ninth or "deathbed edition" in 1891 – 92. Americans at first were slow to accept Whitman's unconventionally open verse forms, his sexual frankness, and his gregarious egoism. The poet of boundless faith in American democracy, Whitman tempered his vision by his experiences as a volunteer hospital nurse during the Civil War (described in his poems *Drum-Taps* and his wartime letters). After the war, he held secretarial jobs to support himself, and lost one such job when his employer's scandalized eye fell upon the *Leaves.* In old age, a semi-invalid after a stroke, Whitman made his home in Camden, New Jersey. Before he died he saw his work finally winning respect and worldwide acceptance. Whitman's influence on later American poetry has been profound, both by the example of his open forms and by his bold encompassing of subject matter that had formerly been considered unpoetic. (In "Song of the Exposition," read aloud at an industrial show in New York, the poet exclaims of his Muse: "She's here, install'd amid the kitchen ware!")

Richard Wilbur

Richard Wilbur, born in 1917 in New York City, was graduated from Amherst College, then served in the army in World War II. He has taught English at Harvard, Wellesley, Wesleyan, and Smith. With his first two collections, *The Beautiful Changes* (1947) and *Ceremony* (1950), Wilbur acquired a high reputation for a poetry of sensitivity, wit, grace, and command of traditional forms. Besides writing poetry, for which he has received many prizes, including two Pulitzer Prizes and a National Book Award, Wilbur has edited the poetry of Shakespeare and Poe. He has written song lyrics for *Candide,* a Broadway musical by Lillian Hellman and Leonard Bernstein (1956); *Loudmouse,* a story for children (1963); and *Responses,* literary criticism (1976); and he has translated plays of Moliere and Racine into wonderfully skillful English verse. He divides his time between Cummington, Massachusetts, where he has a home adjacent to an apple orchard, and Key West, Florida. In 1987 he was named United States Poet Laureate by the Library of Congress. His *New and Collected Poems* (1988) gathers most of his original work in poetry.

William Carlos Williams

William Carlos Williams (1883 – 1963) was born in Rutherford, New Jersey, where he remained in later life as a practicing pediatrician. While taking his M.D. degree at the University of Pennsylvania, he made friends with the poets Ezra Pound and H.D. (Hilda Doolittle). Surprisingly prolific for a busy doctor, Williams wrote (besides poetry) novels and short stories, plays, criticism, and essays in history (*In the American Grain,* 1939). He kept a fliptop desk in his office and between patients would haul out his typewriter and dash off poems. His encouragement of younger poets, among them Allen Ginsberg (whose doctor he was when Ginsberg was a baby), and the long-sustained example of his formally open poetry made him an appealing father figure to the generation of the Beat poets and the Black Mountain poets — Ginsberg, Gary Snyder, and Robert Creeley. But he also had great influence on Robert Lowell, and on a whole younger generation of American poets in our day. Williams believed in truthtelling about ordinary life, championed plain speech "out of the mouths of Polish mothers," and insisted that there can be "no ideas but in things." Combining poetry with prose (including documents and statistics), his long poem in five parts, *Paterson* (1946 – 58) explores the past, present, and future of the New Jersey industrial city near which Williams lived for most of his days.

Yvor Winters

Arthur Yvor Winters (1900 – 1968) is as well remembered for his controversial books of criticism as for his poetry. (As a critic, Winters championed tradition, morality, reason, and certain little-read poets such as Elizabeth Daryush and

Frederick Goddard Tuckerman.) Born in Chicago, he returned to that city for high school and college after spending his childhood in California and Oregon. During his first year at the University of Chicago, he contracted tuberculosis and moved to Santa Fe, New Mexico, where he remained for his health until 1925. From 1928 until his retirement in 1966, he taught at Stanford University. He was married to poet and novelist Janet Lewis. Described as an Imagist for his first book of verse, *The Immobile Wind* (1921), Winters later abandoned free verse for strict traditional forms. Though the audience for his poems was never large, he exerted a powerful formative influence on the work of many poets he taught. For his poetry, see *Collected Poems* (1978); for his criticism, *In Defense of Reason* (1947), *The Function of Criticism* (1957), and *Forms of Discovery* (1968).

William Wordsworth

William Wordsworth (1770 – 1850) was born in England's Lake District, whose landscapes and people were to inform many of his poems. As a young man he visited France, sympathized with the Revolution, and met a young French-woman who bore him a child. The Reign of Terror prevented him from returning to France, and he and Annette Vallon never married. With his sister Dorothy (1771 – 1855), his lifelong intellectual companion and the author of remarkable journals, he settled in Dorsetshire. Later they moved to Grasmere, in the Lake District, where Wordsworth lived the rest of his life. In 1798 his friendship with Samuel Taylor Coleridge resulted in their joint publication of *Lyrical Ballads*, a book credited with introducing Romanticism to English poetry. (Wordsworth contributed "Tintern Abbey" and other poems; Coleridge, "Kubla Khan," "Christabel," and "The Rime of the Ancient Mariner.") To the second edition of 1800, Wordsworth supplied a preface calling for a poetry written "in the real language of men." Time brought him a small official job, a conventional marriage, a swing from left to right in his political sentiments, and appointment as poet laureate. Although he kept on writing, readers have generally preferred his earlier poems. *The Prelude,* a long poem-memoir completed in 1805, did not appear till after the poet's death. One of the most original of writers, Wordsworth — especially for his poems of nature and simple rustics — occupies a popular place in English poetry, much like that of Robert Frost in America.

James Wright

James Wright (1927 – 1980) was born in Martins Ferry, Ohio. After taking his doctorate at the University of Washington, where he studied with Theodore Roethke, he taught at the University of Minnesota, Macalester College, and Hunter College in New York. His first book, *A Green Wall* (1957), in the Yale Series of Younger Poets, established him as a traditional formalist of great skill. With Robert Bly, by whom he was persuaded to branch out of traditional forms, he translated the poems of Cesar Valejo, Pablo Neruda, and George Trakl. In 1972 he received the Pulitzer Prize for his *Collected Poems.* Wright was a memorable teacher, a great quoter of poetry from memory, and a fine critic. "I try and say how I love my country and how I despise the way it is treated," he declared. "I try and speak of the beauty and again of the ugliness in the lives of the poor and neglected."

Sir Thomas Wyatt

Sir Thomas Wyatt (1503? – 1542) was both poet and man of action: diplomat, soldier, and courtier. He was born in his father's castle in Kent, England, and as a boy he was sent to court. In 1516 he entered St. John's College, Cambridge. Wyatt twice saw the inside of prison when he slipped from the favor of King Henry VIII. He is thought to have been a lover of Anne Boleyn, later the King's wife, a fact that perhaps affects some of his remarkable love lyrics. A prominent man in Tudor England, Wyatt carried out diplomatic missions, served as ambassador to Spain, was a member of Parliament and the king's privy council, and was Commander of the Fleet. Wyatt's mission to Italy in 1527 had great consequence for English poetry, for he brought back knowledge of the works of Petrarch and other Italian love poets. In imitation of them, Wyatt wrote some of the first sonnets in our language — also lyrics, rondels, satires, and psalms.

William Butler Yeats

William Butler Yeats (1865 – 1939), poet and playwright, an Irishman of English ancestry, was born in Dublin, the son of painter John Butler Yeats. For a time he studied art himself and was irregularly schooled in Dublin and in London. Early in life Yeats sought to transform Irish folklore and legend into mellifluous poems. He overcame shyness to take an active part in cataclysmic events: he became involved in the movement for an Irish nation (partly drawn into it by his unrequited love for Maud Gonne, a crusading nationalist) and in founding the Irish Literary Theatre (1898) and the Irish National Theatre, which in 1904 moved to the renowned Abbey Theatre in Dublin. Dublin audiences were difficult: in 1899 they jeered Yeats's first play, *The Countess Cathleen,* for portraying a woman who, defying the church, sells her soul to the devil to buy bread for starving peasants. Eventually Yeats retired from the fray, to write plays given in drawing rooms, like *Purgatory.* After the establishment of the Irish Free State, Yeats served as a senator (1922 – 28). His lifelong interest in the occult culminated in his writing of *A Vision* (1937), a view of history as governed by the phases of the moon; Yeats believed the book inspired by spirit masters who dictated communications to his wife, Georgie Hyde-Lees. Had Yeats stopped writing in 1900, he would be remembered as an outstanding minor Victorian. Instead, he went on to become one of the most influential poets of the twentieth century.

CRITICISM: ON POETRY

What is a modern Poet's fate?
To write his thoughts upon a slate —
The Critic spits on what is done,
Gives it a wipe — and all is gone.
>   — Thomas Hood, "To the Reviewers"

The critical power is of lower rank than the creative. True, but in assenting to this proposition, one or two things are to be kept in mind. It is undeniable that the exercise of a creative power, that a free creative activity, is the true function of man; it is proved to be so by man's finding in it his true happiness. But it is undeniable, also, that men may have the sense of exercising this free creative activity in other ways than in producing great works of literature or art; if it were not so, all but a very few men would be shut out from the true happiness of all men; they may have it in well-doing, they may have it in learning, they may have it even in criticizing.
>   — Matthew Arnold, "The Function of Criticism"

"A poem is a pheasant," said Wallace Stevens. Studying poetry, you may find it useful at times to have before you the exact words of a critic who has described that elusive, easily startled bird. Here then are nineteen critical insights. Some are unfamiliar; others are among the best-known, most stimulating remarks about poetry ever made. Included are a few remarks by poets, such as Robert Frost's to his friend about the "sound of sense," which Frost called "the most important thing I know." May they widen your own thinking about poetry and perhaps give you something tough to argue with. Some are controversial. Socrates' case against poets, for instance, remains a fresh and lively opinion still debatable even after twenty-three-hundred-odd years. Nor do these critics chime in perfect harmony. You may hear a certain jangling in their views.

After each passage, its source is indicated. Should one of these ideas capture your interest, why settle for the excerpt given here?

Plato (427? – 347? B.C.)

INSPIRATION[1]   (ABOUT 390 B.C.)

Ion: The world agrees with me in thinking that I do speak better and have more to say about Homer than any other man. But I do not speak equally well about others — tell me the reason for this.

---

[1]Translated by Benjamin Jowett.

Socrates: I perceive, Ion; and I will proceed to explain to you what I imagine to be the reason for this. The gift which you possess of speaking excellently about Homer is not an art, but, as I was just saying, an inspiration; there is a divinity moving you, like that contained in the stone which Euripides calls a magnet, but which is commonly known as the stone of Heraclea. This stone not only attracts iron rings, but also imparts to them a similar power of attracting other rings; and sometimes you may see a number of pieces of iron and rings suspended from one another so as to form quite a long chain: and all of them derive their power of suspension from the original stone. In like manner the Muse first of all inspires men herself; and from these inspired persons a chain of other persons is suspended, who take the inspiration. For all good poets, epic as well as lyric, compose their beautiful poems not by art, but because they are inspired and possessed. And as the Corybantian revelers when they dance are not in their right mind, so the lyric poets are not in their right mind when they are composing their beautiful strains: but when falling under the power of music and meter they are inspired and possessed; like Bacchic maidens who draw milk and honey from the rivers when they are under the influence of Dionysus but not when they are in their right mind. And the soul of the lyric poet does the same, as they themselves say; for they tell us that they bring songs from honeyed fountains, culling them out of the gardens and dells of the Muses; they, like the bees, winging their way from flower to flower. And this is true. For the poet is a light and winged and holy thing, and there is no invention in him until he has been inspired and is out of his senses, and the mind is no longer in him: when he has not attained to this state, he is powerless and is unable to utter his oracles. Many are the noble words in which poets speak concerning the actions of men; but like yourself when speaking about Homer, they do not speak of them by any rules of art: they are simply inspired to utter that to which the Muse impels them, and that only; and when inspired, one of them will make dithyrambs, another hymns of praise, another choral strains, another epic or iambic verses — and he who is good at one is not good at any other kind of verse: for not by art does the poet sing, but by power divine. Had he learned by rules of art, he would have known how to speak not of one theme only, but of all; and therefore God takes away the minds of poets, and uses them as his ministers, as he also uses diviners and holy prophets, in order that we who hear them may know them to be speaking not of themselves who utter these priceless words in a state of unconsciousness, but that God himself is the speaker, and that through them he is conversing with us. And Tynnichus the Chalcidian affords a striking instance of what I am saying: he wrote nothing that any one would care to remember but the famous paean which is in every one's mouth, one of the finest poems ever written, simply an invention of the Muses, as he himself says. For in this way the God would seem to indicate to us and not allow us to doubt that these beautiful poems are not human, or the work of man, but divine and the work of God; and that the poets are only the interpreters of the Gods by whom they are severally possessed. Was not this the lesson which the God intended to teach when by the mouth of the worst of poets he sang the best of songs? Am I not right, Ion?

Ion

INSPIRATION. Plato records a dialogue between his master, the philosopher Socrates (469 B.C. – 399 B.C.) and Ion, a young man of Athens. *Corybantian revellers:* The Corybants, priests or attendants of the nature goddess Cybele, deity of the ancient peoples of Asia Minor, were given to orgiastic rites and frenzied dances. *Bacchic maidens:* attendants of the god of wine and fertility, called Dionysus by the Greeks, Bacchus by the Romans. *Muses:* In Greek mythology, nine sister goddesses who presided over poetry and song, the arts and sciences.

Plato (427? – 347? B.C.)

SOCRATES BANISHES POETS FROM HIS IDEAL STATE[2]

(ABOUT 373 B.C.)

Socrates: Hear and judge: The best of us, I conceive, when we listen to a passage of Homer, or one of the tragedians, in which he represents some pitiful hero who is drawling out his sorrows in a long oration, or weeping, and smiting his breast — the best of us, you know, delight in giving way to sympathy, and are in raptures at the excellence of the poet who stirs our feelings most.

Glaucon: Yes, of course I know.

Socrates: But when any sorrow of our own happens to us, then you may observe that we pride ourselves on the opposite quality — we would fain be quiet and patient; this is the manly part, and the other which delighted us in the recitation is now deemed to be the part of a woman.

Glaucon: Very true.

Socrates: Now can we be right in praising and admiring another who is doing that which any one of us would abominate and be ashamed of in his own person?

Glaucon: No, that is certainly not reasonable.

Socrates: Nay, quite reasonable from one point of view.

Glaucon: What point of view?

Socrates: If you consider that when in misfortune we feel a natural hunger and desire to relieve our sorrow by weeping and lamentation, and that this feeling which is kept under control in our own calamities is satisfied and delighted by the poets; — the better nature in each of us, not having been sufficiently trained by reason or habit, allows the sympathetic element to break loose because the sorrow is another's; and the spectator fancies that there can be no disgrace to himself in praising and pitying any one who comes telling him what a good man he is, and making a fuss about his troubles; he thinks that

[2]Translated by Benjamin Jowett.

the pleasure is a gain, and why should he be supercilious and lose this and the poem too? Few persons ever reflect, as I should imagine, that from the evil of other men something of evil is communicated to themselves. And so the feeling of sorrow which has gathered strength at the sight of the misfortunes of others is with difficulty repressed in our own.

Glaucon: How very true!

Socrates: And does not the same hold also of the ridiculous? There are jests which you would be ashamed to make yourself, and yet on the comic stage, or indeed in private, when you hear them, you are greatly amused by them, and are not at all disgusted at their unseemliness; — the case of pity is repeated; — there is a principle in human nature which is disposed to raise a laugh, and this which you once restrained by reason, because you were afraid of being thought a buffoon, is now let out again; and having stimulated the risible faculty at the theater, you are betrayed unconsciously to yourself into playing the comic poet at home.

Glaucon: Quite true.

Socrates: And the same may be said of lust and anger and all the other affections, of desire and pain and pleasure, which are held to be inseparable from every action — in all of them poetry feeds and waters the passions instead of drying them up; she lets them rule, although they ought to be controlled, if mankind are ever to increase in happiness and virtue.

Glaucon: I cannot deny it.

Socrates: Therefore, Glaucon, whenever you meet with any of the eulogists of Homer declaring that he has been the educator of Hellas, and that he is profitable for education and for the ordering of human things, and that you should take him up again and again and get to know him and regulate your whole life according to him, we may love and honor those who say these things — they are excellent people, as far as their lights extend; and we are ready to acknowledge that Homer is the greatest of poets and first of tragedy writers; but we must remain firm in our conviction that hymns to the gods and praises of famous men are the only poetry which ought to be admitted into our State. For if you go beyond this and allow the honeyed muse to enter, either in epic or lyric verse, not law and the reason of mankind, which by common consent have ever been deemed best, but pleasure and pain will be the rulers in our State.

Glaucon: That is most true.

Socrates: And now since we have reverted to the subject of poetry, let this our defense serve to show the reasonableness of our former judgment in sending away out of our State an art having the tendencies which we have described; for reason constrained us. But that she may not impute to us any harshness or want of politeness, let us tell her that there is an ancient quarrel between philosophy and poetry; of which there are many proofs, such as the saying of 'the yelping hound howling at her lord,' or of one 'mighty in the vain talk of fools,' and 'the mob of sages circumventing Zeus,' and the 'subtle thinkers who are beggars after all'; and there are innumerable other signs of ancient enmity between them. Notwithstanding this, let us assure our sweet friend and the sister arts of imitation, that if she will only prove her title to exist in a well-ordered State we shall be delighted to receive her — we are very conscious of her charms; but we may not on that account betray the truth.

The Republic, X

Aristotle (384 – 322 B.C.)

TWO CAUSES OF POETRY[3]   (ABOUT 330 B.C.)

Poetry in general seems to have sprung from two causes, each of them lying deep in our nature. First, the instinct of imitation is implanted in man from childhood, one difference between him and other animals being that he is the most imitative of living creatures; and through imitation he learns his earliest lessons; and no less universal is the pleasure felt in things imitated. We have evidence of this in the facts of experience. Objects which in themselves we view with pain, we delight to contemplate when reproduced with minute fidelity: such as the forms of the most ignoble animals and of dead bodies. The cause of this again is, that to learn gives the liveliest pleasure, not only to philosophers but to men in general; whose capacity, however, of learning is more limited. Thus the reason why men enjoy seeing a likeness is, that in contemplating it they find themselves learning or inferring, and saying perhaps, "Ah, that is he." For if you happen not to have seen the original, the pleasure will be due not to the imitation as such, but to the execution, the coloring, or some such other cause.

Imitation, then, is one instinct of our nature. Next, there is the instinct for "harmony" and rhythm, meters being manifestly sections of rhythm. Persons, therefore, starting with this natural gift developed by degrees their special aptitudes, till their rude improvisations gave birth to Poetry.

Poetics, IV

Samuel Johnson (1709 – 1784)

THE BUSINESS OF A POET   1759

The business of a poet is to examine, not the individual, but the species; to remark general properties and large appearances; he does not number the streaks of the tulip, or describe the different shades in the verdure of the forest. He is to exhibit in his portraits of nature such prominent and striking features as recall the original to every mind, and must neglect the minuter discriminations, which one may have remarked and another have neglected, for those characteristics which are alike obvious to vigilance and carelessness.

[3]Translated by S. H. Butcher.

But the knowledge of nature is only half the task of a poet; he must be acquainted likewise with all the modes of life. His character requires that he estimate the happiness and misery of every condition, observe the power of all the passions in all their combinations, and trace the changes of the human mind as they are modified by various institutions and accidental influences of climate or custom, from the sprightliness of infancy to the despondency of decrepitude. He must divest himself of the prejudices of his age or country; he must consider right and wrong in their abstracted and variable state; he must disregard present laws and opinions, and rise to general and transcendental truths, which will always be the same.

The History of Rasselas,
Prince of Abyssinia

William Wordsworth (1770 – 1850)

EMOTION RECOLLECTED IN TRANQUILLITY   1800

I have said that poetry is the spontaneous overflow of powerful feelings: it takes its origin from emotion recollected in tranquillity: the emotion is contemplated till, by a species of reaction, the tranquillity gradually disappears, and an emotion, kindred to that which was before the subject of contemplation, is gradually produced, and does itself actually exist in the mind. In this mood successful composition generally begins, and in a mood similar to this it is carried on; but the emotion, of whatever kind, and in whatever degree, from various causes, is qualified by various pleasures, so that in describing any passions whatsoever, which are voluntarily described, the mind will, upon the whole, be in a state of enjoyment. If Nature be thus cautious to preserve in a state of enjoyment a being so employed, the Poet ought to profit by the lesson held forth to him, and ought especially to take care, that, whatever passions he communicates to his Reader, those passions, if his Reader's mind be sound and vigorous, should always be accompanied with an overbalance of pleasure. Now the music of harmonious metrical language, the sense of difficulty over-come, and the blind association of pleasure which has been previously received from works of rhyme or meter of the same or similar construction, an indistinct perception perpetually renewed of language closely resembling that of real life, and yet, in the circumstance of meter, differing from it so widely — all these imperceptibly make up a complex feeling of delight, which is of the most important use in tempering the painful feeling always found intermingled with powerful descriptions of the deeper passions. This effect is always produced in pathetic and impassioned poetry; while, in lighter compositions, the ease and gracefulness with which the Poet manages his numbers are themselves con-fessedly a principal source of the gratification of the Reader. All that it is *necessary* to say, however, upon this subject, may be effected by affirming, what few persons will deny, that, of two descriptions, either of passions, manners, or characters, each of them equally well executed, the one in prose and the other in verse, the verse will be read a hundred times where the prose is read once.

Preface to *Lyrical Ballads,*
second edition

EMOTION RECOLLECTED IN TRANQUILLITY. For information on Wordsworth's methods of composition in his poem "I Wandered Lonely as a Cloud," see page 21.

Samuel Taylor Coleridge (1772 – 1834)

IMAGINATION   1817

What is poetry? — is so nearly the same question with, what is a poet? — that the answer to the one is involved in the solution of the other. For it is a distinction resulting from the poetic genius itself, which sustains and modifies the images, thoughts, and emotions of the poet's own mind.

The poet, described in ideal perfection, brings the whole soul of man into activity, with the subordination of its faculties to each other according to their relative worth and dignity. He diffuses a tone and spirit of unity, that blends, and (as it were) *fuses,* each into each, by that synthetic and magical power, to which I would exclusively appropriate the name of Imagination. This power, first put in action by the will and understanding, and retained under their irremissive, though gentle and unnoticed, control, *laxis effertur habenis°,* reveals itself in the balance or reconcilement of opposite or discordant qualities; of sameness, with difference; of the general with the concrete; the idea with the image; the individual with the representative; the sense of novelty and freshness with old and familiar objects; a more than usual state of emotion with more than usual order; judgment ever awake and steady self-possession, with enthusiasm and feeling profound and vehement; and while it blends and harmonizes the natural and the artificial, still subordinates art to nature; the manner to the matter; and our admiration of the poet to our sympathy with the poetry.

Biographia Literaria: or, Biographical Sketches
of My Literary Life and Opinions, Chapter XIV

THAT SYNTHETIC AND MAGICAL POWER. The Latin phrase *laxis effertur habenis* means "is driven with reins relaxed."

Percy Bysshe Shelley (1792 – 1822)

UNACKNOWLEDGED LEGISLATORS   (1821)

The most unfailing herald, companion, and follower of the awakening of a great people to work a beneficial change in opinion or institution, is poetry. At such periods there is an accumulation of the power of communicating and receiving intense and impassioned conceptions respecting man and nature. The persons in whom this power resides, may often, as far as regards many portions of their nature, have little apparent correspondence with that spirit of good of which they are the ministers. But even whilst they deny and abjure, they are yet compelled to serve, the power which is seated on the throne of their own soul. It is impossible to read the compositions of the most celebrated writers of the present day without being startled with the electric life which burns within their words. They measure the circumference and sound the depths of human nature with a comprehensive and all-penetrating spirit, and they are themselves perhaps the most sincerely astonished at its manifestations; for it is less their spirit than the spirit of the age. Poets are the hierophants of an unapprehended inspiration; the mirrors of the gigantic shadows which futurity casts upon the present; the words which express what they understand not; the trumpets which sing to battle, and feel not what they inspire; the influence which is moved not, but moves. Poets are the unacknowledged legislators of the world.

A Defense of Poetry

Ralph Waldo Emerson (1803 – 1882)

METER-MAKING ARGUMENT   1844

I took part in a conversation the other day concerning a recent writer of lyrics, a man of subtle mind, whose head appeared to be a music-box of delicate tunes and rhythms, and whose skill and command of language we could not sufficiently praise. But when the question arose whether he was not only a lyrist but a poet, we were obliged to confess that he is plainly a contemporary, not an eternal man. He does not stand out of our low limitations, like a Chimborazo under the line°, running up from a torrid base through all the climates of the globe, with belts of the herbage of every latitude on its high and mottled sides; but this genius is the landscape-garden of a modern house adorned with fountains and statues, with well-bred men and women standing and sitting in the walks and terraces. We hear, through all the varied music, the ground-tone of conventional life. Our poets are men of talents who sing, and not the children of music. The argument is secondary, the finish of the verses is primary.

For it is not meters, but a meter-making argument that makes a poem, — a thought so passionate and alive that like the spirit of a plant or an animal it has an architecture of its own, and adorns nature with a new thing. The thought and the form are equal in the order of time, but in the order of genesis the thought is prior to the form. The poet has a new thought; he has a whole new experience to unfold; he will tell us how it was with him, and all men will be the richer in his fortune. For the experience of each new age requires a new confession, and the world seems always waiting for its poet.

The Poet

METER-MAKING ARGUMENT. *Chimborazo under the line:* mountain in Ecuador, south of the Equator.

Edgar Allan Poe (1809 – 1849)

A LONG POEM DOES NOT EXIST
1848

I hold that a long poem does not exist. I maintain that the phrase, "a long poem," is simply a flat contradiction in terms.

I need scarcely observe that a poem deserves its title only inasmuch as it excites, by elevating the soul. The value of the poem is in the ratio of its elevative excitement. But all excitements are, through a psychal necessity, transient. That degree of excitement which would entitle a poem to be so called at all cannot be sustained throughout a composition of any great length. After the lapse of half an hour, at the very utmost, its flags — fails — a revulsion ensues — and then the poem is in effect, and in fact, no longer such.

The Poetic Principle

Robert Frost (1874 – 1963)

THE SOUND OF SENSE
(1913)

I alone of English writers have consciously set myself to make music out of what I may call the sound of sense. Now it is possible to have sense without the sound of sense (as in much prose that is supposed to pass muster but makes very dull reading) and the sound of sense without sense (as in Alice in Wonderland which makes anything but dull reading). The best place to get the abstract sound of sense is from voices behind a door that cuts off the words. Ask yourself how these sentences would sound without the words in which they are embodied:

> You mean to tell me you can't read?
> I said no such thing.
> Well read then.
> You're not my teacher.
>
>   .   .   .
>
> He says it's too late.
> Oh, say!
> Damn an Ingersoll watch anyway.
>
>   .   .   .
>
> One-two-three — go!
> No good! Come back — come back.
> Haslam go down there and make those kids get out of the track.
>
>   .   .   .

Those sounds are summoned by the [audial] imagination and they must be positive, strong, and definitely and unmistakably indicated by the context. The reader must be at no loss to give his voice the posture proper to the sentence. The simple declarative sentence used in making a plain statement is one sound.

But Lord love ye it mustn't be worked to death. It is against the law of nature that whole poems should be written in it. If they are written they won't be read. The sound of sense, then. You get that. It is the abstract vitality of our speech. It is pure sound — pure form. One who concerns himself with it more than the subject is an artist. But remember we are still talking merely of the raw material of poetry. An ear and an appetite for these sounds of sense is the first qualification of a writer, be it of prose or verse. But if one is to be a poet he must learn to get cadences by skillfully breaking the sounds of sense with all their irregularity of accent across the regular beat of the meter. Verse in which there is nothing but the beat of the meter furnished by the accents of the polysyllabic words we call doggerel. Verse is not that. Neither is it the sound of sense alone. It is a resultant from those two. There are only two or three meters that are worth anything. We depend for variety on the infinite play of accents in the sound of sense. The high possibility of emotional expression all lets in this mingling of sense-sound and word-accent. A curious thing. And all this has its bearing on your prose, me boy. Never if you can help it write down a sentence in which the voice will not know how to posture *specially.*

Letter to John T. Bartlett, from *Selected Letters
of Robert Frost,* ed. Lawrance Thompson
(New York: Holt, 1964)

Wallace Stevens (1879 – 1955)

PROVERBS   1957

The poet makes silk dresses out of worms.

After one has abandoned a belief in God, poetry is that essence which takes its place as life's redemption.

All poetry is experimental poetry.

One reads poetry with one's nerves.

A poet looks at the world as a man looks at a woman.

Aristotle is a skeleton.

Thought tends to collect in pools.

Poetry must resist the intelligence almost successfully.

One cannot spend one's time in being modern when there are so many more important things to be.

Adagia, *Opus Posthumous*

William Carlos Williams (1883 – 1963)

THE RHYTHM PERSISTS   (1913?)

No action, no creative action is complete but a period from a greater action going in rhythmic course. . . . Imagination creates an image, point by point, piece by piece, segment by segment — into a whole, living. But each part as it plays into its neighbor, each segment into its neighbor segment and every part into every other, causing the whole — exists naturally in rhythm, and as there are waves there are tides and as there are ridges in the sand there are bars after bars. . . .

I do not believe in *vers libre*, this contradiction in terms. Either the motion continues or it does not continue, either there is rhythm or no rhythm. *Vers libre* is prose. In the hands of Whitman it was a good tool, a kind of synthetic chisel — the best he had. In his bag of chunks even lie some of the pieces of rhythmic life of which we must build. This is honor enough. *Vers libre* is finished — Whitman did all that was necessary with it. Verse has nothing to gain here and all to lose. . . .

Each piece of work, rhythmic in whole, is then in essence an assembly of tides, waves, ripples — in short, of greater and lesser rhythmic particles regularly repeated or destroyed.

Essay "Speech Rhythm" quoted by Mike Weaver,
William Carlos Williams, The American Background
(New York: Cambridge University Press, 1971)

Ezra Pound (1885 – 1972)

POETRY AND MUSIC   1934

The great lyric age lasted while Campion made his own music, while Lawes set Waller's verses, while verses, if not actually sung or set to music, were at least made with the intention of going to music.

Music rots when it gets *too far* from the dance. Poetry atrophies when it gets too far from music.

ABC of Reading

T. S. Eliot (1888 – 1965)

It is not in his personal emotions, the emotions provoked by particular events in his life, that the poet is in any way remarkable or interesting. His particular emotions may be simple, or crude, or flat. The emotion in his poetry will be a very complex thing, but not with the complexity of the emotions of people who have very complex or unusual emotions in life. One error, in fact, of eccentricity in poetry is to seek for new human emotions to express; and in this search for novelty in the wrong place it discovers the perverse. The business of the poet is not to find new emotions, but to use the ordinary ones and, in working them up into poetry, to express feelings which are not in actual emotions at all. And emotions which he has never experienced will serve his turn as well as those familiar to him. Consequently, we must believe that "emotion recollected in tranquillity" is an inexact formula. For it is neither emotion, nor recollection, nor, without distortion of meaning, tranquillity. It is a concentration, and a new thing resulting from the concentration, of a very great number of experiences which to the practical and active person would not seem to be experiences at all; it is a concentration which does not happen consciously or of deliberation. These experiences are not "recollected," and they finally unite in an atmosphere which is "tranquil" only in that it is a passive attending upon the event. Of course this is not quite the whole story. There is a great deal, in the writing of poetry, which must be conscious and deliberate. In fact, the bad poet is usually unconscious where he ought to be conscious, and conscious where he ought to be unconscious. Both errors tend to make him "personal." Poetry is not a turning loose of emotion, but an escape from emotion; it is not the expression of personality, but an escape from personality. But, of course, only those who have personality and emotions know what it means to want to escape from these things.

Tradition and the Individual Talent

Yvor Winters (1900 – 1968)

I cannot grasp the contemporary notion that the traditional virtues of style are incompatible with a poetry of modern subject matter; it appears to rest on the fallacy of expressive form, the notion that the form of the poem should express the matter. This fallacy results in the writing of chaotic poetry about the traffic; of loose poetry about our sprawling nation; of semi-conscious poetry about our semi-conscious states. But the matter of poetry is and always has been chaotic; it is raw nature. To let the form of the poem succumb to its matter is and always will be the destruction of poetry and may be the destruction of intelligence.

Before Disaster

Randall Jarrell (1914 – 1965)

ON THE CHARGE THAT MODERN POETRY IS OBSCURE   1953

That the poet, the modern poet, is, understandably enough, for all sorts of good reasons, more obscure than even he has any imaginable right to be — this is one of those great elementary (or, as people say nowadays, *elemental*) attitudes about which it is hard to write anything that is not sensible and gloomily commonplace; one might as well talk on faith and works, on heredity and environment, or on that old question: why give the poor bath-tubs when they only use them to put coal in? Anyone knows enough to reply to this question: "They don't; and, even if they did, *that's* not the reason you don't want to help pay for the tubs." Similarly, when someone says, "I don't read modern poetry because it's all stuff that nobody on earth can understand," I know enough to be able to answer, though not aloud: "It isn't; and, even if it were, *that's* not the reason you don't read it." . . . And people who have inherited the custom of not reading poets justify it by referring to the obscurity of the poems they have never read — since most people decide that poets are obscure very much as legislators decide that books are pornographic: by glancing at a few fragments someone has strung together to disgust them. When a person says accusingly that he can't understand Eliot, his tone implies that most of his happiest hours are spent at the fireside among worn copies of the *Agamemnon, Phèdre,* and the Symbolic Books of William Blake; and it is melancholy to find, as one commonly will, that for months at a time he can be found pushing eagerly through the pages of *Gone with the Wind* or *Forever Amber.*°

The Obscurity of the Poet,
Poetry and the Age

ON THE CHARGE THAT MODERN POETRY IS OBSCURE. *Forever Amber:* novel by Kathleen Winsor, a best-seller in its day (1945). Much of its action takes place in bed.

Sylvia Plath (1932 – 1963)

THE MAGIC MOUNTAINS   1957

The artist's life nourishes itself on the particular, the concrete: that came to me last night as I despaired about writing poems on the concept of the seven deadly sins and told myself to get rid of the killing idea: this must be a great work of philosophy. Start with the mat-green fungus in the pine woods yesterday: words about it, describing it — and a poem will come. Daily, simply, and then it won't lower in the distance, an untouchable object. Write about the cow, Mrs. Spaulding's heavy eyelids, the smell of vanilla flavoring in a brown bottle. That's where the magic mountains begin.

Journals

'HOW DO WE MAKE A POEM?'   1982

Let us begin with one of the shortest poetic texts in the English language, "Elegy" by W. S. Merwin:

Who would I show it to

One line, one sentence, unpunctuated, but proclaimed an interrogative by its grammar and syntax — what makes it a poem? Certainly without its title it would not be a poem; but neither would the title alone constitute a poetic text. Nor do the two together simply make a poem by themselves. Given the title and the text, the *reader* is encouraged to make a poem. He is not forced to do so, but there is not much else he can do with this material, and certainly nothing else so rewarding. (I will use the masculine pronoun here to refer to the reader, not because all readers are male but because I am, and my hypothetical reader is not a pure construct but an idealized version of myself.)

How do we make a poem out of this text? There are only two things to work on, the title and the question posed by the single, colloquial line. The line is not simply colloquial, it is prosaic; with no words of more than one syllable, concluded by a preposition, it is within the utterance range of every speaker of English. It is, in a sense, completely intelligible. But in another sense it is opaque, mysterious. Its three pronouns — who, I, it — pose problems of reference. Its conditional verb phrase — would . . . show to — poses a problem of situation. The context that would supply the information required to make that simple sentence meaningful as well as intelligible is not there. It must be supplied by the reader.

To make a poem of this text the reader must not only know English, he must know a poetic code as well: the code of the funeral elegy, as practiced in English from the Renaissance to the present time. The "words on the page" do not constitute a poetic "work," complete and self-sufficient, but a "text," a sketch or outline that must be completed by the active participation of a reader equipped with the right sort of information. In this case part of that information consists of an acquaintance with the elegiac tradition: its procedures, assumptions, devices, and values. One needs to know works like Milton's "Lycidas," Shelley's "Adonais," Tennyson's "In Memoriam," Whitman's "When Lilacs Last in the Dooryard Bloomed," Thomas's "Refusal to Mourn the Death by Fire of a Child in London," and so on, in order to "read" this simple poem properly. In fact, it could be argued that the more elegies one can bring to bear on a reading of this one, the better, richer poem this one becomes. I would go even further, suggesting that a knowledge of the critical tradition — of Dr. Johnson's objections to "Lycidas," for instance, or Wordsworth's critique of poetic diction — will also enhance one's reading of this poem. For the poem is, of course, an anti-elegy, a refusal not simply to mourn, but to write a sonorous, eloquent, mournful, but finally acquiescent, accepting — in a word, "elegiac" — poem at all.

Reading the poem involves, then, a special knowledge of its tradition. It also involves a special interpretive skill. The forms of the short, written poem as they have developed in English over the past few centuries can be usefully seen as compressed, truncated, or fragmented imitations of other verbal forms, especially the play, story, public oration, and personal essay. The reasons for this are too complicated for consideration here, but the fact will be apparent to all who reflect upon the matter. Our short poems are almost always elliptical version of what can easily be conceived of as dramatic, narrative, oratorical, or meditative texts. Often, they are combinations of these and other modes of address. To take an obvious example, the dramatic monologue in the hands of Robert Browning is like a speech from a play (though usually more elongated than most such speeches). But to "read" such a monologue we must imagine the setting, the situation, the context, and so on. The dramatic monologue is "like" a play but gives us less information of certain sorts than a play would, requiring us to provide that information by decoding the clues in the monologue itself in the light of our understanding of the generic model. Most short poems work this way. They require both special knowledge and special skills to be "read."

To understand "Elegy" we must construct a situation out of the clues provided. The "it" in "Who would I show it to" is of course the elegy itself. The "I" is the potential writer of the elegy. The "Who" is the audience for the poem. But the verb phrase "would . . . show to" indicates a condition contrary to fact. Who would I show it to *if* I were to write it? This implies in turn that for the potential elegiac poet there is one person whose appreciation means more than that of all the rest of the potential audience for the poem he might write, and it further implies that the death of this particular person is the one imagined in the poem. If this person were dead, the poet suggests, so would his inspiration be dead. With no one to write for, no poem would be forthcoming. This poem is not only a "refusal to mourn," like that of Dylan Thomas, it is a refusal to elegize. The whole elegiac tradition, like its cousin the funeral oration, turns finally away from mourning toward acceptance, revival, renewal, a return to the concerns of life, symbolized by the very writing of the poem. Life goes on; there *is* an audience; and the mourned person will live through accomplishments, influence, descendants, and also (not least) in the elegiac poem itself. Merwin rejects all that. *If* I wrote an elegy for X, the person for whom I have always written, X would not be alive to read it; therefore, there is no reason to write an elegy for the one person in my life who most deserves one; therefore, there is no reason to write any elegy, anymore, ever. Finally, and of course, this poem called "Elegy" is not an elegy.

Semiotics and Interpretation

Sandra M. Gilbert (b. 1936) and **Susan Gubar** (b. 1944)

THE FREEDOM OF EMILY DICKINSON   1985

[Emily Dickinson] defined herself as a *woman* writer, reading the works of female precursors with special care, attending to the implications of novels like Charlotte Brontë's *Jane Eyre*, Emily Brontë's *Wuthering Heights*, and George Eliot's *Middlemarch* with the same absorbed delight that characterized her devotion to Elizabeth Barrett Browning's *Aurora Leigh*. Finally, then, the key to her enigmatic identity as a "supposed person" who was called the "Myth of Amherst" may rest, not in investigations of her questionable romance, but in studies of her unquestionably serious reading as well as in analyses of her disquietingly powerful writing. Elliptically phrased, intensely compressed, her poems are more linguistically innovative than any other nineteenth-century verses, with the possible exception of some works by Walt Whitman and Gerard Manley Hopkins, her two most radical male contemporaries. Throughout her largely secret but always brilliant career, moreover, she confronted precisely the questions about the individual and society, time and death, flesh and spirit, that major precursors from Milton to Keats had faced. Dreaming of "Amplitude and Awe," she recorded sometimes vengeful, sometimes mystical visions of social and personal transformation in poems as inventively phrased and imaginatively constructed as any in the English language.

Clearly such accomplishments required not only extraordinary talent but also some measure of freedom. Yet because she was the unmarried daughter of conservative New Englanders, Dickinson was obliged to take on many household tasks; as a nineteenth-century New England wife, she would have had the same number of obligations, if not more. Some of these she performed with pleasure; in 1856, for instance, she was judge of a bread-baking contest, and in 1857 she won a prize in that contest. But as Higginson's "scholar," as a voracious reader and an ambitious writer, Dickinson had to win herself time for "Amplitude and Awe," and it is increasingly clear that she did so through a strategic withdrawal from her ordinary world. A story related by her niece Martha Dickinson Bianchi reveals that the poet herself knew from the first what both the price and the prize might be: on one occasion, said Mrs. Bianchi, Dickinson took her up to the room in which she regularly sequestered herself, and, mimicking locking herself in, "thumb and forefinger closed on an imaginary key," said "with a quick turn of her wrist, 'It's just a turn — and freedom, Matty!' "

In the freedom of her solitary, but not lonely, room, Dickinson may have become what her Amherst neighbors saw as a bewildering "myth." Yet there, too, she created myths of her own. Reading the Brontës and Barrett Browning, studying Transcendentalism and the Bible, she contrived a theology which is powerfully expressed in many of her poems. That it was at its most hopeful a female-centered theology is revealed in verses like those she wrote about the women artists she admired, as well as in more general works like her gravely pantheistic address to the "Sweet Mountains" who "tell me no lie," with its definition of the hills around Amherst as "strong Madonnas" and its description of the writer herself as "The Wayward Nun — beneath the Hill — / Whose service is to You — ." As Dickinson's admirer and descendant Adrienne Rich has accurately observed, this passionate poet consistently chose to confront her society — to "have it out" — "on her own premises."

Introduction to Emily Dickinson,
The Norton Anthology of Literature by Women

SUPPLEMENT: WRITING

Writing about Literature

All of us have some powers of reasoning and perception. And when we come to a story, a poem, or a play, we can do little other than to trust whatever powers we have, like one who enters a shadowy room, clutching a decent candle.

After all, in the study of literature, common sense (poet Gerard Manley Hopkins said) is never out of place. For most of a class hour, a renowned English professor rhapsodized about the arrangement of the contents of W. H. Auden's *Collected Poems.* Auden, he claimed, was a master of thematic continuity, who had brilliantly placed the poems in the best possible order, in which (to the ingenious mind) they complemented each other. Near the end of the hour, his theories were punctured — with a great inaudible pop — when a student, timidly raising a hand, pointed out that Auden had arranged the poems in the book not according to theme but in alphabetical order according to the first word of each poem. The professor's jaw dropped: "Why didn't you say that sooner?" The student was apologetic: "I — I was afraid I'd sound too *ordinary.*"

Emerson makes a similar point in his essay, "The American Scholar": "Meek young men grow up in libraries, believing it their duty to accept the views which Cicero, which Locke, which Bacon have given; forgetful that Cicero, Locke, and Bacon were only young men in libraries when they wrote these books." Don't be afraid to state a conviction, though it seems obvious. Does it matter that you may be repeating something that, once upon a time or even just the other day, has been said before? There are excellent old ideas as well as new.

Some Approaches to Literature

Most writers of critical essays follow a few familiar approaches to stories, poems, and plays. Underlying each of these four approaches is a specific way of regarding the nature of a work of literature.

1. *The Work by Itself.* This view assumes a story, poem, or play to be an individual entity, existing on its page, which we can read and understand in its own right, without necessarily studying the life of its author, or the age in which it was written, or its possible effect on its readers. This is the approach in most papers written in response to college assignments; to study just the work (and not its backgrounds or its influence) does not require the student to spend prolonged time doing research in a library. The three common ways of writing a paper discussed in this book — explication, analysis, and comparison and contrast — deal mainly with the work of literature in itself.

2. *The Work as Imitation of Life.* Aristotle called the art of writing a tragedy *mimesis:* the imitation or re-creation of an action that is serious and complete in itself. From this classic theory in the *Poetics* comes the view that a work of literature in some ways imitates the world or the civilization in which it was produced. We can say that Ibsen's play *A Doll House* places before our eyes actors whose lifelike speeches and movements represent members of an upper-middle-class society in provincial Norway in the late nineteenth century and that the play reflects their beliefs and attitudes. Not only the subject and theme of a work imitate life in this view: John Ciardi remarked that the heroic couplet, dominant stanza form in poetry read by educated people in eighteenth-century England, reflects, in its exact form and its use of antitheses, the rhythms of the minuet — another contemporary form, fashionable also among the well-to-do: "now on this hand, now on that." The writer considering literature as imitation usually studies the world that the literary work imitates. He or she goes into the ideas underlying the writer's society, showing how the themes, assumptions, and conventions of the writer's work arose out of that time and that place. Obviously, this analysis takes more research than one can do for a weekly paper; it is usually the approach taken for a book or a dissertation, or perhaps an honors thesis or a term paper. (The other two approaches we will mention also take research.) Reasonably short studies of the relation between the work and its world are, however, possible: "World War II as Seen in Henry Reed's 'Naming of Parts' "; "Faulkner's 'Barn Burning': A Mirror of Mississippi?"

3. *The Work as Expression.* In this view, a work of literature expresses the feelings of the person who wrote it; therefore, to study it, one studies the author's life. Typical paper topics: "*A Glass Menagerie* and the Early Life of Tennessee Williams"; "Sylvia Plath's Lost Father and Her View of Him in 'Daddy.' " To write any truly deep-reaching biographical criticism takes research, clearly, but one could write a term paper on topics such as these by reading a biography.

Biographical criticism fell into temporary disrepute around 1920, when T. S. Eliot questioned the assumption that a poem must be a personal statement of the poet's thoughts and emotions.[1] Eliot and other critics did much to clear the air of speculation that "To Autumn" may have been shaped by what Keats had had for breakfast. Evidently, in any search for what went on in an author's

---

[1] See Eliot's essay "Tradition and the Individual Talent," in *Selected Essays* (New York: Harcourt, 1932).

mind, and for the influence of life upon work, absolute certainty is unattainable. Besides, such an approach can be grossly reductive — holding, for example, that Shakespeare was sad when he wrote his tragedies and especially happy when he wrote *A Midsummer Night's Dream.* Still, some works do gain in meaning from even a slight knowledge of the author's biography. In reading *Moby-Dick,* it helps to know that Herman Melville served aboard a whaling vessel.

4. *The Work as Influence.* From this perspective, a literary work is a force that affects people. It stirs responses in them, rouses their emotions, perhaps argues for ideas that change their minds. The artist, said Tolstoi in a famous pronouncement *(What Is Art?),* "hands on to others those feelings he himself has felt, that they too may be moved, and experience them." Part of the function of art, Tolstoi continued, is to enlighten and to lead its audience into an acceptance of better moral attitudes (religious faith, or a sense of social justice). The critic who takes this approach generally deals with the ideas that a literary work imparts and the reception of those ideas by a particular audience: "Did *Uncle Tom's Cabin* Cause the Civil War?"; "The Early Reception of Allen Ginsberg's *Howl*"; "Ed Bullins's Plays and Their Newly Proud Black Audience." As you can see, this whole approach is closely related to viewing a literary work as an imitation of life. Still another way of discussing a work's influence is to trace its effect upon other writers: "Robert Frost's Debt to Emily Dickinson"; "*Moby-Dick* and William Faulkner's *The Bear:* Two Threatened Wildernesses."

BEGINNING

Offered a choice of literary works to write about, you probably will do best if, instead of choosing what you think will impress your instructor, you choose what appeals to you. And how to find out what appeals? Whether you plan to write a short paper that requires no research beyond the story or poem or play itself, or a long term paper that will take you to the library, the first stage of your project is reading — and note taking. To concentrate your attention, one time-honored method is to read with a pencil, marking (if the book is yours) passages that stand out in importance, jotting brief notes in a margin ("*Key symbol — this foreshadows the ending*"; "*Dramatic irony*"; "*IDIOT!!!*"; or other possibly useful remarks). In a long story or poem or play, some students asterisk passages that cry for comparison; for instance, all the places in which they find the same theme or symbol. Later, at a glance, they can review the highlights of a work and, when writing a paper about it, quickly refer to evidence. This method shoots holes in a book's resale value, but many find the sacrifice worthwhile. Patient souls who dislike butchering a book prefer to take notes on looseleaf notebook paper, holding one sheet beside a page in the book and giving it the book's page number. Later, in writing a paper, they can place book page and companion note page together again. This method has the advantage of affording a lot of room for note taking; it is a good one for short poems closely packed with complexities.

But by far the most popular method of taking notes (besides writing on the pages of books) is to write on index cards — the 3 × 5 kind, for brief notes and titles; 5 × 8 cards for longer notes. Write on one side only; notes on the back of the card usually get overlooked later. Cards are easy to shuffle and, in organizing your material, to deal. To save work, instead of copying out on a card the title and author of a book you're taking a note from, just keep a numbered list of the books you're using. Then, when making a note, you need write only the book's identifying number on the card in order to identify your source. (Later, when writing footnotes, you can translate the number into title, author, and other information.)

Now that coin-operated photocopy machines are to be found in many libraries, you no longer need to spend hours copying by hand whole poems and longer passages. If accuracy is essential (surely it is) and if a poem or passage is long enough to be worth the investment of a few cents, you can lay photocopied material into place in your paper with transparent tape or rubber cement. The latest copyright law permits students and scholars to reproduce books and periodicals in this fashion; it does not, however, permit making a dozen or more copies for public sale.

Certain literary works, because they offer intriguing difficulties, have attracted professional critics by the score. On library shelves, great phalanxes of critical books now stand at the side of James Joyce's complex novels *Ulysses* and *Finnegans Wake,* and T. S. Eliot's allusive poem *The Waste Land.* The student who undertakes to study such works seriously is well advised to profit from the critics' labors. Chances are, too, that even in discussing a relatively uncomplicated work you will want to seek the aid of the finest critics. If you quote them, quote them exactly, in quotation marks, and give them credit. When employed in any but the most superlative student paper, a brilliant phrase (or even a not-so-brilliant sentence) from a renowned critic is likely to stand out like a golf ball in a garter snake's midriff, and most English instructors are likely to recognize it. If you rip off the critic's words, then go ahead and steal the whole essay, for good critics write in seamless unities. Then, when apprehended, you can exclaim — like the student whose term paper was found to be the work of a well-known scholar — "I've been robbed! That paper cost me twenty dollars!" But of course the worst rip-off is the one the student inflicted on himself, having got nothing for his money out of a college course but a little practice in touch typing.

Taking notes on your readings, you will want to jot down the title of every book you might refer to in your paper, and the page number of any passage you might wish to quote. Even if you summarize a critic's idea in your own words, rather than quote, you have to give credit to your source. Nothing is cheaper to give than proper credit. Certainly it's easier to take notes while you read than to have to run back to the library during the final typing.

Choose a topic appropriate to the assigned length of your paper. How do you know the probable length of your discussion until you write it? When in doubt, you are better off to define your topic narrowly. Your paper will be stronger if you go deeper into your subject than if you choose some gigantic subject and then find yourself able to touch on it only superficially. A thorough explication of a short story is hardly possible in a paper of 250 words. There are, in truth, four-line poems whose surface 250 words might only begin to scratch. A profound topic ("The Character of Shakespeare's Hamlet") might overflow a book; but a topic more narrowly defined ("Hamlet's Views of Acting"; "Hamlet's Puns") might result in a more nearly manageable term paper. You can narrow and focus a large topic while you work your way into it. A general interest in "Hemingway's Heroes" might lead you, in reading, taking notes, and thinking further, to the narrower topic, "Jake Barnes: Spokesman for Hemingway's Views of War."

Many student writers find it helpful, in defining a topic, to state an emerging idea for a paper in a provisional **thesis sentence:** a summing-up of the one main idea or argument that the paper will embody. (A thesis sentence is for your own use; you don't have to implant it in your paper unless your instructor asks for it.) A good statement of a thesis is not just a disembodied subject; it comes with both subject and verb. ("The Downfall of Oedipus Rex" is not yet a complete idea for a paper; "What Caused the Downfall of Oedipus Rex?" is.) A thesis sentence may help you see for yourself what the author is *saying about* a subject. Not a full thesis, and not a sentence, "The Isolation of Laura in *The Glass Menagerie* might be a decent title for a paper. But it isn't a useful thesis because it doesn't indicate what one might say about that isolation (nor what Tennessee Williams is saying about it). It may be obvious that isolation isn't desirable, but a clearer and more workable thesis sentence might be, "In *The Glass Menagerie,* the playwright shows how Laura's isolation leads her to take refuge in a world of dreams."

DISCOVERING AND PLANNING

Writing is not likely to proceed in a straight line. Like thought, it often goes by fits and starts, by charges and retreats and mopping-up operations. All the while you take notes, you discover material to write about; all the while you tool over your topic in your mind, you plan. It is the nature of ideas, those headstrong things, to happen in any order they desire. While you continue to plan, while you write a draft, and while you revise, expect to keep discovering new thoughts — perhaps the best thoughts of all. If you do, be sure to let them in.

Topic in hand (which may get drastically changed as you continue), you begin to sort out your miscellaneous notes, thoughts, and impressions. If you can see that you haven't had enough ideas, you may wish to **brainstorm** — to set yourself, say, fifteen minutes in which to write down as fast as you can all the ideas on your topic that come into your head, without worrying whether they are going to be useful. (You can look over the results and decide that later.) Another method of discovery is to **freewrite:** to write rapidly and uncritically, letting your thoughts tumble onto paper as fast as your pen, typewriter, or word processor can capture them. Sometimes these methods will goad the unconscious into coming up with unexpectedly good ideas; at least, you will generate more potentially useful raw material.

To outline or not to outline? Unless your topic, by its nature, suggests some obvious way to organize your paper ("An Explication of a Wordsworth Sonnet" might mean simply working through the poem line by line), then some kind of outline will probably help. In high school or other prehistoric times, you perhaps learned how to construct a beautiful outline, laid out with Roman numerals, capital letters, Arabic numerals, and lower-case letters. It was a thing of beauty and symmetry, and possibly even had something to do with paper writing. But if now you are skeptical of the value of outlining, reflect: not every outline needs to be detailed and elaborate. Some students, of course, find it helpful to outline in detail — particularly if they are planning a long term paper involving several literary works, comparing and contrasting several aspects of them. For a 500-word analysis of a short story's figures of speech, though, all you might need is a simple list of points to make, scribbled down in the order in which you will make them. This order is probably not, of course, the order in which the points first occurred to you. Thoughts, when they first come to mind, can be a confused rabble.

While granting the need for order in a piece of writing, the present writer confesses that he is a reluctant outliner. His tendency (or curse) is to want to keep whatever random thoughts occur to him; to polish his prose right then and there; and finally to try to juggle his disconnected paragraphs into something like logical order. The usual result is that he has large blocks of illogical thought left over. This process is wasteful, and if you can learn to live with an outline, then you belong to the legion of the blessed, and will never know the pain of scrapping pages that cost you hours. On the other hand, you will never know the joy of meandering — of bursting into words and surprising yourself. As novelist E. M. Forster remarked, "How do I know what I think until I see what I say?"

An outline, if you use one, is not meant to stand as an achievement in itself. It should — as Ezra Pound said literary criticism ought to do — consume itself and disappear. Here is a once-valuable outline not worth keeping — a very informal one that enabled a student to organize the paper comparing "Design" by Robert Frost with "Wing-Spread" by Abbie Huston Evans that appears on page 000. Before he wrote, the student simply jotted down the points he had in mind. Looking over this "mess of garbage" (as he then regarded it), he could see that, among his scattered thoughts, two topics predominated. One was about figures of speech and about connotations, and these ideas he decided to join under the heading LANGUAGE. His other emerging idea had to do with the two poets' quite different themes. Having perceived that his thoughts weren't totally jumbled, he then proceeded through his list, numbering with the same numbers any ideas that seemed to go together, and so arranging them in the order he wanted to follow. His outline then looked like this:

```
Wing-Spread good, Design better

Frost is in the sonnet tradition

Themes — Evans: "Be small."

          Frost: "Is there any design in universe?"

Evans's word cable — suggests suspension bridge

Is Evans thinking of serpent in Eden?

Figures of speech — Evans doesn't use many —

          gives the moth a gender

Frost's words — more connotations in 'em

Frost's puns
```

Labeling with "A" the two points about words full of connotations, and with "B" the two points about figures of speech, the student indicated to himself that these points were to be taken up together. He found, as you can see in the finished essay, two ideas that didn't seem to relate to his purpose. These were the points about Frost's being in the sonnet tradition and about Evans's possible interest in the Garden of Eden serpent. Reluctantly but wisely, he decided to leave them out. These ideas might have led him to make interesting comments on the individual poems, but would not have got him to *compare* the poems, as the assignment asked. Having made this rough outline, he felt encouraged to return to the two poems; and, on rereading them, noticed some further points, which now fell readily into his plan. One of these points was that Frost's poem also contains similes. He added it to his outline and so remembered it.

DRAFTING AND REVISING

Seated at last, or striking some other businesslike stance,[1] you prepare to write, only to find yourself besieged with petty distractions. All of a sudden you remember a friend you had promised to call, some dry cleaning you were supposed to pick up, a neglected Coke (in another room) growing warmer and flatter by the minute. If your paper is to be written, you have one course of action: to collar these thoughts and for the moment banish them.

When first you draft your paper — that is, when you write it out in the rough — you will probably do best to write rapidly. At this early stage, you don't need to be fussy about spelling, grammar, and punctuation. To be sure, those picayune details matter, but you can worry about them later on, when you are **editing** (combing through your draft repairing grammar, cutting excess words, making small verbal improvements) and **proofreading** (going over your

---

[1]R. H. Super of the University of Michigan wrote a definitive biography of Walter Savage Landor while standing up, typing on a machine atop a filing cabinet.

finished paper line by line, checking it for typographical or other mistakes). Right now, it is more important to get your thoughts down on paper in a steady flow than to keep taking time out to check spellings in the dictionary. Forge ahead, and don't be too nastily self-critical. Perhaps when you write your draft you won't even want to look at all those notes on your reading that you collected so industriously. When you come to a place where a note will fit, you might just insert a reminder to yourself, such as SEE CARD 19, or SEE ARISTOTLE ON COMEDY.

Let us admit that writing about literature is a fussier kind of writing than turning out a narrative essay called, "My Most Exciting Experience." You may need to draft some of your paper slowly and painstakingly. You'll find yourself coping with all sorts of small problems, many of them simple and mechanical. What, for instance, will you call the author whose work you are dealing with? Decide at the outset. Most critics favor the author's last name alone: "Dickinson implies . . ." ("Miss Dickinson" or "Ms. Dickinson" may sound fussily polite; "Emily," too chummy.) Will you include footnotes in your paper and, if so, do you know how they work? (Some pointers on handling the pesky things will come in a few pages.)

You will want to give credit to any critics who helped you out, and properly to do so is to be painstaking. To paraphrase a critic, you do more than just rearrange the critic's words and phrases; you translate them into language of your own. Say you wish to refer to an insight of Randall Jarrell, who comments on the images of spider, flower, and moth in Robert Frost's poem "Design":

> Notice how the *heal-all,* because of its name, is the one flower in all the world picked to be the altar for this Devil's Mass; notice how holding up the moth brings something ritual and hieratic, a ghostly, ghastly formality to this priest and its sacrificial victim. . . .

It would be incorrect to say, without quotation marks:

> Frost picks the <u>heal-all</u> as the one flower in all the world to be the altar for this Devil's Mass. There is a ghostly, ghastly formality to the spider holding up the moth, like a priest holding a sacrificial victim.

That rewording, although not exactly in Jarrell's language, manages to steal his memorable phrases without giving him credit. Nor is it sufficient just to list Jarrell's essay in a bibliography at the end of your paper. If you do, you are still a crook; you merely point to the scene of your crime. What is needed, clearly, is to think through Jarrell's words to the point he is making; and if you want to keep any of his striking phrases (and why not?), put them in quotation marks:

> As Randall Jarrell points out, Frost portrays the spider as a kind of priest in a Mass, or Black Mass, elevating the moth like an object for sacrifice, with "a ghostly, ghastly formality."

To be scrupulous in your acknowledgment, tell where you found your quotation from Jarrell, citing the book and the page. (See "Documenting Your Sources," page 000.) But unless your instructor expects you to write such a formal, documented paper, the passage as it now stands would make sufficiently clear your source, and your obligation.

One more word of Dutch-uncle warning. In this book you are offered a vocabulary with which to discuss literature: a flurry of terms such as *irony*, *symbol*, and *image*, printed in **boldface** when first introduced. In your writing you may decide to enlist a few of them. And yet, critical terminology — especially if unfamiliar — can tempt a beginning critic to sling it about. Nothing can be less sophisticated, or more misleading, than a technical term grandly misapplied: "The *myth-symbolism* of this *rime scheme* leaves one aghast." Far better to choose plain words you're already at ease with. Your instructor, no doubt, has met many a critical term and is not likely to be impressed by the mere sight of another one. Knowingly selected and placed, a critical term can help sharpen a thought and make it easier to handle. Clearly it is less cumbersome to refer to the *tone* of a story than to have to say, "the way the author makes you feel that she feels about what she is talking about." But the paper-writer who declares, "The tone of this poem is full of ironic imagery," fries words to a hash — mixed up and indigestible.

When you write your first draft, by the way, leave plenty of space between lines and enormous margins. Then, when later thoughts come to you, you can easily squeeze them in.

Does any writer write with perfection on first try, and drop ideas with a single shot? Some writers have claimed to do so — among them the English novelist Anthony Trollope, who thought it "unmanly" not to write a thought right the first time. Jack Kerouac, leading novelist of the beat generation of the 1950s, believed in spontaneous prose. He used to write entire novels on uncut ribbons of teletype paper, thus saving himself the interruption of stopping at the bottom of each page. His specialty, though, was fiction of ecstasy and hallucination, not essays in explication, or comparison and contrast. For most of us, however, good writing is largely a matter of revising — of going back over our first thoughts word by word. Painstaking revision is more than a matter of tidying grammar and spelling: in the process of reconsidering our words, we sometimes discover fresher and sharper ideas. "Writing and rewriting," says John Updike, "are a constant search for what one is saying."

To achieve effective writing, you have to have the courage to be wild. Aware that no reader need see your rough drafts, you can treat them mercilessly — scissor them apart, rearrange their pieces, reassemble them into a stronger order, using staples or tape or glue. The art of revising calls for a textbook in itself, but here are a few simple suggestions:

1. Insofar as your deadline allows, be willing to revise as many times as need be.

2. Don't think of revision as the simple chore of fixing up spelling mistakes. That's proofreading, and it comes last. When you revise, be willing to

cut and slash, to discover new insights, to move blocks of words around so that they follow in a stronger order. Stand ready to question your whole approach to a work of literature, to entertain the notion of throwing everything you have written into the wastebasket and starting over again.

3. At this stage, you may find it helpful to enlist outside advice — from your instructor, from your roommate or your mate, from any friend who will read your rough draft and give you a reaction. If you can enlist such a willing reader, ask: What isn't clear to you?

4. If you (or your willing reader) should find any places that aren't readily understandable, single them out for rewriting. After all, you don't need to revise a whole draft if only parts of it need work. Try rewriting any especially troublesome passage or paragraph.

5. Short, skimpy paragraphs of ore or two sentences may indicate places that call for more thought, or more material. Can you supply them with more evidence, more explanation, more example and illustration?

6. A time-tested method of revising is to lay aside your manuscript for a while, forget about it, and then after a long interval (the Roman poet Horace recommended nine years, but obviously that won't do), go back to it for a fresh look. If you have time, take a nap or a walk, or at least a yawn and a stretch before you take yet another look.

7. When your paper is in a *last* draft — that's the time to edit it. Once you have your ideas in firm shape, you can check those uncertain spellings, look up the agreement of verbs in a grammar book or handbook, make your pronouns and numbers agree, cut needless words, pull out a weak word and send in a stronger one. Back when you were drafting, to get prematurely fussy about such small things might have frozen you up. But once you feel satisfied that you have made yourself clear, you can be as fussy as you like.

If you type your papers, it is a great help to become a reasonably expert typist — one whose method is other than the Christopher Columbus method (to discover a key and land on it). Then you can revise while you retype. All to what end? "Each clear sentence," according to Robert Russell, "is that much ground stripped clean of the undergrowth of one's own confusion. Sometimes it's thrilling to feel you have written even a single paragraph that makes sense."[2]

THE FORM OF YOUR FINISHED PAPER

Now that you have smoothed your final draft as fleck-free as you can, your instructor may have specific advice for the form of your finished paper. If none is forthcoming, it is only reasonable

1. to choose standard letter-size (8½ × 11) paper;
2. to give your name at the top of your title page;

[2]*To Catch an Angel* (New York: Vanguard, 1962) 301.

3. to leave an inch or more of margin on all four sides of each page, and a few inches of blank paper or an additional sheet after your conclusion, so that your instructor can offer comment;

4. to doublespace, or (if you handwrite) to use paper with widely spaced lines.

And what of titles of works discussed: when to put them in quotation marks, when to underline them? One rule of thumb is that titles of works shorter than book length rate quotation marks (poems, short stories, articles); but titles of books (including book-length poems: *The Odyssey*), plays, and periodicals take underlining. (In a manuscript to be set in type, an underline is a signal to the compositor to use *italics*.)

DOCUMENTING YOUR SOURCES

When you quote from other writers, when you lift their information, when you summarize or paraphrase their ideas, make sure you give them their due. Document everything you take. Identify the writer by name; cite the very book, magazine, newspaper, pamphlet, letter, or other source you are using, and the page or pages you are indebted to.

By so doing, you invite your readers to go to your original source and check up on you. Most readers won't bother, of course, but at least your invitation enlists their confidence. Besides, the duty to document keeps you carefully looking at your sources — and so helps keep your writing accurate and responsible.

The latest and most efficient way for writers to document their sources is that recommended in the *MLA Handbook for Writers of Research Papers,* 3rd ed. (New York: Modern Language Association of America, 1988). In the long run, whether you write an immense term paper citing a hundred sources or a short paper citing only three or four, the MLA's advice will save you and your reader time and trouble.

These pointers cannot take the place of the *MLA Handbook* itself; but the gist of the method is this. Begin by listing your sources: all the works from which you're going to quote, summarize, paraphrase, or take information. Later on, when you type up your paper in finished form, you're going to *end* it with a neat copy of this list (once called a *bibliography,* now entitled *Works Cited*). But right now, in writing your paper, every time you refer to one of these works, you need give only enough information to help a reader locate it in your Works Cited. Usually, you can just give (in parentheses) an author's last name and a page citation. You incorporate this information right in the text of your paper, most often at the end of a sentence:

```
One recent investigation has suggested that few people
who submit poems to small literary magazines bother to
read those magazines; or indeed, bother to read poems by
anybody else (Horton 108-09).
```

Say you will want to cite *two* books or magazine articles by Horton — how to tell them apart? In your text, condense the title of each article into a word or two.

> One recent investigation has shown that few people who submit poems to small literary magazines bother to read those magazines (Horton, "Magazines" 108-09).

If you have mentioned the name of the author in the body of your paper, you need give only the page number:

> As a recent investigator, Louise Horton, has suggested, few people who submit poems to small literary magazines bother to read those magazines (108-09).

The beauty of this method is that you don't have to stop every two minutes to write a footnote identifying your source in full detail. At the end of your paper, in your list of works cited, your reader can find a fuller description of your source — in this case, a magazine article:

> Horton, Louise. "Who Reads Small Literary Magazines and What Good Do They Do?" Texas Review Spring/Summer 1984: 108-13.

It's imperative to keep citations in your text brief and snappy, lest they hinder the flow of your prose. You may wish to append a note supplying a passage of less important (yet possibly valuable) information or making careful qualifying statements ("On the other hand, not every expert agrees. John Binks finds that poets are often a little magazine's only cash customers; while Molly MacGuire maintains that . . ."). If you want to put in some such aside, and suspect that you couldn't give it in your text without interrupting your paper awkwardly, then cast it into a **footnote** (a note placed at the bottom of a page) or an **endnote** (a note placed at the end of a paper). Given a choice, most writers prefer endnotes. Far easier to collect all the notes at the end of a paper than to use footnotes — as any writer knows who has had to retype pages and pages again and again, to make the footnotes fit.[1]

How do you drop in such notes? The number of each consecutive note comes (following any punctuation) after the last word of a sentence. So that the number will stand out, you roll your typewriter carriage up a click (or order your word-processor to do a superscript), thus lifting the number slightly above the usual level of your prose.

> as other observers have claimed.[1]

---

[1]Nowadays, some word-processing programs make life easier for footnoters by helping to format each footnote and by automatically dropping it in at the bottom of its page.

When you come to type the footnote or endnote itself, skip five spaces, elevate the number again, skip a space, and proceed.

[1]John Binks, to name only one such observer, finds . . .

Although now useful mainly for such slightly longwinded asides, footnotes and endnotes are time-honored ways to document *all* sources in a research paper. Indeed, some instructors still prefer them to the new MLA guidelines, and urge students to use such notes to indicate every writer cited. Though such notes take more work, they have the advantage of hiding dull data away from your reader's eyes, enabling you to end sentences with powerful bangs and inconspicuous note numbers instead of whimpering parentheses (Glutz-Finnegan, *Lesser Corollary* 1029 – 30). Besides, in a brief paper containing only one citation or two, to use footnotes or endnotes may be simpler and less showy than to compile a Works Cited list that has only two entries.

Large-mindedly, the *MLA Handbook* tolerates the continued use of footnotes and endnotes for documentation — indeed, offers advice for their preparation, which we will follow here. If you do use footnotes or endnotes to document all your sources, here is how to format them. A note identifying a magazine article looks like this:

[16]Louise Horton, "Who Reads Small Literary Magazines and What Good Do They Do?" Texas Review Spring/Summer 1984: 108-09.

Notice that, in notes, the author's first name comes first. (In a list of Works Cited, you work differently: you put last name first, so that you can readily arrange your list of authors in easy-to-consult alphabetical order.) A footnote or endnote for a reference to a book (and not a magazine article) looks like this:

[17]Elizabeth Frank, Louise Bogan: A Portrait (New York: Knopf, 1985) 59-60.

Should you return later to cite another place in Frank's book, you need not repeat all its information. Just write:

[18]Frank 192.

If in your paper you refer to *two* books by Elizabeth Frank, give the full title of each in the first note citing it. Then, if you cite it again, use a shortened form of its title:

[19]Frank, Bogan 192.

Your readers should not have to interrupt their reading of your essay to glance down at a note simply to find out whom you are quoting. It is poor form to write:

Dylan Thomas's poem "Fern Hill" is a memory of the poet's childhood: of his Aunt Ann Jones's farm, where he

spent his holidays. "Time, which has an art to throw dust
on all things, broods over the poem."[1] The farm, indeed,
is a lost paradise — a personal garden of Eden.

---

[1]William York Tindall, A Reader's Guide to Dylan
Thomas (New York: Noonday, 1962) 268.

That is annoying, because the reader has to stop reading and look at the
footnote to find out who made that resonant statement about Time brooding
over the poem. A better way:

"Time," as William York Tindall has observed, "which has
an art to throw dust on all things, broods over the
poem."[1]

---

[1]A Reader's Guide to Dylan Thomas (New York: Noonday,
1962) 268.

What to do now but hand in your paper? "And good riddance," you may
feel, after such an expenditure of thinking, time, and energy. But a good paper
is not only worth submitting, it is worth keeping. If you return to it, after a
while, you may find to your surprise that it will preserve and even renew what
you have learned.

KEEPING A JOURNAL

The essay is not, of course, the only medium in which you can write your
responses to literature. Many instructors ask students to keep a **journal:** a
day-to-day account of what they read and how they react to it. A great advantage in keeping a journal is that you can express your thoughts and feelings
immediately, before they grow cold. You can set down all your miscellaneous
reactions to what you read, whether or not they fit into a paper topic. (If you
have to write a paper later on, your journal just might suggest topics galore.)
Depending on what your instructor thinks essential, your journal may take in
all your reading for the course; or you may concentrate on the work of some
writer or writers, or on one kind of story. As you read (or afterward), you can
jot down anything you notice that you wish to remember. Does a theme in a
story, or a line of dialogue, strike you forcefully? Make a note of it. Does
something in the story not make sense? Record your bewilderment. Your
journal is personal: a place for you to sound off, to express your feelings. Don't
just copy your class notes into it; don't simply quote the stories. Mere length
of your entries will not impress your instructor, either: try for insights. A
paragraph or two will probably suffice to set down your main reactions to most
stories. In keeping a journal (a kind of writing primarily for yourself), you don't

rewrite; and so you need not feel obliged to polish your prose. Your aim is to store information without delay: to wrap words around your reactions and observations.

Keeping a journal will be satisfying only if you keep it up to date. Record your feelings and insights while you still have a story freshly in mind. Get weeks behind and have to grind out a journal from scratch, the night before it is due, and the whole project will decay into meaningless drudgery. But faithfully do a little reading and a little writing every day or so, and you will find yourself keeping track of the life of your mind. When your journal is closed, you will have a lively record not only of the literature you have read, but also of your involvement with it.

Robert Wallace (b. 1932)

THE GIRL WRITING HER ENGLISH PAPER   1979

lies on one hip by the fire,
blond, in jeans.

The wreckage of her labor, elegant as Eden
or petals from a tree,
surrounds her —   5

a little farm, smoke rising from the ashtray,
book, notebooks, papers, fields;
a poem's furrows.

If the lights were to go out suddenly,
stars would be overhead,   10
the edge of the wood still and dark.

Writing about a Poem

Assignment: a paper about a poem. You can approach it as a grim duty, of course: any activity can so be regarded. For Don Juan, in Spanish legend, even the act of love became a chore. But the act of writing, like the act of love, is much easier if your feelings take part in it. Write about anything you dislike and don't understand, and you not only set yourself the labors of Hercules, but you guarantee your reader discouragingly hard labor, too.

To write about a poem informatively, you need first to experience it. It helps to live with the poem for as long as possible: there is little point in trying to encompass the poem in a ten-minute tour of inspection on the night before the paper falls due. However challenging, writing about poetry has immediate rewards, and to mention just one, the poem you spend time with and write about is going to mean much more to you than poems skimmed ever do.

Most of the problems you will meet in writing about a poem will be the same ones you meet in writing about a play or a story: finding a topic, organizing your thoughts, writing, revising. For general advice on writing papers about any kind of literature, see "Writing about Literature" on page 461. In a few ways, however, a poem requires a different approach. In this chapter we will deal briefly with some of them, and will offer a few illustrations of papers that students have written. These papers may not be works of inimitable genius, but they are pretty good papers, the likes of which most students can write with a modest investment of time and care.

Briefer than most stories and most plays, lyric poems *look* easier to write about. They call, however, for your keenest attention. You may find that, before you can discuss a short poem, you will have to read it slowly and painstakingly, with your mind (like your pencil) sharp and ready. Unlike a play or a short story, a lyric poem tends to have very little plot, and perhaps you will find little to say about what happens in it. In order to understand a poem, you'll need to notice elements other than narrative: the connotations or suggestions of its words, surely, and the rhythm of phrases and lines. The subtleties of language, almost apart from story, are so essential to a poem (and so elusive) that Robert Frost was moved to say, "Poetry is what gets lost in translation." Once in a while, of course, you'll read a story whose prose abounds in sounds, rhythms, figures of speech, imagery, and other elements you expect of poetry. Certain novels of Herman Melville and William Faulkner contain paragraphs that, if extracted, seem in themselves prose poems — so lively are they in their word-play, so rich in metaphor. But such writing is exceptional, and the main business of most fiction is to get a story told. An extreme case of a fiction writer who didn't want his prose to sound poetic is Georges Simenon, best known for his mystery novels, who said that whenever he noticed in his manuscript any word or phrase that called attention to itself, he struck it out. That method of writing would never do for a poet, who revels in words and phrases that fix themselves in memory. It is safe to say that, in order to write well about a poem, you have to read it carefully enough to remember at least part of it word for word.

Let's consider three commonly useful approaches to writing about poetry.

EXPLICATING

In an **explication** (literally, "an unfolding") of a poem, a writer explains the entire poem in detail, unraveling any complexities to be found in it. This method is a valuable one in approaching a lyric poem, especially if the poem is rich in complexities (or in suggestions worth rendering explicit). Most poems that you'll ever be asked to explicate are short enough to discuss thoroughly within a limited time; fully to explicate a long and involved work, such as John Milton's epic *Paradise Lost*, might require a lifetime. (To explicate a short passage of Milton's long poem would be a more usual course assignment.)

All the details or suggestions in a poem that a sensitive and intelligent reader might consider, the writer of an explication considers and tries to unfold. These might include allusions, the denotations or connotations of words, the possible meanings of symbols, the effects of certain sounds and rhythms and formal elements (rime schemes, for instance), the sense of any statements that contain irony, and other particulars. Not intent on ripping a poem to pieces, the author of a useful explication instead tries to show how each part contributes to the whole.

An explication is easy to organize. You can start with the first line of the poem and keep working straight on through. An explication should not be confused with a paraphrase. A paraphrase simply puts the words of the poem into other words; it is a sort of translation, useful in getting at the plain prose sense and therefore especially helpful in clarifying a poem's main theme. Perhaps in writing an explication you will wish to do some paraphrasing; but an explication (unlike a paraphrase) does not simply restate: it explains a poem, in great detail.

Here, for example, is a famous poem by Robert Frost, followed by a student's concise explication. (The assignment was to explain whatever in "Design" seemed most essential, in not more than 750 words.)

Robert Frost (1874 – 1963)*

DESIGN   1936

I found a dimpled spider, fat and white,
On a white heal-all, holding up a moth
Like a white piece of rigid satin cloth —
Assorted characters of death and blight
Mixed ready to begin the morning right,   5
Like the ingredients of a witches' broth —
A snow-drop spider, a flower like a froth,
And dead wings carried like a paper kite.

What had that flower to do with being white,
The wayside blue and innocent heal-all?   10
What brought the kindred spider to that height,
Then steered the white moth thither in the night?
What but design of darkness to appall? —
If design govern in a thing so small.

An Unfolding of Robert Frost's "Design"

"I always wanted to be very observing," Robert Frost once said, after reading his poem "Design" to an audience. Then he added, "But I have always been afraid of my own observations" (Cook 126-27). What could he have observed that could scare him? Let's observe the poem close up.

Starting with the title, "Design," any reader of this poem will find it full of meaning. As Webster's New World Dictionary defines design, the word can denote among other things a plan, or "purpose; intention; aim." Some arguments for the existence of God (I remember from Sunday School) are based on the "argument from design": that because the world shows a systematic order, there must be a Designer who made it. But the word <u>design</u> can also mean "a secret or sinister scheme" — such as we attribute to a "designing person." As we shall see, Frost's poem incorporates all of these meanings. His poem raises the old philosophic question of whether there is a Designer, an evil Designer, or no Designer at all. Frost probably read William James on this question, as a critic has shown convincingly (Poirier 245-50).

Like many other sonnets, the poem is divided into two parts. The first eight lines draw a picture centering on the spider, who at first seems almost jolly. It is <u>dimpled</u> and <u>fat</u> like a baby, or Santa Claus. It stands on a wild flower whose name, <u>heal-all,</u> seems an irony: a heal-all is supposed to cure any disease, but it certainly has no power to restore life to the dead moth. (Later, in line ten, we learn that the heal-all used to be blue. Presumably it has died and become bleached-looking.) In this second line we discover, too, that the spider has hold of another creature. Right away we might feel sorry for the moth, were it not for the simile applied to it in line three: "Like a white piece of rigid satin cloth." Suddenly the moth becomes not a creature but a piece of fabric — lifeless and dead — and yet <u>satin</u> has connotations also beautiful. For me satin, used in rich ceremonial costumes such as coronation gowns and brides' dresses, has a formality and luxury about it. Besides, there is great accuracy in the word: the smooth and slightly plush surface of satin is like the powder-smooth surface of moths' wings. But this "cloth," rigid and white, could be the lining to Dracula's coffin.

In the fifth line an invisible hand enters. The characters are "mixed" like ingredients in an evil potion. Some force doing the mixing is behind the scene. The characters in themselves are innocent enough, but when brought together and concocted, their whiteness and look of <u>rigor mortis</u> are overwhelming. There is something diabolical in the spider's feast. The "morning right" echoes the word <u>rite,</u> a ritual — in this case apparently a Black Mass or a Witches' Sabbath. The simile in line seven ("a flower like a froth") is more ambiguous and harder to describe. A froth is white, foamy, and delicate — something found on a brook in the woods or on a beach after a wave recedes. However, in the natural world, froth also can be ugly: the foam on a dead dog's mouth. The dualism in nature — its beauty and its horror — is there in that one simile.

So far, the poem has portrayed a small, frozen scene, with the dimpled killer holding its victim as innocently as a boy holds a kite. Already, Frost has hinted that Nature may be, as Radcliffe Squires suggests, "nothing but an ash-white plain without love or faith or hope, where ignorant appetites cross by chance" (87). Now, in the last six lines of the sonnet, Frost comes out and directly states his theme. What else could bring these deathly pale, stiff things together "but design of darkness to appall?" The question is clearly rhetorical, meant to be answered, "Why, nothing but that, of course!" I take the next-to-last line to mean, "What except a design so dark and sinister that we're appalled by it?" "Appall," by the way, is the second pun in the poem: it sounds like <u>a pall</u> or shroud. <u>Steered</u> carries the suggestion of a steering-wheel or rudder that some pilot had to control. Like the word <u>brought,</u> it implies that some Captain charted the paths of spider, heal-all, and moth, so that they arrived together.

Having suggested that the universe is in the hands of that sinister Captain (Fate? the Devil?), Frost adds a note of doubt. The Bible tells us that "His eye is on the sparrow," but at the moment the poet doesn't seem sure.

Maybe, he hints, when things in the universe drop below a certain size, they pass completely out of the Designer's notice. When creatures are that little, maybe He doesn't bother to govern them, but just lets them run wild. And possibly the same idiotic chance is all that governs human lives. Maybe we're not even sinners in the hands of an angry God, but amazingly are nothing but little dicce being slung. And that — because it is even more senseless — is the worst suspicion of all.

Works Cited

Cook, Reginald. <u>Robert Frost: A Living Voice.</u> Amherst: U of Massachusetts P, 1974.

Poirier, Richard. <u>Robert Frost: The Work of Knowing.</u> New York: Oxford UP, 1977.

Squires, Radcliffe. <u>The Major Themes of Robert Frost.</u> Ann Arbor: U of Michigan P, 1963.

This excellent paper, while finding something worth unfolding in every line in Frost's poem, does so without seeming mechanical. Notice that, although the student proceeds through the poem from the title to the last line, she takes up points when necessary, in any sequence. In paragraph two, the writer looks ahead to the end of the poem and briefly states its main theme. (She does so in order to relate this theme to the poem's title.) In the third paragraph, she deals with the poem's *later* image of the heal-all, relating it to the first image. Along the way, she comments on the form of the poem ("Like many other sonnets"), on its similes and puns, its denotations and connotations.

Incidentally, this paper demonstrates good use of manuscript form, following the *MLA Handbook*, 2nd ed. Brief references (in parentheses) tell us where the writer found Frost's remarks before an audience, name the critic (Poirier) who showed that Frost had read the philosopher William James, and give page numbers for these sources and for another, a book by Radcliffe Squires. At the end of the paper, a list of these works cited uses abbreviations for *University* and *Press* that the *MLA Handbook* recommends (but doesn't insist upon). This paper demonstrates, too, how to make final corrections without retyping. In the last paragraph, notice how the student legibly added a word and neatly changed another word by crossing it out and writing a substitute above it. In her next-to-last sentence, the writer clearly transposes two letters with a handy mark ( ), deletes a word, and strikes out a superfluous letter.

It might seem that to work through a poem line by line is a lockstep task; and yet there can be high excitement in it. Randall Jarrell once wrote an explication of "Design" in which he managed to convey such excitement. In the following passage taken from it, see if you can sense the writer's joy in his work. (Don't, incidentally, feel obliged to compare the quality of your own insights with Jarrell's, nor the quality of your own prose. Be fair to yourself: unlike most students, Jarrell had the advantage of being an excellent poet and a gifted critic; besides, he had read and pondered Frost for years before he wrote his essay, and as a teacher he probably had taught "Design" many times.)

Frost's details are so diabolically good that it seems criminal to leave some unremarked; but notice how *dimpled, fat,* and *white* (all but one; all but one) come from our regular description of any baby; notice how the *heal-all,* because of its name, is the one flower in all the world picked to be the altar for this Devil's Mass; notice how *holding up* the moth brings something ritual and hieratic, a ghostly, ghastly formality, to this priest and its sacrificial victim; notice how terrible to the fingers, how full of the stilling rigor of death, that *white piece of rigid satin cloth* is. And *assorted characters of death and blight* is, like so many things in this poem, sharply ambiguous: *a mixed bunch of actors* or *diverse representative signs.* The tone of the phrase *assorted characters of death and blight* is beautifully developed in the ironic Breakfast-Club-calisthenics, Radio-Kitchen heartiness of *mixed ready to begin the morning right* (which assures us, so unreassuringly, that this isn't any sort of Strindberg *Spook Sonata,* but hard fact), and concludes in the *ingredients* of the witches' broth, giving the soup a sort of cuddly shimmer that the cauldron in *Macbeth* never had; the *broth,* even, is brought to life — we realize that witches' broth *is* broth, to be supped with a long spoon.[1]

Evidently, Jarrell's cultural interests are broad: ranging from August Strindberg's ground-breaking modern classic down to the Breakfast Club (a once-popular radio program that cheerfully exhorted its listeners to march around their tables). And yet breadth of knowledge, however much it deepens and enriches Jarrell's writing, isn't all that he brings to the reading of poetry. For him, an explication isn't a dull plod, but a voyage of discovery. His prose — full of figures of speech (*diabolically good, cuddly shimmer*) — conveys the apparent delight he takes in showing off his findings. Such a joy, of course, can't be acquired deliberately. But it can grow, the more you read and study poetry.

ANALYZING

An **analysis** of a poem, like a news commentator's analysis of a crisis in the Middle East or a chemist's analysis of an unknown fluid, separates its subject into elements, as a means to understanding that subject — to see what composes it. Usually, the writer of such an essay singles out one of those elements

[1]From *Poetry and the Age* (New York: Knopf, 1953).

for attention: "Imagery of Light and Darkness in Frost's 'Design' "; "The Character of Satan in *Paradise Lost.*"

Like explication, analysis can be particularly useful in dealing with a short poem. Unlike explication (which inches through a poem line by line), analysis often suits a long poem too, because it allows the writer to discuss just one manageable element in the poem. A good analysis casts intense light upon a poem from one direction. If you care enough about a poem, and about some perspective on it — its theme, say, or its symbolism, or its singability — writing an analysis can enlighten and give pleasure.

In this book you probably have met a few brief analyses: the discussion of connotations in John Masefield's "Cargoes" (page 65), for instance, or the examination of symbols in T. S. Eliot's "The *Boston Evening Transcript*" (page 206). In fact, most of the discussions in this book are analytic. Temporarily, we have separated the whole art of poetry into elements such as tone, irony, literal meaning, suggestions, imagery, figures of speech, sound, rhythm, and so on. No element of a poem, of course, exists apart from all the other elements. Still, by taking a closer look at particular elements, one at a time, we see them more clearly and more easily study them.

Long analyses of metrical feet, rime schemes, and indentations tend to make ponderous reading: such formal and technical elements are perhaps the hardest to discuss engagingly. And yet formal analysis (at least a little of it) can be interesting and illuminating: it can measure the very pulse beat of lines. If you do care about the technical side of poetry, then write about it, by all means. You will probably find it helpful to learn the terms for the various meters, stanzas, fixed forms, and other devices, so that you can summon them to your aid with confidence. Here is a short formal analysis of "Design" by a student who evidently cares for technicalities yet who manages not to be a bore in talking about them. Concentrating on the sonnet form of Frost's poem, the student actually casts light upon the poem in its entirety.

The Design of "Design"

For "Design," the sonnet form has at least two
advantages. First, as in most strict sonnets, the argument
of the poem falls into two parts. In the octave Frost draws
his pale still-life of spider, flower, and moth; then in the
sestet he contemplates the meaning of it. The sestet deals
with a more general idea: the possible existence of a
vindictive deity who causes the spider to catch the moth, and
no doubt also causes other suffering. Frost weaves his own
little web. The unwary reader is led into the poem by its

opening story, and pretty soon is struggling with more than he expected. Even the rime scheme, by the way, has something to do with the poem's meaning. The word <u>white</u> ends the first line of the sestet. The same sound is echoed in the rimes that follow. All in all, half the lines in the poem end in an "ite." It seems as if Frost places great weight on the whiteness of his little scene, for the riming words both introduce the term <u>white</u> and keep reminding us of it.

A sonnet has a familiar design, and that is its second big advantage to this particular poem. In a way, writing "Design" as a sonnet almost seems a foxy joke. (I can just imagine Frost chuckling to himself, wondering if anyone will get it.) A sonnet, being a classical form, is an orderly world with certain laws in it. There is ready-made irony in its containing a meditation on whether there is any order in the universe at large. Obviously there's design in back of the poem, but is there any design to insect life, or human life? Whether or not the poet can answer this question (and it seems he can't), at least he discovers an order writing the poem. Actually, that is just what Frost said a poet achieves: "a momentary stay against confusion."[1]

Although design clearly governs in this poem — in "this thing so small" — the design isn't entirely predictable. The poem starts out as an Italian sonnet, with just two riming sounds; then (unlike an Italian sonnet) it keeps the "ite" rimes going. It ends in a couplet, like a Shakespearean sonnet. From these unexpected departures from the pattern of the Italian sonnet announced in the opening lines, I get the impression that Frost's poem is somewhat like the larger universe. It looks perfectly orderly, until you notice the small details in it.

[1]Robert Frost, "The Figure a Poem Makes," preface, <u>Complete Poems of Robert Frost</u> (New York: Holt, 1949) vi.

Unlike the student paper on pages 478 – 481, that documented its references (inside parentheses), "The Design of 'Design'" uses an endnote to cite its one outside source. (In so doing, it follows the form for such notes suggested in the *MLA Handbook, 2nd ed.*) To do so seems sensible here. This writer doesn't need a list of works cited, for such a list might have looked skimpy, like a one-car funeral. (In the endnote, by the way, *Holt* is a short, MLA-recommended contraction for the full name of the publisher: Holt, Rinehart, and Winston, Inc.)

COMPARING AND CONTRASTING

To write a **comparison** of two poems, you place them side by side and point out their likenesses; to write a **contrast,** you point out their differences. If you wish, you can combine the two methods in the same paper. For example, even though you may emphasize similarities you may also call attention to differences, or vice versa.

Such a paper makes most sense if you pair two poems that have much in common. It would be possible to compare William McGonagall's unintentionally comic poem "The Albion Battleship Calamity" with John Milton's profound "Lycidas," but comparison would be difficult, perhaps futile. Though both poems are in English, the two seem hopelessly remote from each other in diction, in tone, in complexity, and in worth.

Having found, however, a couple of poems that throw light on each other, you then go on in your paper to show further, unsuspected resemblances — not just the ones that are obvious (" 'Design' and 'Wing-Spread' are both about bugs"). The interesting resemblances are ones that take thinking to discover. Similarly, you may want to show noteworthy differences — besides those your reader will see without any help.

In comparing two poems, you may be tempted to discuss one of them and be done with it, then spend the latter half of your paper discussing the other. This simple way of organizing an essay can be dangerous if it leads you to keep the two poems in total isolation from each other. The whole idea of such an assignment, of course, is to get you to do some comparing. There is nothing wrong in discussing all of poem A first, then discussing poem B — *if* in discussing B you keep looking back at A. Another procedure is to keep comparing the two poems all the way through your paper — dealing first, let's say, with their themes; then with their metaphors; and finally, with their respective merits.

More often than not, a comparison is an analysis: a study of a theme common to two poems, for instance; or of two poets' similar fondness for the myth of Eden. But you also can evaluate poems by comparing and contrasting them: placing them side by side in order to decide which poet deserves the brighter laurels. Here, for example, is a paper that considers "Design" and "Wing-Spread," a poem of Abbie Huston Evans (first printed in 1938, two years later than Frost's poem). By comparing and contrasting the two poems for (1) their language and (2) their themes, this student shows us reasons for his evaluation.

"Wing-Spread" Does a Dip

The midge spins out to safety
Through the spider's rope;
But the moth, less lucky,
Has to grope.

Mired in glue-like cable   5
See him foundered swing
By the gap he opened
With his wing,

Dusty web enlacing
All that blue and beryl.   10
In a netted universe
Wing-spread is peril.

— Abbie Huston Evans

"Wing-Spread," quoted above, is a good poem, but it is not in the same class with "Design." Both poets show us a murderous spider and an unlucky moth, but there are two reasons for Robert Frost's superiority. One is his more suggestive use of language, the other is his more memorable theme.

Let's start with language. "Design" is full of words and phrases rich in suggestions. "Wing-Spread," by comparison, contains few. To take just one example, Frost's "dimpled spider, fat and white" is certainly a more suggestive description. Actually, Evans doesn't describe her spider; she just says, "the spider's rope." (I have to hand Evans the palm for showing us the spider and moth in action. In Frost's view, they are dead and petrified — but I guess that is the impression he is after.) In "Design," the spider's dimples show that it is like a chubby little kid, who further turns out to be a kite-flier. This seems an odd, almost freaky way to look at a spider. I find it more refreshing than Evans's view (although I like her word cable, suggesting that the spider's web is a kind of suspension bridge). Frost's word-choice — his harping on white — paints a more striking scene than Evans's slightly vague "All that blue and beryl." Except for her personification of the moth in her second stanza, Evans doesn't go in for any figures of speech, and even that one isn't a clear personification — she simply gives the moth a sex by referring to it as "him." Frost's striking metaphors, similes, and puns (right, appall) show him, as usual, to be a master of figures of speech. He calls the moth's wings "satin cloth" and "a paper kite"; Evans just refers in line 8 to a moth's wing. As far as the language of the two poems goes, you might as well compare a vase full of with flowers and a single flower stuck in a vase. (That is a poor metaphor, since Frost's poem contains only one flower, but I hope you will know what I mean.)

In fairness to Evans, I would say that she picks a pretty good solitary flower. And her poem has powerful sounds: short lines with the riming words coming at us again and again very frequently. In theme, however, "Wing-Spread" seems much more narrow than "Design." The first time I read Evans's poem all I felt was: Ho hum, the moth too was wide and got stuck. The second time I read it, I figured that she is saying something with a universal application. This comes out in line 11, in "a netted universe." That is the most interesting phrase in her poem, one that you can think about. Netted makes me imagine the universe as being full of nets rigged by someone who is fishing for us. Maybe, like Frost, Evans sees an evil plan operating. She does not, though, investigate it. She says that the midge escapes because it is tiny. On the other hand, things with wide wing-spreads get stuck. Her theme as I read it is, "Be small and inconspicuous if you want to survive," or maybe, "Isn't it too bad that in this world the big beautiful types crack up and die, while the miserable little puny punks keep sailing?" Now, that is a valuable idea. I have often thought that very same thing myself. But Frost's closing note ("If design govern in a thing so small") is really devastating, because it raises a huge uncertainty. "Wing-Spread" leaves us with not much besides a moth stuck in a web, and a moral. In both language and theme, "Design" climbs to a higher altitude.

How to Quote a Poem

Preparing to discuss a short poem, it is a good idea to emulate the student who wrote on "Wing-Spread" and to quote the whole text of the poem at the beginning of your paper, with its lines numbered. Then you can refer to it with ease, and your instructor, without having to juggle a book, can follow you.

Quoted to illustrate some point, memorable lines can add interest to your paper, and good commentators on poetry tend to be apt quoters, helping their readers to experience a word, a phrase, a line, or a passage that otherwise might be neglected. However, to quote from poetry is slightly more awkward than to quote from prose. There are lines to think about — important and meaningful units whose shape you will need to preserve. If you are quoting more than a couple of lines, it is good policy to arrange your quotation just as its lines occur in the poem, white space and all:

> At the outset, the poet tells us of his discovery of
>
>> a dimpled spider, fat and white,
>> On a white heal-all, holding up a moth
>> Like a white piece of rigid satin cloth —
>
> and implies that the small killer is both childlike and sinister.

But if you are quoting less than two lines of verse, it would seem wasteful of paper to write:

> The color white preoccupies Frost. The spider is
>
>> fat and white,
>> On a white heal-all
>
> and even the victim moth is pale, too.

In such a case, it saves space to transform Frost's line arrangement into prose:

```
The color white preoccupies Frost. The spider is "fat and
white, / On a white heal-all" — and even the victim moth is
pale, too.
```

Here, a diagonal (/) indicates the writer's respect for where the poet's lines begin and end. Some writers prefer to note line-breaks without diagonals, just by keeping the initial capital letter of a line (if there is any): "fat and white, On a white heal-all. . . ." Incidentally, the ellipsis (. . .) in that last remark indicates that words are omitted from the end of Frost's sentence; the fourth dot is a period. Some writers — meticulous souls — also stick in an ellipsis at the *beginning* of a quotation, if they're leaving out words from the beginning of a sentence in the original:

```
The color white preoccupies Frost in his description
of the spider ". . . fat and white, / On a white heal-
all. . . ."
```

Surely there's no need for an initial ellipsis, though, if you begin quoting at the beginning of a sentence. No need for a final ellipsis, either, if your quotation goes right to the end of a sentence in the original. If it is obvious that only a phrase is being quoted, no need for an ellipsis in any case:

```
The speaker says he "found a dimpled spider" and he goes
on to portray it as a kite-flying boy.
```

If you leave out whole lines, indicate the omission by an ellipsis all by itself on a line:

```
The midge spins out to safety
Through the spider's rope;
        .  .  .
In a netted universe
Wing-spread is peril.
```

Before You Begin

Ready at last to write, you will have spent considerable time in reading, thinking, and feeling. After having chosen your topic, you probably will have taken a further look at the poem or poems you have picked, letting further thoughts and feelings come to you. The quality of your paper will depend, above all, upon the quality of your readiness to write.

Exploring a poem, a sensitive writer handles it with care and affection as though it were a living animal, and, done with it, leaves it still alive. The unfeeling writer, on the other hand, disassembles the poem in a dull, mechanical way, like someone with a blunt ax filling an order for one horse-skeleton.

Again, to write well is a matter of engaging your feelings. Writing to a deadline, on an assigned topic, you easily can sink into a drab, workaday style, especially if you regard the poet as some uninspired builder of chicken-coops who hammers themes and images into place, and then slaps the whole thing with a coat of words. Certain expressions, if you lean on them habitually, may tempt you to think of the poet in that way. Here, for instance, is a discussion — by a plodding writer — of Robert Frost's poem.

> The symbols Frost <u>uses</u> in "Design" are very
>
> successful. Frost makes the spider <u>stand</u> <u>for</u> Nature. He
>
> <u>wants</u> us to see Nature as blind and cruel. He also <u>employs</u>
>
> good sounds. He <u>uses</u> a lot of <u>i</u>'s because he is <u>trying</u> <u>to</u>
>
> make you think of falling rain.

(Underscored words are worth questioning.) What's wrong with that comment? While understandable, the words *uses* and *employs* seem to lead the writer to see Frost only as a conscious tool-manipulator. To be sure, Frost in a sense "uses" symbols, but did he grab hold of them and lay them into his poem? For all we know, perhaps the symbols arrived quite unbidden, and used the poet. To write a good poem, Frost maintained, a poet himself has to be surprised. (How, by the way, can we hope to know what a poet *wants* to do? And there isn't much point in saying that the poet is *trying to* do something. He has already done it, if he has written a good poem.) At least, it is likely that Frost didn't plan to fulfill a certain quota of *i*-sounds. Writing his poem, not by following a blueprint but probably by bringing it slowly to the surface of his mind (like Elizabeth Bishop's hooked fish), Frost no doubt had enough to do without trying to engineer the reactions of his possible audience. Like all true symbols, Frost's spider doesn't *stand for* anything. The writer would be closer to the truth to say that the spider *suggests* or *reminds us* of Nature, or of certain forces in the natural world. (Symbols just hint, they don't indicate.)

After the student discussed the paper in a conference, he rewrote the first two sentences like this:

> The symbols in Frost's "Design" are highly effective.
>
> The spider, for instance, suggests the blindness and
>
> cruelty of Nature. Frost's word-sounds, too, are part of
>
> the meaning of his poem, for the <u>i</u>'s remind the reader of
>
> falling rain.

Not every reader of "Design" will hear rain falling, but the student's revision probably comes closer to describing the experience of the poem most of us know.

In writing about poetry, an occasional note of self-doubt can be useful: now and then a *perhaps* or a *possibly*, an *it seems* or a modest *I suppose.* Such expressions may seem timid shilly-shallying, but at least they keep the writer from thinking, "I know all there is to know about this poem."

Facing the showdown with your empty sheaf of paper, however, you can't worry forever about your critical vocabulary. To do so is to risk the fate of the centipede in a bit of comic verse, who was running along efficiently until someone asked, "Pray, which leg comes after which?," whereupon "He lay distracted in a ditch/Considering how to run." It is a safe bet that your instructor is human. Your main task as a writer is to communicate to another human being your sensitive reading of a poem.

Suggestions for Writing

Topics for Brief Papers (250 – 500 words)

1. Write a concise *explication* of a short poem of your choice, or one suggested by your instructor. In a paper this brief, probably you won't have room to explain everything in the poem; explain what you think most needs explaining. (An illustration of one such explication appears on page 478.)

2. Write an *analysis* of a short poem, first deciding which one of its elements to deal with. (An illustration of such an analysis appears on page 483.) For examples, here are a few specific topics:

   "Kinds of Irony in Hardy's 'The Workbox' "

   "The Attitude of the Speaker in Marvell's 'To His Coy Mistress' "

   "The Theme of Pastan's 'Ethics.' "

   "An Extended Metaphor in Yeats's 'Long-Legged Fly.' " (Explain the one main comparison that the poem makes and show how the whole poem makes it. Other likely possibilities for a paper on extended metaphor: Baca's "Spliced Wire," Chappell's "Skin Flick," Dickinson's "Because I could not stop for Death," Dove's "Daystar," Frost's "The Silken Tent," Lowell's "Skunk Hour," Rich's "Aunt Jennifer's Tigers.")

   "The Rhythms of Plath's 'Daddy' "

   (To locate any of these poems, see the Index to Authors, Titles, and Quotations at the back of this book.)

3. Select a poem in which the main speaker is a character who for any reason interests you. You might consider, for instance, Betjeman's "In Westminster Abbey," Browning's "Soliloquy of the Spanish Cloister," Dove's "Daystar," or Eliot's "Love Song of J. Alfred Prufrock." Then write a brief profile of this character, drawing only on what the poem tells you (or reveals). What is the character's approximate age? Situation in life? Attitude toward self? Attitude toward others? General personality? Do you find this character admirable?

4. Although each of these poems tells a story, what happens in the poem isn't necessarily obvious: Cummings's "anyone lived in a pretty how town," Eliot's "Love Song of J. Alfred Prufrock," Digges's "For *The Daughters of Hannah* Bible Class . . . ," Stafford's "At the Klamath Berry Festival," Winters's "At the San Francisco Airport," James Wright's "A Blessing." Choose one of these poems and in a paragraph sum up what you think happens in it. Then in a second paragraph ask yourself: what, *besides* the element of story, did you consider in order to understand the poem?

5. Think of someone you know (or someone you can imagine) whose attitude toward poetry in general is dislike. Suggest a poem for that person to read — a poem that you like — and, addressing your skeptical reader, point out whatever you find to enjoy in it, that you think the skeptic just might enjoy too.

6. Keeping in mind what Coleridge and Jarrell have to say about "obscurity" in poetry (see their statements in Criticism: On Poetry, pages 447 and 453), write a brief defense of some poem you like against the possible charge that it is obscure.

TOPICS FOR MORE EXTENSIVE PAPERS (600 – 1,000 WORDS)

1. Write an explication of a poem short enough for you to work through line by line — for instance, Emily Dickinson's "My Life had stood – a loaded Gun" or MacLeish's "The End of the World." As if offering your reading experience to a friend who hadn't read the poem before, try to point out all the leading difficulties you encountered, and set forth in detail your understanding of any lines that contain such difficulties.

2. Write an explication of a longer poem — for instance, Eliot's "Love Song of J. Alfred Prufrock," Hardy's "Convergence of the Twain," Rich's "Trying to Talk with a Man," or Steven's "Peter Quince at the Clavier." Although you will not be able to go through every line of the poem, explain what you think most needs explaining.

3. In this book, you will find from five to twelve poems by each of these poets: Blake, Dickinson, Donne, Eliot, Frost, Hardy, Hopkins, Housman, Hughes, Keats, Roethke, Shakespeare, Stevens, Tennyson, Whitman, William Carlos Williams, Wordsworth, Wilbur, and Yeats; and multiple selections for many more. (See Index to Authors, Titles, and Quotations.) After you read a few poems by a poet who interests you, write an analysis of *more than one* of the poet's poems. To do this, you will need to select just one characteristic theme (or other element) to deal with — something typical of the poet's work, not found only in a single poem. Here are a few specific topics for such an analysis:

"What Angers William Blake? A Look at Three Poems of Protest"

"How Emily Dickinson's Lyrics Resemble Hymns"

"The Humor of Robert Frost"

"Folk Elements in the Poetry of Langston Hughes"

"John Keats's Sensuous Imagery"

"The Vocabulary of Music in Poems of Wallace Stevens"

"Non-free Verse: Patterns of Sound in Three Poems of William Carlos Williams"

4. Compare and contrast two poems in order to evaluate them: which is more satisfying and effective poetry? To make a meaningful comparison, be sure to choose two poems that genuinely have much in common: perhaps a similar theme or subject. (For an illustration of such a paper, see the one given in this chapter. For suggestions of poems to compare, see the Anthology.)

5. Evaluate by the method of comparison two versions of a poem: early and late drafts, perhaps, or two translations from another language. For parallel versions to work on, see Chapter Fourteen, "Alternatives."

6. If the previous topic appeals to you, consider this. In 1912, twenty-four years before he printed "Design," Robert Frost sent a correspondent this early version:

IN WHITE

A dented spider like a snow drop white
On a white Heal-all, holding up a moth
Like a white piece of lifeless satin cloth —
Saw ever curious eye so strange a sight? —

Portent in little, assorted death and blight   5
Like ingredients of a witches' broth? —
The beady spider, the flower like a froth,
And the moth carried like a paper kite.

What had that flower to do with being white,
The blue prunella every child's delight.   10
What brought the kindred spider to that height?
(Make we no thesis of the miller's plight.)
What but design of darkness and of night?
Design, design! Do I use the word aright?

Compare "In White" with "Design." In what respects is the finished poem superior?

Topics for Long Papers (1,500 words or More)

1. Write a line-by-line explication of a poem rich in matters to explain, or a longer poem that offers ample difficulty. While relatively short, Donne's "A Valediction: Forbidding Mourning" or Hopkins's "The Windhover" are poems that will take a good bit of time to explicate; but even a short, apparently simple poem such as Frost's "Stopping by Woods on a Snowy Evening" can provide more than enough to explicate thoughtfully in a longer paper.

2. Write an analysis of the work of one poet (as suggested above, in the third topic for more extensive papers) in which you go beyond this book to read an entire collection of that poet's work.

3. Write an analysis of a certain theme (or other element) that you find in the work of two or more poets. It is probable that in your conclusion you will want to set the poets' work side by side, comparing or contrasting it, and perhaps making some evaluation. Sample topics:

   "Langston Hughes, Gwendolyn Brooks, and Dudley Randall as Prophets of Social Change."

   "What It Is to Be a Woman: The Special Knowledge of Sylvia Plath, Anne Sexton, and Adrienne Rich."

   "Language of Science in Some Poems of Eberhart, Merrill, and Ammons"

4. Taking a passage from "Criticism: On Poetry," see what light it will cast on a poem that interests you. You might test Gray's "Elegy" by Poe's dictum that there is no such thing as a long poem. (Does the "Elegy" flag in intensity?) Or try reading several poems of Robert Frost, looking for the "sound of sense" (which Frost explains in his letter to John Bartlett on page 449).

Writing a Poem

How Does a Poem Begin?

After you have read much poetry and (as Keats said) "traveled in the realms of gold," it is natural to want to write a poem. And why shouldn't you? Whether or not you aspire ever to publish your work, the attempt itself offers profound satisfactions; and it offers, too, a way to become a finer reader of poetry. To learn how to carry a football may not equip you to play for the Oilers, but it may help you appreciate the timing and skill of an Earl Campbell. In a roughly similar way, you may find yourself better able to perceive the artistry of an excellent sonnet from having written a sonnet of your own — even a merely acceptable one.

Poems, like new comets, tend to arrive mysteriously. Sometimes they go burning right past a serious, hard-working poet only to dawn, as though by accident, upon a madman, an idler, or a child. This may be why no one has ever devised a formula for synthesizing memorable poems. "A good poet," said Randall Jarrell, "is someone who manages, in a lifetime of standing out in thunderstorms, to be struck by lightning five or six times." In this view, poetic inspiration, like grace, is something beyond human control. Still, most of the best lightning bolts tend to strike those poets who keep waiting patiently, writing and rewriting and discarding, keeping their lightning rods lifted as they work. As Louis Pasteur said — speaking of scientists — "Chance favors the prepared mind."

Teachers of creative writing do not promise to create poets. All they can try to create is an atmosphere in which good poems may be written, given a hearing, and perhaps rendered stronger and more concise. As a member of a class or writing workshop, you have certain advantages. At least, you have companions in your struggles and chagrins. You may even find a sympathetic audience.

Even though the writing of poetry cannot be taught with great efficiency, some knowledge useful to poets can be imparted. What does a poet need to know? Half-jokingly, W. H. Auden once proposed a College for Bards with this curriculum:

1. In addition to English, at least one ancient language, probably Greek or Hebrew, and two modern languages would be required.

2. Thousands of lines of poetry in these languages would be learned by heart.

3. The library would contain no books of literary criticism, and the only critical exercise required of students would be the writing of parodies.

4. Courses in prosody, rhetoric, and comparative philology would be required of all students, and every student would have to select three courses out of courses in mathematics, natural history, geology, meteorology, archeology, mythology, liturgics, and cooking.

5. Every student would be required to look after a domestic animal and cultivate a garden plot.[1]

Auden, though he pokes fun at the notion of systematically training poets, makes constructive suggestions. He would have the aspiring poet study languages and something besides literature, and store up some poetry in memory. William Butler Yeats, too, thought that poets learn mainly by reading the work of other poets. There can be no "singing school" except the study of great poems — monuments, Yeats calls them, of the human soul's magnificence. (See "Sailing to Byzantium," page 257.)

Begin by reading. Don't limit yourself to poems assigned for college credit. Until you explore poetry more widely and roam around in it, how will you know what kind you most care to write? Pick up current poetry magazines. Read an **anthology** of contemporary poets or a **collection** of poems by a contemporary. (An *anthology* represents the work of many poets; a *collection* gathers a single poet's poems.) Crack open a survey of older literature. Browse in bookshops. Lift some dust from library stacks. Read methodically or read by whim. Whatever poetry you come to love may nourish a poem you will write.

As you read, make your own personal, selective anthology. Don't let in a poem of Tennyson just because your instructor thinks it is great stuff, let it in only because you cherish it. Instead of just banging out Xerox copies of the poems you admire, you would do well to copy them by hand into a book with blank pages, or to type them on looseleaf notebook paper. By doing so, you'll pay close attention to them, and you'll grow accustomed to seeing excellent poetry (no matter whose) flow from your fingertips. If you would please the ghost of W. H. Auden, you'll say aloud the poems from your personal anthology until you can say them by heart. The suggestion that you memorize poetry may

---

[1]"The Poet and the City" in *The Dyer's Hand* (New York: Random, 1962).

strike you as boring, but its benefits may be surprising. You just might transfer some poetry from your head down to your viscera and into your bones. Then, the music of words, especially their rhythms, will become part of you. Your own work may well prove richer for knowing poetry on a deeper level than that of the mind and eye.

It would save time, of course, not to read anything, but simply to look into your heart and write. And yet, because poetry is (among other things) an art of choosing words and arranging them, the usual result of just looking into one's heart and writing is a lot of words hastily chosen and stodgily arranged. "But," the novice might protest, "why should I read Keats and Yeats and the Beats? I don't want to be influenced by all those old birds — I want to be myself!" Excellent poets, though they may be bundles of influences, are still themselves. In truth, when you are starting out, you can learn a great deal by deliberately imitating the work of any excellent poets you deeply love. Spenser studied Chaucer; Keats studied Spenser; Tennyson and Stevens studied Keats. (Auden said he began by imitating Thomas Hardy, because Hardy's work looked imitable.) If you borrow any mannerisms from your models, they will probably disappear as soon as you gain in confidence. Although the novice poet is sometimes urged, "Discover your own voice!" such advice can lead to a painful self-consciousness. Your own voice is probably the last thing to concern yourself about. Certainly it would be a mistake to settle on any one particular voice or style before you have practiced singing in many registers. Imitate whomever you choose, and see what you can do best. Try a Levertovian lyric or a Miltonic meditation. Let out a Whitmanic yawp. Express what you feel in the strongest words you can find, and your voice will take care of itself. It will be your own, in the end, though Donne or Emily Dickinson went into the training of it.

From your reading, you will probably notice that long-lasting poems — those that remain in print after a century or more — tend to express powerful feelings. "In poetry," as Ezra Pound observed, "only emotion endures." Certainly, to name only one instance, the ballad of "Edward" remains vital after hundreds of years, still brimming with sorrow and hate. Asked by a student, "What shall I write about?" Karl Shapiro replied, "Praise something — anything!" — and that is good advice. Although it is possible to write a memorable poem out of piddling, nugatory feelings (or a poem about being unable to feel anything, like Eliot's "The *Boston Evening Transcript*"), a poem written out of love, or loathing, is more likely to radiate energy. (One of John Donne's most energetic poems begins with the impassioned outburst, "For God's sake hold your tongue, and let me love.")

Very often, beginning to write a poem is a process of discovering, and opening, some deep resource of feeling. You have to search within yourself; no map can lead you to such a discovery. Whatever quickens your imagination is your resource. It may be a dream or a nightmare. It may be the memory of some moving experience. At times, your resource may lie in some unexpected place. You might want to write — as Whitman, Keats, and Elizabeth Bishop did — a deeply felt poem about a spider, a piece of ancient pottery, or a filling station.

This is not to say that you can mechanically cram your past life into your poetry-mill and grind it into poems. Although poems may rise from your experience, sometimes in becoming a poem the experience will "suffer a sea change / Into something rich and strange" (like the drowned man's bones in the song in Shakespeare's *Tempest*). You have to leave room for your imagination freely to operate, to transform the raw matter of experience however it will. You will probably limit and constrict your poetry if you regard it as a diary to be kept — as a complete and faithful transcript of what happens to you. Your imagination may yearn to improve upon the literal truth for the sake of the truth of art. Inevitably, a successful poem (even one that sticks to the facts) will be more than journalism. It will be, as Robert Frost memorably described it, "a performance in words."

If it takes feelings to write a memorable poem, yet in poetry the hardest thing to do is to talk about those feelings directly. Readers grow weary of poets who bleat, "Woe is me! I'm so lonely! How miserably sterile I feel!" But probably no reader has ever failed to sympathize with the poet who begins, "Western wind, when wilt thou blow, / The small rain down can rain?" Such a poem does not *discuss* the poet's feelings. It utters them, and it points to objects in the world that invite the reader to feel similarly.

Drink or drugs, by the way, seem of little aid to poets in search of inspiration. The trouble with trying to write while stoned (according to one contemporary) is that poetry may seem too far below you to be worth noticing. Coleridge's visionary "Kubla Khan," though possibly inspired by an opium dream, was written by daylight, after the poet for years had stored his mind with descriptions of exotic landscapes in accounts of travel and exploration. In this regard, the poet Robert Wallace has made an excellent suggestion: "Get high on what you write." Some poets try to prod the unconscious by natural means. Donald Hall has testified to the advantages of rising before dawn and writing poetry when thoughts seem fruitful, being close to dream. (However, some writers who try Hall's method find themselves staring sleepily at blank paper.)

Novice poets sometimes begin a poem in a language clouded not with dream, but with gaseous abstraction:

> Indifferent cosmos!
> O ye cryptic force!
> Don't you notice our pitiful human
> Agonies and sufferings?
> Are we mere tools of careless, crushing Fate?

Far better for a poet to open his eyes and begin with whatever small object he sees:

> I found a dimpled spider, fat and white,
> On a white heal-all, holding up a moth . . .

Unlike the novice's complaint about the indifference of the universe, Robert Frost's lines on a similar theme are many times more inviting — more striking, more definite.

Poetry, then, tends to inhere not in abstract editorial stands, but in particulars. William Carlos Williams's brief poem about eating the plums in the ice box (page 39) may not be great, but it is human, and hard to forget. Sources of poems may lie before your eyes. Although poets can learn from reading other poets' work, they can also learn from the testimony of their own senses. In the best poems, as the following poem reminds us, there is always a quality that cannot be distilled from schools and libraries: a freshness that comes only from contact with the living world.

Frederick Morgan (b. 1922)

THE MASTER   1982

When Han Kan was summoned
to the imperial capital
it was suggested he sit at the feet of
the illustrious senior court painter
to learn from him the refinements of the art.   5

"No, thank you," he replied,
"I shall apprentice myself to the stables."

And he installed himself and his brushes amid the dung and the flies,
and studied the horses — their bodies' keen alertness —
eye-sparkle of one, another's sensitive stance,   10
the way a third moved graceful in his bulk —
and painted at last the emperor's favorite,
the charger named "Nightshining White,"

whose likeness after centuries still dazzles.

The advice of W. Somerset Maugham to aspiring novelists may be useful to poets, too: Keep a notebook of memorable things you observe, of revealing bits of conversation you overhear. Jot them down for no purpose except to gain skill in recording them. Don't feel duty-bound to work this material into anything you write. It will serve its purpose, even though none of it proves of any further use to you.

All right, then, how is your poem to begin? Some poets begin with something to say, then strive for the best way of saying it. Others start with nothing much in mind. In the grip of strong but perhaps woolly and indefinite feelings, they play around with words until they discover to their surprise that they have said something. Evidently, a poem can arise from any adequate provocation. T. S. Eliot, speaking of the habits of poets in general, but probably referring to his own, said that at times a rhythm will begin to course through a poet's mind even before there are words to embody it. Some poets begin from a memorable image; Ezra Pound said he began writing "In a Station of the Metro" from being haunted by a glimpse of a woman's face. Following still another procedure, Dylan Thomas and many other poets have taken some promising line or phrase that swam to mind, and without knowing where it might lead, have trustingly gone on with it. Clearly, what matters isn't whether you begin with an idea or an emotion, a rhythm or an image, a phrase or a line. What matters is that, somehow, you begin.

Plunge in and blunder about. Why be afraid of a blank sheet of paper? You're writing only a first draft. No one is judging you. True poets, as they start to write a poem, don't worry whether a reader will find it admirable. They are too busy finding the words for an idea (or emotion, or rhythm) before it can get away. If you begin to write in a state of high excitement, by all means keep going until you simmer down. Let the words flow. Are some of them not the right ones? Have you misspelled something? No matter, you can make repairs later. Go on with your task and, whatever you do, don't stop to congratulate yourself on your splendid workmanship, or to contemplate the poetic process. The point may be expressed in this "Ars Poetica," or poem about how poetry is written:

> The goose that laid the golden egg
> Died looking up its crotch
> To find out how its sphincter worked.
> Would you lay well? Don't watch.

Later on, of course, you will want to examine your first draft critically; but for now, write as though you were divinely inspired and sustained. When you revise and try to amend your faults, you can view yourself as the lowest sinner. When you write a first draft, you are (with any luck) bringing something out of obscure depths, raising it to the surface. It may mean more than you consciously know. If you are going ahead blindly — that is, if you have begun to write without any burning idea in mind — let the poem choose its own direction. See where it wants to go. Be reluctant to bark orders to it.

A quite different method of composition, which some poets find fruitful, is to compose a poem entirely in the mind, revolving it around and around, saying it over to oneself and trying to perfect it before setting it down on paper. The result tends to have a certain seamless consistency. This method, though, will probably work only for poets who write short poems in rime and meter — devices that help to hold a poem in the mind — or for those with excellent memories.

In a first draft, it is usually a good idea to write everything out in great detail, even at the risk of driveling. If, when you revise, you discover that changes are necessary, it is generally easier to delete than to amplify. A common reason for failure — for the poem that nobody knows what to make of, or feels any positive reaction toward — is mistakenly to assume that the reader is as thoroughly grounded in the facts behind the poem as the poet is. Sometimes, however, a reader will fail to grasp a poem because some vital bit of knowledge still lies within the poet's mind, folded like a green bud. In your first draft, spell out the background of the poem. Define its setting, flesh out any people in it. Show us how they relate to one another, and why they behave the way they do. Perhaps you will only set down a lot of unnecessary explanation, but when you revise, you will then have all the matter arrayed before you, and you can easily see what to cut, or to retain.

Special challenges face anyone who writes a poem in meter and rime. Most students who attempt a traditionally formal poem, such as a ballad or a sonnet, quickly discover that to write skillfully in meter and rime is difficult. Thwarted by the requirements of strict form, they feel hindered from saying what they want to say. "This straitjacket isn't for me," they conclude hastily.

True, writing a poem in rime is at first and odd and unsettling experience. It is like walking blindfolded down a dark road with your hand in the hand of an inexorable guide. With the conscious, lighted portion of your mind, you may want to express some idea. But a line that ends in *year* must be followed by another ending in *atmosphere, beer, bier, bombardier, cashier, deer, friction-gear, frontier,* or some other word that probably would not have occurred if the rime scheme had not suggested it. As Rolfe Humphries once pointed out, rime sometimes "makes you think of better things than you would all by yourself." Far from being a coldly rational process of filling a form with wordage, to write a riming poem is to pit yourself against (or to enter into a playful relationship with) some of the wildest and most chaotic forces of the unconscious.

Learn to write a decent poem in rimed stanzas, and you will have at your fingertips certain skills useful in writing poems of any kind. You will know, for instance, how to condense a thought to its gist, from having wrestled with metrical lines that allow you only so many syllables. In revising and finishing your poem, you will become an old hand at replacing stumbling words and phrases with rhythmic ones, at choosing words for their sounds as well as their senses. This won't be easy. Although the iambic rhythm is native to English, learning to speak in it with ease and grace is almost like learning a foreign language. Alexander Pope's observation remains accurate:

True ease in writing comes from art, not chance,
As those move easiest who have learned to dance.

With practice, the day will come when a rime or a metrical line will spring to your lips almost thoughtlessly. And then, even if you decide to write poetry in *open* forms, you will do so from choice, not from inability to do otherwise. Proponents of closed form or open form sometimes assume that their favorite kind of form is intrinsically superior; but in truth, the form of an excellent poem, whether open or closed, is whatever the poem requires. The poet's task is to discover it.

Whatever your formal preference, it is probably a mistake to try to plan out the direction of your poetic career, and then grimly oblige yourself to go in it. Better to write a hundred poems and place them in a row, and see where they have taken you. Your life will shape what you write, and the words you write in. Richard Hugo, speaking hyperbolically, has argued that the study of poetry writing fulfills a unique function: "Creative writing is the last class you can go where your life as an individual is important."[2] Professors of mathematics, natural history, and geology might well argue that individual lives matter in their disciplines, too; but Hugo is surely right in at least one regard. Writing a poem calls for a kind of knowledge that only a poet can provide.

By the way, if a poem doesn't come to you all in one sitting, don't despair. Forget about it for a while. It may need more time to gather its forces. Many poets carefully save their fragments: lines and passages that arrive easily, but which do not immediately want to go anywhere. In dry seasons, when inspiration is scarce, they can look back over their notebooks, and sometimes a fragment will spring to life at last, and grow into an entire poem. Try this and see if you have any luck with it. For many, being a poet is like being a beggar: like standing with outstretched bowl by the side of a road, hoping for charity. Thankful poets keep whatever a passing Muse may throw, whether it is a Brasher doubloon or only a bent bottlecap.

ON BLOTTING OUT LINES

Your first draft is done, and the excitement of writing it has cooled. Your next step is to take a step back from it.

A hard but necessary part of being a poet is to try to see your work through a reader's eyes. How to reread it with detachment? The advice of the Roman poet Horace — to put aside a poem for nine years — may seem too discouraging. At least, you can put your poem aside for a week, or even overnight. You may then take a more nearly objective look at it. To help distance yourself from it, try reading it aloud — at least to yourself. Friends may be asked for their criticism, but it is a rare friend who is also a competent critic of poetry. Probably it is best to try to cultivate your own faculties for tough and demanding self-criticism.

Told that his friend Shakespeare in writing his plays never blotted out a line, Ben Jonson wished he had blotted a thousand. (Scholars, by the way, think that even Shakespeare blotted many lines.) Although there is a school of thought that holds for total spontaneity in writing, and for leaving words just the way they land on a page, most poets probably feel that second thoughts, too, can be spontaneous, and often more memorable. If you regard your first draft as holy writ, and refuse to make any changes in it, you may be preserving a work of genius, but more probably you will be passing up your chance to write a good poem. Poets usually don't mind revision; in fact, they find the task fascinating. "What happiness!" exclaimed Yeats, in a letter to a friend, on facing months of demanding rewriting. (It was Yeats, incidentally, who pointed out that, no less than the original act of writing a poem, the act of revision may be inspired.) A contemporary poet, James Dickey, says he writes a poem over and over in many ways. "After I've tried every possible way I can think of,"

[2]Quoted by Harriet Heyman, "Eleven American Poets," *Life* (Apr. 1981), 89.

he explains, "I finally get maybe not absolutely the right poem, but the poem that is less wrong than the others."[3]

Is there not a danger that much revision will drain the life out of a poem — or cause it to become ornate and needlessly complicated? Perhaps; but more often, the poem that seems beautifully simple, as if casually dropped from the lips, is the result of hard work; while the poem that the poet didn't retouch makes difficult reading. As you can tell from the two versions Yeats made of his "Old Pensioner," the one written a half-century later, far from lacking in life, seems the more youthful and spontaneous. (For this and other illustrations of poets' revisions, see pages 232 – 235.)

Working on your second draft, you have the leisure to look up spellings and to verify information. For the poet who is stuck for a rime, a riming dictionary will suggest some likely — and some outlandish — possibilities. When in such a fix, you will probably do better to proceed down the alphabet (*air, bear, bare, care, dare* . . .) and discover a rime among common words you know already. Rimes will strike your reader as reached-for and strange if you enlist them from far beyond your vocabulary.

Some poets make a typewritten first draft, then revise in longhand. When additions, deletions, and substitutions accumulate and the page becomes too crosshatched to decipher, they type a fresh version (keeping the old version just in case they botch the revision and want to go back to the original and start over). Some poets — Richard Wilbur is one — prefer to keep working on a single poem till it is done; others simultaneously revise many poems, going around and making fresh moves like a chess master playing all comers.

In your first draft, when you were trying to include everything essential, you could allow yourself a multitude of words. But in revising and striving for concision, you have to select what is essential and decide what to leave out. Ask yourself whether every line — every word — deserves the room it occupies. Does it *do* anything? To decide, imagine your poem without the word or line. Begin your inspection with your opening lines. Are they valuable, or do they only delay the reader's entry into something more essential? What if, instead, the poem began with some line that now comes later? Opening lines, of course, don't have to be sensational, but there is much to be said for a beginning that stops the reader in his tracks and hangs on to him:

> You do not do, you do not do
> Any more, black shoe
> In which I have lived like a foot . . .

(To quote Sylvia Plath's brilliant opening to "Daddy.") Samuel Johnson, that down-to-earth critic, insisted that a writer's first duty is to excite the reader of his work "to *read it through,*" and to that purpose, it helps to be interesting. Don't be afraid to be obvious. Go ahead and say, if necessary, "I started Early – Took my Dog – /And visited the Sea," or whatever will begin a story,

---

[3] *Self-Interviews,* edited by Barbara and James Reiss (New York: Doubleday, 1970) 64.

or clearly set forth a situation. Excellent poems may be clear and yet be profound — like bodies of water.

Here are some other questions to ask yourself while you revise:

1. Does this poem express what I feel? Does it claim to feel more than I do — that is, is it sentimental? Or does it hang back, afraid to declare itself? (If it does, see if you can persuade the feelings out into the open.) The advice of W. D. Snodgrass is worth remembering:

> Our only hope as artists is to continually ask ourselves, "Am I writing what I *really* think? Not what is acceptable; not what my favorite intellectual would think in this situation; not what I wish I felt. Only what I cannot help thinking."[4]

2. Somewhere in its first half-dozen lines, does the poem offer the reader any temptation to go on reading? If so, something will have been begun: perhaps a story, dramatic situation, metaphor, or intriguing perplexity. To recognize it, you will need to put yourself into the reader's seat. One veteran teacher of poetry-writing, John Ciardi, placed great weight on engaging a reader early. Ciardi sometimes penciled a line underneath the line in the poem at which, out of boredom or disgust, he quit reading.

3. Is there anything in my poem that doesn't make sense to me? (*Careful! Such a difficulty may not be a fault!*) Does the difficulty come in stating something I feel to be valuable, or is it just an unsuccessful attempt to say something unimportant or needlessly explanatory? If it is the latter, away with it.

Here is some further advice, from Ezra Pound:

> Use no superfluous word, no adjective which does not reveal something.
>
> Don't use such an expression as 'dim lands *of peace.*' It dulls the image. It mixes an abstraction with the concrete. It comes from the writer's not realizing that the natural object is always the *adequate* symbol.
>
> Go in fear of abstractions. Do not retell in mediocre verse what has already been done in good prose. Don't think any intelligent person is going to be deceived when you try to shirk all the difficulties of the unspeakably difficult art of good prose by chopping your composition into line lengths. . . .
>
> Don't be 'viewy' — leave that to the writers of pretty little philosophic essays. Don't be descriptive; remember that the painter can describe a landscape much better than you can, and that he has to know a deal more about it.
>
> When Shakespeare talks of the 'Dawn in russet mantle clad' he presents something which the painter does not present. There is in this line of his nothing that one can call description; he presents. . . .
>
> If you are using a symmetrical form, don't put in what you want to say and then fill up the remaining vacuums with slush.[5]

[4]"Finding a Poem," *In Radical Pursuit* (New York: Harper, 1974) 32.
[5]Excerpts from "A Retrospect," *Literary Essays of Ezra Pound,* ed. T. S. Eliot (New York: New Directions, 1954) 4 – 6.

In Pound's view, a poet ought to pay attention to vivid detail, and usually that is good advice. But like all general advice to poets, it is not to be followed absolutely. Some details may point us nowhere. They distract us from what matters, and they will need to be cut. Thomas Hardy probably wouldn't have improved "Channel Firing" by naming the brand of beer Parson Thirdly preferred, nor by describing the picture on its label.

Evidently, the details to render vividly are the ones that mean the most. Unless you agree with Edgar Allan Poe that a short intense poem is the only true poem (see page 449), revision isn't a matter of polishing an entire poem to a level of high intensity. Long poems, said T. S. Eliot in "The Music of Poetry," naturally contain prosaic passages as well as intensely "poetic" ones. See the advice of Yeats on the need for deliberately putting in a bit of dullness now and again.

Of all the skills a poet has, one of the most valuable is to know where to end lines. If your poem happens to be written in meter and rime, where to end lines is clearly suggested for you: lines end on riming words, or they end when their metrical expectation has been fulfilled. (An iambic pentameter line stops on its tenth syllable, give or take a syllable or two.) But in "free verse" or formally open poetry, you do not have any guidance other than your mind and eye and ear. To place your line breaks effectively calls for much care during revision, and at all times, a certain sensibility. Because the ending of a line compels your readers to make a slight pause — at least a moment for their eyes to relocate at the beginning of the next line — the placement of these pauses is a great resource to you. If most of your lines end on strong words (such as verbs and nouns), the effect is different from that of slicing your lines after weak words (such as articles — *a, the* — or prepositions). To see this truth for yourself, study the ways in which lines end in William Carlos Williams's "The Dance" (page 185).

Early in life, William Carlos Williams decided that it seemed pretentious to begin each line with a capital. Such avoidance of convention is neither right nor wrong, and your choice depends on the effect you are after. Any evident attempt to defy convention calls attention to itself. Say "i think, therefore i am," and you aren't necessarily being modest. The effect is as though you were to print the letter *I* in red. E. E. Cummings, who favored the small letter *i*, was, according to many who knew him, an egotist.

When should you declare your poem done? Never, according to the French poet Paul Valéry, who said that a poem is never finished, only abandoned in despair. Other poets feel a definite sense of completion — as did Yeats, to whom a poem came shut with a click. But if you hear no such click, just stop when you see no more verbiage to prune, no more weak words to tighten.

If by now a title for your poem hasn't occurred to you, you may want to consider one. Some poets, to be sure, dispense with any title — as was the usual practice of Cummings and Emily Dickinson. To a reader, however, a title may be a help. If a poem is difficult, its title can show the reader how to take hold of it. An explicit title can supply needed background, tell us who is speaking, or explain a dramatic situation. By calling his poem "Soliloquy of the Spanish Cloister," Robert Browning indicates that we listen in on the thoughts of a single character, a monk in a religious order. Even a flatly indicative title ("Stopping by a Market in Pismo Beach to Buy Wine for a Wedding Present") may be more helpful to a reader than a merely decorative title ("Subterfuge with Sea-green Raisins"). Some poems, however, seem to thrive under titles that intrigue or tantalize without telling everything: "The Portent," "Disillusion-ment of Ten O'Clock," "Daystar," "The Listeners."

REACHING AN AUDIENCE

Few contemporary poets seem to follow the custom of Emily Dickinson and store their poems in the family attic. Most poets want to share their work with the world, and some, as soon as they have written a first poem, rush to send it to a magazine. Hopes of instant acclaim, of course, often meet with disap-pointment. "Don't imagine," Ezra Pound warned, "that you can please the expert before you have spent at least as much effort on the art of verse as the average piano teacher spends on the art of music." Nevertheless, if you master your art, it is reasonable to expect that sooner or later people will listen to it.

In a writing class, you already have an audience: your fellow students, your instructor. Still, some beginning poets feel reluctant to display their work even to friendly eyes. They have an uncomfortable sense, at first, that they are being asked to parade their inmost emotions in public, while at the same time they risk being ridiculed for their weak artistry. That is why a writing class needs to agree that the poems its members share are to be regarded as works of the imagination, not as personal diaries. As for the risk of ridicule, nobody expects the beginner to be T. S. Eliot. Probably you will find your fellow students reading your poems as considerately and sympathetically as (they trust) you'll read theirs. As for your instructor, don't worry. He or she has seen worse poems.

If you *enjoy* reading your poems aloud, live audiences may be yours for the asking. Does your campus have a coffeehouse or other room in which to hold readings? Audience responses, while sometimes misleading, can encourage you. Be aware, however, that audiences like to laugh together, and often prefer funny, outrageous, immediately understandable poems to more difficult, subtle ones that require more than one hearing. If any of your fellow student poets are interested, it may be even more valuable to form a small group for mutual criticism and support.

Some novice poets crave early publication, and some who hurry into print are later sorry. Should the day arrive, however, when, tired of staring at a tall stack of beautiful finished poems, you just have to break into print, why not begin near home? Submit poems to your campus literary magazine, if there is any. If there isn't, can you see about starting one? Another alternative is to bring out your own magazine of limited circulation, with the aid of a mimeo-graph or a copier. Eventually, you may decide that your work belongs in magazines of wider readership — but first, make sure it is ready. Unlike your fellow students and your instructor, who know you personally and are likely to sympathize with your creative labors, the editor of a national magazine, to whom you are only a licked stamp, cares for nothing but what you can show on cold white paper. A writing class may deal patiently with a faulted poem, taking time to rummage it for meaning, but the glance of an overworked editor will be more cursory. A bungled opening, a cliché, a line of bombast or sentiment, and back goes the manuscript with a rejection slip. Not that this threat should discourage you. Just realize that, in trying to print your poems, you'll be venturing forth into a crowded marketplace.

At the moment, American poetry seems in the throes of an inflation: Karl Shapiro, somewhat grimly, has called it a "poetry glut." For a number of reasons (including, no doubt, the popularity of creative writing programs), thousands of people today are trying to throng into print. Perhaps, in a world of social-security numbers sorted out into zip-code areas, they feel nameless, and so hope to make a lasting name — however small — by writing poetry. Whatever the explanation, in the latest *Directory of American Poets and Fiction Writers*, 3,918 published poets are listed — an incomplete listing at that.[6] Although the ranks of poets are thick, recent years have seen a dwindling in the number of paying markets for a poem. Few magazines currently sold on newsstands regularly print poetry: *The Atlantic, The New Yorker, Yankee* — the list expires.

Still, poets need not consign their work to their attics. Lately, in noncommercial publishing, there has been a tremendous explosion of energy. As the latest *International Directory of Little Magazines and Small Presses* will indicate,[7] literary publishers now number in the thousands. **Little magazines,** periodicals edited and published as labors of love, exist not to turn a profit but to turn up new writing. A few such magazines, thick and printed handsomely, appear on more or less regular schedules. The majority, less expensively produced, usually lag behind their declared frequencies. Most little magazines, if well established, reach an audience of perhaps 500 to 5,000.[8]

Read a magazine before sending it your work; if need be, write off (and pay) for a sample copy. There is no sense in offering, say, a pastoral elegy in heroic couplets to the radically experimental *Hanging Loose*, or a pornographic punk rock song to *The American Scholar*. Decent respect for editors requires that along with your poems you enclose a stamped, self-addressed envelope; send

[6] 1987 – 88 edition (New York: Poets & Writers, 1987).
[7] Edited by Len Fulton and Ellen Ferber, and published annually by Dustbooks, Box 100, Paradise, CA 95969. It may be in the reference department of your library.
[8] Among the heftier and more faithfully appearing little magazines are *Antaeus, Boulevard, Grand Street, Hudson Review, Paris Review, Ploughshares,* and *Threepenny Review;* also those reviews subsidized by universities (*Georgia Review, Massachusetts Review, TriQuarterly, Sewanee Review,* and others). *Poetry,* which printed the early poems of Eliot, Frost, Marianne Moore, and Stevens, still issues monthly from Chicago, as essential as ever. The influential *American Poetry Review,* a bimonthly in tabloid newspaper format, claims the largest circulation of any little magazine: according to one report, more than 20,000.

original copies, not carbons or Xeroxes; and submit a poem to one magazine at a time.

Delmore Schwartz once made a brilliant observation: a poet is wise to write as much and to publish as little as possible. With so many noncommercial publishers, it is a safe bet that any halfway competent poet who persists in licking stamps will break into print sooner or later. Yet the difficulty for poets today is not merely to be printed, but to be read. Ours seems a time of more good voices than good listeners. It is, besides, an age of disagreement and diversity. Ask any published poets what they think of poetry, and they will probably tell you that most poetry now being printed, other than their own, is bad or mediocre. But ask any six poets (selected at random) which other poets among their contemporaries they admire, and you will receive six lists of names with little duplication. To add to the confusion about what is excellent (or, some might say, to add to the merriment), most literary critics, as if discouraged by the vastness of the task of keeping up with contemporary poetry, have folded their practices. (To be sure, a very few brave and overworked critics of contemporary poetry are still operating.) Some poets feel that, since criticism isn't a help to them anyhow, who needs it? Still, without critics, who used to be poets' most devoted readers, it is more difficult for excellence to be recognized. Two truths seem evident. It is hard for a new poet today to gain an audience and a reputation. And yet, in the last few years, despite all odds, several excellent new poets have succeeded in doing so.

If you are a dedicated poet, and your work truly deserves your dedication, you'll keep faith that you will eventually find your audience. You'll listen to the voice of your Muse, not to the siren warblings of the marketplace. (In John Ciardi's view, it is hardly possible to prostitute your talent for poetry, anyway, there being so few paying customers.) You will become a severer critic of your own work than your fellow students or your instructor. Although when you send out your poems to the handsome magazines you'll have to elbow through a crowd, you can be sure that, among contenders for immortality, there can no more be any rivalry than there is among gold prospectors. That is, when poets strike paydirt and achieve renown, it is usually because they have stalwart backs, eyes for a gleam, and likely claims, not because they know someone at the assay office.

Apparently, poets are not paid in bullion. In fact, nowhere in the English-speaking world at the moment is the writing of poems a full-time paying occupation. Most poets survive by other honest trades (such as teaching), receiving nothing or almost nothing for their poems, making a spare dollar from an occasional reading. Still, most derive ample compensation. No one has better summed up the payment of being a poet than John Keats, in a letter to a friend: "I should write for the mere yearning and fondness I have for the beautiful, even if my night's labors should be burnt every morning and no eye shine upon them." For any poet so intently dedicated, writing a poem is today — as it always has been — its own considerable, immediate reward.

Suggestions for Writing

Doing finger exercises is generally less fruitful to a poet than trying to write poems. Here are a few suggestions that might result in poems, if they arouse any responses in you.

1. Try to recall, and recapture in a poem, some experience that deeply moved you. The experience does not have to be anything world-shaking or traumatic; it might be as small as a memory from early childhood, a chance meeting with someone, a visit to a beach, the realization that some ordinary object is beautiful.

2. Try writing a poem in a voice *remote* from your own — speaking, say, as a character in history or fiction or film; an ordinary citizen in a different place or time; a child; an octogenarian. (For one famous illustration of a poet's speaking through a mask or persona, see Robert Browning's "Soliloquy of the Spanish Cloister," page 296. Presumably Browning set himself a problem: What would a hate-filled, envious monk think and mutter about a devout brother? Then, having imagined such a character, the poet found the character some artful and appropriate words.)

3. Attempt a poem in which you convey the joy of performing some simple, familiar, routine act: running, driving a car, peeling an orange, stroking a cat, changing a baby — or whatever you like to do.

4. Here is an experiment suggested by Ezra Pound: Write words to a well-known tune "in such a way that the words will not be distorted when one sings them."

5. Here is a suggestion that Nancy Willard has given to her student poets: Write a poem that responds to another poem. (First, find a poem you feel strongly compelled to respond to.)

6. Find, in a current magazine, or anthology, a poem that strikes you as silly, pretentious, or simple-minded. Write a take-off on it.

7. The aim of the following experiment is to lead you to wrestle with arbitrary difficulties. Observe some limitation that may seem to you pointless, but which might set up a certain tension within your poem — provide a bottle (to echo Richard Wilbur) for your genie to try to burst out of. For instance, write a poem entirely in simple declarative subject-plus-verb sentences. Write a poem that is all one metaphor (like, for example, Emily Dickinson's "Because I could not stop for Death" or Whitman's "A Noiseless Patient Spider." Write a poem in blank verse (the form of Tennyson's "Ulysses"). Or, as Theodore Roethke was fond of asking his students to do, write a poem without adjectives.

8. Write a poem in praise of someone you admire, allowing yourself no general terms (*beautiful, wonderful,* etc.); try to describe the person in language so specific that a reader, too, will find your subject admirable.

9. Write a curse in verse: a damnation of someone or something you can't abide.

10. From an opening line (or lines) supplied by your instructor, try to develop a poem. Then compare the result with poems developed by others from the same beginning.

11. In verse (whether rimed or open), write a letter to a friend. For neoclassical examples, see the works of Swift and Pope (the latter's "Epistle to Dr. Arbuthnot" and other epistles in particular); for less formal contemporary examples, see Richard Hugo's collection *31 Letters and 13 Dreams* (New York: Norton, 1977) — mostly verse-letters to fellow poets.

12. Write a poem in the form of a dialogue between two people. (Christina Rossetti's "Uphill," page 213, may help illustrate such an exchange of speeches.)

13. Intently observe something for twenty or thirty minutes, then write a poem full of images through which your reader, too, can apprehend it. An excellent object for scrutiny would be any small living thing that will stand still long enough: an animal, bird, tropical fish, insect, or plant.

14. In a bookstore or library, select a book of poems that appeals to you. Take it home and read it thoroughly. If you have chosen well, the book may quicken your feelings and encourage you, too, to devote yourself to words. See if you can write a poem suggested or inspired by it — not necessarily an imitation.

References

LITERARY ACKNOWLEDGMENTS

"Night Driving" from *Flight and Pursuit, Poems* by Dick Allen. Copyright © 1987 by Dick Allen. Reprinted by permission of Louisiana State University Press.

"Spring Coming" is reprinted from *Collected Poems, 1951–1971,* by A. R. Ammons, by permission of W.W. Norton & Company, Inc. Copyright © 1972 by A. R. Ammons.

"At North Farm" from *A Wave* by John Ashbery. Copyright © 1984 by John Ashbery. All rights reserved. Reprinted by permission of Viking Penguin, a division of Penguin Books USA, Inc. Originally appeared in *The New Yorker.*

"All Bread" from *Selected Poems II: Poems Selected and New 1976–1986* by Margaret Atwood. Copyright © 1987 by Margaret Atwood. Reprinted by permission of Houghton Mifflin Company and Oxford University Press Canada.

Margaret Atwood, "you fit into me" from *Power Politics* (Toronto: House of Anansi Press, 1971). Reprinted by permission.

"James Watt" from *Academic Graffiti,* by W. H. Auden. Copyright © 1960 by W. H. Auden. Reprinted by permission of Random House, Inc.

"As I Walked Out One Evening," "Musee des Beaux Arts" and "The Unknown Citizen" Copyright 1940 and renewed 1968 by W. H. Auden. Reprinted from *W. H. Auden: Collected Poems,* edited by Edward Mendelson, by permission of Random House, Inc. and Faber and Faber Ltd.

"Spliced Wire" from *What's Happening* by Jimmy Santiago Baca. Copyright © 1982 by Jimmy Santiago Baca. Reprinted by permission of Curbstone Press.

"Readers and listeners praise my books" from *Earthenware: XLIV Epigrams from Martial,* translated by R. L. Barth. Copyright © 1988 by R. L. Barth. Reprinted by permission.

"Sir Christopher Wren" from *Clerihews Complete* by E. C. Bentley. © E. C. Bentley. Reprinted by permission of Curtis Brown London.

"In Westminster Abbey" from *Collected Poems* by John Betjeman (Houghton Mifflin Company, 1959). Reprinted by permission of John Murray Publishers Ltd.

"Haiku Ambulance" from *The Pill Versus the Springhill Mine Disaster* by Richard Brautigan. Copyright © 1965 by Richard Brautigan. Reprinted by permission of Houghton Mifflin Company/Seymour Lawrence.

"One Art" from *The Complete Poems 1927–1979* by Elizabeth Bishop. Copyright © 1979, 1983 by Alice Helen Methfessel. Reprinted by permission of Farrar, Straus and Giroux, Inc.

"Belfast Tune" from *To Urania* by Joseph Brodsky. Copyright © 1981, 1982, 1983, 1984, 1985, 1987, 1988 by Joseph Brodsky. Reprinted by permission of Farrar, Straus & Giroux, Inc.

"A Black Wedding Song" from *To Disembark* by Gwendolyn Brooks. Copyright © 1981 by Gwendolyn Brooks. Reprinted by permission of Third World Press, Chicago.

"The Bean Eaters" from *Selected Poems* by Gwendolyn Brooks. Copyright © 1944, 1945, 1949, 1959, 1960, 1963 by Gwendolyn Brooks Blakely. Reprinted by permission of the author.

"We Real Cool" and "The Rites for Cousin Vit" from *Blacks* by Gwendolyn Brooks (Chicago: The David Company). Copyright © 1987 by Gwendolyn Brooks Blakely. Reprinted by permission of the author.

"The Habit of Imperfect Rhyming" from *Collected Poems, 1915–1967* by Kenneth Burke. Copyright © 1968 Kenneth Burke. Reprinted by permission of The University of California Press.

"Skin Flick" from *The World Between the Eyes* by Fred Chappell. Copyright © 1971 by Fred Chappell. Reprinted by permission of Louisiana State University Press.

G. K. Chesterton, "The Donkey," *The Wild Knight and Other Poems* (London: J. M. Dent & Sons Ltd.).

"In Place of a Curse" from *Selected Poems* by John Ciardi. Copyright © 1984 by John Ciardi. Reprinted by permission of The University of Arkansas Press.

"winnie song" copyright © 1987 by Lucille Clifton. Reprinted from *Next: New Poems* by Lucille Clifton with the permission of BOA Editions, Ltd.

From "Some River Rhymes" by William Cole from *Light Year '85* edited by Robert Wallace (Cleveland, Ohio: Bits Press, 1984). Reprinted by permission of the author.

"Scott Huff" from *New and Collected Poems* by Leo Connellan (New York: Paragon House). Copyright © 1989 by Leo Connellan. Reprinted by permission of the author.

"Oh No" reprinted with permission of Charles Scribner's Sons, an imprint of Macmillan Publishing Company, from *For Love: Poems 1950–1960* by Robert Creeley. Copyright © 1962 by Robert Creeley.

"For a Lady I Know" from *On These I Stand* by Countee Cullen. Copyright 1925 by Harper & Row, Publishers, Inc.; renewed 1953 by Ida M. Cullen. Reprinted by permission of GRM Associates, Inc., as agents for the Estate of Ida M. Cullen.

"anyone lived in a pretty how town" and "a politician is an arse upon" are reprinted from *Complete Poems, 1913–1962* by E. E. Cummings, by permission of Liveright Publishing Corporation. Copyright © 1923, 1925, 1931, 1935, 1938, 1939, 1940, 1944, 1945, 1946, 1947, 1948, 1949, 1950, 1951, 1952, 1953, 1954, 1955, 1956, 1957, 1958, 1959, 1960, 1961, 1962 by the Trustees for the E. E. Cummings Trust. Copyright © 1961, 1963, 1968 by Marion Morehouse Cummings.

"Buffalo Bill's" and "in Just-" reprinted from *Tulips and Chimneys* by E. E. Cummings, edited by George James Firmage, by permission of Liveright

"Cargoes" reprinted with permission of Macmillan Publishing Company from *Poems* by John Masefield (New York: Macmillan, 1953).

"Thoughts on Capital Punishment" from *Stanyan Street and Other Sorrows* by Rod McKuen. Copyright 1954, © 1960, 1962, 1963, 1964, 1965, 1966 by Rod McKuen. Reprinted by permission of Random House, Inc.

"Laboratory Poem" reprinted with permission of Atheneum Publishers, an imprint of Macmillan Publishing Company from *The Country of A Thousand Years of Peace* by James Merrill. Copyright © 1958, 1970 by James Merrill. Originally appeared in *Poetry*.

"Elegy" reprinted with permission of Atheneum Publishers, an imprint of Macmillan Publishing Company from *The Carrier of Ladders* by W. S. Merwin. Copyright © 1970 by W. S. Merwin.

"Song of Man Chipping an Arrowhead" reprinted with permission of Atheneum Publishers, an imprint of Macmillan Publishing Company from *Writings to an Unfinished Accompaniment* by W. S. Merwin. Copyright © 1972, 1973 by W. S. Merwin. Originally appeared in *Poetry*.

"The Farmer's Bride" from *Collected Poems and Prose* by Charlotte Mew, edited by Val Warner. Copyright © 1981 The Estate of Charlotte Mew. Reprinted by permission of Carcanet Press Ltd.

"Reason" from *Poems 1930–1960* by Josephine Miles. Copyright © 1960 by Indiana University Press. Reprinted by permission.

"Counting-out Rhyme" by Edna St. Vincent Millay. From *Collected Poems*, Harper & Row. Copyright © 1928, 1955 by Edna St. Vincent Millay and Norma Millay Ellis. Reprinted by permission.

"Recuerdo" by Edna St. Vincent Millay. From *Collected Poems* (Harper & Row). Copyright 1922, 1950 by Edna St. Vincent Millay. Reprinted by permission.

"The Mind is an Enchanting Thing" and "The Wood-Weasel" reprinted with permission of Macmillan Publishing Company from *Collected Poems* by Marianne Moore. Copyright 1944 and renewed 1972, by Marianne Moore.

"The Master" from *Northbrook* by Frederick Morgan. Copyright © 1982 by Frederick Morgan. Reprinted by permission of University of Illinois Press.

"Shall I Compare Thee to a Summer's Day" (from "Modified Sonnets") reprinted with permission of Atheneum Publishers, an imprint of Macmillan Publishing Company from *A Swim Off the Rocks* by Howard Moss. Copyright © 1976 by Howard Moss.

"The Snow Globe" from *The Collected Poems of Howard Nemerov.* Copyright © 1977 by Howard Nemerov. Reprinted by permission of the author.

First four lines from "Carnation Milk" reprinted with permission of Atheneum Publishers, an imprint of Macmillan Publishing Company, from *Confessions of an Advertising Man* by David Ogilvy. Copyright © 1963, 1987 by David Ogilvy, Trustee.

From *From This Condensery: The Complete Writing of Lorine Niedecker*, edited by Robert J. Bertholf. Copyright © Cid Corman, Literary executor of Lorine Niedecker Estate. Reprinted by permission.

"The One Girl at the Boys Party" from *The Dead and the Living*, by Sharon Olds. Copyright © 1983 by Sharon Olds. Reprinted by permission of Alfred A. Knopf, Inc.

"Rain in Ohio" from *American Primitive* by Mary Oliver. Copyright © 1981 by Mary Oliver. First appeared in the *Atlantic Monthly*. Reprinted by permission of Little, Brown and Company.

"La Chute" by Charles Olson. Reprinted by permission of Richard H. Schimmelpfeng for the Estate of Charles Olson.

"Anthem for Doomed Youth" and "Dulce et Decorum Est" from *Collected Poems* by Wilfred Owen. Copyright 1946, 1963 by Chatto & Windus Ltd. Reprinted by permission of New Directions Publishing Corporation, The Hogarth Press and the Estate of Wilfred Owen.

"Ethics" is reprinted from *Waiting For My Life,* Poems by Linda Pastan, by permission of the author and W. W. Norton & Company, Inc. Copyright © 1981 by Linda Pastan.

"A Sensual, For Ezra Pound" and "Rain," copyright © 1989 by Emanuel di Pasquale. Reprinted from *Genesis* by Emanuel di Pasquale with the permission of BOA Editions, Ltd.

First six lines from "III Hiang Niao" reprinted by permission of the publishers from Ezra Pound, *Shih-Ching: The Classic Anthology Defined by Confucius*; Cambridge, Mass.: Harvard University Press. Copyright 1954 by the President and Fellows of Harvard College.

From *ABC of Reading* by Ezra Pound. Copyright 1934 by Ezra Pound. Reprinted by permission of New Directions Publishing Corporation.

"A Retrospect" from *Literary Essays* by Ezra Pound. Copyright 1935 by Ezra Pound. Reprinted by permission of New Directions Publishing Corporation.

"In a Station of the Metro" and "The River-Merchant's Wife: A Letter" from *Personae* by Ezra Pound. Copyright 1926 by Ezra Pound. Reprinted by permission of New Directions Publishing Corporation.

"Old Witherington" from *A Litany of Friends: New and Selected Poems* by Dudley Randall. Copyright © 1981 by Dudley Randall. Reprinted by permission of the author.

"The Bells for John Whiteside's Daughter" from *Selected Poems, Third Edition, Revised and Enlarged,* by John Crowe Ransom. Copyright 1924 by Alfred A. Knopf, Inc. and renewed 1952 by John Crowe Ransom. Reprinted by permission of Alfred A. Knopf, Inc.

"Aunt Jennifer's Tigers," "The Ninth Symphony of Beethoven Understood at Last as a Sexual Message," and "Trying to Talk with a Man" are reprinted from *The Fact of a Doorframe,* Poems Selected and New, 1950–1984, by Adrienne Rich, by permission of W. W. Norton & Company, Inc. Copyright © 1984 by Adrienne Rich. Copyright © 1975, 1978 by W. W. Norton & Company, Inc. Copyright © 1981 by Adrienne Rich.

"Naming of Parts" from *A Map of Verona* by Henry Reed (1946). Reprinted by permission of John Tydeman.

"A Dawn in a Tree of Birds" from *New Poems* by Kenneth Rexroth. Copyright © 1974 by Kenneth Rexroth. Reprinted by permission of New Directions Publishing Corporation.

"The Lazy Man's Haiku" by John Ridland. Reprinted by permission of the author.

From "Elegy for My Aunt" by John Ridland. Reprinted by permission of the author.

"Waiting for You with the Swallows" from *Keeping Company* by Gibbons Ruark. Copyright © 1983 by The Johns Hopkins University Press. Reprinted by permission.

"Fog" from *Chicago Poems* by Carl Sandburg, copyright 1916 by Holt, Rinehart and Winston, Inc. and renewed 1944 by Carl Sandburg, reprinted by permission of Harcourt Brace Jovanovich, Inc.

From "crickets" from *Works* by Aram Saroyan. Copyright © 1966 by Aram Saroyan. Reprinted by permission of the author.

From *Semiotics and Interpretation* by Robert

Photo Credits

364 Rollie McKenna/Courtesy Harper & Row
     Publishers, Inc., New York
365 Coris De Rachewiltz/Courtesy New
     Directions Publishing Corporation
366 Billy Williams
369 Colleen McKay Courtesy W. W. Norton &
     Company
371 Courtesy University of Washington
373 UPI/Bettmann Newsphotos
375 National Portrait Gallery, London
382 Hulton Picture Library/The Bettmann
     Archive

386 The Bettmann Archive
387 UPI/Bettmann Newsphotos
388 The Bettmann Archive
394 National Archives
395 AP/Wide World
398 John D. Schiff/Courtesy
     New Directions Publishing
     Corporation
400 The Bettmann Archive
401 AP/Wide World
404 Pirie MacDonald/The Royal
     Photographic Society

Index of First Lines

Index of Authors and Titles

To the Student

As publishers, we realize that one way to improve education is to improve textbooks. We also realize that you, the student, largely determine the success or failure of textbooks. Although the instructor assigns them, the student buys and uses them. If enough of you don't like a book and make your feelings known, the chances are your instructor will not assign it again.

Usually only instructors are asked about the quality of a text; their opinion alone is considered as revisions are planned or as new books are developed. Now, we would like to ask you about X. J. Kennedy's *An Introduction to Poetry, 7th Edition*: how you liked or disliked it; why it was interesting or dull; if it taught you anything. Please fill in this form and return it to us at: Scott, Foresman/Little, Brown, English Editor, Higher Education Division, 1900 E. Lake Ave., Glenview, Illinois 60025.

School:_____

Instructor's name:_____

Title of course:_____

1. Did you find this book too easy?_____ too difficult?_____

   about right?_____

2. Which chapters did you find the most interesting?_____

   _____

3. Which chapters did you find least interesting?_____

   _____

4. Which poems did you like most?_____

   _____

5. Were there any poems you particularly disliked?_____

   _____

6. Which statement comes closest to expressing your feelings about reading and studying literature? (Please check one, or supply your own statement.)

   _____ Love to read literature. It's my favorite subject.

   _____ Usually enjoy reading most literature.

   _____ Can take it or leave it.

_____ Usually find little of interest in most literature.

_____ Literature just is not for me.

Other: _____

7. Did you find this book helped you to enjoy poetry any more than you did?

_____

8. Were the supplements "Writing about Literature," "Writing about a Poem," and

"Writing a Poem" very useful? _____ somewhat useful? _____

of no help? _____

9. In the sections about writing papers, do you prefer to see examples of writing by

students? _____ or by professional critics? _____

10. Do you intend to keep this book for your personal library? Yes _____

No _____

11. Any other comments or suggestions: _____

_____

_____

_____

12. May we quote you in our efforts to promote this book? Yes _____

No _____

Date: _____

Signature (optional): _____

Address (optional): _____